THE LIFE OF
SAMUEL JOHNSON, LL.D.

HESTER THRALE PIOZZI
by Robert Edge Pine
in the collection of Courage Barclay & Simonds, Ltd.

THE LIFE OF
SAMUEL JOHNSON
LL.D.

BY JAMES BOSWELL, ESQ.

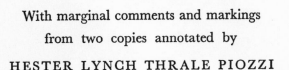

With marginal comments and markings
from two copies annotated by
HESTER LYNCH THRALE PIOZZI

Prepared for publication
with an Introduction by
EDWARD G. FLETCHER

IN THREE VOLUMES
III

THE HERITAGE PRESS
NEW YORK

The special contents of this edition are copyright © 1963
by The George Macy Companies, Inc.

THE LIFE OF
SAMUEL JOHNSON, LL.D.

THE LIFE OF
SAMUEL JOHNSON
LL.D.

ON Wednesday, April 15, I dined with Dr. Johnson at Mr. Dilly's, and was in high spirits, for I had been a good part of the morning with Mr. Orme, the able and eloquent historian of Hindostan, who expressed a great admiration of Johnson. 'I do not care (said he,) on what subject Johnson talks; but I love better to hear him talk than any body. He either gives you new thoughts, or a new colouring. It is a shame to the nation that he has not been more liberally rewarded. Had I been George the Third, and thought as he did about America, I would have given Johnson three hundred a year for his "Taxation no Tyranny," alone.' I repeated this, and Johnson was much pleased with such praise from such a man as Orme.

At Mr. Dilly's to-day were Mrs. Knowles, the ingenious Quaker lady,[1] Miss Seward, the poetess of Lichfield, the Reverend Dr. Mayo, and the Rev. Mr. Beresford, Tutor to the Duke of Bedford. Before dinner Dr. Johnson seized upon Mr. Charles Sheridan's[2] 'Account of the late Revolution in Sweden,' and seemed to read it ravenously, as if he devoured it, which was to all appearance his method of studying. 'He knows how to read better than any one (says Mrs. Knowles); he gets at the substance of a book directly; he tears out the heart of it.' He kept it wrapt up in the tablecloth in his lap during the time of dinner, from an avidity to have one entertainment in readiness, when he should have finished another; resembling (if I may use so coarse a simile) a dog who holds a bone in his paws in

a *It was no Mistake . . . as* Pictures *they are futile: so are Miss Linwood's: The Moth, the Sunshine every thing may destroy the beautiful Work—Alas! 1817* [H]

on the Contrary it is a plain f . . . but Mr. Lysons said it should be sutile—I car'd not which it was; I knew he wrote futile. Against Mrs. Knowles I could have no malice, I knew her not. [I]

[1] Dr. Johnson, describing her needlework in one of his letters to Mrs. Thrale, vol. i. p. 326, uses the learned word *sutile;* which Mrs. Thrale has mistaken, and made the phrase injurious by writing '*futile* pictures.'[a]

[2] [The elder brother of R. B. Sheridan, Esq. He died in 1806. MALONE.]

reserve, while he eats something else which has been thrown to him.[a]

The subject of cookery having been very naturally introduced at a table where Johnson, who boasted of the niceness of his palate, owned that 'he always found a good dinner,' he said, 'I could write a better book of cookery than has ever yet been written; it should be a book upon philosophical principles. Pharmacy is now made much more simple. Cookery may be made so too. A prescription which is now compounded of five ingredients, had formerly fifty in it. So in cookery, if the nature of the ingredients be well known, much fewer will do. Then, as you cannot make bad meat good, I would tell what is the best butcher's meat, the best beef, the best pieces; how to choose young fowls; the proper seasons of different vegetables; and then how to roast and boil and compound.' DILLY. 'Mrs. Glasse's "Cookery," which is the best, was written by Dr. Hill. Half the trade[1] know this.' JOHNSON. 'Well, Sir. This shews how much better the subject of cookery may be treated by a philosopher. I doubt if the book be written by Dr. Hill; for, in Mrs. Glasse's "Cookery," which I have looked into, salt-petre and sal-prunella are spoken of as different substances, whereas sal-prunella is only salt-petre burnt on charcoal; and Hill could not be ignorant of this.[b] However, as the greatest part of such a book is made by transcription, this mistake may have been carelessly adopted. But you shall see what a Book of Cookery I shall make: I shall agree with Mr. Dilly for the copy-right.' MISS SEWARD. 'That would be Hercules with the distaff indeed.' JOHNSON. 'No, Madam. Women can spin very well; but they cannot make a good book of Cookery.'

JOHNSON. 'O! Mr. Dilly—you must know that an English Benedictine Monk at Paris[c] has translated "The Duke of Berwick's Memoirs," from the original French, and has sent them to me to sell. I offered them to Strahan, who sent them back with this answer:—"That the first book he had published was the Duke of Berwick's Life, by

Marginal notes:

[a] *just so.* [H]

[b] *Bravo Johnson!* [H]

underlined: *Benedictine Monk* [I]
[c] *I think Mrs. Gibbes conversed with this very Man at Paris in this very Year 1817.* [H]
I suppose Wilkes, whom they called No. 45 in the Convent—Father Prior was a Mr. Cowley—it was not him I shd: think. [I]

[1] As Physicians are called *the Faculty*, and Counsellors at Law *the Profession*, the Booksellers of London are denominated *the Trade*. Johnson disapproved of these denominations.

which he had lost: and he hated the name."—Now I honestly tell you, that Strahan has refused them; but I also honestly tell you, that he did it upon no principle, for he never looked into them.' DILLY. 'Are they well translated, Sir?' JOHNSON. 'Why, Sir, very well—in a style very current and very clear. I have written to the Benedictine to give me an answer upon two points—What evidence is there that the letters are authentick? (for if they are not authentick, they are nothing;)—And how long will it be before the original French is published? For if the French edition is not to appear for a considerable time, the translation will be almost as valuable as an original book. They will make two volumes in octavo; and I have undertaken to correct every sheet as it comes from the press.' Mr. Dilly desired to see them, and said he would send for them. He asked Dr. Johnson, if he would write a Preface to them. JOHNSON. 'No, Sir. The Benedictines were very kind to me, and I'll do what I undertook to do; but I will not mingle my name with them. I am to gain nothing by them. I'll turn them loose upon the world, and let them take their chance.' DR. MAYO. 'Pray, Sir, are Ganganelli's letters authentick?' JOHNSON. 'No, Sir. Voltaire put the same question to the editor of them, that I did to Macpherson—Where are the originals?'

Mrs. Knowles affected to complain that men had much more liberty allowed them than women. JOHNSON. 'Why, Madam, women have all the liberty they should wish to have. We have all the labour and the danger, and the women all the advantage. We go to sea, we build houses, we do every thing, in short, to pay our court to the women.' MRS. KNOWLES. 'The Doctor reasons very wittily, but not convincingly. Now, take the instance of building; the mason's wife, if she is ever seen in liquor, is ruined; the mason may get himself drunk as often as he pleases, with little loss of character; nay, may let his wife and children starve.' JOHNSON. 'Madam, you must consider, if the mason does get himself drunk, and let his wife and children starve, the parish will oblige him to find security for their maintenance. We have different modes of restraining evil. Stocks for the men, a ducking-stool for women, and a pound for beasts. If we require more perfection from women than from ourselves, it is doing them honour. And women have not the same temptations that we have; they may always live in virtuous company; men must mix in the world indiscriminately. If a woman has no inclination to do what is wrong, being secured from it is no restraint to her. I am at liberty to walk into the Thames; but if I were to try it, my friends would restrain me in Bedlam, and I should be obliged to them.' MRS. KNOWLES. 'Still, Doctor, I cannot help thinking it a hardship that more indulgence is allowed to men than to women. It gives a superiority to men, to which I do not see how they are entitled.' JOHNSON. 'It is plain, Madam, one or other must have the superiority. As Shakspeare says, "If two men ride on a horse, one must ride behind."'

underlined:
panniers, the horse [H]

DILLY. 'I suppose, Sir, Mrs. Knowles would have them ride in panniers, one on each side.'[a] JOHNSON. 'Then, Sir, the horse would throw them both.'[b] MRS. KNOWLES.

[a] *comical.* [H]

[b] *'Your Horse! your Horse is an Ass Sir' from Congreve would have been the proper Reply.* [H]

'Well, I hope that in another world the sexes will be equal.' BOSWELL. 'That is being too ambitious, Madam. *We* might as well desire to be equal with the angels. We shall all, I hope, be happy in a future state, but we must not expect to be all happy in the same degree. It is enough, if we be happy according to our several capacities. A worthy carman will get to heaven as well as Sir Isaac Newton.

underlined:
carman, Isaac Newton [H]

Yet, though equally good, they will not have the same degrees of happiness.'[c] JOHNSON. 'Probably not.'[1]

[c] *I should expect the Carman to sit higher—if their Piety & Virtue were equal; The Knight had Opportunities of learning his Duty better, and Dick had Temptations which could not have assail'd Sir Isaac. No, No; Aristocracy will end on this Side the great Gulph I hope. Jesus Christ came to preach to the Poor, not to the Philosophers.* [H]

Upon this subject I had once before sounded him, by mentioning the late Reverend Mr. Brown, of Utrecht's, image; that a great and small glass, though equally full, did not hold an equal quantity; which he threw out to refute David Hume's saying, that a little miss, going to dance at a ball, in a fine new dress, was as happy as a great oratour, after having made an eloquent and applauded speech. After some thought, Johnson said,[2] 'I come over to the parson.' As an instance of coincidence of thinking, Mr. Dilly told me, that Dr. King, a late dissenting minister in London, said to him, upon the happiness in a

[1] [See on this question Bishop Hall's Epistles, Dec. iii. Epist. 6, 'Of the different degrees of heavenly glory, and of our mutual knowledge of each other above.' MALONE.]

[2] [See vol. i. p. 361, where also this subject is discussed. MALONE.]

future state of good men of different capacities, 'A pail does not hold so much as a tub; but, if it be equally full, it has no reason to complain. Every Saint in heaven will have as much happiness as he can hold.' Mr. Dilly thought this a clear, though a familiar illustration of the phrase, 'One star differeth from another in brightness.'

Dr. Mayo having asked Johnson's opinion of Soame Jenyns's 'View of the Internal Evidence of the Christian Religion;'—JOHNSON. 'I think it a pretty book; not very theological indeed; and there seems to be an affectation of ease and carelessness, as if it were not suitable to his character to be very serious about the matter.' BOSWELL. 'He may have intended this to introduce his book the better among genteel people, who might be unwilling to read too grave a treatise. There is a general levity in the age. We have physicians now with bag-wigs; may we not have airy divines, at least somewhat less solemn in their appearance than they used to be?' JOHNSON. 'Jenyns might mean as you say.' BOSWELL. '*You* should like his book, Mrs. Knowles, as it maintains, as you *friends* do, that courage is not a Christian virtue.' MRS. KNOWLES. 'Yes, indeed, I like him there; but I cannot agree with him, that friendship is not a Christian virtue.' JOHNSON. 'Why, Madam, strictly speaking, he is right. All friendship is preferring the interest of a friend, to the neglect, or, perhaps, against the interest of others; so that an old Greek said, "He that has *friends* has *no friend*." Now Christianity recommends universal benevolence,—to consider all men as our brethren; which is contrary to the virtue of friendship, as described by the ancient philosophers. Surely, Madam, your sect must approve of this; for, you call all men *friends*.' MRS. KNOWLES. 'We are commanded to do good to all men,[a] "but especially to them who are of the household of Faith."' JOHNSON. 'Well, Madam. The household of Faith is wide enough.' MRS. KNOWLES. 'But, Doctor, our Saviour had twelve Apostles, yet there was *one* whom he *loved*. John was called "the disciple whom JESUS loved."'[b] JOHNSON. (with eyes sparkling benignantly) 'Very well, indeed, Madam. You have said very well.' BOSWELL. 'A fine application. Pray, Sir, had you ever thought of it?' JOHNSON. 'I had not, Sir.'[c]

[a] *besides* this *Text* 'Now *Jesus loved Mary & her Sister & Lazarus.*' ... *& when he saw the Distress'd Family Jesus wept.* [1]

[b] *and Jesus loved Martha & her Sister, & Lazarus.* [H]

underlined: *I had not, Sir* [H]

[c] *I wonder, & it escaped Porteus too.* [H]

From this pleasing subject, he, I know not how or why, made a sudden transition to one upon which he was a violent aggressor; for he said, 'I am willing to love all mankind, *except an American:*' and his inflammable corruption bursting into horrid fire, he 'breathed out threatenings and slaughter;' calling them, 'Rascals— Robbers—Pirates;' and exclaiming, he'd 'burn and destroy them.' Miss Seward, looking to him with mild but steady astonishment, said, 'Sir, this is an instance that we are always most violent against those whom we have injured.'—He was irritated still more by this delicate and keen reproach; and roared out another tremendous volley, which one might fancy could be heard across the Atlantick. During this tempest I sat in great uneasiness, lamenting his heat of temper; till, by degrees, I diverted his attention to other topicks.

DR. MAYO, (to Dr. Johnson.) 'Pray, Sir, have you read Edwards, of New England, on Grace?' JOHNSON. 'No, Sir.' BOSWELL. 'It puzzled me so much as to the freedom of the human will, by stating, with wonderful acute ingenuity, our being actuated by a series of motives which we cannot resist, that the only relief I had was to forget it.' MAYO. 'But he makes the proper distinction between moral and physical necessity.' BOSWELL. 'Alas, Sir, they come both to the same thing. You may be bound as hard by chains when covered by leather, as when the iron appears. The argument for the moral necessity of human actions is always, I observe, fortified by supposing universal prescience to be one of the attributes of the Deity.' JOHNSON. 'You are surer that you are free, than you are of prescience; you are surer that you can lift up your finger or not as you please, than you are of any conclusion from a deduction of reasoning. But let us consider a little the objection from prescience. It is certain I am either to go home to-night or not; that does not prevent my freedom.' BOSWELL. 'That it is certain you are *either* to go home or not, does not prevent your freedom: because the liberty of choice between the two is compatible with that certainty. But if *one* of these events be certain *now*, you have no *future* power of volition. If it be certain you are to go home to-night, you *must* go home.' JOHNSON. 'If I am

well acquainted with a man, I can judge with great probability how he will act in any case, without his being
restrained by my judging. GOD may have this probability
increased to certainty.' BOSWELL. 'When it is increased
to *certainty*, freedom ceases, because that cannot be certainly foreknown, which is not certain at the time; but if
it be certain at the time, it is a contradiction in terms to
maintain that there can be afterwards any *contingency*
dependent upon the exercise of will or any thing else.'
JOHNSON. 'All theory is against the freedom of the will;[a]   [a] *certainly* [H]
all experience for it.'—I did not push the subject any
farther. I was glad to find him so mild in discussing a
question of the most abstract nature, involved with
theological tenets, which he generally would not suffer to
be in any degree opposed.[1]

He, as usual, defended luxury: 'You cannot spend   marginal line:
money in luxury without doing good to the poor. Nay,   *He, as . . . the poor*
you do more good to them by spending it in luxury, you   [H]
make them exert industry, whereas by giving it, you keep
them idle. I own, indeed, there may be more virtue in
giving it immediately in charity, than in spending it in
luxury; though there may be pride in that too.' Miss
Seward asked, if this was not Mandeville's doctrine of
'private vices publick benefits.' JOHNSON. 'The fallacy
of that book is, that Mandeville defines neither vices nor
benefits. He reckons among vices every thing that gives
pleasure. He takes the narrowest system of morality,
monastick morality, which holds pleasure itself to be a   underlined:
vice, such as eating salt with our fish, because it makes it   *perfectly innocent* [H]
eat better; and he reckons wealth as a publick benefit,   [b] *Is it perfectly Inno-*
which is by no means always true. Pleasure of itself is not   *cent to spend 50 L. in*
a vice. Having a garden, which we all know to be per-   *fine Shrubs wch. might*
fectly innocent, is a great pleasure.[b] At the same time, in   *make 5 families happy?*
this state of being there are many pleasures vices, which   [H]
however are so immediately agreeable that we can hardly   [c] *So it will.* [H]
abstain from them. The happiness of Heaven will be, that   [d] *I am* not at all displeasure and virtue will be perfectly consistent.[c] Mandeville   *turbed by it: I know*
                                                            & feel that 'tis the
                                                            same Thing to me: *I*
                                                            must work out my Sal-
[1] If any of my readers are disturbed by this thorny question,[d] I beg leave   *vation with Fear &*
to recommend to them Letter 69 of Montesquieu's *Lettres Persannes;* and the   *Trembling, whether I*
late Mr. John Palmer of Islington's Answer to Dr. Priestley's mechanical   *am, or am not Predes-*
arguments for what he absurdly calls 'Philosophical necessity.'   *tinated to it:—It comes*
                                                            to the same Thing. [I]

puts the case of a man who gets drunk at an alehouse; and says it is a publick benefit, because so much money is got by it to the publick. But it must be considered, that all the good gained by this, through the gradation of alehouse-keeper, brewer, maltster, and farmer, is over-balanced by the evil caused to the man and his family by his getting drunk. This is the way to try what is vicious, by ascertaining whether more evil than good is produced by it upon the whole, which is the case in all vice. It may happen that good is produced by vice, but not as vice; for instance, a robber may take money from its owner, and give it to one who will make a better use of it. Here is good produced; but not by the robbery as robbery, but as translation of property. I read Mandeville forty, or, I believe, fifty years ago. He did not puzzle me; he opened my views into real life very much. No, it is clear that the happiness of society depends on virtue. In Sparta, theft was allowed by general consent; theft, therefore, was *there* not a crime, but then there was no security; and what a life must they have had, when there was no security. Without truth there must be a dissolution of society. As it is, there is so little truth, that we are almost afraid to trust our ears; but how should we be, if falsehood were multiplied ten times! Society is held together by communication and information; and I remember this remark of Sir Thomas Brown's, "Do the devils lie? No; for then Hell could not subsist."'

a *Hannah More* [H]
Hannah More I think [I]

b *She wrote Odes (in those Days) to Garrick's Dog Dragon—* [H]

Talking of Miss ————,[a] a literary lady, he said, 'I was obliged to speak to Miss Reynolds, to let her know that I desired she would not flatter me so much.' Somebody now observed, 'She flatters Garrick.'[b] JOHNSON. 'She is in the right to flatter Garrick. She is in the right for two reasons; first, because she has the world with her, who have been praising Garrick these thirty years; and secondly, because she is rewarded for it by Garrick. Why should she flatter *me?* I can do nothing for her. Let her carry her praise to a better market. (Then turning to Mrs. Knowles.) You, Madam, have been flattering me all the evening; I wish you would give Boswell a little now. If you knew his merit as well as I do, you would say a great deal; he is the best travelling companion in the world.'

Somebody mentioned the Reverend Mr. Mason's prosecution of Mr. Murray, the bookseller, for having inserted
in a collection of 'Gray's Poems,' only fifty lines, of which
Mr. Mason had still the exclusive property, under the
statute of Queen Anne; and that Mr. Mason has persevered, notwithstanding his being requested to name his
own terms of compensation.[1] Johnson signified his displeasure at Mr. Mason's conduct very strongly; but
added, by way of shewing that he was not surprized
at it, 'Mason's a Whig.' MRS. KNOWLES, (not hearing
distinctly:) 'What! a Prig, Sir?' JOHNSON. 'Worse,
Madam; a Whig! But he is both!'

I expressed a horrour at the thought of death. MRS.
KNOWLES. 'Nay, thou should'st not[a] have a horrour for
what is the gate of life.' JOHNSON. (standing upon the
hearth rolling about, with a serious, solemn, and somewhat gloomy air:) 'No rational man can die without
uneasy apprehension.' MRS. KNOWLES. 'The Scriptures
tell us, "The righteous shall have *hope* in his death."'[b]
JOHNSON. 'Yes, Madam; that is, he shall not have
despair. But, consider, his hope of salvation must be
founded on the terms on which it is promised that the
mediation of our SAVIOUR shall be applied to us,—
namely, obedience; and where obedience has failed, then,
as suppletory to it, repentance. But what man can say that
his obedience has been such, as he would approve of in
another, or even in himself upon close examination, or
that his repentance has not been such as to require being
repented of? No man can be sure that his obedience and
repentance will obtain salvation.' MRS. KNOWLES. 'But
divine intimation of acceptance may be made to the soul.'
JOHNSON. 'Madam, it may; but I should not think the
better of a man who should tell me on his deathbed, he
was sure of salvation. A man cannot be sure himself that
he has divine intimation of acceptance; much less can he
make others sure that he has it.' BOSWELL. 'Then, Sir,
we must be contented to acknowledge that death is a
terrible thing.' JOHNSON. 'Yes, Sir. I have made no
approaches to a state which can look on it as not terrible.'

[1] See 'A Letter to W. Mason, A. M. from J. Murray, Bookseller in London;'
2d edition, p. 20.

underlined:
not [I]

[a] *Then you see She
did think courage a
Xtian Virtue* [I]

[b] *but who are* the
Righteous? [H]

MRS. KNOWLES. (seeming to enjoy a pleasing serenity in the persuasion of benignant divine light:) 'Does not St. Paul say, "I have fought the good fight of faith, I have finished my course; henceforth is laid up for me a crown of life"?' JOHNSON. 'Yes, Madam; but here was a man inspired, a man who had been converted by supernatural interposition.' BOSWELL. 'In prospect death is dreadful; but in fact we find that people die easy.' JOHNSON. 'Why, Sir, most people have not *thought* much of the matter, so cannot *say* much, and it is supposed they die easy. Few believe it certain they are then to die; and those who do, set themselves to behave with resolution, as a man does who is going to be hanged:—he is not the less unwilling to be hanged.' MISS SEWARD. 'There is one mode of the fear of death, which is certainly absurd: and that is the dread of annihilation, which is only a pleasing sleep without a dream.' JOHNSON. 'It is neither pleasing, nor sleep; it is nothing. Now mere existence is so much better than nothing, that one would rather exist even in pain, than not exist.' BOSWELL. 'If annihilation be nothing, then existing in pain is not a comparative state, but is a positive evil, which I cannot think we should choose. I must be allowed to differ here, and it would lessen the hope of a future state founded on the argument, that the Supreme Being, who is good as he is great, will hereafter compensate for our present sufferings in this life. For if existence, such as we have it here, be comparatively a good, we have no reason to complain, though no more of it should be given to us. But if our only state of existence were in this world, then we might with some reason complain that we are so dissatisfied with our enjoyments compared with our desires.' JOHNSON. 'The lady confounds annihilation, which is nothing, with the apprehension of it, which is dreadful. It is in the apprehension of it that the horrour of annihilation consists.'

Of John Wesley, he said, 'He can talk well on any subject.' BOSWELL. 'Pray, Sir, what has he made of his story of a ghost?' JOHNSON. 'Why, Sir, he believes it; but not on sufficient authority. He did not take time enough to examine the girl. It was at Newcastle, where the ghost was said to have appeared to a young woman several

queried:
existence is so much better etc. [H]

times, mentioning something about the right to an old house, advising application to be made to an attorney, which was done; and, at the same time, saying the attorney would do nothing, which proved to be the fact. "This, (says John) is a proof that a ghost knows our thoughts." Now (laughing) it is not necessary to know our thoughts, to tell that an attorney will sometimes do nothing. Charles Wesley, who is a more stationary man, does not believe the story. I am sorry that John did not take more pains to enquire into the evidence for it.' MISS SEWARD, (with an incredulous smile:) 'What, Sir! about a ghost?' JOHNSON, (with solemn vehemence:) 'Yes, Madam: this is a question which, after five thousand years, is yet undecided; a question, whether in theology or philosophy, one of the most important that can come before the human understanding.'

Mrs. Knowles mentioned, as a proselyte to Quakerism, Miss ————, a young lady well known to Dr. Johnson, for whom he had shewn much affection; while she ever had, and still retained, a great respect for him. Mrs. Knowles at the same time took an opportunity of letting him know 'that the amiable young creature was sorry at finding that he was offended at her leaving the Church of England and embracing a simpler faith;' and, in the gentlest and most persuasive manner, solicited his kind indulgence for what was sincerely a matter of conscience. JOHNSON, (frowning very angrily,) 'Madam, she is an odious wench. She could not have any proper conviction that it was her duty to change her religion, which is the most important of all subjects, and should be studied with all care, and with all the helps we can get. She knew no more of the Church which she left, and that which she embraced, than she did of the difference between the Copernican and Ptolemaick systems.'[a] MRS. KNOWLES. 'She had the New Testament before her.' JOHNSON. 'Madam, she could not understand the New Testament, the most difficult book in the world, for which the study of a life is required.' MRS. KNOWLES. 'It is clear as to essentials.' JOHNSON. 'But not as to controversial points. The heathens were easily converted, because they had nothing to give up; but we ought not, without very strong

[a] *Very True—I dare say She had no settled Notions about the Matter.* [H]

conviction indeed, to desert the religion in which we have
been educated. That is the religion given you, the religion
in which it may be said Providence has placed you. If you
live conscientiously in that religion, you may be safe. But
errour is dangerous indeed, if you err when you choose a
religion for yourself.' MRS. KNOWLES. 'Must we then
go by implicit faith?' JOHNSON. 'Why, Madam, the
greatest part of our knowledge is implicit faith, and as to
religion, have we heard all that a disciple of Confucius, all
that a Mahometan, can say for himself?' He then rose
again into passion, and attacked the young proselyte in
the severest terms of reproach, so that both the ladies
seemed to be much shocked.[1]

We remained together till it was pretty late. Notwithstanding occasional explosions of violence, we were all
delighted upon the whole with Johnson. I compared him
at this time to a warm West-Indian climate, where you
have a bright sun, quick vegetation, luxuriant foliage,
luscious fruits; but where the same heat sometimes produces thunder, lightning, and earthquakes, in a terrible
degree.

April 17, being Good-Friday, I waited on Johnson, as
usual. I observed at breakfast that although it was a part
of his abstemious discipline on this most solemn fast, to
take no milk in his tea, yet when Mrs. Desmoulins inad-
vertently poured it in, he did not reject it. I talked of the
strange indecision of mind, and imbecility in the common
occurrences of life, which we may observe in some people.
JOHNSON. 'Why, Sir, I am in the habit of getting others

[1] Mrs. Knowles, not satisfied with the fame of her needlework, the 'sutile
pictures' mentioned by Johnson, in which she has indeed displayed much
dexterity, nay, with the fame of reasoning better than women generally do,
as I have fairly shewn her to have done, communicated to me a Dialogue of
considerable length, which after many years had elapsed, she wrote down
as having passed between Dr. Johnson and her at this interview. As I had
not the least recollection of it, and did not find the smallest trace of it in my
Record taken at the time, I could not in consistency with my firm regard to
authenticity, insert it in my work. It has, however, been published in 'The
Gentleman's Magazine' for June 1791. It chiefly relates to the principles of
the sect called Quakers; and no doubt the lady appears to have greatly the
advantage of Dr. Johnson in argument as well as expression. From what I
have now stated, and from the internal evidence of the paper itself, any one
who may have the curiosity to peruse it, will judge whether it was wrong in
me to reject it, however willing to gratify Mrs. Knowles.

to do things for me.' BOSWELL. 'What, Sir! have you that weakness?' JOHNSON. 'Yes, Sir. But I always think afterwards I should have done better for myself.'

I told him that at a gentleman's house where there was thought to be such extravagance or bad management, that he[a] was living much beyond his income, his lady had objected to the cutting of a pickled mango, and that I had taken an opportunity to ask the price of it, and found it was only two shillings; so here was a very poor saving. JOHNSON. 'Sir, that is the blundering œconomy of a narrow understanding. It is stopping one hole in a sieve.'[b]

I expressed some inclination to publish an account of my *Travels* upon the continent of Europe, for which I had a variety of materials collected. JOHNSON. 'I do not say, Sir, you may not publish your travels; but I give you my opinion, that you would lessen yourself by it. What can you tell of countries so well known as those upon the continent of Europe, which you have visited?' BOSWELL. 'But I can give an entertaining narrative, with many incidents, anecdotes, *jeux d'esprit*, and remarks, so as to make very pleasant reading.' JOHNSON. 'Why, Sir, most modern travellers in Europe who have published their travels, have been laughed at: I would not have you added to the number.[1] The world is now not contented to be merely entertained by a traveller's narrative; they want to learn something. Now some of my friends asked me, why I did not give some account of my travels in France. The reason is plain; intelligent readers had seen more of France than I had. *You* might have liked my travels in France, and THE CLUB might have liked them; but upon the whole, there would have been more ridicule than good produced by them.' BOSWELL. 'I cannot agree with you, Sir. People would like to read what you say of any thing. Suppose a face has been painted by fifty painters before; still we love to see it done by Sir Joshua.' JOHNSON. 'True, Sir, but Sir Joshua cannot paint a face when he has not time to look on it.' BOSWELL. 'Sir, a sketch of any sort by him is valuable. And, Sir, to talk to you in your own style (raising my voice, and shaking my

---

[1] I believe, however, I shall follow my own opinion; for the world has shewn a very flattering partiality to my writings, on many occasions.[c]

marginal line:
JOHNSON. '*Yes . . .
for myself* [H]

[a] *I suppose Langton*
[H]

marginal line:
*narrow understanding
. . . a sieve* [H]

[b] *That's very comical
& very just.—and so it
is stopping one Hole in
a Sieve.* [I]

[c] *So it has truly.* [I]

head,) you *should* have given us your travels in France. I am *sure* I am right, and *there's an end on't.*'

I said to him that it was certainly true, as my friend Dempster had observed in his letter to me upon the subject, that a great part of what was in his 'Journey to the Western Islands of Scotland,' had been in his mind before he left London. JOHNSON. 'Why, yes, Sir, the topicks were; and books of travels will be good in proportion to what a man has previously in his mind; his knowing what to observe; his power of contrasting one mode of life with another. As the Spanish proverb says, "He, who would bring home the wealth of the Indies, must carry the wealth of the Indies with him." So it is in travelling; a man must carry knowledge with him, if he would bring home knowledge.' BOSWELL. 'The proverb, I suppose, Sir, means, he must carry a large stock with him to trade with.' JOHNSON. 'Yes, Sir.'

It was a delightful day: as we walked to St. Clement's church, I again remarked that Fleet-street was the most cheerful scene in the world. 'Fleet-street (said I,) is in my mind more delightful than Tempé.' JOHNSON. 'Ay, Sir; but let it be compared with Mull.'

There was a very numerous congregation to-day at St. Clement's church, which Dr. Johnson said he observed with pleasure.

And now I am to give a pretty full account of one of the most curious incidents in Johnson's life, of which he himself has made the following minute on this day; 'In my return from church, I was accosted by Edwards, an old fellow-collegian, who had not seen me since 1729. He knew me, and asked if I remembered one Edwards; I did not at first recollect the name, but gradually as we walked along, recovered it, and told him a conversation that had passed at an alehouse between us. My purpose is to continue our acquaintance.'[1]

It was in Butcher-row that this meeting happened. Mr. Edwards, who was a decent-looking elderly man in grey clothes, and a wig of many curls, accosted Johnson with familiar confidence, knowing who he was, while Johnson returned his salutation with a courteous formality, as to a

marginal line:
Tempé.'JOHNSON...
with Mull [H]

[1] Prayers and Meditations, p. 164.

stranger. But as soon as Edwards had brought to his recollection their having been at Pembroke-College together
nine-and-forty years ago, he seemed much pleased, asked
where he lived, and said he should be glad to see him in
Bolt-court. EDWARDS. 'Ah, Sir! we are old men now.'
JOHNSON, (who never liked to think of being old:) 'Don't
let us discourage one another.' EDWARDS. 'Why, Doctor,
you look stout and hearty, I am happy to see you so; for
the newspapers told us you were very ill.' JOHNSON. 'Ay,
Sir, they are always telling lies of *us old fellows.*'

Wishing to be present at more of so singular a conversation as that between two fellow-collegians, who had
lived forty years in London without ever having chanced
to meet, I whispered to Mr. Edwards that Dr. Johnson
was going home, and that he had better accompany him
now. So Edwards walked along with us, I eagerly assisting
to keep up the conversation. Mr. Edwards informed Dr.
Johnson that he had practised long as a solicitor in Chancery, but that he now lived in the country upon a little
farm, about sixty acres, just by Stevenage in Hertford-
shire, and that he came to London (to Barnard's Inn,
No. 6,) generally twice a week. Johnson appearing to me
in a reverie, Mr. Edwards addressed himself to me, and
expatiated on the pleasure of living in the country.
BOSWELL. 'I have no notion of this, Sir. What you have
to entertain you, is, I think, exhausted in half an hour.'
EDWARDS. 'What? don't you love to have hope realized?
I see my grass, and my corn, and my trees growing. Now,
for instance, I am curious to see if this frost has not nipped
my fruit-trees.' JOHNSON, (who we did not imagine was
attending:) 'You find, Sir, you have fears as well as hopes.'
—So well did he see the whole, when another saw but
the half of a subject.

When we got to Dr. Johnson's house, and were seated
in his library, the dialogue went on admirably. EDWARDS.
'Sir, I remember you would not let us say *prodigious* at
College. For even then, Sir, (turning to me,) he was
delicate in language, and we all feared him.'[1] JOHNSON,

----

[1] Johnson said to me afterwards, 'Sir, they respected me for my literature;
and yet it was not great but by comparison. Sir, it is amazing how little
literature there is in the world.'

(to Edwards:) 'From your having practised the law long, Sir, I presume you must be rich.' EDWARDS. 'No, Sir: I got a good deal of money; but I had a number of poor relations to whom I gave a great part of it.' JOHNSON. 'Sir, you have been rich in the most valuable sense of the word.' EDWARDS. 'But I shall not die rich.' JOHNSON. 'Nay, sure, Sir, it is better to *live* rich, than to *die* rich.' EDWARDS. 'I wish I had continued at College.' JOHNSON. 'Why do you wish that, Sir?' EDWARDS. 'Because I think I should have had a much easier life than mine has been. I should have been a parson, and had a good living, like Bloxham and several others, and lived comfortably.' JOHNSON. 'Sir, the life of a parson, of a conscientious clergyman, is not easy. I have always considered a clergyman as the father of a larger family than he is able to maintain. I would rather have Chancery suits upon my hands than the cure of souls. No, Sir, I do not envy a clergyman's life as an easy life, nor do I envy the clergyman who makes it an easy life.'—Here taking himself up all of a sudden, he exclaimed, 'O! Mr. Edwards! I'll convince you that I recollect you. Do you remember our drinking together at an alehouse near Pembroke gate? At that time, you told me of the Eton boy, who, when verses on our SAVIOUR's turning water into wine were prescribed as an exercise, brought up a single line, which was highly admired:

marginal line: *time, you . . . when verses* [H]

"Vidit et erubuit lympha pudica DEUM,"[1]

marginal line: *Videt et . . . pudica* DEUM [H]

and I told you of another fine line in "Camden's Remains,"

[1] [This line has frequently been attributed to Dryden, when a King's Scholar at Westminster. But neither Eton nor Westminster have in truth any claim to it, the line being borrowed, with a slight change, (as Mr. Bindley has observed to me), from an Epigram by Richard Crashaw, which was published in his EPIGRAMMATA SACRA, first printed at Cambridge without the authour's name, in 1634, 8vo.—The original is much more elegant than the copy, the water being personified, and the word on which the point of the Epigram turns, being reserved to the close of the line:

'JOANN. 2.

'Aquæ in vinum versæ.

'Unde rubor vestris et non sua purpura lymphis?
Quæ rosa mirantes tam nova mutat aquas?
Numen, convivæ, præsens agnoscite numen,
Nympha pudica DEUM vidit, et *erubuit*.' MALONE.]

an eulogy upon one of our Kings, who was succeeded by
his son, a prince of equal merit:

"Mira cano, Sol occubuit, nox nulla secuta est."'

marginal line:
*Mira cano . . . secuta
est* [H]

EDWARDS. 'You are a philosopher, Dr. Johnson. I
have tried too in my time to be a philosopher; but, I don't
know how, cheerfulness was always breaking in.'—Mr.
Burke, Sir Joshua Reynolds, Mr. Courtenay, Mr. Malone,
and, indeed, all the eminent men to whom I have mentioned this, have thought it an exquisite trait of character.
The truth is, that philosophy, like religion, is too generally
supposed to be hard and severe, at least so grave as to
exclude all gaiety.

EDWARDS. 'I have been twice married, Doctor. You,
I suppose, have never known what it was to have a wife.'
JOHNSON. 'Sir, I have known what it was to have a wife,
and (in a solemn tender faultering tone) I have known
what it was to *lose a wife*.—It had almost broke my heart.'

EDWARDS. 'How do you live, Sir? For my part, I must
have my regular meals, and a glass of good wine. I find
I require it.' JOHNSON. 'I now drink no wine, Sir. Early
in life I drank wine: for many years I drank none. I then
for some years drank a great deal.' EDWARDS. 'Some
hogsheads, I warrant you.' JOHNSON. 'I then had a severe
illness, and left it off, and I have never begun it again. I
never felt any difference upon myself from eating one
thing rather than another, nor from one kind of weather
rather than another. There are people, I believe, who feel
a difference; but I am not one of them. And as to regular
meals, I have fasted from the Sunday's dinner to the
Tuesday's dinner, without any inconvenience. I believe
it is best to eat just as one is hungry: but a man who is in
business, or a man who has a family, must have stated
meals. I am a straggler. I may leave this town and go to
Grand Cairo, without being missed here, or observed
there.' EDWARDS. 'Don't you eat supper, Sir?' JOHN-
SON. 'No, Sir.' EDWARDS. 'For my part, now, I consider
supper as a turnpike through which one must pass, in
order to get to bed.'[1]

queried:
I am not etc. [H]

[1] I am not absolutely sure but this was my own suggestion, though it is
truly in the character of Edwards.

JOHNSON. 'You are a lawyer, Mr. Edwards. Lawyers know life practically. A bookish man should always have them to converse with. They have what he wants.' EDWARDS. 'I am grown old: I am sixty-five.' JOHNSON. 'I shall be sixty-eight next birth-day. Come, Sir, drink water, and put in for a hundred.'

Mr. Edwards mentioned a gentleman who had left his whole fortune to Pembroke College. JOHNSON. 'Whether to leave one's whole fortune to a College be right, must depend upon circumstances. I would leave the interest of the fortune I bequeathed to a College to my relations or my friends, for their lives. It is the same thing to a College, which is a permanent society, whether it gets the money now or twenty years hence; and I would wish to make my relations or friends feel the benefit of it.'

This interview confirmed my opinion of Johnson's most humane and benevolent heart. His cordial and placid behaviour to an old fellow collegian, a man so different from himself; and his telling him that he would go down to his farm and visit him, shewed a kindness of disposition very rare at an advanced age. He observed, 'how wonderful it was that they had both been in London forty years, without having ever once met, and both walkers in the street too!' Mr. Edwards, when going away, again recurred to his consciousness of senility, and looking full in Johnson's face, said to him, 'You'll find in Dr. Young,

"O my coevals! remnants of yourselves."'

marginal line:
Johnson did . . . off seemingly [H]

Johnson did not relish this at all; but shook his head with impatience. Edwards walked off seemingly highly pleased with the honour of having been thus noticed by Dr. Johnson. When he was gone, I said to Johnson, I thought him but a weak man. JOHNSON. 'Why, yes, Sir. Here is a man who has passed through life without experience: yet I would rather have him with me than a more sensible

marginal line:
who will . . . Dr. Johnson [H]

man who will not talk readily. This man is always willing to say what he has to say.' Yet Dr. Johnson had himself by no means that willingness which he praised so much, and I think so justly: for who has not felt the painful effect of the dreary void, when there is a total silence in a company, for any length of time; or, which is as bad, or perhaps worse, when the conversation is with difficulty kept up by a perpetual effort?

Johnson once observed to me, 'Tom Tyers described me the best: "Sir, (said he,) you are like a ghost: you never speak till you are spoken to."'

The gentleman whom he thus familiarly mentioned, was Mr. Thomas Tyers, son of Mr. Jonathan Tyers, the founder of that excellent place of publick amusement, Vauxhall Gardens, which must ever be an estate to its proprietor, as it is peculiarly adapted to the taste of the English nation; there being a mixture of curious shew,—gay exhibition,—musick, vocal and instrumental, not too refined for the general ear;—for all which only a shilling is paid;[1] and, though last, not least, good eating and drinking for those who choose to purchase that regale. Mr. Thomas Tyers was bred to the law; but having a handsome fortune, vivacity of temper, and eccentricity of mind, he could not confine himself to the regularity of practice. He therefore ran about the world with a pleasant carelessness, amusing every body by his desultory conversation. He abounded in anecdote, but was not sufficiently attentive to accuracy. I therefore cannot venture to avail myself much of a biographical sketch of Johnson which he published, being one among the various persons ambitious of appending their names to that of my illustrious friend. That sketch is, however, an entertaining little collection of fragments. Those which he published of Pope and Addison are of higher merit; but his fame must chiefly rest upon his 'Political Conferences,' in which he introduces several eminent persons delivering their sentiments in the way of dialogue, and discovers a considerable share of learning, various knowledge, and discernment of character. This much may I be allowed to say of a man who was exceedingly obliging to me, and who lived with Dr. Johnson in as easy a manner as almost any of his very numerous acquaintance.

marginal line:
Tyers, the . . . ever be [H]

marginal line:
world with . . . He abounded [H]

---

[1] In summer, 1792, additional and more expensive decorations having been introduced, the price of admission was raised to two shillings. I cannot approve of this. The company may be more select; but a number of the honest commonalty are, I fear, excluded from sharing in elegant and innocent entertainment. An attempt to abolish the one-shilling gallery at the playhouse has been very properly counteracted.

Mr. Edwards had said to me aside, that Dr. Johnson should have been of a profession. I repeated the remark to Johnson that I might have his own thoughts on the subject. JOHNSON. 'Sir, it *would* have been better that I had been of a profession. I ought to have been a lawyer.' BOSWELL. 'I do not think, Sir, it would have been better, for we should not have had the English Dictionary.' JOHNSON. 'But you would have had Reports.' BOSWELL. 'Ay; but there would not have been another, who could have written the Dictionary. There have been many very good Judges. Suppose you had been Lord Chancellor; you would have delivered opinions with more extent of mind, and in a more ornamented manner, than perhaps any Chancellor ever did, or ever will do. But, I believe, causes have been as judiciously decided as you could have done.' JOHNSON. 'Yes, Sir. Property has been as well settled.'

Johnson, however, had a noble ambition floating in his mind, and had, undoubtedly, often speculated on the possibility of his supereminent powers being rewarded in this great and liberal country by the highest honours of the state. Sir William Scott informs me, that upon the death of the late Lord Lichfield, who was Chancellor of the University of Oxford, he said to Johnson, 'What a pity it is, Sir, that you did not follow the profession of the law. You might have been Lord Chancellor of Great Britain, and attained to the dignity of the peerage; and now that the title of Lichfield, your native city, is extinct, you might have had it.' Johnson, upon this, seemed much agitated; and, in an angry tone, exclaimed, 'Why will you vex me by suggesting this, when it is too late.'

But he did not repine at the prosperity of others. The late Dr. Thomas Leland told Mr. Courtenay that when Mr. Edmund Burke shewed Johnson his fine house and lands near Beaconsfield, Johnson coolly said, '*Non equidem invideo; miror magis.*'[1a]

a *Johnson's Name will outlive that of Burke.* [H]

That is true   *I was with him—I suppose Mr Burke told it to Dr. Deland—for he was not present.* [I]

[1] I am not entirely without suspicion that Johnson may have felt a little momentary envy; for no man loved the good things of this life better than he did; and he could not but be conscious that he deserved a much larger share of them, than he ever had. I attempted in a news-paper to comment on the above passage in the manner of Warburton, who must be allowed to have shewn uncommon ingenuity, in giving to any authour's text whatever

Yet no man had a higher notion of the dignity of literature than Johnson, or was more determined in maintaining the respect which he justly considered as due to it. Of this, besides the general tenor of his conduct in society, some characteristical instances may be mentioned.

He told Sir Joshua Reynolds, that once when he dined in a numerous company of booksellers, where the room being small, the head of the table, at which he sat, was almost close to the fire, he persevered in suffering a great deal of inconvenience from the heat, rather than quit his place, and let one of them sit above him.[a]

[a] *comical enough!* [H & I]

Goldsmith, in his diverting simplicity, complained one day, in a mixed company, of Lord Camden. 'I met him (said he) at Lord Clare's house in the country, and he took no more notice of me than if I had been an ordinary man.' The company having laughed heartily, Johnson stood forth in defence of his friend.[b] 'Nay, Gentlemen, (said he,) Dr. Goldsmith is in the right. A nobleman ought to have made up to such a man as Goldsmith; and I think it is much against Lord Camden that he neglected him.'

[b] *but the Company laughed very properly at Goldsmith for saying so* [I]

Nor could he patiently endure to hear, that such respect as he thought due only to higher intellectual qualities, should be bestowed on men of slighter, though perhaps more amusing, talents. I told him, that one morning, when I went to breakfast with Garrick, who was very vain of his intimacy with Lord Camden, he accosted me thus:— 'Pray, now, did you—did you meet a little lawyer turning the corner, eh?'—'No, Sir, (said I.) Pray what do you mean by the question?'—'Why, (replied Garrick, with an

meaning he chose it should carry. As this imitation may amuse my readers, I shall here introduce it:

'No saying of DR. JOHNSON's has been more misunderstood than his applying to MR. BURKE when he first saw him at his fine place at Beaconsfield, *Non equidem invideo; miror magis*. These two celebrated men had been friends for many years before Mr. Burke entered on his parliamentary career. They were both writers, both members of THE LITERARY CLUB; when, therefore, Dr. Johnson saw Mr. Burke in a situation so much more splendid than that to which he himself had attained, he did not mean to express that he thought it a disproportionate prosperity; but while he, as a philosopher, asserted an exemption from envy, *non equidem invideo*, he went on in the words of the poet, *miror magis;* thereby signifying, either that he was occupied in admiring what he was glad to see; or, perhaps, that considering the general lot of men of superiour abilities, he wondered, that Fortune, who is represented as blind, should, in this instance, have been so just.'

affected indifference, yet as if standing on tip-toe,) Lord Camden has this moment left me. We have had a long walk together.' JOHNSON. 'Well, Sir, Garrick talked very properly. Lord Camden *was* a *little lawyer* to be associating so familiarly with a player.'

Sir Joshua Reynolds observed, with great truth, that Johnson considered Garrick to be as it were his *property*. He would allow no man either to blame or to praise Garrick in his presence, without contradicting him.[a]

Having fallen into a very serious frame of mind, in which mutual expressions of kindness passed between us, such as would be thought too vain in me to repeat, I talked with regret of the sad inevitable certainty that one of us must survive the other. JOHNSON. 'Yes, Sir, that is an affecting consideration. I remember Swift, in one of his letters to Pope, says, "I intend to come over, that we may meet once more; and when we must part, it is what happens to all human beings."' BOSWELL. 'The hope that we shall see our departed friends again must support the mind.' JOHNSON. 'Why, yes, Sir.'[1] BOSWELL. 'There is a strange unwillingness to part with life, independent of serious fears as to futurity. A reverend friend of ours (naming him) tells me, that he feels an uneasiness at the thoughts of leaving his house, his study, his books.' JOHNSON. 'This is foolish in *****. A man need not be uneasy on these grounds; for, as he will retain his consciousness, he may say with the philosopher, *Omnia mea mecum porto.*' BOSWELL. 'True, Sir: we may carry our books in our heads; but still there is something painful in the thought of leaving for ever what has given us pleasure. I remember, many years ago, when my imagination was warm, and I happened to be in a melancholy mood, it distressed me to think of going into a state of being in which Shakspeare's poetry did not exist.[b] A lady whom I then much admired, a very amiable woman, humoured my fancy, and relieved me by saying, "The first thing you will meet in the other world, will be an elegant copy of Shakspeare's works presented to you."' Dr Johnson smiled benignantly at this, and did not appear to disapprove of the notion.

b *& Virgil's Sacred Work shall die . . . says Cowley. I am not so sure however that we may not repeat Virgil, as I am that we shall not see the Pictures of Raphael or Coreggio. They must be taken from us I fear—The Verses may be remember'd.* [H]

[1] [See on the same subject, vol. ii, p. 13. MALONE.]

We went to St. Clement's church again in the afternoon, and then returned and drank tea and coffee in Mrs. Williams's room; Mrs. Desmoulins doing the honours of the tea-table. I observed that he would not even look at a proof-sheet of his 'Life of Waller' on Good-Friday.

Mr. Allen, the printer, brought a book on agriculture, which was printed, and was soon to be published. It was a very strange performance, the authour having mixed in it his own thoughts upon various topicks, along with his remarks on plowing, sowing, and other farming operations. He seemed to be an absurd profane fellow, and had introduced in his books many sneers at religion, with equal ignorance and conceit. Dr. Johnson permitted me to read some passages aloud. One was that he resolved to work on Sunday, and did work, but he owned he felt *some* weak compunction; and he had this very curious reflection:— 'I was born in the wilds of Christianity, and the briars and thorns still hang about me.' Dr. Johnson could not help laughing at this ridiculous image, yet was very angry at the fellow's impiety. 'However, (said he,) the Reviewers will make him hang himself.' He, however, observed, 'that formerly there might have been a dispensation obtained for working on Sunday in the time of harvest.' Indeed in ritual observances, were all the ministers of religion what they should be, and what many of them are, such a power might be wisely and safely lodged with the Church.

On Saturday, April 18, I drank tea with him. He praised the late Mr. Duncombe,[1] of Canterbury, as a pleasing man. 'He used to come to me; I did not seek much after *him*. Indeed I never sought much after any body.' BOSWELL. 'Lord Orrery, I suppose.' JOHNSON. 'No, Sir; I never went to him but when he sent for me.' BOSWELL.'Richardson?' JOHNSON. 'Yes, Sir. But I sought after George Psalmanazar the most. I used to go and sit with him at an alehouse in the city.'

I am happy to mention another instance which I discovered of his *seeking after* a man of merit. Soon after the Honourable Daines Barrington had published his excellent

---

[1] [William Duncombe, Esq. He married the sister of John Hughes, the poet; was the authour of two tragedies, and other ingenious productions; and died Feb. 26, 1769, aged 79. MALONE.]

'Observations on the Statutes,'[1] Johnson waited on that worthy and learned gentleman; and, having told him his name, courteously said, 'I have read your book, Sir, with great pleasure, and wish to be better known to you.' Thus began an acquaintance, which was continued with mutual regard as long as Johnson lived.

Talking of a recent seditious delinquent, he said, 'They should set him in the pillory, that he may be punished in a way that would disgrace him.' I observed, that the pillory does not always disgrace. And I mentioned an instance of a gentleman, who I thought was not dishonoured by it.[a] JOHNSON. 'Ay, but he was, Sir. He could not mouth and strut as he used to do, after having been there. People are not willing to ask a man to their tables, who has stood in the pillory.'

marginal line: *punished in . . . always disgrace* [H]

[a] *Dr. Shebbears I suppose.* [H]

The gentleman who had dined with us at Dr. Percy's[2] came in. Johnson attacked the Americans with intemperate vehemence of abuse. I said something in their favour; and added, that I was always sorry, when he talked on that subject. This, it seems, exasperated him; though he said nothing at the time. The cloud was charged with sulphureous vapour, which was afterwards to burst in thunder.—We talked of a gentleman who was running out his fortune in London; and I said, 'We must get him out of it. All his friends must quarrel with him, and that will soon drive him away.' JOHNSON. 'Nay, Sir, we'll send *you* to him. If your company does not drive a man out of his house, nothing will.' This was a horrible shock, for which there was no visible cause. I afterwards asked him, why he had said so harsh a thing. JOHNSON. 'Because, Sir, you made me angry about the Americans.' BOSWELL. 'But why did you not take your revenge directly?' JOHNSON. (smiling) 'Because, Sir, I had nothing ready. A man cannot strike till he has his weapons.' This was a candid and pleasant confession.

two exclamation points: *we'll send* etc. [H]

He shewed me to-night his drawing-room, very genteelly fitted up, and said, 'Mrs. Thrale sneered, when I talked of my having asked you and your lady to live at my

---

[1] [4to. 1766. The worthy authour died many years after Johnson, March 13, 1800, aged about 74. MALONE.]

[2] See vol. ii. p. 479.

house. I was obliged to tell her, that you would be in as respectable a situation in my house as in hers. Sir, the insolence of wealth will creep out.' BOSWELL. 'She has a little both of the insolence of wealth, and the conceit of parts.' JOHNSON. 'The insolence of wealth is a wretched thing; but the conceit of parts has some foundation. To be sure, it should not be. But who is without it?' BOSWELL. 'Yourself, Sir.' JOHNSON. 'Why, I play no tricks: I lay no traps.' BOSWELL. 'No, Sir. You are six feet high, and you only do not stoop.'

We talked of the numbers of people that sometimes have composed the household of great families. I mentioned that there were a hundred in the family of the present Earl of Eglintoune's father. Dr. Johnson seeming to doubt it, I began to enumerate. 'Let us see: my Lord and my Lady two.' JOHNSON.'Nay, Sir, if you are to count by twos, you may be long enough.' BOSWELL. 'Well, but now I add two sons and seven daughters, and a servant for each, that will make twenty; so we have the fifth part already.' JOHNSON. 'Very true. You get at twenty pretty readily; but you will not so easily get further on. We grow to five feet pretty readily; but it is not so easy to grow to seven.'

On Sunday, April 19, being Easter-day, after the solemnities of the festival in St. Paul's Church, I visited him, but could not stay to dinner. I expressed a wish to have the arguments for Christianity always in readiness, that my religious faith might be as firm and clear as any proposition whatever, so that I need not be under the least uneasiness, when it should be attacked. JOHNSON. 'Sir, you cannot answer all objections. You have demonstration for a First Cause: you see he must be good as well as powerful, because there is nothing to make him otherwise, and goodness of itself is preferable. Yet you have against this, what is very certain, the unhappiness of human life. This, however, gives us reason to hope for a future state of compensation, that there may be a perfect system. But of that we were not sure, till we had a positive revelation.' I told him, that his 'Rasselas' had often made me unhappy; for it represented the misery of human life so well, and so convincingly to a thinking mind, that if at any time the impression wore off, and I felt myself easy, I began to suspect some delusion.

On Monday, April 20, I found him at home in the morning. We talked of a gentleman who we apprehended was gradually involving his circumstances by bad management.[a] JOHNSON. 'Wasting a fortune is evaporation by a thousand imperceptible means. If it were a stream, they'd stop it. You must speak to him. It is really miserable. Were he a gamester, it could be said he had hopes of winning. Were he a bankrupt in trade, he might have grown rich; but he has neither spirit to spend, nor resolution to spare. He does not spend fast enough to have pleasure from it. He has the crime of prodigality, and the wretchedness of parsimony. If a man is killed in a duel, he is killed as many a one has been killed; but it is a sad thing for a man to lie down and die; to bleed to death, because he has not fortitude enough to sear the wound, or even to stitch it up.' I cannot but pause a moment to admire the fecundity of fancy, and choice of language, which in this instance, and, indeed, on almost all occasions, he displayed. It was well observed by Dr. Percy, now Bishop of Dromore,[b] 'The conversation of Johnson is strong and clear, and may be compared to an antique statue, where every vein and muscle is distinct and bold. Ordinary conversation resembles an inferiour cast.'

On Saturday, April 25, I dined with him at Sir Joshua Reynolds's, with the learned Dr. Musgrave,[1] Counsellor Leland of Ireland, son to the historian, Mrs. Cholmondeley, and some more ladies. 'The Project,' a new poem, was read to the company by Dr. Musgrave. JOHNSON. 'Sir, it has no power. Were it not for the well-known names with which it is filled, it would be nothing: the names carry the poet, not the poet the names.' MUSGRAVE. 'A temporary poem always entertains us.' JOHNSON. 'So does an account of the criminals hanged yesterday entertain us.'

He proceeded;—'Demosthenes Taylor, as he was called, (that is, the Editor of Demosthenes) was the most silent man, the merest statue of a man that I have ever seen. I

[a] *Langton I suppose* [H]

[b] *So it was well observed—& in Percy's Way.* [H]

---

[1] [Samuel Musgrave, M.D. Editor of the Euripides, and authour of 'Dissertations on the Grecian Mythology,' &c. published in 1782, after his death, by the learned Mr. Tyrwhitt. MALONE.]

once dined in company with him, and all he said during
the whole time was no more than *Richard*. How a man
should say only Richard, it is not easy to imagine. But it
was thus: Dr. Douglas was talking of Dr. Zachary Grey,
and ascribing to him something that was written by Dr.
Richard Grey. So, to correct him, Taylor said, "*Richard.*"

marginal line:
*Richard Grey . . . Tay-
lor said* [H]

Mrs. Cholmondeley, in a high flow of spirits, exhibited
some lively sallies of hyperbolical compliment to Johnson,
with whom she had been long acquainted and was very
easy. He was quick in catching the *manner* of the moment,
and answered her somewhat in the style of the hero of a
romance, 'Madam, you crown me with unfading laurels.'

I happened, I know not how, to say that a pamphlet
meant a prose piece. JOHNSON. 'No, Sir. A few sheets of
poetry unbound are a pamphlet,[1] as much as a few sheets
of prose.' MUSGRAVE. 'A pamphlet may be understood to
mean a poetical piece in Westminster-Hall, that is, in
formal language; but in common language, it is understood to mean prose.' JOHNSON. (and here was one of the
many instances of his knowing clearly and telling exactly
how a thing is,) 'A pamphlet is understood in common
language to mean prose, only from this, that there is so
much more prose written than poetry; as when we say a
book, prose is understood for the same reason, though a
book may as well be in poetry as in prose. We understand
what is most general, and we name what is less frequent.'

We talked of a lady's verses on Ireland. MISS REY-
NOLDS. 'Have you seen them, Sir?' JOHNSON. 'No,
Madam, I have seen a translation from Horace, by one of
her daughters. She shewed it me.' MISS REYNOLDS.
'And how was it, Sir?' JOHNSON. 'Why, very well for a
young Miss's verses;—that is to say, compared with excellence, nothing; but, very well, for the person who wrote
them. I am vexed at being shewn verses in that manner.'
MISS REYNOLDS. 'But if they should be good, why not
give them hearty praise?' JOHNSON. 'Why, Madam,

---

[1] [Dr. Johnson is here perfectly correct, and is supported by the usage of
preceding writers.[a] So in MUSARUM DELICIÆ, a collection of poems, 8vo.
1656, (the writer is speaking of Suckling's play entitled AGLAURA, printed
in folio):

'This great voluminous PAMPHLET may be said,
To be like one, that hath more hair than head.' MALONE.]

[a] *whatever is slight
enough to be tied to-
gether* par un filet [I]

because I have not then got the better of my bad humour from having been shewn them. You must consider, Madam; before-hand they may be bad, as well as good. Nobody has a right to put another under such a difficulty, that he must either hurt the person by telling the truth, or hurt himself by telling what is not true.' BOSWELL. 'A man often shews his writings to people of eminence, to obtain from them, either from their good-nature, or from their not being able to tell the truth firmly, a commendation, of which he may afterwards avail himself.' JOHNSON. 'Very true, Sir. Therefore the man, who is asked by an authour, what he thinks of his work, is put to the torture, and is not obliged to speak the truth; so that what he says is not considered as his opinion; yet he has said it, and cannot retract it; and this authour, when mankind are hunting him with a cannister at his tail, can say, "I would not have published, had not Johnson, or Reynolds, or Musgrave, or some other good judge commended the work." Yet I consider it as a very difficult question in conscience, whether one should advise a man not to publish a work, if profit be his object; for the man may say, "Had it not been for you, I should have had the money." Now you cannot be sure; for you have only your own opinion, and the publick may think very differently.' SIR JOSHUA REYNOLDS. 'You must upon such an occasion have two judgements; one as to the real value of the work, the other as to what may please the general taste at the time.' JOHNSON. 'But you can be *sure* of neither; and therefore I should scruple much to give a suppressive vote. Both Goldsmith's comedies were once refused; his first by Garrick, his second by Colman, who was prevailed on at last by much solicitation, nay, a kind of force, to bring it on. His "Vicar of Wakefield" I myself did not think would have had much success. It was written and sold to a bookseller, before his "Traveller;" but published after; so little expectation had the bookseller from it. Had it been sold after the "Traveller," he might have had twice as much money for it, though sixty guineas was no mean price. The bookseller had the advantage of Goldsmith's reputation from "The Traveller" in the sale, though Goldsmith had it not in selling the copy.'

marginal line:
under such . . . by telling [H]

marginal lines:
time.' JOHNSON . . .
second by [H]

Sir Joshua Reynolds. 'The Beggar's Opera affords a proof how strangely people will differ in opinion about a literary performance. Burke thinks it has no merit.' Johnson. 'It was refused by one of the houses; but I should have thought it would succeed, not from any great excellence in the writing, but from the novelty, and the general spirit and gaiety of the piece, which keeps the audience always attentive, and dismisses them in good humour.'

We went to the drawing-room, where was a considerable increase of company. Several of us got round Dr. Johnson, and complained that he would not give us an exact catalogue of his works, that there might be a complete edition. He smiled, and evaded our entreaties. That he intended to do it, I have no doubt, because I have heard him say so; and I have in my possession an imperfect list, fairly written out, which he entitles *Historia Studiorum*. I once got from one of his friends a list, which there was pretty good reason to suppose was accurate, for it was written down in his presence by this friend, who enumerated each article aloud, and had some of them mentioned to him by Mr. Levett, in concert with whom it was made out; and Johnson, who heard all this, did not contradict it. But when I shewed a copy of this list to him, and mentioned the evidence for its exactness, he laughed and said, 'I was willing to let them go on as they pleased, and never interfered.' Upon which I read it to him, article by article, and got him positively to own or refuse; and then, having obtained certainty so far, I got some other articles confirmed by him directly, and afterwards, from time to time, made additions under his sanction.

His friend, Edward Cave, having been mentioned, he told us, 'Cave used to sell ten thousand of "The Gentleman's Magazine;" yet such was then his minute attention and anxiety that the sale should not suffer the smallest decrease, that he would name a particular person who he heard had talked of leaving off the Magazine, and would say, "Let us have something good next month."'

It was observed, that avarice was inherent in some dispositions. Johnson. 'No man was born a miser, because no man was born to possession. Every man is born

marginal line: *he told . . . his minute* [H]

marginal line: *particular person . . . us have* [H]

queried: *is born* etc. [H]

cupidus—desirous of getting; but not *avarus*—desirous of keeping.' BOSWELL. 'I have heard old Mr. Sheridan maintain, with much ingenuity, that a complete miser is a happy man; a miser who gives himself wholly to the one passion of saving.' JOHNSON. 'That is flying in the face of all the world, who have called an avaricious man a *miser*, because he is miserable. No, Sir, a man who both spends and saves money is the happiest man, because he has both enjoyments.'

The conversation having turned on *Bon-Mots*, he quoted, from one of the *Ana*, an exquisite instance of flattery in a maid of honour in France, who being asked by the Queen what o'clock it was, answered, 'What your Majesty pleases.' He admitted that Mr. Burke's classical pun upon Mr. Wilkes's being carried on the shoulders of the mob,

'———— ———— numerisque fertur
Lege solutus,'

was admirable; and though he was strangely unwilling to allow to that extraordinary man the talent of wit,[1] he also laughed with approbation at another of his playful conceits; which was, that 'Horace has in one line given a description of a good desirable manour:

"Est *modus* in rebus, sunt certi denique *fines;*"[2]

that is to say, a *modus* as to the tithes, and certain *fines*.'

He observed, 'A man cannot with propriety speak of himself, except he relates simple facts; as, "I was at Richmond:" or what depends on mensuration; as, "I am six feet high." He is sure he has been at Richmond; he is sure

marginal line:
because he . . . man,
because [H]

marginal line:
quoted, from . . . was,
answered [H]

[1] See this question fully investigated in the Notes upon my 'Journal of a Tour to the Hebrides,' edit. 3, p. 21, *et seq*. And here, as a lawyer mindful of the maxim *Suum cuique tribuito*, I cannot forbear to mention, that the additional Note beginning with 'I find since the former edition,' is not mine, but was obligingly furnished by Mr. Malone, who was so kind as to superintend the press while I was in Scotland, and the first part of the second edition was printing. He would not allow me to ascribe it to its proper authour; but, as it is exquisitely acute and elegant, I take this opportunity, without his knowledge, to do him justice.

[2] [This, as both Mr. Bindley and Dr. Kearney have observed to me, is the motto to 'An Enquiry into Customary Estates and Tenant's Rights, &c.— with some considerations for restraining excessive *fines*.' By Everard Fleetwood, Esq. 8vo. 1731. But it is, probably, a mere coincidence. Mr. Burke perhaps never saw that pamphlet. MALONE.]

he is six feet high: but he cannot be sure he is wise, or that
he has any other excellence. Then, all censure of a man's
self is oblique praise. It is in order to shew how much he
can spare. It has all the invidiousness of self-praise, and
all the reproach of falsehood.' BOSWELL. 'Sometimes it
may proceed from a man's strong consciousness of his
faults being observed. He knows that others would throw
him down, and therefore he had better lie down softly of
his own accord.'

marginal line:
excellence. Then . . .
much he [H]

On Tuesday, April 28, he was engaged to dine at
General Paoli's, where, as I have already observed, I was
still entertained in elegant hospitality, and with all the
ease and comfort of a home. I called on him, and accompanied him in a hackney-coach. We stopped first at the
bottom of Hedge-lane, into which he went to leave a letter,
'with good news for a poor man in distress,' as he told me.
I did not question him particularly as to this. He himself
often resembled Lady Bolingbroke's lively description of
Pope: that 'he was *un politique aux choux et aux raves.*' He
would say, 'I dine to-day in Grosvenor-square;' this
might be with a Duke; or, perhaps, 'I dine to-day at the
other end of the town;' or, 'A gentleman of great eminence
called on me yesterday.'—He loved thus to keep things
floating in conjecture: *Omne ignotum pro magnifico est.* I
believe I ventured to dissipate the cloud, to unveil the
mystery, more freely and frequently than any of his friends.
We stopped again at Wirgman's, the well-known *toy-shop*,
in St. James's-Street, at the corner of St. James's-Place, to
which he had been directed, but not clearly, for he searched
about some time, and could not find it at first; and said,
'To direct one only to a corner shop is *toying* with one.' I
supposed he meant this as a play upon the word *toy;* it was
the first time that I knew him stoop to such sport. After he
had been some time in the shop, he sent for me to come out
of the coach, and help him to choose a pair of silver buckles,
as those he had were too small. Probably this alteration in
dress had been suggested by Mrs. Thrale,[a] by associating
with whom, his external appearance was much improved.
He got better cloaths; and the dark colour, from which he
never deviated, was enlivened by metal buttons. His wigs,
too, were much better; and during their travels in France,

marginal line:
*any of . . . James's-
Street* [H]

[a] *by Mr. Thrale it
was,—not by his Wife.*
[H]

*no truly—it was Mr.
Thrale & not his Wife
who attempted such
Corrections. He would
no more have suffer'd
me to have chosen his
Coat than the very
Youngest of my Chil-
dren.* [I]

he was furnished with a Paris-made wig, of handsome construction. This choosing of silver buckles was a negociation: 'Sir, (said he,) I will not have the ridiculous large ones now in fashion; and I will give no more than a guinea for a pair.' Such were the *principles* of the business; and, after some examination he was fitted. As we drove along, I found him in a talking humour, of which I availed myself. BOSWELL. 'I was this morning in Ridley's shop, Sir; and was told, that the collection called "*Johnsoniana*" has sold very much.' JOHNSON. 'Yet the "Journey to the Hebrides" has not had a great sale.'[1] BOSWELL. 'That is strange.' JOHNSON. 'Yes, Sir; for in that book I have told the world a great deal that they did not know before.'

BOSWELL. 'I drank chocolate, Sir, this morning with Mr. Eld;[a] and, to my no small surprize, found him to be a *Staffordshire Whig*, a being which I did not believe had existed.' JOHNSON. 'Sir, there are rascals in all countries.' BOSWELL. 'Eld said, a Tory was a creature, generated between a non-juring parson and one's grandmother.' JOHNSON. 'And I have always said, the first Whig was the Devil.' BOSWELL. 'He certainly was, Sir.[b] The Devil was impatient of subordination; he was the first who resisted power:

"Better to reign in Hell, than serve in Heaven."'

At General Paoli's were Sir Joshua Reynolds, Mr. Langton, Marchese Gherardi of Lombardy, and Mr. John Spottiswoode the younger, of Spottiswoode,[2] the solicitor. At this time fears of an invasion were circulated; to obviate which, Mr. Spottiswoode observed, that Mr. Fraser the engineer, who had lately come from Dunkirk, said, that

marginal line:
Sir; for . . . know before [H]

underlined:
Mr. Eld, Eld [H]
[a] *I think I saw this Gentleman's death in a Newspaper The Age 87 in this very year 1817;—or was his Son the Man? They were both very odd Mortals 50 or 60 Years ago.* [H]
marginal lines:
a Tory . . . Sir. The [H]
underlined:
was [I]

[b] *yes; & Milton (who was Whig enough himself,) makes that ye. Subject of his Poem.* [I]

marginal line:
that four . . . sold very [H]

marginal line:
voce ILK . . . *his estate* [H]

---

[1] Here he either was mistaken, or had a different notion of an extensive sale from what is generally entertained; for the fact is, that four thousand copies of that excellent work were sold very quickly. A new edition has been printed since his death, besides that in the collection of his works.

[Another edition has just been printed since Mr. Boswell wrote the above, besides repeated editions in the general collection of his works during the last twenty years. MALONE.]

[2] In the phraseology of Scotland, I should have said, 'Mr. John Spottiswoode the younger, *of that ilk*.' Johnson knew that sense of the word very well, and has thus explained it in his Dictionary, *voce* ILK—'It also signifies "the same;" as, *Mackintosh of that ilk*, denotes a gentleman whose surname and the title of his estate are the same.'

the French had the same fears of us. JOHNSON. 'It is thus
that mutual cowardice keeps us in peace. Were one half of
mankind brave, and one half cowards, the brave would be
always beating the cowards. Were all brave, they would
lead a very uneasy life; all would be continually fighting:
but being all cowards, we go on very well.'

We talked of drinking wine. JOHNSON. 'I require wine,
only when I am alone. I have then often wished for it, and
often taken it.' SPOTTISWOODE. 'What, by way of a
companion, Sir?' JOHNSON. 'To get rid of myself, to send
myself away. Wine gives great pleasure; and every pleasure
is of itself a good. It is a good, unless counterbalanced by
evil. A man may have a strong reason not to drink wine;
and that may be greater than the pleasure. Wine makes a
man better pleased with himself. I do not say that it makes
him more pleasing to others. Sometimes it does. But the
danger is, that while a man grows better pleased with
himself, he may be growing less pleasing to others.[1] Wine
gives a man nothing. It neither gives him knowledge nor
wit; it only animates a man, and enables him to bring
out what a dread of the company has repressed. It only
puts in motion what has been locked up in frost. But this
may be good, or it may be bad.' SPOTTISWOODE. 'So,
Sir, wine is a key which opens a box; but this box may be
either full or empty?'[a] JOHNSON. 'Nay, Sir, conversation
is the key: wine is a pick-lock, which forces open the box,
and injures it. A man should cultivate his mind so as to
have that confidence and readiness without wine, which
wine gives.' BOSWELL. 'The great difficulty of resisting
wine is from benevolence. For instance, a good worthy
man asks you to taste his wine, which he has had twenty
years in his cellar.' JOHNSON. 'Sir, all this notion about
benevolence arises from a man's imagining himself to be
of more importance to others, than he really is. They
don't care a farthing whether he drinks wine or not.'
SIR JOSHUA REYNOLDS. 'Yes, they do for the time.'

[a] *Wine — says   the
Orator   in   Esdras—
enables a Man to speak
with his Talent.* [H]

[1] It is observed in Waller's Life, in the *Biographia Britannica*, that he drank
only water; and that while he sat in a company who were drinking wine,
'he had the dexterity to accommodate his discourse to the pitch of theirs as
it *sunk*.'[b] If excess in drinking be meant, the remark is acutely just. But
surely a moderate use of wine gives a gaiety of spirits which water-drinkers
know not.

[b] *The Frolickers of
that Day, said they
would keep Company
with no one who drank
Water — except Ned
Waller.* [H]

JOHNSON. 'For the time!—If they care this minute, they forget it the next. And as for the good worthy man; how do you know he is good and worthy? No good and worthy man will insist upon another man's drinking wine. As to the wine twenty years in the cellar,—of ten men, three say this, merely because they must say something;—three are telling a lie, when they say they have had the wine twenty years;—three would rather save the wine;—one, perhaps, cares. I allow it is something to please one's company; and people are always pleased with those who partake pleasure with them. But after a man has brought himself to relinquish the great personal pleasure which arises from drinking wine, any other consideration is a trifle. To please others by drinking wine, is something, only, if there be nothing against it. I should, however, be sorry to offend worthy men:

> 'Curst be the verse, how well so e'er it flow,
>   That tends to make one worthy man my foe."'

BOSWELL. 'Curst be the *spring*, the *water*.' JOHNSON. 'But let us consider what a sad thing it would be, if we were obliged to drink or do any thing else that may happen to be agreeable to the company where we are.' LANGTON. 'By the same rule you must join with a gang of cut-purses.' JOHNSON. 'Yes, Sir: but yet we must do justice to wine; we must allow it the power it possesses. To make a man pleased with himself, let me tell you, is doing a very great thing:

> "Si patriæ volumus, si NOBIS vivere cari."'

I was at this time myself a water-drinker, upon trial, by Johnson's recommendation. JOHNSON. 'Boswell is a bolder combatant than Sir Joshua; he argues for wine without the help of wine; but Sir Joshua with it.' SIR JOSHUA REYNOLDS. 'But to please one's company is a strong motive.' JOHNSON. (who, from drinking only water, supposed every body who drank wine to be elevated,) 'I won't argue any more with you, Sir. You are too far gone.' SIR JOSHUA. 'I should have thought so indeed, Sir, had I made such a speech as you have now done.' JOHNSON. (drawing himself in, and, I really

index sign: JOHNSON. (*drawing himself in* etc. [1]

thought blushing,) 'Nay, don't be angry. I did not mean to offend you.'[a] SIR JOSHUA. 'At first the taste of wine was disagreeable to me; but I brought myself to drink it, that I might be like other people. The pleasure of drinking wine is so connected with pleasing your company, that altogether there is something of social goodness in it.' JOHNSON. 'Sir, this is only saying the same thing over again.' SIR JOSHUA. 'No, this is new.' JOHNSON. 'You put it in new words, but it is an old thought.[b] This is one of the disadvantages of wine, it makes a man mistake words for thoughts.' BOSWELL. 'I think it is a new thought; at least, it is in a new *attitude*.' JOHNSON. 'Nay, Sir, it is only in a new coat; or an old coat with a new facing. (Then laughing heartily) It is the old dog in a new doublet.—An extraordinary instance, however, may occur where a man's patron will do nothing for him, unless he will drink: *there* may be a good reason for drinking.'

I mentioned a nobleman, who I believed was really uneasy, if his company would not drink hard. JOHNSON. 'That is from having had people about him whom he has been accustomed to command.' BOSWELL. 'Supposing I should be *tête-à-tête* with him at table.' JOHNSON. 'Sir, there is no more reason for your drinking with *him*, than his being sober with *you*.' BOSWELL. 'Why, that is true; for it would do him less hurt to be sober, than it would do me to get drunk.' JOHNSON. 'Yes, Sir; and from what I have heard of him, one would not wish to sacrifice himself to such a man. If he must always have somebody to drink with him, he should buy a slave, and then he would be sure to have it. They who submit to drink as another pleases, make themselves his slaves.' BOSWELL. 'But, Sir, you will surely make allowance for the duty of hospitality. A gentleman who loves drinking, comes to visit me.' JOHNSON. 'Sir, a man knows whom he visits; he comes to the table of a sober man.' BOSWELL. 'But, Sir, you and I should not have been so well received in the Highlands and Hebrides, if I had not drunk with our worthy friends. Had I drunk water only as you did, they would not have been so cordial.' JOHNSON. 'Sir William Temple mentions, that in his travels through the Netherlands he had two or three gentlemen with him; and when a bumper was

underlined:
you [H]

[a] *he never would offend Reynolds, he had his Reason.* [H]

[b] *& a new Thought is a very uncommon Thing in Conversation even of witty Men. A new Thought is like a New Coin, It has more Glitter, but not more Weight than the Expression we have long been used to.* [H]

necessary, he put it on *them*. Were I to travel again through the islands, I would have Sir Joshua with me to take the bumpers.' BOSWELL. 'But, Sir, let me put a case. Suppose Sir Joshua should take a jaunt into Scotland; he does me the honour to pay me a visit at my house in the country; I am overjoyed at seeing him; we are quite by ourselves; shall I unsociably and churlishly let him sit drinking by himself? No, no, my dear Sir Joshua, you shall not be treated so, I *will* take a bottle with you.'

The celebrated Mrs. Rudd being mentioned. JOHNSON. 'Fifteen years ago I should have gone to see her.' SPOT-TISWOODE. 'Because she was fifteen years younger?' JOHNSON. 'No, Sir; but now they have a trick of putting every thing into the news-papers.'

He begged of General Paoli to repeat one of the introductory stanzas of the first book of Tasso's 'Jerusalem,' which he did, and then Johnson found fault with the simile of sweetening the edges of a cup for a child, being transferred from Lucretius into an epick poem. The General said he did not imagine Homer's poetry was so ancient as is supposed, because he ascribes to a Greek colony circumstances of refinement not found in Greece itself at a later period, when Thucydides wrote. JOHNSON. 'I recollect but one passage quoted by Thucydides from Homer, which is not to be found in our copies of Homer's works; I am for the antiquity of Homer, and think that a Grecian colony by being nearer Persia might be more refined than the mother country.'

On Wednesday, April 29, I dined with him at Mr. Allan Ramsay's, where were Lord Binning, Dr. Robertson the historian, Sir Joshua Reynolds, and the Honourable Mrs. Boscawen, widow of the Admiral, and mother of the present Viscount Falmouth; of whom, if it be not presumptuous in me to praise her, I would say, that her manners are the most agreeable, and her conversation the best,[a] of any lady with whom I ever had the happiness to be acquainted. Before Johnson came we talked a good deal of him. Ramsay said, he had always found him a very polite man, and that he treated him with great respect, which he did very sincerely. I said, I worshipped him. ROBERTSON. 'But some of you spoil him: you should not

[a] *She was a Woman much liked for her Conversation.* [H]
She was an eminently pleasing Converser. [I]

worship him; you should worship no man.' BOSWELL.
'I cannot help worshipping him, he is so much superiour
to other men.' ROBERTSON. 'In criticism, and in wit and
conversation, he is no doubt very excellent; but in other
respects he is not above other men; he will believe any
thing, and will strenuously defend the most minute circumstance connected with the Church of England.' BOSWELL.
'Believe me, Doctor, you are much mistaken as to this; for
when you talk with him calmly in private, he is very liberal
in his way of thinking.' ROBERTSON. 'He and I have
been always very gracious; the first time I met him was one
evening at Strahan's, when he had just had an unlucky
altercation with Adam Smith, to whom he had been so
rough, that Strahan, after Smith was gone, had remon-
strated with him, and told him that I was coming soon,
and that he was uneasy to think that he might behave in
the same manner to me. "No, no, Sir, (said Johnson) I
warrant you Robertson and I shall do very well." Accordingly he was gentle and good-humoured and courteous
with me, the whole evening; and he has been so upon
every occasion that we have met since. I have often said,
(laughing) that I have been in a great measure indebted
to Smith for my good reception.' BOSWELL. 'His power
of reasoning is very strong, and he has a peculiar art of
drawing characters, which is as rare as good portrait
painting.' SIR JOSHUA REYNOLDS. 'He is undoubtedly
admirable in this; but, in order to mark the characters
which he draws, he overcharges them, and gives people
more than they really have, whether of good or bad.'

marginal line:
he draws . . . or bad [H]

No sooner did he, of whom we had been thus talking so
easily, arrive, than we were all as quiet as a school upon
the entrance of the head-master;[a] and were very soon sat
down to a table covered with such variety of good things,
as contributed not a little to dispose him to be pleased.

[a] *Ay, Ay; so they did I
dare say—sit as quiet*
[H]

RAMSAY. 'I am old enough to have been a contemporary of Pope. His poetry was highly admired in his life-
time, more a great deal than after his death.' JOHNSON.
'Sir, it has not been less admired since his death; no
authours ever had so much fame in their own life-time as
Pope and Voltaire; and Pope's poetry has been as much
admired since his death as during his life; it has only not

marginal line:
*fame in . . . and Vol-
taire* [H]

been as much talked of, but that is owing to its being now more distant, and people having other writings to talk of. Virgil is less talked of than Pope, and Homer is less talked of than Virgil; but they are not less admired. We must read what the world reads at the moment. It has been maintained that this superfetation, this teeming of the press in modern times, is prejudicial to good literature, because it obliges us to read so much of what is of inferiour value, in order to be in the fashion; so that better works are neglected for want of time, because a man will have more gratification of his vanity in conversation, from having read modern books, than from having read the best works of antiquity. But it must be considered, that we have now more knowledge generally diffused; all our ladies read now, which is a great extension. Modern writers are the moons of literature; they shine with reflected light, with light borrowed from the ancients. Greece appears to me to be the fountain of knowledge; Rome of elegance.' RAMSAY. 'I suppose Homer's "Iliad" to be a collection of pieces which had been written before his time. I should like to see a translation of it in poetical prose, like the book of Ruth or Job.' ROBERTSON. 'Would you, Dr. Johnson, who are master of the English language, but try your hand upon a part of it.' JOHNSON. 'Sir, you could not read it without the pleasure of verse.'[1]

marginal line: *upon a . . . could not* [H]

We talked of antiquarian researches. JOHNSON. 'All that is really *known* of the ancient state of Britain is contained in a few pages. We *can* know no more than what the old writers have told us, yet what large books have we upon it, the whole of which, excepting such parts as are taken from those old writers, is all a dream, such as Whitaker's "Manchester." I have heard Henry's "History of Britain" well spoken of; I am told it is carried on in separate divisions, as the civil, the military, the religious history; I wish much to have one branch well done, and that is the history of manners, of common life.' ROBERTSON. 'Henry should have applied his attention to that alone, which is

[1] This experiment, which Madame Dacier made in vain, has since been tried in our own language, by the editor of 'Ossian,' and we must either think very meanly of his abilities, or allow that Dr. Johnson was in the right. And Mr. Cowper, a man of real genius, has miserably failed in his blank verse translation.

enough for any man; and he might have found a great deal
scattered in various books, had he read solely with that
view. Henry erred in not selling his first volume at a
moderate price to the booksellers, that they might have
pushed him on till he had got reputation. I sold my "History of Scotland" at a moderate price, as a work by which
the booksellers might either gain or not; and Cadell has
told me, that Miller and he have got six thousand pounds
by it. I afterwards received a much higher price for my
writings. An authour should sell his first work for what
the booksellers will give, till it shall appear whether he
is an authour of merit, or, which is the same thing as to
purchase-money, an authour who pleases the publick.'

marginal line:
*authour should . . . is
an* [H]

Dr. Robertson expatiated on the character of a certain
nobleman; that he was one of the strongest-minded men
that ever lived; that he would sit in company quite sluggish, while there was nothing to call forth his intellectual
vigour; but the moment that any important subject was
started, for instance, how this country is to be defended
against a French invasion, he would rouse himself, and
shew his extraordinary talents with the most powerful
ability and animation. JOHNSON. 'Yet this man cut his
own throat.[a] The true strong and sound mind is the mind
that can embrace equally great things and small. Now I
am told the King of Prussia will say to a servant, "Bring
me a bottle of such a wine, which came in such a year; it
lies in such a corner of the cellars." I would have a man
great in great things, and elegant in little things.' He said
to me afterwards, when we were by ourselves, 'Robertson
was in a mighty romantick humour, he talked of one
whom he did not know; but I *downed* him with the
King of Prussia.'—'Yes, Sir, (said I,) you threw a *bottle*
at his head.'

underlined:
cut his own throat [I]
[a] *Yorke I suppose.* [H]
was it Charles Yorke?
[I]

marginal line:
of the . . . to me [H]

An ingenious gentleman was mentioned, concerning
whom both Robertson and Ramsay agreed that he had a
constant firmness of mind; for after a laborious day, and
amidst a multiplicity of cares and anxieties, he would sit
down with his sisters[b] and be quite cheerful and good-
humoured. Such a disposition, it was observed, was the
happy gift of nature. JOHNSON. 'I do not think so; a man
has from nature a certain portion of mind; the use he

underlined:
sisters [I]
[b] *his Sisters!! who was
this Man? Dr. Lisle?*
[I]

makes of it depends upon his own free will. That a man has always the same firmness of mind, I do not say: because every man feels his mind less firm at one time than another; but I think, a man's being in a good or bad humour depends upon his will.'—I, however, could not help thinking that a man's humour is often uncontroulable by his will.

queried:
I think etc. [H]

Johnson harangued against drinking wine. 'A man, (said he,) may choose whether he will have abstemiousness and knowledge, or claret and ignorance.' Dr. Robertson, (who is very companionable,) was beginning to dissent as to the proscription of claret. JOHNSON: (with a placid smile.) 'Nay, Sir, you shall not differ with me; as I have said that the man is most perfect who takes in the most things, I am for knowledge and claret.' ROBERTSON: (holding a glass of generous claret in his hand.) 'Sir, I can only drink your health.' JOHNSON. 'Sir, I should be sorry if *you* should be ever in such a state as to be able to do nothing more.' ROBERTSON. 'Dr. Johnson, allow me to say, that in one respect I have the advantage of you; when you were in Scotland you would not come to hear any of our preachers, whereas, when I am here, I attend your publick worship without scruple, and indeed, with great satisfaction.' JOHNSON. 'Why, Sir, that is not so extraordinary: the King of Siam sent ambassadors to Louis the Fourteenth; but Louis the Fourteenth sent none to the King of Siam.'[1]

two marginal lines:
only drink . . . as to [H]

marginal line:
*extraordinary: the . . .
of Siam* [H]

Here my friend for once discovered a want of knowledge or forgetfulness; for Louis the Fourteenth did send an embassy[a] to the King of Siam,[2] and the Abbé Choisi, who was employed in it, published an account of it in two volumes.

[a] *It was more* Mission *than Embassy.* [H]

Next day, Thursday, April 30, I found him at home by himself. JOHNSON. 'Well, Sir, Ramsay gave us a splendid dinner. I love Ramsay. You will not find a man in whose conversation there is more instruction, more information,

[1] Mrs. Piozzi confidently mentions this as having passed in Scotland. 'Anecdotes,' p. 62.

[2] [The Abbé de Choisi was sent by Louis XIV. on an embassy to the King of Siam in 1683, with a view, it has been said, to convert the King of that country to Christianity. MALONE.]

and more elegance, than in Ramsay's.' BOSWELL. 'What
I admire in Ramsay, is his continuing to be so young.'
JOHNSON. 'Why, yes, Sir, it is to be admired. I value
myself upon this, that there is nothing of the old man in
my conversation. I am now sixty-eight, and I have no
more of it than at twenty-eight.' BOSWELL. 'But, Sir,
would not you wish to know old age? He who is never an
old man, does not know the whole of human life; for old
age is one of the divisions of it.' JOHNSON. 'Nay, Sir,
what talk is this?' BOSWELL. 'I mean, Sir, the Sphinx's
description of it:—morning, noon, and night. I would
know night, as well as morning and noon.' JOHNSON.
'What, Sir, would you know what it is to feel the evils of
old age? Would you have the gout? Would you have
decrepitude?'—Seeing him heated, I would not argue any
farther; but I was confident that I was in the right. I
would, in due time, be a Nestor, an elder of the people;
and there *should* be some difference between the conversation of twenty-eight and sixty-eight.[1] A grave picture
should not be gay. There is a serene, solemn, placid old
age. JOHNSON. 'Mrs. Thrale's mother said of me what
flattered me much. A clergyman[a] was complaining of want
of society in the country where he lived, and said, "They
talk of *runts;*" (that is, young cows.)[2] "Sir, (said Mrs.
Salusbury,) Mr. Johnson would learn to talk of runts;"
meaning that I was a man who would make the most of
my situation, whatever it was.' He added, 'I think myself
a very polite man.'

[1] [Johnson clearly meant, (what the authour has often elsewhere mentioned,) that he had none of the listlessness of old age, that he had the same
activity and energy of mind as formerly; not that a man of sixty-eight might
dance in a publick assembly with as much propriety as he could at twenty-
eight.[b] His conversation, being the product of much various knowledge,
great acuteness, and extraordinary wit, was equally well suited to every
period of life; and as in his youth it probably did not exhibit any unbecoming
levity, so certainly in his later years it was totally free from the garrulity and
querulousness of old age.[c] MALONE.]

[2] [Such is the signification of this word in Scotland, and it should seem in
Wales. (See Skinner in *v.*) But the heifers of Scotland and Wales, when
brought to England, being always smaller than those of this country, the
word *runt* has acquired a secondary sense, and generally signifies a heifer
diminutive in size, small beyond the ordinary growth of that animal; and
in this sense alone the word is acknowledged by Dr. Johnson, in his
Dictionary. MALONE.]

marginal line:
*old man . . . twenty-
eight* [H]

[a] *poor dear Dr. Delap
of Lewes in Sussex.* [I]

underlined:
dance [H]

[b] *If he could dance as
well & look as Young—
why not? 'Tis done in
France every day.* [H]

[c] *—was not Johnson
querulous?—in whom
else would such queru-
lousness have been en-
dured?* [H]

On Saturday, May 2, I dined with him at Sir Joshua Reynolds's, where there was a very large company, and a great deal of conversation; but owing to some circumstance which I cannot now recollect, I have no record of any part of it, except that there were several people there by no means of the Johnsonian school; so that less attention was paid to him than usual, which put him out of humour; and upon some imaginary offence from me, he attacked me with such rudeness, that I was vexed and angry,[a] because it gave those persons an opportunity of enlarging upon his supposed ferocity, and ill treatment of his best friends. I was so much hurt, and had my pride so much roused, that I kept away from him for a week; and, perhaps, might have kept away much longer, nay, gone to Scotland without seeing him again,[b] had not we fortunately met and been reconciled. To such unhappy chances are human friendships liable.

On Friday, May 8, I dined with him at Mr. Langton's. I was reserved and silent, which I suppose he perceived, and might recollect the cause. After dinner, when Mr. Langton was called out of the room, and we were by ourselves, he drew his chair near to mine, and said, in a tone of conciliating courtesy, 'Well, how have you done?' BOSWELL. 'Sir, you have made me very uneasy by your behaviour to me when we were last at Sir Joshua Reynolds's. You know, my dear Sir, no man has a greater respect and affection for you, or would sooner go to the end of the world to serve you. Now to treat me so—.' He insisted that I had interrupted him, which I assured him was not the case; and proceeded—'But why treat me so before people who neither love you nor me?' JOHNSON. 'Well, I am sorry for it. I'll make it up to you twenty different ways, as you please.' BOSWELL. 'I said to-day to Sir Joshua, when he observed that you *tossed* me sometimes—I don't care how often, or how high he tosses me, when only friends are present, for then I fall upon soft ground: but I do not like falling on stones, which is the case when enemies are present.—I think this a pretty good image, Sir.' JOHNSON. 'Sir, it is one of the happiest I have ever heard.'[c]

The truth is, there was no venom in the wounds which

[a] *I have forgotten what past, but it must have been much indeed if Boswell was really angry in good earnest. Witness Page 342 of this very Volume.* [p. 24 of this volume] [H]

[b] *not* he! [I]

[c] *Oh that would make all up.* [H]

he inflicted at any time, unless they were irritated by some malignant infusion by other hands. We were instantly as cordial again as ever, and joined in hearty laugh at some ludicrous but innocent peculiarities of one of our friends. BOSWELL. 'Do you think, Sir, it is always culpable to laugh at a man to his face?' JOHNSON. 'Why, Sir, that depends upon the man and the thing. If it is a slight man, and a slight thing, you may; for you take nothing valuable from him.'

He said, 'I read yesterday Dr. Blair's sermon on Devotion, from the text, "*Cornelius, a devout man.*" His doctrine is the best limited, the best expressed: there is the most warmth without fanaticism, the most rational transport. There is one part of it which I disapprove, and I'd have him correct it; which is, that "he who does not feel joy in religion is far from the kingdon of Heaven!" There are many good men whose fear of GOD predominates over their love. It may discourage. It was rashly said. A noble sermon it is indeed. I wish Blair would come over to the Church of England.'

When Mr. Langton returned to us, the 'flow of talk' went on. An eminent authour being mentioned;—JOHNSON. 'He is not a pleasant man. His conversation is neither instructive nor brilliant. He does not talk as if impelled by any fullness of knowledge or vivacity of imagination. His conversation is like that of any other sensible man. He talks with no wish either to inform or to hear, but only because he thinks it does not become ——— ———[a] to sit in a company and say nothing.'

Mr. Langton having repeated the anecdote of Addison having distinguished between his powers in conversation and in writing, by saying 'I have only nine-pence in my pocket; but I can draw for a thousand pounds;'—JOHNSON. 'He had not that retort ready, Sir; he had prepared it before-hand.' LANGTON: (turning to me.) 'A fine surmise. Set a thief to catch a thief.'

Johnson called the East-Indians barbarians. BOSWELL. 'You will except the Chinese, Sir?' JOHNSON. 'No, Sir.' BOSWELL. 'Have they not arts?' JOHNSON. 'They have pottery.' BOSWELL. 'What do you say to the written characters of their language?' JOHNSON. 'Sir, they have

marginal line: *does not . . . His conversation* [H]

[a] *a Who was this Man?* [H]

James Harris perhaps [I]

marginal line: *nine-pence . . . that retort* [H]

marginal line: LANGTON: (*turning . . . a thief* [H]

not an alphabet. They have not been able to form what all other nations have formed.' BOSWELL. 'There is more learning in their language than in any other, from the immense number of their characters.' JOHNSON. 'It is only more difficult from its rudeness; as there is more labour in hewing down a tree with a stone than with an axe.'

He said, 'I have been reading Lord Kames's "Sketches of the History of Man." In treating of severity of punishment, he mentions that of Madame Lapouchin, in Russia, but he does not give it fairly; for I have looked at *Chappe D'Auteroche*, from whom he has taken it. He stops where it is said that the spectators thought her innocent, and leaves out what follows; that she nevertheless was guilty. Now this is being as culpable as one can conceive, to misrepresent fact in a book, and for what motive? It is like one of those lies which people tell, one cannot see why. The woman's life was spared; and no punishment was too great for the favourite of an Empress, who had conspired to dethrone her mistress.' BOSWELL. 'He was only giving a picture of the lady in her sufferings.' JOHNSON. 'Nay, don't endeavour to palliate this. Guilt is a principal feature in the picture. Kames is puzzled with a question that puzzled me when I was a very young man. Why is it that the interest of money is lower, when money is plentiful; for five pounds has the same proportion of value to a hundred pounds when money is plentiful, as when it is scarce? A lady explained it to me. " It is (said she) because when money is plentiful there are so many more who have money to lend, that they bid down one another. Many have then a hundred pounds; and one says,—Take mine rather than another's, and you shall have it at four *per cent*."' BOSWELL. 'Does Lord Kames decide the question?' JOHNSON. 'I think he leaves it as he found it.' BOSWELL. 'This must have been an extraordinary lady who instructed you, Sir. May I ask who she was?' JOHNSON. 'Molly Aston,[1] Sir, the sister of those ladies with whom you dined at Lichfield.———I shall be at home to-morrow.' BOSWELL. 'Then let us dine by ourselves at the Mitre, to keep up the old custom, "the custom of

[1] Johnson had an extraordinary admiration of this lady, notwithstanding she was a violent Whig. In answer to her high-flown speeches for *Liberty*, he

the manor," custom of the Mitre.' JOHNSON. 'Sir, so it shall be.'

On Saturday, May 9, we fulfilled our purpose of dining by ourselves at the Mitre, according to the old custom. There was, on these occasions, a little circumstance of kind attention to Mrs. Williams, which must not be omitted. Before coming out, and leaving her to dine alone, he gave her the choice of a chicken, a sweetbread, or any other little nice thing, which was carefully sent to her from the tavern ready-drest.

Our conversation to-day, I know not how, turned, I think, for the only time at any length, during our long acquaintance, upon the sensual intercourse between the sexes, the delight of which he ascribed chiefly to imagination. 'Were it not for imagination, Sir, (said he,) a man would be as happy in the arms of a chambermaid as of a Duchess. But such is the adventitious charm of fancy, that we find men who have violated the best principles of society, and ruined their fame and their fortune, that they might possess a woman of rank.' It would not be proper to record the particulars of such a conversation in moments of unreserved frankness, when nobody was present on whom it could have any hurtful effect. That subject, when philosophically treated, may surely employ the mind in a curious discussion, and as innocently, as anatomy; provided that those who do treat it, keep clear of inflammatory incentives.

addressed to her the following Epigram, of which I presume to offer a translation:

> 'Liber ut esse velim, suasisti pulchra Maria,
> Ut maneam liber, pulchra Maria vale.'

> Adieu, Maria! since you'd have me free;
> For, who beholds thy charms, a slave must be.

marginal line:
Liber ut . . . Maria
vale [H]

A correspondent of 'The Gentleman's Magazine,' who subscribes himself SCIOLUS, to whom I am indebted for several excellent remarks, observes, 'The turn of Dr. Johnson's lines to Miss Aston, whose Whig principles he had been combating, appears to me to be taken from an ingenious epigram in the "*Menagiana*," (vol. iii. p. 376, edit. 1716) on a young lady who appeared at a masquerade, *habillé en Jesuite*, during the fierce contentions of the followers of Molinos and Jansenius concerning free-will:

> "On s'étonne ici que Caliste
> Ait pris l'habit de Moliniste.
> Puisque cette jeune beauté
> Ote à chacun sa liberté
> N'est-ce pas une Janseniste?"'

'From grave to gay, from lively to severe,'—we were soon engaged in very different speculation; humbly and reverently considering and wondering at the universal mystery of all things, as our imperfect faculties can now judge of them. 'There are (said he) innumerable questions to which the inquisitive mind can in this state receive no answer: Why do you and I exist? Why was this world created? Since it was to be created, why was it not created sooner?'

On Sunday, May 10, I supped with him at Mr. Hoole's, with Sir Joshua Reynolds. I have neglected the memorial of this evening, so as to remember no more of it than two particulars; one that he strenuously opposed an argument by Sir Joshua, that virtue was preferable to vice, considering this life only; and that a man would be virtuous were it only to preserve his character: and that he expressed much wonder at the curious formation of the bat, a mouse with wings; saying, that it 'was almost as strange a thing in physiology, as if the fabulous dragon could be seen.'

On Tuesday, May 12, I waited on the Earl of Marchmont, to know if his Lordship would favour Dr. Johnson with information concerning Pope, whose Life he was about to write. Johnson had not flattered himself with the hopes of receiving any civility from this nobleman; for he said to me, when I mentioned Lord Marchmont as one who could tell him a great deal about Pope,—'Sir, he will tell *me* nothing.' I had the honour of being known to his Lordship, and applied to him of myself, without being commissioned by Johnson. His Lordship behaved in the most polite and obliging manner, promised to tell all he recollected about Pope, and was so very courteous as to say, 'Tell Dr. Johnson I have a great respect for him, and am ready to shew it in any way I can. I am to be in the city to-morrow, and will call at his house as I return.' His Lordship however asked, 'Will he write the Lives of the Poets impartially? He was the first that brought Whig and Tory into a Dictionary. And what do you think of the definition of Excise? Do you know the history of his aversion to the word *transpire?*' Then taking down the folio Dictionary, he shewed it with this censure on its secondary sense: 'To escape from secrecy to notice; a sense lately innovated from France, without necessity.' The truth was, Lord Bolingbroke, who left the Jacobites, first used it; therefore it was to be condemned. He should have shewn what word would do for it, if it was unnecessary.' I afterwards put the question to Johnson: 'Why, Sir, (said he,) *get abroad.*' BOSWELL.'That, Sir, is using two words.' JOHNSON. 'Sir, there is no end of this. You may as well insist to have a word for old age.' BOSWELL. 'Well, Sir, *Senectus.*' JOHNSON. 'Nay, Sir, to insist always that there should be one word to express a thing in English, because there is one in another language, is to change the language.'

I availed myself of this opportunity to hear from his Lordship many particulars both of Pope and Lord Bolingbroke, which I have in writing.

I proposed to Lord Marchmont, that he should revise Johnson's Life of Pope: 'So (said his Lordship) you would put me in a dangerous situation. You know he knocked down Osborne, the bookseller.'

Elated with the success of my spontaneous exertion to procure material and respectable aid to Johnson for his very favourite work, 'The Lives of the Poets,' I hastened down to Mr. Thrale's at Streatham, where he now was, that I might insure his being at home next day; and after dinner, when I thought he would receive the good news in the best humour, I announced it eagerly: 'I have been at work for you to-day, Sir. I have been with Lord Marchmont. He bade me tell you, he has a great respect for you, and will call on you to-morrow, at one o'clock, and communicate all he knows about Pope.'—Here I paused, in full expectation that he would be pleased with this intelligence, would praise my active merit, and would be alert to embrace such an offer from a nobleman. But whether I had shewn an over-exultation, which provoked his spleen, or whether he was seized with a suspicion that I had obtruded him on Lord Marchmont, and humbled him too much; or whether there was any thing more than an unlucky fit of ill-humour, I know not; but to my surprise, the result was,—JOHNSON. 'I shall not be in town to-morrow. I don't care to know about Pope.' MRS. THRALE: (surprised as I was, and a little angry.) 'I suppose, Sir,

Mr. Boswell thought, that as you are to write Pope's
Life, you would wish to know about him.' JOHNSON.
'Wish! why yes. If it rained knowledge, I'd hold out my
hand; but I would not give myself the trouble to go in
quest of it.' There was no arguing with him at the moment. Some time afterwards he said, 'Lord Marchmont
will call on me, and then I shall call on Lord Marchmont.'
Mrs. Thrale was uneasy at his unaccountable caprice; and
told me, that if I did not take care to bring about a meeting
between Lord Marchmont and him, it would never take
place, which would be a great pity. I sent a card to his
Lordship, to be left at Johnson's house, acquainting him,
that Dr. Johnson could not be in town next day, but would
do himself the honour of waiting on him at another time.—
I give this account fairly, as a specimen of that unhappy
temper with which this great and good man had occasionally to struggle, from something morbid in his constitution.
Let the most censorious of my readers suppose himself to
have a violent fit of the tooth-ach, or to have received a
severe stroke on the shin-bone, and when in such a state to
be asked a question; and if he has any candour, he will not
be surprised at the answers which Johnson sometimes gave
in moments of irritation, which, let me assure them, is
exquisitely painful. But it must not be erroneously supposed
that he was, in the smallest degree, careless concerning
any work which he undertook, or that he was generally
thus peevish. It will be seen that in the following year
he had a very agreeable interview with Lord Marchmont
at his Lordship's house; and this very afternoon he soon
forgot any fretfulness, and fell into conversation as usual.

I mentioned a reflection having been thrown out against
four Peers for having presumed to rise in opposition to the
opinion of the twelve Judges, in a cause in the House of
Lords, as if that were indecent. JOHNSON. 'Sir, there is no
ground for censure. The Peers are Judges themselves: and
supposing them really to be of a different opinion, they
might from duty be in opposition to the Judges, who were
there only to be consulted.'

In this observation I fully concurred with him; for
unquestionably, all the Peers are vested with the highest
judicial powers; and when they are confident that they

understand a cause, are not obliged, nay, ought not to
acquiesce in the opinion of the ordinary Law Judges, or
even in that of those who from their studies and experience
are called the Law Lords. I consider the Peers in general
as I do a Jury, who ought to listen with respectful attention
to the sages of the law; but, if after hearing them, they have
a firm opinion of their own, are bound, as honest men, to
decide accordingly. Nor is it so difficult for them to understand even law questions, as is generally thought; provided
they will bestow sufficient attention upon them. This
observation was made by my honoured relation the late
Lord Cathcart, who had spent his life in camps and courts;
yet assured me, that he could form a clear opinion upon
most of the causes that came before the House of Lords,
'as they were so well enucleated in the Cases.'

Mrs. Thrale told us, that a curious clergyman of our
acquaintance[a] had discovered a licentious stanza, which
Pope had originally in his 'Universal Prayer,' before the
stanza,

[a] *Doctor Lort.* [H & I]

> 'What conscience dictates to be done,
>   Or warns us not to do,' &c.

It was this:

> 'Can sins of moment claim the rod
>   Of everlasting fires?
>   And that offend great Nature's GOD,
>   Which Nature's self inspires?'

and that Dr. Johnson observed, 'it had been borrowed
from *Guarini.*' There are, indeed, in *Pastor Fido*, many such
flimsy superficial reasonings, as that in the last two lines
of this stanza.

BOSWELL. 'In that stanza of Pope's, "*rod of fires,*" is
certainly a bad metaphor.' MRS. THRALE. 'And "sins
of *moment*" is a faulty expression; for its true import is
momentous, which cannot be intended.' JOHNSON. 'It must
have been written "of *moments.*" Of *moment*, is *momentous;*
of *moments, momentary.* I warrant you, however, Pope wrote
this stanza, and some friend struck it out. Boileau wrote
some such thing, and Arnaud struck it out, saying, "*Vous
gagnerez deux ou trois impies, et perdrez je ne scais combien des
honnettes gens.*" These fellows want to say a daring thing,

marginal line:
of moments . . . *of*
moments [H]

and don't know how to go about it. Mere poets know no
more of fundamental principles than—.' Here he was
interrupted somehow. Mrs. Thrale mentioned Dryden.
JOHNSON. 'He puzzled himself about predestination.—
How foolish was it in Pope to give all his friendship to
Lords, who thought they honoured him by being with him;
and to choose such Lords as Burlington, and Cobham, and
Bolingbroke! Bathurst was negative, a pleasing man; and
I have heard no ill of Marchmont;—and then always
saying, "I do not value you for being a Lord;" which was
a sure proof that he did. I never say, I do not value Boswell
more for being born to an estate, because I do not care.'
BOSWELL. 'Nor for being a Scotchman?' JOHNSON.
'Nay, Sir, I do value you more for being a Scotchman.
You are a Scotchman without the faults of Scotchmen. You
would not have been so valuable as you are had you not
been a Scotchman.'

Talking of divorces, I asked if Othello's doctrine was
not plausible;

> 'He that is robb'd, not wanting what is stolen,
> Let him not know't, and he's not robb'd at all.'

Dr. Johnson and Mrs. Thrale joined against this. JOHNSON.
'Ask any man if he'd wish not to know of such an injury.'
BOSWELL. 'Would you tell your friend to make him
unhappy?' JOHNSON. 'Perhaps, Sir, I should not; but that
would be from prudence on my own account. A man
would tell his father.' BOSWELL. 'Yes; because he would
not have spurious children to get any share of the family
inheritance.' MRS. THRALE. 'Or he would tell his
brother.' BOSWELL. 'Certainly his *elder* brother.' JOHN-
SON. 'You would tell your friend of a woman's infamy, to
prevent his marrying a whore: there is the same reason
to tell him of his wife's infidelity, when he is married, to
prevent the consequences of imposition. It is a breach of
confidence not to tell a friend.' BOSWELL. 'Would you
tell Mr. ———?' (naming a gentleman[a] who assuredly
was not in the least danger of such a miserable disgrace,
though married to a fine woman.) JOHNSON. 'No, Sir;
because it would do no good: he is so sluggish, he'd never
go to parliament and get through a divorce.'[b]

He said of one of our friends,[a] 'He is ruining himself without pleasure. A man who loses at play, or who runs out his fortune at court, makes his estate less, in hopes of making it bigger: (I am sure of this word, which was often used by him:) but it is a sad thing to pass through the quagmire of parsimony, to the gulph of ruin. To pass over the flowery path of extravagance, is very well.'

Amongst the numerous prints pasted on the walls of the dining-room at Streatham, was Hogarth's 'Modern Midnight Conversation.' I asked him what he knew of Parson Ford, who makes a conspicuous figure in the riotous group. JOHNSON. 'Sir, he was my acquaintance and relation, my mother's nephew. He had purchased a living in the country, but not simoniacally. I never saw him but in the country. I have been told he was a man of great parts; very profligate, but I never heard he was impious.' BOSWELL. 'Was there not a story of his ghost having appeared?' JOHNSON. 'Sir, it was believed. A waiter at the Hummums, in which house Ford died, had been absent for some time, and returned, not knowing that Ford was dead. Going down to the cellar, according to the story, he met him; going down again, he met him a second time. When he came up, he asked some of the people of the house what Ford could be doing there. They told him Ford was dead. The waiter took a fever, in which he lay for some time. When he recovered, he said he had a message to deliver to some women from Ford; but he was not to tell what, or to whom. He walked out; he was followed; but somewhere about St. Paul's they lost him. He came back, and said he had delivered the message, and the women exclaimed, "Then we are all undone!" Dr. Pellet, who was not a credulous man, enquired into the truth of this story, and he said, the evidence was irresistible. My wife went to the Hummums; (it is a place where people get themselves cupped.) I believe she went with intention to hear about this story of Ford. At first they were unwilling to tell her; but, after they had talked to her, she came away satisfied that it was true. To be sure, the man had a fever; and this vision may have been the beginning of it.[b] But if the message to the women, and their behaviour upon

[a] as this was. [H]

marginal line:
is a ... over the [H]

[b] the Waiter was delirious I doubt not, but did he die? [H]

it, were true as related, there was something supernatural. That rests upon his word; and there it remains.'

After Mrs. Thrale was gone to bed, Johnson and I sat up late. We resumed Sir Joshua Reynolds's argument on the preceding Sunday, that a man would be virtuous, though he had no other motive than to preserve his character. JOHNSON. 'Sir, it is not true; for, as to this world, vice does not hurt a man's character.' BOSWELL. 'Yes, Sir, debauching a friend's wife will.' JOHNSON. 'No, Sir. Who thinks the worse of ———ᵃ for it?' BOSWELL. 'Lord ———ᵇ was not his friend.' JOHNSON. 'That is only a circumstance, Sir; a slight distinction. He could not get into the house but by Lord ———.ᶜ A man is chosen Knight of the shire, not the less for having debauched ladies.' BOSWELL. 'What, Sir, if he debauched the ladies of gentlemen in the county, will not there be a general resentment against him?' JOHNSON. 'No, Sir. He will lose those particular gentlemen; but the rest will not trouble their heads about it.' (warmly.) BOSWELL. 'Well, Sir, I cannot think so.' JOHNSON. 'Nay, Sir, there is no talking with a man who will dispute what every body knows, (angrily.) Don't you know this?' BOSWELL. 'No, Sir; and I wish to think better of your country than you represent it. I knew in Scotland a gentleman obliged to leave it for debauching a lady; and in one of our counties an Earl's brother lost his election, because he had debauched the lady of another Earl in that county, and destroyed the peace of a noble family.'

Still he would not yield. He proceeded: 'Will you not allow, Sir, that vice does not hurt a man's character so as to obstruct his prosperity in life, when you know that ———ᵈ was loaded with wealth and honours; a man who had acquired his fortune by such crimes, that his consciousness of them impelled him to cut his own throat?' BOSWELL. 'You will recollect, Sir, that Dr. Robertson said, he cut his throat because he was weary of still life; little things not being sufficient to move his great mind.' JOHNSON, (very angry.) 'Nay, Sir, what stuff is this? You have no more this opinion after Robertson said it, than before. I know nothing more offensive than repeating what one knows to be foolish things, by way of

ᵃ *Beauclerc* [H]

Beauclerc I guess [I]

ᵇ *Bolingbroke* [H & I]

ᶜ *I don't know whether I am right—'tis all guess-work* now *1808.*

30 Years gone, will carry Memory with them. [I]

ᵈ *Lord Clive* [H]

I cannot think who not Charles Yorke certainly   Ld: Clive it was [I]

marginal line: *he cut . . . Sir, what* [H]

continuing a dispute, to see what a man will answer,—to
make him your butt!' (angrier still.) BOSWELL. 'My dear
Sir, I had no such intention as you seem to suspect; I had
not indeed. Might not this nobleman have felt every thing
"weary, stale, flat, and unprofitable," as Hamlet says?'
JOHNSON. 'Nay, if you are to bring in gabble, I'll talk no
more. I will not, upon my honour.'—My readers will
decide upon this dispute.

Next morning I stated to Mrs. Thrale at breakfast before
he came down, the dispute of last night as to the influence
of character upon success in life. She said he was certainly
wrong; and told me, that a Baronet lost an election in
Wales,[a] because he had debauched the sister of a gentleman in the county, whom he made one of his daughters
invite as her companion at his seat in the country, when
his lady and his other children were in London. But she
would not encounter Johnson upon the subject.

I staid all this day with him at Streatham. He talked a
great deal in very good humour.

Looking at Messrs. Dilly's splendid edition of Lord
Chesterfield's miscellaneous works, he laughed, and said,
'Here are now two speeches ascribed to him, both of
which were written by me: and the best of it is, they have
found out that one is like Demosthenes, and the other
like Cicero.'[b]

He censured Lord Kames's 'Sketches of the History of
Man,' for misrepresenting Clarendon's account of the
appearance of Sir George Villiers's ghost, as if Clarendon
were weakly credulous; when the truth is, that Clarendon
only says, that the story was upon a better foundation of
credit, than usually such discourses are founded upon; nay,
speaks thus of the person who was reported to have seen
the vision, 'the poor man, *if he had been at all waking;*'
which Lord Kames has omitted. He added, 'in this book
it is maintained that virtue is natural to man, and, that
if we would but consult our own hearts, we should be
virtuous. Now, after consulting our own hearts all we can,
and with all the helps we have, we find how few of us are
virtuous. This is saying a thing which all mankind know
not to be true.' BOSWELL. 'Is not modesty natural?'
JOHNSON. 'I cannot say, Sir, as we find no people quite

[a] *It was Sir Nicholas Bayley.—he married pretty Miss Paget, & his Son was the late Earl of Uxbridge; Father to this Marquis, who lost his Leg at Waterloo . . . after marrying the Wife of one of the Wellesleys. She was originally Lady Charlotte Cadogan 1817.* [H]
  & very true   I told him—it was Sir Nicholas Bayly [I]

index sign: *her companion etc.* [H]

[b] *Comical!* [H]

in a state of nature; but I think, the more they are taught, the more modest they are. The French are a gross, ill-bred, untaught people; a lady there will spit on the floor and rub it with her foot.[a] What I gained by being in France was, learning to be better satisfied with my own country. Time may be employed to more advantage from nineteen to twenty-four, almost in any way than in travelling; when you set travelling against mere negation, against doing nothing, it is better to be sure; but how much more would a young man improve were he to study during those years. Indeed, if a young man is wild, and must run after women and bad company, it is better this should be done abroad, as, on his return, he can break off such connections, and begin at home a new man, with a character to form, and acquaintances to make. How little does travelling supply to the conversation of any man who has travelled; how little to Beauclerk!' BOSWELL. 'What say you to Lord ———?'[b] JOHNSON. 'I never but once heard him talk of what he had seen, and that was of a large serpent in one of the Pyramids of Egypt.' BOSWELL. 'Well, I happened to hear him tell the same thing, which made me mention him.'[c]

I talked of a country life.—JOHNSON. 'Were I to live in the country, I would not devote myself to the acquisition of popularity; I would live in a much better way, much more happily; I would have my time at my own command.' BOSWELL. 'But, Sir, is it not a sad thing to be at a distance from all our literary friends?' JOHNSON. 'Sir, you will by and by have enough of this conversation, which now delights you so much.'

As he was a zealous friend of subordination, he was at all times watchful to repress the vulgar cant against the manners of the great; 'High people, Sir, (said he,) are the best; take a hundred ladies of quality, you'll find them better wives, better mothers,[d] more willing to sacrifice their own pleasure to their children, than a hundred other women. Tradeswomen (I mean the wives of tradesmen) in the city, who are worth from ten to fifteen thousand pounds, are the worst creatures upon the earth, grossly ignorant, and thinking viciousness fashionable. Farmers, I think, are often worthless fellows. Few lords will cheat;

[a] *So She will* [I]

[b] *was it Lord Palmer-stone!* [I]

[c] *Who was He?* [H]
Oh Dear—& now I do not know who this *was.* [I]

marginal line:
against the . . . women. Tradeswomen [H]

[d] *It is true I think* [H]

marginal line:
thinking viciousness . . . cheating into [H]

and, if they do, they'll be ashamed of it: farmers cheat and are not ashamed of it: they have all the sensual vices too of the nobility, with cheating into the bargain. There is as much fornication and adultery amongst farmers as amongst noblemen.'[a] BOSWELL. 'The notion of the world, Sir, however, is, that the morals of women of quality are worse than those in lower stations.' JOHNSON. 'Yes, Sir, the licentiousness of one woman of quality makes more noise than that of a number of women in lower stations; then, Sir, you are to consider the malignity of women in the city against women of quality, which will make them believe any thing of them, such as that they call their coachmen to bed. No, Sir, so far as I have observed, the higher in rank, the richer ladies are, they are the better instructed, and the more virtuous.'

This year the Reverend Mr. Horne published his 'Letter to Mr. Dunning, on the English Particle;' Johnson read it, and though not treated in it with sufficient respect, he had candour enough to say to Mr. Seward, 'Were I to make a new edition of my Dictionary, I would adopt several[1] of Mr. Horne's etymologies; I hope they did not put the dog in the pillory for his libel; he has too much literature for that.'

On Saturday, May 16, I dined with him at Mr. Beau-clerk's with Mr. Langton, Mr. Steevens, Dr. Higgins, and some others. I regret very feelingly every instance of my remissness in recording his *memorabilia;* I am afraid it is the condition of humanity (as Mr. Windham, of Norfolk, once observed to me, after having made an admirable speech in the House of Commons, which was highly applauded, but which he afterwards perceived might have been better:) 'that we are more uneasy from thinking of our wants, than happy in thinking of our acquisitions.'[b] This is an un-reasonable mode of disturbing our tranquillity, and should be corrected; let me then comfort myself with the large treasure of Johnson's conversation which I have preserved for my own enjoyment and that of the world, and let me

marginal line:
the bargain ... amongst noblemen [H]

[a] So there is—perhaps a little more. [H]

marginal line:
ladies are . . . more virtuous [H]

underlined:
more uneasy . . . our acquisitions [H]

[b] no need of Mr Wynd-ham to tell us that What need of Books those Truths to tell Which Folks perceive who cannot spell? And must we Specta-cles apply, To see, what hurts our naked Eye? [H]

Doubtless Mr. Wind-ham said true [I]

marginal line:
In Mr. . . . . or, the [H]

---

[1] In Mr. Horne Tooke's enlargement of that 'Letter,' which he has since published with the title of '"Επεα πτεροεντα ; or, the Diversions of Purley;' he mentions this compliment, as if Dr. Johnson, instead of *several* of his etymologies had said *all.* His recollection having thus magnified it, shews how ambitious he was of the approbation of so great a man.

exhibit what I have upon each occasion, whether more or less, whether a bulse, or only a few sparks of a diamond.

He said, 'Dr. Mead lived more in the broad sunshine of life than almost any man.'

The disaster of General Burgoyne's army was then the common topick of conversation. It was asked why piling their arms was insisted upon as a matter of such consequence, when it seemed to be a circumstance so inconsiderable in itself. JOHNSON. 'Why, Sir, a French authour says, "*Il y a beaucoup de puerilités dans la guerre.*" All distinctions are trifles, because great things can seldom occur, and those distinctions are settled by custom. A savage would as willingly have his meat sent to him in the kitchen, as eat it at the table here: as men become civilized, various modes of denoting honourable preference are invented.'

marginal line:
as eat . . . preference are [H]

He this day made the observations upon the similarity between 'Rasselas' and 'Candide', which I have inserted in its proper place, when considering his admirable philosophical Romance. He said '*Candide*' he thought had more power in it than any thing that *Voltaire* had written.

marginal line:
He said . . . excellence is [H]

He said, 'The lyrical part of Horace never can be perfectly translated; so much of the excellence is in the numbers and the expression. Francis has done it the best; I'll take his, five out of six, against them all.'

On Sunday, May 17, I presented to him Mr. Fullarton, of Fullarton, who has since distinguished himself so much in India, to whom he naturally talked of travels, as Mr. Brydone accompanied him in his tour to Sicily and Malta. He said, 'The information which we have from modern travellers is much more authentick than what we had from ancient travellers; ancient travellers guessed; modern travellers measure. The Swiss admit that there is but one errour in Stanyan. If Brydone were more attentive to his Bible, he would be a good traveller.'

He said, 'Lord Chatham was a Dictator; he possessed the power of putting the State in motion; now there is no power; all order is relaxed.' BOSWELL. 'Is there no hope of a change to the better?' JOHNSON. 'Why, yes, Sir, when we are weary of this relaxation. So the City of London will appoint its Mayors again by seniority.' BOSWELL. 'But is not that taking a mere chance for having a good or a bad Mayor?' JOHNSON. 'Yes, Sir; but the evil of competition is greater than that of the worst Mayor that can come; besides, there is no more reason to suppose that the choice of a rabble will be right, than that chance will be right.'

On Tuesday, May 19, I was to set out for Scotland in the evening. He was engaged to dine with me at Mr. Dilly's; I waited upon him to remind him of his appointment and attend him thither; he gave me some salutary counsel, and recommended vigorous resolution against any deviation from moral duty. BOSWELL. 'But you would not have me to bind myself by a solemn obligation?' JOHNSON. (much agitated) 'What! a vow—O, no, Sir, a vow is a horrible thing, it is a snare for sin. The man who cannot go to heaven without a vow—may go—' Here, standing erect in the middle of his library, and rolling grand, his pause was truly a curious compound of the solemn and the ludicrous; he half-whistled in his usual way, when pleasant, and he paused as if checked by religious awe.—Methought he would have added—to Hell—but was restrained. I humoured the dilemma. 'What! Sir, (said I,) "*In cœlum jusseris ibit?*"' alluding to his imitation of it,

'And bid him go to Hell, to Hell he goes.'

I had mentioned to him a slight fault in his noble 'Imitation of the Tenth Satire of Juvenal,' a too near recurrence of the verb *spread*, in his description of the young Enthusiast at College:

'Through all his veins the fever of renown,
Spreads from the strong contagion of the gown;
O'er Bodley's dome his future labours *spread*,
And Bacon's mansion trembles o'er his head.'

He had desired me to change *spreads* to *burns*, but for perfect authenticity, I now had it done with his own hand.[1] I thought this alteration not only cured the fault, but was more poetical, as it might carry an allusion to the shirt by which Hercules was inflamed.[a]

[a] *every Fever burns I believe; but Bozzy could think only on Nessus's dirty shirt or Dr. Johnson's.* [H]

[1] The slip of paper on which he made the correction, is deposited by me in the noble library to which it relates, and to which I have presented other pieces of his hand-writing.

We had a quiet comfortable meeting at Mr. Dilly's;
nobody there but ourselves. Mr. Dilly mentioned some
body having wished that Milton's 'Tractate on Education'
should be printed along with his Poems in the edition of
the English Poets then going on. JOHNSON. 'It would be
breaking in upon the plan; but would be of no great consequence. So far as it would be any thing, it would be
wrong. Education in England has been in danger of being
hurt by two of its greatest men, Milton and Locke. Milton's
plan is impracticable, and I suppose has never been tried.
Locke's, I fancy, has been tried often enough, but is very
imperfect; it gives too much to one side, and too little to
the other; it gives too little to literature.—I shall do what
I can for Dr. Watts; but my materials are very scanty. His
poems are by no means his best works; I cannot praise his
poetry itself highly; but I can praise its design.'

My illustrious friend and I parted with assurances of
affectionate regard.

I wrote to him on the 25th of May, from Thorpe, in
Yorkshire, one of the seats of Mr. Bosville, and gave him
an account of my having passed a day at Lincoln, unexpectedly, and therefore without having any letters of
introduction, but that I had been honoured with civilities
from the Rev. Mr. Simpson, an acquaintance of his,
and Captain Broadley, of the Lincolnshire Militia; but
more particularly from the Rev. Dr. Gordon, the Chancellor, who first received me with great politeness as a
stranger, and, when I informed him who I was, entertained me at his house with the most flattering attention;
I also expressed the pleasure with which I had found that
our worthy friend, Langton, was highly esteemed in his
own county town.

'TO DR. SAMUEL JOHNSON

'MY DEAR SIR,   'Edinburgh, June 18, 1778

* * * * *

'SINCE my return to Scotland, I have been again at
Lanark, and have had more conversation with Thomson's
sister. It is strange that Murdoch, who was his intimate
friend, should have mistaken his mother's maiden name,

which he says was Hume, whereas Hume was the name of
his grandmother by the mother's side. His mother's name
was Beatrix Trotter,[1] a daughter of Mr. Trotter of Fogo, a
small proprietor of land. Thomson had one brother, whom
he had with him in England as his amanuensis; but he was
seized with a consumption, and having returned to Scotland, to try what his native air would do for him, died
young. He had three sisters, one married to Mr. Bell,
minister of the parish of Strathaven; one to Mr. Craig,
father of the ingenious architect, who gave the plan of the
New Town of Edinburgh; and one to Mr. Thomson,
master of the grammar-school at Lanark. He was of a
humane and benevolent disposition; not only sent valuable
presents to his sisters, but a yearly allowance in money,
and was always wishing to have it in his power to do them
more good. Lord Lyttleton's observation, that "he loathed
much to write," was very true. His letters to his sister Mrs.
Thomson, were not frequent, and in one of them he says,
"All my friends who know me, know how backward I am
to write letters; and never impute the negligence of my
hand to the coldness of my heart." I send you a copy of the
last letter which she had from him; she never heard that
he had any intention of going into holy orders. From this
late interview with his sister, I think much more favourably
of him, as I hope you will. I am eager to see more of
your Prefaces to the Poets: I solace myself with the few
proof-sheets which I have.

marginal line:
observation, that . . .
very true [H]

'I send another parcel of Lord Hailes's "Annals," which
you will please to return to me as soon as you conveniently
can. He says, "he wishes you would cut a little deeper;"
but he may be proud that there is so little occasion to
use the critical knife. I ever am, my dear Sir,

'Your faithful and affectionate,
'Humble servant,
'JAMES BOSWELL'

Mr. Langton has been pleased, at my request, to
favour me with some particulars of Dr. Johnson's visit to

---

[1] Dr. Johnson was by no means attentive to minute accuracy in his 'Lives
of the Poets;' for notwithstanding my having detected this mistake, he
continued it.

Warley-camp, where this gentleman was at the time stationed as a Captain in the Lincolnshire militia. I shall give them in his own words in a letter to me.

'It was in the summer of the year 1778, that he complied with my invitation to come down to the Camp at Warley, and he staid with me about a week; the scene appeared, notwithstanding a great degree of ill health that he seemed to labour under, to interest and amuse him, as agreeing with the disposition that I believe you know he constantly manifested towards enquiring into subjects of the military kind. He sate, with a patient degree of attention, to observe the proceedings of a regimental court-martial, that happened to be called, in the time of his stay with us; and one night, as late as at eleven o'clock, he accompanied the Major of the regiment in going what are styled the *Rounds*, where he might observe the forms of visiting the guards, for the seeing that they and their sentries are ready in their duty on their several posts. He took occasion to converse at times on military topicks, once in particular, that I see the mention of, in your "Journal of a Tour to the Hebrides," which lies open before me,[1] as to gun-powder; which he spoke of to the same effect, in part, that you relate.

'On one occasion, when the regiment were going through their exercise, he went quite close to the men at one of the extremities of it, and watched all their practices attentively; and, when he came away, his remark was, "The men indeed do load their musquets and fire with wonderful celerity." He was likewise particular in requiring to know what was the weight of the musquet balls in use, and within what distance they might be expected to take effect when fired off.

'In walking among the tents, and observing the difference between those of the officers and private men, he said, that the superiority of accommodation of the better conditions of life, to that of the inferiour ones, was never exhibited to him in so distinct a view. The civilities paid to him in the camp were, from the gentlemen of the Lincolnshire regiment, one of the officers of which accommodated him with a tent in which he slept; and from General Hall, who very courteously invited him to dine with him, where he

[1] Third Edition, p. 111.

appeared to be very well pleased with his entertainment, and the civilities he received on the part of the General;[1] the attention likewise of the General's aid-de-camp, Captain Smith, seemed to be very welcome to him, as appeared by their engaging in a great deal of discourse together. The gentlemen of the East-York regiment like-wise, on being informed of his coming, solicited his company at dinner, but by that time he had fixed his departure, so that he could not comply with the invitation.'

'TO JAMES BOSWELL, ESQ.

'SIR,

'I HAVE received two letters from you, of which the second complains of the neglect shown to the first. You must not tie your friends to such punctual correspondence. You have all possible assurances of my affection and esteem; and there ought to be no need of reiterated professions. When it may happen that I can give you either counsel or comfort, I hope it will never happen to me that I should neglect you; but you must not think me criminal or cold, if I say nothing when I have nothing to say.

'You are now happy enough. Mrs. Boswell is recovered; and I congratulate you upon the probability of her long life. If general approbation will add any thing to your enjoyment, I can tell you that I have heard you mentioned as *a man whom every body likes*. I think life has little more to give.

'————————[a] has gone to his regiment. He has laid down his coach, and talks of making more contractions of his expence: how he will succeed, I know not. It is difficult to reform a household gradually; it may be better done by a system totally new. I am afraid he has always something to hide. When we pressed him to go to ————————, he objected the necessity of attending his navigation; yet he could talk of going to Aberdeen, a place not much nearer his navigation. I believe he cannot bear the thought of living at ———————— in a state of diminution; and of appearing among the gentlemen of the neighbourhood *shorn of his beams*. This is natural, but it is cowardly. What I told him of the increasing expence of a growing family, seems to

[a] *Langton I fancy* [H]

[1] When I one day at Court expressed to General Hall my sense of the honour he had done my friend, he politely answered, 'Sir, I did *myself* honour.'

have struck him. He certainly had gone on with very
confused views, and we have, I think, shown him that he

^a They were always teizing the Man . . . whether benefiting him —I know not. [H & I]

is wrong;^a though, with the common deficience of advisers,
we have not shown him how to do right.

'I wish you would a little correct or restrain your
imagination, and imagine that happiness, such as life
admits, may be had at other places as well as London.
Without asserting Stoicism,[1] it may be said, that it is our
business to exempt ourselves as much as we can from the
power of external things. There is but one solid basis of
happiness: and that is, the reasonable hope of a happy
futurity. This may be had every where.

'I do not blame your preference to London to other
places, for it is really to be preferred, if the choice is free;
but few have the choice of their place, or their manner of
life; and mere pleasure ought not to be the prime motive
of action.

^b Poor Henrietta! [I]

'Mrs. Thrale, poor thing, has a daughter.^b Mr. Thrale
dislikes the times, like the rest of us. Mrs. Williams is sick;
Mrs. Desmoulins is poor. I have miserable nights. Nobody
is well but Mr. Levett.

'I am, dear Sir,

'Your most, &c.

'London, July 3, 1778.'

'SAM. JOHNSON'

In the course of this year there was a difference between
him and his friend Mr. Strahan; the particulars of which
it is unnecessary to relate. Their reconciliation was
communicated to me in a letter from Mr. Strahan in the
following words:

'The notes I shewed you that past between him and me
were dated in March last. The matter lay dormant till
July 27, when he wrote to me as follows:

"TO WILLIAM STRAHAN, ESQ.

"SIR,

"IT would be very foolish for us to continue strangers
any longer. You can never by persistency make wrong

---

[1] [I suspect that this is a misprint, and that Johnson wrote 'without
affecting Stoicism;'—but the original letter being burned in a mass of papers
in Scotland, I have not been able to ascertain whether my conjecture is well
founded or not. The expression in the text, however, may be justified.
MALONE.]

right. If I resented too acrimoniously, I resented only to
yourself. Nobody ever saw or heard what I wrote. You
saw that my anger was over, for in a day or two I came to
your house. I have given you a longer time; and I hope
you have made so good use of it, as to be no longer on evil
terms with,[a] Sir,

" Your, &c.

"Sam. Johnson" [H]

a *The Quarrels* must
prove him querulous.

'On this I called upon him: and he has since dined
with me.'

After this time, the same friendship as formerly continued between Dr. Johnson and Mr. Strahan. My friend
mentioned to me a little circumstance of his attention,
which, though we may smile at it, must be allowed to have
its foundation in a nice and true knowledge of human life.
'When I write to Scotland (said he,) I employ Strahan to
frank my letters, that he may have the consequence of
appearing a Parliament-man among his countrymen.'

'to captain langton,[1] warley-camp

'DEAR SIR,

'When I recollect how long ago I was received with
so much kindness at Warley Common, I am ashamed that
I have not made some enquiries after my friends.

'Pray how many sheep-stealers did you convict? and
how did you punish them? When are you to be cantoned
in better habitations? The air grows cold, and the ground
damp. Longer stay in the camp cannot be without much
danger to the health of the common men, if even the
officers can escape.

'You see that Dr. Percy is now Dean of Carlisle; about
five hundred a year, with a power of presenting himself
to some good living. He is provided for.

'The Session of the Club is to commence with that of
the parliament. Mr. Banks desires to be admitted; he will
be a very honourable accession.

---

[1] Dr. Johnson here addresses his worthy friend, Bennet Langton, Esq. by
his title as Captain of the Lincolnshire militia, in which he has since been
most deservedly raised to the rank of Major.

'Did the King please you? The Coxheath men, I think, have some reason to complain: Reynolds says your camp is better than theirs.

' I hope you find yourself able to encounter this weather. Take care of your own health: and, as you can, of your men. Be pleased to make my compliments to all the gentlemen whose notice I have had, and whose kindness I have experienced.

'I am, dear Sir,

'Your most humble servant,

'October 31, 1778.'   'SAM. JOHNSON'

I wrote to him on the 18th of August, the 18th of September, and the 6th of November; informing him of my having had another son born, whom I had called James; that I had passed some time at Auchinleck; that the Countess of Loudoun, now in her ninety-ninth year, was as fresh as when he saw her, and remembered him with respect; and that his mother by adoption, the Countess of Eglintoune, had said to me, 'Tell Mr. Johnson I love him exceedingly;' that I had again suffered much from bad spirits; and that as it was very long since I heard from him, I was not a little uneasy.

index sign and underlined:
ninety-ninth [H]

The continuance of his regard for his friend Dr. Burney, appears from the following letters:

'TO THE REVEREND DR. WHEELER, OXFORD

'DEAR SIR,

'DR. BURNEY, who brings this paper, is engaged in a History of Musick; and having been told by Dr. Markham of some MSS. relating to his subject, which are in the library of your College, is desirous to examine them. He is my friend; and therefore I take the liberty of entreating your favour and assistance in his enquiry: and can assure you, with great confidence, that if you knew him he would not want any intervenient solicitation to obtain the kindness of one who loves learning and virtue as you love them.

'I have been flattering myself all the summer with the hope of paying my annual visit to my friends; but something has obstructed me: I still hope not to be long without seeing you. I should be glad of a little literary talk; and glad to shew you, by the frequency of my visits, how eagerly I love it, when you talk it.

'I am, dear Sir,

'Your most humble servant,

'London, November 2, 1778.' 'SAM. JOHNSON'

'TO THE REVEREND DR. EDWARDS, OXFORD

'SIR,

'THE bearer, DR. BURNEY, has had some account of a Welsh Manuscript in the Bodleian library, from which he hopes to gain some materials for his History of Musick; but being ignorant of the language, is at a loss where to find assistance. I make no doubt but you, Sir, can help him through his difficulties, and therefore take the liberty of recommending him to your favour, as I am sure you will find him a man worthy of every civility that can be shewn, and every benefit that can be conferred.

'But we must not let Welsh drive us from Greek. What comes of Xenophon? If you do not like the trouble of publishing the book, do not let your commentaries be lost; contrive that they may be published somewhere.

'I am, Sir,

'Your humble servant,

'London, November 2, 1778.' 'SAM. JOHNSON'

These letters procured Dr. Burney great kindness and friendly offices from both of these gentlemen, not only on that occasion, but in future visits to the university. The same year Dr. Johnson not only wrote to Dr. Joseph Warton in favour of Dr. Burney's youngest son,[a] who was to be placed in the college of Winchester, but accompanied him when he went thither.

We surely cannot but admire the benevolent exertions of this great and good man, especially when we consider how grievously he was afflicted with bad health and how uncomfortable his home was made by the perpetual jarring of those whom he charitably accommodated under his roof. He has sometimes suffered me to talk jocularly of his group of females, and call them his *Seraglio*. He thus mentions

[a] *That was* Dick *mentioned in Piozzi's Anecdotes.* [H]

Richard Burney I wonder what became of him! Death became of him or to him A:D: 1809. [I]

them, together with honest Levett, in one of his letters to
Mrs. Thrale;[1] 'Williams hates every body; Levett hates
Desmoulins, and does not love Williams; Desmoulins hates
them both; Poll[2] loves none of them.'

'TO JAMES BOSWELL, ESQ.

'DEAR SIR,

'IT is indeed a long time since I wrote, and I think
you have some reason to complain; however, you must not
let small things disturb you, when you have such a fine
addition to your happiness as a new boy, and I hope your
lady's health restored by bringing him. It seems very
probable that a little care will now restore her, if any
remains of her complaints are left.

'You seem, if I understand your letter, to be gaining
ground at Auchinleck, an incident that would give me
great delight.   * * * * * *

'When any fit of anxiety or gloominess, or perversion of
mind, lays hold upon you, make it a rule not to publish it
by complaints, but exert your whole care to hide it; by endeavouring to hide it, you will drive it away. Be always busy.

'The CLUB is to meet with the parliament; we talk of
electing Banks, the traveller;[a] he will be a reputable
member.

[a] & he is dead now 1820—his Travels are done. [H]

'Langton has been encamped with his company of
militia on Warley-common; I spent five days amongst
them; he signalized himself as a diligent officer, and has
very high respect in the regiment. He presided when I was
there at a court-martial; he is now quartered in Hertford-
shire; his lady and little ones are in Scotland. Paoli came
to the camp, and commended the soldiers.

'Of myself I have no great matters to say, my health
is not restored, my nights are restless and tedious. The
best night that I have had these twenty years was at
Fort-Augustus.

'I hope soon to send you a few lives to read.

'I am, dear Sir,
'Your most affectionate,

'November 21, 1778.'   'SAM. JOHNSON'

[1] Vol. ii. p. 38.   [2] Miss Carmichael.

About this time the Rev. Mr. John Hussey, who had been some time in trade, and was then a clergyman of the church of England,[a] being about to undertake a journey to Aleppo, and other parts of the East, which he accomplished, Dr. Johnson, (who had long been in habits of intimacy with him,) honoured him with the following letter:

underlined: *then* [H]

[a] *did he change his Religious Opinions? This could not sure be Father Hussey who died Titular Bishop of Waterford.* [H]

'TO MR. JOHN HUSSEY

'DEAR SIR,

'I HAVE sent you the "Grammar," and have left you two books more, by which I hope to be remembered: write my name in them; we may perhaps see each other no more, you part with my good wishes, nor do I despair of seeing you return. Let no opportunities of vice corrupt you; let no bad example seduce you; let the blindness of Mahometans confirm you in Christianity. God bless you.

'I am, dear Sir,
'Your affectionate humble servant,

'December 29, 1778.'   'SAM. JOHNSON'

Johnson this year expressed great satisfaction at the publication of the first volume of 'Discourses to the Royal Academy,' by Sir Joshua Reynolds, whom he always considered as one of his literary school. Much praise indeed is due to those excellent Discourses, which are so universally admired, and for which the authour received from the Empress of Russia a gold snuff-box, adorned with her profile in *bas relief*, set in diamonds; and containing what is infinitely more valuable, a slip of paper, on which are written with her Imperial Majesty's own hand, the following words: '*Pour le Chevalier Reynolds en temoignage du contentement que j'ai ressentie à la lecture de ses excellens discours sur la peinture.*'

In 1779, Johnson gave the world a luminous proof that the vigour of his mind in all its faculties, whether memory, judgement, or imagination, was not in the least abated; for this year came out the first four volumes of his 'Prefaces, biographical and critical, to the most eminent of the English Poets,'* published by the booksellers of London. The remaining volumes came out in the year 1780. The

marginal line:
the decision . . . the
perpetuity [H]

Poets were selected by the several booksellers who had the honorary copy right, which is still preserved among them by mutual compact, notwithstanding the decision of the House of Lords against the perpetuity of Literary Property. We have his own authority,[1] that by his recommendation the poems of Blackmore, Watts, Pomfret, and Yalden, were added to the collection. Of this work I shall speak more particularly hereafter.

On the 22d of January, I wrote to him on several topicks, and mentioned that as he had been so good as to permit me to have the proof sheets of his 'Lives of the Poets,' I had written to his servant, Francis, to take care of them for me.

'MR. BOSWELL TO DR. JOHNSON

'MY DEAR SIR,   'Edinburgh, Feb. 2, 1779

'GARRICK's death is a striking event; not that we should be surprised with the death of any man, who has lived sixty-two years;[2] but because there was a *vivacity* in our late celebrated friend, which drove away the thoughts of *death* from any association with *him*. I am sure you will be tenderly affected with his departure; and I would wish to hear from you upon the subject. I was obliged to him in my days of effervescence in London, when poor Derrick was my governour; and since that time I received many civilities from him. Do you remember how pleasing it was, when I received a letter from him at Inverary, upon our first return to civilized living after our Hebridean journey. I shall always remember him with affection as well as admiration.

'On Saturday last, being the 30th of January, I drank coffee and old port, and had solemn conversation with the Reverend Mr. Falconer, a nonjuring bishop, a very learned and worthy man. He gave two toasts, which you will believe I drank with cordiality, Dr. Samuel Johnson, and

[1] Life of Watts.

[2] [On Mr. Garrick's Monument in Lichfield Cathedral, he is said to have died, 'aged 64 years.' But it is a mistake, and Mr. Boswell is perfectly correct. Garrick was baptized at Hereford, Feb. 28, 1716–17, and died at his house in London, Jan. 20, 1779. The inaccuracy of lapidary inscriptions is well known. MALONE.]

Flora Macdonald. I sat about four hours with him, and it was really as if I had been living in the last century. The Episcopal Church of Scotland, though faithful to the royal house of Stuart, has never accepted of any *congé d'élire*, since the Revolution; it is the only true Episcopal Church in Scotland, as it has its own succession of bishops. For as to the episcopal clergy who take the oaths to the present government, they indeed follow the rites of the Church of England, but, as Bishop Falconer observed, "they are not *Episcopals;* for they are under no bishop, as a bishop cannot have authority beyond his diocese." This venerable gentleman did me the honour to dine with me yesterday, and he laid his hands upon the heads of my little ones. We had a good deal of curious literary conversation, particularly about Mr. Thomas Ruddiman, with whom he lived in great friendship.

marginal line:
Episcopal Church . . . only true [H]

'Any fresh instance of the uncertainty of life makes one embrace more closely a valuable friend. My dear and much respected Sir, may GOD preserve you long in this world while I am in it.

'I am ever,
'Your much obliged,
'And affectionate humble servant,
'JAMES BOSWELL'

On the 23d of February I wrote to him again, complaining of his silence, as I had heard he was ill, and had written to Mr. Thrale for information concerning him; and I announced my intention of soon being again in London.

'TO JAMES BOSWELL, ESQ.

'DEAR SIR,
'WHY should you take such delight to make a bustle, to write to Mr. Thrale that I am negligent, and to Francis to do what is so very unnecessary. Thrale, you may be sure, cared not about it;[a] and I shall spare Francis the trouble, by ordering a set both of the Lives and Poets to dear Mrs. Boswell,[1] in acknowledgement of her marmalade.

underlined:
cared not about it [H]
a *To be sure he did not.* [H]

[1] He sent a set elegantly bound and gilt, which was received as a very handsome present.

Persuade her to accept them, and accept them kindly. If I thought she would receive them scornfully, I would send them to Miss Boswell, who, I hope, has yet none of her mamma's ill-will to me.

'I would send sets of Lives, four volumes, to some other friends, to Lord Hailes first. His second volume lies by my bed-side; a book surely of great labour, and to every just thinker of great delight. Write me word to whom I shall send besides; would it please Lord Auchinleck? Mrs. Thrale waits in the coach.[a]

a which he cared no more for, than her Husband cared about Boswell's anxiety. [H]

'I am, dear Sir, &c.

'March 13, 1779.'   'SAM. JOHNSON'

This letter crossed me on the road to London, where I arrived on Monday, March 15, and next morning at a late hour, found Dr. Johnson sitting over his tea, attended by Mrs. Desmoulins, Mr. Levett, and a clergyman,[b] who had come to submit some poetical pieces to his revision. It is wonderful what a number and variety of writers, some of them even unknown to him, prevailed on his good-nature to look over their works, and suggest corrections and improvements. My arrival interrupted, for a little while, the important business of this true representative of Bayes; upon its being resumed, I found that the subject under immediate consideration was a translation, yet in manuscript, of the *Carmen Seculare* of Horace, which had this year been set to musick, and performed as a publick entertainment in London, for the joint benefit of Monsieur Philidor and Signor Baretti. When Johnson had done reading, the authour asked him bluntly, 'If upon the whole it was a good translation?' Johnson, whose regard for truth was uncommonly strict, seemed to be puzzled for a moment, what answer to make; as he certainly could not honestly commend the performance: with exquisite address he evaded the question thus, 'Sir, I do not say that it may not be made a very good translation.' Here nothing whatever in favour of the performance was affirmed, and yet the writer was not shocked. A printed 'Ode to the Warlike Genius of Britain' came next in review; the bard[c] was a lank bony figure, with short black hair; he was writhing himself in agitation, while Johnson read, and shewing his

underlined: *clergyman* [H]

b Was it Dr Delap? [H]

marginal line: *representative of . . . I found* [H]

c Mr. Tasker [I]

teeth in a grin of earnestness, exclaimed in broken sentences, and in a keen sharp tone, 'Is that poetry, Sir?—Is it Pindar?' JOHNSON. 'Why, Sir, there is here a great deal of what is called poetry.' Then, turning to me, the poet cried, 'My muse has not been long upon the town, and (pointing to the Ode) it trembles under the hand of the great critick.' Johnson, in a tone of displeasure, asked him, 'Why do you praise Anson?' I did not trouble him by asking his reason for this question. He proceeded, 'Here is an errour, Sir; you have made Genius feminine.'— 'Palpable, Sir; (cried the enthusiast) I know it. But (in a lower tone) it was to pay a compliment to the Duchess of Devonshire, with which her Grace was pleased. She is walking across Coxheath, in the military uniform, and I suppose her to be the Genius of Britain.' JOHNSON. 'Sir, you are giving a reason for it; but that will not make it right. You may have a reason why two and two should make five; but they will still make but four.'

Although I was several times with him in the course of the following days, such it seems were my occupations, or such my negligence, that I have preserved no memorial of his conversation till Friday, March 26, when I visited him. He said he expected to be attacked on account of his 'Lives of the Poets.' 'However (said he) I would rather be attacked than unnoticed. For the worst thing you can do to an authour is to be silent as to his works. An assault upon a town is a bad thing; but starving it is still worse; an assault may be unsuccessful, you may have more men killed than you kill; but if you starve the town, you are sure of victory.'

index sign: *the worst thing* etc. [H]

Talking of a friend of ours associating with persons of very discordant principles and characters; I said he was a very universal man, quite a man of the world. JOHNSON. 'Yes, Sir; but one may be so much a man of the world, as to be nothing in the world. I remember a passage in Goldsmith's "Vicar of Wakefield," which he was afterwards fool enough to expunge: "I do not love a man who is zealous for nothing."' BOSWELL. 'That was a fine passage.' JOHNSON. 'Yes, Sir: there was another fine passage too, which he struck out: "When I was a young man, being anxious to distinguish myself, I was perpetually starting

two marginal lines: *to expunge* . . . *fine passage* [H]

new propositions. But I soon gave this over; for, I found that generally what was new was false."'[1] I said I did not like to sit with people of whom I had not a good opinion. JOHNSON. 'But you must not indulge your delicacy too much; or you will be a *tête-à-tête* man all your life.'

During my stay in London this spring, I find I was unaccountably negligent in preserving Johnson's sayings, more so than at any time when I was happy enough to have an opportunity of hearing his wisdom and wit. There is no help for it now. I must content myself with presenting such scraps as I have. But I am nevertheless ashamed and vexed to think how much has been lost. It is not that there was a bad crop this year; but that I was not sufficiently careful in gathering it in. I, therefore, in some instances, can only exhibit a few detached fragments.

Talking of the wonderful concealment of the authour of the celebrated letters signed *Junius;* he said, 'I should have believed Burke to be Junius, because I know no man but Burke who is capable of writing these letters; but Burke spontaneously denied it to me. The case would have been different, had I asked him if he was the authour; a man so questioned, as to an anonymous publication, may think he has a right to deny it.'

He observed that his old friend, Mr. Sheridan, had been honoured with extraordinary attention in his own country, by having had an exception made in his favour in an Irish Act of Parliament concerning insolvent debtors. 'Thus to be singled out (said he) by a legislature, as an object of public consideration and kindness, is a proof of no common merit.'

At Streatham, on Monday, March 29, at breakfast, he maintained that a father had no right to controul the inclinations of his daughter in marriage.[a]

On Wednesday, March 31, when I visited him, and confessed an excess of which I had very seldom been guilty:

---

[a] *Some of his Auditors were however of [the] Opinion, that Children might controul their Parents in Marriage.* [H]

he always did say so; & it is express'd,— at least implied in his Rambler. [I]

[1] [Dr. Burney, in a note introduced in a former page, has mentioned this circumstance, concerning Goldsmith, as communicated to him by Dr. Johnson; not recollecting that it occurred here. His remark, however, is not wholly superfluous, as it ascertains that the words which Goldsmith had put into the mouth of a fictitious character in 'The Vicar of Wakefield,' and which, as we learn from Dr. Johnson, he afterwards expunged, related, like many other passages in his Novel, to himself. MALONE.]

that I had spent a whole night in playing at cards, and that I could not look back on it with satisfaction: instead of a harsh animadversion, he mildly said, 'Alas, Sir, on how few things can we look back with satisfaction.'

On Thursday, April 1, he commended one of the Dukes of Devonshire for 'a dogged veracity.'[1] He said too, 'London is nothing to some people; but to a man whose pleasure is intellectual, London is the place. And there is no place where economy can be so well practised as in London: more can be had here for the money, even by ladies, than any where else. You cannot play tricks with your fortune in a small place; you must make an uniform appearance. Here a lady may have well-furnished apartments, and elegant dress, without any meat in her kitchen.'

I was amused by considering with how much ease and coolness he could write or talk to a friend, exhorting him not to suppose that happiness was not to be found as well in other places as in London; when he himself was at all times sensible of its being, comparatively speaking, a heaven upon earth. The truth is, that by those who from sagacity, attention, and experience, have learnt the full advantage of London, its pre-eminence over every other place, not only for variety of enjoyment, but for comfort, will be felt with a philosophical exultation. The freedom from remark and petty censure, with which life may be passed there, is a circumstance which a man who knows the teazing restraint of a narrow circle must relish highly. Mr. Burke, whose orderly and amiable domestick habits might make the eye of observation less irksome to him than to most men, said once very pleasantly, in my hearing, 'Though I have the honour to represent Bristol, I should not like to live there; I should be obliged to be so much *upon my good behaviour.*' In London, a man may live in splendid society at one time, and in frugal retirement at another, without animadversion. There, and there alone, a man's own house is truly his *castle*, in which he can be in perfect safety from intrusion whenever he pleases. I never shall forget how well this was expressed to me one day by Mr. Meynell: 'The chief advantage of London (said he) is, that a man is always *so near his burrow.*'

marginal line: *but to . . . where economy* [H]

marginal line: *can be . . . your fortune* [H]

marginal line: *he himself . . . The truth* [H]

marginal line: *remark and . . . and amiable* [H]

marginal line: *very pleasantly . . . much upon* [H]

marginal line: *retirement at . . . his castle* [H]

marginal line: *The chief . . . that a* [H]

[1] See vol. ii. p. 409.

He said of one of his old acquaintances, 'He is very fit for a travelling governour.' He knows French very well. He is a man of good principles; and there would be no danger that a young gentleman should catch his manner; for it is so very bad, that it must be avoided. In that respect he would be like the drunken Helot.'[a]

[a] *I guess not who it was.* [H]

A gentleman has informed me, that Johnson said of the same person, 'Sir, he has the most *inverted* understanding of any man whom I have ever known.'[b]

[b] *I have a notion it was the Revd Mr. Mence: of whom I once heard Dr. Johnson say to Old Burney—Sir—Mence is a Man who should be stuck upon a Pole, & a large Writing under him—to say Do nothing as Mence does it.* [H]

Oh Dear! who could that be? was it Mr. Mence? [I]

On Friday, April 2, being Good-Friday, I visited him in the morning as usual; and finding that we insensibly fell into a train of ridicule upon the foibles of one of our friends, a very worthy man, I, by way of a check, quoted some good admonition from 'The Government of the Tongue,' that very pious book. It happened also remarkably enough, that the subject of the sermon preached to us to-day by Dr. Burrows, the rector of St. Clement Danes, was the certainty that at the last day we must give an account of 'the deeds done in the body;' and amongst various acts of culpability he mentioned evil-speaking. As we were moving slowly along in the crowd from church, Johnson jogged my elbow and said, 'Did you attend to the sermon?'—'Yes, Sir, (said I,) it was very applicable to *us*.' He, however, stood upon the defensive. 'Why, Sir, the sense of ridicule is given us, and may be lawfully used. The authour of "The Government of the Tongue" would have us treat all men alike.'

In the interval between morning and evening service, he endeavoured to employ himself earnestly in devotional exercise; and, as he has mentioned in his 'Prayers and Meditations,'[1] gave me '*Les Pensées de Pascal*,' that I might not interrupt him. I preserve the book with reverence. His presenting it to me is marked upon it with his own hand, and I have found in it a truly divine unction. We went to church again in the afternoon.

On Saturday, April 3, I visited him at night, and found him sitting in Mrs. Williams's room, with her, and one who he afterwards told me was a natural son[2] of the second

---

[1] Page 173.

[2] [Mr. Mauritius Lowe, a painter, in whose favour Johnson, some years afterwards, wrote a kind letter to Sir Joshua Reynolds. MALONE.]

Lord Southwell. The table had a singular appearance, being covered with a heterogeneous assemblage of oysters and porter for his company, and tea for himself. I mentioned my having heard an eminent physician, who was himself a Christian, argue in favour of universal toleration, and maintain, that no man could be hurt by another man's differing from him in opinion. JOHNSON. 'Sir, you are to a certain degree hurt by knowing that even one man does not believe.'

On Easter-day, after solemn service at St. Paul's, I dined with him: Mr. Allen the printer was also his guest. He was uncommonly silent; and I have not written down any thing, except a single curious fact, which, having the sanction of his inflexible veracity, may be received as a striking instance of human insensibility and inconsideration. As he was passing by a fishmonger who was skinning an eel alive, he heard him 'curse it, because it would not lye still.'[a]

On Wednesday, April 7, I dined with him at Sir Joshua Reynolds's. I have not marked what company was there. Johnson harangued upon the qualities of different liquors; and spoke with great contempt of claret, as so weak, that 'a man would be drowned by it before it made him drunk.' He was persuaded to drink one glass of it, that he might judge, not from recollection, which might be dim, but from immediate sensation. He shook his head, and said, 'Poor stuff! No, Sir, claret is the liquor for boys; port for men; but he who aspires to be a hero (smiling) must drink brandy. In the first place, the flavour of brandy is most grateful to the palate; and then brandy will do soonest for a man what drinking *can* do for him. There are, indeed, few who are able to drink brandy. That is a power rather to be wished for than attained. And yet, (proceeded he) as in all pleasure hope is a considerable part, I know not but fruition comes too quick by brandy. Florence wine I think the worst; it is wine only to the eye; it is wine neither while you are drinking it, nor after you have drunk it; it neither pleases the taste, nor exhilarates the spirits.'[b] I reminded him how heartily he and I used to drink wine together, when we were first acquainted; and how I used to have a head-ache after sitting up with him.

[a] *This is a common Book Story, & in every Mouth: was it really True once & did Johnson witness it??* [I]

[b] *Povero   Aleatico! Povero   Monte Pulciano!* [H]

marginal line:
stroke at . . . into it [H]

marginal line:
ache?' JOHNSON . . .
a true [H]

He did not like to have this recalled, or, perhaps, thinking that I boasted improperly, resolved to have a witty stroke at me; 'Nay, Sir, it was not the *wine* that made your head-ache, but the *sense* that I put into it.' BOSWELL. 'What, Sir! will sense make the head ache?' JOHNSON. 'Yes, Sir, (with a smile) when it is not used to it.'—No man who has a true relish of pleasantry could be offended at this; especially if Johnson in a long intimacy had given him repeated proofs of his regard and good estimation. I used to say, that as he had given me a thousand pounds in praise, he had a good right now and then to take a guinea from me.^a

^a *a good Joke . . . but I remember the Guineas better than the Bank Bill.* [H]

On Thursday, April 8, I dined with him at Mr. Allan Ramsay's, with Lord Graham and some other company. We talked of Shakspeare's witches. JOHNSON. 'They are beings of his own creation; they are a compound of malignity and meanness, without any abilities: and are quite different from the Italian magician. King James says in his "Dæmonology," "Magicians command the devils: witches are their servants." The Italian magicians are elegant beings.' RAMSAY. 'Opera witches, not Drury-lane witches.'—JOHNSON observed that abilities might be employed in a narrow sphere, as in getting money, which he said he believed no man could do, without vigorous parts, though concentrated to a point. RAMSAY. 'Yes, like a strong horse in a mill; he pulls better.'

marginal line:
Dæmonology" "Magicians . . . are elegant [H]

Lord Graham, while he praised the beauty of Loch-lomond, on the banks of which is his family seat, complained of the climate, and said he could not bear it. JOHNSON. 'Nay, my Lord, don't talk so: you may bear it well enough. Your ancestors have borne it more years than I can tell.' This was a handsome compliment to the antiquity of the House of Montrose. His Lordship told me afterwards, that he had only affected to complain of the climate; lest, if he had spoken as favourably of his country as he really thought, Dr. Johnson might have attacked it. Johnson was very courteous to Lady Margaret Macdonald. 'Madam, (said he,) when I was in the Isle of Sky, I heard of the people running to take the stones off the road, lest Lady Margaret's horse should stumble.'

Lord Graham commended Dr. Drummond at Naples

as a man of extraordinary talents; and added, that he had
a great love of liberty. JOHNSON. 'He is *young*, my Lord;
(looking to his Lordship with an arch smile) all *boys* love
liberty, till experience convinces them they are not so fit
to govern themselves as they imagined. We are all agreed
as to our own liberty; we would have as much of it as we
can get; but we are not agreed as to the liberty of others:
for in proportion as we take, others must lose. I believe we
hardly wish that the mob should have liberty to govern
us. When that was the case some time ago, no man was at
liberty not to have candles in his windows.' RAMSAY.
'The result is, that order is better than confusion.' JOHN-
SON. 'The result is, that order cannot be had but by
subordination.'

On Friday, April 16, I had been present at the trial of
the unfortunate Mr. Hackman, who, in a fit of frantick
jealous love, had shot Miss Ray, the favourite of a nobleman. Johnson, in whose company I dined to-day with
some other friends, was much interested by my account of
what passed, and particularly with his prayer for the
mercy of heaven. He said, in a solemn fervid tone, 'I hope
he *shall* find mercy.'

This day a violent altercation arose between Johnson
and Beauclerk, which having made much noise at the
time, I think it proper, in order to prevent any future
misrepresentation, to give a minute account of it.

In talking of Hackman, Johnson argued, as Judge
Blackstone had done, that his being furnished with two
pistols was a proof that he meant to shoot two persons.
Mr. Beauclerk said, 'No; for that every wise man who
intended to shoot himself, took two pistols, that he might
be sure of doing it at once. Lord————'s cook
shot himself with one pistol,[a] and lived ten days in great
agony. Mr. ————,[b] who loved buttered muffins, but
durst not eat them because they disagreed with his
stomach, resolved to shoot himself; and then he eat three
buttered muffins for breakfast, before shooting himself,
knowing that he should not be troubled with indigestion;
he had two charged pistols; one was found lying charged
upon the table by him, after he had shot himself with the
other.'—'Well, (said Johnson, with an air of triumph,)

[a] *I never heard the Story* [I]

exclamation point: Mr. ———— etc. [H]

[b] *nor of this Man* [I]

you see here one pistol was sufficient.' Beauclerk replied smartly, 'Because it happened to kill him.' And either then or a very little afterwards, being piqued at Johnson's triumphant remark, added, 'This is what you don't know, and I do.' There was then a cessation of the dispute; and some minutes intervened, during which, dinner and the glass went on cheerfully; when Johnson suddenly and abruptly exclaimed, 'Mr. Beauclerk, how came you to talk so petulantly to me, as "This is what you don't know, but what I know"? One thing *I* know, which *you* don't seem to know, that you are very uncivil.' BEAUCLERK. 'Because *you* began by being uncivil, (which you always are.)' The words in parentheses were, I believe, not heard by Dr. Johnson. Here again there was a cessation of arms. Johnson told me, that the reason why he waited at first some time without taking any notice of what Mr. Beauclerk said, was because he was thinking whether he should resent it. But when he considered that there were present a young Lord and an eminent traveller, two men of the world with whom he had never dined before, he was apprehensive that they might think they had a right to take such liberties with him as Beauclerk did, and therefore resolved he would not let it pass; adding, 'that he would not appear a coward.' A little while after this, the conversation turned on the violence of Hackman's temper. Johnson then said, 'It was his business to *command* his temper, as my friend, Mr. Beauclerk, should have done some time ago.' BEAUCLERK. 'I should learn of *you*, Sir.' JOHNSON. 'Sir, you have given *me* opportunities enough of learning, when I have been in *your* company. No man loves to be treated with contempt.'[a] BEAUCLERK. (with a polite inclination towards Johnson) 'Sir, you have known me twenty years, and however I may have treated others, you may be sure I could never treat you with contempt.' JOHNSON. 'Sir, you have said more than was necessary.' Thus it ended; and Beauclerk's coach not having come for him till very late, Dr. Johnson and another gentleman sat with him a long time after the rest of the company were gone; and he and I dined at Beauclerk's on the Saturday se'nnight following.

[a] *This last was a good Hit.* [H]

After this tempest had subsided, I recollect the following particulars of his conversation:

'I am always for getting a boy forward in his learning; for that is a sure good. I would let him at first read *any* English book which happens to engage his attention; because you have done a great deal, when you have brought him to have entertainment from a book. He'll get better books afterwards.'

underlined:
when you . . . books afterwards. [H]

'Mallet, I believe, never wrote a single line of his projected Life of the Duke of Marlborough. He groped for materials; and thought of it, till he had exhausted his mind. Thus it sometimes happens that men entangle themselves in their own schemes.'

'To be contradicted, in order to force you to talk, is mighty unpleasing. You *shine*, indeed, but it is by being *ground*.'ᵃ

ᵃ *very good.* [H]

Of a gentleman who made some figure among the *Literati* of his time, (Mr. Fitzherbert,) he said, 'What eminence he had was by a felicity of manner: he had no more learning than what he could not help.'

On Saturday, April 24, I dined with him at Mr. Beauclerk's, with Sir Joshua Reynolds, Mr. Jones, (afterwards Sir William,) Mr. Langton, Mr. Steevens, Mr. Paradise, and Dr. Higgins. I mentioned that Mr. Wilkes had attacked Garrick to me, as a man who had no friend. JOHNSON. 'I believe he is right, Sir. Οι φιλοι, ου φιλος. —He had friends, but no friend.[1] Garrick was so diffused, he had no man to whom he wished to unbosom himself. He found people always ready to applaud him, and that always for the same thing: so he saw life with great uniformity.' I took upon me, for once, to fight with Goliath's weapons, and play the sophist.—'Garrick did not need a friend, as he got from every body all he wanted. What is a friend? One who supports you and comforts you, while others do not. Friendship, you know, Sir, is the cordial drop, "to make the nauseous draught of life go down:" but if the draught be not nauseous, if it be all sweet, there is no occasion for that drop.' JOHNSON. 'Many men would not be content to live so. I hope I should not. They would wish to have an intimate friend, with whom they might

underlined:
Sir. Οι . . . *man to* [H]

[1] See p. 5 of this vol. and vol. i. p. 137.

compare minds, and cherish private virtues.' One of the company mentioned Lord Chesterfield, as a man who had no friend. JOHNSON. 'There were more materials to make friendship in Garrick, had he not been so diffused.' BOSWELL. 'Garrick was pure gold, but beat out to thin leaf. Lord Chesterfield was tinsel.' JOHNSON. 'Garrick was a very good man, the cheerfulest man of his age; a decent liver in a profession which is supposed to give indulgence to licentiousness; and a man who gave away freely, money acquired by himself. He began the world with a great hunger for money; the son of a half-pay officer, bred in a family whose study was to make four-pence do as much as others made four-pence-halfpenny do. But, when he had got money, he was very liberal.' I presumed to animadvert on his eulogy on Garrick, in his 'Lives of the Poets.' 'You say, Sir, his death eclipsed the gaiety of nations.' JOHNSON. 'I could not have said more nor less. It is the truth; *eclipsed*, not *extinguished;* and his death *did* eclipse; it was like a storm.' BOSWELL. 'But why nations? Did his gaiety extend further than his own nation?' JOHNSON. 'Why, Sir, some exaggeration must be allowed. Besides, nations may be said—if we allow the Scotch to be a nation, and to have gaiety,—which they have not. *You* are an exception, though. Come, gentlemen, let us candidly admit that there is one Scotchman who is cheerful.' BEAUCLERK. 'But he is a very unnatural Scotchman.' I, however, continued to think the compliment to Garrick hyperbolically untrue. His acting had ceased some time before his death; at any rate he had acted in Ireland but a short time, at an early period of his life, and never in Scotland. I objected also to what appears an anticlimax of praise, when contrasted with the preceding panegyrick,— 'and diminished the publick stock of harmless pleasure!'—'Is not *harmless pleasure* very tame?' JOHNSON. 'Nay, Sir, harmlesss pleasure is the highest praise. Pleasure is a word of dubious import; pleasure is in general dangerous, and pernicious to virtue; to be able therefore to furnish pleasure that is harmless, pleasure pure and unalloyed, is as great a power as man can possess.' This was, perhaps, as ingenious a defence as could be made; still, however, I was not satisfied.

two marginal lines:
BOSWELL. *'Garrick . . . tinsel.'* JOHN-
SON [H]

marginal line:
Sir, his . . . his death
[H]

queried:
if we allow etc. [H]

A celebrated wit[a] being mentioned, he said, 'One may say of him as was said of a French wit, *Il n'a de l'esprit que contre Dieu.* I have been several times in company with him, but never perceived any strong power of wit. He produces a general effect by various means; he has a cheerful countenance and a gay voice.[b] Besides his trade is wit. It would be as wild in him to come into company without merriment, as for a highwayman to take the road without his pistols.'

Talking of the effects of drinking, he said, 'Drinking may be practised with great prudence; a man who exposes himself when he is intoxicated, has not the art of getting drunk; a sober man who happens occasionally to get drunk, readily enough goes into a new company, which a man who has been drinking should never do. Such a man will undertake any thing; he is without skill in inebriation. I used to slink home when I had drunk too much. A man accustomed to self-examination will be conscious when he is drunk, though an habitual drunkard will not be conscious of it. I knew a physician, who for twenty years was not sober;[c] yet in a pamphlet, which he wrote upon fevers, he appealed to Garrick and me for his vindication from a charge of drunkenness. A bookseller (naming him)[d] who got a large fortune by trade, was so habitually and equably drunk, that his most intimate friends never perceived that he was more sober at one time than another.'

Talking of celebrated and successful irregular practisers in physick, he said, 'Taylor[1] was the most ignorant man I ever knew, but sprightly; Ward, the dullest. Taylor challenged me once to talk Latin with him; (laughing.) I quoted some of Horace, which he took to be a part of my own speech. He said a few words well enough.' BEAU-CLERK. 'I remember, Sir, you said, that Taylor was an instance how far impudence could carry ignorance.'— Mr. Beauclerk was very entertaining this day, and told us a number of short stories in a lively elegant manner, and with that air of *the world*, which has I know not what impressive effect, as if there were something more than is expressed, or than perhaps we could perfectly understand. As Johnson and I accompanied Sir Joshua Reynolds in

---

[1] [The Chevalier Taylor, the celebrated Oculist. MALONE.]

Marginal notes:

[a] *I cannot think who this was. Perhaps Sir Charles Hanbury Williams* [I]

[b] *Was it Wilkes? Wilkes had a Face too ugly ever to look chearful.* [H]

underlined: *physician* [I]

[c] *Poor Dr. James.* [H & I]

[d] *Andrew Millar I believe.* [I]

marginal line: *by trade . . . he was* [H]

marginal line: *how far . . . ignorance.' —Mr.* [H]

his coach, Johnson said, 'There is in Beauclerk a predominance over his company, that one does not like. But he is a man who has lived so much in the world, that he has a short story on every occasion; he is always ready to talk, and is never exhausted.'

Johnson and I passed the evening at Miss Reynolds's, Sir Joshua's sister. I mentioned that an eminent friend of ours, talking of the common remark, that affection descends, said, that 'this was wisely contrived for the preservation of mankind; for which it was not so necessary that there should be affection from children to parents, as from parents to children; nay, there would be no harm in that view though children should at a certain age eat their parents.' JOHNSON. 'But, Sir, if this were known generally to be the case, parents would not have affection for children.' BOSWELL. 'True, Sir; for it is in expectation of a return that parents are so attentive to their children;[a] and I know a very pretty instance of a little girl of whom her father was very fond, who once when he was in a melancholy fit, and had gone to bed, persuaded him to rise in good humour by saying, "My dear papa, please to get up, and let me help you on with your clothes, that I may learn to do it when you are an old man."'

underlined:
expectation, return [H]
 [a] *They must be silly Parents Sure,—of no Experience at all—* Scotch *Parents attentive to Interest even while fondling their babies. What Nonsense!* [H]

Soon after this time a little incident occurred, which I will not suppress, because I am desirous that my work should be, as much as is consistent with the strictest truth, an antidote to the false and injurious notions of his character, which have been given by others, and therefore I infuse every drop of genuine sweetness into my biographical cup.

'TO DR. JOHNSON

'MY DEAR SIR,

'I AM in great pain with an inflamed foot, and obliged to keep my bed, so am prevented from having the pleasure to dine at Mr. Ramsay's to-day, which is very hard; and my spirits are sadly sunk. Will you be so friendly as to come and sit an hour with me in the evening. I am ever

'Your most faithful,

'And affectionate humble servant,

'South Audley-street,   'JAMES BOSWELL'
Monday, April 26.'

'TO MR. BOSWELL

'MR. JOHNSON laments the absence of Mr. Boswell, and will come to him.'

'Harley-street.'[a]

[a] *This date* must *be false: Mr. Thrale died not till 1781 . . . and Johnson was never in Harley Street but with* his Widow. [H]

He came to me in the evening, and brought Sir Joshua Reynolds. I need scarcely say, that their conversation, while they sat by my bedside, was the most pleasing opiate to pain that could have been administered.

Johnson being now better disposed to obtain information concerning Pope than he was last year,[1] sent by me to my Lord Marchmont, a present of those volumes of his 'Lives of the Poets,' which were at this time published, with a request to have permission to wait on him; and his Lordship, who had called on him twice, obligingly appointed Saturday, the first of May, for receiving us.

On that morning Johnson came to me from Streatham, and after drinking chocolate, at General Paoli's, in South-Audley-street, we proceeded to Lord Marchmont's in Curzon-street. His Lordship met us at the door of his library, and with great politeness said to Johnson, 'I am not going to make an encomium upon *myself*, by telling you the high respect I have for *you*, Sir.' Johnson was exceedingly courteous; and the interview, which lasted about two hours, during which the Earl communicated his anecdotes of Pope, was as agreeable as I could have wished. When we came out, I said to Johnson, that considering his Lordship's civility, I should have been vexed if he had again failed to come. 'Sir, (said he,) I would rather have given twenty pounds than not have come.' I accompanied him to Streatham, where we dined, and returned to town in the evening.

On Monday, May 3, I dined with him at Mr. Dilly's; I pressed him this day for his opinion on the passage in Parnell, concerning which I had in vain questioned him in several letters, and at length obtained it in *due form of law*.

[1] See p. 47 of this volume.

CASE for Dr. JOHNSON's Opinion;
3d of May, 1779.

'PARNELL, in his "Hermit," has the following
passage:

"To clear this doubt, to know the world by sight,
To find if *books* and *swains* report it right:
(For yet by *swains alone* the world he knew,
Whose feet came wand'ring o'er the nightly dew.)"

Is there not a contradiction in its being *first* supposed that
the Hermit knew *both* what books and swains reported of
the world; yet *afterwards* said, that he knew it by swains
alone?

'*I think it an inaccuracy.—He mentions two instructors in
the first line, and says he had only one in the next.*'[1]

This evening I set out for Scotland.

'TO MRS. LUCY PORTER, IN LICHFIELD

'DEAR MADAM,

'MR. GREEN has informed me that you are much
better; I hope I need not tell you that I am glad of it. I
cannot boast of being much better; my old nocturnal
complaint still pursues me, and my respiration is difficult,
though much easier than when I left you the summer
before last. Mr. and Mrs. Thrale are well;[a] Miss has been
a little indisposed; but she is got well again. They have,

underlined:
Mr., Mrs. *Thrale* [H]
[a] *& were living either
at Southwark or Streat-
ham. never in Harley
Street.* [H]

[1] 'I do not (says Mr. Malone,) see any difficulty in this passage, and
wonder that Dr. Johnson should have acknowledged it to be *inaccurate*. The
Hermit, it should be observed, had no actual experience of the world whatsoever: all his knowledge concerning it had been obtained in two ways: from
books, and from the *relations* of those country swains, who had seen a little of
it. The plain meaning, therefore, is, "To clear his doubts concerning Providence, and to obtain some knowledge of the world by actual experience;
to see whether the accounts furnished by books, or by the oral communications of swains, were just representations of it; [I say *swains*,] for his oral or
vivâ voce information had been obtained from that part of mankind *alone*, &c."
The word *alone* here does not relate to the whole of the preceding line, as has
been supposed, but by a common licence, to the words,—*of all mankind,*
which are understood, and of which it is restrictive.'
Mr. Malone, it must be owned, has shewn much critical ingenuity in his
explanation of this passage. His interpretation, however, seems to me much

since the loss of their boy, had two daughters; but they seem likely to want a son.

'I hope you had some books which I sent you. I was sorry for poor Mrs. Adey's death, and am afraid you will be sometimes solitary; but endeavour, whether alone or in company, to keep yourself cheerful. My friends likewise die very fast; but such is the state of man. I am, dear love,

'Your most humble servant,

'May 4, 1779.'   'SAM. JOHNSON'

He had, before I left London, resumed the conversation concerning the appearance of a ghost at Newcastle upon Tyne, which Mr. John Wesley believed, but to which Johnson did not give credit. I was, however, desirous to examine the question closely, and at the same time wished to be made acquainted with Mr. John Wesley; for though I differed from him in some points, I admired his various talents, and loved his pious zeal. At my request, therefore, Dr. Johnson gave me a letter of introduction to him.

'TO THE REVEREND MR. JOHN WESLEY

'SIR,

'MR. BOSWELL, a gentleman who has been long known to me, is desirous of being known to you, and has asked this recommendation, which I give him with great willingness, because, I think it very much to be wished that worthy and religious men should be acquainted with each other.

'I am, Sir,
'Your most humble servant,

'May 3, 1779.'   'SAM. JOHNSON'

too recondite. The *meaning* of the passage may be certain enough; but surely the expression is confused, and one part of it contradictory to the other.[a]

[But why *too recondite?*—When a meaning is given to a passage by understanding words in an uncommon sense, the interpretation may be said to be *recondite*, and, however ingenious, may be suspected not to be sound; but when words are explained in their ordinary acceptation, and the explication which is fairly deduced from them without any force or constraint is also perfectly justified by the context, it surely may be safely accepted; and the calling such an explication *recondite*, when *nothing else can be said against it*, will not make it the less just. MALONE.]

[a] *Parnell was an Irishman, & made a Blunder* [1]

Mr. Wesley being in the course of his ministry at Edinburgh, I presented this letter to him, and was very politely received. I begged to have it returned to me, which was accordingly done.—His state of the evidence as to the ghost, did not satisfy me.

I did not write to Johnson, as usual, upon my return to my family; but tried how he would be affected by my silence.[a] Mr. Dilly sent me a copy of a note which he received from him on the 13th of July, in these words:

[a] *Oh! that was a deep Device.* [H]

'TO MR. DILLY

'SIR,

'SINCE Mr. Boswell's departure, I have never heard from him; please to send word what you know of him, and whether you have sent my books to his lady. I am, &c.

'SAM JOHNSON'

My readers will not doubt that his solicitude about me was very flattering.

'TO JAMES BOSWELL, ESQ.

'DEAR SIR,

'WHAT can possibly have happened, that keeps us two such strangers to each other? I expected to have heard from you when you came home; I expected afterwards. I went into the country and returned; and yet there is no letter from Mr. Boswell. No ill I hope has happened; and if ill should happen, why should it be concealed from him who loves you? Is it a fit of humour, that has disposed you to try who can hold out longest without writing? If it be, you have the victory. But I am afraid of something bad; set me free from my suspicions.

'My thoughts are at present employed in guessing the reason of your silence: you must not expect that I should tell you any thing, if I had any thing to tell.[b] Write, pray write to me, and let me know what is, or what has been the cause of this long interruption.

[b] *very true, he never did tell him any thing for fear of misrepresentation.* [H]

'I am, dear Sir,

'Your most affectionate humble servant,

'July 13, 1779.'   'SAM. JOHNSON'

'TO DR. SAMUEL JOHNSON

'MY DEAR SIR,   'Edinburgh, July 17, 1779

'WHAT may be justly denominated a supine indolence of mind, has been my state of existence since I last returned to Scotland. In a livelier state I had often suffered severely from long intervals of silence on your part; and I had even been chid by you for expressing my uneasiness. I was willing to take advantage of my insensibility, and while I could bear the experiment, to try whether your affection for me would, after an unusual silence on my part, make you write first. This afternoon I have had a very high satisfaction by receiving your kind letter of enquiry, for which I most gratefully thank you. I am doubtful if it was right to make the experiment; though I have gained by it. I was beginning to grow tender, and to upbraid myself, especially after having dreamt two nights ago that I was with you. I and my wife, and my four children, are all well. I would not delay one post to answer your letter, but as it is late, I have not time to do more. You shall soon hear from me, upon many and various particulars; and I shall never again put you to any test. I am, with veneration, my dear Sir,

> 'Your most obliged
> 'And faithful humble servant,
>
> 'JAMES BOSWELL'

On the 22d of July, I wrote to him again; and gave him an account of my last interview with my worthy friend, Mr. Edward Dilly, at his brother's house at Southill in Bedfordshire, where he died soon after I parted from him, leaving me a very kind remembrance of his regard.

I informed him that Lord Hailes, who had promised to furnish him with some anecdotes for his 'Lives of the Poets,' had sent me three instances of Prior's borrowing from *Gombauld*, in '*Recueil des Poetes*,' tome 3. Epigram 'To John I owed great obligation,' p. 25. 'To the Duke of Noailles,' p. 32. 'Sauntering Jack and idle Joan,' p. 25.

My letter was a pretty long one, and contained a variety

of particulars; but he, it should seem, had not attended to it; for his next to me was as follows:

'TO JAMES BOSWELL, ESQ.

'MY DEAR SIR,

'ARE you playing the same trick again, and trying who can keep silence longest? Remember that all tricks are either knavish or childish: and that it is as foolish to make experiments upon the constancy of a friend, as upon the chastity of a wife.

'What can be the cause of this second fit of silence, I cannot conjecture; but after one trick, I will not be cheated by another, nor will harass my thoughts with conjectures about the motives of a man who, probably, acts only by caprice. I therefore suppose you are well, and that Mrs. Boswell is well too; and that the fine summer has restored Lord Auchinleck. I am much better than you left me; I think I am better than when I was in Scotland.

'I forgot whether I informed you that poor Thrale has been in great danger. Mrs. Thrale likewise has miscarried, and been much indisposed. Every body else is well; Langton is in camp. I intend to put Lord Hailes's description of Dryden[1] into another edition, and, as I know his accuracy, wish he would consider the dates, which I could not always settle to my own mind.

^a *Helas!* [1]

'Mr. Thrale goes to Brighthelmstone,^a about Michaelmas, to be jolly and ride a hunting. I shall go to town, or perhaps to Oxford. Exercise and gaiety, or rather carelessness, will, I hope, dissipate all remains of his malady; and I likewise hope by the change of place, to find some opportunities of growing yet better myself. I am, dear Sir,

'Your humble servant,

'Streatham, Sept. 9, 1779.'   'SAM. JOHNSON'

My readers will not be displeased at being told every slight circumstance of the manner in which Dr. Johnson

---

[1] Which I communicated to him from his Lordship, but it has not yet been published. I have a copy of it.

[The few notices concerning Dryden, which Lord Hailes had collected, the authour afterwards gave me. MALONE.]

contrived to amuse his solitary hours. He sometimes employed himself in chymistry, sometimes in watering and pruning a vine, sometimes in small experiments, at which those who may smile, should recollect that they are moments which admit of being soothed only by trifles.[1]

On the 20th of September I defended myself against his suspicion of me, which I did not deserve; and added, 'Pray let us write frequently. A whim strikes me, that we should send off a sheet once a week, like a stage-coach, whether it be full or not; nay, though it should be empty. The very sight of your hand-writing would comfort me; and were a sheet to be thus sent regularly, we should much oftener convey something, were it only a few kind words.'

My friend, Colonel James Stuart, second son of the Earl of Bute, who had distinguished himself as a good officer of the Bedfordshire militia, had taken a publick-spirited resolution to serve his country in its difficulties, by raising a regular regiment, and taking the command of it himself. This, in the heir of the immense property of Wortley, was highly honourable. Having been in Scotland recruiting, he obligingly asked me to accompany him to Leeds, then the head-quarters of his corps; from thence to London for a short time, and afterwards to other places to which the regiment might be ordered. Such an offer, at a time of the year, when I had full leisure, was very pleasing; especially as I was to accompany a man of sterling good sense, information, discernment, and conviviality, and was to have a second crop, in one year, of London and Johnson. Of this I informed my illustrious friend, in characteristical warm terms, in a letter dated the 30th of September, from Leeds.

On Monday, October 4, I called at his house before he

---

[1] In one of his manuscript Diaries, there is the following entry, which marks his curious minute attention: 'July 26, 1768. I shaved my nail by accident in whetting the knife, about an eighth of an inch from the bottom, and about a fourth from the top. This I measure that I may know the growth of nails; the whole is about five-eighths of an inch.'

Another of the same kind appears, 'Aug. 7, 1779. *Partem brachii dextri carpo proximam et cutem pectoris circa mamillam dextram rasi, ut notum fieret quanto temporis pili renovarentur.*'

And, 'Aug. 15, 1783. I cut from the vine 41 leaves, which weighed five oz. and a half, and eight scruples:—I lay them upon my book-case, to see what weight they will lose by drying.'

was up. He sent for me to his bed-side, and expressed his satisfaction at this incidental meeting, with as much vivacity as if he had been in the gaiety of youth. He called briskly, 'Frank, go and get coffee, and let us breakfast *in splendour*.'

During this visit to London I had several interviews with him, which it is unnecessary to distinguish particularly. I consulted him as to the appointment of guardians to my children, in case of my death. 'Sir, (said he,) do not appoint a number of guardians. When there are many, they trust one to another, and the business is neglected. I would advise you to choose only one; let him be a man of respectable character, who, for his own credit, will do what is right; let him be a rich man, so that he may be under no temptation to take advantage; and let him be a man of business,[a] who is used to conduct affairs with ability and expertness, to whom, therefore, the execution of the trust will not be burdensome.'

underlined:
him be a rich man, a man of business [H]

[a] *on those Considerations he advised Mr. Thrale to choose Mr. Cator*. [H]

On Sunday, October 10, we dined together at Mr. Strahan's. The conversation having turned on the prevailing practice of going to the East-Indies in quest of wealth;—JOHNSON. 'A man had better have ten thousand pounds at the end of ten years passed in England, than twenty thousand pounds at the end of ten years passed in India, because you must compute what you *give* for money; and a man who has lived ten years in India, has given up ten years of social comfort and all those advantages which arise from living in England. The ingenious Mr. Brown, distinguished by the name of *Capability Brown*, told me, that he was once at the seat of Lord Clive, who had returned from India with great wealth; and that he shewed him at the door of his bed-chamber a large chest, which he said he had once had full of gold; upon which Brown observed, "I am glad you can bear it so near your bed-chamber."'

marginal line:
Brown, distinguished . . . bed-chamber [H]

We talked of the state of the poor in London.—JOHNSON. 'Saunders Welch, the Justice, who was once High-Constable of Holborn, and had the best opportunities of knowing the state of the poor, told me, that I under-rated the number, when I computed that twenty a week, that is, above a thousand a year, died of hunger; not absolutely of immediate hunger; but of the wasting and other diseases which are the consequences of hunger. This happens only in so large a place as London, where people are not known. What we are told about the great sums got by begging, is not true: the trade is overstocked. And, you may depend upon it, there are many who cannot get work. A particular kind of manufacture fails: those who have been used to work at it, can, for some time, work at nothing else. You meet a man begging; you charge him with idleness: he says, "I am willing to labour. Will you give me work?"—"I cannot."—"Why, then you have no right to charge me with idleness."[a]

*marginal line:
so large . . . sums got
[H]*

[a] I think all this true & just 'spite of the Wise ones [H]

We left Mr. Strahan's at seven, as Johnson had said he intended to go to evening prayers. As we walked alone, he complained of a little gout in his toe, and said, 'I shan't go to prayers to-night; I shall go to-morrow. Whenever I miss church on a Sunday, I resolve to go another day. But I do not always do it.' This was a fair exhibition of that vibration between pious resolutions and indolence, which many of us have too often experienced.

I went home with him, and we had a long quiet conversation.

I read him a letter from Dr. Hugh Blair concerning Pope, (in writing whose life he was now employed,) which I shall insert as a literary curiosity.[1]

'TO JAMES BOSWELL, ESQ.

'DEAR SIR,

'IN the year 1763, being at London, I was carried by Dr. John Blair, Prebendary of Westminster, to dine at old

[1] The Rev. Dr. Law, Bishop of Carlisle, in the Preface to his valuable edition of Archbishop King's 'Essay on the Origin of Evil,' mentions that the principles maintained in it had been adopted by Pope in his 'Essay on Man;' and adds, 'The fact, notwithstanding such denial (Bishop Warburton's) might have been strictly verified by an unexceptionable testimony, *viz.* that of the late Lord Bathurst, who saw the very same system of the τὸ βέλτιον (taken from the Archbishop) in Lord Bolingbroke's own hand, lying before Pope, while he was composing his Essay.' This is respectable evidence; but that of Dr. Blair is more direct from the fountain-head, as well as more full. Let me add to it that of Dr. Joseph Warton: 'The late Lord Bathurst repeatedly assured me that he had read the whole scheme of "the Essay on Man," in the hand-writing of Bolingbroke, and drawn up in a series of propositions, which Pope was to versify and illustrate.' Essay on the Genius and Writings of Pope, vol. ii. p. 62.

Lord Bathurst's; where we found the late Mr. Mallet, Sir James Porter, who had been Ambassadour at Constantinople, the late Dr. Macaulay, and two or three more. The conversation turning on Mr. Pope, Lord Bathurst told us, that "The Essay on Man" was originally composed by Lord Bolingbroke in prose, and that Mr. Pope did no more than put it into verse: that he had read Lord Bolingbroke's manuscript in his own hand-writing; and remembered well, that he was at a loss whether most to admire the elegance of Lord Bolingbroke's prose, or the beauty of Mr. Pope's verse. When Lord Bathurst told this, Mr. Mallet bade me attend, and remember this remarkable piece of information; as, by the course of Nature, I might survive his Lordship, and be a witness of his having said so. The conversation was indeed too remarkable to be forgotten. A few days after, meeting with you, who were then also at London, you will remember that I mentioned to you what had passed on this subject, as I was much struck with this anecdote. But what ascertains my recollection of it, beyond doubt, is, that being accustomed to keep a journal of what passed when I was at London, which I wrote out every evening, I find the particulars of the above information, just as I have now given them, distinctly marked; and am thence enabled to fix this conversation to have passed on Friday, the 22d of April, 1763.

'I remember also distinctly, (though I have not for this the authority of my journal,) that the conversation going on concerning Mr. Pope, I took notice of a report which had been sometimes propagated that he did not understand Greek. Lord Bathurst said to me that he knew that to be false; for that part of the Iliad was translated by Mr. Pope in his house in the country; and that in the mornings when they assembled at breakfast, Mr. Pope used frequently to repeat, with great rapture, the Greek lines which he had been translating, and then to give them his version of them, and to compare them together.

marginal line:
assembled at . . . them
together [H]

'If these circumstances can be of any use to Dr. Johnson, you have my full liberty to give them to him. I beg you will, at the same time, present to him my most respectful compliments, with best wishes for his success and fame in all his literary undertakings. I am, with great respect, my dearest Sir,

'Your most affectionate,

'Broughton Park,   'And obliged humble servant,
Sept. 21, 1779.'
                                'HUGH BLAIR'

JOHNSON. 'Depend upon it, Sir, this is too strongly stated. Pope may have had from Bolingbroke the philosophick *stamina* of his Essay; and admitting this to be true, Lord Bathurst did not intentionally falsify. But the thing is not true in the latitude that Blair seems to imagine; we are sure that the poetical imagery, which makes a great part of the poem, was Pope's own. It is amazing, Sir, what deviations there are from precise truth, in the account which is given of almost every thing. I told Mrs. Thrale, "You have so little anxiety about truth, that you never tax your memory with the exact thing." Now what is the use of the memory to truth, if one is careless of exactness? Lord Hailes's "Annals of Scotland" are very exact; but they contain mere dry particulars. They are to be considered as a Dictionary. You know such things are there; and may be looked at when you please. Robertson paints; but the misfortune is, you are sure he does not know the people whom he paints; so you cannot suppose a likeness. Characters should never be given by an historian, unless he knew the people whom he describes, or copies from those who knew them.'

marginal line:
Mrs. Thrale . . . the exact [H]

BOSWELL. 'Why, Sir, do people play this trick which I observe now, when I look at your grate, putting the shovel against it to make the fire burn?' JOHNSON. 'They play the trick, but it does not make the fire burn.[1] *There* is a better; (setting the poker perpendicularly up at right angles with the grate.) In days of superstition they thought, as it made a cross with the bars, it would drive away the witch.'

BOSWELL. 'By associating with you, Sir, I am always getting an accession of wisdom. But perhaps a man, after knowing his own character—the limited strength of his own mind, should not be desirous of having too much

---

[1] [It certainly does make the fire burn: by repelling the air, it throws a blast on the fire, and so performs the part in some degree of a blower or bellows. KEARNEY.]

wisdom, considering, *quid valeant humeri*, how little he can carry.' JOHNSON. 'Sir, be as wise as you can; let a man be *aliis lætus, sapiens sibi:*

> "Though pleas'd to see the dolphins play,
> I mind my compass and my way."[1]

marginal line:
man is . . . others think
[H]

You may be wise in your study in the morning, and gay in company at a tavern in the evening. Every man is to take care of his own wisdom and his own virtue, without minding too much what others think.'

He said, 'Dodsley first mentioned to me the scheme of an English Dictionary; but I had long thought of it.' BOSWELL. 'You did not know what you were undertaking.' JOHNSON. 'Yes, Sir, I knew very well what I was undertaking,—and very well how to do it,—and have done it very well.' BOSWELL. 'An excellent climax! and it *has* availed you. In your Preface you say, "What would it avail me in this gloom of solitude?" You have been agreeably mistaken.'

In his Life of Milton, he observes, 'I cannot but remark a kind of respect, perhaps unconsciously, paid to this great man by his biographers: every house in which he resided is historically mentioned, as if it were an injury to neglect naming any place that he honoured by his presence.' I had, before I read this observation, been desirous of shewing that respect to Johnson, by various enquiries. Finding him this evening in a very good humour, I prevailed on him to give me an exact list of his places of residence, since he entered the metropolis as an authour, which I subjoin in a note.[2]

marginal line:
residence, since . . . an
authour [H]

I mentioned to him a dispute between a friend of mine and his lady, concerning conjugal infidelity, which my friend had maintained was by no means so bad in the husband, as in the wife. JOHNSON. 'Your friend was in the right, Sir. Between a man and his Maker it is a different

---

[1] The Spleen, a Poem.

[2] 1. Exeter-street, off Catherine-street, Strand. 2. Greenwich. 3. Woodstock-street, near Hanover-square. 4. Castle-street, Cavendish-square, No. 6. 5. Strand. 6. Boswell-Court. 7. Strand, again. 8. Bow-street. 9. Holborn. 10. Fetter-lane. 11. Holborn, again. 12. Gough-Square. 13. Staple-Inn. 14. Gray's-Inn. 15. Inner Temple-lane, No. 1. 16. Johnson's-court, No. 7. 17. Bolt-court, No. 8.

question: but between a man and his wife, a husband's infidelity is nothing. They are connected by children, by fortune, by serious considerations of community. Wise married women don't trouble themselves about infidelity in their husbands.' BOSWELL. 'To be sure there is a great difference between the offence of infidelity in a man and that of his wife.' JOHNSON. 'The difference is boundless. The man imposes no bastards upon his wife.'[a]

Here it may be questioned, whether Johnson was entirely in the right. I suppose it will not be controverted that the difference in the degree of criminality is very great, on account of consequences: but still it may be maintained that, independent of moral obligation, infidelity is by no means a light offence in a husband; because it must hurt a delicate attachment, in which a mutual constancy is implied, with such refined sentiments as Massinger has exhibited in his play of 'The Picture.'—Johnson probably at another time would have admitted this opinion. And let it be kept in remembrance, that he was very careful not to give any encouragement to irregular conduct. A gentleman, not adverting to the distinction made by him upon this subject, supposed a case of singular perverseness in a wife, and heedlessly said, 'That then he thought a husband might do as he pleased with a safe conscience.' JOHNSON. 'Nay, Sir, this is wild indeed (smiling;) you must consider that fornication is a crime in a single man; and you cannot have more liberty by being married.'

He this evening expressed himself strongly against the Roman Catholics; observing, 'In every thing in which they differ from us, they are wrong.' He was even against the invocation of Saints; in short, he was in the humour of opposition.

Having regretted to him that I had learnt little Greek, as is too generally the case in Scotland; that I had for a long time hardly applied at all to the study of that noble language, and that I was desirous of being told by him what method to follow; he recommended to me as easy helps, Sylvanus's 'First Book of the Iliad;' Dawson's 'Lexicon to the Greek New Testament;' and 'Hesiod,' with *Pasoris Lexicon* at the end of it.

On Tuesday, October 12, I dined with him at Mr.

queried:
a husband's infidelity
etc. [H]

[a] Sometimes *he does:*
Johnson knew a Man
who did; & the Lady
took very tender Care of
them. [H]

marginal line:
such refined . . . probably
at [H]

marginal line:
the Greek . . . Hesiod,'
with [H]

Ramsay's, with Lord Newhaven, and some other company, none of whom I recollect, but a beautiful Miss Graham,[1] a relation of his Lordship's, who asked Dr. Johnson to hob or nob with her. He was flattered by such pleasing attention, and politely told her, he never drank wine; but if she would drink a glass of water, he was much at her service. She accepted. 'Oho, Sir! (said Lord Newhaven) you are caught.' JOHNSON. 'Nay, I do not see *how I am caught;* but if I am caught, I don't want to get free again. If I am caught, I hope to be kept.' Then when the two glasses of water were brought, smiling placidly to the young lady, he said, 'Madam, let us *reciprocate.*'

Lord Newhaven and Johnson carried on an argument for some time, concerning the Middlesex election. Johnson said, 'Parliament may be considered as bound by law, as a man is bound where there is nobody to tie the knot. As it is clear that the House of Commons may expel, and expel again and again, why not allow of the power to incapacitate for that parliament, rather than have a perpetual contest kept up between parliament and the people.' Lord Newhaven took the opposite side; but respectfully said, 'I speak with great deference to you, Dr. Johnson; I speak to be instructed.' This had its full effect on my friend. He bowed his head almost as low as the table, to a complimenting nobleman; and called out, 'My Lord, my Lord, I do not desire all this ceremony; let us tell our minds to one another quietly.' After the debate was over, he said, 'I have got lights on the subject to-day, which I had not before.' This was a great deal from him, especially as he had written a pamphlet upon it.

He observed, 'The House of Commons was originally not a privilege of the people, but a check, for the Crown, on the House of Lords. I remember, Henry the Eighth wanted them to do something; they hesitated in the morning, but did it in the afternoon. He told them, "It is well you did; or half your heads should have been upon Temple-bar." But the House of Commons is now no longer under the power of the Crown, and therefore must be bribed.' He added, 'I have no delight in talking of publick affairs.'

marginal line:
afternoon. He . . .
Temple-bar [H]

---

[1] Now the Lady of Sir Henry Dashwood, Bart.

Of his fellow-collegian, the celebrated Mr. George Whitefield, he said, 'Whitefield never drew as much attention as a mountebank does; he did not draw attention by doing better than others, but by doing what was strange. Were Astley to preach a sermon standing upon his head on a horse's back, he would collect a multitude to hear him; but no wise man would say he had made a better sermon for that. I never treated Whitefield's ministry with contempt; I believe he did good. He had devoted himself to the lower classes of mankind, and among them he was of use. But when familiarity and noise claim the praise due to knowledge, art, and elegance, we must beat down such pretensions.'

two marginal lines: was of . . . elegance, we [H]

What I have preserved of his conversation during the remainder of my stay in London at this time, is only what follows: I told him that when I objected to keeping company with a notorious infidel, a celebrated friend of ours said to me, 'I do not think that men who live laxly in the world, as you and I do, can with propriety assume such an authority. Dr. Johnson may, who is uniformly exemplary in his conduct. But it is not very consistent to shun an infidel to-day, and get drunk to-morrow.' JOHNSON. 'Nay, Sir, this is sad reasoning. Because a man cannot be right in all things, is he to be right in nothing? Because a man sometimes gets drunk, is he therefore to steal? This doctrine would very soon bring a man to the gallows.'

After all, however, it is a difficult question how far sincere Christians should associate with the avowed enemies of religion; for in the first place, almost every man's mind may be more or less "corrupted by evil communications;" secondly, the world may very naturally suppose that they are not really in earnest in religion, who can easily bear its opponents; and thirdly, if the profane find themselves quite well received by the pious, one of the checks upon an open declaration of their infidelity, and one of the probable chances of obliging them seriously to reflect, which their being shunned would do, is removed.

He, I know not why, shewed upon all occasions an aversion to go to Ireland, where I proposed to him that we should make a tour. JOHNSON. 'It is the last place where I should wish to travel.' BOSWELL. 'Should you not like

to see Dublin, Sir?' JOHNSON. 'No, Sir; Dublin is only
a worse capital.' BOSWELL. 'Is not the Giant's-causeway
worth seeing?' JOHNSON. 'Worth seeing? yes; but not
worth going to see.'

Yet he had a kindness for the Irish nation, and thus
generously expressed himself to a gentleman from that
country, on the subject of an UNION which artful Politi-
cians have often had in view—'Do not make an union with
us, Sir. We should unite with you, only to rob you.[a] We
should have robbed the Scotch, if they had had any thing
of which we could have robbed them.'

Of an acquaintance of ours, whose manners and every
thing about him, though expensive, were coarse, he said,
'Sir, you see in him vulgar prosperity.'

A foreign minister of no very high talents, who had been
in his company for a considerable time quite overlooked,
happened luckily to mention that he had read some of his
'*Rambler*' in Italian, and admired it much. This pleased
him greatly; he observed that the title had been translated,
Il Genio errante, though I have been told it was rendered
more ludicrously, *Il Vagabondo;* and finding that this
minister gave such a proof of his taste, he was all attention
to him, and on the first remark which he made, however simple, exclaimed, 'The Ambassadour[b] says well—
His Excellency observes—' And then he expanded and
enriched the little that had been said, in so strong a manner,
that it appeared something of consequence. This was exceedingly entertaining to the company who were present,
and many a time afterwards it furnished a pleasant topick
of merriment: '*The Ambassadour says well*,' became a laughable term of applause, when no mighty matter had been
expressed.

I left London on Monday, October 18, and accompanied Colonel Stuart to Chester, where his regiment was
to lye for some time.

'MR. BOSWELL TO DR. JOHNSON

'MY DEAR SIR,   'Chester, October 22, 1779

'IT was not till one o'clock on Monday morning that
Colonel Stuart and I left London; for we chose to bid a

Marginal notes:

marginal line:
seeing?' JOHNSON
... to see [H]

index sign:
We should have robbed
etc. [?]

[a] *excellent.* [H]

[b] *If he means Prince
Gonzaga he was Am-
bassador from no Place*
[I]

cordial adieu to Lord Mountstuart, who was to set out on that day on his embassy to Turin. We drove on excellently, and reached Lichfield in good time enough that night. The Colonel had heard so preferable a character of the George, that he would not put up at the Three Crowns, so that I did not see our host, Wilkins. We found at the George as good accommodation as we could wish to have, and I fully enjoyed the comfortable thought that *I was in Lichfield again.* Next morning it rained very hard; and as I had much to do in a little time, I ordered a post-chaise, and between eight and nine sallied forth to make a round of visits. I first went to Mr. Green, hoping to have had him to accompany me to all my other friends, but he was engaged to attend the Bishop of Sodor and Man, who was then lying at Lichfield very ill of the gout. Having taken a hasty glance at the additions to Green's museum, from which it was not easy to break away, I next went to the Friery, where I at first occasioned some tumult in the ladies, who were not prepared to receive *company* so early: but my *name*, which has by wonderful felicity come to be closely associated with yours, soon made all easy; and Mrs. Cobb and Miss Adey re-assumed their seats at the breakfast table, which they had quitted with some precipitation. They received me with the kindness of an old acquaintance; and after we had joined in a cordial chorus to *your* praise, Mrs. Cobb gave *me* the high satisfaction of hearing that you said, "Boswell is a man who I believe never left a house without leaving a wish for his return." And she afterwards added, that she bid you tell me, that if ever I came to Lichfield, she hoped I would take a bed at the Friery. From thence I drove to Peter Garrick's,[1] where I also found a very flattering welcome. He appeared to me to enjoy his usual cheerfulness; and he very kindly asked me to come when I could, and pass a week with him. From Mr. Garrick's, I went to the Palace to wait on Mr. Seward. I was first entertained by his lady[a] and daughter, he himself being in bed with a cold, according to his valetudinary custom. But he desired to see me; and I found him dressed in his black gown, with a white flannel night-gown above

underlined:
lady [1]

[a] *of whom I never heard till now.* [1]

---

[1] [This gentleman survived his brother David many years; and died at Lichfield, Dec. 12, 1795, ætat. 86. A. CHALMERS.]

it; so that he looked like a Dominican Friar. He was good-humoured and polite; and under his roof too my reception was very pleasing. I then proceeded to Stow-hill, and first paid my respects to Mrs. Gastrell, whose conversation I was not willing to quit. But my sand-glass was now beginning to run low, as I could not trespass too long on the Colonel's kindness, who obligingly waited for me; so I hastened to Mrs. Aston's,[1] whom I found much better than I feared I should; and there I met a brother-in-law of these ladies, who talked much of you, and very well too, as it appeared to me. It then only remained to visit Mrs. Lucy Porter, which I did, I really believe, with sincere satisfaction on both sides. I am sure I was glad to see her again; and, as I take her to be very honest, I trust she was glad to see me again; for she expressed herself so, that I could not doubt of her being in earnest. What a great key-stone of kindness, my dear Sir, were you that morning! for we were all held together by our common attachment to you. I cannot say that I ever passed two hours with more self-complacency that I did those two at Lichfield. Let me not entertain any suspicion that this is idle vanity. Will not you confirm me in my persuasion, that he who finds himself so regarded has just reason to be happy?

'We got to Chester about midnight on Tuesday; and here again I am in a state of much enjoyment. Colonel Stuart and his officers treat me with all the civility I could wish; and I play my part admirably. *Lætus aliis, sapiens sibi*, the classical sentence which you, I imagine, invented the other day, is exemplified in my present existence. The Bishop, to whom I had the honour to be known several years ago, shews me much attention; and I am edified by his conversation. I must not omit to tell you, that his Lordship admires, very highly, your Prefaces to the Poets. I am daily obtaining an extension of agreeable acquaintance, so that I am kept in animated variety; and the study of the place itself, by the assistance of books, and of the Bishop, is sufficient occupation. Chester pleases my fancy more than any town I ever saw. But I will not enter upon it at all in this letter.

exclamation point:
Chester etc. [H]

[1] [A maiden sister of Johnson's favourite, Molly Aston, who married Captain Brodie, of the Navy. MALONE.]

'How long I shall stay here I cannot yet say. I told a very pleasing young lady,[1] niece to one of the Prebendaries, at whose house I saw her, "I have come to Chester, Madam, I cannot tell how; and far less can I tell how I am to get away from it." Do not think me too juvenile. I beg it of you, my dear Sir, to favour me with a letter while I am here, and add to the happiness of a happy friend, who is ever, with affectionate veneration,

'Most sincerely yours,
'JAMES BOSWELL'

'If you do not write directly, so as to catch me here, I shall be disappointed. Two lines from you will keep my lamp burning bright.'

'TO JAMES BOSWELL, ESQ.

'DEAR SIR,

'WHY should you importune me so earnestly to write? Of what importance can it be to hear of distant friends, to a man who finds himself welcome wherever he goes, and makes new friends faster than he can want them? If to the delight of such universal kindness of reception, any thing can be added by knowing that you retain my good-will, you may indulge yourself in the full enjoyment of that small addition.

'I am glad that you made the round of Lichfield with so much success: the oftener you are seen, the more you will be liked. It was pleasing to me to read that Mrs. Aston was so well, and that Lucy Porter was so glad to see you.

'In the place where you now are, there is much to be observed; and you will easily procure yourself skilful directors. But what will you do to keep away the *black dog* that worries you at home? If you would, in compliance with your father's advice, enquire into the old tenures and old charters of Scotland, you would certainly open to yourself many striking scenes of the manners of the middle ages. The feudal system, in a country half-barbarous, is naturally productive of great anomalies in civil life. The

[1] Miss Letitia Barnston.

knowledge of past times is naturally growing less in all cases not of publick record; and the past time of Scotland is so unlike the present, that it is already difficult for a Scotch-man to image the economy of his grandfather. Do not be tardy nor negligent; but gather up eagerly what can yet be found.[1]

'We have, I think, once talked of another project, a History of the late insurrection in Scotland, with all its incidents. Many falsehoods are passing into uncontra-dicted history. Voltaire, who loved a striking story, has told what he could not find to be true.

'You may make collections for either of these projects, or for both, as opportunities occur, and digest your mate-rials at leisure. The great direction which Burton has left to men disordered like you, is this, *Be not solitary; be not idle:* which I would thus modify;—If you are idle, be not solitary; if you are solitary, be not idle.

'There is a letter for you, from

'Your humble servant,

'London, October 27, 1779.'   'SAM. JOHNSON'

TO DR. SAMUEL JOHNSON

'MY DEAR SIR,   'Carlisle, Nov. 7, 1779

'THAT I should importune you to write to me at Chester, is not wonderful, when you consider what an avidity I have for delight; and that the *amor* of pleasure, like the *amor nummi*, increases in proportion with the quan-tity which we possess of it. Your letter, so full of polite kindness and masterly counsel, came like a large treasure upon me, while already glittering with riches. I was quite enchanted at Chester, so that I could with difficulty quit it. But the enchantment was the reverse of that of Circé; for so far was there from being any thing sensual in it, that I was *all mind*. I do not mean all reason only; for my fancy

---

[1] I have a valuable collection made by my Father, which, with some additions and illustrations of my own, I intend to publish. I have some hereditary claim to be an Antiquary; not only from my Father, but as being descended, by the mother's side, from the able and learned Sir John Skene, whose merit bids defiance to all the attempts which have been made to lessen his fame.

was kept finely in play. And why not?—If you please I will
send you a copy, or an abridgement of my Chester journal,
which is truly a log-book of felicity.

'The Bishop treated me with a kindness which was very
flattering. I told him, that you regretted you had seen so
little of Chester. His Lordship bade me tell you, that he
should be glad to shew you more of it. I am proud to find
the friendship with which you honour me is known in so
many places.

'I arrived here late last night. Our friend the Dean has
been gone from hence some months; but I am told at my
inn, that he is very *populous* (popular.) However, I found
Mr. Law, the Archdeacon, son to the Bishop, and with
him I have breakfasted and dined very agreeably. I got
acquainted with him at the assizes here, about a year and
a half ago; he is a man of great variety of knowledge, uncommon genius, and, I believe, sincere religion. I received
the holy sacrament in the Cathedral in the morning, this
being the first Sunday in the month; and was at prayers
there in the morning. It is divinely cheering to me to think
that there is a Cathedral so near Auchinleck; and I now
leave Old England in such a state of mind as I am thankful
to God for granting me.

'The *black dog* that worries me at home I cannot but
dread; yet as I have been for some time past in a military
train, I trust I shall *repulse* him. To hear from you will
animate me like the sound of a trumpet; I therefore hope,
that soon after my return to the northern field, I shall
receive a few lines from you.

'Colonel Stuart did me the honour to escort me in his
carriage to shew me Liverpool, and from thence back again
to Warrington, where we parted.[1] In justice to my valuable
wife, I must inform you she wrote to me, that as I was so
happy, she would not be so selfish as to wish me to return
sooner than business absolutely required my presence. She
made my clerk write to me a post or two after to the same
purpose, by commission from her; and this day a kind

---

[1] His regiment was afterwards ordered to Jamaica, where he accompanied
it, and almost lost his life by the climate. This impartial order I should think
a sufficient refutation of the idle rumour that 'there was still something
behind the throne greater than the throne itself.'

letter from her met me at the Post-Office here, acquainting
me that she and the little ones were well, and expressing
all their wishes for my return home. I am, more and more,
my dear Sir,

'Your affectionate,

'And obliged humble servant,

'JAMES BOSWELL'

'TO JAMES BOSWELL, ESQ.

'DEAR SIR,

'YOUR last letter was not only kind but fond. But I
wish you to get rid of all intellectual excesses, and neither
to exalt your pleasures, nor aggravate your vexations,
beyond their real and natural state. Why should you not
be as happy at Edinburgh as at Chester? *In culpa est animus,
qui se non effugit usquam.* Please yourself with your wife and
children, and studies, and practice.

'I have sent a petition[1] from Lucy Porter, with which I
leave it to your discretion whether it is proper to comply.
Return me her letter, which I have sent, that you may
know the whole case, and not be seduced to anything that
you may afterwards repent. Miss Doxy perhaps you know
to be Mr. Garrick's niece.

'If Dean Percy can be popular at Carlisle, he may be
very happy. He has in his disposal two livings, each equal,
or almost equal in value to the deanery; he may take one
himself, and give the other to his son.

'How near is the Cathedral to Auchinleck, that you are
so much delighted with it? It is, I suppose, at least an
hundred and fifty miles off. However, if you are pleased,
it is so far well.

'Let me know what reception you have from your father,
and the state of his health. Please him as much as you can,
and add no pain to his last years.

'Of our friends here I can recollect nothing to tell you.
I have neither seen nor heard of Langton. Beauclerk is just
returned from Brighthelmston, I am told, much better. Mr.
Thrale and his family are still there; and his health is said
to be visibly improved; he has not bathed, but hunted.

[1] Requesting me to enquire concerning the family of a gentleman who
was then paying his addresses to Miss Doxy.

'At Bolt-court there is much malignity, but of late little open hostility.[1] I have had a cold, but it is gone.

'Make my compliments to Mrs. Boswell, &c.

'I am, Sir,
'Your humble servant,
'London, Nov. 13, 1779.'   'SAM. JOHNSON'

On November 22, and December 21, I wrote to him from Edinburgh, giving a very favourable report of the family of Miss Doxy's lover;—that after a good deal of enquiry I had discovered the sister of Mr. Francis Stewart, one of his amanuenses when writing his Dictionary;—that I had, as desired by him, paid her a guinea for an old pocket-book of her brother's which he had retained; and that the good woman, who was in very moderate circumstances, but contented and placid, wondered at his scrupulous and liberal honesty, and reccived the guinea as if sent her by Providence.—That I had repeatedly begged of him to keep his promise to send me his letter to Lord Chesterfield, and that this *memento*, like *Delenda est Carthago*, must be in every letter that I should write to him, till I had obtained my object.

In 1780, the world was kept in impatience for the completion of his 'Lives of the Poets,' upon which he was employed so far as his indolence allowed him to labour.

I wrote to him on January 1, and March 13, sending him my notes of Lord Marchmont's information concerning Pope;—complaining that I had not heard from him for almost four months, though he was two letters in my debt; —that I had suffered again from melancholy;—hoping that he had been in so much better company, (the Poets,) that he had not time to think of his distant friends; for if that were the case, I should have some recompence for my uneasiness;—that the state of my affairs did not admit of my coming to London this year; and begging he would return me Goldsmith's two poems, with his lines marked.

His friend Dr. Lawrence having now suffered the greatest affliction to which a man is liable, and which Johnson himself had felt in the most severe manner; Johnson wrote to him in an admirable strain of sympathy and pious consolation.

[1] See page 65.

'TO DR. LAWRENCE

'DEAR SIR,

'AT a time when all your friends ought to shew their kindness, and with a character which ought to make all that know you your friends, you may wonder that you have yet heard nothing from me.

'I have been hindered by a vexatious and incessant cough, for which within these ten days I have been bled once, fasted four or five times, taken physick five times, and opiates, I think six. This day it seems to remit.

'The loss, dear Sir, which you have lately suffered, I felt many years ago, and know therefore how much has been taken from you, and how little help can be had from consolation. He that outlives a wife whom he has long loved, sees himself disjoined from the only mind that has the same hopes, and fears, and interest; from the only companion with whom he has shared much good or evil; and with whom he could set his mind at liberty, to retrace the past or anticipate the future. The continuity of being is lacerated; the settled course of sentiment and action is stopped; and life stands suspended and motionless, till it is driven by external causes into a new channel. But the time of suspense is dreadful.

'Our first recourse in this distressed solitude, is, perhaps for want of habitual piety, to a gloomy acquiescence in necessity. Of two mortal beings, one must lose the other; but surely there is a higher and better comfort to be drawn from the consideration of that Providence which watches over all, and a belief that the living and the dead are equally[a] in the hands of GOD, who will reunite those whom he has separated; or who sees that it is best not to reunite.[b]

underlined:
living, dead, equally [I]

[a] *God is not the God of the* Dead *but of the* Living. *Blest be his Name for the Assurance of it.* [I]

[b] *just so.* [H]

'I am, dear Sir,

'Your most affectionate,

'And most humble servant,

'January 20, 1780.'   'SAM. JOHNSON'

'TO JAMES BOSWELL, ESQ.

'DEAR SIR,

'WELL, I had resolved to send you the Chesterfield letter, but I will write once again without it. Never impose tasks upon mortals. To require two things is the way to have them both undone.

For the difficulties which you mention in your affairs, I am sorry; but difficulty is now very general: it is not therefore less grievous, for there is less hope of help. I pretend not to give you advice, not knowing the state of your affairs; and general counsels about prudence and frugality would do you little good. You are, however, in the right not to increase your own perplexity by a journey hither; and I hope that by staying at home you will please your father.

'Poor dear Beauclerk[1]—*nec, ut soles, dabis joca.* His wit and his folly, his acuteness and maliciousness, his merriment and reasoning, are now over. Such another will not often be found among mankind. He directed himself to be buried by the side of his mother, an instance of tenderness which I hardly expected. He has left his children to the care of Lady Di, and if she dies, of Mr. Langton, and of Mr. Leicester his relation, and a man of good character. His library has been offered to sale to the Russian ambassador.

'Dr. Percy, notwithstanding all the noise of the newspapers, has had no literary loss.[2] Clothes and moveables were burnt to the value of about one hundred pounds; but his papers, and I think his books, were all preserved.

'Poor Mr. Thrale has been in extreme danger from an apoplectical disorder, and recovered, beyond the expectation of his physicians; he is now at Bath, that his mind may be quiet, and Mrs. Thrale and Miss are with him.

'Having told you what has happened to your friends, let me say something to you of yourself. You are always complaining of melancholy, and I conclude from those complaints that you are fond of it. No man talks of that which he is desirous to conceal, and every man desires to conceal that of which he is ashamed. Do not pretend to deny it; *manifestum habemus furem;* make it an invariable and obligatory law to yourself, never to mention your own

---

[1] [The Hon. Topham Beauclerk died March 11, 1780. His Library was sold by publick auction in April and May 1781, for £5011. MALONE.]

[2] By a fire in Northumberland-house, where he had an apartment in which I have passed many an agreeable hour.

mental diseases; if you are never to speak of them you will think on them but little, and if you think little of them, they will molest you rarely. When you talk of them, it is plain that you want either praise or pity; for praise there is no room, and pity will do you no good; therefore, from this hour speak no more, think no more, about them.

'Your transaction with Mrs. Stewart gave me great satisfaction; I am much obliged to you for your attention. Do not lose sight of her; your countenance may be of great credit, and of consequence of great advantage to her. The memory of her brother is yet fresh in my mind; he was an ingenious and worthy man.

'Please to make my compliments to your lady and to the young ladies. I should like to see them, pretty loves.

'I am, dear Sir,

'Your's affectionately,

'April 8, 1780.'   'SAM. JOHNSON'

Mrs. Thrale being now at Bath with her husband, the correspondence between Johnson and her was carried on briskly. I shall present my readers with one of her original letters to him at this time, which will amuse them probably more than those well-written but studied epistles which she has inserted in her collection, because it exhibits the easy vivacity of their literary intercourse. It is also of value as a key to Johnson's answer, which she has printed by itself, and of which I shall subjoin extracts.

'MRS. THRALE TO DR. JOHNSON[a]

'I HAD a very kind letter from you yesterday, dear Sir, with a most circumstantial date. You took trouble with my circulating letter, Mr. Evans writes me word, and I thank you sincerely for so doing; one might do mischief else not being on the spot.

'Yesterday's evening was passed at Mrs. Montagu's: there was Mr. Melnoth; I do not like him *though*, nor he me; it was expected we should have pleased each other; he is, however, just Tory enough to hate the bishop of Peterborough[1] for Whiggism, and Whig enough to abhor you for Toryism.

[1] Dr. John Hinchliffe.

[a] *This is the famous Letter with which Mr. Boswell threatened us all so; He bought it of Francis the Black for half a Crown to have a little Teizing in his Power.* [H]

for this Letter he gave a Bribe to the Blackamoore of ½ a Crown & Then made a Bustle & a Rout as if he had got a great Prize; It is a complete Nothing.[I]

'Mrs. Montagu flattered him finely; so he had a good afternoon on't. This evening we spend at a concert. Poor Queeney's[1] sore eyes have just released her: she had a long confinement, and could neither read nor write, so my master[2] treated her very good-naturedly with the visits of a young woman in this town, a taylor's daughter, who professes musick,[a] and teaches so as to give six lessons a day to ladies, at five and threepence a lesson. Miss Burney says, she is a great performer; and I respect the wench for getting her living so prettily; she is very modest and pretty-mannered, and not seventeen years old.

'You live in a fine whirl indeed; if I did not write regularly, you would half forget me, and that would be very wrong, for I *felt* my regard for you in my *face* last night, when the criticisms were going on.

'This morning it was all connoisseurship; we went to see some pictures painted by a gentleman-artist, Mr. Taylor, of this place; my master makes one every where, and has got a good dawling companion to ride with him now. * * * * * * *. He looks well enough, but I have no notion of health for a man whose mouth cannot be sewed up. Burney and I and Queeney teaze him every meal he eats, and Mrs. Montagu is quite serious with him; but what *can* one do? He will eat, I think, and if he does eat I know he will not live; it makes me very unhappy, but I must bear it. Let me always have your friendship. I am, most sincerely, dear Sir,

'Your faithful servant,

'Bath, Friday, April 28.'   'H. L. T.'

'DR. JOHNSON TO MRS. THRALE

'DEAREST MADAM,

'MR. THRALE never will live abstinently, till he can persuade himself to live by rule.[3] * * * * * * * * *. Encourage, as you can, the musical girl.

'Nothing is more common than mutual dislike, where

---

[1] A kind of nick-name given to Mrs. Thrale's eldest daughter, whose name being *Esther* she might be assimilated to a *Queen*.[b]

[2] Mr. Thrale.

[3] I have taken the liberty to leave out a few lines.

[a] *Jenny Guest now Mrs. Miles* [H]

Jenny Guest, now the justly famous Mrs. Miles. [I]

[b] *What Nonsense! it was a mere Pet Name for a Baby too long continued* [I]

mutual approbation is particularly expected. There is often on both sides a vigilance not over-benevolent; and as attention is strongly excited, so that nothing drops unheeded, any difference in taste or opinion, and some difference where there is no restraint will commonly appear, immediately generates dislike.

'Never let criticisms operate on your face or your mind; it is very rarely that an authour is hurt by his cricks. The blaze of reputation cannot be blown out, but it often dies in the socket; a very few names may be considered as perpetual lamps that shine unconsumed. From the authour of "Fitzosborne's Letters" I cannot think myself in much danger, I met him only once about thirty years ago, and in some small dispute reduced him to whistle; having not seen him since, that is the last impression. Poor Moore, the fabulist, was one of the company.

'Mrs. Montagu's long stay, against her own inclination, is very convenient. You would, by your own confession, want a companion: and she is *par pluribus;* conversing with her you may *find variety in one.*'

'London, May 1, 1780.'

On the 2d of May I wrote to him, and requested that we might have another meeting somewhere in the North of England, in the autumn of this year.

From Mr. Langton I received soon after this time a letter, of which I extract a passage, relative both to Mr. Beauclerk and Dr. Johnson.

'The melancholy information you have received concerning Mr. Beauclerk's death is true. Had his talents been directed in any sufficient degree as they ought, I have always been strongly of opinion that they were calculated to make an illustrious figure; and that opinion, as it had been in part formed upon Dr. Johnson's judgement, receives more and more confirmation by hearing, what since his death, Dr. Johnson has said concerning them; a few evenings ago, he was at Mr. Vesey's, where Lord Althorpe, who was one of a numerous company there, addressed Dr. Johnson on the subject of Mr. Beauclerk's death, saying "Our CLUB has had a great loss since we met last." He replied, "A loss, that perhaps the whole nation could not repair!" The Doctor then went on to speak of his endowments, and particularly extolled the wonderful ease with which he uttered what was highly excellent. He said, that "no man ever was so free when he was going to say a good thing, from a *look* that expressed that it was coming;[a] or, when he had said it, from a look that expressed that it had come." At Mr. Thrale's, some days before when we were talking on the same subject, he said, referring to the same idea of his wonderful facility, "That Beauclerk's talents were those which he had felt himself more disposed to envy, than those of any whom he had known."

'On the evening I have spoken of above, at Mr. Vesey's, you would have been much gratified, as it exhibited an instance of the high importance in which Dr. Johnson's character is held, I think even beyond any I ever before was witness to. The company consisted chiefly of ladies, among whom were the Duchess Dowager of Portland, the Duchess of Beaufort, whom I suppose from her rank, I must name before her mother, Mrs. Boscawen, and her eldest sister Mrs. Lewson, who was likewise there; Lady Lucan, Lady Clermont,[b] and others of note both for their station and understandings. Among the gentlemen were Lord Althorpe, whom I have before named, Lord Macartney, Sir Joshua Reynolds, Lord Lucan, Mr. Wraxal,[c] whose book you have probably seen, "*The Tour to the Northern Parts of Europe;*" a very agreeable ingenious man; Dr. Warren, Mr. Pepys,[d] the Master in Chancery, whom I believe you know, and Dr. Barnard, the Provost of Eton. As soon as Dr. Johnson was come in, and had taken the chair, the company began to collect round him till they became not less than four, if not five, deep; those behind standing, and listening over the heads of those that were sitting near him. The conversation for some time was chiefly between Dr. Johnson and the Provost of Eton, while the others contributed occasionally their remarks. Without attempting to detail the particulars of the conversation, which perhaps if I did, I should spin my account out to a tedious length, I thought, my dear Sir, this general account of the respect with which our valued friend was attended to, might be acceptable.'

[a] *Yes: Beauclerck was first upon the languid List of Ton People. Dr. Johnson who was all Emphasis himself, felt epris of such a Character; a Man of Quality who disdained Effort in Conversation —to which He never came unprepared.* [H]

I fancy this strong Praise helped to bring up the Mode of speaking in a Monotonous Tone, and putting on a Face of Vacant Insipidity as The Ton-Talkers have been doing these last 20 Years — not recollecting that Mr. Beauclerc had much to say, & they have nothing. [I]

[b] *All dead* [H]

underlined: *Wraxal* [H]
[c] *Alive.* [H]

underlined: *Pepys* [H]
[d] *Alive.* [H]

'TO THE REVEREND DR. FARMER

'SIR,   'May 25, 1780

'I KNOW your disposition to second any literary
attempt, and therefore venture upon the liberty of entreating you to procure from College or University
registers, all the dates or other informations which they
can supply relating to Ambrose Philips, Broome, and
Gray, who were all of Cambridge, and of whose lives I am
to give such accounts as I can gather. Be pleased to forgive
this trouble from, Sir,

'Your most humble servant,

'SAM. JOHNSON'

While Johnson was thus engaged in preparing a delightful literary entertainment for the world, the tranquillity
of the metropolis of Great Britain was unexpectedly
disturbed, by the most horrid series of outrage that ever
disgraced a civilized country. A relaxation of some of the
severe penal provisions against our fellow-subjects of the
Catholick communion had been granted by the legislature
with an opposition so inconsiderable, that the genuine
mildness of Christianity united with liberal policy, seemed
to have become general in this island. But a dark and
malignant spirit of persecution soon shewed itself, in an
unworthy petition for the repeal of the wise and humane
statute. That petition was brought forward by a mob, with
the evident purpose of intimidation, and was justly
rejected. But the attempt was accompanied and followed
by such daring violence as is unexampled in history. Of
this extraordinary tumult, Dr. Johnson has given the
following concise, lively, and just account in his 'Letters
to Mrs. Thrale.'[1]

'On Friday,[2] the good Protestants met in Saint George's-
Fields, at the summons of Lord George Gordon, and
marching to Westminster, insulted the Lords and Commons, who all bore it with great tameness. At night the

[1] Vol. ii. p. 143, *et seq.* I have selected passages from several letters,
without mentioning dates.
[2] June 2.

outrages began by the demolition of the mass-house by Lincoln's-Inn.'

'An exact journal of a week's defiance of government I cannot give you. On Monday Mr. Strahan, who had been insulted, spoke to Lord Mansfield, who had I think been insulted too, of the licentiousness of the populace; and his Lordship treated it as a very slight irregularity. On Tuesday night they pulled down Fielding's house,[1] and burnt his goods in the street. They had gutted on Monday Sir George Savile's house, but the building was saved. On Tuesday evening, leaving Fielding's ruins, they went to Newgate to demand their companions, who had been seized demolishing the chapel. The keeper could not release them but by the Mayor's permission, which he went to ask; at his return he found all the prisoners released, and Newgate in a blaze. They then went to Bloomsbury, and fastened upon Lord Mansfield's house, which they pulled down; and as for his goods, they totally burnt them. They have since gone to Caen-wood, but a guard was there before them. They plundered some Papists, I think, and burnt a mass-house in Moor-fields the same night.'

'On Wednesday I walked with Dr. Scot to look at Newgate, and found it in ruins, with the fire yet glowing. As I went by, the Protestants were plundering the Sessions-house at the Old-Bailey. There were not, I believe, a hundred; but they did their work at leisure, in full security, without sentinels, without trepidation, as men lawfully employed, in full day. Such is the cowardice of a commercial place. On Wednesday they broke open the Fleet, and the King's-Bench, and the Marshalsea, and Wood-street Compter, and Clerkenwell Bridewell, and released all the prisoners.'

'At night they set fire to the Fleet, and to the King's-Bench, and I know not how many other places; and one might see the glare of conflagration fill the sky from many parts. The sight was dreadful. Some people were

---

[1] [This is not quite correct. Sir John Fielding was, I think, then dead. It was Justice Hyde's house in St. Martin's-street, Leicester-Fields, that was gutted, and his goods burnt in the street. BLAKEWAY.]

threatened: Mr. Strahan advised me to take care of myself. Such a time of terrour you have been happy in not seeing.'

'The King said in council, "That the magistrates had not done their duty, but that he would do his own;" and a proclamation was published, directing us to keep our servants within doors, as the peace was now to be preserved by force. The soldiers were sent out to different parts, and the town is now [*June* 9,] at quiet.'

index sign:
to seize etc. [1]

'The soldiers are stationed so as to be every where within call: there is no longer any body of rioters, and the individuals are hunted to their holes, and led to prison; Lord George was last night sent to the Tower. Mr. John Wilkes was this day in my neighbourhood, to seize the publisher of a seditious paper.'

'Several chapels have been destroyed, and several inoffensive Papists have been plundered, but the high sport was to burn the gaols. This was a good rabble trick. The debtors and the criminals were all set at liberty; but of the criminals, as has always happened, many are already retaken; and two pirates have surrendered themselves, and it is expected that they will be pardoned.'

'Government now acts again with its proper force; and we are all under the protection of the King and the law. I thought that it would be agreeable to you and my master to have my testimony to the public security; and that you would sleep more quietly when I told you that you are safe.'

'There has, indeed, been an universal panick, from which the King was the first that recovered. Without the concurrence of his ministers, or the assistance of the civil magistrate, he put the soldiers in motion, and saved the town from calamities, such as a rabble's government must naturally produce.'

'The publick has escaped a very heavy calamity. The rioters attempted the Bank on Wednesday night, but in no great number; and like other thieves, with no great resolution. Jack Wilkes headed the party that drove them away. It is agreed, that if they had seized the Bank on Tuesday, at the height of the panick, when no resistance had been prepared, they might have carried irrecoverably away whatever they had found. Jack, who was always zealous for order and decency, declares, that if he be trusted with power, he will not leave a rioter alive. There is, however, now no longer any need of heroism or bloodshed; no blue ribband[1] is any longer worn.'[a]

Such was the end of this miserable sedition, from which London was delivered by the magnanimity of the Sovereign himself. Whatever some may maintain, I am satisfied that there was no combination or plan, either domestick or foreign; but that the mischief spread by a gradual contagion of frenzy, augmented by the quantities of fermented liquors, of which the deluded populace possessed themselves in the course of their depredations.

I should think myself very much to blame, did I here neglect to do justice to my esteemed friend Mr. Akerman, the keeper of Newgate, who long discharged a very important trust with an uniform intrepid firmness, and at the same time a tenderness and a liberal charity, which entitle him to be recorded with distinguished honour.

Upon this occasion, from the timidity and negligence of magistracy on the one hand, and the almost incredible exertions of the mob on the other, the first prison of this great country was laid open, and the prisoners set free; but that Mr. Akerman, whose house was burnt, would have prevented all this, had proper aid been sent him in due time, there can be no doubt.

Many years ago, a fire broke out in the brick part which was built as an addition to the old gaol of Newgate. The prisoners were in consternation and tumult, calling out, 'We shall be burnt—we shall be burnt! Down with the gate!—down with the gate!' Mr. Akerman hastened to them, shewed himself at the gate, and having, after some confused vociferation of 'Hear him—hear him!' obtained a silent attention, he then calmly told them, that the gate must not go down; that they were under his care, and that they should not be permitted to escape: but that he could assure them, they need not be afraid of being burnt, for that the fire was not in the prison, properly so called,

[a] *I forget now, who was the Member of Parliament that tore the blue Ribbon from Lord George's Hat, calling it this Ensign of Sedition: & swearing solemnly that he would run Lord George thro' the body the first Moment the Mob . . . or any Deputy from the out Door Rabble should break in, & That Menace saved the house of Commons. 1817.* [H]

[1] [Lord George Gordon and his followers, during these outrages, wore blue ribbands in their hats. MALONE.]

which was strongly built with stone; and that if they would engage to be quiet, he himself would come in to them, and conduct them to the further end of the building, and would not go out till they gave him leave. To this proposal they agreed; upon which Mr. Akerman, having first made them fall back from the gate, went in, and with a determined resolution ordered the outer turnkey upon no account to open the gate, even though the prisoners (though he trusted they would not) should break their word, and by force bring himself to order it. 'Never mind me, (said he,) should that happen.' The prisoners peaceably followed him, while he conducted them through passages of which he had the keys, to the extremity of the gaol, which was most distant from the fire. Having by this very judicious conduct fully satisfied them that there was no immediate risk, if any at all, he then addressed them thus: 'Gentlemen, you are now convinced that I told you true. I have no doubt that the engines will soon extinguish this fire; if they should not, a sufficient guard will come, and you shall be all taken out and lodged in the Compters. I assure you, upon my word and honour, that I have not a farthing insured. I have left my house that I might take care of you. I will keep my promise, and stay with you if you insist upon it; but if you will allow me to go out and look after my family and property, I shall be obliged to you.'[a] Struck with his behaviour, they called out, 'Master Akerman, you have done bravely; it was very kind in you: by all means go and take care of your own concerns.' He did so accordingly, while they remained, and were all preserved.

^a *Oh! he was a fine Creature.* [H]

Johnson has been heard to relate the substance of this story with high praise,[b] in which he was joined by Mr. Burke. My illustrious friend, speaking of Mr. Akerman's kindness to his prisoners, pronounced this eulogy upon his character:—'He who has long had constantly in his view the worst of mankind, and is yet eminent for the humanity of his disposition, must have had it originally in a great degree, and continued to cultivate it very carefully.'

^b *It is a very fine Story.* [I]

In the course of this month my brother David waited upon Dr. Johnson, with the following letter of introduction, which I had taken care should be lying ready on his arrival in London.

'TO DR. SAMUEL JOHNSON

'MY DEAR SIR,   'Edinburgh, April 29, 1780

'THIS will be delivered to you by my brother David, on his return from Spain. You will be glad to see the man who vowed to "stand by the old castle of Auchinleck, with heart, purse, and sword;" that romantick family solemnity devised by me, of which you and I talked with complacency upon the spot. I trust that twelve years of absence have not lessened his feudal attachment; and that you will find him worthy of being introduced to your acquaintance.

'I have the honour to be,
'With affectionate veneration,
'My dear Sir,
'Your most faithful humble servant,
'JAMES BOSWELL'

Johnson received him very politely, and has thus mentioned him in a letter to Mrs. Thrale:[1] 'I have had with me a brother of Boswell's, a Spanish merchant,[2] whom the war has driven from his residence at Valencia; he is gone to see his friends, and will find Scotland but a sorry place after twelve years' residence in a happier climate. He is a very agreeable man, and speaks no Scotch.'

'TO DR. BEATTIE, AT ABERDEEN
'SIR,

'MORE years[3] than I have any delight to reckon, have past since you and I saw one another: of this, however, there is no reason for making any reprehensory complaint: —*Sic fata ferunt*. But methinks there might pass some small interchange of regard between us. If you say, that I ought to have written, I now write; and I write to tell you, that I have much kindness for you and Mrs. Beattie; and that I wish your health better, and your life long. Try change of air, and come a few degrees Southwards; a softer climate may do you both good; winter is coming in; and London will be warmer, and gayer, and busier, and more fertile of amusement, than Aberdeen.

[1] Vol. ii. p. 163. Mrs. Piozzi has omitted the name, she best knows why.[a]   [a] *I never heard his Name.* [H]
[2] Now settled in London.
[3] I had been five years absent from London. BEATTIE.

'My health is better; but that will be little in the balance, when I tell you that Mrs. Montagu has been very ill, and is, I doubt, now but weakly.[a] Mr. Thrale has been very dangerously disordered; but is much better, and I hope will totally recover. He has withdrawn himself from business the whole summer. Sir Joshua and his sister are well; and Mr. Davies has got great success as an authour,[1] generated by the corruption of a bookseller. More news I have not to tell you, and therefore you must be contented with hearing, what I know not whether you much wish to hear,[2] that I am, Sir,

'Your most humble servant,

'Bolt-court, Fleet-street,   'SAM. JOHNSON'
August 21, 1780.'

a Mrs. Montagu outlived Johnson many Years. [H]

'TO JAMES BOSWELL, ESQ.

'DEAR SIR,

'I FIND you have taken one of your fits of taciturnity, and have resolved not to write till you are written to; it is but a peevish humour, but you shall have your way.

'I have sat at home in Bolt-court, all the summer, thinking to write the Lives, and a great part of the time only thinking. Several of them, however, are done, and I still think to do the rest.

'Mr. Thrale and his family have, since his illness, passed their first time at Bath, and then at Brighthelmston; but I have been at neither place. I would have gone to Lichfield if I could have had time, and I might have had time if I had been active; but I have missed much, and done little.

'In the late disturbances, Mr. Thrale's house and stock were in great danger; the mob was pacified at their first invasion, with about fifty pounds in drink and meat; and at their second, were driven away by the soldiers. Mr.

---

[1] Meaning his entertaining 'Memoirs of David Garrick, Esq.' of which Johnson (as Davies informed me) wrote the first sentence: thus giving, as it were, the key-note to the performance. It is, indeed, very characteristic of its authour, beginning with a maxim, and proceeding to illustrate.—'All excellence has a right to be recorded. I shall, therefore, think it superfluous to apologize for writing the life of a man, who, by an uncommon assemblage of private virtues, adorned the highest eminence in a publick profession.'

[2] I wish he had omitted the suspicion expressed here, though I believe he meant nothing but jocularity; for, though he and I differed sometimes in opinion, he well knew how much I loved and revered him.[b] BEATTIE.

b To be sure he did [J]

Strahan got a garrison into his house, and maintained them a fortnight; he was so frighted, that he removed part of his goods. Mrs. Williams took shelter in the country.

'I know not whether I shall get a ramble this autumn; it is now about the time when we were travelling. I have, however, better health than I had then, and hope you and I may yet shew ourselves on some part of Europe, Asia, or Africa.[1] In the mean time let us play no trick, but keep each other's kindness by all means in our power.

'The bearer of this is Dr. Dunbar of Aberdeen, who has written and published a very ingenious book,[2] and who I think has a kindness for me, and will, when he knows you, have a kindness for you.

'I suppose your little ladies are grown tall; and your son has become a learned young man. I love them all, and I love your naughty lady, whom I never shall persuade to love me. When the Lives are done, I shall send them to complete her collection, but must send them in paper, as for want of a pattern, I cannot bind them to fit the rest.

'I am, Sir,
'Yours most affectionately,
'London, Aug. 21, 1780.'   'SAM. JOHNSON'

This year he wrote to a young clergyman in the country the following very excellent letter, which contains valuable advice to Divines in general:

'DEAR SIR,
'NOT many days ago Dr. Lawrence shewed me a letter, in which you make mention of me: I hope, therefore, you will not be displeased that I endeavour to preserve your good-will by some observations which your letter suggested to me.

---

[1] It will no doubt be remarked how he avoids the *rebellious* land of America. This puts me in mind of an anecdote for which I am obliged to my worthy social friend, Governour Richard Penn: 'At one of Miss E. Hervey's[a] assemblies, Dr. Johnson was following her up and down the room; upon which Lord Abingdon observed to her, "Your great friend is very fond of you; you can go no where without him."—"Ay, (said she,) he would follow me to any part of the world."—"Then (said the Earl,) ask him to go with you to *America*."'

[2] 'Essays on the History of Mankind.'

underlined: *Miss E.* [1]

[a] *Miss* crossed out; *Lady* written in the margin [H]

Lady Emily Hervey [1]

'You are afraid of falling into some improprieties in the daily service by reading to an audience that requires no exactness. Your fear, I hope, secures you from danger. They who contract absurd habits are such as have no fear. It is impossible to do the same thing very often, without some peculiarity of manner: but that manner may be good or bad, and a little care will at least preserve it from being bad: to make it good, there must, I think, be something of natural or casual felicity, which cannot be taught.

'Your present method of making your sermons seems very judicious. Few frequent preachers can be supposed to have sermons more their own than yours will be. Take care to register, somewhere or other, the authours from whom your several discourses are borrowed; and do not imagine that you shall always remember, even what perhaps you now think it impossible to forget.

'My advice, however, is, that you attempt, from time to time, an original sermon; and in the labour of composition, do not burden your mind with too much at once; do not exact from yourself at one effort of excogitation, propriety of thought and elegance of expression. Invent first, and then embellish. The production of something, where nothing was before, is an act of greater energy than the

^a *how clever all this is!!* [I]

expansion or decoration of the thing produced.^a Set down diligently your thoughts as they rise in the first words that occur; and when you have matter, you will easily give it form; nor, perhaps, will this method be always necessary;

^b *as his own did.* [H]

for by habit, your thoughts and diction will flow together.^b

'The composition of sermons is not very difficult: the divisions not only help the memory of the hearer, but direct the judgement of the writer: they supply sources of invention, and keep every part in its proper place.

'What I like least in your letter is your account of the manners of your parish; from which I gather, that it has been long neglected by the parson. The Dean of Carlisle,¹ who was then a little rector in Northamptonshire, told me, that it might be discerned whether or not there was a clergyman resident in a parish, by the civil or savage manner of the people. Such a congregation as yours stands in need of much reformation; and I would not have you

---

¹ Dr. Percy, now Bishop of Dromore.

think it impossible to reform them. A very savage parish
was civilized by a decayed gentlewoman, who came among
them to teach a petty school. My learned friend, Dr.
Wheeler, of Oxford, when he was a young man, had the
care of a neighbouring parish for fifteen pounds a year,
which he was never paid; but he counted it a convenience,
that it compelled him to make a sermon weekly. One
woman he could not bring to the communion; and when
he reproved or exhorted her, she only answered, that she
was no scholar. He was advised to set some good woman
or man of the parish, a little wiser than herself, to talk to
her in a language level to her mind. Such honest, I may
call them holy, artifices, must be practised by every clergyman; for all means must be tried by which souls may be
saved. Talk to your people, however, as much as you can;
and you will find, that the more frequently you converse
with them upon religious subjects, the more willingly they
will attend, and the more submissively they will learn. A
clergyman's diligence always makes him venerable. I
think I have now only to say, that in the momentous work
you have undertaken, I pray GOD to bless you.

> 'I am, Sir,
> 'Your most humble servant,

'Bolt-court, Aug. 30, 1780.'   'SAM. JOHNSON'

My next letters to him were dated August 24, September
6, and October 1, and from them I extract the following
passages:

'My brother David and I find the long indulged fancy
of our comfortable meeting again at Auchinleck, so well
realized, that it in some degree confirms the pleasing hope
of O! preclarum diem! in a future state.'

'I beg that you may never again harbour a suspicion of
my indulging a peevish humour, or playing tricks; you
will recollect, that when I confessed to you, that I had once
been intentionally silent to try your regard, I gave you my
word and honour that I would not do so again.'

'I rejoice to hear of your good state of health; I pray
GOD to continue it long. I have often said, that I would

willingly have ten years added to my life, to have ten taken from yours; I mean, that I would be ten years older to have you ten years younger. But let me be thankful for the years during which I have enjoyed your friendship, and please myself with the hopes of enjoying it many years to come in this state of being, trusting always, that in another state, we shall meet never to be separated. Of this we can form no notion; but the thought, though indistinct, is delightful, when the mind is calm and clear.'

'The riots in London were certainly horrible; but you give me no account of your own situation during the barbarous anarchy. A description of it by Dr. JOHNSON would be a great painting;[1] you might write another "LONDON, A POEM."

'I am charmed with your condescending affectionate expression, "let us keep each other's kindness by all the means in our power;" my revered Friend! how elevating is it to my mind, that I am found worthy to be a companion of Dr. Samuel Johnson! All that you have said in grateful praise of Mr. Walmsley, I have long thought of you; but we are both Tories, which has a very general influence upon our sentiments. I hope that you will agree to meet me at York, about the end of this month; or if you will come to Carlisle, that would be better still, in case the Dean be there. Please to consider, that to keep each other's kindness, we should every year have that free and intimate communication of mind which can be had only when we are together. We should have both our solemn and our pleasant talk.'

'I write now for the third time, to tell you that my desire for our meeting this autumn is much increased. I wrote to 'Squire Godfrey Bosville, my Yorkshire Chief, that I should, perhaps, pay him a visit, as I was to hold a conference with Dr. Johnson at York. I give you my word and honour that I said not a word of his inviting you; but he wrote to me as follows:

'"I need not tell you I shall be happy to see you here the latter end of this month, as you propose; and I shall likewise be in hopes that you will persuade Dr. Johnson to finish the conference here. It will add to the favour of your

---

[1] I had not seen his Letters to Mrs. Thrale.

own company, if you prevail upon such an associate, to assist your observations. I have often been entertained with his writings, and I once belonged to a club of which he was a member, and I never spent an evening there, but I heard something from him well worth remembering."

'We have thus, my dear Sir, good comfortable quarters in the neighbourhood of York, where you may be assured we shall be heartily welcome. I pray you then resolve to set out; and let not the year 1780 be a blank in our social calendar, and in that record of wisdom and wit, which I keep with so much diligence, to your honour, and the instruction and delight of others.'

Mr. Thrale had now another contest for the representation in parliament of the borough of Southwark, and Johnson kindly lent him his assistance, by writing advertisements and letters for him. I shall insert one as a specimen:*

'TO THE WORTHY ELECTORS OF THE BOROUGH
OF SOUTHWARK

'GENTLEMEN,

'A NEW Parliament being now called, I again solicit the honour of being elected for one of your representatives; and solicit it with the greater confidence, as I am not conscious of having neglected my duty, or of having acted otherwise than as becomes the independent representative of independent constituents; superiour to fear, hope, and expectation, who has no private purposes to promote, and whose prosperity is involved in the prosperity of his country. As my recovery from a very severe distemper is not yet perfect, I have declined to attend the Hall, and hope an omission so necessary will not be harshly censured.

'I can only send my respectful wishes, that all your deliberations may tend to the happiness of the kingdom, and the peace of the borough.

'I am, Gentlemen,
'Your most faithful
'And obedient servant,

'Southwark, Sept, 5, 1780.'   'HENRY THRALE'

['TO THE RIGHT HONOURABLE LADY SOUTHWELL,[1]
DUBLIN
'MADAM,

'AMONG the numerous addresses of condolence which your great loss must have occasioned, be pleased to receive this from one whose name perhaps you have never heard, and to whom your Ladyship is known only by the reputation of your virtue, and to whom your Lord was known only by his kindness and beneficence.

'Your Ladyship is now again summoned to exert that piety of which you once gave, in a state of pain and danger, so illustrious an example; and your Lord's beneficence may be still continued by those, who with his fortune inherit his virtues.

'I hope to be forgiven the liberty which I shall take of informing your Ladyship, that Mr. Mauritius Lowe, a son of your late Lord's father,[2] had, by recommendation to your Lord, a quarterly allowance of ten pounds, the last of which, due July 26, he has not received: he was in hourly hope of his remittance, and flattered himself that on October 26, he should have received the whole half year's

[1] [Margaret, the second daughter, and one of the co-heiresses of Arthur Cecil Hamilton, Esq. She was married in 1741 to Thomas George, the third Baron, and first Viscount, Southwell, and lived with him in the most perfect connubial felicity till September, 1780, when Lord Southwell died; a loss which she never ceased to lament to the hour of her own dissolution, in her eighty-first year, August 16, 1802.—The 'illustrious example of piety and fortitude' to which Dr. Johnson alludes, was the submitting, when passed her fiftieth year, to an extremely painful surgical operation, which she endured with extraordinary firmness and composure, not allowing herself to be tied to her chair, nor uttering a single moan.—This slight tribute of affection to the memory of these two most amiable and excellent persons, who were not less distinguished by their piety, beneficence, and unbounded charity, than by a suavity of manners which endeared them to all who knew them, it is hoped, will be forgiven from one who was honoured by their kindness and friendship from his childhood. MALONE.]

[2] [Thomas, the second Lord Southwell, who was born Jan. 7, 1698–9, and died in London, Nov. 18, 1766. Johnson was well acquainted with this nobleman, and said, 'he was the highest bred man, without insolence, that he was ever in company with.' See *post*, p. 264. His younger brother, Edmund Southwell, lived in intimacy with Johnson for many years. (See an account of him in Hawkins's Life of Johnson, p. 405.) He died in London, Nov. 22, 1772.

In opposition to the Knight's unfavourable representation of this gentleman, to whom I was indebted for my first introduction to Johnson, I take this opportunity to add, that he appeared to me a pious man, and was very fond of leading the conversation to religious subjects. MALONE.]

bounty, when he was struck with the dreadful news of his benefactor's death.

'May I presume to hope, that his want, his relation, and his merit, which excited his Lordship's charity, will continue to have the same effect upon those whom he has left behind; and that, though he has lost one friend, he may not yet be destitute. Your Ladyship's charity cannot easily be exerted where it is wanted more; and to a mind like yours, distress is a sufficient recommendation.

'I hope to be allowed the honour of being,

'Madam,

'Your Ladyship's

'Most humble Servant,

'Bolt-court, Fleet-street,
  London, Sept, 9, 1780.'   'SAM. JOHNSON']

On his birth-day, Johnson has this note: 'I am now beginning the seventy-second year of my life, with more strength of body and greater vigour of mind, than I think is common at that age.' But still he complains of sleepless nights and idle days, and forgetfulness, or neglect of resolutions. He thus pathetically expresses himself: 'Surely I shall not spend my whole life with my own total disapprobation.'[1]

Mr. Macbean, whom I have mentioned more than once, as one of Johnson's humble friends, a deserving but unfortunate man, being now oppressed by age and poverty, Johnson solicited the Lord Chancellor Thurlow, to have him admitted into the Charter-house.[2] I take the liberty

[1] Prayers and Meditations, p. 185.

[2] [Mr. Alexander Macbean, on Lord Thurlow's nomination, was admitted into the Chartreux in April, 1781; on which occasion Dr. Johnson, with that benevolence by which he was uniformly actuated, wrote the following letter, which, for the sake of connexion, may properly be introduced here:

'TO THE REV. DR. VYSE, AT LAMBETH

'REV. SIR,

'THE bearer is one of my old friends, a man of great learning, whom the Chancellor has been pleased to nominate to the Chartreux. He attends his Grace the Archbishop, to take the oath required, and being a modest scholar, will escape embarrassment, if you are so kind as to introduce him, by which you will do a kindness to a man of great merit, and add another to those favours, which have already been conferred by you on,

'Sir,

'Your most humble servant,

'Bolt-court, Fleet-street,   'SAM. JOHNSON'
  April 10, 1781.'   MALONE]

to insert his Lordship's answer, as I am eager to embrace every occasion of augmenting the respectable notion which should ever be entertained of my illustrious friend:

'TO DR. SAMUEL JOHNSON

'SIR,   'London, October 24, 1780

'I HAVE this moment received your letter dated the 19th, and returned from Bath.

'In the beginning of the summer I placed one in the Chartreux, without the sanction of a recommendation so distinct and so authoritative as yours of Macbean; and I am afraid, that according to the establishment of the House, the opportunity of making the charity so good amends will not soon recur. But whenever a vacancy shall happen, if you'll favour me with notice of it, I will try to recommend him to the place, even though it should not be my turn to nominate.

'I am, Sir, with great regard,
'Your most faithful
'And obedient servant,

'THURLOW'

'TO JAMES BOSWELL, ESQ.

'DEAR SIR,

'I AM sorry to write you a letter that will not please you, and yet it is at last what I resolve to do. This year must pass without an interview; the summer has been foolishly lost, like many other of my summers and winters. I hardly saw a green field, but staid in town to work, without working much.

'Mr. Thrale's loss of health has lost him the election; he is now going to Brighthelmstone, and expects me to go with him; and how long I shall stay, I cannot tell. I do not much like the place, but yet I shall go and stay while my stay is desired. We must, therefore, content ourselves with knowing what we know as well as man can know the mind of man, that we love one another, and that we wish each other's happiness, and that the lapse of a year cannot lessen our mutual kindness.

'I was pleased to be told that I accused Mrs. Boswell unjustly, in supposing that she bears me ill-will. I love you so much, that I would be glad to love all that love you, and that you love; and I have love very ready for Mrs. Boswell, if she thinks it worthy of acceptance. I hope all the young ladies and gentlemen are well.

'I take a great liking to your brother. He tells me that his father received him kindly, but not fondly: however, you seem to have lived well enough at Auchinleck, while you staid. Make your father as happy as you can.

'You lately told me of your health: I can tell you in return, that my health has been for more than a year past, better than it has been for many years before. Perhaps it may please GOD to give us some time together before we are parted.

             'I am, dear Sir,
                'Yours, most affectionately,
'Oct. 17, 1780.'   'SAM. JOHNSON'

['TO THE REVEREND DR. VYSE, AT LAMBETH

'SIR,

'I hope you will forgive the liberty I take, in soliciting your interposition with his Grace the Archbishop: my first petition was successful, and I therefore venture on a second.

'The Matron of the Chartreux is about to resign her place, and Mrs. Desmoulins, a daughter of the late Dr. Swinfen,[1] who was well known to your father, is desirous of succeeding her. She has been accustomed by keeping a boarding-school to the care of children, and I think is very likely to discharge her duty. She is in great distress, and therefore may properly receive the benefit of a charitable foundation. If you wish to see her, she will be willing to give an account of herself.

'If you shall be pleased, Sir, to mention her favourably to his Grace, you will do a great act of kindness to, Sir,

                'Your most obliged,
                  'And most humble Servant,
'Dec. 30, 1780.'   'SAM. JOHNSON']

            [1] [See vol. i. p. 40. MALONE.]

Being disappointed in my hopes of meeting Johnson this year, so that I could hear none of his admirable sayings, I shall compensate for this want by inserting a collection of them, for which I am indebted to my worthy friend Mr. Langton, whose kind communications have been separately interwoven in many parts of this work. Very few articles of this collection were committed to writing by himself, he not having that habit; which he regrets, and which those who know the numerous opportunities he had of gathering the rich fruits of *Johnsonian* wit and wisdom, must ever regret. I however found, in conversation with him, that a good store of JOHNSONIANA was treasured in his mind; and I compared it to Herculaneum, or some old Roman field, which, when dug, fully rewards the labour employed. The authenticity of every article is unquestionable. For the expression, I, who wrote them down in his presence, am partly answerable.

'Theocritus is not deserving of very high respect as a writer; as to the pastoral part, Virgil is very evidently superiour. He wrote, when there had been a larger influx of knowledge into the world than when Theocritus lived. Theocritus does not abound in description, though living in a beautiful country: the manners painted are coarse and gross. Virgil has much more description, more sentiment, more of nature, and more of art. Some of the most excellent parts of Theocritus are, where Castor and Pollux, going with the other Argonauts, land on the Bebrycian coast, and there fall into a dispute with Amycus, the King of that country: which is as well conducted as Euripides could have done it; and the battle is well related. Afterwards they carry off a woman, whose two brothers come to recover her, and expostulate with Castor and Pollux on their injustice; but they pay no regard to the brothers, and a battle ensues, where Castor and his brother are triumphant.—Theocritus seems not to have seen that the brothers have their advantage in their argument over his Argonaut heroes—"The Sicilian Gossips"[a] is a piece of merit.'

'Callimachus is a writer of little excellence. The chief thing to be learned from him is his account of Rites and Mythology; which, though desirable to be known for the

underlined:
Sicilian Gossips [H]

[a] *Bob Lloyd has En-glish'd it beautifully. Après tout—La Nature est comme la nature. It will please in every age & in ev'ry Language.* [H]

Lloyd has done it charmingly into En-glish. [I]

sake of understanding other parts of ancient authours, is the least pleasing or valuable part of their writings.'

'Mattaire's account of the Stephani is a heavy book. He seems to have been a puzzle-headed man, with a large share of scholarship, but with little geometry or logick in his head, without method, and possessed of little genius. He wrote Latin verses from time to time, and published a set in his old age, which he called "*Senilia;*" in which he shews so little learning or taste in writing, as to make *Carteret* a dactyl.—In matters of genealogy it is necessary to give the bare names as they are; but in poetry, and in prose of any elegance in the writing, they require to have inflection given to them.—His book of the Dialects is a sad heap of confusion; the only way to write on them is to tabulate them with Notes, added at the bottom of the page, and references.'

'It may be questioned, whether there is not some mistake as to the methods of employing the poor, seemingly on a supposition that there is a certain portion of work left undone for want of persons to do it; but if that is otherwise, and all the materials we have are actually worked up, or all the manufactures we can use or dispose of are already executed, then what is given to the poor, who are to be set at work, must be taken from some who now have it: as time must be taken for learning, (according to Sir William Petty's observation); a certain part of those very materials that, as it is, are properly worked up, must be spoiled by the unskilfulness of novices. We may apply to well-meaning, but misjudging persons in particulars of this nature, what Giannone said to a monk, who wanted what he called to *convert* him: "*Tu sei santo, ma tu non sei filosofo.*"—It is an unhappy circumstance that one might give away five hundred pounds a year to those that importune in the streets, and not do any good.'

'There is nothing more likely to betray a man into absurdity, than *condescension;* when he seems to suppose his understanding too powerful for his company.'

'Having asked Mr. Langton if his father and mother had sat for their pictures, which he thought it right for each generation of a family to do, and being told they had opposed it, he said, "Sir, among the anfractuosities of the

human mind, I know not if it may not be one, that there
is a superstitious reluctance to sit for a picture." [a]

[a] *If this was true—how would Portrait Painters make Fortunes?* [H]

'John Gilbert Cooper related that soon after the publication of his Dictionary, Garrick being asked by Johnson what people said of it, told him, that among other animadversions, it was objected that he cited authorities which were beneath the dignity of such a work, and mentioned Richardson. "Nay, (said Johnson,) I have done worse than that: I have cited *thee*, David." [b]

[b] *Bravo.* [H]

'Talking of expence, he observed, with what munificence a great merchant will spend his money, both from his having it at command, and from his enlarged views by calculation of a good effect upon the whole. "Whereas (said he) you will hardly ever find a country gentleman, who is not a good deal disconcerted at an unexpected occasion for his being obliged to lay out ten pounds." '

'When in good humour, he would talk of his own writings with a wonderful frankness and candour, and would even criticise them with the closest severity. One day, having read over one of his Ramblers, Mr. Langton asked him, how he liked that paper; he shook his head, and answered, "too wordy." At another time, when one was reading his tragedy of "Irene," to a company at a house in the country, he left the room: and somebody having asked him the reason of this, he replied, "Sir, I thought it had been better." '

'Talking of a point of delicate scrupulosity of moral conduct, he said to Mr. Langton, "Men of harder minds than ours will do many things from which you and I would shrink; yet, Sir, they will, perhaps, do more good in life than we. But let us try to help one another. If there be a wrong twist, it may be set right. It is not probable that two people can be wrong the same way." '

'Of the Preface to Capel's Shakspeare, he said, "If the man would have come to me, I would have endeavoured to 'endow his purposes with words;' for as it is, 'he doth gabble monstrously.' " '

'He related, that he had once in a dream a contest of wit with some other person, and that he was very much mortified by imagining that his opponent had the better of him. "Now, (said he,) one may mark here the effect of sleep in weakening the power of reflection; for had not my judgement failed me, I should have seen, that the wit of this supposed antagonist, by whose superiority I felt myself depressed, was as much furnished by me, as that which I thought I had been uttering in my own character.""ᵃ   ᵃ *Just so.* [H]

'One evening in company, an ingenious and learned gentleman read to him a letter of compliment which he had received from one of the Professors of a Foreign University. Johnson, in an irritable fit, thinking there was too much ostentation, said, "I never receive any of these tributes of applause from abroad. One instance I recollect of a foreign publication, in which mention is made of *l'illustre Lockman.*"'[1]

'Of Sir Joshua Reynolds, he said, "Sir, I know no man who has passed through life with more observation than Reynolds."'

'He repeated to Mr. Langton, with great energy, in the Greek, our SAVIOUR's gracious expression concerning the forgiveness of Mary Magdalen,[2] "'Η πίστις σου σέσωκέ σε· πορεύου εἰς εἰρήνην. Thy faith hath saved thee; go in peace."[3] He said, "the manner of this dismission is exceedingly affecting."'

'He thus defined the difference between physical and moral truth: "Physical truth, is, when you tell a thing as it actually is. Moral truth, is, when you tell a thing sincerely and precisely as it appears to you. I say such a one walked across the street; if he really did so, I told a physical truth. If I thought so, though I should have been mistaken, I told a moral truth."'[4]

'Huggins, the translator of Ariosto, and Mr. Thomas Warton, in the early part of his literary life, had a dispute concerning that poet, of whom Mr. Warton, in his "Observations on Spenser's Fairy Queen," gave some account which Huggins attempted to answer with violence, and

[1] Secretary to the British Herring Fishery, remarkable for an extraordinary number of occasional verses, not of eminent merit.

[2] It does not appear that the woman forgiven was Mary Magdalen.ᵇ KEARNEY.]

ᵇ *I never heard it was except in this Page.* [H]

[3] Luke vii. 50.

[4] [This account of the difference between moral and physical truth is in Locke's 'Essay on Human Understanding,' and many other books. KEARNEY.]

It plainly (to me) appears that it was not. [I]

said, "I will *militate* no longer against his *nescience*."
Huggins was master of the subject, but wanted expression.
Mr. Warton's knowledge of it was then imperfect, but his
manner lively and elegant. Johnson said, "It appears to
me, that Huggins has ball without powder, and Warton
powder without ball."'

'Talking of the Farce of "High Life below Stairs," he
said, "Here is a Farce, which is really very diverting,
when you see it acted; and yet one may read it, and not
know that one has been reading any thing at all."'

'He used at one time to go occasionally to the green-
room of Drury-lane Theatre, where he was much regarded
by the players, and was very easy and facetious with them.
He had a very high opinion of Mrs. Clive's comick powers,
and conversed more with her than with any of them. He
said, "Clive, Sir, is a good thing to sit by; she always
understands what you say." And she said of him, "I love
to sit by Dr. Johnson: he always entertains me." One
night, when "The Recruiting Officer" was acted, he said
to Mr. Holland, who had been expressing an apprehension
that Dr. Johnson would disdain the works of Farquhar;
"No, Sir, I think Farquhar a man whose writings have
considerable merit."'

'His friend Garrick was so busy in conducting the drama,
that they could not have so much intercourse as Mr.
Garrick used to profess an anxious wish that there should
be.[1] There might, indeed, be something in the contemptuous severity as to the merit of acting, which his old
preceptor nourished in himself, that would mortify Garrick
after the great applause which he received from the
audience. For though Johnson said of him, "Sir, a man
who has a nation to admire him every night, may well
be expected to be somewhat elated;" yet he would treat
theatrical matters with a ludicrous slight. He mentioned
one evening, "I met David coming off the stage, drest in
a woman's riding hood, when he acted in The Wonder;
I came full upon him, and I believe he was not pleased."'

'Once he asked Tom Davies, whom he saw drest in a
fine suit of clothes, "And what art thou to-night?"

---

[1] [In a letter written by Johnson to a friend in Jan. 1742-3, he says, 'I
never see Garrick.' MALONE.]

Tom answered, "The Thane of Ross;" (which it will be recollected is a very inconsiderable character.) "O brave!" said Johnson.'

'Of Mr. Longley, at Rochester, a gentleman of very considerable learning, whom Dr. Johnson met there, he said, "My heart warms towards him. I was surprised to find in him such a nice acquaintance with the metre in the learned languages: though I was somewhat mortified that I had it not so much to myself, as I should have thought."'

'Talking of the minuteness with which people will record the sayings of eminent persons, a story was told, that when Pope was on a visit to Spence at Oxford, as they looked from the window they saw a Gentleman Commoner, who was just come in from riding, amusing himself with whipping at a post. Pope took occasion to say, "That young gentleman seems to have little to do." Mr. Beauclerk observed, "Then, to be sure, Spence turned round and wrote that down;" and went on to say to Dr. Johnson, "Pope, Sir, would have said the same of you, if he had seen you distilling." JOHNSON. "Sir, if Pope had told me of my distilling, I would have told him of his grotto."'

'He would allow no settled indulgence of idleness upon principle, and always repelled every attempt to urge excuses for it. A friend one day suggested, that it was not wholesome to study soon after dinner. JOHNSON. "Ah, Sir, don't give way to such a fancy. At one time of my life I had taken it into my head that it was not wholesome to study between breakfast and dinner."'

'Mr. Beauclerk one day repeated to Dr. Johnson, Pope's lines,

> "Let modest Foster, if he will, excel
> Ten metropolitans in preaching well:"

Then asked the Doctor, "Why did Pope say this?" JOHNSON. "Sir, he hoped it would vex somebody."'

'Dr. Goldsmith, upon occasion of Mrs. Lennox's bringing out a play,[1] said to Dr. Johnson at the CLUB, that a

---

[1] [Probably 'The Sisters,' a comedy performed one night only, at Covent Garden, in 1769. Dr. Goldsmith wrote an excellent epilogue to it.—Mrs. Lennox, whose maiden name was Ramsay, died in London in distressed circumstances, in her eighty-fourth year, January 4, 1804.[a] MALONE.]

[a] *Poor Thing! She deserved saving better than Beauclerc.* [H] *Poor Charlotte!* [I]

person had advised him to go and hiss it, because she had attacked Shakspeare in her book called "Shakspeare Illustrated." JOHNSON. "And did not you tell him that he was a rascal?" GOLDSMITH. "No, Sir, I did not. Perhaps he might not mean what he said." JOHNSON. "Nay, Sir, if he lied, it is a different thing." Colman slily said, (but it is believed Dr. Johnson did not hear him,) "Then the proper expression should have been,—Sir, if you don't lie, you're a rascal."'

'His affection for Topham Beauclerk was so great, that when Beauclerk was labouring under that severe illness which at last occasioned his death, Johnson said, (with a voice faultering with emotion,) "Sir, I would walk to the extent of the diameter of the earth to save Beauclerk."'

'One night at the CLUB he produced a translation of an Epitaph which Lord Elibank had written in English, for his lady, and requested of Johnson to turn it into Latin for him. Having read *Domina de North et Gray*, he said to Dyer,[1] "You see, Sir, what barbarisms we are compelled to make use of, when modern titles are to be specifically mentioned in Latin inscriptions." When he had read it once aloud, and there had been a general approbation expressed by the company, he addressed himself to Mr. Dyer in particular and said, "Sir, I beg to have your judgement, for I know your nicety." Dyer then very properly desired to read it over again; which having done, he pointed out an incongruity in one of the sentences. Johnson immediately assented to the observation, and said, "Sir, this is owing to an alteration of a part of the sentence, from the form in which I had first written it; and I believe, Sir, you may have remarked, that the making a partial change, without a due regard to the general structure of the sentence, is a very frequent cause of errour in composition."'

'Johnson was well acquainted with Mr. Dossie, authour of a treatise on Agriculture; and said of him, "Sir, of the objects which the Society of Arts have chiefly in view, the chymical effects of bodies operating upon other bodies, he knows more than almost any man." Johnson, in order to give Mr. Dossie his vote to be a member of this Society,

marginal note: exclamation point: *Johnson said* etc. [H]

---

[1] [See vol. i. p. 367. MALONE.]

paid up an arrear which had run on for two years. On this occasion he mentioned a circumstance, as characteristick of the Scotch. "One of that nation, (said he,) who had been a candidate, against whom I had voted, came up to me with a civil salutation. Now, Sir, this is their way. An Englishman would have stomached it, and been sulky, and never have taken further notice of you; but a Scotchman, Sir, though you vote nineteen times against him, will accost you with equal complaisance after each time, and the twentieth time, Sir, he will get your vote."'

'Talking on the subject of toleration, one day when some friends were with him in his study, he made his usual remark, that the State has a right to regulate the religion of the people, who are the children of the State. A clergyman having readily acquiesced in this, Johnson, who loved discussion, observed, "But, Sir, you must go round to other States than our own. You do not know what a Bramin has to say for himself.[1] In short, Sir, I have got no further than this: Every man has a right to utter what he thinks truth, and every other man has a right to knock him down for it. Martyrdom is the test."'

marginal line:
acquiesced in . . . discussion, observed [H]
underlined:
who loved discussion [H]

'A man, he observed, should begin to write soon; for, if he waits till his judgement is matured, his inability, through want of practice to express his conceptions, will make the disproportion so great between what he sees, and what he can attain, that he will probably be discouraged from writing at all. As a proof of the justness of this remark, we may instance what is related of the great Lord Granville;[2] that after he had written his letter giving an account of the battle of Dettingen, he said, "Here is a letter, expressed in terms not good enough for a tallow-chandler to have used."'

'Talking of a Court-martial that was sitting upon a very momentous publick occasion, he expressed much doubt of an enlightened decision; and said, that perhaps there was not a member of it, who in the whole course of his life, had ever spent an hour by himself in balancing probabilities.'

marginal line:
Here Lord . . . discovered the [H]

[1] Here Lord Macartney remarks, 'A Bramin or any cast of the Hindoos will neither admit you to be of their religion, nor be converted to yours:— a thing which struck the Portuguese with the greatest astonishment, when they first discovered the East Indies.'

[2] [John, the first Earl Granville, who died January 2, 1763. MALONE.]

'Goldsmith one day brought to the CLUB a printed Ode, which he, with others, had been hearing read by its authour in a publick room, at the rate of five shillings each for admission. One of the company having read it aloud, Dr. Johnson said, "Bolder words and more timorous meaning, I think, never were brought together."'

queried twice:
they are etc. (H)

'Talking of Gray's Odes, he said, "They are forced plants, raised in a hot-bed; and they are poor plants; they are but cucumbers after all." A gentleman present, who had been running down Ode-writing in general, as a bad species of poetry, unluckily said, "Had they been literally cucumbers, they had been better things than Odes."— "Yes, Sir, (said Johnson,) for a *hog*."'

'His distinction of the different degrees of attainment of learning was thus marked upon two occasions. Of Queen Elizabeth he said, "She had learning enough to have given dignity to a bishop;" and of Mr. Thomas Davies he said, "Sir, Davies has learning enough to give credit to a clergyman."'

'He used to quote, with great warmth, the saying of Aristotle recorded by Diogenes Laertius; that there was the same difference between one learned and unlearned, as between the living and the dead.'

'It is very remarkable, that he retained in his memory very slight and trivial, as well as important, things. As an instance of this, it seems that an inferiour domestick[a] of the Duke of Leeds had attempted to celebrate his Grace's marriage in such homely rhymes as he could make; and this curious composition having been sung to Dr. Johnson, he got it by heart, and used to repeat it in a very pleasant manner.[b] Two of the stanzas were these:

[a] *his Porter.* [I]

[b] *he used to bid Baretti repeat it—who was particularly fond of it.* [H & I]

underlined:
lady [H]

[c] *I fancy I was the Lady whose Uncle Sir Thomas Salusbury used to repeat it for ever— The Song was made by the Porter of that Duke of Leeds who married Lady Mary Godolphin.* [H & I]

"When the Duke of Leeds shall married be
To a fine young lady of high quality,
How happy will that gentlewoman be
In his Grace of Leeds's good company.

She shall have all that's fine and fair,
And the best of silk and satin shall wear;
And ride in a coach to take the air,
And have a house in St. James's-square."[1]

[1] The correspondent of the Gentleman's Magazine who subscribes himself Sciolus, furnishes the following supplement:

'A lady of my acquaintance remembers to have heard her uncle[c] sing

To hear a man of the weight and dignity of Johnson, repeating such humble attempts at poetry, had a very amusing effect. He, however, seriously observed of the last stanza repeated by him, that it nearly comprised all the advantages that wealth can give.'

'An eminent foreigner, when he was shewn the British Museum, was very troublesome with many absurd enquiries. "Now there, Sir, (said he,) is the difference between an Englishman and a Frenchman. A Frenchman must be always talking, whether he knows any thing of the matter or not; an Englishman is content to say nothing, when he has nothing to say." '

'His unjust contempt for foreigners was, indeed, extreme. One evening, at Old Slaughter's coffee-house, when a number of them were talking loud about little matters, he said, "Does not this confirm old Meynell's observation —*For any thing I see, foreigners are fools?*"'

'He said, that once, when he had a violent tooth-ach, a Frenchman accosted him thus: *Ah, Monsieur, vous étudiez trop.*'

marginal line: tooth-ach, a ... étudiez trop [H]

'Having spent an evening at Mr. Langton's with the Reverend Dr. Parr, he was much pleased with the conversation of that learned gentleman; and, after he was gone, said to Mr. Langton, "Sir, I am obliged to you for having asked me this evening. Parr is a fair man.[1] I do not know

those homely stanzas more than forty-five years ago. He repeated the second thus:

> "She shall breed young lords and ladies fair,
> And ride abroad in a coach and three pair,
> And the best, &c.
> And have a house, &c."

And remembered a third which seems to have been the introductory one, and is believed to have been the only remaining one:

> " When the Duke of Leeds shall have made his choice
> Of a charming young lady that's beautiful and wise,
> She'll be the happiest young gentlewoman under the skies,
> As long as the sun and moon shall rise,
> And how happy shall, &c."'

It is with pleasure I add that this stanza could never be more truly applied than at this present time [1792.]

[1] [When the Corporation of Norwich applied to Johnson to point out to them a proper master for their Grammar-School, he recommended Dr. Parr, on his ceasing to be usher to Sumner at Harrow. BURNEY.]

when I have had an occasion of such free controversy. It
is remarkable how much of a man's life may pass without
meeting with any instance of this kind of open discussion."'

'We may fairly institute a criticism between Shakspeare
and Corneille, as they both had, though in a different
degree, the lights of a latter age. It is not so just between
the Greek dramatick writers and Shakspeare. It may be
replied to what is said by one of the remarkers on Shakspeare, that though Darius's shade had *prescience*, it does
not necessarily follow that he had all *past* particulars
revealed to him.'

'Spanish plays, being wildly and improbably farcical,
would please children here, as children are entertained
with stories full of prodigies; their experience not being
sufficient to cause them to be so readily startled at deviations from the natural course of life. The machinery of the
Pagans is uninteresting to us: when a Goddess appears in
Homer or Virgil, we grow weary; still more so in the
Grecian tragedies, as in that kind of composition a nearer
approach to Nature is intended. Yet there are good reasons
for reading romances; as—the fertility of invention, the
beauty of style and expression, the curiosity of seeing with
what kind of performances the age and country in which
they were written was delighted: for it is to be apprehended, that at the time when very wild improbable tales
were well received, the people were in a barbarous state,
and so on the footing of children, as has been explained.'

marginal line:
tragedies, as . . . are
good [H]

'It is evident enough that no one who writes now can
use the Pagan deities and mythology; the only machinery,
therefore, seems that of ministering spirits, the ghosts of
the departed, witches, and fairies, though these latter, as
the vulgar superstition concerning them (which, while in
its force, infected at least the imagination of those that had
more advantage in education, though their reason set them
free from it,) is every day wearing out, seem likely to be
of little further assistance in the machinery of poetry. As I
recollect, Hammond introduces a hag or witch into one
of his love elegies, where the effect is unmeaning and
disgusting.'[a]

underlined:
hag [H]

[a] *Otway's Hag is a*
very fine one: completely
what you see every day.
Yet he makes it impress
you at the 50th Read-
ing.   Oh seen for
ever, yet for ever new,
can be applied only
to Otways Hag. [H]

'The man who uses his talent of ridicule in creating or
grossly exaggerating the instances he gives, who imputes

absurdities that did not happen, or when a man was a little ridiculous, describes him as having been very much so, abuses his talents greatly. The great use of delineating absurdities is, that we may know how far human folly can go; the account, therefore, ought of absolute necessity to be faithful. A certain character (naming the person) as to the general cast of it, is well described by Garrick, but a great deal of the phraseology he uses in it, is quite his own, particularly in the proverbial comparisons, "obstinate as a pig," &c. but I don't know whether it might not be true of Lord ———,[a] that from a too great eagerness of praise and popularity, and a politeness carried to a ridiculous excess, he was likely, after asserting a thing in general, to give it up again in parts. For instance, if he had said Reynolds was the first of painters, he was capable enough of giving up, as objections might happen to be severally made, first, his outline,—then the grace in form,—then the colouring,—and lastly, to have owned that he was such a mannerist, that the disposition of his pictures was all alike.'

[a] *Corke* [H & I]

'For hospitality, as formerly practised, there is no longer the same reason; heretofore the poorer people were more numerous, and from want of commerce, their means of getting a livelihood more difficult; therefore the supporting them was an act of great benevolence; now that the poor can find maintenance for themselves, and their labour is wanted, a general undiscerning hospitality tends to ill, by withdrawing them from their work to idleness and drunkenness. Then, formerly rents were received in kind, so that there was a great abundance of provisions in possession of the owners of the lands, which since the plenty of money afforded by commerce, is no longer the case.'

'Hospitality to strangers and foreigners in our country is now almost at an end; since, from the increase of them that come to us; there have been a sufficient number of people that have found an interest in providing inns and proper accommodations, which is in general a more expedient method for the entertainment of travellers. Where the travellers and strangers are few, more of that hospitality subsists, as it has not been worth while to provide places of accommodation. In Ireland, there is still hospitality to strangers, in some degree; in Hungary and Poland, probably more.'

'Colman, in a note on his translation of Terence, talking of Shakspeare's learning, asks, "What says Farmer to this? What says Johnson?" Upon this he observed, "Sir, let Farmer answer for himself: *I* never engaged in this controversy. I always said, Shakspeare had Latin enough to grammaticise his English." '

'A clergyman, whom he characterised as one who loved to say little oddities, was affecting one day, at a Bishop's table, a sort of slyness and freedom not in character, and repeated, as if part of "The Old Man's Wish," a song by Dr. Walter Pope, a verse bordering on licentiousness. Johnson rebuked him in the finest manner, by first shewing him that he did not know the passage he was aiming at, and thus humbling him: "Sir, that is not the song: it is thus." And he gave it right. Then looking stedfastly on him, "Sir, there is a part of that song which I should wish to exemplify in my own life:

"May I govern my passions with absolute sway!" '

a Bentley said Barnes had about as much Greek as an Athenian Blacksmith [1]

'Being asked if Barnes knew a good deal of Greek,[a] he answered, "I doubt, Sir, he was *unoculus inter cæcos*." [1]

'He used frequently to observe, that men might be very eminent in a profession, without our perceiving any particular power of mind in them in conversation. "It seems strange (said he) that a man should see so far to the right, who sees so short a way to the left. Burke is the only man whose common conversation corresponds with the general fame which he has in the world. Take up whatever topick you please, he is ready to meet you." '

'A gentleman, by no means deficient in literature, having discovered less acquaintance with one of the Classicks than Johnson expected, when the gentleman left the room, he observed, "You see, now, how little any body

---

[1] [Johnson, in his Life of Milton, after mentioning that great poet's extraordinary fancy that the world was in its decay, and that his book was to be written in an age too late for heroick poesy, thus concludes: 'However inferiour to the heroes who were born in better ages, he might still be great among his contemporaries, with the hope of growing every day greater in the dwindle of posterity; he might still be a giant among the pigmies, *the one-eyed monarch of the blind.*' J. BOSWELL.]

reads." Mr. Langton happening to mention his having read a good deal in Clenardus's Greek Grammar, "Why, Sir, (said he,) who is there in this town who knows any thing of Clenardus[1] but you and I?" And upon Mr. Langton's mentioning that he had taken the pains to learn by heart the Epistle of St. Basil, which is given in that Grammar as a praxis, "Sir, (said he,) I never made such an effort to attain Greek."'

'Of Dodsley's "Publick Virtue, a Poem," he said, "It was fine *blank;* (meaning to express his usual contempt for blank verse): however, this miserable poem did not sell, and my poor friend Doddy said, Publick Virtue was not a subject to interest the age."'

'Mr. Langton, when a very young man, read Dodsley's "Cleone, a Tragedy," to him, not aware of his extreme impatience to be read to. As it went on he turned his face to the back of his chair, and put himself into various attitudes, which marked his uneasiness. At the end of an act, however, he said, "Come, let's have some more, let's go into the slaughter-house again, Lanky. But I am afraid there is more blood than brains." Yet he afterwards said, "When I heard you read it, I thought higher of its power of language: when I read it myself, I was more sensible of its pathetick effect;"[a] and then he paid it a compliment which many will think very extravagant. "Sir, (said he,) if Otway had written this play, no other of his pieces would have been remembered." Dodsley himself, upon this being repeated to him, said, "It was too much:"[b] it must be remembered, that Johnson always appeared not to be sufficiently sensible of the merit of Otway.'[2]

'Snatches of reading (said he) will not make a Bentley

[a] *I saw at Lyons a pathetic Pantomime called Sophie de Brabant—a Dance—Tragedie Ballet. The Story was the same to Cleone, & I cried for an Hour together.* [I]
underlined: *too much* [H]

[b] *a good deal too much; because poor Cleone has been long forgotten: while the orphan & Venice Preserved, hold their Places on the Stage. 1820.* [H]

[1] [Nicholas Clenard, who was born in Brabant, and died at Grenada in 1542, was a great traveller and linguist. Besides his Greek Grammar, (of which an improved edition was published by Vossius, at Amsterdam in 1626,) he wrote a Hebrew Grammar, and an account of his travels in various countries, in Latin, (Epistolarum Libri duo, 8vo. 1556,) a very rare work, of which there is a copy in the Bodleian Library. His Latin (says the authour of Nouveau Dictionnaire Historique, 1789,) would have been more pure, if he had not known so many languages. Malone.]

[2] [This assertion concerning Johnson's insensibility to the pathetick powers of Otway, is too *round.* I once asked him, whether he did not think Otway frequently tender: when he answered, 'Sir, he is all tenderness.' Burney.]

or a Clarke. They are, however, in a certain degree advantageous. I would put a child into a library (where no unfit books are) and let him read at his choice. A child should not be discouraged from reading any thing that he takes a liking to, from a notion that it is above his reach. If that be the case, the child will soon find it out and desist; if not, he of course gains the instruction; which is so much the more likely to come, from the inclination with which he takes up the study.'

'Though he used to censure carelessness with great vehemence, he owned, that he once, to avoid the trouble of locking up five guineas, hid them, he forgot where, so that he could not find them.'

'A gentleman who introduced his brother to Dr. Johnson, was earnest to recommend him to the Doctor's notice, which he did by saying, "When we have sat together some time, you'll find my brother grow very entertaining." — "Sir, (said Johnson,) I can wait." '

'When the rumour was strong that we should have a war, because the French would assist the Americans, he rebuked a friend with some asperity for supposing it, saying, "No, Sir, national faith is not yet sunk so low." '

'In the latter part of his life, in order to satisfy himself whether his mental faculties were impaired, he resolved that he would try to learn a new language, and fixed upon the Low Dutch, for that purpose, and this he continued till he had read about one half of "Thomas à Kempis;" and finding that there appeared no abatement of his power of acquisition, he then desisted, as thinking the experiment had been duly tried. Mr. Burke justly observed, that this was not the most vigorous trial, Low Dutch being a language so near to our own; had it been one of the languages entirely different, he might have been very soon satisfied.'

'Mr. Langton and he having gone to see a Freemason's funeral procession, when they were at Rochester, and some solemn musick being played on French-horns, he said, "This is the first time that I have ever been affected by musical sounds;" adding, "that the impression made upon him was of a melancholy kind." Mr. Langton saying, that this effect was a fine one'—JOHNSON. "Yes, if it softens the mind so as to prepare it for the reception of salutary feelings, it may be good: but inasmuch as it is melancholy *per se*, it is bad."' [1]

'Goldsmith had long a visionary project, that some time or other when his circumstances should be easier, he would go to Aleppo, in order to acquire a knowledge, as far as might be, of any arts peculiar to the East, and introduce them into Britain. When this was talked of in Dr. Johnson's company, he said, "Of all men Goldsmith is the most unfit to go out upon such an enquiry; for he is utterly ignorant of such arts as we already possess, and consequently could not know what would be accessions to our present stock of mechanical knowledge. Sir, he would bring home a grinding-barrow, which you see in every street in London, and think that he had furnished a wonderful improvement."'

'Greek, Sir, (said he,) is like lace; every man gets as much of it as he can.' [2]

'When Lord Charles Hay, after his return from America, was preparing his defence to be offered to the Court-Martial which he had demanded, having heard Mr. Langton as high in expressions of admiration of Johnson, as he usually was, he requested that Dr. Johnson might be introduced to him; and Mr. Langton having mentioned it to Johnson, he very kindly and readily agreed; and being presented by Mr. Langton to his Lordship, while under arrest, he saw him several times; upon one of which occasions Lord Charles read to him what he had prepared, which Johnson signified his approbation of, saying, "It is a very good soldierly defence." Johnson said that he had advised his Lordship, that as it was in vain to contend with those who were in possession of power, if they would offer him the rank of Lieutenant-General, and a government, it would be better judged to desist from urging his complaints. It is well known that his Lordship died before the sentence was made known.'

---

[1] [The French-horn, however, is so far from being melancholy *per se*, that when the strain is light, and in the field, there is nothing so cheerful! It was the funeral occasion, and probably the solemnity of the strain, that produced the plaintive effect here mentioned. BURNEY.]

[2] [It should be remembered, that this was said twenty-five or thirty years ago, when lace was very generally worn.'[a] MALONE.]

[a] *so die away our Bons Mots, if they are not classical; Duration can be expected from Learning only — not Wit. 1820.* [H]

'Johnson one day gave high praise to Dr. Bentley's verses[1] in Dodsley's Collection, which he recited with his usual energy. Dr. Adam Smith, who was present, observed in his decisive professorial manner, "Very well—Very well." Johnson, however, added, "Yes, they *are* very well, Sir; but you may observe in what manner they are well. They

[1] Dr. Johnson, in his Life of Cowley, says, that these are 'the only English verses which Bentley is known to have written.' I shall here insert them, and hope my readers will apply them.[a]

underlined:
apply them [H]
to whom, or to what?
[H]

[a] *& these are imitated from some Stanzas written by Evelyn— The Author of the pretty Book de Re Rustica* [I]

'Who strives to mount Parnassus' hill,
    And thence poetick laurels bring,
Must first acquire due force and skill,
    Must fly with swan's or eagle's wing.

Who Nature's treasures would explore,
    Her mysteries and arcana know;
Must high as lofty Newton soar,
    Must stoop as delving Woodward low.

[b] *Seldon* corrected to
Selden [H]

Who studies ancient laws and rites,
    Tongues, arts, and arms, and history;
Must drudge, like Seldon,[b] days and nights,
    And in the endless labour die.

Who travels in religious jars,
    (Truth mixt with errour, shades with rays,)
Like Whiston, wanting pyx or stars,
    In ocean wide or sinks or strays.

But grant, our hero's hope long toil
    And comprehensive genius crown,
All sciences, all arts his spoil,
    Yet what reward, or what renown?

Envy, innate in vulgar souls,
    Envy steps in and stops his rise;
Envy with poison'd tarnish fouls
    His lustre, and his worth decries.

He lives inglorious or in want,
    To college and old books confin'd:
Instead of learn'd, he's call'd pedant,
    Dunces advanc'd, he's left behind:
Yet left content, a genuine Stoick he,
    Great without patron, rich without South Sea.'

[A different, and probably a more accurate copy of these spirited verses is to be found in 'The Grove, or a Collection of Original Poems and Translations,' &c. 1721. In this miscellany the last stanza, which in Dodsley's copy is unquestionably uncouth, is thus exhibited:

'*Inglorious or by wants inthrall'd*,
    To college and old books confin'd,
A pedant from his learning call'd,
    Dunces advanc'd, he's left behind.'   J. BOSWELL]

are the forcible verses of a man of a strong mind, but not accustomed to write verse; for there is some uncouthness in the expression." [1]

'Drinking tea one day at Garrick's with Mr. Langton, he was questioned if he was not somewhat of a heretick as to Shakspeare; said Garrick, "I doubt he is a little of an infidel."—"Sir, (said Johnson) I will stand by the lines I have written on Shakspeare in my Prologue at the opening of your Theatre." Mr. Langton suggested, that in the line

> "And panting Time toil'd after him in vain;"

Johnson might have had in his eye the passage in the "Tempest," [a] where Prospero says of Miranda,

> "——— She will outstrip all praise,
> And make it halt behind her."

Johnson said nothing. Garrick then ventured to observe, "I do not think that the happiest line in the praise of Shakspeare." Johnson exclaimed (smiling,) "Prosaical rogues! next time I write, I'll make both time and space pant." [2]

marginal notes:
marginal line:
Johnson) I . . . in the [H]

[a] *rather the Winter's Tale* [I]

marginal line:
Prosaical rogues . . . space pant [H]

---

[1] The difference between Johnson and Smith is apparent even in this slight instance. Smith was a man of extraordinary application, and had his mind crowded with all manner of subjects; but the force, acuteness, and vivacity of Johnson were not to be found there. He had book-making so much in his thoughts, and was so chary of what might be turned to account in that way, that he once said to Sir Joshua Reynolds, that he made it a rule when in company, never to talk of what he understood. Beauclerk had for a short time a pretty high opinion of Smith's conversation. Garrick, after listening to him for a while, as to one of whom his expectations had been raised, turned slyly to a friend, and whispered him, 'What say you to this? —eh? *flabby,* I think.'

[2] I am sorry to see in the 'Transactions of the Royal Society of Edinburgh,' Vol II, 'An Essay on the Character of Hamlet,' written, I should suppose, by a very young man, though called 'Reverend;' who speaks with pre- sumptuous petulance of the first literary character of his age. Amidst a cloudy confusion of words, (which hath of late too often passed in Scotland for *Metaphysicks,*) he thus ventures to criticise one of the noblest lines in our language:—'Dr. Johnson has remarked, that "time toiled after him in vain." But I should apprehend, that this is *entirely to mistake the character.* Time toils after *every great man,* as well as after Shakspeare. The *workings* of an ordinary mind *keep pace,* indeed, with time; they move no faster; *they have their beginning, their middle, and their end;* but superiour natures can *reduce these into a point.* They do not, indeed, *suppress* them; but they *suspend,* or they *lock them up in the breast.*' The learned Society, under whose sanction such gabble is ushered into the world, would do well to offer a premium to any one who will discover its meaning.

two marginal lines:
literary character . . .
for Metaphysicks [H]

'It is well known that there was formerly a rude custom for those who were sailing upon the Thames, to accost each other as they passed, in the most abusive language they could invent, generally, however, with as much satirical humour as they were capable of producing. Addison gives a specimen of this ribaldry, in Number 383 of "The Spectator," when Sir Roger de Coverly and he are going to Spring-garden. Johnson was once eminently successful in this species of contest; a fellow having attacked him with some coarse raillery, Johnson answered him thus, "Sir, your wife, *under pretence of keeping a bawdy-house*, is a receiver of stolen goods." One evening when he and Mr. Burke and Mr. Langton were in company together, and the admirable scolding of Timon of Athens was mentioned, this instance of Johnson's was quoted, and thought to have at least equal excellence.'

'As Johnson always allowed the extraordinary talents of Mr. Burke, so Mr. Burke was fully sensible of the wonderful powers of Johnson. Mr. Langton recollects having passed an evening with both of them, when Mr. Burke repeatedly entered upon topicks which it was evident he would have illustrated with extensive knowledge and richness of expression; but Johnson always seized upon the conversation, in which, however, he acquitted himself in a most masterly manner. As Mr. Burke and Mr. Langton were walking home, Mr. Burke observed that Johnson had been very great that night; Mr. Langton joined in this, but added, he could have wished to hear more from another person; (plainly intimating that he meant Mr. Burke.) "O, no, (said Mr. Burke) it is enough for me to have rung the bell to him."'

marginal line:
counting money . . . *to*
count [H]
underlined:
I [H]

'Beauclerk having observed to him of one of their friends, that he was aukward at counting money, "Why, Sir," said Johnson, "I am likewise aukward at counting money. But then, Sir, the reason is plain; I have had very little money to count."'

'He had an abhorrence of affectation. Talking of old Mr. Langton, of whom he said, "Sir, you will seldom see such a gentleman, such are his stores of literature, such his knowledge in divinity, and such his exemplary life;" he added, "and Sir, he has no grimace, no gesticulation, no burst of admiration on trivial occasions; he never embraces you with an overacted cordiality."'

marginal line:
trivial occasions . . .
overacted cordiality [H]

'Being in company with a gentleman who thought fit to maintain Dr. Berkeley's ingenious philosophy, that nothing exists but as perceived by some mind; when the gentleman was going away, Johnson said to him, "Pray, Sir, don't leave us; for we may perhaps forget to think of you, and then you will cease to exist."'

marginal line:
to him . . . to exist [H]

'Goldsmith, upon being visited by Johnson one day in the Temple, said to him with a little jealousy of the appearance of his accommodation, "I shall soon be in better chambers than these." Johnson at the same time checked him and paid him a handsome compliment, implying that a man of his talents should be above attention to such distinctions, — "Nay, Sir, never mind that: *Nil te quæsiveris extra.*"'

'At the time when his pension was granted to him, he said, with a noble literary ambition, "Had this happened twenty years ago, I should have gone to Constantinople to learn Arabick, as Pococke did."'

'As an instance of the niceness of his taste, though he praised West's translation of Pindar, he pointed out the following passages as faulty, by expressing a circumstance so minute as to detract from the general dignity which should prevail:

"Down then from thy glittering *nail*,
     Take, O Muse, thy Dorian lyre."'

'When Mr. Vesey[1] was proposed as a member of the LITERARY CLUB, Mr. Burke began by saying, that he was a man of gentle manners. "Sir, said Johnson, you need say no more. When you have said a man of gentle manners, you have said enough."'

'The late Mr. Fitzherbert told Mr. Langton, that Johnson said to him, "Sir, a man has no more right to *say* an uncivil thing, than to *act* one; no more right to say a rude thing to another than to knock him down."'

marginal line:
Johnson said . . . no
more [H]

'My dear friend Dr. Bathurst, (said he with a warmth of approbation) declared, he was glad that his father, who was a West-India planter, had left his affairs in total ruin,

[1] [The Right Honourable Agmondesham Vesey was elected a member of the LITERARY CLUB in 1773, and died August 11th, 1786. MALONE.]

because, having no estate, he was not under the temptation of having slaves.'

marginal line:
*Richardson had ... them
introduced* [H]

'Richardson had little conversation, except about his own works, of which Sir Joshua Reynolds said he was always willing to talk, and glad to have them introduced. Johnson, when he carried Mr. Langton to see him, professed that he could bring him out into conversation, and

ᵃ underlined,   cor-
rected to *roar,* and
queried: *rear* [H]

used this allusive expression, "Sir, I can make him *rear*."ᵃ But he failed; for in that interview Richardson said little else than that there lay in the room a translation of his Clarissa into German.'[1]

'Once when somebody produced a newspaper in which there was a letter of stupid abuse of Sir Joshua Reynolds, of which Johnson himself came in for a share,—"Pray, said he, let us have it read aloud from beginning to end;" which being done, he with a ludicrous earnestness, and not directing his look to any particular person, called out, "Are we alive after all this satire!"'

'He had a strong prejudice against the political character of Secker, one instance of which appeared at Oxford, where he expressed great dissatisfaction at his varying the old established toast, "Church and King." "The Archbishop of Canterbury," said he, (with an affected smooth smiling grimace) "drinks, 'Constitution in Church and

underlined:
literary lady [H]

ᵇ *I wonder if it was
Hannah More, It was
certainly not H. L. P.*
[H]

underlined:
*Clarissa, King's
brother's* [H]

ᶜ *The present King of
France Louis dixhuit
... who likewise de-
lighted in reading Field-
ing's Tom: Jones ...
he asked Dr. Browne
Mill—as they walked
on the Crescent at Bath
—If Prior Park had
belonged to the Man
who was believed The
Allworthy of Tom
Jones? but Louis dix-
huit is a universal
Reader 1820.* [H]

State.'" Being asked what difference there was between the two toasts, he said, "Why, Sir, you may be sure he meant something." Yet when the life of that prelate, prefixed to his sermons by Dr. Porteus and Dr. Stinton, his chaplains, first came out, he read it with the utmost avidity,

[1] A literary ladyᵇ has favoured me with a characteristick anecdote of Richardson. One day at his country house at Northend, where a large company was assembled at dinner, a gentleman who was just returned from Paris, willing to please Mr. Richardson, mentioned to him a very flattering circumstance,—that he had seen his Clarissa lying on the King's brother's table.ᶜ Richardson observing that part of the company were engaged in talking to each other, affected then not to attend to it: but by and by, when there was a general silence, and he thought that the flattery might be fully heard, he addressed himself to the gentleman, 'I think, Sir, you were saying something about,'—pausing in a high flutter of expectation. The gentleman provoked at his inordinate vanity, resolved not to indulge it, and with an exquisitely sly air of indifference answered, 'A mere trifle, Sir, not worth repeating.' The mortification of Richardson was visible, and he did not speak ten words more the whole day. Dr. Johnson was present, and appeared to enjoy it much.

and said, "It is a life well written, and that well deserves to be recorded."'

'Of a certain noble Lord, he said, "Respect him, you could not; for he had no mind of his own. Love him you could not; for that which you could do with him, every one else could."'

'Of Dr. Goldsmith he said, "No man was more foolish when he had not a pen in his hand, or more wise when he had."'

marginal line:
Of Dr. . . . he had [H]

'He told in his lively manner the following literary anecdote: "Green and Guthrie, an Irishman and a Scotchman, undertook a translation of Duhalde's history of China. Green said of Guthrie, that he knew no English, and Guthrie of Green, that he knew no French; and these two undertook to translate Duhalde's history of China. In this translation there was found,—'the twenty-sixth day of the new moon.' Now, as the whole age of the moon is but twenty-eight days, the moon, instead of being new, was nearly as old as it could be. The blunder arose from their mistaking the word *neuvième*, ninth, for *nouvelle*, or *neuve*, new."'

marginal line:
arose from . . . *neuve, new* [H]

'Talking of Dr. Blagden's copiousness and precision of communication, Dr. Johnson said, "Blagden, Sir, is a delightful fellow."'

'On occasion of Dr. Johnson's publishing his pamphlet of "The False Alarm," there came out a very angry answer (by many supposed to be by Mr. Wilkes.) Dr. Johnson determined on not answering it; but, in conversation with Mr. Langton mentioned a particular or two, which if he *had* replied to it, he might perhaps have inserted.—In the answerer's pamphlet, it had been said with solemnity, "Do you consider, Sir, that a House of Commons is to the people as a creature is to its Creator." To this question, said Dr. Johnson, I could have replied, that —in the first place—the idea of a CREATOR must be such as that he has a power to unmake or annihilate his creature.'

'Then it cannot be conceived that a creature can make laws for its CREATOR.'[1]

[1] His profound adoration of the GREAT FIRST CAUSE was such as to set him above that 'Philosophy and vain deceit,' with which men of narrow conceptions have been infected. I have heard him strongly maintain that

'Depend upon it, said he, that if a man *talks* of his misfortunes, there is something in them that is not disagreeable to him;[a] for where there is nothing but pure misery, there never is any recourse to the mention of it.'

'A man must be a poor beast, that should *read* no more in quantity than he could *utter* aloud.'

'Imlac in "Rasselas," I spelt with a *c* at the end, because it is less like English, which should always have the Saxon *k* added to the *c*.'[1]

'Many a man is mad in certain instances, and goes through life without having it perceived;—for example, a madness has seized a person, of supposing himself obliged literally to pray continually; had the madness turned the opposite way, and the person thought it a crime ever to pray, it might, not improbably, have continued unobserved.'

'He apprehended that the delineation of *characters* in the end of the first Book of the "Retreat of the ten thousand" was the first instance of the kind that was known.'

'Supposing (said he) a wife to be of a studious or argumentative turn, it would be very troublesome: for instance, —if a woman should continually dwell upon the subject of the Arian heresy.'

'No man speaks concerning another, even suppose it be in his praise, if he thinks he does not hear him, exactly as he would, if he thought he was within hearing.'

' "The applause of a single human being is of great consequence:" This he said to me with great earnestness of manner, very near the time of his decease, on occasion of having desired me to read a letter addressed to him from some person in the North of England; which when I had done, and he asked me what the contents were, as I thought being particular upon it might fatigue him, it being of great length, I only told him in general that it was highly in his praise;—and then he expressed himself as above.'

'He mentioned with an air of satisfaction what Baretti had told him; that, meeting, in the course of his studying

'what is right is not so from any natural fitness, but because GOD wills it to be right;' and it is certainly so, because he has predisposed the relations of things so, as that which he wills must be right.

[1] I hope the authority of the great Master of our language will stop that curtailing innovation, by which we see *critic, public,* &c. frequently written instead of *critick, publick,* &c.

English, with an excellent paper in the Spectator, one of four that were written by the respectable Dissenting Minister Mr. Grove of Taunton, and observing the genius and energy of mind that it exhibits, it greatly quickened his curiosity to visit our country; as he thought, if such were the lighter periodical essays of our authours, their productions on more weighty occasions must be wonderful indeed!'

'He observed once, at Sir Joshua Reynolds's, that a beggar in the street will more readily ask alms from a *man*, though there should be no marks of wealth in his appearance, than from even a well-dressed *woman;*[1a] which he accounted for from the great degree of carefulness as to money, that is to be found in women; saying farther upon it, that, the opportunities in general that they possess of improving their condition are much fewer than men have; and adding, as he looked round the company, which consisted of men only,—there is not one of us who does not think he might be richer, if he would use his endeavour.'

'He thus characterised an ingenious writer of his acquaintance: "Sir, he is an enthusiast by rule."'

' "*He may hold up that* SHIELD *against all his enemies;*"— was an observation on Homer, in reference to his description of the shield of Achilles, made by Mrs. Fitzherbert, wife to his friend Mr. Fitzherbert of Derbyshire, and respected by Dr. Johnson as a very fine one. He had in general a very high opinion of that lady's understanding.'

'An observation of Bathurst's may be mentioned, which Johnson repeated, appearing to acknowledge it to be well founded; namely, it was somewhat remarkable how seldom, on occasion of coming into the company of any new person, one felt any wish or inclination to see him again.'

This year the Reverend Dr. Franklin having published a translation of 'Lucian,' inscribed to him the *Demonax* thus:

'To DR. SAMUEL JOHNSON, the Demonax of the present age, this piece is inscribed by a sincere admirer of his respectable talents,   'THE TRANSLATOR'

a *The Man has more Money in his Pocket, & his Money is his own. The Woman is commonly responsible for her Expences to a Father, a Brother or a Husband. She must give in her Acct. on Monday Morns— & mention her Shilling given to the Beggar ... for doing which She will receive a Check, & be told it was ill bestowed.* [H]

marginal line:
He thus ... by rule [H]

[1] Sterne is of a direct contrary opinion. See his 'Sentimental Journey,' Article, '*The Mystery.*'

Though upon a particular comparison of Demonax and Johnson, there does not seem to be a great deal of similarity between them, this Dedication is a just compliment from the general character given by Lucian of the ancient Sage, 'ἄριστον ὧν οἶδα ἐγὼ φιλοσόφων γενόμενον, the best philosopher whom I have ever seen or known.'

In 1781, Johnson at last completed his 'Lives of the Poets,' of which he gives this account: 'Some time in March I finished the "Lives of the Poets," which I wrote in my usual way, dilatorily and hastily, unwilling to work, and working with vigour and haste.'[1] In a memorandum previous to this, he says of them: 'Written, I hope, in such a manner as may tend to the promotion of piety.'[2]

This is the work, which of all Dr. Johnson's writings will perhaps be read most generally, and with most pleasure. Philology and biography were his favourite pursuits, and those who lived most in intimacy with him, heard him upon all occasions, when there was a proper opportunity, take delight in expatiating upon the various merits of the English Poets: upon the niceties of their characters, and the events of their progress through the world which they contributed to illuminate. His mind was so full of that kind of information, and it was so well arranged in his memory, that in performing what he had undertaken in this way, he had little more to do than to put his thoughts upon paper; exhibiting first each Poet's life, and then subjoining a critical examination of his genius and works. But when he began to write, the subject swelled in such a manner, that instead of prefaces to each poet, of no more than a few pages, as he had originally intended,[3] he produced an ample, rich, and most entertaining view of them in every respect. In this he resembled Quintilian,

[1] Prayers and Meditations, p. 190.

[2] Ibid. 174.

[3] His design is thus announced in his *Advertisement:* 'The Booksellers having determined to publish a body of English Poetry, I was persuaded to promise them a preface to the works of each authour; an undertaking, as it was then presented to my mind, not very tedious or difficult.

'My purpose was only to have allotted to every poet an Advertisement, like that which we find in the French Miscellanies, containing a few dates, and a general character; but I have been led beyond my intention, I hope by the honest desire of giving useful pleasure.'

who tells us, that in the composition of his Institutions of
Oratory, '*Latiùs se tamen aperiente materiâ, plus quàm impone-
batur oneris sponte suscepi.*' The booksellers, justly sensible
of the great additional value of the copy-right, presented
him with another hundred pounds, over and above two
hundred, for which his agreement was to furnish such
prefaces as he thought fit.

This was, however, but a small recompence for such a
collection of biography, and such principles and illustrations of criticism, as, if digested and arranged in one
system, by some modern Aristotle or Longinus, might
form a code upon that subject, such as no other nation
can shew. As he was so good as to make me a present of
the greatest part of the original, and indeed only manuscript of this admirable work, I have an opportunity of
observing with wonder the correctness with which he
rapidly struck off such glowing composition. He may be
assimilated to the Lady in Waller, who could impress
with 'Love at first sight:'

> 'Some other nymphs with colours faint,
>   And pencil slow, may Cupid paint,
>   And a weak heart in time destroy;
> She has a stamp, and prints the boy.'

That he, however, had a good deal of trouble, and some
anxiety in carrying on the work, we see from a series of
letters to Mr. Nichols the printer,[1] whose variety of literary

marginal line:
*arranged in . . . that
subject* [H]

---

[1] Thus:—'In the Life of Waller, Mr. Nichols will find a reference to the
Parliamentary History, from which a long quotation is to be inserted. If Mr.
Nichols cannot easily find the book, Mr. Johnson will send it from Streatham.'

'Clarendon is here returned.'

'By some accident, I laid *your* note upon Duke up so safely, that I cannot
find it. Your informations have been of great use to me. I must beg it
again; with another list of our authours, for I have laid that with the other.
I have sent Stepney's Epitaph. Let me have the revises as soon as can be.
Dec. 1778.'

'I have sent Philips, with his Epitaphs, to be inserted. The fragment of a
preface is hardly worth the impression, but that we may seem to do something. It may be added to the Life of Philips. The Latin page is to be added
to the Life of Smith. I shall be at home to revise the two sheets of Milton.
March 1, 1779.'

'Please to get me the last edition of Hughes's Letters; and try to get Dennis
upon Blackmore, and upon Cato, and any thing of the same writer against
Pope. Our materials are defective.'

enquiry and obliging disposition, rendered him useful to
Johnson. Mr. Steevens appears, from the papers in my
possession, to have supplied him with some anecdotes and
quotations; and I observe the fair hand of Mrs. Thrale as
one of his copyists of select passages. But he was principally
indebted to my steady friend Mr. Isaac Reed, of Staple-
inn, whose extensive and accurate knowledge of English
literary History I do not express with exaggeration,
when I say it is wonderful; indeed his labours have
proved it to the world; and all who have the pleasure of
his acquaintance can bear testimony to the frankness of
his communications in private society.

It is not my intention to dwell upon each of Johnson's
'Lives of the Poets,' or attempt an analysis of their merits,
which, were I able to do it, would take up too much room
in this work; yet I shall make a few observations upon
some of them, and insert a few various readings.

The Life of COWLEY he himself considered as the best
of the whole, on account of the dissertation which it
contains on the *Metaphysical Poets*. Dryden, whose critical
abilities were equal to his poetical, had mentioned them
in his excellent Dedication of his Juvenal, but had barely
mentioned them. Johnson has exhibited them at large,
with such happy illustration from their writings, and in
so luminous a manner, that indeed he may be allowed the
full merit of novelty, and to have discovered to us, as it
were, a new planet in the poetical hemisphere.

It is remarked by Johnson, in considering the works of a

'As Waller professed to have imitated Fairfax, do you think a few pages of
Fairfax would enrich our edition? Few readers have seen it, and it may
please them. But it is not necessary.'

'An account of the Lives and Works of some of the most eminent English
Poets. By, &c.—"The English Poets, biographically and critically considered, by SAM. JOHNSON."—Let Mr. Nichols take his choice, or make
another to his mind. May, 1781.'

'You somehow forgot the advertisement for the new edition. It was not
enclosed. Of Gay's Letters I see not that any use can be made, for they give
no information of any thing. That he was a member of a Philosophical
Society is something; but surely he could be but a corresponding member.
However, not having his life here, I know not how to put it in, and it is of
little importance.'

See several more in 'The Gentleman's Magazine,' 1785. The Editor of
that Miscellany, in which Johnson wrote for several years, seems justly to
think that every fragment of so great a man is worthy of being preserved.

poet,[1] that 'amendments are seldom made without some token of a rent;' but I do not find that this is applicable to prose.[2] We shall see that though his amendments in this work are for the better, there is nothing of the *pannus assutus;* the texture is uniform: and indeed, what had been there at first, is very seldom unfit to have remained.

Various Readings[3] *in the Life of* COWLEY

'All [future votaries of] *that may hereafter pant for* solitude.
'To conceive and execute the [agitation or perception] *pains and the pleasures* of other minds.
'The wide effulgence of [the blazing] *a summer* noon.'

In the Life of WALLER, Johnson gives a distinct and animated narrative of publick affairs in that variegated period, with strong yet nice touches of character; and having a fair opportunity to display his political principles, does it with an unqualified manly confidence, and satisfies his readers how nobly he might have executed a *Tory History* of his country.

So easy is his style in these Lives, that I do not recollect more than three uncommon or learned words: one, when giving an account of the approach of Waller's mortal disease, he says, 'he found his legs grow *tumid;*'[a] by using the expression his legs *swelled*, he would have avoided this; and there would have been no impropriety in its being followed by the interesting question to his physician, 'What that *swelling* meant?' Another, when he mentions that Pope had *emitted* proposals; when *published* or *issued* would have been more readily understood; and a third, when he calls Orrery and Dr. Delany, writers both undoubtedly *veracious;* when *true, honest,* or *faithful,* might have been used. Yet, it must be owned, that none of these are *hard* or *too big* words: that custom would make them seem as easy as any others; and that a language is richer and capable of

underlined:
tumid [H]

[a] *common enough I think.* [H]

---

[1] Life of Sheffield.

[2] [See, however, p. 134 of this volume, where the same remark is made, and Johnson is there speaking of *prose*. In his Life of Dryden, his observations on the Opera of 'King Arthur,' furnish a striking instance of the truth of this remark. MALONE.]

[3] The original reading is enclosed in crotchets, and the present one is printed in Italicks.

more beauty of expression, by having a greater variety of synonimes.

His dissertation upon the unfitness of poetry for the awful subjects of our holy religion, though I do not entirely agree with him, has all the merit of originality, with uncommon force and reasoning.

Various Readings in the Life of WALLER

'Consented to [the insertion of their names] *their own nomination.*

'[After] *paying* a fine of ten thousand pounds.

'Congratulating Charles the Second on his [coronation] *recovered right.*

'He that has flattery ready for all whom the vicissitudes of the world happen to exalt, must be [confessed to degrade his powers] *scorned as a prostituted mind.*

'The characters by which Waller intended to distinguish his writings are [elegance] *sprightliness* and dignity.

'Blossoms to be valued only as they [fetch] *foretell* fruits.

'Images such as the superficies of nature [easily] *readily* supplies.

'[His] *Some* applications [are sometimes] *may be thought* too remote and unconsequential.

'His images are [sometimes confused] *not always distinct.*'

Against his Life of MILTON, the hounds of Whiggism have opened in full cry. But of Milton's great excellence as a poet, where shall we find such a blazon as by the hand of Johnson? I shall select only the following passage concerning 'PARADISE LOST':

'Fancy can hardly forbear to conjecture with what temper Milton surveyed the silent progress of his work, and marked his reputation stealing its way in a kind of subterraneous current, through fear and silence. I cannot but conceive him calm and confident, little disappointed, not at all dejected, relying on his own merit with steady consciousness, and waiting without impatience, the vicissitudes of opinion, and the impartiality of a future generation.'

Indeed even Dr. Towers, who may be considered as one of the warmest zealots of *The Revolution Society* itself, allows, that 'Johnson has spoken in the highest terms of the abilities of that great poet, and has bestowed on his principal poetical compositions, the most honourable encomiums.'[1]

That a man, who venerated the Church and Monarchy as Johnson did, should speak with a just abhorrence of Milton as a politician, or rather as a daring foe to good polity, was surely to be expected; and to those who censure him, I would recommend his commentary on Milton's celebrated complaint of his situation, when by the lenity of Charles the Second, 'a lenity of which (as Johnson well observes) the world has had perhaps no other example, he, who had written in justification of the murder of his Sovereign, was safe under an *Act of Oblivion*.' 'No sooner is he safe than he finds himself in danger, *fallen on evil days and evil tongues, with darkness and with dangers compassed round*. This darkness, had his eyes been better employed, had undoubtedly deserved compassion; but to add the mention of danger, was ungrateful and unjust. He was fallen, indeed, on *evil days;* the time was come in which regicides could no longer boast their wickedness. But of *evil tongues* for Milton to complain, required impudence at least equal to his other powers; Milton, whose warmest advocates must allow, that he never spared any asperity of reproach, or brutality of insolence.'

I have, indeed, often wondered how Milton, 'an acrimonious and surly Republican,'[2]—'a man who in his domestick relations was so severe and arbitrary,'[3] and

[1] See 'An Essay on the Life, Character, and Writings of Dr. Samuel Johnson,' London, 1787; which is very well written, making a proper allowance for the democratical bigotry of its authour: whom I cannot however but admire for his liberality in speaking thus of my illustrious friend:

'He possessed extraordinary powers of understanding, which were much cultivated by study, and still more by meditation and reflection. His memory was remarkably retentive, his imagination uncommonly vigorous, and his judgement keen and penetrating. He had a strong sense of the importance of religion; his piety was sincere, and sometimes ardent: and his zeal for the interests of virtue was often manifested in his conversation and in his writings. The same energy which was displayed in his literary productions was exhibited also in his conversation, which was various, striking, and instructive; and perhaps no man ever equalled him for nervous and pointed repartees.

'His Dictionary, his moral Essays, and his productions in polite literature, will convey useful instruction, and elegant entertainment, as long as the language in which they are written shall be understood.'

[2] Johnson's Life of Milton. [3] *Ibid.*

whose head was filled with the hardest and most dismal tenets of Calvinism, should have been such a poet; should not only have written with sublimity, but with beauty, and even gaiety; should have exquisitely painted the sweetest sensations of which our nature is capable; imaged the delicate raptures of connubial love; nay, seemed to be animated with all the spirit of revelry. It is a proof that in the human mind the departments of judgement and imagination, perception and temper, may sometimes be divided by strong partitions; and that the light and shade in the same character may be kept so distinct as never to be blended.[1]

In the Life of Milton, Johnson took occasion to maintain his own and the general opinion of the excellence of rhyme over blank verse, in English poetry; and quotes this apposite illustration of it by 'an ingenious critick,' that *it seems to be verse only to the eye*.[2] The gentleman whom he thus characterises, is (as he told Mr. Seward) Mr. Lock, of Norbury Park, in Surrey, whose knowledge and taste in the fine arts is universally celebrated; with whose elegance of manners the writer of the present work has felt himself much impressed, and to whose virtues a common friend, who has known him long, and is not much addicted to flattery, gives the highest testimony.

Various Readings in the Life of MILTON

'I cannot find any meaning but this which [his most bigoted advocates] *even kindness and reverence* can give.

'[Perhaps no] *scarcely any* man ever wrote so much, and praised so few.

'A certain [rescue] *preservative* from oblivion.

'Let me not be censured for this digression, as [contracted] *pedantick* or paradoxical.

'Socrates rather was of opinion, that what we had to

marginal line:
footnote 1 [H]

[1] Mr. Malone thinks it is rather a proof that he felt nothing of those cheerful sensations which he has described: that on these topicks it is the *poet*, and not the *man*, that writes.

[2] One of the most natural instances of the effect of blank verse occurred to the late Earl of Hopeton. His Lordship observed one of his shepherds poring in the fields upon Milton's 'Paradise Lost;' and having asked him what book it was, the man answered, 'An't please your Lordship, this is a very odd sort of an authour: he would fain rhyme, but cannot get at it.'

marginal line:
Paradise Lost . . . at it
[H]

learn was how to [obtain and communicate happiness] *do good and avoid evil.*

'Its elegance [who can exhibit?] *is less attainable.*'

I could, with pleasure, expatiate upon the masterly execution of the Life of DRYDEN, which we have seen[1] was one of Johnson's literary projects at an early period, and which it is remarkable, that after desisting from it, from a supposed scantiness of materials, he should, at an advanced age, have exhibited so amply.

His defence of that great poet against the illiberal attacks upon him, as if his embracing the Roman Catholick communion had been a time-serving measure, is a piece of reasoning at once able and candid. Indeed, Dryden himself, in his 'Hind and Panther,' hath given such a picture of his mind, that they who know the anxiety for repose as to the awful subject of our state beyond the grave, though they may think his opinion ill-founded, must think charitably of his sentiment:

'BUT, gracious GOD, how well dost thou provide
For erring judgements an unerring guide!
Thy throne is darkness in the abyss of light,
A blaze of glory that forbids the sight.
O! teach me to believe thee thus conceal'd,
And search no farther than thyself reveal'd;
But Her alone for my director take,
Whom thou hast promis'd never to forsake.
My thoughtless youth was wing'd with vain desires;
My manhood long misled by wand'ring fires,
Follow'd false lights; and when their glimpse was gone,
My pride struck out new sparkles of her own.
Such was I, such by nature still I am;
Be thine the glory and be mine the shame.
Good life be now my task: my doubts are done;
What more could shock my faith than Three in One?'

In drawing Dryden's character, Johnson has given, though I suppose unintentionally, some touches of his own. Thus: 'The power that predominated in his intellectual operations was rather strong reason than quick sensibility.

[1] See vol. ii. page 312.

Upon all occasions that were presented, he studied rather than felt; and produced sentiments not such as Nature enforces, but meditation supplies. With the simple and elemental passions as they spring separate in the mind, he seems not much acquainted. He is, therefore, with all his variety of excellence, not often pathetick;[1a] and had so little sensibility of the power of effusions purely natural, that he did not esteem them in others.'—It may indeed be observed, that in all the numerous writings of Johnson, whether in prose or verse, and even in his Tragedy, of which the subject is the distress of an unfortunate Princess, there is not a single passage that ever drew a tear.[b]

underlined:
often [H]
[a] *never* [H]

[b] *Perfectly true* [I]

Various Readings in the Life of DRYDEN

'The reason of this general perusal, Addison has attempted to [find in] *derive from* the delight which the mind feels in the investigation of secrets.

'His best actions are but [convenient] *inability of* wickedness.

'When once he had engaged himself in disputation, [matter] *thoughts* flowed in on either side.

'The abyss of an un-ideal [emptiness] *vacancy*.

'These, like [many other harlots,] *the harlots of other men*, had his love though not his approbation.

'He [sometimes displays] *descends to display* his knowledge with pedantick ostentation.

'French words which [were then used in] *had then crept into* conversation.'

The Life of Pope was written by Johnson *con amore*, both from the early possession which that writer had taken of his mind, and from the pleasure which he must have felt, in for ever silencing all attempts to lessen his poetical fame, by demonstrating his excellence, and pronouncing the following triumphant eulogium:—'After all this, it is surely superfluous to answer the question that has once been asked, Whether Pope was a poet? otherwise than by asking in return, if Pope be not a poet, where is poetry to be found? To circumscribe poetry by a definition, will

[c] *Where? The End of his Preface to the Dictionary certainly does call a Reader to lament with & for the Author —but it was mere Autobiographical Pathos: Johnson neither felt nor Could excite Concern for others— unless they wanted a Dinner: he laughed at distresses of Sentiment.* [H]

Where? [I]

[1] [It seems to me, that there are many pathetick passages in Johnson's works, both prose and verse.[c] KEARNEY.]

only shew the narrowness of the definer; though a definition which shall exclude Pope will not easily be made. Let
us look round upon the present time, and back upon the
past; let us enquire to whom the voice of mankind has
decreed the wreath of poetry; let their productions be
examined, and their claims stated, and the pretensions
of Pope will be no more disputed.'

I remember once to have heard Johnson say, 'Sir, a
thousand years may elapse before there shall appear
another man with a power of versification equal to that
of Pope.' That power must undoubtedly be allowed its
due share in enhancing the value of his captivating
composition.

Johnson who had done liberal justice to Warburton in
his edition of Shakspeare, which was published during the
life of that powerful writer, with still greater liberality
took an opportunity, in the Life of Pope, of paying the
tribute due to him when he was no longer in 'high place,'
but numbered with[a] the dead.[1]

a *with* crossed out; *among* written in; comment: *Bozzy had no Ear.* [H]

[1] Of Johnson's conduct towards Warburton, a very honourable notice is
taken by the Editor of 'Tracts by Warburton, and a Warburtonian, not
admitted into the Collection of their respective Works.' After an able and
'fond, though not undistinguishing,' consideration of Warburton's character, he says, 'In two immortal works, Johnson has stood forth in the
foremost rank of his admirers. By the testimony of such a man, impertinence
must be abashed, and malignity itself must be softened. Of literary merit,
Johnson, as we all know, was a sagacious but a most severe judge. Such was
his discernment, that he pierced into the most secret springs of human
actions: and such was his integrity, that he always weighed the moral
characters of his fellow-creatures in the "balance of the sanctuary." He was
too courageous to propitiate a rival, and too proud to truckle to a superiour.
Warburton he knew, as I know him, and as every man of sense and virtue
would wish to be known,—I mean, both from his own writings, and from
the writings of those who dissented from his principles or who envied his
reputation. But, as to favours, he had never received or asked any from the
Bishop of Gloucester: and, if my memory fails me not, he had seen him only
once, when they met almost without design, conversed without much effort,
and parted without any lasting impression of hatred or affection.[b] Yet, with
all the ardour of sympathetick genius, Johnson had done that spontaneously
and ably, which, by some writers, had been before attempted injudiciously,
and which, by others, from whom more successful attempts might have been
expected, has not *hitherto* been done at all. He spoke well of Warburton,
without insulting those whom Warburton despised. He suppressed not the
imperfections of this extraordinary man, while he endeavoured to do justice
to his numerous and transcendental excellencies. He defended him when
living, amidst the clamours of his enemies; and praised him when dead,
amidst the *silence of his friends.*'[c]

b '*I met Warburton last Night;*' *said he to me when he came home—and before we parted, he patted me.*' [I]

c *Who is this excellent Writer? known as it appears—to every body except H. L. P.* [H]

Having availed myself of this editor's eulogy on my departed friend, for

It seems strange, that two such men as Johnson and Warburton, who lived in the same age and country, should not only not have been in any degree of intimacy, but been almost personally unacquainted. But such instances, though we must wonder at them, are not rare. If I am rightly informed, after a careful enquiry, they never met but once, which was at the house of Mrs. French,[a] in London, well known for her elegant assemblies, and bringing eminent characters together. The interview proved to be mutually agreeable.

underlined:
French [H]

[a] *Murphy's Aunt.* [H]

I am well informed, that Warburton said of Johnson, 'I admire him, but I cannot bear his style:' and that Johnson being told of this, said, 'That is exactly my case as to him.' The manner in which he expressed his admiration of the fertility of Warburton's genius and of the variety of his materials, was, 'The table is always full, Sir. He brings things from the north, and the south, and from every quarter. In his "Divine Legation," you are always entertained. He carries you round and round, without carrying you forward to the point; but then you have no wish to be carried forward.' He said to the Reverend Mr. Strahan, 'Warburton is perhaps the last man who has written with a mind full of reading and reflection.'

It is remarkable, that in the Life of Broome, Johnson takes notice of Dr. Warburton's using a mode of expression which he himself used, and that not seldom, to the great offence of those who did not know him. Having occasion to mention a note, stating the different parts which were

which I warmly thank him, let me not suffer the lustre of his reputation, honestly acquired by profound learning and vigorous eloquence, to be tarnished by a charge of illiberality. He has been accused of invidiously dragging again into light certain writings of a person respectable by his talents, his learning, his station, and his age, which were published a great many years ago, and have since, it is said, been silently given up by their authour. But when it is considered that these writings were not *sins of youth*, but deliberate works of one well-advanced in life, overflowing at once with flattery to a great man of great interest in the Church, and with unjust and acrimonious abuse of two men of eminent merit; and that, though it would have been unreasonable to expect an humiliating recantation, no apology whatever has been made in the cool of the evening, for the oppressive fervour of the heat of the day; no slight relenting indication has appeared in any note,

[b] *I do not understand this—either: who was wounded—& in what Cause?* [H]

or any corner of later publications; is it not fair to understand him as superciliously persevering? When he allows the shafts to remain in the wounds, and will not stretch forth a lenient hand, is it wrong, is it not generous to become an indignant avenger?[b]

executed by the associated translators of 'The Odyssey,' he says, 'Dr. Warburton told me, in his warm language, that he thought the relation given in the note *a lie*.' The language is *warm* indeed; and, I must own, cannot be justified in consistency with a decent regard to the established forms of speech. Johnson had accustomed himself to use the word *lie*, to express a mistake or an errour in relation; in short, when the *thing was not so as told*, though the relater did not *mean* to deceive. When he thought there was intentional falsehood in the relater, his expression was, 'He *lies*, and he *knows* he *lies*.'

Speaking of Pope's not having been known to excel in conversation, Johnson observes, that 'traditional memory retains no sallies of raillery, or sentences of observation; nothing either pointed or solid, wise or merry; and that one apophthegm only is recorded.' In this respect, Pope differed widely from Johnson, whose conversation was, perhaps, more admirable than even his writings, however excellent. Mr. Wilkes has, however, favoured me with one repartee of Pope, of which Johnson was not informed. Johnson, after justly censuring him for having 'nursed in his mind a foolish dis-esteem of Kings,' tells us, 'yet a little regard shewn him by the Prince of Wales melted his obduracy; and he had not much to say when he was asked by his Royal Highness, *how he could love a Prince, while he disliked Kings?*' The answer which Pope made, was, 'The young lion is harmless, and even playful; but when his claws are full grown, he becomes cruel, dreadful, and mischievous.'[a]

a *&* this *borrowed from Shakespeare*. [H]

But although we have no collection of Pope's sayings, it is not therefore to be concluded, that he was not agreeable in social intercourse; for Johnson has been heard to say, that 'the happiest conversation is that of which nothing is distinctly remembered, but a general effect of pleasing impression.' The late Lord Somerville,[1] who saw much both of great and brilliant life, told me, that he had dined

---

[1] [James Lord Somerville, who died in 1766. MALONE.]

Let me here express my grateful remembrance of Lord Somerville's kindness to me, at a very early period. He was the first person of high rank, that took particular notice of me in the way most flattering to a young man fondly ambitious of being distinguished for his literary talents; and by the honour of his encouragement made me think well of myself, and aspire to

in company with Pope, and that after dinner the *little man*, as he called him, drank his bottle of Burgundy, and was exceedingly gay and entertaining.

I cannot withhold from my great friend a censure of at least culpable inattention, to a nobleman, who, it has been shewn, behaved to him with uncommon politeness. He says, 'Except Lord Bathurst, none of Pope's noble friends were such as that a good man would wish to have his intimacy with them known to posterity.' This will not apply to Lord Mansfield, who was not ennobled in Pope's life-time; but Johnson should have recollected, that Lord Marchmont was one of those noble friends. He includes his Lordship along with Lord Bolingbroke, in a charge of neglect of the papers which Pope left by his will; when, in truth, as I myself pointed out to him, before he wrote that poet's life, the papers were 'committed to *the sole care and judgement* of Lord Bolingbroke, unless he (Lord Boling-broke) shall not survive me;' so that Lord Marchmont had no concern whatever with them. After the first edition of the Lives, Mr. Malone, whose love of justice is equal to his accuracy, made, in my hearing, the same remark to Johnson; yet he omitted to correct the erroneous statement.[1] These particulars I mention, in the belief that there was only forgetfulness in my friend; but I owe this much to the Earl of Marchmont's reputation, who, were there no other memorials, will be immortalized by that line of Pope, in the verses on his Grotto:

'And the bright flame was shot through Marchmont's soul.'

Various Readings in the Life of POPE

'[Somewhat free] *sufficiently bold* in his criticism.
'All the gay [niceties] *varieties* of diction.

deserve it better. He had a happy art of communicating his varied know-ledge of the world, in short remarks and anecdotes, with a quiet pleasant gravity that was exceedingly engaging. Never shall I forget the hours which I enjoyed with him at his apartments in the Royal Palace of Holy-Rood House, and at his seat near Edinburgh, which he himself had formed with an elegant taste.

[1] [This neglect, however, assuredly did not arise from any ill-will towards Lord Marchmont, but from inattention; just as he neglected to correct his statement concerning the family of Thomson, the poet, after it had been shewn to be erroneous. MALONE.]

'Strikes the imagination with far [more] *greater* force.

'It is [probably] *certainly* the noblest version of poetry which the world has ever seen.

'Every sheet enabled him to write the next with [less trouble] *more facility*.

'No man sympathizes with [vanity depressed] *the sorrows of vanity*.

'It had been [criminal] *less easily excused*.

'When he [threatened to lay down] *talked of laying down* his pen.

'Society [is so named emphatically in opposition to] *politically regulated, is a state contra-distinguished from* a state of nature.

'A fictitious life of an [absurd] *infatuated* scholar.

'A foolish [contempt, disregard,] *disesteem* of Kings.

'His hopes and fears, his joys and sorrows [were like those of other mortals] *acted strongly upon his mind*.

'Eager to pursue knowledge and attentive to [accumulate] *retain it*.

'A mind [excursive] *active*, ambitious, and adventurous.

'In its [noblest] *widest* searches still longing to go forward.

'He wrote in such a manner as might expose him to few [neglects] *hazards*.

'The [reasonableness] *justice* of my determination.

'A [favourite] *delicious* employment of the poets.

'More terrifick and more powerful [beings] *phantoms* perform on the stormy ocean.

'The inventor of [those] *this* petty [beings] *nation*.

'The [mind] *heart* naturally loves truth.'

In the Life of ADDISON we find an unpleasing account of his having lent Steele a hundred pounds, and 'reclaimed his loan by an execution.' In the new edition of the *Biographia Britannica*, the authenticity of this anecdote is denied. But Mr. Malone has obliged me with the following note concerning it:—

'Many persons having doubts concerning this fact, I applied to Dr. Johnson, to learn on what authority he asserted it. He told me, he had it from Savage, who lived in intimacy with Steele, and who mentioned, that Steele

told him the story with tears in his eyes.—Ben Victor,
Dr. Johnson said, likewise informed him of this remarkable
transaction, from the relation of Mr. Wilkes the comedian,
who was also an intimate of Steele's.[1]—Some in defence
of Addison, have said, that "the act was done with the
good-natured view of rousing Steele, and correcting that
profusion which always made him necessitous."—"If that
were the case, (said Johnson,) and that he only wanted to
alarm Steele, he would afterwards have *returned* the money
to his friend, which it is not pretended he did."—"This,
too, (he added,) might be retorted by an advocate for
Steele, who might allege, that he did not repay the loan
intentionally, merely to see whether Addison would be
mean and ungenerous enough to make use of legal process
to recover it. But of such speculations there is no end: we
cannot dive into the hearts of men; but their actions are
open to observation."[a]

'I then mentioned to him that some people thought that
Mr. Addison's character was so pure, that the fact, *though
true*, ought to have been suppressed. He saw no reason for
this. "If nothing but the bright side of characters should be
shewn, we should sit down in despondency, and think it
utterly impossible to imitate them in *any thing*. The sacred
writers (he observed) related the vicious as well as the
virtuous actions of men; which had this moral effect, that
it kept mankind from *despair*, into which otherwise they
would naturally fall, were they not supported by the
recollection that others had offended like themselves, and
by penitence and amendment of life had been restored to
the favour of Heaven." '[2]

'March 15, 1781.'   'E. M.'

The last paragraph of this note is of great importance;
and I request that my readers may consider it with

[a] *For what Men say I
daily hear, & what
Men do I see;
But that which in
their Hearts they
hould—Oh that is
hid frae me.*
Scots Proverb. [H]
*For what Men say I
hear full plain, &
what Men do, I
see:
But what 'tis in their
hearts they hold,—
Oh that is hid
from me*
Says some old Verse [1]

[1] [The late Mr. Burke informed me, in 1792, that Lady Dorothea Prim-
rose, who died at a great age, I think in 1768, and had been well acquainted
with Steele, told him the same story. MALONE.]

[2] [I have since observed, that Johnson has further enforced the propriety
of exhibiting the faults of virtuous and eminent men in their true colours, in
the last paragraph of the 164th Number of his RAMBLER.

'It is particularly the duty of those who consign illustrious names to
posterity, to take care lest their readers be misled by ambiguous examples.

particular attention. It will be afterwards referred to in this work.

Various Readings in the Life of ADDISON

'[But he was our first example] *He was, however, one of our earliest examples* of correctness.

'And [overlook] *despise* their masters.

'His instructions were such as the [state] *character* of his [own time] *readers* made [necessary] *proper*.

'His purpose was to [diffuse] *infuse* literary curiosity by gentle and unsuspected conveyance [among] *into* the gay, the idle, and the wealthy.

'Framed rather for those that [wish] *are learning* to write.

'Domestick [manners] *scenes*.'

In his Life of PARNELL, I wonder that Johnson omitted to insert an Epitaph which he had long before composed for that amiable man, without ever writing it down, but which he was so good as, at my request, to dictate to me, by which means it has been preserved.

'*Hic requiescit* THOMAS PARNELL, *S. T. P.*

> *Qui sacerdos pariter et poeta,*
> *Utrasque partes ita implevit,*
> *Ut neque sacerdoti suavitas poetæ,*
> *Nec poetæ sacerdotis sanctitas, deesset.*'

Various Readings in the Life of PARNELL

'About three years [after] *afterwards*.

'[Did not much want] *was in no great need of* improvement.

'But his prosperity *did not last long* [was clouded with that which took away all his powers of enjoying either profit or pleasure, the death of his wife, whom he is said

That writer may be justly condemned as an enemy to goodness, who suffers fondness or interest to confound right with wrong, or to shelter the faults which even the wisest and the best have committed, from that ignominy which guilt ought always to suffer, and with which it should be more deeply stigmatized, when dignified by its neighbourhood to uncommon worth; since we shall be in danger of beholding it without abhorrence, unless its turpitude be laid open, and the eye secured from the deception of surrounding splendour.' MALONE.]

to have lamented with such sorrow, as hastened his end.[1]]
His end, whatever was the cause, was now approaching.

'In the Hermit, the [composition] *narrative*, as it is less
airy, is less pleasing.'

In the Life of BLACKMORE, we find that writer's reputation generously cleared by Johnson from the cloud of
prejudice which the malignity of contemporary wits had
raised around it. In the spirited exertion of justice, he has
been imitated by Sir Joshua Reynolds, in his praise of the
architecture of Vanburgh.

We trace Johnson's own character in his observations on
Blackmore's 'magnanimity as an authour.'—'The incessant attacks of his enemies, whether serious or merry,
are never discovered to have disturbed his quiet, or to
have lessened his confidence in himself.' Johnson, I recollect, once told me, laughing heartily, that he understood
it had been said of him, 'He *appears* not to feel; but when
he is *alone*, depend upon it, he *suffers sadly*.' I am as certain
as I can be of any man's real sentiments, that he *enjoyed*
the perpetual shower of little hostile arrows, as evidences
of his fame.

Various Readings in the Life of BLACKMORE

'To [set] *engage* poetry [on the side] *in the cause* of virtue.
'He likewise [established] *enforced* the truth of Revelation.
'[Kindness] *benevolence* was ashamed to favour.
'His practice, which was once [very extensive] *invidiously
great*.
'There is scarcely any distemper of dreadful name [of]
which he has not [shewn] *taught his reader* how [it is to be
opposed] *to oppose*.
'Of this [contemptuous] *indecent* arrogance.
'[He wrote] *but produced* likewise a work of a different
kind.
'At least [written] *compiled* with integrity.

[1] I should have thought that Johnson, who had felt the severe affliction
from which Parnell never recovered, would have preserved this passage.

[He omitted it, doubtless, because he afterwards learned that however he
[a] *by Dramdrinking*[1] might have lamented his wife, his end was hastened by other means.[a]
MALONE.]

'Faults which many tongues [were desirous] *would have made haste* to publish.

'But though he [had not] *could not boast of* much critical knowledge.

'He [used] *waited for* no felicities of fancy.

'Or had ever elated his [mind] *views* to that ideal perfection which every [mind] *genius* born to excel is condemned always to pursue and never to overtake.

'The [first great] *fundamental* principle of wisdom and of virtue.'

Various Readings in the Life of PHILIPS

'His dreadful [rival] *antagonist* Pope.

'They [have not often much] *are not loaded with* thought.

'In his translation from Pindar, he [will not be denied to have reached] *found the art of reaching* all the obscurity of the Theban bard.'

Various Readings in the Life of CONGREVE

'Congreve's conversation must surely have been *at least* equally pleasing with his writings.

'It apparently [requires] *pre-supposes* a familiar knowledge of many characters.

'Reciprocation of [similes] *conceits*.

'The dialogue is quick and [various] *sparkling*.

'Love for Love; a comedy [more drawn from life] *of nearer alliance to life*.

'The general character of his miscellanies is, that they shew little wit and [no] *little* virtue.

'[Perhaps] *certainly* he had not the fire requisite for the higher species of lyrick poetry.'

Various Readings in the Life of TICKELL

'[Longed] *long wished* to peruse it.

'At the [accession] *arrival* of King George.

'Fiction [unnaturally] *unskilfully* compounded of Grecian deities and Gothick fairies.'

Various Readings in the Life of AKENSIDE

'For [another] *a different* purpose.

'[A furious] *an unnecessary* and outrageous zeal.

'[Something which] *what* he called and thought liberty.
'A [favourer of innovation] *lover of contradiction.*
'Warburton's [censure] *objections.*
'His rage [for liberty] *of patriotism.*
'Mr. Dyson with [a zeal] *an ardour* of friendship.'

In the Life of LYTTELTON, Johnson seems to have been not favourably disposed towards that nobleman. Mrs. Thrale suggests that he was offended by *Molly Aston's* preference of his Lordship to him.[1a] I can by no means join in the censure bestowed by Johnson on his Lordship, whom he calls 'poor Lyttelton,' for returning thanks to the Critical Reviewers, for having 'kindly commended' his '*Dialogues of the Dead.*' Such 'acknowledgements (says my friend) never can be proper, since, they must be paid either for flattery or for justice.' In my opinion, the most upright man, who has been tried on a false accusation, may, when he is acquitted, make a bow to his jury. And when those, who are so much the arbiters of literary merit,

a *I never said so. I believe Ld Lyttelton & Molly Aston were not acquainted. It was Miss Boothby whose Preference he profess'd to have been jealous of:—and so I said in the Anecdotes   H. L. P.* [H]

[1] Let not my readers smile to think of Johnson's being a candidate for female favour; Mr. Peter Garrick assured me that he was told by a lady, that in her opinion Johnson was 'a very *seducing man.*'[b] Disadvantages of person and manner may be forgotten, where intellectual pleasure is communicated to a susceptible mind; and that Johnson was capable of feeling the most delicate and disinterested attachment, appears from the following letter, which is published by Mrs. Thrale, with some others to the same person, of which the excellence is not so apparent:

b *no no:* [H]

'TO MISS BOOTHBY

'DEAREST MADAM,   'January, 1755

'THOUGH I am afraid your illness leaves you little leisure for the reception of airy civilities, yet I cannot forbear to pay you my congratulations on the new year; and to declare my wishes that your years to come may be many and happy. In this wish, indeed, I include myself, who have none but you on whom my heart reposes; yet surely I wish your good, even though your situation were such as should permit you to communicate no gratifications to, dearest, dearest Madam,

'Your, &c.

'SAM. JOHNSON'

c *very True* [I]

[There is here a slight mistake in the text. It was not Molly Aston, but Hill Boothby, for whose affections Johnson and Lord Lyttelton were rival candidates.[c] See Mrs. Piozzi's 'Anecdotes,' p. 160. After mentioning the death of Mrs. Fitzherbert, (who was a daughter of Mr. Meynell of Bradley in Derbyshire,) and Johnson's high admiration of her, she adds, 'The friend of this lady, Miss Boothby, succeeded her in the management of Mr. Fitzherbert's family, and in the esteem of Dr. Johnson; though he told me, she pushed her piety to bigotry, her devotion to enthusiasm; that she somewhat disqualified herself for the duties of *this* life, by her perpetual aspirations after

as in a considerable degree to influence the publick opinion, review an authour's work, *placido lumine,* when I am afraid mankind in general are better pleased with severity, he may surely express a grateful sense of their civility.

Various Readings in the Life of LYTTELTON

'He solaced [himself] *his grief* by writing a long poem to her memory.

'The production rather [of a mind that means well than thinks vigorously] *as it seems of leisure than of study, rather effusions than compositions.*

'His last literary [work] *production.*

'[Found the way] *undertook* to persuade.'

As the introduction to his critical examination of the genius and writings of YOUNG, he did Mr. Herbert Croft, then a Barrister of Lincoln's Inn, now a clergyman, the

the *next:* such was, however, the purity of her mind, he said, and such the graces of her manner, that Lord Lyttelton and he used to strive for her preference with an emulation that occasioned hourly disgust, and ended in lasting animosity. You may see (said he to me, when the Poets' Lives were printed,) that dear Boothby is at my heart still.'

index sign: *used to strive* etc. [H]

Miss Hill Boothby, who was the only daughter of Brook Boothby, Esq. and his wife, Elizabeth Fitzherbert, was somewhat older than Johnson. She was born October 27, 1708, and died January 16, 1756. Six Letters addressed to her by Johnson in the year 1755, are printed in Mrs. Piozzi's Collection; and a Prayer composed by him on her death may be found in his 'Prayers and Meditations.' His affection for her induced him to preserve and bind up in a volume thirty-three of her Letters, which were purchased from the widow of his servant, Francis Barber, and published by R. Phillips, in 1805.[a]

[a] *I wish I had seen them.* [H]

But highly as he valued this lady, his attachment to Miss *Molly* Aston, (afterwards Mrs. Brodie,) appears to have been still more ardent. He burned (says Mrs. Piozzi,) many letters in the last week, [of his life,] I am told, and those written by his mother drew from him a flood of tears, when the paper they were written on was all consumed. Mr. Sastres saw him cast a melancholy look upon their ashes, which he took up and examined, to see if a word was still legible.—Nobody has ever mentioned what became of Miss Aston's letters, though he once told me himself, they should be the last papers he would destroy, and added these lines with a very faultering voice:

'Then from his closing eyes thy form shall part,
And the last pang shall tear thee from his heart;[b]
Life's idle business at one gasp be o'er,
The muse forgot, and thou beloved no more.'

underlined:
last, pang, tear;
[b] *with Emphasis.* [H]

Additions to Mrs. Piozzi's Collection of
Dr. Johnson's Letters. MALONE.]

honour to adopt a Life of Young written by that gentleman, who was the friend of Dr. Young's son, and wished
to vindicate him from some very erroneous remarks to his
prejudice. Mr. Croft's performance was subjected to the
revision of Dr. Johnson, as appears from the following note
to Mr. John Nichols:[1]

'This Life of Dr. Young was written by a friend of his
son. What is crossed with black is expunged by the authour,
what is crossed with red is expunged by me. If you find
any thing more that can be well omitted, I shall not be
sorry to see it yet shorter.'

It has always appeared to me to have a considerable
share of merit, and to display a pretty successful imitation
of Johnson's style. When I mentioned this to a very
eminent literary character,[2] he opposed me vehemently,
exclaiming, 'No, no, it is *not* a good imitation of Johnson;
it has all his pomp without his force; it has all the nodosi-
ties of the oak without its strength.' This was an image so
happy, that one might have thought he would have been
satisfied with it; but he was not. And setting his mind
again to work, he added, with exquisite felicity, 'It has
all the contortions of the Sybil, without the inspiration.'

Mr. Croft very properly guards us against supposing
that Young was a gloomy man; and mentions, that 'his
parish was indebted to the good-humour of the authour
of the "*Night Thoughts*" for an Assembly and a Bowling
Green.' A letter from a noble foreigner is quoted, in which
he is said to have been 'very pleasant in conversation.'

Mr. Langton, who frequently visited him, informs me,
that there was an air of benevolence in his manner, but
that he could obtain from him less information than he
had hoped to receive from one who had lived so much in
intercourse with the brightest men of what has been called
the Augustan age of England; and that he shewed a
degree of eager curiosity concerning the common occurrences that were then passing, which appeared somewhat
remarkable in a man of such intellectual stores, of such an
advanced age, and who had retired from life with declared
disappointment in his expectations.

marginal line:
*without his . . . oak
without* [H]

marginal line:
*again to . . . the in-
spiration* [H]
marginal line:
*Mr. Croft . . . and
mentions* [H]

[1] Gentleman's Magazine, vol. iv. p. 10.
[2] [The late Mr. Burke. MALONE.]

An instance at once of his pensive turn of mind, and his cheerfulness of temper, appeared in a little story, which he himself told to Mr. Langton, when they were walking in his garden: 'Here (said he) I had put a handsome sun-dial, with this inscription, *Eheu fugaces!* which (speaking with a smile) was sadly verified, for by the next morning my dial had been carried off.'[1]

It gives me much pleasure to observe, that however Johnson may have casually talked, yet when he sits, as 'an ardent judge zealous to his trust, giving sentence' upon the excellent works of Young, he allows them the high praise to which they are justly entitled. 'The *Universal Passion* (says he) is indeed a very great performance,—his distichs have the weight of solid sentiment, and his points the sharpness of resistless truth.'

marginal line: weight of ... resistless truth [H]

But I was most anxious concerning Johnson's decision upon 'NIGHT THOUGHTS,' which I esteem as a mass of the grandest and richest poetry that human genius has ever produced: and was delighted to find this character of that work: 'In his "NIGHT THOUGHTS," he has exhibited a very wide display of original poetry, variegated with deep reflection and striking allusions: a wilderness of thought, in which the fertility of fancy scatters flowers of every hue and of every odour. This is one of the few poems in which blank verse could not be changed for rhime, but with disadvantage.' And afterwards, 'Particular lines are not to be regarded; the power is in the whole; and in the whole there is a magnificence like that ascribed to Chinese plantation, the magnificence of vast extent and endless diversity.'

marginal line: as a ... delighted to [H]

But there is in this Poem not only all that Johnson so well brings in view, but a power of the *Pathetick* beyond almost any example that I have seen. He who does not feel his nerves shaken, and his heart pierced by many passages in this extraordinary work, particularly by that most affecting one, which describes the gradual torment

---

[1] The late Mr. James Ralph told Lord Macartney, that he passed an evening with Dr. Young at Lord Melcombe's (then Mr. Doddington) at Hammersmith. The Doctor happening to go out into the garden, Mr. Doddington observed to him, on his return, that it was a dreadful night, as in truth it was, there being a violent storm of rain and wind. 'No, Sir, (replied the Doctor) it is a very fine night. THE LORD is abroad.'[a]

[a] *I like this rocking of the Battlements* [I]

suffered by the contemplation of an object of affectionate attachment visibly and certainly decaying into dissolution, must be of a hard and obstinate frame.

To all the other excellencies of 'NIGHT THOUGHTS' let me add the great and peculiar one, that they contain not only the noblest sentiments of virtue, and contemplations on immortality, but the *Christian Sacrifice*, the *Divine Propitiation*, with all its interesting circumstances, and consolations to 'a wounded spirit,' solemnly and poetically displayed in such imagery and language, as cannot fail to exalt, animate, and soothe the truly pious. No book whatever can be recommended to young persons, with better hopes of seasoning their minds with *vital religion*, than 'YOUNG'S NIGHT THOUGHTS.'

In the Life of SWIFT, it appears to me that Johnson had a certain degree of prejudice against that extraordinary man, of which I have elsewhere had occasion to speak. Mr. Thomas Sheridan imputed it to a supposed apprehension in Johnson, that Swift had not been sufficiently active in obtaining for him an Irish degree when it was solicited,[1] but of this there was not sufficient evidence; and let me not presume to charge Johnson with injustice, because he did not think so highly of the writings of this authour, as I have done from my youth upwards. Yet that he had an unfavourable bias is evident, were it only from that passage in which he speaks of Swift's practice of saving, as, 'first ridiculous and at last detestable;' and yet after some examination of circumstances, finds himself obliged to own, that 'it will perhaps appear that he only liked one mode of expence better than another, and saved merely that he might have something to give.'

One observation which Johnson makes in Swift's Life, should be often inculcated: 'It may be justly supposed, that there was in his conversation what appears so frequently in his letters, an affectation of familiarity with the great, an ambition of momentary equality, sought and enjoyed by the neglect of those ceremonies which custom has established as the barriers between one order of society and another. This transgression of regularity was by himself and his admirers termed greatness of soul; but a great

exclamation point: *an Irish degree* etc. [H]

[1] See vol. i. page 81.

mind disdains to hold any thing by courtesy, and therefore never usurps what a lawful claimant may take away. He that encroaches on another's dignity, puts himself in his power; he is either repelled with helpless indignity, or endured by clemency and condescension.'

Various Readings in the Life of SWIFT

'Charity may be persuaded to think that it might be written by a man of *a* peculiar [opinions] *character*, without ill intention.

'He did not [disown] *deny* it.

'[To] *by* whose kindness it is not unlikely that he was [indebted for] *advanced to* his benefices.

'[With] *for* this purpose he had recourse to Mr. Harley.

'Sharpe, whom he [represents] *describes* as "the harmless tool of others' hate."

'Harley was slow because he was [irresolute] *doubtful*.

'When [readers were not many] *we were not yet a nation of readers*.

'[Every man who] *he that could say he* knew him.

'Every man of known influence has so many [more] petitions [than] *which* [he can] *cannot* grant, that he must necessarily offend more than he [can gratify] *gratifies*.

'Ecclesiastical [preferments] *benefices*.

'Swift [procured] *contrived* an interview.

'[As a writer] *In his works* he has given very different specimens.

'On all common occasions he habitually [assumes] *affects* a style of [superiority] *arrogance*.

'By the [omission] *neglect* of those ceremonies.

'That their merits filled the world [and] *or that* there was no [room for] *hope of* more.'

I have not confined myself to the order of the 'Lives,' in making my few remarks. Indeed a different order is observed in the original publication, and in the collection of Johnson's Works. And should it be objected, that many of my various readings are inconsiderable, those who make an objection will be pleased to consider, that such small particulars are intended for those who are nicely critical in composition, to whom they will be an acceptable selection.

'Spence's Anecdotes,' which are frequently quoted and referred to in Johnson's 'Lives of the Poets,' are in a manuscript collection, made by the Reverend Mr. Joseph Spence,[1] containing a number of particulars concerning eminent men. To each anecdote is marked the name of the person on whose authority it is mentioned. This valuable collection is the property of the Duke of Newcastle, who upon the application of Sir Lucas Pepys, was pleased to permit it to be put into the hands of Dr. Johnson, who I am sorry to think made but an awkward return. 'Great assistance (says he) has been given me by Mr. Spence's Collection, of which I consider the communication as a favour worthy of publick acknowledgement;' but he has not owned to whom he was obliged; so that the acknowledgement is unappropriated to his Grace.

While the world in general was filled with admiration of Johnson's 'Lives of the Poets,' there were narrow circles in which prejudice and resentment were fostered, and from which attacks of different sorts issued against him.[2] By some violent Whigs he was arraigned of injustice to Milton; by some Cambridge men of depreciating Gray; and his expressing with a dignified freedom what he really thought of George, Lord Lyttelton, gave offence to some of the friends of that nobleman, and particularly produced a declaration of war against him from Mrs. Montagu, the ingenious Essayist on Shakspeare, between whom and his Lordship a commerce of reciprocal compliments had long been carried on. In this war the smallest powers in alliance with him were of course led to engage, at least on the defensive, and thus I for one, was excluded from the enjoyment of 'A Feast of Reason,' such as Mr. Cumberland

[1] [The Rev. Joseph Spence, A. M. Rector of Great Harwood in Buckinghamshire, and Prebendary of Durham, died at Byfleet in Surrey, August 20, 1768. He was a fellow of New College in Oxford, and held the office of Professor of Poetry in that University from 1728 to 1738. MALONE.]

[2] From this disreputable class, I except an ingenious, though not satisfactory defence of HAMMOND, which I did not see till lately, by the favour of its authour, my amiable friend, the Reverend Mr. Bevil, who published it without his name. It is a juvenile performance, but elegantly written, with classical enthusiasm of sentiment, and yet with a becoming modesty, and great respect for Dr. Johnson.

has described, with a keen, yet just and delicate pen, in his 'OBSERVER.' These minute inconveniencies gave not the least disturbance to Johnson. He nobly said, when I talked to him of the feeble, though shrill outcry which had been raised, 'Sir, I considered myself as entrusted with a certain portion of truth. I have given my opinion sincerely; let them shew where they think me wrong.'

While my friend is thus contemplated in the splendour derived from his last and perhaps most admirable work, I introduce him with peculiar propriety as the correspondent of WARREN HASTINGS! a man whose regard reflects dignity even upon JOHNSON; a man, the extent of whose abilities was equal to that of his power; and who, by those who are fortunate enough to know him in private life, is admired for his literature and taste, and beloved for the candour, moderation, and mildness of his character. Were I capable of paying a suitable tribute of admiration to him, I should certainly not withhold it at a moment[1] when it is not possible that I should be suspected of being an interested flatterer. But how weak would be my voice after that of the millions whom he governed. His condescending and obliging compliance with my solicitation, I with humble gratitude acknowledge; and while by publishing his letter to me, accompanying the valuable communication, I do eminent honour to my great friend, I shall entirely disregard any invidious suggestions, that as I in some degree participate in the honour, I have, at the same time, the gratification of my own vanity in view.

'TO JAMES BOSWELL, ESQ.

'SIR,   'Park-lane, Dec. 2, 1790

'I HAVE been fortunately spared the troublesome suspense of a long search, to which, in performance of my promise, I had devoted this morning, by lighting upon the objects of it among the first papers that I laid my hands on: my veneration for your great and good friend, Dr. Johnson, and the pride, or I hope something of a better sentiment, which I indulge in possessing such memorials

[1] January, 1791.

of his good will towards me, having induced me to bind
them in a parcel containing other select papers, and labelled
with the titles appertaining to them. They consist but of
three letters, which I believe were all that I ever received
from Dr. Johnson. Of these, one, which was written in
quadruplicate, under the different dates of its respective
dispatches, has already been made publick, but not from
any communication of mine. This, however, I have joined
to the rest; and have now the pleasure of sending them to
you, for the use to which you informed me it was your
desire to destine them.

'My promise was pledged with the condition, that if the
letters were found to contain any thing which should
render them improper for the publick eye, you would
dispense with the performance of it. You will have the
goodness, I am sure, to pardon my recalling this stipu-
lation to your recollection, as I shall be loth to appear
negligent of that obligation which is always implied in an
epistolary confidence. In the reservation of that right I
have read them over with the most scrupulous attention,
but have not seen in them the slightest cause on that
ground to withhold them from you. But, though not on
that, yet on another ground I own I feel a little, yet but a
little, reluctance to part with them: I mean on that of my
own credit, which I fear will suffer by the information
conveyed by them, that I was early in the possession of
such valuable instructions for the beneficial employment
of the influence of my late station, and (as it may seem)
have so little availed myself of them. Whether I could, if it
were necessary, defend myself against such an imputation,
it little concerns the world to know. I look only to the
effect which these relicks may produce, considered as
evidences of the virtues of their authour: and believing
that they will be found to display an uncommon warmth
of private friendship, and a mind ever attentive to the
improvement and extension of useful knowledge, and
solicitous for the interests of mankind, I can cheerfully
submit to the little sacrifice of my own fame, to contribute
to the illustration of so great and venerable a character.
They cannot be better applied, for that end, than by being
entrusted to your hands. Allow me, with this offering, to

infer from it a proof of the very great esteem with which I have the honour to profess myself, Sir,

'Your most obedient
'And most humble servant,

'WARREN HASTINGS'

'*P.S.* At some future time, and when you have no further occasion for these papers, I shall be obliged to you if you will return them.'

The last of the three letters thus graciously put into my hands, and which has already appeared in publick, belongs to this year; but I shall previously insert the first two in the order of their dates. They altogether form a grand group in my biographical picture.

'TO THE HONOURABLE WARREN HASTINGS, ESQ.

'SIR,

'THOUGH I have had but little personal knowledge of you, I have had enough to make me wish for more; and though it be now a long time since I was honoured by your visit, I had too much pleasure from it to forget it. By those whom we delight to remember, we are unwilling to be forgotten; and therefore I cannot omit this opportunity of reviving myself in your memory by a letter which you will receive from the hands of my friend Mr. Chambers;[1] a man, whose purity of manners and vigour of mind are sufficient to make every thing welcome that he brings.

'That this is my only reason for writing, will be too apparent by the uselessness of my letter to any other purpose. I have no questions to ask; not that I want curiosity after either the ancient or present state of regions, in which have been seen all the power and splendour of wide-extended empire; and which, as by some grant of natural superiority, supply the rest of the world with almost all that pride desires, and luxury enjoys. But my knowledge of them is too scanty to furnish me with proper topicks of enquiry; I can only wish for information; and

[1] Afterwards Sir Robert Chambers, one of his Majesty's Judges in India.

hope, that a mind comprehensive like yours will find leisure, amidst the cares of your important station, to enquire into many subjects of which the European world either thinks not at all, or thinks with deficient intelligence and uncertain conjecture. I shall hope, that he who once intended to increase the learning of his country by the introduction of the Persian language, will examine nicely the traditions and histories of the East; that he will survey the wonders of its ancient edifices, and trace the vestiges of its ruined cities; and that, at his return, we shall know the arts and opinions of a race of men, from whom very little has been hitherto derived.

'You, Sir, have no need of being told by me, how much may be added by your attention and patronage to experimental knowledge and natural history. There are arts of manufacture practised in the countries in which you preside, which are yet very imperfectly known here, either to artificers or philosophers. Of the natural productions, animate and inanimate, we yet have so little intelligence, that our books are filled, I fear, with conjectures about things which an Indian peasant knows by his senses.

'Many of those things my first wish is to see; my second to know, by such accounts as a man like you will be able to give.

'As I have not skill to ask proper questions, I have likewise no such access to great men as can enable me to send you any political information. Of the agitations of an unsettled government, and the struggles of a feeble ministry, care is doubtless taken to give you more exact accounts than I can obtain. If you are inclined to interest yourself much in publick transactions, it is no misfortune to you to be so distant from them.

'That literature is not totally forsaking us, and that your favourite language is not neglected, will appear from the book,[1] which I should have pleased myself more with sending, if I could have presented it bound: but time was wanting. I beg, however, Sir, that you will accept it from a man very desirous of your regard; and that if you think me able to gratify you by any thing more important, you will employ me.

[1] Jones's 'Persian Grammar.'

'I am now going to take leave, perhaps a very long leave, of my dear Mr. Chambers. That he is going to live where you govern, may justly alleviate the regard of parting:^a and the hope of seeing both him and you again, which I am not willing to mingle with doubt, must at present, comfort as it can, Sir,

underlined:
alleviate, regard [H]

^a *alleviate the Regard an odd Expression Regard cannot be alle-viated* [H]

'Your most humble servant,

'March 30, 1774.'   'SAM. JOHNSON'

TO THE SAME

'SIR,

'BEING informed that by the departure of a ship, there is now an opportunity of writing to Bengal, I am unwilling to slip out of your memory by my own negligence, and therefore take the liberty of reminding you of my existence, by sending you a book which is not yet made publick.

'I have lately visited a region less remote, and less illustrious than India, which afforded some occasions for speculation. What has occurred to me, I have put into the volume,¹ of which I beg your acceptance.

'Men in your station seldom have presents totally disinterested; my book is received, let me now make my request.

'There is, Sir, somewhere within your government, a young adventurer, one Chauncey Lawrence, whose father is one of my oldest friends. Be pleased to shew the young man what countenance is fit, whether he wants to be restrained by your authority, or encouraged by your favour. His father is now President of the College of Physicians, a man venerable for his knowledge, and more venerable for his virtue.

underlined:
one [H]

'I wish you a prosperous government, a safe return, and a long enjoyment of plenty and tranquillity.

'I am, Sir,
'Your most obedient,
'And most humble servant,

'London, Dec. 20, 1774.'   'SAM. JOHNSON'

¹ 'Journey to the Western Islands of Scotland.'

'SIR,   'Jan. 9, 1781

'AMIDST the importance and multiplicity of affairs
in which your great office engages you, I take the liberty
of recalling your attention for a moment to literature, and
will not prolong the interruption by an apology which
your character makes needless.

'Mr. Hoole, a gentleman long known, and long esteemed
in the India-House, after having translated Tasso, has
undertaken Ariosto. How well he is qualified for his
undertaking he has already shewn. He is desirous, Sir, of
your favour in promoting his proposals, and flatters me
by supposing that my testimony may advance his interest.

'It is a new thing for a clerk of the India-House to
translate poets;—it is new for a Governor of Bengal to
patronize learning. That he may find his ingenuity rewarded, and that learning may flourish under your
protection, is the wish of, Sir,

'Your most humble servant,

'SAM. JOHNSON'

I wrote to him in February, complaining of having been
troubled by a recurrence of the perplexing question of
Liberty and Necessity; and mentioning that I hoped soon
to meet him again in London.

'TO JAMES BOSWELL, ESQ.

'DEAR SIR,

'I HOPED you had got rid of all this hypocrisy of misery.
What have you to do with Liberty and Necessity? Or what
more than to hold your tongue about it? Do not doubt but
I shall be most heartily glad to see you here again, for I
love every part about you but your affectation of distress.

'I have at last finished my Lives, and have laid up for
you a load of copy, all out of order, so that it will amuse
you a long time to set it right. Come to me, my dear Bozzy,
and let us be as happy as we can. We will go again to the
Mitre, and talk old times over.

'I am, dear Sir,

'Your's affectionately,

'March 14, 1781.'   'SAM. JOHNSON'

On Monday, March 19, I arrived in London, and on Tuesday, the 20th, met him in Fleet-street, walking, or rather indeed moving along; for his peculiar march is thus described in a very just and picturesque manner, in a short Life[1] of him published very soon after his death:—'When he walked the streets, what with the constant roll of his head, and the concomitant motion of his body, he appeared to make his way by that motion, independent of his feet.' That he was often much stared at while he advanced in this manner, may easily be believed; but it was not safe to make sport of one so robust as he was. Mr. Langton saw him one day, in a fit of absence, by a sudden start, drive the load off a porter's back, and walk forward briskly, without being conscious of what he had done. The porter was very angry, but stood still, and eyed the huge figure with much earnestness, till he was satisfied that his wisest course was to be quiet, and take up his burthen again.

Our accidental meeting in the street after a long separation, was a pleasing surprize to us both. He stepped aside with me into Falcon-court, and made kind enquiries about my family, and as we were in a hurry going different ways, I promised to call on him next day; he said he was engaged to go out in the morning. 'Early, Sir?' said I. JOHNSON. 'Why, Sir, a London morning does not go with the sun.'

I waited on him next evening, and he gave me a great portion of his original manuscript of his 'Lives of the Poets,' which he had preserved for me.

I found on visiting his friend, Mr. Thrale, that he was now very ill, and had removed, I suppose by the solicitation of Mrs. Thrale, to a house in Grosvenor-square.[a] I was sorry to see him sadly changed in his appearance.

He told me I might now have the pleasure to see Dr. Johnson drink wine again, for he had lately returned to it. When I mentioned this to Johnson, he said, 'I drink it now sometimes, but not socially.' The first evening that I was

underlined:
Mrs. Thrale [H]

[a] *spiteful again; he went by Direction of his Physicians where they could easiest attend to him.* [H]

No truly. [I]

---

[1] Published by Kearsley, with this well-chosen motto:

'———— ———— From his cradle
He was a SCHOLAR, and a ripe and good one:
And to add greater honours to his age
Than man could give him; he died fearing Heaven.'[b]
SHAKSPEARE

[b] *Heaven* crossed out; *God* written in [I]

with him at Thrale's, I observed he poured a large quantity of it into a glass, and swallowed it greedily. Every thing about his character and manners was forcible and violent; there never was any moderation; many a day did he fast, many a year did he refrain from wine; but when he did eat, it was voraciously; when he did drink wine, it was copiously.[a] He could practise abstinence, but not temperance.

Mrs. Thrale and I had a dispute, whether Shakspeare or Milton had drawn the most admirable picture of a man.[1] I was for Shakspeare; Mrs. Thrale for Milton; and after a fair hearing, Johnson decided for my opinion.[2]

I told him of one of Mr. Burke's playful sallies upon Dean Marlay:[3] 'I don't like the Deanery of *Ferns*, it sounds so like a *barren* title.'—'Dr. *Heath* should have it;' said I. Johnson laughed, and condescending to trifle in the same mode of conceit, suggested Dr. *Moss*.

He said, 'Mrs. Montagu has dropt me. Now, Sir, there are people whom one should like very well to drop, but would not wish to be dropped by.' He certainly was vain of the society of ladies, and could make himself very

underlined:
copiously [H]
[a] *and pour'd Capillaire into it.* [H]

[1] Shakspeare makes Hamlet thus describe his father:

> 'See what a grace was seated on this brow:
> Hyperion's curls, the front of Jove himself,
> An eye like Mars, to threaten and command;
> A station like the herald, Mercury,
> New-lighted on a heaven-kissing hill;
> A combination, and a form, indeed,
> Where every God did seem to set his seal,
> To give the world assurance of a man.'

Milton thus pourtrays our first parent, Adam:

> 'His fair large front and eye sublime declar'd
> Absolute rule; and hyacinthin locks
> Round from his parted forelock manly hung
> Clust'ring, but not beneath his shoulders broad.'[b]

[b] *Milton kept his Head closer to the* Man; *Shakespeare was more excursive; he heaped on Ornaments.—after all, his is a more Dramatic,* — Milton's *a more Epic Description. Both were best as the Children say.* [H]

[The latter part of this description, 'but not beneath,' &c. may very probably be ascribed to Milton's prejudices in favour of the Puritans, who had a great aversion to *long* hair. MALONE.]

[2] [It is strange, that the picture drawn by the unlearned Shakspeare, should be full of classical images, and that by the learned Milton, void of them—Milton's description appears to be more picturesque. KEARNEY.]

[3] [Dr. Richard Marlay, afterwards Lord Bishop of Waterford; a very amiable, benevolent, and ingenious man. He was chosen a member of the LITERARY CLUB in 1777, and died in Dublin, July 2, 1802, in his 75th year. MALONE.]

agreeable to them, when he chose it; Sir Joshua Reynolds
agreed with me that he could. Mr. Gibbon, with his usual
sneer, controverted it, perhaps in resentment of Johnson's
having talked with some disgust of his ugliness, which one
would think a *philosopher* would not mind. Dean Marlay
wittily observed, 'A lady may be vain, when she can turn
a wolf-dog into a lap-dog.'

The election for Ayrshire, my own county, was this
spring tried upon a petition, before a Committee of the
House of Commons. I was one of the Counsel for the sitting
member, and took the liberty of previously stating different
points to Johnson, who never failed to see them clearly,
and to supply me with some good hints. He dictated to me
the following note upon the registration of deeds:

'ALL laws are made for the convenience of the community; what is legally done, should be legally recorded,
that the state of things may be known, and that wherever
evidence is requisite, evidence may be had. For this
reason, the obligation to frame and establish a legal register
is enforced by a legal penalty, which penalty is the want
of that perfection and plenitude of right which a register
would give. Thence it follows, that this is not an objection merely legal; for the reason on which the law stands
being equitable, makes it an equitable objection.'

'This (said he) you must enlarge on, when speaking to
the Committee. You must not argue there, as if you were
arguing in the schools; close reasoning will not fix their
attention; you must say the same thing over and over
again, in different words. If you say it but once, they miss
it in a moment of inattention. It is unjust, Sir, to censure
lawyers for multiplying words, when they argue; it is
often *necessary* for them to multiply words.'

His notion of the duty of a member of Parliament, sitting
upon an election-committee, was very high; and when he
was told of a gentleman upon one of those committees,
who read the news-papers part of the time, and slept the
rest, while the merits of a vote were examined by the
counsel; and as an excuse, when challenged by the chairman for such behaviour, bluntly answered, 'I had made

up my mind upon that case;'—Johnson, with an indignant contempt, said, 'If he was such a rogue as to make up his mind upon a case without hearing it, he should not have been such a fool as to tell it.'—'I think (said Mr. Dudley Long, now North) the Doctor has pretty plainly made him out to be both rogue and fool.'

Johnson's profound reverence for the Hierarchy made him expect from Bishops the highest degree of decorum; he was offended even at their going to taverns: 'A bishop (said he) has nothing to do at a tippling-house. It is not indeed immoral in him to go to a tavern; neither would it be immoral in him to whip a top in Grosvenor-square: but, if he did, I hope the boys would fall upon him, and apply the whip to *him*. There are gradations in conduct; there is morality,—decency,—propriety. None of these should be violated by a bishop. A bishop should not go to a house where he may meet a young fellow leading out a wench.' BOSWELL. 'But, Sir, every tavern does not admit women.' JOHNSON. 'Depend upon it, Sir, any tavern will admit a well-drest man and a well-drest woman; they will not perhaps admit a woman whom they see every night walking by their door, in the street. But a well-drest man may lead in a well-drest woman to any tavern in London. Taverns sell meat and drink, and will sell them to any body who can eat and can drink. You may as well say, that a mercer will not sell silks to a woman of the town.'

He also disapproved of bishops going to routs, at least of their staying at them longer than their presence commanded respect. He mentioned a particular bishop. 'Poh! (said Mrs. Thrale,) the Bishop of ——a is never minded at a rout.' BOSWELL. 'When a bishop places himself in a situation where he has no distinct character, and is of no consequence, he degrades the dignity of his order.' JOHNSON. 'Mr. Boswell, Madam, has said it as correctly as it could be.'

Nor was it only in the dignitaries of the Church that Johnson required a particular decorum and delicacy of behaviour; he justly considered that the clergy, as persons set apart for the sacred office of serving at the altar, and impressing the minds of men with the awful concerns of a

a *St. Asaph* [H]

future state, should be somewhat more serious than the generality of mankind, and have a suitable composure of manners. A due sense of the dignity of their profession, independent of higher motives, will ever prevent them from losing their distinction in an indiscriminate sociality; and did such as affect this, know how much it lessens them in the eyes of those whom they think to please by it, they would feel themselves much mortified.

Johnson, and his friend, Beauclerk, were once together in company with several clergymen, who thought that they should appear to advantage, by assuming the lax jollity of *men of the world;* which, as it may be observed in similar cases, they carried to noisy excess. Johnson, who they expected would be *entertained,* sat grave and silent for some time; at last, turning to Beauclerk, he said, by no means in a whisper, 'This merriment of parsons is mighty offensive.'

Even the dress of a clergyman should be in character, and nothing can be more despicable than conceited attempts at avoiding the appearance of the clerical order; attempts, which are as ineffectual as they are pitiful. Dr. Porteus, now Bishop of London, in his excellent charge when presiding over the diocese of Chester, justly animadverts upon this subject; and observes of a reverend fop, that he 'can be but *half a beau.*'[a]

[a] Did Sophy Streatfield teach him that? [1]

Addison, in 'The Spectator,' has given us a fine portrait of a clergyman, who is supposed to be a member of his *Club;* and Johnson has exhibited a model, in the character of Mr. Mudge,[1] which has escaped the collectors of his works, but which he owned to me, and which indeed he shewed to Sir Joshua Reynolds at the time when it was written. It bears the genuine marks of Johnson's best manner, and is as follows:

'The Reverend Mr. *Zachariah Mudge,* Prebendary of Exeter, and Vicar of St. Andrew's in Plymouth; a man equally eminent for his virtues and abilities, and at once beloved as a companion and reverenced as a pastor. He had that general curiosity to which no kind of knowledge is indifferent or superfluous; and that general benevolence by which no order of men is hated or despised.

---

[1] See vol. i. p. 267.

'His principles both of thought and action were great and comprehensive. By a solicitous examination of objections, and judicious comparison of opposite arguments, he attained what enquiry never gives but to industry and perspicuity, a firm and unshaken settlement of conviction. But his firmness was without asperity; for, knowing with how much difficulty truth was sometimes found, he did not wonder that many missed it.

'The general course of his life was determined by his profession; he studied the sacred volumes in the original languages; with what diligence and success his *Notes upon the Psalms* give sufficient evidence. He once endeavoured to add the knowledge of Arabick to that of Hebrew; but finding his thoughts too much diverted from other studies, after some time desisted from his purpose.

'His discharge of parochial duties was exemplary. How his *Sermons* were composed, may be learned from the excellent volume which he has given to the publick; but how they were delivered, can be known only to those that heard them; for as he appeared in the pulpit, words will not easily describe him.[a] His delivery, though unconstrained, was not negligent, and though forcible, was not turbulent; disdaining anxious nicety of emphasis, and laboured artifice of action, it captivated the hearer by its natural dignity, it roused the sluggish, and fixed the volatile, and detained the mind upon the subject, without directing it to the speaker.[b]

'The grandeur and solemnity of the preacher did not intrude upon his general behaviour; at the table of his friends he was a companion communicative and attentive, of unaffected manners, of manly cheerfulness, willing to please, and easy to be pleased. His acquaintance was universally solicited, and his presence obstructed no enjoyment which religion did not forbid. Though studious he was popular; though argumentative he was modest; though inflexible he was candid; and though metaphysical yet orthodox.'[1]

On Friday, March 30, I dined with him at Sir Joshua

marginal notes:

marginal line: given to ... the speaker [1]

[a] *all this is not only applicable but seems written on purpose as if descriptive of George Henry Glasse 1808.* [1]

[b] *That is indeed Perfection: I think George Henry Glasse came nearest to it.* [H]

[1] 'London Chronicle,' May 2, 1769. This respectable man is there mentioned to have died on the 3d of April, that year, at Cofflect, the seat of Thomas Veale, Esq. in his way to London.

Reynolds's, with the Earl of Charlemont, Sir Annesley Stewart, Mr. Eliot, of Port-Eliot, Mr. Burke, Dean Marlay, Mr. Langton; a most agreeable day, of which I regret that every circumstance is not preserved; but it is unreasonable to require such a multiplication of felicity.

Mr. Eliot, with whom Dr. Walter Harte had travelled, talked to us of his 'History of Gustavus Adolphus,' which he said was a very good book in the German translation. JOHNSON. 'Harte was excessively vain. He put copies of his book in manuscript into the hands of Lord Chesterfield and Lord Granville, that they might revise it. Now how absurd was it to suppose that two such noblemen would revise so big a manuscript. Poor man! he left London the day of the publication of his book, that he might be out of the way of the great praise he was to receive; and he was ashamed to return, when he found how ill his book had succeeded. It was unlucky in coming out on the same day with Robertson's "History of Scotland." His husbandry, however, is good.' BOSWELL. 'So he was fitter for that than for heroick history: he did well, when he turned his sword into a plough-share.'

Mr. Eliot mentioned a curious liquor peculiar to his country, which the Cornish fishermen drink. They call it *Mahogany;* and it is made of two parts gin, and one part treacle, well beaten together. I begged to have some of it made, which was done with proper skill by Mr. Eliot. I thought it very good liquor; and said it was a counterpart of what is called *Athol Porridge* in the Highlands of Scotland, which is a mixture of whisky and honey. Johnson said, 'that must be a better liquor than the Cornish, for both its component parts are better.' He also observed, '*Mahogany* must be a modern name; for it is not long since the wood called mahogany was known in this country.' I mentioned his scale of liquors:—claret for boys,—port for men,—brandy for heroes. 'Then (said Mr. Burke) let me have claret: I love to be a boy; to have the careless gaiety of boyish days.' JOHNSON. 'I should drink claret too, if it would give me that; but it does not: it neither makes boys men, nor men boys. You'll be drowned by it, before it has any effect upon you.'

I ventured to mention a ludicrous paragraph in the

news-papers, that Dr. Johnson was learning to dance of Vestris. Lord Charlemont, wishing to excite him to talk, proposed in a whisper, that he should be asked, whether it was true. 'Shall I ask him?' said his Lordship. We were, by a great majority, clear for the experiment. Upon which his Lordship very gravely, and with a courteous air said, 'Pray, Sir, is it true that you are taking lessons of Vestris?' This was risking a good deal, and required the boldness of a General of Irish Volunteers to make the attempt. Johnson was at first startled, and in some heat answered, 'How can your Lordship ask so simple a question?'[a] But immediately recovering himself, whether from unwillingness to be deceived, or to appear deceived, or whether from real good humour, he kept up the joke: 'Nay, but if any body were to answer the paragraph, and contradict it, I'd have a reply, and would say, that he who contradicted it was no friend either to Vestris or me. For why should not Dr. Johnson add to his other powers a little corporeal agility? Socrates learnt to dance at an advanced age, and Cato learnt Greek at an advanced age. Then it might proceed to say, that this Johnson, not content with dancing on the ground, might dance on the rope; and they might introduce the elephant dancing on the rope. A nobleman[1] wrote a play, called "Love in a hollow Tree." He found out that it was a bad one, and therefore wished to buy up all the copies, and burn them. The Duchess of Marlborough had kept one; and when he was against her at an election, she had a new edition of it printed, and prefixed to it, as a frontispiece, an elephant dancing on a rope; to shew, that his Lordship's writing comedy was as aukward as an elephant dancing on a rope.'

On Sunday, April 1, I dined with him at Mr. Thrale's, with Sir Philip Jennings Clerk and Mr. Perkins,[2] who had the superintendance of Mr. Thrale's brewery, with a salary of five hundred pounds a year. Sir Philip had the appearance of a gentleman of ancient family, well advanced in life. He wore his own white hair in a bag of goodly size, a black velvet coat, with an embroidered waistcoat, and very rich laced ruffles; which Mrs. Thrale

[a] *was he not right in hating to be so treated? & would he not have been right to have lov'd me better than any of them? because I never did make a Lyon of him.* [H]

---

[1] William, the first Viscount Grimston.   [2] See vol. ii. p. 112.

said were old fashioned, but which, for that reason, I thought the more respectable, more like a Tory; yet Sir Philip was then in Opposition in Parliament. 'Ah, Sir, (said Johnson,) ancient ruffles and modern principles do not agree.' Sir Philip defended the opposition to the American war ably and with temper, and I joined him. He said, the majority of the nation was against the ministry. JOHNSON. '*I*, Sir, am against the ministry; but it is for having too little of that, of which Opposition thinks they have too much. Were I minister, if any man wagged his finger against me, he should be turned out; for that which it is in the power of Government to give at pleasure to one or to another, should be given to the supporters of Government. If you will not oppose at the expence of losing your place, your opposition will not be honest, you will feel no serious grievance; and the present opposition is only a contest to get what others have. Sir Robert Walpole acted as I would do. As to the American war, the *sense* of the nation is *with* the ministry. The majority of those who can *understand* is with it; the majority of those who can only *hear*, is against it; and as those who can only hear are more numerous than those who can understand, and Opposition is always loudest, a majority of the rabble will be for Opposition.'

This boisterous vivacity entertained us: but the truth in my opinion was, that those who could understand the best were against the American war, as almost every man now is, when the question has been coolly considered.

Mrs. Thrale gave high praise to Mr. Dudley Long, (now North). JOHNSON. 'Nay, my dear lady, don't talk so. Mr. Long's character is very *short*. It is nothing. He fills a chair. He is a man of genteel appearance, and that is all.[1] I know nobody who blasts by praise as you do: for whenever there is exaggerated praise, every body is set against a character. They are provoked to attack it. Now

[1] Here Johnson condescended to play upon the words *Long* and *short*. But little did he know that, owing to Mr. Long's reserve in his presence, he was talking thus of a gentleman distinguished amongst his acquaintance, for acuteness of wit, one to whom I think the French expression, '*Il pétille d'esprit*,' is particularly suited. He has gratified me by mentioning that he heard Dr. Johnson say, 'Sir, if I were to lose Boswell, it would be a limb amputated.'

there is Pepys;[1] you praised that man with such disproportion, that I was incited to lessen him, perhaps more
than he deserves. His blood is upon your head.[a] By the
same principle, your malice defeats itself; for your censure
is too violent. And yet (looking to her with a leering smile)
she is the first woman in the world, could she but restrain
that wicked tongue of hers;—she would be the only woman,
could she but command that little whirligig.'

Upon the subject of exaggerated praise I took the liberty
to say, that I thought there might be very high praise
given to a known character which deserved it, and therefore it would not be exaggerated. Thus, one might say of
Mr. Edmund Burke, he is a very wonderful man. JOHN-
SON. 'No, Sir, you would not be safe, if another man had
a mind perversely to contradict. He might answer, "Where
is all the wonder? Burke is, to be sure, a man of uncommon
abilities, with a great quantity of matter in his mind, and
a great fluency of language in his mouth. But we are not
to be stunned and astonished by him." So you see, Sir,
even Burke would suffer, not from any fault of his own,
but from your folly.'

Mrs. Thrale mentioned a gentleman who had acquired
a fortune of four thousand a year in trade, but was absolutely miserable, because he could not talk in company;[b]
so miserable, that he was impelled to lament his situation
in the street to ******, whom he hates, and who he knows
despises him. 'I am a most unhappy man (said he). I am
invited to conversations. I go to conversations; but, alas!
I have no conversation.'[c]—JOHNSON. 'Man commonly
cannot be successful in different ways. This gentleman has
spent, in getting four thousand pounds a year, the time in
which he might have learnt to talk; and now he cannot
talk.' Mr. Perkins made a shrewd and droll remark: 'If he
had got his four thousand a year as a mountebank, he
might have learnt to talk at the same time that he was
getting his fortune.'[d]

[1] William Weller Pepys, Esq. one of the Masters in the High Court of
Chancery, and well known in polite circles. My acquaintance with him is
not sufficient to enable me to speak of him from my own judgement. But I
know that both at Eton and Oxford he was the intimate friend of the late
Sir James Macdonald, the *Marcellus* of Scotland, whose extraordinary talents,
learning, and virtues, will ever be remembered with admiration and regret.

---

underlined:
*His blood . . . your
head* [H & I]

[a] *an Expression he
would not have used;—
no, not for Worlds.* [H]
   *an Expression Dr.
Johnson would not
have taken 100.£ to
have used.* [I]

[b] *I have forgotten who
this man was com-
pletely—no Recollection
of him.* [H]

underlined:
no [I]

[c] *how comical! I have
forgotten who he was.*
[I]

[d] *excellent. Bravo Perkins! I remember noth-
ing of all this.* [H]
   Bravo! [I]

Some other gentlemen came in. The conversation concerning the person whose character Dr. Johnson had treated so slightingly, as he did not know his merit, was resumed. Mrs. Thrale said, 'You think so of him, Sir, because he is quiet, and does not exert himself with force. You'll be saying the same thing of Mr. ***** there, who sits as quiet—.' This was not well bred; and Johnson did not let it pass without correction. 'Nay, Madam, what right have you to talk thus? Both Mr. ***** and I have reason to take it ill. *You* may talk so of Mr. *****; but why do you make *me* do it? Have I said any thing against Mr. *****? You have *set* him, that I might shoot him: but I have not shot him.'[a]

One of the gentlemen said, he had seen three folio volumes of Dr. Johnson's sayings collected by me. 'I must put you right, Sir, (said I;) for I am very exact in authenticity. You could not see folio volumes, for I have none: you might have seen some in quarto and octavo. This is an inattention which one should guard against.' JOHNSON. 'Sir, it is a want of concern about veracity. He does not know that he saw *any* volumes. If he had seen them he could have remembered their size.'

Mr. Thrale appeared very lethargick to-day. I saw him again on Monday evening, at which time he was not thought to be in immediate danger; but early in the morning of Wednesday the 4th, he expired. Johnson was in the house, and thus mentions the event: 'I felt almost the last flutter of his pulse, and looked for the last time upon the face that for fifteen years had never been turned upon me but with respect and benignity.'[1] Upon that day there was a *Call* of the LITERARY CLUB; but Johnson apologised for his absence by the following note:

'MR. JOHNSON knows that Sir Joshua Reynolds and the other gentlemen will excuse his incompliance with the Call, when they are told that Mr. Thrale died this morning.'

'Wednesday.'

[a] *Who could the Men be?* [I]

---

[1] Prayers and Meditations, p. 191.

[Johnson's expressions on this occasion remind us of Isaac Walton's eulogy on Whitgift, in his Life of Hooker.—'He lived . . . to be present at the expiration of her [Q. Elizabeth's] last breath, and to behold the closing of those eyes that had long looked upon him with reverence and affection.' KEARNEY.]

Mr. Thrale's death was a very essential loss to Johnson, who, although he did not foresee all that afterwards happened, was sufficiently convinced that the comforts which Mr. Thrale's family afforded him, would now in a great measure cease. He, however, continued to shew a kind attention to his widow and children as long as it was acceptable: and he took upon him, with a very earnest concern, the office of one of his executors, the importance of which seemed greater than usual to him, from his circumstances having been always such, that he had scarcely any share in the real business of life. His friends of the CLUB were in hopes that Mr. Thrale might have made a liberal provision for him for his life, which, as Mr. Thrale left no son, and a very large fortune, it would have been highly to his honour to have done; and, considering Dr. Johnson's age, could not have been of long duration; but he bequeathed him only two hundred pounds, which was the legacy given to each of his executors. I could not but be somewhat diverted by hearing Johnson talk in a pompous manner of his new office, and particularly of the concerns of the brewery, which it was at last resolved should be sold. Lord Lucan tells a very good story, which, if not precisely exact, is certainly characteristical: that when the sale of Thrale's brewery was going forward, Johnson appeared bustling about, with an ink-horn and pen in his buttonhole, like an excise-man; and on being asked what he really considered to be the value of the property which was to be disposed of, answered, 'We are not here to sell a parcel of boilers and vats, but the potentiality of growing rich beyond the dreams of avarice.'

On Friday, April 6, he carried me to dine at a club, which, at his desire, had been lately formed at the Queen's Arms, in St. Paul's Church-yard. He told Mr. Hoole, that he wished to have a *City Club*, and asked him to collect one; but, said he, 'Don't let them be *patriots*.' The company were to-day very sensible, well-behaved men. I have preserved only two particulars of his conversation. He said he was glad Lord George Gordon had escaped, rather than that a precedent should be established for hanging a man for *constructive treason;* which, in consistency with his true, manly, constitutional Toryism, he considered would be a dangerous engine of arbitrary power. And upon its being mentioned that an opulent and very indolent Scotch nobleman, who totally resigned the management of his affairs to a man of knowledge and abilities, had claimed some merit by saying, 'The next best thing to managing a man's own affairs well, is being sensible of incapacity, and not attempting it, but having full confidence in one who can do it.' JOHNSON. 'Nay, Sir, this is paltry. There is a middle course. Let a man give application; and depend upon it he will soon get above a despicable state of helplessness, and attain the power of acting for himself.'

On Saturday, April 7, I dined with him at Mr. Hoole's with Governour Bouchier and Captain Orme, both of whom had been long in the East-Indies; and being men of good sense and observation, were very entertaining. Johnson defended the oriental regulation of different *casts* of men,[1] which was objected to as totally destructive of the hopes of rising in society by personal merit. He shewed that there was a *principle* in it sufficiently plausible by analogy. 'We see (said he) in metals that there are different species; and so likewise in animals, though one species may not differ very widely from another, as in the species of dogs,—the cur, the spaniel, the mastiff. The Bramins are the mastiffs of mankind.'[a]

On Thursday, April 12, I dined with him at a Bishop's,[b] where were Sir Joshua Reynolds, Mr. Berenger, and some more company. He had dined the day before at another Bishop's. I have unfortunately recorded none of his conversation at the Bishop's where we dined together: but I have preserved his ingenious defence of his dining twice abroad in Passion-week; a laxity, in which I am convinced he would not have indulged himself at the time when he wrote his solemn paper in 'The Rambler,' upon that awful season. It appeared to me, that by being much more in company, and enjoying more luxurious living, he had contracted a keener relish for pleasure, and was consequently less rigorous in his religious rites. This he would

[a] *how Mastiffs!! poor gentle Souls.* [I]

underlined: *Bishop's, another Bishop's* [H]

[b] *Well! I do think it was out of Rule for a Bishop to make Dinners on holy Thursday. It would shock a foreign Romanist to hear of it. Who was the Bishop I wonder! But there were Two it seems.* [H]

---

[1] [Rajapouts, the military cast; the Bramins, pacifick and abstemious. KEARNEY.]

not acknowledge; but he reasoned with admirable sophistry, as follows: 'Why, Sir, a Bishop's calling company together in this week, is, to use the vulgar phrase, not *the thing*. But you must consider laxity is a bad thing; but preciseness is also a bad thing; and your general character may be more hurt by preciseness than by dining with a Bishop in Passion-week. There might be a handle for reflection. It might be said, "He refuses to dine with a Bishop in Passion-week, but was three Sundays absent from church."' BOSWELL. 'Very true, Sir. But suppose a man to be uniformly of good conduct, would it not be better that he should refuse to dine with a Bishop in this week, and so not encourage a bad practice by his example?' JOHNSON. 'Why, Sir, you are to consider whether you might not do more harm by lessening the influence of a Bishop's character by your disapprobation in refusing him, than by going to him.'

'TO MRS. LUCY PORTER, IN LICHFIELD

'DEAR MADAM,

'LIFE is full of troubles. I have just lost my dear friend Thrale. I hope he is happy; but I have had a great loss. I am otherwise pretty well. I require some care of myself, but that care is not ineffectual; and when I am out of order, I think it often my own fault.

'The spring is now making quick advances. As it is the season in which the whole world is enlivened and invigorated, I hope that both you and I shall partake of its benefits. My desire is to see Lichfield; but being left executor to my friend, I know not whether I can be spared; but I will try, for it is now long since we saw one another, and how little we can promise ourselves many more interviews, we are taught by hourly examples of mortality. Let us try to live so as that mortality may not be an evil. Write to me soon, my dearest; your letters will give me great pleasure.

'I am sorry that Mr. Porter has not had his box; but by sending it to Mr. Mathias, who very readily undertook its conveyance, I did the best I could, and perhaps before now he has it.

'Be so kind as to make my compliments to my friends; I have a great value for their kindness, and hope to enjoy it before summer is past. Do write to me. I am, dearest love,

'Your most humble servant,

'London, April 12, 1781.'   'SAM. JOHNSON'

On Friday, April 13, being Good-Friday, I went to St. Clement's church with him as usual. There I saw again his old fellow-collegian, Edwards, to whom I said, 'I think, Sir, Dr. Johnson and you meet only at Church.'— 'Sir, (said he,) it is the best place we can meet in, except Heaven, and I hope we shall meet there too.' Dr. Johnson told me, that there was very little communication between Edwards and him, after their unexpected renewal of acquaintance. 'But (said he, smiling) he met me once, and said, "I am told you have written a very pretty book called *The Rambler*." I was unwilling that he should leave the world in total darkness, and sent him a set.'

Mr. Berenger[1] visited him to-day, and was very pleasing. We talked of an evening society for conversation at a house in town, of which we were all members, but of which Johnson said, 'It will never do, Sir. There is nothing served about there, neither tea, nor coffee, nor lemonade, nor any thing whatever; and depend upon it, Sir, a man does not love to go to a place from whence he comes out exactly as he went in.' I endeavoured for argument's sake, to maintain that men of learning and talents might have very good intellectual society, without the aid of any little gratifications of the senses. Berenger joined with Johnson, and said, that without these any meeting would be dull and insipid. He would therefore have all the slight refreshments; nay, it would not be amiss to have some cold meat, and a bottle of wine upon a side-board. 'Sir, (said Johnson to me, with an air of triumph,) Mr. Berenger knows the world. Every body loves to have good things furnished to them without any trouble. I told Mrs. Thrale once, that as she did not choose to have card-tables, she should have a profusion of the best sweetmeats, and she

---

[1] [Richard Berenger, Esq. many years Gentleman of the Horse to his present Majesty, and authour of 'The History and Art of Horsemanship,' in two volumes, 4to. 1771. MALONE.]

would be sure to have company enough come to her.' I agreed with my illustrious friend upon this subject; for it has pleased GOD to make man a composite animal, and where there is nothing to refresh the body, the mind will languish.

On Sunday, April 15, being Easter-day, after solemn worship in St. Paul's church, I found him alone; Dr. Scott, of the Commons, came in. He talked of its having been said, that Addison wrote some of his best papers in 'The Spectator,' when warm with wine. Dr. Johnson did not seem willing to admit this. Dr. Scott, as a confirmation of it, related, that Blackstone, a sober man, composed his 'Commentaries' with a bottle of port before him; and found his mind invigorated and supported in the fatigue of his great Work, by a temperate use of it.

I told him, that in a company where I had lately been, a desire was expressed to know his authority for the shocking story of Addison's sending an execution into Steele's house.[1] 'Sir, (said he,) it is generally known; it is known to all who are acquainted with the literary history of that period: it is as well known, as that he wrote "Cato."' Mr. Thomas Sheridan once defended Addison to me, by alleging that he did it in order to cover Steele's goods from other creditors, who were going to seize them.

We talked of the difference between the mode of education at Oxford, and that in those Colleges where instruction is chiefly conveyed by lectures. JOHNSON. 'Lectures were once useful; but now, when all can read and books are so numerous, lectures are unnecessary. If your attention fails, and you miss a part of the lecture, it is lost; you cannot go back as you do upon a book.' Dr. Scott agreed with him. 'But yet (said I) Dr. Scott, you yourself gave lectures at Oxford.' He smiled. 'You laughed (then said I) at those who came to you.'

Dr. Scott left us, and soon afterwards we went to dinner. Our company consisted of Mrs. Williams, Mrs. Desmoulins, Mr. Levett, Mr. Allen, the printer, [Mr. Macbean,] and Mrs. Hall, sister of the Reverend Mr. John Wesley, and resembling him, as I thought, both in figure and manner. Johnson produced now, for the first time, some

[1] See this explained, pp. 165, 166, of this volume.

handsome silver salvers, which he told me he had bought fourteen years ago; so it was a great day. I was not a little amused by observing Allen perpetually struggling to talk in the manner of Johnson,[a] like the little frog in the fable blowing himself up to resemble the stately ox.

I mentioned a kind of religious Robinhood Society, which met every Sunday evening at Coachmakers'-hall, for free debate; and that the subject for this night was, the text which relates, with other miracles, which happened at our SAVIOUR's death, 'And the graves were opened, and many bodies of the saints which slept arose, and came out of the graves after his resurrection, and went into the holy city, and appeared unto many.' Mrs. Hall said it was a very curious subject, and she should like to hear it discussed. JOHNSON. (somewhat warmly.) 'One would not go to such a place to hear it,—one would not be seen in such a place—to give countenance to such a meeting.' I, however, resolved that I would go. 'But, Sir, (said she to Johnson,) I should like to hear *you* discuss it.' He seemed reluctant to engage in it. She talked of the resurrection of the human race in general, and maintained that we shall be raised with the same bodies. JOHNSON. 'Nay, Madam, we see that it is not to be the same body; for the Scripture uses the illustration of grain sown, and we know that the grain which grows is not the same with what is sown. You cannot suppose that we shall rise with a diseased body; it is enough if there be such a sameness as to distinguish identity of person.' She seemed desirous of knowing more, but he left the question in obscurity.

Of apparitions,[1] he observed, 'A total disbelief of them is adverse to the opinion of the existence of the soul between death and the last day; the question simply is,

---

[1] [As this subject frequently recurs in these volumes, the reader may be led erroneously to suppose that Dr. Johnson was so fond of such discussions, as frequently to introduce them. But the truth is, that the authour himself delighted in talking concerning ghosts, and what he has frequently denominated *the mysterious;* and therefore took every opportunity of *leading* Johnson to converse on such subjects. MALONE.]

[The authour of this work was most undoubtedly fond of *the mysterious*, and perhaps upon some occasions may have directed the conversation to those topics, when they would not spontaneously have suggested themselves to Johnson's mind; but that *he* also had a love for speculations of that nature, may be gathered from his writings throughout. J. BOSWELL.]

whether departed spirits ever have the power of making themselves perceptible to us: a man who thinks he has seen an apparition, can only be convinced himself; his authority will not convince another; and his conviction, if rational, must be founded on being told something which cannot be known but by supernatural means.'

He mentioned a thing as not unfrequent, of which I had never heard before,—being *called*,[a] that is, hearing one's name pronounced by the voice of a known person at a great distance, far beyond the possibility of being reached by any sound uttered by human organs. 'An acquaintance, on whose veracity I can depend, told me, that walking home one evening to Kilmarnock, he heard himself called from a wood, by the voice of a brother who had gone to America; and the next packet brought accounts of that brother's death.' Macbean asserted that this inexplicable *calling* was a thing very well known. Dr. Johnson said, that one day at Oxford, as he was turning the key of his chamber, he heard his mother distinctly call—*Sam*.[b] She was then at Lichfield; but nothing ensued. This phenomenon is, I think, as wonderful as any other mysterious fact, which many people are very slow to believe, or rather, indeed, reject with an obstinate contempt.

Some time after this, upon his making a remark which escaped my attention, Mrs. Williams and Mrs. Hall were both together striving to answer him. He grew angry, and called out loudly, 'Nay, when you both speak at once, it is intolerable.' But checking himself, and softening, he said, 'This one may say, though you *are* ladies.' Then he brightened into gay humour, and addressed them in the words of one of the songs in 'The Beggar's Opera,'

'But two at a time there's no mortal can bear.'

'What, Sir, (said I,) are you going to turn Captain Macheath?' There was something as pleasantly ludicrous in this scene as can be imagined. The contrast between Macheath, Polly, and Lucy—and Dr. Samuel Johnson, blind, peevish Mrs. Williams, and lean, lank, preaching Mrs. Hall, was exquisite.

I stole away to Coachmakers'-hall, and heard the difficult text of which we had talked, discussed with great

underlined:
never heard before [H]
[a]*Milton mentions it & airy Tongues that Syllable Men's Names &c* [H]
—*of airy Tongues That Syllable Men's Names   Milton* [I]

[b] *he told me the same Thing. A Gentleman—since I possess'd these books;—a Man of the highest Gradation of Intellect . . . a Friend here at Bath told me he had himself been so called. he told me in August   1817* [H]

So he told me [I]

decency, and some intelligence, by several speakers. There
was a difference of opinion as to the appearance of ghosts
in modern times, though the arguments for it, supported
by Mr. Addison's authority, preponderated. The immediate subject of debate was embarrassed by the *bodies* of
the saints having been said to rise, and by the question
what became of them afterwards:—did they return again
to their graves? or were they translated to heaven? Only
one evangelist mentions the fact,[1] and the commentators
whom I have looked at do not make the passage clear.
There is, however, no occasion for our understanding it
farther, than to know that it was one of the extraordinary
manifestations of divine power, which accompanied the
most important event that ever happened.

On Friday, April 20, I spent with him one of the happiest
days that I remember to have enjoyed in the whole course
of my life. Mrs. Garrick, whose grief for the loss of her
husband was, I believe, as sincere as wounded affection
and admiration could produce, had this day, for the first
time since his death, a select party of his friends to dine
with her. The company was, Miss Hannah More, who
lived with her, and whom she called her Chaplain;[a] Mrs.
Boscawen,[2] Mrs. Elizabeth Carter, Sir Joshua Reynolds,
Dr. Burney, Dr. Johnson, and myself. We found ourselves
very elegantly entertained at her house in the Adelphi,
where I have passed many a pleasing hour with him 'who
gladdened life.' She looked well, talked of her husband
with complacency, and while she cast her eyes on his
portrait, which hung over the chimney-piece, said, that
'death was now the most agreeable object to her.'[b] The
very semblance of David Garrick was cheering. Mr.
Beauclerk, with happy propriety, inscribed under that
fine portrait of him, which by Lady Diana's kindness is
now the property of my friend Mr. Langton, the following
passage from his beloved Shakspeare:

'———————— A merrier man,
Within the limit of becoming mirth,
I never spent an hour's talk withal.
His eye begets occasion for his wit;

index sign:
a select party etc. [H]

underlined:
Chaplain [H & I]

[a] —*odd enough if She
did so call her, because
their Religious Opin-
ions were so* widely
different. [H]

I suppose in Con-
tempt; for Mrs. Gar-
rick was a Romanist.
[I]

[b] *She yet lives—1817.
even yet—1820.* [H]

[1] St. Matthew, chap. xxvii. v. 52, 53.   [2] See p. 36 of this volume.

For every object that the one doth catch,
The other turns to a mirth-moving jest;
Which his fair tongue (Conceit's expositor)
Delivers in such apt and gracious words,
That aged ears play truant at his tales,
And younger hearings are quite ravished;
So sweet and voluble is his discourse.'

We were all in fine spirits; and I whispered to Mrs.
Boscawen, 'I believe this is as much as can be made of
life.' In addition to a splendid entertainment, we were
regaled with Lichfield ale, which had a peculiar appropriate value. Sir Joshua, and Dr. Burney, and I, drank
cordially of it to Dr. Johnson's health; and though he
would not join us, he as cordially answered, 'Gentlemen,
I wish you all as well as you do me.'[a]

The general effect of this day dwells upon my mind in
fond remembrance; but I do not find much conversation
recorded. What I have preserved shall be faithfully given.

One of the company mentioned Mr. Thomas Hollis, the
strenuous Whig, who used to send over Europe presents
of democratical books, with their boards stamped with
daggers and caps of liberty. Mrs. Carter said, 'He was
a bad man: he used to talk uncharitably.' JOHNSON.
'Poh! poh! Madam; who is the worse for being talked of
uncharitably? Besides, he was a dull poor creature as ever
lived: and I believe he would not have done harm to a
man whom he knew to be of very opposite principles to
his own. I remember once at the Society of Arts, when an
advertisement was to be drawn up, he pointed me out as
the man who could do it best. This, you will observe, was
kindness to me. I however slipt away and escaped it.'

Mrs. Carter having said of the same person, 'I doubt
he was an Atheist.' JOHNSON. 'I don't know that. He
might, perhaps, have become one, if he had had time to
ripen, (smiling.) He might have *exuberated* into an Atheist.'

Sir Joshua Reynolds praised 'Mudge's[1] Sermons.'
JOHNSON. 'Mudge's Sermons are good, but not practical.
He grasps more sense than he can hold; he takes more
corn than he can make into meal; he opens a wide prospect,

[1] See page 187 of this volume.

but it is so distant, it is indistinct. I love "Blair's Sermons."
Though the dog is a Scotchman, and a Presbyterian, and
every thing he should not be, I was the first to praise them.
Such was my candour.' (smiling.) MRS. BOSCAWEN.
'Such his great merit, to get the better of all your prejudices.' JOHNSON. 'Why, Madam, let us compound the
matter; let us ascribe it to my candour, and his merit.'

In the evening we had a large company in the drawing-
room; several ladies, the Bishop of Killaloe, Dr. Percy,
Mr. Chamberlayne of the Treasury,[a] &c. &c. Somebody
said, the life of a mere literary man could not be very
entertaining. JOHNSON. 'But it certainly may. This is a
remark which has been made, and repeated, without
justice; why should the life of a literary man be less entertaining than the life of any other man? Are there not as
interesting varieties in such a life? As *a literary life* it may
be very entertaining.'[b] BOSWELL. 'But it must be better
surely, when it is diversified with a little active variety—
such as his having gone to Jamaica;—or—his having gone
to the Hebrides.' Johnson was not displeased at this.

Talking of a very respectable authour,[c] he told us a
curious circumstance in his life, which was, that he had
married a printer's devil. REYNOLDS. 'A printer's devil,
Sir! Why, I thought a printer's devil was a creature with
a black face and in rags.' JOHNSON. 'Yes, Sir. But I
suppose he had her face washed, and put clean clothes on
her. (Then looking very serious, and very earnest.) And
she did not disgrace him;—the woman had a bottom of
good sense.' The word *bottom* thus introduced, was so
ludicrous when contrasted with his gravity, that most of us
could not forbear tittering and laughing; though I recollect that the Bishop of Killaloe kept his countenance with
perfect steadiness, while Miss Hannah More slyly hid her
face behind a lady's back who sat on the same settee with
her. His pride could not bear that any expression of his
should excite ridicule, when he did not intend it; he
therefore resolved to assume and exercise despotick power,
glanced sternly around, and called out in a strong tone,
'Where's the merriment?' Then collecting himself, and
looking awful, to make us feel how he could impose
restraint, and as it were searching his mind for a still more

[a] *who jump'd out of a Window afterwards.* [H & I]

[b] *to literary People it may: not to Readers who want a Story Book I suppose.* [H]

[c] *Who was this King Cophetua? I forget if ever I knew. was it Richardson?* [I]

ludicrous word, he slowly pronounced, 'I say the *woman* was *fundamentally* sensible;' as if he had said, hear this now, and laugh if you dare. We all sat composed as at a funeral.

He and I walked away together; we stopped a little while by the rails of the Adelphi, looking on the Thames, and I said to him with some emotion, that I was now thinking of two friends we had lost, who once lived in the buildings behind us, Beauclerk and Garrick. 'Ay, Sir, (said he, tenderly,) and two such friends as cannot be supplied.'

For some time after this day I did not see him very often, and of the conversation which I did enjoy, I am sorry to find I have preserved but little. I was at this time engaged in a variety of other matters, which required exertion and assiduity, and necessarily occupied almost all my time.

One day, having spoken very freely of those who were then in power, he said to me, 'Between ourselves, Sir, I do not like to give opposition the satisfaction of knowing how much I disapprove of the ministry.' And when I mentioned that Mr. Burke had boasted how quiet the nation was in George the Second's reign, when Whigs were in power, compared with the present reign, when Tories governed;—'Why, Sir, (said he,) you are to consider that Tories having more reverence for government, will not oppose with the same violence as Whigs, who being unrestrained by that principle, will oppose by any means.'

This month he lost not only Mr. Thrale, but another friend, Mr. William Strahan, Junior, printer, the eldest son of his old and constant friend, Printer to his Majesty.

'TO MRS. STRAHAN

'DEAR MADAM,

'THE grief which I feel for the loss of a very kind friend, is sufficient to make me know how much you suffer by the death of an amiable son: a man, of whom I think it may be truly said, that no one knew him who does not lament him. I look upon myself as having a friend, another friend, taken from me.

'Comfort, dear Madam, I would give you, if I could; but I know how little the forms of consolation can avail.

Let me, however, counsel you not to waste your health in unprofitable sorrow, but go to Bath, and endeavour to prolong your own life; but when we have all done all that we can, one friend must in time lose the other.

'I am, dear Madam,
'Your most humble servant,

'April 23, 1781.'   'SAM. JOHNSON'

On Tuesday, May 8, I had the pleasure of again dining with him and Mr. Wilkes, at Mr. Dilly's. No *negociation* was now required to bring them together; for Johnson was so well satisfied with the former interview, that he was very glad to meet Wilkes again, who was this day seated between Dr. Beattie and Dr. Johnson; (between *Truth* and *Reason*, as General Paoli said, when I told him of it.) WILKES. 'I have been thinking, Dr. Johnson, that there should be a bill brought into parliament that the controverted elections for Scotland should be tried in that country, at their own Abbey of Holy-Rood House, and not here; for the consequence of trying them here is, that we have an inundation of Scotchmen, who come up and never go back again. Now here is Boswell, who is come upon the election for his own county, which will not last a fortnight.' JOHNSON. 'Nay, Sir, I see no reason why they should be tried at all; for, you know, one Scotchman is as good as another.' WILKES. 'Pray, Boswell, how much may be got in a year by an Advocate at the Scotch bar?' BOSWELL. 'I believe, two thousand pounds.' WILKES. 'How can it be possible to spend that money in Scotland?' JOHNSON. 'Why, Sir, the money may be spent in England; but there is a harder question. If one man in Scotland gets possession of two thousand pounds, what remains for all the rest of the nation?' WILKES. 'You know, in the last war, the immense booty which Thurot carried off by the complete plunder of seven Scotch isles; he re-embarked with *three and six-pence*.' Here again Johnson and Wilkes joined in extravagant sportive raillery upon the supposed poverty of Scotland, which Dr. Beattie and I did not think it worth our while to dispute.

The subject of quotation being introduced, Mr. Wilkes censured it as pedantry. JOHNSON. 'No, Sir, it is a good thing; there is a community of mind in it. Classical quotation is the *parole* of literary men all over the world.' WILKES. 'Upon the continent they all quote the vulgate Bible. Shakspeare is chiefly quoted here; and we quote also Pope, Prior, Butler, Waller, and sometimes Cowley.'

We talked of Letter-writing. JOHNSON. 'It is now become so much the fashion to publish letters, that, in order to avoid it, I put as little into mine as I can.' BOSWELL. 'Do what you will, Sir, you cannot avoid it. Should you even write as ill as you can, your letters would be published as curiosities:

> "Behold a miracle! instead of wit,
>   See two dull lines with Stanhope's pencil writ."'

He gave us an entertaining account of *Bet Flint*, a woman of the town, who, with some eccentrick talents and much effrontery, forced herself upon his acquaintance. 'Bet (said he) wrote her own Life in verse,[1] which she brought to me, wishing that I would furnish her with a Preface to it. (Laughing.) I used to say of her, that she was generally slut and drunkard;—occasionally, whore and thief. She had, however, genteel lodgings, a spinnet on which she played, and a boy that walked before her chair. Poor Bet was taken up on a charge of stealing a counterpane, and tried at the Old Bailey. Chief Justice ———, who loved a wench, summed up favourably, and she was acquitted.[2] After which, Bet said, with a gay and satisfied

---

[1] Johnson, whose memory was wonderfully retentive, remembered the first four lines of this curious production, which have been communicated to me by a young lady of his acquaintance:

> 'When first I drew my vital breath,
>   A little minikin I came upon earth;
> And then I came from a dark abode,
>   Into this gay and gaudy world.'[a]

[a] *not exact but very like* [1]

[2] [The account which Johnson had received on this occasion, was not quite accurate. BET was tried at the Old Bailey in September 1758, not by the Chief Justice here alluded to, (who however tried another cause on the same day,) but before Sir William Moreton, Recorder; and she was acquitted, not in consequence of any *favourable summing up* of the Judge, but because the Prosecutrix, Mary Walthow, could not prove that the goods charged to have been stolen, [a counterpane, a silver spoon, two napkins, &c.] were her property.

BET does not appear to have lived at that time in a very *genteel* style; for she paid for her ready-furnished *room* in Meard's Court, Dean Street, Soho,

air, "Now that the counterpane is *my own*, I shall make a petticoat of it."' [a]

Talking of oratory, Mr. Wilkes described it as accompanied with all the charms of poetical expression. JOHNSON. 'No, Sir; oratory is the power of beating down your adversary's arguments, and putting better in their place.' —WILKES. 'But this does not move the passions.' JOHNSON. 'He must be a weak man, who is to be so moved.' WILKES. (naming a celebrated orator) 'Amidst all the brilliancy of ——'s[b] imagination, and the exuberance of his wit, there is a strange want of *taste*. It was observed of Apelles's Venus,[1] that her flesh seemed as if she had been nourished by roses: his oratory would sometimes make one suspect that he eats potatoes and drinks whisky.'

Mr. Wilkes observed, how tenacious we are of forms in this country; and gave as an instance, the vote of the House of Commons for remitting money to pay the army in America *in Portugal pieces*, when, in reality, the remittance is made not in Portugal money, but in our specie. JOHNSON. 'Is there not a law, Sir, against exporting the current coin of the realm?' WILKES. 'Yes, Sir; but might not the House of Commons, in case of real evident necessity, order our own current coin to be sent into our own colonies?'—Here Johnson, with that quickness of recollection which distinguished him so eminently, gave the *Middlesex Patriot* an admirable retort upon his own ground. 'Sure, Sir, *you* don't think a *resolution of the House of Commons* equal to *the law of the land*.' WILKES. (at once perceiving the application) 'GOD forbid, Sir.'—To hear what had been treated with such violence in 'The False Alarm,' now turned into pleasant repartee, was extremely agreeable. Johnson went on:—'Locke observes well, that a prohibition to export the current coin is impolitick; for when the balance of trade happens to be against a state, the current coin *must* be exported.'

from which these articles were alleged to be stolen, only *five shillings* a week.
　Mr. James Boswell took the trouble to examine the Sessions Paper, to ascertain these particulars.[c] MALONE.]

　[1] [Mr. Wilkes mistook the objection of Euphranor to the Theseus of Parrhasius for a description of the Venus of Apelles. Vide Plutarch. '*Bellone an pace clariores Athenienses.*'[d] KEARNEY.]

---

[a] *I remember this Stuff perfectly—he ended all with an odd ludicrous Sigh—& I loved Bet Flint! So comically.* [I]

[b] *Burke's* [H]
　Burke [I]

marginal line:
sometimes make . . . drinks whisky [H]

[c] *astonishing!* [H]

[d] *very true* [I]

Mr. Beauclerk's great library was this season sold in London by auction. Mr. Wilkes said, he wondered to find in it such a numerous collection of sermons; seeming to think it strange that a gentleman of Mr. Beauclerk's character in the gay world, should have chosen to have many compositions of that kind. JOHNSON. 'Why, Sir, you are to consider, that sermons make a considerable branch of English literature; so that a library must be very imperfect if it has not a numerous collection of sermons:[1] and in all collections, Sir, the desire of augmenting them grows stronger in proportion to the advance in acquisition; as motion is accelerated by the continuance of the *impetus*. Besides, Sir, (looking at Mr. Wilkes with a placid but significant smile,) a man may collect sermons with intention of making himself better by them. I hope Mr. Beauclerk intended that some time or other that should be the case with him.'

Mr. Wilkes said to me, loud enough for Dr. Johnson to hear, 'Dr. Johnson should make me a present of his

---

[1] Mr. Wilkes probably did not know that there is in an English sermon the most comprehensive and lively account of that entertaining faculty, for which he himself was so much admired. It is in Dr. Barrow's first volume, and fourteenth sermon, '*Against foolish Talking and Jesting.*' My old acquaintance, the late Corbyn Morris, in his ingenious 'Essay on Wit, Humour, and Ridicule,' calls it 'a *profuse* description of Wit:' but I do not see how it could be curtailed, without leaving out some good circumstance of discrimination. As it is not generally known, and may perhaps dispose some to read sermons, from which they may receive real advantage, while looking only for entertainment, I shall here subjoin it.

'But first (says the learned preacher) it may be demanded, what the thing we speak of is? Or what this facetiousness (or *wit*, as he calls it before) doth import? To which questions I might reply, as Democritus did to him that asked the definition of a man, "'Tis that which we all see and know." Any one better apprehends what it is by acquaintance, than I can inform him by description. It is, indeed, a thing so versatile and multiform, appearing in so many shapes, so many postures, so many garbs, so variously apprehended by several eyes and judgements, that it seemeth no less hard to settle a clear and certain notion thereof, than to make a portrait of Proteus, or to define the figure of the fleeting air. Sometimes it lieth in pat allusion to a known story, or in seasonable application of a trivial saying, or in forging an apposite tale; sometimes it playeth in words and phrases, taking advantage from the ambiguity of their sense, or the affinity of their sound: sometimes it is wrapped in a dress of humourous expression: sometimes it lurketh under an old similitude: sometimes it is lodged in a sly question, in a smart answer, in a quirkish reason, in a shrewd intimation, in cunningly diverting or cleverly retorting an objection: sometimes it is couched in a bold scheme of speech, in a tart irony, in a lusty hyperbole, in a startling metaphor, in a

"Lives of the Poets," as I am a poor patriot, who cannot afford to buy them.' Johnson seemed to take no notice of this hint; but in a little while, he called to Mr. Dilly, 'Pray, Sir, be so good as to send a set of my Lives to Mr. Wilkes, with my compliments.' This was accordingly done; and Mr. Wilkes paid Dr. Johnson a visit, was courteously received, and sat with him a long time.

The company gradually dropped away. Mr. Dilly himself was called down stairs upon business; I left the room for some time; when I returned, I was struck with observing Dr. Samuel Johnson and John Wilkes, Esq. literally *tête-à-tête;* for they were reclined upon their chairs, with their heads leaning almost close to each other, and talking earnestly, in a kind of confidential whisper, of the personal quarrel between George the Second and the King of Prussia. Such a scene of perfectly easy sociality between two such opponents in the war of political controversy, as that which I now beheld, would have been an excellent subject for a picture. It presented to my mind the happy

plausible reconciling of contradictions, or in acute nonsense: sometimes a scenical representation of persons or things, a counterfeit speech, a mimical look or gesture, passeth for it: sometimes an affected simplicity, sometimes a presumptuous bluntness giveth it being: sometimes it riseth only from a lucky hitting upon what is strange: sometimes from a crafty wresting obvious matter to the purpose. Often it consisteth in one knows not what, and springeth up one can hardly tell how. Its ways are unaccountable, and inexplicable; being answerable to the numberless rovings of fancy, and windings of language. It is, in short, a manner of speaking out of the simple and plain way, (such as reason teacheth and proveth things by,) which by a pretty surprising uncouthness in conceit or expression, doth affect and amuse the fancy, stirring in it some wonder, and breeding some delight thereto. It raiseth admiration, as signifying a nimble sagacity of apprehension, a special felicity of invention, a vivacity of spirit, and reach of wit more than vulgar; it seeming to argue a rare quickness of parts, that one can fetch in remote conceits applicable; a notable skill, that he can dextrously accommodate them to the purpose before him; together with a lively briskness of humour, not apt to damp those sportful flashes of imagination. (Whence in Aristotle such persons are termed ἐπιδέξιοι, dextrous men, and εὔστροφοι, men of facile or versatile manners, who can easily turn themselves to all things, or turn all things to themselves.) It also procureth delight, by gratifying curiosity with its rareness, as semblance of difficulty: (as monsters, not for their beauty, but their rarity: as juggling tricks, not for their use, but their abstruseness, are beheld with pleasure:) by diverting the mind from its road of serious thoughts; by instilling gaiety and airiness of spirit; by provoking to such dispositions of spirit in way of emulation or complaisance; and by seasoning matters, otherwise distasteful or insipid, with an unusual and thence grateful tang.'

days which are foretold in Scripture, when the lion shall lie down with the kid.[1]

After this day there was another pretty long interval, during which Dr. Johnson and I did not meet. When I mentioned it to him with regret, he was pleased to say, 'Then, Sir, let us live double.'

About this time it was much the fashion for several ladies to have evening assemblies, where the fair sex might participate in conversation with literary and ingenious men, animated by a desire to please. These societies were denominated *Blue-stocking Clubs*, the origin of which title being little known, it may be worth while to relate it. One of the most eminent members of those societies, when they first commenced, was Mr. Stillingfleet,[2] whose dress was remarkably grave, and in particular it was observed, that he wore blue stockings. Such was the excellence of his conversation, that his absence was felt as so great a loss, that it used to be said, 'We can do nothing without the *blue-stockings;*' and thus by degrees the title was established. Miss Hannah More has admirably described a *Blue-stocking Club*, in her '*Bas Bleu*,' a poem in which many of the persons who were most conspicuous there are mentioned.[a]

[a] *& which Dr. Johnson commended exceedingly.* [H]

Johnson was prevailed with to come sometimes into these circles, and did not think himself too grave even for the lively Miss Monckton (now Countess of Corke) who used to have the finest *bit of blue* at the house of her mother, Lady Galway. Her vivacity enchanted the Sage, and they used to talk together with all imaginable ease. A singular instance happened one evening, when she insisted that some of Sterne's writings were very pathetick. Johnson bluntly denied it. 'I am sure (said she) they have affected me.'—'Why (said Johnson, smiling, and rolling himself about,) that is, because, dearest, you're a dunce.' When she sometime afterwards mentioned this to him, he said with equal truth and politeness; 'Madam, if I had thought so, I certainly should not have said it.'

queried:
Why (said *Johnson* etc. [H]

marginal line:
politeness; 'Madam . . . I certainly [H]

Another evening Johnson's kind indulgence towards me

---

[1] When I mentioned this to the Bishop of Killaloe, 'With the *goat*,' said his Lordship. Such, however, was the engaging politeness and pleasantry of Mr. Wilkes, and such the social good humour of the Bishop, that when they dined together at Mr. Dilly's, where I also was, they were mutually agreeable.

[2] Mr. Benjamin Stillingfleet, authour of tracts relating to natural history, &c.

had a pretty difficult trial. I had dined at the Duke of
Montrose's with a very agreeable party, and his Grace,
according to his usual custom, had circulated the bottle
very freely. Lord Graham and I went together to Miss
Monckton's, where I certainly was in extraordinary spirits,
and above all fear or awe. In the midst of a great number
of persons of the first rank, amongst whom I recollect with
confusion, a noble lady of the most stately decorum, I
placed myself next to Johnson, and thinking myself now
fully his match, talked to him in a loud and boisterous
manner, desirous to let the company know how I could
contend with *Ajax*. I particularly remember pressing him
upon the value of the pleasures of the imagination, and as
an illustration of my argument, asking him, 'What, Sir,
supposing I were to fancy that the ——[a] (naming the most
charming Duchess in his Majesty's dominions) were in
love with me, should I not be very happy?' My friend with
much address, evaded my interrogatories, and kept me as
quiet as possible; but it may easily be conceived how he
must have felt.[1] However, when a few days afterwards I

[a] *Duchess of Devon-
shire* [H & I]

two marginal lines:
*kept me . . . However,
when* [H]

---

[1] Next day I endeavoured to give what had happened the most ingenious
turn I could, by the following verses:

TO THE HONOURABLE MISS MONCKTON

Not that with th' excellent Montrose
   I had the happiness to dine;
Not that I late from table rose,
   From Graham's wit, from generous wine.

It was not these alone which led
   On sacred manners to encroach:
And made me feel what most I dread,
   JOHNSON's just frown, and self-reproach.

But when I enter'd, not abash'd,
   From your bright eyes were shot such rays,
At once intoxication flash'd
   And all my frame was in a blaze!

But not a brilliant blaze I own,
   Of the dull smoke I'm yet asham'd;
I was a dreary ruin grown,
   And not enlighten'd though inflam'd.

Victim at once to wine and love,
   I hope, MARIA, you'll forgive;
While I invoke the powers above,
   That henceforth I may wiser live.

The lady was generously forgiving, returned me an obliging answer, and
I thus obtained an *Act of Oblivion*, and took care never to offend again.

waited upon him and made an apology, he behaved with the most friendly gentleness.

While I remained in London this year, Johnson and I dined together at several places. I recollect a placid day at Dr. Butter's, who had now removed from Derby to Lower Grosvenor-street, London; but of his conversation on that and other occasions during this period, I neglected to keep any regular record, and shall therefore insert here some miscellaneous articles which I find in my Johnsonian notes.

His disorderly habits, when 'making provision for the day that was passing over him,' appear from the following anecdote, communicated to me by Mr. John Nichols:—'In the year 1763, a young bookseller, who was an apprentice to Mr. Whiston, waited on him with a subscription to his "Shakspeare:" and observing that the Doctor made no entry in any book of the subscriber's name, ventured diffidently to ask, whether he would please to have the gentleman's address, that it might be properly inserted in the printed list of subscribers.—"*I shall print no List of Subscribers;*" said Johnson, with great abruptness; but almost immediately recollecting himself, added, very complacently, "Sir, I have two very cogent reasons for not printing any list of subscribers;—one, that I have lost all the names,—the other, that I have spent all the money."'

marginal line:
that I . . . the money [H]

Johnson could not brook appearing to be worsted in argument, even when he had taken the wrong side, to shew the force and dexterity of his talents. When, therefore, he perceived that his opponent gained ground, he had recourse to some sudden mode of robust sophistry. Once when I was pressing upon him with visible advantage, he stopped me thus:—'My dear Boswell, let's have no more of this; you'll make nothing of it. I'd rather have you whistle a Scotch tune.'

marginal line:
Care, however . . . and illustrate [H]

Care, however, must be taken to distinguish between Johnson when he 'talked for victory,' and Johnson when he had no desire but to inform and illustrate.—'One of Johnson's principal talents (says an eminent friend of his)[1] was shewn in maintaining the wrong side of an argument, and in a splendid perversion of the truth.—If you could

[1][The late Right Hon. William Gerrard Hamilton. MALONE.]

contrive to have his fair opinion on a subject, and without
any bias from personal prejudice, or from a wish to be
victorious in argument, it was wisdom itself, not only
convincing, but overpowering.'

He had, however, all his life habituated himself to
consider conversation as a trial of intellectual vigour
and skill: and to this, I think, we may venture to ascribe
that unexampled richness and brilliancy which appeared
in his own. As a proof at once of his eagerness for colloquial
distinction, and his high notion of this eminent friend, he
once addressed him thus: '——, we now have been several
hours together; and you have said but one thing for which
I envied you.'

He disliked much all speculative desponding considerations, which tended to discourage men from diligence and
exertion. He was in this like Dr. Shaw, the great traveller,
who Mr. Daines Barrington told me, used to say, 'I hate a
cui bono man.'[a] Upon being asked by a friend what he
should think of a man who was apt to say *non est tanti;* —
'That he's a stupid fellow, Sir, (answered Johnson): What
would these *tanti* men be doing the while?' When I in a
low-spirited fit, was talking to him with indifference of the
pursuits which generally engage us in a course of action,
and enquiring a *reason* for taking so much trouble; 'Sir,
(said he, in an animated tone) it is driving on the system
of life.'

He told me, that he was glad that I had, by General
Oglethorpe's means, become acquainted with Dr. Shebbeare. Indeed that gentleman, whatever objections were
made to him, had knowledge and abilities much above the
class of ordinary writers, and deserves to be remembered
as a respectable name in literature, were it only for his
admirable 'Letters on the English Nation,' under the
name of 'Battista Angeloni, a Jesuit.'

Johnson and Shebbeare[1] were frequently named together, as having in former reigns had no predilection for
the family of Hanover. The authour of the celebrated
'Heroick Epistle to Sir William Chambers,' introduces
them in one line, in a list of those 'who tasted the sweets

---

[1] I recollect a ludicrous paragraph in the news-papers, that the King had
pensioned both a *He*-bear and a *She*-bear.

marginal line:
*bias from . . . but over-
powering* [H]

[a] *so do I.* [I]

marginal line:
footnote 1 [H]

of his present Majesty's reign.' Such was Johnson's candid
relish of the merit of that satire, that he allowed Dr.
Goldsmith, as he told me, to read it to him from beginning
to end, and did not refuse his praise to its execution.

Goldsmith could sometimes take adventurous liberties
with him, and escape unpunished. Beauclerk told me, that
when Goldsmith talked of a project for having a third
Theatre in London solely for the exhibition of new plays,
in order to deliver authours from the supposed tyranny of
managers, Johnson treated it slightingly, upon which
Goldsmith said, 'Ay, ay, this may be nothing to you, who
can now shelter yourself behind the corner of a pension;'
and Johnson bore this with good-humour.

Johnson praised the Earl of Carlisle's Poems, which his
Lordship had published with his name, as not disdaining
to be a candidate for literary fame. My friend was of
opinion, that when a man of rank appeared in that
character, he deserved to have his merit handsomely
allowed.[1] In this I think he was more liberal than Mr.
William Whitehead, in his 'Elegy to Lord Villiers,' in
which, under the pretext of 'superiour toils, demanding all

---

[1] Men of rank and fortune, however, should be pretty well assured of
having a real claim to the approbation of the publick, as writers, before they
venture to stand forth. Dryden in his preface to 'All for Love,' thus expresses
himself:

'Men of pleasant conversation (at least esteemed so) and endued with a
trifling kind of fancy, perhaps helped out by a smattering of Latin, are
ambitious to distinguish themselves from the herd of gentlemen, by their
poetry:
             "*Rarus enim fermè sensus communis in illa
             Fortuna.*"———

And is not this a wretched affectation, not to be contented with what fortune
has done for them, and sit down quietly with their estates, but they must call
their wits in question, and needlessly expose their nakedness to publick view?
Not considering that they are not to expect the same approbation from sober
men, which they have found from their flatterers after the third bottle. If a
little glittering in discourse has passed them on us for witty men, where was
the necessity of undeceiving the world? Would a man, who has an ill title to
an estate, but yet is in possession of it, would he bring it out of his own accord
to be tried at Westminster? We who write, if we want the talents, yet have
the excuse that we do it for a poor subsistence; but what can be urged in
their defence, who, not having the vocation of poverty to scribble, out of
mere wantonness take pains to make themselves ridiculous? Horace was
certainly in the right where he said, "That no man is satisfied with his own
condition." A Poet is not pleased, because he is not rich; and the rich are
discontented because the poets will not admit them of their number.'

their care,' he discovers a jealousy of the great paying their court to the Muses:

'———— to the chosen few
    Who dare excel, thy fost'ring aid afford,
Their arts, their magick powers, with honours due
Exalt;—but be thyself what they record.'

Johnson had called twice on the Bishop of Killaloe before his Lordship set out for Ireland, having missed him the first time. He said, 'It would have hung heavy on my heart if I had not seen him. No man ever paid more attention to another than he has done to me;[1] and I have neglected him,[a] not wilfully, but from being otherwise occupied. Always, Sir, set a high value on spontaneous kindness. He whose inclination prompts him to cultivate your friendship of his own accord, will love you more than one whom you have been at pains to attach to you.'

a *The Charade on his name is Johnson's.* [1]
marginal line: *from being . . . whose inclination* [H]
index sign: *He whose inclination* etc. [H]

Johnson told me, that he was once much pleased to find that a carpenter, who lived near him, was very ready to shew him some things in his business which he wished to see: 'It was paying (said he) respect to literature.'

I asked him, if he was not dissatisfied with having so small a share of wealth, and none of those distinctions in the state which are the objects of ambition. He had only a pension of three hundred a year. Why was he not in such circumstances as to keep his coach? Why had he not some considerable office? JOHNSON. 'Sir, I have never complained of the world; nor do I think that I have reason to

---

[1] This gave me very great pleasure, for there had been once a pretty smart altercation between Dr. Barnard and him, upon a question, whether a man could improve himself after the age of forty-five;[b] when Johnson in a hasty humour, expressed himself in a manner not quite civil. Dr. Barnard made it the subject of a copy of pleasant verses, in which he supposed himself to learn different perfections from different men. They concluded with delicate irony:

b *why You are 45 Yourself — and may surely improve quoth Johnson.* [1]

'Johnson shall teach me how to place
In fairest light each borrow'd grace;
    From him I'll learn to write:
Copy his clear familiar style,
And by the roughness of his file
    Grow, like *himself, polite*.'

underlined: *clear familiar* [1]

I know not whether Johnson ever saw the Poem, but I had occasion to find that as Dr. Barnard and he knew each other better, their mutual regard increased.

complain. It is rather to be wondered at that I have so much. My pension is more out of the usual course of things than any instance that I have known. Here, Sir, was a man avowedly no friend to Government at the time, who got a pension without asking for it. I never courted the great; they sent for me; but I think they now give me up. They are satisfied: they have seen enough of me.' Upon my observing that I could not believe this; for they must certainly be highly pleased by his conversation; conscious of his own superiority, he answered, 'No, Sir; great Lords and great Ladies don't love to have their mouths stopped.' This was very expressive of the effect which the force of his understanding and brilliancy of his fancy could not but produce; and, to be sure, they must have found themselves strangely diminished in his company. When I warmly declared how happy I was at all times to hear him;—'Yes, Sir, (said he); but if you were Lord Chancellor, it would not be so: you would then consider your own dignity.'

There was much truth and knowledge of human nature in this remark. But certainly one should think, that in whatever elevated state of life a man who *knew* the value of the conversation of Johnson might be placed, though he might prudently avoid a situation in which he might appear lessened by comparison; yet he would frequently gratify himself in private with the participation of the rich intellectual entertainment which Johnson could furnish. Strange, however, is it, to consider how few of the great sought his society; so that if one were disposed to take occasion for satire on that account, very conspicuous objects present themselves. His noble friend, Lord Elibank, well observed, that if a great man procured an interview with Johnson, and did not wish to see him more, it shewed a mere idle curiosity, and a wretched want of relish for extraordinary powers of mind. Mrs. Thrale justly and wittily accounted for such conduct by saying, that Johnson's conversation was by much too strong for a person accustomed to obsequiousness and flattery; it was *mustard in a young child's mouth!*

One day, when I told him that I was a zealous Tory, but not enough 'according to knowledge,' and should be obliged to him for 'a reason,' he was so candid, and

marginal line:
to be . . . warmly declared [H]

two marginal lines:
Chancellor, it . . . own dignity [H]

index sign:
Mrs. Thrale etc. [I]

expressed himself so well, that I begged of him to repeat what he had said, and I wrote down as follows:

OF TORY AND WHIG

'A wise Tory and a wise Whig, I believe, will agree. Their principles are the same, though their modes of thinking are different. A high Tory makes government unintelligible: it is lost in the clouds. A violent Whig makes it impracticable: he is for allowing so much liberty to every man, that there is not power enough to govern any man. The prejudice of the Tory is for establishment; the prejudice of the Whig is for innovation. A Tory does not wish to give more real power to Government; but that Government should have more reverence. Then they differ as to the church. The Tory is not for giving more legal power to the Clergy, but wishes they should have a considerable influence, founded on the opinion of mankind: the Whig is for limiting and watching them with a narrow jealousy.'

'TO MR. PERKINS
'SIR,

'However often I have seen you, I have hitherto forgotten the note, but I have now sent it: with my good wishes for the prosperity of you and your partner,[1] of whom, from our short conversation, I could not judge otherwise than favourably.

'I am, Sir,
'Your most humble servant,

'June 2, 1781.'   'SAM. JOHNSON'

On Saturday, June 2, I set out for Scotland, and had promised to pay a visit, in my way, as I sometimes did, at Southill, in Bedfordshire, at the hospitable mansion of 'Squire Dilly, the elder brother of my worthy friends, the booksellers, in the Poultry. Dr. Johnson agreed to be of the party this year, with Mr. Charles Dilly and me, and to go

[1] Mr. Barclay, a descendant of Robert Barclay, of Ury, the celebrated apologist of the people called Quakers, and remarkable for maintaining the principles of his venerable progenitor, with as much of the elegance of modern manners, as is consistent with primitive simplicity.

and see Lord Bute's seat at Luton Hoe. He talked little to us in the carriage, being chiefly occupied in reading Dr. Watson's[1] second volume of 'Chemical Essays,' which he liked very well, and his own 'Prince of Abyssinia,' on which he seemed to be intensely fixed; having told us, that he had not looked at it since it was first finished. I happened to take it out of my pocket this day, and he seized upon it with avidity. He pointed out to me the following remarkable passage: 'By what means (said the prince) are the Europeans thus powerful; or why, since they can so easily visit Asia and Africa for trade or conquest, cannot the Asiaticks and Africans invade their coasts, plant colonies[2] in their ports, and give laws to their natural princes? The same wind that carried them back would bring us thither.' —'They are more powerful, Sir, than we, (answered Imlac,) because they are wiser. Knowledge will always predominate over ignorance, as man governs the other animals. But why their knowledge is more than ours, I know not what reason can be given,[a] but the unsearchable will of the Supreme Being.' He said, 'This, Sir, no man can explain otherwise.'

a They are only wiser now. The Egyptians & the Phonicians were wise once when Gauls and Britons were in a State of Savage Nature. As the Earth rolls round, one Side will get into Opacity; whilst the other Side is shone upon. [1]

We stopped at Welwin, where I wished much to see, in company with Johnson, the residence of the author of 'Night Thoughts,' which was then possessed by his son, Mr. Young. Here some address was requisite, for I was not acquainted with Mr. Young, and had I proposed to Dr. Johnson that we should send to him, he would have checked my wish, and perhaps been offended. I therefore concerted with Mr. Dilly, that I should steal away from Dr. Johnson and him, and try what reception I could procure from Mr. Young; if unfavourable, nothing was to be said; but if agreeable, I should return and notify it to them. I hastened to Mr. Young's, found he was at home, sent in word that a gentleman desired to wait upon him,

---

[1] Now Bishop of Llandaff, one of the *poorest* Bishoprics in this Kingdom. His Lordship has written with much zeal to shew the propriety of *equalizing* the revenues of Bishops. He has informed us that he has burnt all his Chemical papers. The friends of our excellent constitution, now assailed on every side, by innovators and levellers, would have less regretted the suppression of some of his Lordship's other writings.

[2] [The Phœnicians and Carthaginians *did* plant colonies in Europe. KEARNEY.]

and was shewn into a parlour, where he and a young
lady, his daughter, were sitting. He appeared to be a
plain, civil, country gentleman; and when I begged pardon for presuming to trouble him, but that I wished much
to see his place, if he would give me leave; he behaved
very courteously, and answered, 'By all means, Sir; we
are just going to drink tea; will you sit down?' I thanked
him, but said, that Dr. Johnson had come with me from
London, and I must return to the inn to drink tea with
him; that my name was Boswell, I had travelled with him
in the Hebrides. 'Sir, (said he,) I should think it a great
honour to see Dr. Johnson here. Will you allow me to send
for him?' Availing myself of this opening, I said that 'I
would go myself and bring him, when he had drunk tea;
he knew nothing of my calling here.' Having been thus
successful, I hastened back to the inn, and informed Dr.
Johnson that 'Mr. Young, son of Dr. Young, the author
of "Night Thoughts," whom I had just left, desired to
have the honour of seeing him at the house where his
father lived.' Dr. Johnson luckily made no enquiry how
this invitation had arisen, but agreed to go, and when we
entered Mr. Young's parlour, he addressed him with a
very polite bow, 'Sir, I had a curiosity to come and see
this place. I had the honour to know that great man, your
father.'[a] We went into the garden, where he found a gravel
walk, on each side of which was a row of trees, planted by
Dr. Young, which formed a handsome Gothick arch; Dr.
Johnson called it a fine grove. I beheld it with reverence.

 We sat some time in the summer-house, on the outside
wall of which was inscribed, '*Ambulantes in horto audiebant
vocem Dei;*' and in reference to a brook by which it is
situated, '*Vivendi rectè qui prorogat horam,*' &c. I said to Mr.
Young, that I had been told his father was cheerful. 'Sir,
(said he) he was too well-bred a man not to be cheerful in
company; but he was gloomy when alone. He never was
cheerful after my mother's death, and he had met with
many disappointments.' Dr. Johnson observed to me
afterwards, 'That this was no favourable account of Dr.
Young; for it is not becoming in a man to have so little
acquiescence in the ways of Providence, as to be gloomy
because he has not obtained as much preferment as he

marginal mark:
father [H]

[a] *a parent that he—
the Young Man, hated.
Addison & Young
knew too much of Life
to be favourites with
Their Families.* [H]

expected; nor to continue gloomy for the loss of his wife. Grief has its time.' The last part of this censure was theoretically made. Practically, we know that grief for the loss of a wife may be continued very long, in proportion as affection has been sincere. No man knew this better than Dr. Johnson.

We went into the church, and looked at the monument erected by Mr. Young to his father. Mr. Young mentioned an anecdote, that his father had received several thousand pounds of subscription-money for his 'Universal Passion,' but had lost it in the South-Sea.[1] Dr. Johnson thought this must be a mistake; for he had never seen a subscription-book.

Upon the road we talked of the uncertainty of profit with which authours and booksellers engage in the publication of literary works. JOHNSON. 'My judgement I have found is no certain rule as to the sale of a book.' BOSWELL. 'Pray, Sir, have you been much plagued with authours sending you their works to revise?' JOHNSON. 'No, Sir; I have been thought a sour surly fellow.' BOSWELL. 'Very lucky for you, Sir,—in that respect.' I must however observe, that notwithstanding what he now said, which he no doubt imagined at the time to be the fact, there was, perhaps, no man who more frequently yielded to the solicitations even of very obscure authours, to read their manuscripts, or more liberally assisted them with advice and correction.

He found himself very happy at 'Squire Dilly's, where there is always abundance of excellent fare, and hearty welcome.

On Sunday, June 3, we all went to Southill church, which is very near to Mr. Dilly's house. It being the first Sunday of the month, the holy sacrament was administered, and I staid to partake of it. When I came afterwards into Dr. Johnson's room, he said, 'You did right to stay and receive the communion; I had not thought of it.' This seemed to imply that he did not choose to approach the altar without a previous preparation, as

ᵃ *You see the Man ever traducing his Father.* [H]

¹ [This assertion is disproved by a comparison of dates.ᵃ The first four satires of Young were published in 1725; The South-sea scheme (which appears to be meant,) was in 1720. MALONE.]

to which good men entertain different opinions, some holding that it is irreverent to partake of that ordinance without considerable premeditation; others, that whoever is a sincere Christian, and in a proper frame of mind to discharge any other ritual duty of our religion, may, without scruple, discharge this most solemn one. A middle notion I believe to be the just one, which is, that communicants need not think a long train of preparatory forms indispensably necessary; but neither should they rashly and lightly venture upon so awful and mysterious an institution. Christians must judge, each for himself, what degree of retirement and self-examination is necessary upon each ocasion.

Being in a frame of mind which, I hope for the felicity of human nature, many experience,—in fine weather,—at the country-house of a friend,—consoled and elevated by pious exercises,—I expressed myself with an unrestrained fervour to my 'Guide, Philosopher, and Friend;' 'My dear Sir, I would fain be a good man; and I am very good now. I fear GOD, and honour the King; I wish to do no ill, and to be benevolent to all mankind.' He looked at me with a benignant indulgence; but took occasion to give me wise and salutary caution. 'Do not, Sir, accustom yourself to trust to *impressions*. There is a middle state of mind between conviction and hypocrisy, of which many are unconscious. By trusting to impressions, a man may gradually come to yield to them, and at length be subject to them, so as not to be a free agent, or what is the same thing in effect, to *suppose* that he is not a free agent. A man who is in that state, should not be suffered to live; if he declares he cannot help acting in a particular way, and is irresistibly impelled, there can be no confidence in him, no more than in a tyger. But, Sir, no man believes himself to be impelled irresistibly; we know that he who says he believes it, lies.[a] Favourable impressions at particular moments, as to the state of our souls, may be deceitful and dangerous. In general no man can be sure of his acceptance with GOD; some, indeed, may have had it revealed to them. St. Paul, who wrought miracles, may have had a miracle wrought on himself, and may have obtained supernatural assurance of pardon, and mercy, and beatitude;

[a] *True; & of late Years Two or three Murderers have pleaded irresistible Impulse. The Footman who killed Mr. & Mrs. Bonar: and another Fellow, who run o' Muck at a whole Family living if I remember rightly at Hoddesdon. There was another Man, but I have forgotten his History. 1820.* [H]

yet St. Paul, though he expresses strong hope, also expresses fear, lest having preached to others, he himself should be a cast-away.'

The opinion of a learned Bishop of our acquaintance, as to there being merit in religious faith, being mentioned;— JOHNSON. 'Why, yes, Sir, the most licentious man, were hell open before him, would not take the most beautiful strumpet to his arms. We must, as the Apostle says, live by faith, not by sight.'

I talked to him of original sin,[1] in consequence of the fall of man, and of the atonement made by our SAVIOUR. After some conversation, which he desired me to remember, he, at my request, dictated to me as follows:

'WITH respect to original sin, the enquiry is not necessary; for whatever is the cause of human corruption, men are evidently and confessedly so corrupt, that all the laws of heaven and earth are insufficient to restrain them from crimes.

'Whatever difficulty there may be in the conception of vicarious punishments, it is an opinion which has had possession of mankind in all ages. There is no nation that has not used the practice of sacrifices. Whoever, therefore, denies the propriety of vicarious punishments, holds an opinion which the sentiments and practice of mankind have contradicted, from the beginning of the world. The great sacrifice for the sins of mankind was offered at the death of the MESSIAH, who is called in scripture, "The Lamb of GOD, that taketh away the sins of the world." To judge of the reasonableness of the scheme of redemption, it must be considered as necessary to the government of the universe, that GOD should make known his perpetual and irreconcileable detestation of moral evil. He might indeed punish, and punish only the offenders; but as the

---

[1] Dr. Ogden, in his second sermon 'On the Articles of the Christian Faith,' with admirable acuteness thus addresses the opposers of that Doctrine, which accounts for the confusion, sin, and misery, which we find in this life: 'It would be severe in GOD, you think, to *degrade* us to such a sad state as this, for the offence of our first parents: but you can allow him to *place* us in it without any inducement. Are our calamities lessened for not being ascribed to Adam? If your condition be unhappy, is it not still unhappy, whatever was the occasion? with the aggravation of this reflection, that if it was as good as it was at first designed, there seems to be somewhat the less reason to look for its amendment.'

end of punishment is not revenge of crimes, but propagation of virtue, it was more becoming the Divine clemency to find another manner of proceeding, less destructive to man, and at least equally powerful to promote goodness. The end of punishment is to reclaim and warn. *That* punishment will both reclaim and warn, which shews evidently such abhorrence of sin in GOD, as may deter us from it, or strike us with dread of vengeance when we have committed it. This is effected by vicarious punishment. Nothing could more testify the opposition between the nature of GOD and moral evil, or more amply display his justice, to men and angels, to all orders and successions of beings, than that it was necessary for the highest and purest nature, even for DIVINITY itself, to pacify the demands of vengeance, by a painful death; of which the natural effect will be, that when justice is appeased, there is a proper place for the exercise of mercy; and that such propitiation shall supply, in some degree, the imperfections of our obedience, and the inefficacy of our repentance: for, obedience and repentance, such as we can perform, are still necessary. Our SAVIOUR has told us, that he did not come to destroy the law but to fulfill: to fulfill the typical law, by the performance of what those types had foreshewn; and the moral law, by precepts of greater purity and higher exaltation.'

[Here he said, 'GOD bless you with it.' I acknowledged myself much obliged to him; but I begged that he would go on as to the propitiation being the chief object of our most holy faith. He then dictated this one other paragraph.]

'The peculiar doctrine of Christianity is, that of an universal sacrifice, and perpetual propitiation. Other prophets only proclaimed the will and the threatenings of GOD. CHRIST satisfied his justice.'

The Reverend Mr. Palmer,[1] Fellow of Queen's College,

---

[1] This unfortunate person, whose full name was Thomas Fysche Palmer' afterwards went to Dundee, in Scotland, where he officiated as minister to a congregation of the sect who call themselves *Unitarians*, from a notion that they distinctively worship one GOD, because they *deny* the mysterious doctrine of the TRINITY. They do not advert that the great body of the Christian Church in maintaining that mystery, maintain also the

Cambridge, dined with us. He expressed a wish that a better provision were made for parish-clerks. JOHNSON. 'Yes, Sir, a parish-clerk should be a man who is able to make a will, or write a letter for any body in the parish.'

I mentioned Lord Monboddo's notion[1] that the ancient Egyptians, with all their learning, and all their arts, were not only black, but woolly-haired. Mr. Palmer asked how did it appear upon examining the mummies? Dr. Johnson approved of this test.

Although upon most occasions I never heard a more strenuous advocate for the advantages of wealth, than Dr. Johnson, he this day, I know not from what caprice, took the other side. 'I have not observed (said he) that men of very large fortunes enjoy any thing extraordinary that makes happiness. What has the Duke of Bedford? What has the Duke of Devonshire? The only great instance that I have ever known of the enjoyment of wealth was that of Jamaica Dawkins, who, going to visit Palmyra, and hearing that the way was infested by robbers, hired a troop of Turkish horse to guard him.'

Dr. Gibbons, the Dissenting minister, being mentioned, he said, 'I took to Dr. Gibbons.' And addressing himself to Mr. Charles Dilly, added, 'I shall be glad to see him. Tell him, if he'll call on me, and dawdle over a dish of tea in an afternoon, I shall take it kind.'

The Reverend Mr. Smith, Vicar of Southill, a very respectable man, with a very agreeable family, sent an invitation to us to drink tea. I remarked Dr. Johnson's very respectful politeness. Though always fond of changing

Unity of the GODHEAD: the 'TRINITY in UNITY!—three persons and ONE GOD.' The Church humbly adores the DIVINITY as exhibited in the holy Scriptures. The Unitarian sect vainly presumes to comprehend and define the ALMIGHTY. Mr. Palmer having heated his mind with political speculations, became so much dissatisfied with our excellent Constitution, as to compose, publish, and circulate writings, which were found to be so seditious and dangerous, that upon being found guilty by a Jury, the Court of Justiciary in Scotland sentenced him to transportation for fourteen years. A loud clamour against this sentence was made by some Members of both Houses of Parliament; but both Houses approved of it by a great majority; and he was conveyed to the settlement for convicts in New South Wales.

[Mr. T. F. Palmer was of Queen's College, in Cambridge, where he took the degree of Master of Arts in 1772, and that of S. T. B. in 1781. He died on his return from Botany Bay, in the year 1803.[a] MALONE.]

[1] Taken from Herodotus.

[a] *When Margarot came home safe; & his old Cat which he took out to Exile with him. I know not who told me the Cat recognized her original Habitation.* [H]

the scene, he said, 'We must have Mr. Dilly's leave. We cannot go from your house, Sir, without your permission.' We all went, and were well satisfied with our visit. I however remember nothing particular, except a nice distinction which Dr. Johnson made with respect to the power of memory, maintaining that forgetfulness was a man's own fault. 'To remember and to recollect (said he) are different things. A man has not the power to recollect what is not in his mind; but when a thing is in his mind he may remember it.'

The remark was occasioned by my leaning back on a chair, which a little before I had perceived to be broken, and pleading forgetfulness as an excuse. 'Sir, (said he,) its being broken was certainly in your mind.'

When I observed that a housebreaker was in general very timorous;—JOHNSON. 'No wonder, Sir; he is afraid of being shot getting *into* a house, or hanged when he has got *out* of it.'[a]

He told us, that he had in one day written six sheets of a translation from the French; adding, 'I should be glad to see it now. I wish that I had copies of all the pamphlets written against me, as it is said Pope had. Had I known that I should make so much noise in the world, I should have been at pains to collect them. I believe there is hardly a day in which there is not something about me in the news-papers.'

On Monday, June 4, we all went to Luton-Hoe, to see Lord Bute's magnificent seat, for which I had obtained a ticket. As we entered the park, I talked in a high style of my old friendship with Lord Mountstuart, and said, 'I shall probably be much at this place.' The Sage, aware of human vicissitudes, gently checked me: 'Don't you be too sure of that.' He made two or three peculiar observations; as when shewn the botanical garden, 'Is not *every* garden a botanical garden?' When told that there was a shrubbery to the extent of several miles; 'That is making a very foolish use of the ground; a little of it is very well.' When it was proposed that we should walk on the pleasure-ground; 'Don't let us fatigue ourselves. Why should we walk there? Here's a fine tree, let's get to the top of it.' But upon the whole, he was very much pleased. He said, 'This

[a] *Comical enough* [H]

is one of the places I do not regret having come to see. It is a very stately place, indeed; in the house magnificence is not sacrificed to convenience, nor convenience to magnificence. The library is very splendid; the dignity of the rooms is very great; and the quantity of pictures is beyond expectation, beyond hope.'

It happened without any previous concert, that we visited the seat of Lord Bute upon the King's birthday; we dined and drank his Majesty's health at an inn, in the village of Luton.

In the evening I put him in mind of his promise to favour me with a copy of his celebrated Letter to the Earl of Chesterfield, and he was at last pleased to comply with this earnest request, by dictating it to me from his memory; for he believed that he himself had no copy. There was an animated glow in his countenance while he thus recalled his high-minded indignation.

He laughed heartily at a ludicrous action in the Court of Session, in which I was Counsel. The Society of *Procurators*, or Attornies, entitled to practise in the inferiour courts at Edinburgh, had obtained a royal charter, in which they had taken care to have their ancient designation of *Procurators* changed into that of *Solicitors*, from a notion, as they supposed, that it was more *genteel;* and this new title they displayed by a publick advertisement for a *General Meeting* at their HALL.

It has been said, that the Scottish nation is not distinguished for humour; and, indeed, what happened on this occasion may in some degree justify the remark; for although this society had contrived to make themselves a very prominent object for the ridicule of such as might stoop to it, the only joke to which it gave rise, was the following paragraph, sent to the news-paper called ' *The Caledonian Mercury.*'

' A correspondent informs us, that the Worshipful Society of *Chaldeans, Cadies,* or *Running-Stationers* of this city are resolved, in imitation, and encouraged by the singular success of their brethren, of an *equally respectable* Society, to apply for a Charter of their Privileges, particularly of the sole privilege of PROCURING, in the most extensive sense of the word, exclusive of chairmen, porters, penny-post men, and other *inferiour* ranks; their brethren the R—y—l S—ll—rs, *alias* P—c—rs, *before the* INFERIOUR Courts of this City, always excepted.

'Should the Worshipful Society be successful, they are farther resolved not to be *puffed up* thereby, but to demean themselves with more equanimity and decency than their *R-y-l, learned,* and *very modest* brethren above mentioned have done, upon their late dignification and exaltation.'

A majority of the members of the Society prosecuted Mr. Robertson, the publisher of the paper, for damages; and the first judgement of the whole Court very wisely dismissed the action: *Solventur risu tabulæ, tu missus abibis.* But a new trial or review was granted upon a petition, according to the forms in Scotland. This petition I was engaged to answer, and Dr. Johnson, with great alacrity furnished me this evening with what follows:

'All injury is either of the person, the fortune, or the fame. Now it is a certain thing, it is proverbially known, that *a jest breaks no bones.* They never have gained half-a-crown less in the whole profession since this mischievous paragraph has appeared; and, as to their reputation, What is their reputation but an instrument of getting money? If, therefore, they have lost no money, the question upon reputation may be answered by a very old position, — *De minimis non curat Prætor.*

'Whether there was, or was not, an *animus injuriandi*, is not worth enquiring, if no *injuria* can be proved. But the truth is, there was no *animus injuriandi.* It was only an *animus irritandi*,[1] which, happening to be exercised upon a *genus irritabile*, produced unexpected violence of resentment. Their irritability arose only from an opinion of their own importance, and their delight in their new exaltation. What might have been borne by a *Procurator*, could not be borne by a *Solicitor.* Your Lordships well know, that *honores mutant mores.* Titles and dignities play strongly on the fancy. As a madman is apt to think himself grown suddenly great, so he that grows suddenly great is apt to borrow a little from the madman. To co-operate with their resentment would be to promote their phrenzy; nor is it

---

[1] Mr. Robertson altered his word to *jocandi*, he having found in Blackstone that to *irritate* is actionable.

possible to guess to what they might proceed, if to the new title of Solicitor should be added the elation of victory and triumph.

'We consider your Lordships as the protectors of our rights, and the guardians of our virtues; but believe it not included in your high office, that you should flatter our vices, or solace our vanity; and, as vanity only dictates this prosecution, it is humbly hoped your Lordships will dismiss it.

'If every attempt, however light or ludicrous, to lessen another's reputation, is to be punished by a judicial sentence, what punishment can be sufficiently severe for him who attempts to diminish the reputation of the Supreme Court of Justice, by reclaiming upon a cause already determined, without any change in the state of the question? Does it not imply hopes that the Judges will change their opinion? Is not uncertainty and inconstancy in the highest degree disreputable to a Court? Does it not suppose, that the former judgement was temerarious or negligent? Does it not lessen the confidence of the publick? Will it not be said, that *jus est aut incognitum, aut vagum?* and will not the consequence be drawn, *misera est servitus?* Will not the rules of action be obscure? Will not he who knows himself wrong to-day, hope that the Courts of Justice will think him right to-morrow? Surely, my Lords, these are attempts of dangerous tendency, which the Solicitors, as men versed in the law, should have foreseen and avoided. It was natural for an ignorant printer to appeal from the Lord Ordinary; but from lawyers, the descendants of lawyers, who have practised for three hundred years, and have now raised themselves to a higher denomination, it might be expected, that they should know the reverence due to a judicial determination; and, having been once dismissed, should sit down in silence.'

I am ashamed to mention, that the Court, by a plurality of voices, without having a single additional circumstance before them, reversed their own judgement, made a serious matter of this dull and foolish joke, and adjudged Mr. Robertson to pay to the Society five pounds (sterling money) and costs of suit. The decision will seem strange to English lawyers.

On Tuesday, June 5, Johnson was to return to London. He was very pleasant at breakfast; I mentioned a friend of mine having resolved never to marry a pretty woman. JOHNSON. 'Sir, it is a very foolish resolution to resolve not to marry a pretty woman. Beauty is of itself very estimable. No, Sir, I would prefer a pretty woman, unless there are objections to her. A pretty woman may be foolish; a pretty woman may be wicked; a pretty woman may not like me. But there is no such danger in marrying a pretty woman as is apprehended; she will not be persecuted if she does not invite persecution. A pretty woman, if she has a mind to be wicked, can find a readier way than another; and that is all.'

I accompanied him in Mr. Dilly's chaise to Shefford, where talking of Lord Bute's never going to Scotland, he said, 'As an Englishman, I should wish all the Scotch gentlemen should be educated in England; Scotland would become a province; they would spend all their rents in England.' This is a subject of much consequence, and much delicacy. The advantage of an English education is unquestionably very great to Scotch gentlemen of talents and ambition; and regular visits to Scotland, and perhaps other means, might be effectually used to prevent them from being totally estranged from their native country, any more than a Cumberland or Northumberland gentleman, who has been educated in the South of England. I own, indeed, that it is no small misfortune for Scotch gentlemen, who have neither talents nor ambition, to be educated in England, where they may be perhaps distinguished only by a nick-name, lavish their fortune in giving expensive entertainments to those who laugh at them, and saunter about as mere idle insignificant hangers-on even upon the foolish great; when, if they had been judiciously brought up at home, they might have been comfortable and creditable members of society.

At Shefford I had another affectionate parting from my revered friend, who was taken up by the Bedford coach and carried to the metropolis. I went with Messieurs Dilly to see some friends at Bedford; dined with the officers of the militia of the county, and next day proceeded on my journey.

'TO BENNET LANGTON, ESQ.

'DEAR SIR,

'How welcome your account of yourself and your
invitation to your new house was to me, I need not tell
you, who consider our friendship not only as formed by
choice, but as matured by time. We have been now long
enough acquainted to have many images in common,
and therefore to have a source of conversation which
neither the learning nor the wit of a new companion
can supply.

'My Lives are now published; and if you will tell me
whither I shall send them, that they may come to you,
I will take care that you shall not be without them.

index sign:
You will etc. [1]

'You will, perhaps, be glad to hear, that Mrs. Thrale

ᵃ *I suppose he was*
neither glad nor sorry.
[H]

is disincumbered of her brewhouse;ᵃ and that it seemed to
the purchaser so far from an evil, that he was content to
give for it an hundred and thirty-five thousand pounds.
Is the nation ruined?

'Please to make my respectful compliments to Lady
Rothes, and keep me in the memory of all the little dear
family, particularly Mrs. Jane.

'I am, Sir,
'Your affectionate humble servant,

'Bolt-court, June 16, 1781.'   'SAM. JOHNSON'

Johnson's charity to the poor was uniform and extensive,
both from inclination and principle. He not only bestowed
liberally out of his own purse, but what is more difficult as
well as rare, would beg from others, when he had proper
objects in view. This he did judiciously as well as humanely.
Mr. Philip Metcalfe tells me, that when he has asked him
for some money for persons in distress, and Mr. Metcalfe
has offered what Johnson thought too much, he insisted
on taking less, saying 'No, no, Sir; we must not *pamper*
them.'

I am indebted to Mr. Malone, one of Sir Joshua
Reynolds's executors, for the following note, which was
found among his papers after his death, and which, we
may presume, his unaffected modesty prevented him

from communicating to me with the other letters from
Dr. Johnson with which he was pleased to furnish me.
However slight in itself, as it does honour to that
illustrious painter, and most amiable man, I am happy
to introduce it.

'TO SIR JOSHUA REYNOLDS

'DEAR SIR,

'IT was not before yesterday that I received your
splendid benefaction. To a hand so liberal in distributing,
I hope nobody will envy the power of acquiring. I am,
dear Sir,

'Your obliged and most humble servant,

'June 23, 1781.'   'SAM. JOHNSON'[1]

'TO THOMAS ASTLE, ESQ.

'SIR,

'I AM ashamed that you have been forced to call so
often for your books, but it has been by no fault on either
side. They have never been out of my hands, nor have I
ever been at home without seeing you; for to see a man so
skilful in the antiquities of my country, is an opportunity
of improvement not willingly to be missed.

[1] [The following Letter was written at this time by Johnson, on receiving
from Mrs. Reynolds, sister to Sir Joshua Reynolds, a copy of her 'Essay on
Taste,' privately printed, but never published.

'TO MRS. FRANCES REYNOLDS

'DEAREST MADAM,

'There is in these [f. pages, or remarks,] such depth of penetration, such
nicety of observation, as Locke or Pascal might be proud of. This I desire
you to believe is my real opinion.

'However, it cannot be published in its present state. Many of your
notions seem not to be very clear in your own mind; many are not sufficiently
developed and expanded for the common reader: it wants every where to
be made smoother and plainer.

'You may by revisal and correction make it a very elegant and a very
curious work.   'I am, my dearest dear,

'Your affectionate and obedient servant,

'Bolt-court, June 28, 1781.'   'SAMUEL JOHNSON'

The lady to whom this letter was addressed, and for whom Dr. Johnson
had a high regard, died in Westminster, at the age of eighty, Nov. 1, 1807.
MALONE.]

'Your notes on Alfred[1] appear to me very judicious and accurate, but they are too few. Many things familiar to you, are unknown to me, and to most others; and you must not think too favourably of your readers; by supposing them knowing, you will leave them ignorant. Measure of land, and value of money, it is of great importance to state with care. Had the Saxons any gold coin?

'I have much curiosity after the manners and transactions of the middle ages, but have wanted either diligence or opportunity, or both. You, Sir, have great opportunities, and I wish you both diligence and success.

'I am, Sir, &c.

'July 17, 1781.'   'SAM. JOHNSON'

The following curious anecdote I insert in Dr. Burney's own words. 'Dr. Burney related to Dr. Johnson the partiality which his writings had excited in a friend of Dr. Burney's, the late Mr. Bewley, well known in Norfolk by the name of the *Philosopher of Massingham;* who, from the Ramblers and Plan of his Dictionary, and long before the authour's fame was established by the Dictionary itself, or any other work, had conceived such a reverence for him, that he earnestly begged Dr. Burney to give him the cover of the first letter he had received from him, as a relick of so estimable a writer. This was in 1755. In 1760, when Dr. Burney visited Dr. Johnson at the Temple in London, where he had then Chambers, he happened to arrive there before he was up; and being shewn into the room where he was to breakfast, finding himself alone, he examined the contents of the apartment, to try whether he could undiscovered steal any thing to send to his friend Bewley, as another relick of the admirable Dr. Johnson. But finding nothing better to his purpose, he cut some bristles off his hearth-broom, and enclosed them in a letter to his country enthusiast, who received them with due reverence. The Doctor was so sensible of the honour done him by a man of genius and science, to whom he was an utter stranger, that he said to Dr. Burney, "Sir, there is no man possessed

---

[1] The Will of King Alfred, alluded to in this letter, from the original Saxon, in the library of Mr. Astle, has been printed at the expence of the University of Oxford.

of the smallest portion of modesty, but must be flattered
with the admiration of such a man. I'll give him a set of
my Lives, if he will do me the honour to accept of them."
In this he kept his word; and Dr. Burney had not only the
pleasure of gratifying his friend with a present more worthy
of his acceptance than the segment from the hearth-
broom, but soon after introducing him to Dr. Johnson
himself in Bolt-court, with whom he had the satisfaction
of conversing a considerable time, not a fortnight before
his death; which happened in St. Martin's-street, during
his visit to Dr. Burney, in the house where the great Sir
Isaac Newton had lived and died before.'

In one of his little memorandum books is the following
minute:

'August 9, 3 P.M. ætat. 72, in the summer-house at
Streatham.

'After innumerable resolutions formed and neglected,
I have retired hither, to plan a life of greater diligence, in
hope that I may yet be useful, and be daily better prepared
to appear before my Creator and my Judge, from whose
infinite mercy I humbly call for assistance and support.

'My purpose is,

'To pass eight hours every day in some serious
employment.

'Having prayed, I purpose to employ the next six weeks
upon the Italian language, for my settled study.'

How venerably pious does he appear in these moments
of solitude, and how spirited are his resolutions for the
improvement of his mind, even in elegant literature, at a
very advanced period of life, and when afflicted with many
complaints.

In autumn he went to Oxford, Birmingham, Lichfield,
and Ashbourne, for which very good reasons might be
given in the conjectural yet positive manner of writers,
who are proud to account for every event which they relate.
He himself, however, says, 'The motives of my journey I
hardly know; I omitted it last year, and am not willing to
miss it again.'[1] But some good considerations arise, amongst
which is the kindly recollection of Mr. Hector, surgeon of
Birmingham. 'Hector is likewise an old friend, the only

[1] Prayers and Meditations, p. 201.

companion of my childhood that passed through the school with me. We have always loved one another; perhaps we may be made better by some serious conversation, of which however I have no distinct hope.'

He says too, 'At Lichfield, my native place, I hope to shew a good example by frequent attendance on publick worship.'

My correspondence with him during the rest of this year was, I know not why, very scanty, and all on my side. I wrote him one letter to introduce Mr. Sinclair, (now Sir John,) the member for Caithness, to his acquaintance; and informed him in another, that my wife had again been affected with alarming symptoms of illness.

In 1782, his complaints increased, and the history of his life this year, is little more than a mournful recital of the variations of his illness, in the midst of which, however, it will appear from his letters, that the powers of his mind were in no degree impaired.

'TO JAMES BOSWELL, ESQ.

'DEAR SIR,

'I sit down to answer your letter on the same day in which I received it, and am pleased that my first letter of the year is to you. No man ought to be at ease while he knows himself in the wrong; and I have not satisfied myself with my long silence. The letter relating to Mr. Sinclair, however, was, I believe, never brought.

'My health has been tottering this last year: and I can give no very laudable account of my time. I am always hoping to do better than I have ever hitherto done.

'My journey to Ashbourne and Staffordshire was not pleasant; for what enjoyment has a sick man visiting the sick? Shall we ever have another frolick like our journey to the Hebrides?

'I hope that dear Mrs. Boswell will surmount her complaints; in losing her you will lose your anchor, and be tost, without stability, by the waves of life.[1] I wish both you and her very many years, and very happy.

[1] The truth of this has been proved by sad experience. [Mrs. Boswell died June 4, 1789. MALONE.]

'For some months past I have been so withdrawn from the world, that I can send you nothing particular. All your friends, however, are well, and will be glad of your return to London.

'I am, dear Sir,
'Your's most affectionately,
'SAM. JOHNSON'

'January 5, 1782.'

At a time when he was less able than he had once been to sustain a shock, he was suddenly deprived of Mr. Levett, which event he thus communicated to Dr. Lawrence.

'SIR,

'OUR old friend, Mr. Levett, who was last night eminently cheerful, died this morning. The man who lay in the same room, hearing an uncommon noise, got up and tried to make him speak, but without effect. He then called Mr. Holder, the apothecary, who, though when he came he thought him dead, opened a vein, but could draw no blood. So has ended the long life of a very useful and very blameless man. I am, Sir,

'Your most humble servant,
'SAM. JOHNSON'

'Jan. 17, 1782.'

In one of his memorandum-books in my possession, is the following entry: 'January 20, Sunday. Robert Levett was buried in the church-yard of Bridewell, between one and two in the afternoon. He died on Thursday 17, about seven in the morning, by an instantaneous death. He was an old and faithful friend; I have known him from about 46. *Commendavi.* May GOD have mercy on him. May he have mercy on me.'

Such was Johnson's affectionate regard for Levett,[1] that he honoured his memory with the following pathetick verses:

'CONDEMN'D to Hope's delusive mine,
    As on we toil from day to day,
By sudden blast or slow decline
    Our social comforts drop away.

[1] See an account of him in 'The Gentleman's Magazine,' Feb. 1785.

Well try'd through many a varying year,
  See LEVETT to the grave descend;
Officious, innocent, sincere,
  Of every friendless name the friend.

Yet still he fills affection's eye,
  Obscurely wise, and coarsely kind;
Nor, letter'd arrogance,[1] deny
  Thy praise to merit unrefin'd.

When fainting Nature call'd for aid,
  And hov'ring Death prepar'd the blow,
His vigorous remedy display'd
  The power of art without the show.

In Misery's darkest caverns known,
  His ready help was ever nigh,
Where hopeless Anguish pour'd his groan,
  And lonely Want retir'd to die.[2]

No summons mock'd by chill delay,
  No petty gains disdain'd by pride;
The modest wants of every day
  The toil of every day supply'd.

His virtues walk'd their narrow round,
  Nor made a pause, nor left a void;
And sure the eternal Master found
  His single talent well employ'd.

The busy day, the peaceful night,
  Unfelt, uncounted, glided by;
His frame was firm, his powers were bright,
  Though now his eightieth year was nigh.

Then, with no throbs of fiery pain,
  No cold gradations of decay,
Death broke at once the vital chain,
  And freed his soul the nearest way.'

[1] In both editions of Sir John Hawkins's Life of Dr. Johnson, 'letter'd
ignorance,' is printed.

[2] Johnson repeated this line to me thus:
      'And Labour steals an hour to die.'
But he afterwards altered it to the present reading.

In one of Johnson's registers of this year, there occurs the following curious passage: 'Jan. 20. The Ministry is dissolved. I prayed with Francis, and gave thanks.'[1a] It has been the subject of discussion, whether there are two distinct particulars mentioned here? Or that we are to understand the giving of thanks to be in consequence of the dissolution of the Ministry? In support of the last of these conjectures may be urged his mean opinion of that Ministry, which has frequently appeared in the course of this work; and it is strongly confirmed by what he said on the subject to Mr. Seward:—'I am glad the Ministry is removed. Such a bunch of imbecility never disgraced a country. If they sent a messenger into the City to take up a printer, the messenger was taken up instead of the printer, and committed by the sitting Alderman. If they sent one army to the relief of another, the first army was defeated and taken before the second arrived. I will not say that what they did was always wrong; but it was always done at a wrong time.'

underlined:
Francis [1]
[a] *comical enough!* [1]

'TO MRS. STRAHAN[b]

'DEAR MADAM,

'MRS. WILLIAMS shewed me your kind letter. This little habitation is now but a melancholy place, clouded with the gloom of disease and death. Of the four inmates, one has been suddenly snatched away; two are oppressed by very afflictive and dangerous illness; and I tried yesterday to gain some relief by a third bleeding, from a disorder which has for some time distressed me, and I think myself to-day much better.

'I am glad, dear Madam, to hear that you are so far recovered as to go to Bath. Let me once more entreat you to stay till your health is not only obtained, but confirmed. Your fortune is such as that no moderate expence deserves your care; and you have a husband, who, I believe, does not regard it. Stay, therefore, till you are quite well. I am, for my part, very much deserted; but complaint is useless.

underlined:
TO MRS. STRAHAN [1]
[b] *A Woman who was —as Dr. Johnson told me;—so consummate a Drunkard, as to lie down in Bed with her heels on the Pillow—by Mistake.* [1]

[1] Prayers and Meditations, p. 209.

I hope GOD will bless you, and I desire you to form the same wish for me. I am, dear Madam,

'Your most humble servant,

'Feb. 4, 1782.'   'SAM. JOHNSON'

'TO EDMOND MALONE, ESQ.

'SIR,

'I HAVE for many weeks been so much out of order, that I have gone out only in a coach to Mrs. Thrale's, where I can use all the freedom that sickness requires. Do not, therefore, take it amiss, that I am not with you and Dr. Farmer. I hope hereafter to see you often. I am, Sir,

'Your most humble servant,

'Feb. 27, 1782.'   'SAM. JOHNSON'

TO THE SAME

'DEAR SIR,

'I HOPE I grow better, and shall soon be able to enjoy the kindness of my friends. I think this wild adherence to Chatterton[1] more unaccountable than the obstinate defence of Ossian. In Ossian there is a national pride, which may be forgiven, though it cannot be applauded. In Chatterton there is nothing but the resolution to say again what has once been said. I am, Sir,

'Your humble servant,

'March 2, 1782.'   'SAM. JOHNSON'

These short letters shew the regard which Dr. Johnson entertained for Mr. Malone, who the more he is known is

[1] [This Note was in answer to one which accompanied one of the earliest pamphlets on the subject of Chatterton's forgery, entitled 'Cursory Observations on the Poems attributed to Thomas Rowley,' &c. Mr. Thomas Warton's very able 'Inquiry' appeared about three months afterwards: and Mr. Tyrwhitt's admirable 'Vindication of his Appendix,' in the summer of the same year, left the believers in this daring imposture nothing but 'the resolution to say again what had been said before.' Daring, however, as this fiction was, and wild as was the adherence to Chatterton, both were greatly exceeded in 1795 and the following year, by a still more audacious imposture,[a] and the pertinacity of one of its adherents, who has immortalized his name by publishing a bulky volume, of which the direct and manifest object was, to prove the authenticity of certain papers attributed to Shakspeare, after the fabricator of the spurious trash had publickly acknowledged the imposture! MALONE.]

[a] *Oh Ireland!! Yes, that was worse still.* [H]

the more highly valued. It is much to be regretted that Johnson was prevented from sharing the elegant hospitality of that gentleman's table, at which he would in every respect have been fully gratified. Mr. Malone, who has so ably succeeded him as an Editor of Shakspeare, has, in his Preface, done great and just honour to Johnson's memory.

'TO MRS. LUCY PORTER, IN LICHFIELD

'DEAR MADAM,

'I WENT away from Lichfield ill, and have had a troublesome time with my breath; for some weeks I have been disordered by a cold, of which I could not get the violence abated, till I had been let blood three times. I have not, however, been so bad but that I could have written, and am sorry that I neglected it.

'My dwelling is but melancholy; both Williams, and Desmoulins, and myself, are very sickly: Frank is not well; and poor Levett died in his bed the other day, by a sudden stroke; I suppose not one minute passed between health and death; so uncertain are human things.

'Such is the appearance of the world about me; I hope your scenes are more cheerful. But whatever befalls us, though it is wise to be serious, it is useless and foolish, and perhaps sinful, to be gloomy. Let us, therefore, keep ourselves as easy as we can; though the loss of friends will be felt, and poor Levett had been a faithful adherent for thirty years.

'Forgive me, my dear love, the omission of writing: I hope to mend that and my other faults. Let me have your prayers.

'Make my compliments to Mrs. Cobb, and Miss Adey, and Mr. Pearson, and the whole company of my friends. I am, my dear,   'Your most humble servant,

'London, March 2, 1782.'   'SAM. JOHNSON'

TO THE SAME

'DEAR MADAM,

'MY last was but a dull letter, and I know not that this will be much more cheerful; I am, however, willing to write, because you are desirous to hear from me.

'My disorder has now begun its ninth week, for it is not yet over. I was last Thursday blooded for the fourth time, and have since found myself much relieved, but I am very tender and easily hurt; so that since we parted I have had but little comfort, but I hope that the spring will recover me; and that in the summer I shall see Lichfield again, for I will not delay my visit another year to the end of autumn.

'I have, by advertising, found poor Mr. Levett's brothers in Yorkshire, who will take the little he has left: it is but little, yet it will be welcome, for I believe they are of very low condition.

'To be sick, and to see nothing but sickness and death, is but a gloomy state; but I hope better times, even in this world, will come, and whatever this world may with-hold or give, we shall be happy in a better state. Pray for me, my dear Lucy.

'Make my compliments to Mrs. Cobb, and Miss Adey, and my old friend, Hetty Bailey, and to all the Lichfield ladies. I am, dear Madam,

'Yours, affectionately,

'Bolt-court, Fleet-street,
March 19, 1782.'

'SAM. JOHNSON'

On the day on which this letter was written, he thus feelingly mentions his respected friend, and physician, Dr. Lawrence:—'Poor Lawrence has almost lost the sense of hearing; and I have lost the conversation of a learned, intelligent, and communicative companion, and a friend whom long familiarity has much endeared. Lawrence is one of the best men whom I have known.—"*Nostrum omnium miserere Deus.*"*[1]*

It was Dr. Johnson's custom when he wrote to Dr. Lawrence concerning his own health to use the Latin language. I have been favoured by Miss Lawrence with one of these letters as a specimen:

T. Lawrencio, *Medico S.*

'Novum *frigus, nova tussis, nova spirandi difficultas, novam sanguinis missionem suadent, quam tamen te inconsulto nolim fieri. Ad te venire vix possum, nec est cur ad me venias.*

[1] Prayers and Meditations, p. 207.

Licere vel non licere uno verbo dicendum est; cætera mihi et Holdero[1] *reliqueris. Si per te licet, imperatur nuncio Holderum ad me deducere.*

'*Maiis Calendis,* 1782.

'*Postquàm tu discesseris quò me vertam?*'[2]

'TO CAPTAIN LANGTON,[3] IN ROCHESTER

'DEAR SIR,

'It is now long since we saw one another; and, whatever has been the reason, neither you have written to me, nor I to you. To let friendship die away by negligence and silence, is certainly not wise. It is voluntarily to throw away one of the greatest comforts of this weary pilgrimage, of which when it is, as it must be, taken finally away, he that travels on alone, will wonder how his esteem could be so little. Do not forget me; you see that I do not forget you. It is pleasing in the silence of solitude to think, that

[1] Mr. Holder, in the Strand, Dr. Johnson's apothecary.

[2] Soon after the above letter, Dr. Lawrence left London, but not before the palsy had made so great a progress as to render him unable to write for himself. The following are extracts from letters addressed by Dr. Johnson to one of his daughters:

'You will easily believe with what gladness I read that you had heard once again that voice to which we have all so often delighted to attend. May you often hear it. If we had his mind, and his tongue, we could spare the rest.

'I am not vigorous, but much better than when dear Dr. Lawrence held my pulse the last time. Be so kind as to let me know, from one little interval to another, the state of his body. I am pleased that he remembers me, and hope that it never can be possible for me to forget him. July 22, 1782.'

'I am much delighted even with the small advances which dear Dr. Lawrence makes towards recovery. If we could have again but his mind, and his tongue in his mind, and his right hand, we should not much lament the rest. I should not despair of helping the swelled hand by electricity, if it were frequently and diligently supplied.

'Let me know from time to time whatever happens; and I hope I need not tell you, how much I am interested in every change. Aug. 26, 1782.'

'Though the account with which you favoured me in your last letter could not give me the pleasure that I wished, yet I was glad to receive it; for my affection to my dear friend makes me desirous of knowing his state, whatever it be. I beg, therefore, that you continue to let me know, from time to time, all that you observe.

'Many fits of severe illness have, for about three months past, forced my kind physician often upon my mind. I am now better; and hope gratitude, as well as distress, can be a motive to remembrance. Bolt-court, Fleet-street, Feb. 4, 1783.'

[3] Mr. Langton being at this time on duty at Rochester, he is addressed by his military title.

there is one at least, however distant, of whose benevolence there is little doubt, and whom there is yet hope of seeing again.

'Of my life, from the time we parted, the history is mournful. The spring of last year deprived me of Thrale, a man whose eye for fifteen years had scarcely been turned upon me but with respect or tenderness; for such another friend, the general course of human things will not suffer man to hope. I passed the summer at Streatham, but there was no Thrale; and having idled away the summer with a weakly body and neglected mind, I made a journey to Staffordshire on the edge of winter. The season was dreary, I was sickly, and found the friends sickly whom I went to see. After a sorrowful sojourn, I returned to a habitation possessed for the present by two sick women, where my dear old friend, Mr. Levett, to whom as he used to tell me, I owe your acquaintance, died a few weeks ago, suddenly in his bed; there passed not, I believe, a minute between health and death. At night, as at Mrs. Thrale's, I was musing in my chamber, I thought with uncommon earnestness, that however I might alter my mode of life, or whithersoever I might remove, I would endeavour to retain Levett about me: in the morning my servant brought me word that Levett was called to another state, a state for which, I think, he was not unprepared, for he was very useful to the poor. How much soever I valued him, I now wish that I had valued him more.[1]

'I have myself been ill more than eight weeks, of a disorder, from which at the expence of about fifty ounces of blood, I hope I am now recovering.

'You, dear Sir, have, I hope, a more cheerful scene; you see George fond of his book, and the pretty misses airy and lively, with my own little Jenny equal to the best: and in whatever can contribute to your quiet or pleasure, you have Lady Rothes ready to concur. May whatever

---

[1] [Johnson has here expressed a sentiment similar to that contained in one of Shenstone's stanzas, to which in his life of that poet he has given high praise:

'I prized every hour that went by,
Beyond all that had pleas'd me before;
But now they are gone and I sigh,
And I grieve that I prized them no more.'

J. BOSWELL.]

you enjoy of good be increased, and whatever you suffer of evil be diminished. I am, dear Sir,

'Your humble servant,

'Bolt-court, Fleet-street,   'SAM. JOHNSON'
    March 20, 1782.'

'TO MR. HECTOR, IN BIRMINGHAM[1]

'DEAR SIR,

'I hope I do not very grossly flatter myself to imagine that you and dear Mrs. Careless[2] will be glad to hear some account of me. I performed the journey to London with very little inconvenience, and came safe to my habitation, where I found nothing but ill health, and, of consequence, very little cheerfulness. I then went to visit a little way into the country, where I got a complaint by a cold which has hung eight weeks upon me, and from which I am, at the expence of fifty ounces of blood, not yet free. I am afraid I must once more owe my recovery to warm weather, which seems to make no advances towards us.

'Such is my health, which will, I hope, soon grow better. In other respects I have no reason to complain. I know not that I have written any thing more generally commended than the Lives of the Poets; and have found the world willing enough to caress me, if my health had invited me to be in much company; but this season I have been almost wholly employed in nursing myself.

'When summer comes I hope to see you again, and will not put off my visit to the end of the year. I have lived so long in London, that I did not remember the difference of seasons.

'Your health, when I saw you, was much improved. You will be prudent enough not to put it in danger. I hope, when we meet again, we shall congratulate each other upon fair prospects of longer life; though what are the pleasures of the longest life, when placed in comparison with a happy death? I am, dear Sir,

'Yours most affectionately,

'London, March 21, 1782.'   'SAM. JOHNSON'

[1] A part of this letter having been torn off, I have, from the evident meaning, supplied a few words and half words at the ends and beginning of lines.   [2] See vol. ii. p. 247.

TO THE SAME

'DEAR SIR, [*Without a date, but supposed to be about this time*]

exclamation point: *In age* etc. [H]

'THAT you and dear Mrs. Careless should have care or curiosity about my health gives me that pleasure which every man feels from finding himself not forgotten. In age we feel again that love of our native place and our early friends, which in the bustle or amusements of middle life, were overborne and suspended.[a] You and I should now naturally cling to one another: we have outlived most of those who could pretend to rival us in each other's kindness. In our walk through life we have dropped our companions, and are now to pick up such as chance may offer us, or to travel on alone. You, indeed, have a sister, with whom you can divide the day: I have no natural friend left; but Providence has been pleased to preserve me from neglect; I have not wanted such alleviations of life as friendship could supply. My health has been, from my twentieth year, such as has seldom afforded me a single day of ease; but it is at least not worse; and I sometimes make myself believe that it is better. My disorders are, however, still sufficiently oppressive.

[a] *Eheu!* [H]
Very fine! [I]

'I think of seeing Staffordshire again this autumn, and intend to find my way through Birmingham, where I hope to see you and dear Mrs. Careless well. I am, Sir,

'Your affectionate friend,

'SAM. JOHNSON'

I wrote to him at different dates; regretted that I could not come to London this spring, but hoped we should meet somewhere in the summer; mentioned the state of my affairs, and suggested hopes of some preferment; informed him, that as 'The Beauties of Johnson' had been published in London, some obscure scribbler had published at Edinburgh, what he called 'The Deformities of Johnson.'

'TO JAMES BOSWELL, ESQ.

'DEAR SIR,

'THE pleasure which we used to receive from each other on Good-Friday and Easter-day, we must be this year content to miss. Let us, however, pray for each other, and hope to see one another yet from time to time with mutual delight. My disorder has been a cold, which impeded the organs of respiration, and kept me many weeks in a state of great uneasiness; but by repeated phlebotomy it is now relieved: and next to the recovery of Mrs. Boswell, I flatter myself, that you will rejoice at mine.

'What we shall do in the summer, it is yet too early to consider. You want to know what you shall do now; I do not think this time of bustle and confusion[1] like to produce any advantage to you. Every man has those to reward and gratify who have contributed to his advancement. To come hither with such expectations at the expence of borrowed money, which, I find you know not where to borrow, can hardly be considered prudent. I am sorry to find, what your solicitations seem to imply, that you have already gone the whole length of your credit. This is to set the quiet of your whole life at hazard. If you anticipate your inheritance, you can at last inherit nothing; all that you receive must pay for the past. You must get a place, or pine in penury, with the empty name of a great estate. Poverty, my dear friend, is so great an evil, and pregnant with so much temptation, and so much misery, that I cannot but earnestly enjoin you to avoid it. Live on what you have; live if you can on less; do not borrow either for vanity or pleasure; the vanity will end in shame, and the pleasure in regret: stay therefore at home, till you have saved money for your journey hither.

'"The Beauties of Johnson" are said to have got money to the collector; if the "Deformities" have the same success, I shall be still a more extensive benefactor.

'Make my compliments to Mrs. Boswell, who is I hope reconciled to me; and to the young people whom I never have offended.

'You never told me the success of your plea against the Solicitors.   I am, dear Sir,

'Your most affectionate,

'London, March 28, 1782.'   'SAM. JOHNSON'

---

[1] [On the preceding day the Ministry had been changed. MALONE.]

Notwithstanding his afflicted state of body and mind this year, the following correspondence affords a proof not only of his benevolence and conscientious readiness to relieve a good man from errour, but by his cloathing one of the sentiments in his 'Rambler' in different language, not inferiour to that of the original, shews his extraordinary command of clear and forcible expression.

A clergyman at Bath wrote to him, that in 'The Morning Chronicle,' a passage in 'The Beauties of Johnson,' article DEATH, had been pointed out as supposed by some readers to recommend suicide, the words being, 'To die is the fate of man; but to die with lingering anguish is generally his folly;' and respectfully suggesting to him, that such an erroneous notion of any sentence in the writings of an acknowledged friend of religion and virtue, should not pass uncontradicted.

Johnson thus answered this clergyman's letter:

'TO THE REVEREND MR. ————, AT BATH

'SIR,

'BEING now in the country in a state of recovery, as I hope, from a very oppressive disorder, I cannot neglect the acknowledgement of your Christian letter. The book called 'The Beauties of Johnson,' is the production of I know not whom; I never saw it but by casual inspection, and considered myself as utterly disengaged from its consequences. Of the passage you mention, I remember some notice in some paper; but knowing that it must be misrepresented, I thought of it no more, nor do I know where to find it in my own books. I am accustomed to think little of newspapers; but an opinion so weighty and serious as yours has determined me to do, what I should without your seasonable admonition, have omitted; and I will direct my thought to be shewn in its true state.[1]

[1] What follows, appeared in the Morning Chronicle of May 29, 1782.—'A correspondent having mentioned, in the Morning Chronicle of December 12, the last clause of the following paragraph, as seeming to favour suicide; we are requested to print the whole passage, that its true meaning may appear, which is not to recommend suicide but exercise.

'Exercise cannot secure us from that dissolution to which we are decreed; but while the soul and body continue united, it can make the association pleasing, and give probable hopes that they shall be disjoined by an easy

If I could find the passage I would direct you to it. I suppose the tenour is this:—"Acute diseases are the immediate and inevitable strokes of Heaven; but of them the pain is short, and the conclusion speedy; chronical disorders, by which we are suspended in tedious torture between life and death, are commonly the effect of our own misconduct and intemperance. To die, &c."—This, Sir, you see is all true and all blameless. I hope some time in the next week, to have all rectified. My health has been lately much shaken; if you favour me with any answer, it will be a comfort to me to know that I have your prayers.

'I am, &c.

'May 15, 1782.'   'SAM. JOHNSON'

This letter, as might be expected, had its full effect, and the clergyman acknowledged it in grateful and pious terms.[1]

The following letters require no extracts from mine to introduce them.

'TO JAMES BOSWELL, ESQ.

'DEAR SIR,

'THE earnestness and tenderness of your letter is such, that I cannot think myself shewing it more respect than it claims, by sitting down to answer it the day on which I received it.

'This year has afflicted me with a very irksome and severe disorder. My respiration has been much impeded, and much blood has been taken away. I am now harassed by a catarrhous cough, from which my purpose is to seek relief by change of air; and I am, therefore, preparing to go to Oxford.

'Whether I did right in dissuading you from coming to London this spring, I will not determine. You have not lost much by missing my company; I have scarcely been well for a single week. I might have received comfort from

separation. It was a principle among the ancients, that acute diseases are from Heaven, and chronical from ourselves; the dart of death, indeed, falls from Heaven, but we poison it by our own misconduct: to die is the fate of man; but to die with lingering anguish is generally his folly.'

index sign: *the dart of death* etc. [H]

[1] The Correspondence may be seen at length in the Gentleman's Magazine, Feb. 1786.

your kindness; but you would have seen me afflicted, and, perhaps, found me peevish. Whatever might have been your pleasure or mine, I know not how I could have honestly advised you to come hither with borrowed money. Do not accustom yourself to consider debt only as an inconvenience; you will find it a calamity.[a] Poverty takes away so many means of doing good, and produces so much inability to resist evil, both natural and moral, that it is by all virtuous means to be avoided. Consider a man whose fortune is very narrow; whatever be his rank by birth, or whatever his reputation by intellectual excellence, what can he do? or what evil can he prevent? That he cannot help the needy is evident; he has nothing to spare. But, perhaps, his advice or admonition may be useful. His poverty will destroy his influence: many more can find that he is poor, than that he is wise; and few will reverence the understanding that is of so little advantage to its owner. I say nothing of the personal wretchedness of a debtor, which, however, has passed into a proverb. Of riches it is not necessary to write the praise. Let it, however, be re-membered, that he who has money to spare, has it always in his power to benefit others; and of such power a good man must always be desirous.[b]

'I am pleased with your account of Easter.[1] We shall meet, I hope, in Autumn, both well and both cheerful; and part each the better for the other's company.

'Make my compliments to Mrs. Boswell, and to the young charmers.

'I am, &c.

'London, June 3, 1782.'   'SAM. JOHNSON'

[a] charming! [H & J]
[b] A very fine Letter. [H]

'TO MR. PERKINS

'DEAR SIR,

'I AM much pleased that you are going a very long journey, which may by proper conduct restore your health and prolong your life.

'Observe these rules:

'1. Turn all care out of your head as soon as you mount the chaise.

---

[1] Which I celebrated in the Church-of-England chapel at Edinburgh, founded by Lord Chief Baron Smith, of respectable and pious memory.

'2. Do not think about frugality; your health is worth more than it can cost.

'3. Do not continue any day's journey to fatigue.

'4. Take now and then a day's rest.

'5. Get a smart sea sickness, if you can.

'6. Cast away all anxiety, and keep your mind easy.

'This last direction is the principal: with an unquiet mind, neither exercise, nor diet, nor physick, can be of much use.ᵃ

'I wish you, dear Sir, a prosperous journey, and a happy recovery.ᵇ I am, dear Sir,

'Your most affectionate, humble servant,

'July 28, 1782.'   'SAM. JOHNSON'

ᵃ *True   True* [1]

ᵇ *This Man's Illness ended in irrecovereable Deafness—he died at a very advanced Age.* [H]

'TO JAMES BOSWELL, ESQ.

'DEAR SIR,

'BEING uncertain whether I should have any call this autumn into the country, I did not immediately answer your kind letter. I have no call; but if you desire to meet me at Ashbourne, I believe I can come thither; if you had rather come to London, I can stay at Streatham: take your choice.

'This year has been very heavy. From the middle of January to the middle of June I was battered by one disorder after another! I am now very much recovered, and hope still to be better. What happiness it is that Mrs. Boswell has escaped.

'My "Lives" are reprinting, and I have forgotten the authour of Gray's character:¹ write immediately, and it may be perhaps yet inserted.

'Of London or Ashbourne you have your free choice; at any place I shall be glad to see you. I am, dear Sir,

'Yours, &c,

'August 24, 1782.'   'SAM. JOHNSON'

On the 30th of August, I informed him that my honoured father had died that morning; a complaint under

¹ The Reverend Mr. Temple, Vicar of St. Gluvias, Cornwall.

which he had long laboured, having suddenly come to a crisis, while I was upon a visit at the seat of Sir Charles Preston, from whence I had hastened the day before, upon receiving a letter by express.

'TO JAMES BOSWELL, ESQ.

'DEAR SIR,

'I HAVE struggled through this year with so much infirmity of body, and such strong impressions of the fragility of life, that death, whenever it appears, fills me with melancholy; and I cannot hear without emotion of the removal of any one, whom I have known, into another state.

'Your father's death had every circumstance that could enable you to bear it; it was at a mature age, and it was expected; and as his general life had been pious, his thoughts had doubtless for many years past been turned upon eternity. That you did not find him sensible must doubtless grieve you; his disposition towards you was undoubtedly that of a kind, though not of a fond father. Kindness, at least actual, is in our power, but fondness is not; and if by negligence or imprudence you had extinguished his fondness, he could not at will rekindle it. Nothing then remained between you but mutual forgiveness of each other's faults, and mutual desire of each other's happiness.

'I shall long to know his final disposition of his fortune.

'You, dear Sir, have now a new station, and have therefore new cares, and new employments. Life, as Cowley seems to say, ought to resemble a well-ordered poem; of which one rule generally received is, that the exordium should be simple, and should promise little. Begin your new course of life with the least shew, and the least expence possible; you may at pleasure encrease both, but you cannot easily diminish them. Do not think your estate your own, while any man can call upon you for money which you cannot pay; therefore, begin with timorous parsimony. Let it be your first care not to be in any man's debt.

'When the thoughts are extended to a future state, the present life seems hardly worthy of all those principles of

marginal line:
is, that . . . *life with*
[H]

index sign:
Do not think etc. [H]

conduct, and maxims of prudence, which one generation
of men has transmitted to another; but upon a closer view,
when it is perceived how much evil is produced, and how
much good is impeded by embarrassment and distress,
and how little room the expedients of poverty leave for
the exercise of virtue, it grows manifest that the boundless
importance of the next life enforces some attention to the
interest of this.[a]

[a] *so it does.* [H]

'Be kind to the old servants, and secure the kindness
of the agents and factors; do not disgust them by asperity,
or unwelcome gaiety, or apparent suspicion. From them
you must learn the real state of your affairs, the characters
of your tenants, and the value of your lands.

'Make my compliments to Mrs. Boswell; I think her
expectations from air and exercise are the best that she
can form. I hope she will live long and happily.

'I forgot whether I told you that Rasay has been here;
we dined cheerfully together. I entertained lately a young
gentleman from Corrichatachin.

'I received your letters only this morning. I am, dear Sir,
                         'Yours, &c.
'London, Sept. 7, 1782.'   'SAM. JOHNSON'

In answer to my next letter, I received one from him
dissuading me from hastening to him as I had proposed;
what is proper for publication is the following paragraph,
equally just and tender:

'One expence, however, I would not have you to spare;
let nothing be omitted that can preserve Mrs. Boswell,
though it should be necessary to transplant her for a time
into a softer climate. She is the prop and stay of your life.
How much must your children suffer by losing her.'

My wife was now so much convinced of his sincere
friendship for me, and regard for her, that, without any
suggestion on my part, she wrote him a very polite and
grateful letter.

'DR. JOHNSON TO MRS. BOSWELL

'DEAR LADY,

'I HAVE not often received so much pleasure as from
your invitation to Auchinleck. The journey thither and

back is, indeed, too great for the latter part of the year; but if my health were fully recovered, I would suffer no little heat and cold, nor a wet or a rough road to keep me from you. I am, indeed, not without hope of seeing Auchinleck again; but to make it a pleasant place I must see its lady well, and brisk, and airy. For my sake, therefore, among many greater reasons, take care, dear Madam, of your health, spare no expence, and want no attendance that can procure ease, or preserve it. Be very careful to keep your mind quiet; and do not think it too much to give an account of your recovery to, Madam,

                          'Yours, &c.
'London, Sept. 7, 1782.'   'SAM. JOHNSON'

'TO JAMES BOSWELL, ESQ.

'DEAR SIR,

    'HAVING passed almost this whole year in a succession of disorders, I went in October to Brighthelmstone, whither I came in a state of so much weakness, that I rested four times in walking between the inn and the lodging. By physick and abstinence I grew better, and am now reasonably easy, though at a great distance from health. I am afraid, however, that health begins, after seventy, and long before, to have a meaning different from that which it had at thirty. But it is culpable to murmur at the established order of the creation, as it is vain to oppose it, he that lives, must grow old; and he that would rather grow old than die, has GOD to thank for the infirmities of old age.

    'At your long silence I am rather angry. You do not since now you are the head of your house, think it worth your while to try whether you or your friend can live longer without writing, nor suspect after so many years of friendship, that when I do not write to you, I forget you. Put all such useless jealousies out of your head, and disdain to regulate your own practice by the practice of another, or by any other principle than the desire of doing right.

    'Your œconomy, I suppose, begins now to be settled; your expences are adjusted to your revenue, and all your people in their proper places. Resolve not to be poor: whatever you have, spend less. Poverty is a great enemy to human happiness; it certainly destroys liberty, and it makes some virtues impracticable, and others extremely difficult.

'Let me know the history of your life, since your accession to your estate. How many houses, how many cows, how much land in your own hand, and what bargains you make with your tenants.

*   *   *   *   *   *

'Of my "Lives of the Poets," they have printed a new edition in octavo, I hear, of three thousand. Did I give a set to Lord Hailes? If I did not, I will do it out of these. What did you make of all your copy?

'Mrs. Thrale and the three Misses are now for the winter, in Argyll-street. Sir Joshua Reynolds has been out of order, but is well again; and I am, dear Sir,

'Your affectionate humble servant,

'London, Dec. 7, 1782.'   'SAM. JOHNSON'

'TO DR. SAMUEL JOHNSON

'DEAR SIR,   'Edinburgh, Dec. 20, 1782

'I WAS made happy by your kind letter, which gave us the agreeable hopes of seeing you in Scotland again.

'I am much flattered by the concern you are pleased to take in my recovery. I am better, and hope to have it in my power to convince you by my attention, of how much consequence I esteem your health to the world and to myself. I remain, Sir, with grateful respect,

'Your obliged and obedient servant,

'MARGARET BOSWELL'

The death of Mr. Thrale had made a very material alteration with respect to Johnson's reception in that family. The manly authority of the husband no longer curbed the lively exuberance of the lady; and as her vanity had been fully gratified, by having the Colossus of Literature attached to her for many years, she gradually became less assiduous to please him. Whether her attachment to him was already divided by another object, I am unable to ascertain; but it is plain that Johnson's penetration was alive to her neglect or forced attention; for on the 6th of October this year we find him making a 'parting use of the library' at Streatham, and pronouncing a prayer, which he composed on leaving Mr. Thrale's family.[1]

'Almighty GOD, Father of all mercy, help me by thy grace, that I may, with humble and sincere thankfulness, remember the comforts and conveniencies which I have enjoyed at this place; and that I may resign them with holy submission, equally trusting in thy protection when Thou givest, and when Thou takest away. Have mercy upon me, O LORD, have mercy upon me.

'To thy fatherly protection, O LORD, I commend this family. Bless, guide, and defend them, that they may so pass through this world, as finally to enjoy in thy presence everlasting happiness, for JESUS CHRIST'S sake. Amen.'

One cannot read this prayer, without some emotions not very favourable to the lady whose conduct occasioned it.

In one of his memorandum-books I find, 'Sunday, went to church at Streatham. *Templo valedixi cum osculo.*'

He met Mr. Philip Metcalfe often at Sir Joshua Reynolds's, and other places, and was a good deal with him at Brighthelmstone this autumn, being pleased at once with his excellent table and animated conversation. Mr. Metcalfe shewed him great respect, and sent him a note that he might have the use of his carriage whenever he pleased. Johnson (3d October, 1782) returned this polite answer:—'Mr. Johnson is very much obliged by the kind offer of the carriage, but he has no desire of using Mr. Metcalfe's carriage, except when he can have the pleasure of Mr. Metcalfe's company.' Mr. Metcalfe could not but be highly pleased that his company was thus valued by Johnson, and he frequently attended him in airings. They also went together to Chichester, and they visited Petworth, and Cowdry, the venerable seat of the Lords Montacute.[2] 'Sir, (said Johnson,) I should like to stay here four-and-twenty hours. We see here how our ancestors lived.'

That his curiosity was still unabated, appears from two letters to Mr. John Nichols, of the 10th and 20th of

[1] Prayers and Meditations, p. 214.

[2] [This venerable mansion has since been totally destroyed by fire. MALONE.]

October this year. In one he says, 'I have looked into your
"Anecdotes," and you will hardly thank a lover of literary
history for telling you, that he has been much informed
and gratified. I wish you would add your own discoveries
and intelligence to those of Dr. Rawlinson, and undertake
the Supplement to Wood. Think of it.' In the other, 'I wish,
Sir, you could obtain some fuller information of Jortin,
Markland, and Thirlby. They were three contemporaries
of great eminence.'

'TO SIR JOSHUA REYNOLDS

'DEAR SIR,

'I HEARD yesterday of your late disorder, and should
think ill of myself if I had heard of it without alarm. I
heard likewise of your recovery, which I sincerely wish to
be complete and permanent. Your country has been in
danger of losing one of its brightest ornaments, and I of
losing one of my oldest and kindest friends; but I hope
you will still live long, for the honour of the nation: and
that more enjoyment of your elegance, your intelligence,
and your benevolence, is still reserved for, dear Sir, your
most affectionate, &c.

'Brighthelmstone,   'SAM. JOHNSON'
   Nov, 14, 1782.'

The Reverend Mr. Wilson having dedicated to him his
'Archæological Dictionary,' that mark of respect was thus
acknowledged:

'TO THE REVEREND MR. WILSON, CLITHEROE,
                LANCASHIRE

'REVEREND SIR,

'THAT I have long omitted to return you thanks for
the honour conferred upon me by your Dedication, I entreat you with great earnestness not to consider as more
faulty than it is. A very importunate and oppressive disorder has for some time debarred me from the pleasures,
and obstructed me in the duties of life. The esteem and
kindness of wise and good men is one of the last pleasures
which I can be content to lose; and gratitude to those

from whom this pleasure is received, is a duty of which I hope never to be reproached with the final neglect. I therefore now return you thanks for the notice which I have received from you, and which I consider as giving to my name not only more bulk, but more weight; not only as extending its superficies, but as increasing its value. Your book was evidently wanted, and will, I hope, find its way into the school, to which, however, I do not mean to confine it; for no man has so much skill in antient rites and practices as not to want it. As I suppose myself to owe part of your kindness to my excellent friend, Dr. Patten, he has likewise a just claim to my acknowledgement, which I hope you, Sir, will transmit. There will soon appear a new edition of my Poetical Biography; if you will accept of a copy to keep me in your mind, be pleased to let me know how it may be conveniently conveyed to you. This present is small, but it is given with good will by, Reverend Sir,

'Your most, &c.

'December 31, 1782.'   'SAM. JOHNSON'

In 1783, he was more severely afflicted than ever, as will appear in the course of his correspondence; but still the same ardour for literature, the same constant piety, the same kindness for his friends, and the same vivacity, both in conversation and writing, distinguished him.

Having given Dr. Johnson a full account of what I was doing at Auchinleck, and particularly mentioned what I knew would please him,—my having brought an old man of eighty-eight from a lonely cottage to a comfortable habitation within my enclosures, where he had good neighbours near to him,—I received an answer in February, of which I extract what follows:

'I am delighted with your account of your activity at Auchinleck, and wish the old gentleman, whom you have so kindly removed, may live long to promote your prosperity by his prayers. You have now a new character and new duties; think on them and practise them.

'Make an impartial estimate of your revenue, and whatever it is, live upon less. Resolve never to be poor. Frugality is not only the basis of quiet, but of beneficence. No man can help others that wants help himself; we must have enough before we have to spare.

'I am glad to find that Mrs. Boswell grows well; and hope that to keep her well, no care nor caution will be omitted. May you long live happily together.

'When you come hither, pray bring with you Baxter's Anacreon. I cannot get that edition in London.'[1]

On Friday, March 21, having arrived in London the night before, I was glad to find him at Mrs. Thrale's house, in Argyll-street, appearances of friendship between them being still kept up. I was shewn into his room, and after the first salutation he said, 'I am glad you are come: I am very ill.' He looked pale, and was distressed with a difficulty of breathing: but after the common enquiries he assumed his usual strong animated style of conversation. Seeing me now for the first time as a *Laird*, or proprietor of land, he began thus: 'Sir, the superiority of a country-gentleman over the people upon his estate is very agreeable: and he who says he does not feel it to be agreeable, lies; for it must be agreeable to have a casual superiority over those who are by nature equal with us.' BOSWELL. 'Yet, Sir, we see great proprietors of land who prefer living in London.' JOHNSON. 'Why, Sir, the pleasure of living in London, the intellectual superiority that is enjoyed there, may counterbalance the other. Besides, Sir, a man may prefer the state of the country-gentleman upon the whole, and yet there may never be a moment when he is willing to make the change, to quit London for it.' He said, 'It is better to have five *per cent.* out of land, than out of money, because it is more secure; but the readiness of transfer, and promptness of interest, make many people rather choose the funds. Nay, there is another disadvantage belonging to land, compared with money. A man is not so much afraid of being a hard creditor, as of being a hard landlord.' BOSWELL. 'Because there is a sort of kindly connection between a landlord and his tenants.' JOHNSON. 'No, Sir; many landlords with us never see their tenants. It is because if a landlord drives away his

---

[1] [Dr. Johnson should seem not to have sought diligently for Baxter's Anacreon, for there are two editions of that book, and they are frequently found in the London Sale-Catalogue. MALONE.]

tenants, he may not get others; whereas the demand for
money is so great, it may always be lent.'

He talked with regret and indignation of the factious
opposition to Government at this time, and imputed it in
a great measure to the Revolution. 'Sir, (said he, in a low
voice, having come nearer to me, while his old prejudices
seemed to be fermenting in his mind,) this Hanoverian
family is *isolée* here. They have no friends. Now the Stuarts
had friends who stuck by them so late as 1745. When the
right of the King is not reverenced, there will not be
reverence for those appointed by the King.'

His observation that the present royal family has no
friends, has been too much justified by the very ungrateful
behaviour of many who were under great obligations to
his Majesty; at the same time there are honourable exceptions; and the very next year after this conversation, and
ever since, the King has had as extensive and generous
support as ever was given to any monarch, and has had
the satisfaction of knowing that he was more and more
endeared to his people.

He repeated to me his verses on Mr. Levett, with an
emotion which gave them full effect; and then he was
pleased to say, 'You must be as much with me as you can.
You have done me good. You cannot think how much
better I am, since you came in.'

He sent a message to acquaint Mrs. Thrale that I was
arrived. I had not seen her since her husband's death. She
soon appeared, and favoured me with an invitation to stay
to dinner, which I accepted. There was no other company
but herself and three of her daughters, Dr. Johnson, and I.
She too said, she was very glad I was come, for she was
going to Bath, and should have been sorry to leave Dr.
Johnson before I came. This seemed to be attentive and
kind; and I who had not been informed of any change,
imagined all to be as well as formerly. He was little inclined
to talk at dinner, and went to sleep after it; but when he
joined us in the drawing-room, he seemed revived, and
was again himself.

Talking of conversation, he said, 'There must, in the first
place, be knowledge, there must be materials;—in the
second place, there must be a command of words;—in

the third place, there must be imagination, to place things in such views as they are not commonly seen in;—and in the fourth place, there must be presence of mind, and a resolution that is not to be overcome by failures; this last is an essential requisite; for want of it many people do not excel in conversation. Now *I* want it; I throw up the game upon losing a trick.' I wondered to hear him talk thus of himself, and said, 'I don't know, Sir, how this may be; but I am sure you beat other people's cards out of their hands.' I doubt whether he heard this remark. While we went on talking triumphantly, I was fixed in admiration, and said to Mrs. Thrale, 'O, for short-hand to take this down!'—'You'll carry it all in your head, (said she;) a long head is as good as short-hand.'

It has been observed and wondered at, that Mr. Charles Fox never talked with any freedom in the presence of Dr. Johnson; though it is well known, and I myself can witness, that his conversation is various, fluent, and exceedingly agreeable. Johnson's own experience, however, of that gentleman's reserve was a sufficient reason for his going on thus: 'Fox never talks in private company; not from any determination not to talk, but because he has not the first motion. A man who is used to the applause of the House of Commons, has no wish for that of a private company. A man accustomed to throw for a thousand pounds, if set down to throw for sixpence, would not be at the pains to count his dice. Burke's talk is the ebullition of his mind; he does not talk from a desire of distinction, but because his mind is full.'

marginal line: *from a . . . is full* [H]

He thus curiously characterised one of our old acquaintance: '*********ᵃ is a good man, Sir; but he is a vain man and a liar. He, however, only tells lies of vanity; of victories, for instance, in conversation, which never happened.' This alluded to a story which I had repeated from that gentleman, to entertain Johnson with its wild bravado: 'This Johnson, Sir, (said he,) whom you are all afraid of, will shrink, if you come close to him in argument, and roar as loud as he. He once maintained the paradox, that there is no beauty but in utility. "Sir, (said I,) what say you to the peacock's tail, which is one of the most beautiful objects in nature, but would have as much utility if its

ᵃ *I suppose 'tis Baretti* [H]
Baretti [I]

feathers were all of one colour." He *felt* what I thus produced, and had recourse to his usual expedient, ridicule; exclaiming, "A peacock has a tail, and a fox has a tail;" and then he burst out into a laugh.—"Well, Sir, (said I, with a strong voice, looking him full in the face,) you have unkennelled your fox; pursue him if you dare." He had not a word to say, Sir.'—Johnson told me, that this was fiction from beginning to end.[1]

After musing for some time, he said, 'I wonder how I should have any enemies; for I do harm to nobody.'[2] BOSWELL. 'In the first place, Sir, you will be pleased to recollect, that you set out with attacking the Scotch; so you got a whole nation for your enemies.' JOHNSON. 'Why, I own, that by my definition of *oats* I meant to vex them.' BOSWELL. 'Pray, Sir, can you trace the cause of your antipathy to the Scotch?' JOHNSON. 'I cannot, Sir.' BOSWELL. 'Old Mr. Sheridan says, it was because they sold Charles the First.' JOHNSON. 'Then, Sir, old Mr. Sheridan has found out a very good reason.'

Surely the most obstinate and sulky nationality, the most determined aversion to this great and good man, must be cured, when he is seen thus playing with one of his prejudices, of which he candidly admitted that he could not tell the reason. It was, however, probably owing to his having had in his view the worst part of the Scottish nation, the needy adventurers, many of whom he thought were advanced above their merits, by means which he did not approve. Had he in his early life been in Scotland, and

[1] Were I to insert all the stories which have been told of contests boldly maintained with him, imaginary victories obtained over him, of reducing him to silence, and of making him own that his antagonist had the better of him in argument, my volumes would swell to an immoderate size. One instance, I find, has circulated both in conversation and in print; that when he would not allow the Scotch writers to have merit, the late Dr. Rose, of Chiswick, asserted, that he could name one Scotch writer, whom Dr. Johnson himself would allow to have written better than any man of the age; and upon Johnson's asking who it was, answered, 'Lord Bute, when he signed the warrant for your pension.' Upon which, Johnson, struck with the repartee, acknowledged that this *was* true. When I mentioned it to Johnson, 'Sir, (said he,) if Rose said this, I never heard it.'

[2] This reflection was very natural in a man of a good heart, who was not conscious of any ill-will to mankind, though the sharp sayings which were sometimes produced by his discrimination and vivacity, which he perhaps did not recollect, were, I am afraid, too often remembered with resentment.

seen the worthy, sensible, independent gentlemen, who live rationally and hospitably at home, he never could have entertained such unfavourable and unjust notions of his fellow-subjects. And accordingly we find, that when he did visit Scotland, in the latter period of his life, he was fully sensible of all that it deserved, as I have already pointed out, when speaking of his 'Journey to the Western Islands.'

Next day, Saturday, March 22, I found him still at Mrs. Thrale's, but he told me that he was to go to his own house in the afternoon. He was better, but I perceived he was but an unruly patient, for Sir Lucas Pepys, who visited him, while I was with him said, 'If you were *tractable*, Sir, I should prescribe for you.'

I related to him a remark which a respectable friend had made to me, upon the then state of Government, when those who had been long in opposition had attained to power, as it was supposed, against the inclination of the Sovereign. 'You need not be uneasy (said this gentleman) about the King. He laughs at them all; he plays them one against another.' JOHNSON. 'Don't think so, Sir. The King is as much oppressed as a man can be. If he plays them one against another, he *wins* nothing.'

I had paid a visit to General Oglethorpe in the morning, and was told by him that Dr. Johnson saw company on Saturday evenings, and he would meet me at Johnson's that night. When I mentioned this to Johnson, not doubting that it would please him, as he had a great value for Oglethorpe, the fretfulness of his disease unexpectedly shewed itself; his anger suddenly kindled, and he said, with vehemence, 'Did not you tell him not to come? Am I to be *hunted* in this manner?' I satisfied him that I could not divine that the visit would not be convenient, and that I certainly could not take it upon me of my own accord to forbid the General.

I found Dr. Johnson in the evening in Mrs. Williams's room, at tea and coffee with her and Mrs. Desmoulins, who were also both ill; it was a sad scene, and he was not in a very good humour. He said of a performance that had lately come out, 'Sir, if you should search all the mad-houses in England, you would not find ten men who would write so, and think it sense.'[a]

a *I think this was* Elphinstone's Martial. [H]
   Elphinstone's Martial [1]

I was glad when General Oglethorpe's arrival was announced, and we left the ladies. Dr. Johnson attended him in the parlour, and was as courteous as ever. The General said, he was busy reading the writers of the middle age. Johnson said they were very curious. OGLETHORPE. 'The House of Commons has usurped the power of the nation's money, and used it tyrannically. Government is now carried on by corrupt influence, instead of the inherent right in the King.' JOHNSON. 'Sir, the want of inherent right in the King occasions all this disturbance. What we did at the Revolution was necessary: but it broke our constitution.'[1] OGLETHORPE. 'My father did not think it necessary.'

On Sunday, March 23, I breakfasted with Dr. Johnson, who seemed much relieved, having taken opium the night before. He however protested against it, as a remedy that should be given with the utmost reluctance, and only in extreme necessity. I mentioned how commonly it was used in Turkey, and that therefore it could not be so pernicious as he apprehended. He grew warm, and said, 'Turks take opium, and Christians take opium; but Russell, in his account of Aleppo, tells us, that it is as disgraceful in Turkey to take too much opium, as it is with us to get drunk. Sir, it is amazing how things are exaggerated. A gentleman was lately telling in a company where I was present, that in France as soon as a man of fashion marries, he takes an opera girl into keeping; and this he mentioned as a general custom.[a] "Pray, Sir, (said I,) how many opera girls may there be?" He answered, "About fourscore."[b] "Well then, Sir, (said I,) you see there can be no more than four-score men of fashion who can do this." '

Mrs. Desmoulins made tea; and she and I talked before him upon a topick which he had once borne patiently from me when we were by ourselves,—his not complaining of the world, because he was not called to some great office,

[a] *That I do remember: it was Colonel Cunningham said it at Brighthelmston* [I]

[b] *Well! that seems quite sufficient for Leaders of the Mode.* [H]

---

[1] I have, in my 'Journal of a Tour to the Hebrides,' fully expressed my sentiments upon this subject. The Revolution was *necessary*, but not a subject for *glory;* because it for a long time blasted the generous feelings of *Loyalty*. And now, when by the benignant effect of time the present Royal Family are established in our *affections*, how unwise is it to revive by celebrations the memory of a shock, which it would surely have been better that our constitution had not required.

nor had attained to great wealth. He flew into a violent passion, I confess with some justice, and commanded us to have done. 'Nobody, (said he) has a right to talk in this manner, to bring before a man his own character, and the events of his life, when he does not choose it should be done. I never have sought the world; the world was not to seek me. It is rather wonderful that so much has been done for me. All the complaints which are made of the world are unjust. I never knew a man of merit neglected: it was generally by his own fault that he failed of success. A man may hide his head in a hole: he may go into the country, and publish a book now and then, which nobody reads, and then complain he is neglected. There is no reason why any person should exert himself for a man who has written a good book: he has not written it for any individual. I may as well make a present to the postman who brings me a letter. When patronage was limited, an authour expected to find a Mæcenas, and complained if he did not find one. Why should he complain? This Mæcenas has others as good as he, or others who have got the start of him.' BOSWELL. 'But, surely, Sir, you will allow that there are men of merit at the bar, who never get practice.' JOHNSON. 'Sir, you are sure that practice is got from an opinion that the person employed deserves it best; so that if a man of merit at the bar does not get practice, it is from errour, not from injustice. He is not neglected. A horse that is brought to market may not be bought, though he is a very good horse: but that is from ignorance, not from inattention.'

There was in this discourse much novelty, ingenuity, and discrimination, such as is seldom to be found. Yet I cannot help thinking that men of merit, who have no success in life, may be forgiven for *lamenting*, if they are not allowed to *complain*. They may consider it as *hard* that their merit should not have its suitable distinction. Though there is no intentional injustice towards them on the part of the world, their merit not having been perceived, they may yet repine against *fortune*, or *fate*, or by whatever name they choose to call the supposed mythological power of *Destiny*. It has, however, occurred to me, as a consolatory thought, that men of merit should consider thus:—'How much harder would it be, if the same persons had both all the merit and all the prosperity. Would not this be a miserable distribution for the poor dunces? Would men of merit exchange their intellectual superiority, and the enjoyments arising from it, for external distinction and the pleasures of wealth? If they would not, let them not envy others, who are poor where they are rich, a compensation which is made to them. Let them look inwards and be satisfied; recollecting with conscious pride what Virgil finely says of the *Corycius Senex,* and which I have, in another place,[1] with truth and sincerity applied to Mr. Burke:

marginal line:
merit exchange . . . not, let [H]

marginal line:
conscious pride . . . Mr. Burke [H]

'*Regum æquabat opes animis.*'

On the subject of the right employment of wealth, Johnson observed, 'A man cannot make a bad use of his money, so far as regards Society, if he does not hoard it; for if he either spends it or lends it out, Society has the benefit. It is in general better to spend money than to give it away; for industry is more promoted by spending money than by giving it away. A man who spends his money is sure he is doing good with it: he is not so sure when he gives it away. A man who spends ten thousand a year will do more good[a] than a man who spends two thousand and gives away eight.'[b]

marginal line:
more promoted . . . he is [H]

[a] *to a Commercial Country.* [H]
[b] *Ay Ay—Mandeville forever.* [H]

In the evening I came to him again. He was somewhat fretful from his illness. A gentleman asked him whether he had been abroad to-day. 'Don't talk so childishly, (said he.) You may as well ask if I hanged myself to-day.' I mentioned politicks. JOHNSON. 'Sir, I'd as soon have a man to break my bones as talk to me of public affairs, internal or external. I have lived to see things all as bad as they can be.'[c]

marginal line:
Don't talk . . . I mentioned [H]

[c] *no, indeed had he not. 1820* [H & I]

Having mentioned his friend, the second Lord Southwell, he said, 'Lord Southwell was the highest-bred man without insolence, that I ever was in company with; the most *qualitied* I ever saw. Lord Orrery was not dignified; Lord Chesterfield was, but he was insolent. Lord ********* is a man of coarse manners, but a man of abilities and information. I don't say he is a man I would

[1] Letter to the People of Scotland against the Attempt to diminish the Number of the Lords of Session, 1785.

set at the head of a nation, though perhaps he may be as good as the next Prime Minister that comes; but he is a man to be at the head of a Club;—I don't say *our* CLUB;— for there's no such Club.' BOSWELL. 'But, Sir, was he not once a factious man?' JOHNSON. 'O yes, Sir, as factious a fellow as could be found: one who was for sinking us all into the mob.' BOSWELL. 'How then, Sir, did he get into favour with the King?' JOHNSON. 'Because, Sir, I suppose he promised the King to do whatever the King pleased.'

He said, 'Goldsmith's blundering speech to Lord Shelburne, which has been so often mentioned, and which he really did make to him, was only a blunder in emphasis:— "I wonder they should call your Lordship *Malagrida*, for Malagrida was a very good man;"—meant, I wonder they should use *Malagrida* as a term of reproach.'

Soon after this time I had an opportunity of seeing, by means of one of his friends, a proof that his talents, as well as his obliging service to authours, were ready as ever. He had revised 'The Village,' an admirable poem, by the Reverend Mr. Crabbe. Its sentiments as to the false notions of rustick happiness and rustick virtue, were quite congenial with his own; and he had taken the trouble not only to suggest slight corrections and variations, but to furnish some lines, when he thought he could give the writer's meaning better than in the words of the manuscript.[1]

On Sunday, March 30, I found him at home in the

marginal line:
*an admirable . . . Mr.
Crabbe* [H]

[1] I shall give an instance, marking the original by Roman, and Johnson's substitution in Italick characters:

'In fairer scenes, where peaceful pleasures spring,
Tityrus, the pride of Mantuan swains, might sing;
But charmed by him, or smitten with his views,
Shall modern poets court the Mantuan muse?
From Truth and Nature shall we widely stray,
Where Fancy leads, or Virgil led the way?'

'*On Mincio's Banks, in Cæsar's bounteous reign,
If Tityrus found the golden age again,
Must sleepy bards the flattering dream prolong,
Mechanick echoes of the Mantuan song?*
From Truth and Nature shall we widely stray,
Where Virgil, not where Fancy, leads the way?'

Here we find Johnson's poetical and critical powers undiminished. I must, however, observe, that the aids he gave to this poem, as to 'The Traveller' and 'Deserted Village' of Goldsmith, were so small as by no means to impair the distinguished merit of the authour.

evening, and had the pleasure to meet with Dr. Brocklesby, whose reading, and knowledge of life, and good spirits, supply him with a never-failing source of conversation. He mentioned a respectable gentleman, who became extremely penurious near the close of his life. Johnson said there must have been a degree of madness about him. 'Not at all, Sir, (said Dr. Brocklesby,) his judgement was entire.' Unluckily, however, he mentioned that although he had a fortune of twenty-seven thousand pounds, he denied himself many comforts, from an apprehension that he could not afford them. 'Nay, Sir, (cried Johnson,) when the judgement is so disturbed that a man cannot count, that is pretty well.'

I shall here insert a few of Johnson's sayings, without the formality of dates, as they have no reference to any particular time or place.

'The more a man extends and varies his acquaintance the better.' This, however, was meant with a just restriction; for, he on another occasion said to me, 'Sir, a man may be so much of every thing, that he is nothing of any thing.'

'Raising the wages of day-labourers is wrong; for it does not make them live better, but only makes them idler, and idleness is a very bad thing for human nature.'

'It is a very good custom to keep a journal for a man's own use; he may write upon a card a day all that is necessary to be written, after he has had experience of life. At first there is a great deal to be written, because there is a great deal of novelty; but when once a man has settled his opinions, there is seldom much to be set down.'

'There is nothing wonderful in the Journal[1] which we

---

[1] [In his Life of Swift, he thus speaks of this Journal:

'In the midst of his power and his politicks, he kept a journal of his visits, his walks, his interviews with ministers, and quarrels with his servant, and transmitted it to Mrs. Johnson and Mrs. Dingley, to whom he knew that whatever befel him was interesting, and no account could be too minute. Whether these diurnal trifles were properly exposed to eyes which had never received any pleasure from the Dean, may be reasonably doubted; they have, however, some odd attractions: the reader finding frequent mention of names which he has been used to consider as important, goes on in hope of information; and as there is nothing to fatigue attention, if he is disappointed, he can hardly complain.'

It may be added, that the reader not only hopes to find, but does find, in this very entertaining Journal, much curious information, respecting persons and things, which he will in vain seek for in other books of the same period. MALONE.]

see Swift kept in London, for it contains slight topicks, and it might soon be written.'

I praised the accuracy of an account-book of a lady whom I mentioned. JOHNSON. 'Keeping accounts, Sir, is of no use when a man is spending his own money, and has nobody to whom he is to account. You won't eat less beef to-day, because you have written down what it cost yesterday.' I mentioned another lady who thought as he did, so that her husband could not get her to keep an account of the expence of the family, as she thought it enough that she never exceeded the sum allowed her. JOHNSON. 'Sir, it is fit she should keep an account, because her husband wishes it; but I do not see its use.' I maintained that keeping an account has this advantage, that it satisfies a man that his money has not been lost or stolen, which he might sometimes be apt to imagine, were there no written state of his expence; and besides, a calculation of economy so as not to exceed one's income, cannot be made without a view of the different articles in figures, that one may see how to retrench in some particulars less necessary than others. This he did not attempt to answer.

Talking of an acquaintance of ours, whose narratives, which abounded in curious and interesting topicks, were unhappily found to be very fabulous; I mentioned Lord Mansfield's having said to me, 'Suppose we believe one *half* of what he tells.' JOHNSON. 'Ay; but we don't know *which* half to believe. By his lying we lose not only our reverence for him, but all comfort in his conversation.' BOSWELL. 'May we not take it as amusing fiction?' JOHNSON. 'Sir, the misfortune is, that you will insensibly believe as much of it as you incline to believe.'

It is remarkable, that notwithstanding their congeniality in politicks, he never was acquainted with a late eminent noble judge, whom I have heard speak of him as a writer, with great respect. Johnson, I know not upon what degree of investigation, entertained no exalted opinion of his Lordship's intellectual character. Talking of him to me one day, he said, 'It is wonderful, Sir, with how little real superiority of mind men can make an eminent figure in publick life.' He expressed himself to the same purpose concerning another law-lord, who, it seems, once took a

marginal line:
JOHNSON. '*Ay ... half to* [H]

marginal line:
said, 'It ... figure in [H]
underlined:
real [H]

fancy to associate with the wits of London; but with so little success, that Foote said, 'What can he mean by coming among us? He is not only dull himself, but the cause of dullness in others.'[a] Trying him by the test of his colloquial powers, Johnson had found him very defective. He once said to Sir Joshua Reynolds, 'This man now has been ten years about town, and has made nothing of it;' meaning as a companion.[1] He said to me, 'I never heard any thing from him in company that was at all striking; and depend upon it, Sir, it is when you come close to a man in conversation, that you discover what his real abilities are: to make a speech in a publick assembly is a knack. Now I honour Thurlow, Sir; Thurlow is a fine fellow; he fairly puts his mind to yours.'

After repeating to him some of his pointed, lively sayings, I said, 'It is a pity, Sir, you don't always remember your own good things, that you may have a laugh when you will.' JOHNSON. 'Nay, Sir, it is better that I forget them, that I may be reminded of them, and have a laugh on their being brought to my recollection.'

When I recalled to him his having said as we sailed up Lochlomond, 'That if he wore any thing fine, it should be *very* fine;' I observed that all his thoughts were upon a great scale. JOHNSON. 'Depend upon it, Sir, every man will have as fine a thing as he can get; as large a diamond for his ring.' BOSWELL. 'Pardon me, Sir: a man of a narrow mind will not think of it, a slight trinket will satisfy him:

"*Nec sufferre queat majoris pondera gemmæ.*"'

I told him I should send him some 'Essays' which I had written,[2] which I hoped he would be so good as to read, and pick out the good ones. JOHNSON. 'Nay, Sir, send me only the good ones: don't make *me* pick them.'

I heard him once say, 'Though the proverb "*Nullum numen abest, si sit prudentia*," does not always prove true, we

---

[1] Knowing as well as I do what precision and elegance of oratory his Lordship can display, I cannot but suspect that his unfavourable appearance in a social circle, which drew such animadversions upon him, must be owing to a cold affectation of consequence, from being reserved and stiff. If it be so, and he might be an agreeable man if he would, we cannot be sorry that he misses his aim.

[2] [Under the title of 'The Hypochondriack.' MALONE.]

marginal line:
not only . . . his collo-
quial [H]
a *This was Wedder-
burne.* [H]
  meaning Wedderburne
[I]

marginal line:
*fairly puts . . . to
yours* [H]

marginal line:
JOHNSON. '*Nay . . .
pick them* [H]

may be certain of the converse of it, *Nullum numen adest, si sit imprudéntia.*[a]

Once, when Mr. Seward was going to Bath, and asked his commands, he said, 'Tell Dr. Harrington that I wish he would publish another volume of the "*Nugæ antiquæ;*"[1] it is a very pretty book.'[2] Mr. Seward seconded this wish, and recommended to Dr. Harrington to dedicate it to Johnson, and take for his motto, what Catullus says to Cornelius Nepos:

> '———— namque tu solebas
> Meas esse aliquid putare NUGAS.'

As a small proof of his kindliness and delicacy of feeling, the following circumstance may be mentioned: One evening when we were in the street together, and I told him I was going to sup at Mr. Beauclerk's, he said, 'I'll go with you.' After having walked part of the way, seeming to recollect something, he suddenly stopped and said, 'I cannot go,—but *I do not love Beauclerk the less.*'

On the frame of his portrait, Mr. Beauclerk had inscribed,

> '———— Ingenium ingens
> Inculto latet hoc sub corpore.'

After Mr. Beauclerk's death, when it became Mr. Langton's property, he made the inscription be defaced. Johnson said complacently, 'It was kind in you to take it off;' and then after a short pause, added, 'and not unkind in him to put it on.'

He said, 'How few of his friends' houses would a man choose to be at, when he is sick!' He mentioned one or two. I recollect only Thrale's.

He observed, 'There is a wicked inclination in most people to suppose an old man decayed in his intellects. If a young or middle-aged man, when leaving a company, does not recollect where he laid his hat, it is nothing; but if

a corrected to *ni sit prudentia* [H]
ni *sit prudentia* [I]

[1] It has since appeared.

[2] [A new and greatly improved edition of this very curious collection was published by Mr. Park in 1804, in two volumes, octavo. In this edition the letters are chronologically arranged, and the account of the Bishops, which was formerly printed from a very corrupt copy, is taken from Sir John Harrington's original manuscript, which he presented to Henry Prince of Wales, and is now in the Royal Library in the Museum. MALONE.]

the same inattention is discovered in an old man, people will shrug up their shoulders, and say, "His memory is going."'

When I once talked to him of some of the sayings which every body repeats, but nobody knows where to find, such as, *Quos* DEUS *vult perdere, prius dementat;* he told me that he was once offered ten guineas to point out from whence *Semel insanivimus omnes* was taken. He could not do it; but many years afterwards met with it by chance in *Johannes Baptista Mantuanus.*[1]

marginal line:
The words ... *insani-vimus omnes* [H]

[1] [The words occur, (as Mr. Bindley observes to me,) in the First Eclogue of Mantuanus, DE HONESTO AMORE, &c.

Id commune malum; semel insanivimus omnes.

With the following elucidation of the other saying—*Quos Deus* (it should rather be—*Quem Jupiter*) *vult perdere, prius dementat,*—Mr. Boswell was furnished by Mr. Richard How, of Apsley, in Bedfordshire, as communicated to that gentleman by his friend Mr. John Pitts, late Rector of Great Brickhill, in Buckinghamshire:

'Perhaps no scrap of Latin whatever has been more quoted than this. It occasionally falls even from those who are scrupulous even to pedantry in their Latinity, and will not admit a word into their compositions, which has not the sanction of the first age. The word *demento* is of no authority, either as a verb active or neuter.—After a long search for the purpose of deciding a bet, some gentlemen of Cambridge found it among the fragments of Euripides, in what edition I do not recollect, where it is given as a translation of a Greek Iambick:

Ον Θεος θελει απολεσαι, πρωτ' αποφρεναι.

marginal line:
age. The ... *of de-ciding* [H]
marginal line:
is given ... *Greek Iambick* [H]

'The above scrap was found in the hand-writing of a suicide of fashion, Sir D. O.,[a] some years ago, lying on the table of the room where he had destroyed himself. The suicide was a man of classical acquirements: he left no other paper behind him.'—

[a] *Sir D'Anvers Osborne* [H]
Sir Danvers Osborne Poor Man! [I]

Another of these proverbial sayings—

Incidit in Scyllam, cupiens vitare Charybdim,

I some years ago, in a Note on a passage in THE MERCHANT OF VENICE, traced to its source. It occurs (with a slight variation) in the ALEXANDREIS of Philip Gualtier, (a poet of the thirteenth century) which was printed at Lyons in 1558. Darius is the person addressed:

marginal line:
in the ... *is the* [H]

————————————Quò tendis inertem,
Rex periture, fugam? nescis, heu! perdite, nescis
Quem fugias: hostes incurris dum fugis hostem;
Incidis in Scyllam, cupiens vitare Charybdim.

The authour of this line was first ascertained by Galleottus Martius, who died in 1476; as is observed in MENAGIANA, vol. iii. p. 130. edit. 1762.— For an account of Philip Gualtier, see Vossius de Poet. Latin. p. 254. fol. 1697.

A line not less frequently quoted than any of the preceding, was suggested for enquiry, several years ago, in a Note on THE RAPE OF LUCRECE:

Solamen miseris socios habuisse doloris:—

But the authour of this verse has not, I believe, been discovered. MALONE.]

I am very sorry that I did not take a note of an eloquent argument in which he maintained that the situation of Prince of Wales was the happiest of any person's in the kingdom, even beyond that of the Sovereign. I recollect only—the enjoyment of hope,—the high superiority of rank, without the anxious cares of government,—and a great degree of power, both from natural influence wisely used, and from the sanguine expectations of those who look forward to the chance of future favour.

Sir Joshua Reynolds communicated to me the following particulars:

Johnson thought the poems published as translations from Ossian, had so little merit, that he said, 'Sir, a man might write such stuff for ever, if he would *abandon* his mind to it.'

He said, 'A man should pass a part of his time with *the laughers*, by which means any thing ridiculous or particular about him might be presented to his view, and corrected.' I observed, he must have been a bold laugher who would have ventured to tell Dr. Johnson of any of his particularities.[1]

Having observed the vain ostentatious importance of many people in quoting the authority of Dukes and Lords, as having been in their company, he said, he went to the other extreme, and did not mention his authority when he should have done it, had it not been that of a Duke or a Lord.

Dr. Goldsmith said once to Dr. Johnson, that he wished for some additional members to the LITERARY CLUB, to give it an agreeable variety; for (said he) there can now be nothing new among us: we have travelled over one another's minds. Johnson seemed a little angry, and said, 'Sir, you have not travelled over *my* mind, I promise you.' Sir Joshua, however, thought Goldsmith right; observing, that 'when people have lived a great deal together, they

marginal lines:
travelled over . . . not travelled [H]
marginal line:
when people . . . every subject [H]

[1] I am happy, however, to mention a pleasing instance of his enduring with great gentleness to hear one of his most striking particularities pointed out:—Miss Hunter, a niece of his friend Christopher Smart, when a very young girl, struck by his extraordinary motions, said to him.[a] 'Pray, Dr. Johnson, why do you make such strange gestures? —'From bad habit, (he replied.) Do you, my dear, take care to guard against bad habits.' This I was told by the young lady's brother at Margate.

index sign:
such strange gestures etc. [H]
[a] *curious. She was as mad as her Uncle Kit I suppose.* [I]

know what each of them will say on every subject. A new understanding, therefore, is desirable; because though it may only furnish the same sense upon a question which would have been furnished by those with whom we are accustomed to live, yet this sense will have a different colouring; and colouring is of much effect in every thing else as well as in painting.'

Johnson used to say that he made it a constant rule to talk as well as he could, both as to sentiment and expression; by which means, what had been originally effort became familiar and easy. The consequence of this, Sir Joshua observed, was, that his common conversation in all companies was such as to secure him universal attention, as something above the usual colloquial style was expected.

Yet, though Johnson had this habit in company, when another mode was necessary, in order to investigate truth, he could descend to a language intelligible to the meanest capacity. An instance of this was witnessed by Sir Joshua Reynolds, when they were present at an examination of a little blackguard boy, by Mr. Saunders Welch, the late Westminster Justice. Welch, who imagined that he was exalting himself in Dr. Johnson's eyes by using big words, spoke in a manner that was utterly unintelligible to the boy; Dr. Johnson perceiving it, addressed himself to the boy, and changed the pompous phraseology into colloquial language. Sir Joshua Reynolds, who was much amused by this proceeding, which seemed a kind of reversing of what might have been expected from the two men, took notice of it to Dr. Johnson, as they walked away by themselves. Johnson said, that it was continually the case; and that he was always obliged to *translate* the Justice's swelling diction, (smiling,) so as that his meaning might be under-stood by the vulgar, from whom information was to be obtained.

Sir Joshua once observed to him, that he had talked above the capacity of some people with whom they had been in company together. 'No matter, Sir, (said Johnson); they consider it as a compliment to be talked to, as if they were wiser than they are. So true is this,

marginal lines:
Sir, (said . . . his audi-ence [H]

Sir, that Baxter made it a rule in every sermon that he preached, to say something that was above the capacity of his audience.'[1]

Johnson's dexterity in retort, when he seemed to be driven to an extremity by his adversary, was very remarkable. Of his power, in this respect, our common friend, Mr. Windham, of Norfolk, has been pleased to furnish me with an eminent instance. However unfavourable to Scotland, he uniformly gave liberal praise to George Buchanan, as a writer. In a conversation concerning the literary merits of the two countries, in which Buchanan was introduced, a Scotchman, imagining that on this ground he should have an undoubted triumph over him, exclaimed, 'Ah, Dr. Johnson, what would you have said of Buchanan, had he been an Englishman?'—'Why, Sir, (said Johnson, after a little pause,) I should *not* have said of Buchanan, had he been an *Englishman*, what I will now say of him as a *Scotchman*,—that he was the only man of genius his country ever produced.'[2]

underlined: *only* [H]

And this brings to my recollection another instance of the same nature. I once reminded him that when Dr. Adam Smith was expatiating on the beauty of Glasgow, he had cut him short by saying, 'Pray, Sir, have you ever seen Brentford?' and I took the liberty to add, 'My dear Sir, surely that was *shocking*.'—'Why, then, Sir, (he replied,) YOU have never seen Brentford.'[a]

marginal line: *Sir, have . . . took the* [H]

[a] *That I do not understand* [I]

Though his usual phrase for conversation was *talk*, yet he made a distinction; for when he once told me that he dined the day before at a friend's house, with 'a very pretty company;' and I asked him if there was good conversation, he answered, 'No, Sir; we had *talk* enough, but no *conversation;* there was nothing *discussed*.'

[1] The justness of this remark is confirmed by the following story, for which I am indebted to Lord Eliot: A country parson, who was remarkable for quoting scraps of Latin in his sermons, having died, one of his parishioners was asked how he liked his successor; 'He is a very good preacher, (was his answer,) but no *latiner*.'

[2] [This prompt and sarcastic retort may not unaptly be compared with Sir Henry Wotton's celebrated answer to a Priest in Italy, who asked him 'Where was your religion to be found, before Luther?'—'My religion was to be found then, where yours is not to be found now, in the written word of GOD.'[b] But Johnson's admirable reply has a sharper edge and perhaps more ingenuity than that of Wotton. MALONE.]

index sign: *yours is not* etc. [H]

[b] *There is another famous Reply recorded —Where was your Religion before Luther's day? Retort. Pray have you washed your Face today? Yes Sir. & Where was your Face early this Morning before you washed it?* [H]

Talking of the success of the Scotch in London, he imputed it in a considerable degree to their spirit of nationality. 'You know, Sir, (said he,) that no Scotchman publishes a book, or has a play brought upon the stage, but there are five hundred people ready to applaud him.'

He gave much praise to his friend, Dr. Burney's elegant and entertaining travels, and told Mr. Seward that he had them in his eye, when writing his 'Journey to the Western Islands of Scotland.'

Such was his sensibility, and so much was he affected by pathetick poetry, that, when he was reading Dr. Beattie's 'Hermit' in my presence, it brought tears into his eyes.[1a]

a *Yes—*
Man lovely Com-
plainer! Man calls thee
to mourn. [H]

He disapproved much of mingling real facts with fiction. On this account he censured a book entitled 'Love and Madness.'

Mr. Hoole told him, he was born in Moorfields, and had received part of his early instruction in Grub-street. 'Sir, (said Johnson, smiling) you have been *regularly* educated.' Having asked who was his instructor, and Mr. Hoole having answered, 'My uncle, Sir, who was a taylor;' Johnson, recollecting himself, said, 'Sir, I knew him; we

marginal line:
him the . . . club in [H]

called him the *metaphysical taylor.* He was of a club in Old-street, with me and George Psalmanazar, and some others; but pray, Sir, was he a good taylor?' Mr. Hoole having answered that he believed he was too mathematical, and

b *a Laputa Taylor.* [H]
very comical; he was
like the Taylor at
Laputa it seems [I]

used to draw squares and triangles on his shop-board,[b] so that he did not excel in the cut of a coat;'—'I am sorry for it, (said Johnson,) for I would have every man to be master of his own business.'

In pleasant reference to himself and Mr. Hoole, as brother authours, he often said, 'Let you and I, Sir, go together, and eat a beef-steak in Grub-street.'

Sir William Chambers, that great Architect,[2] whose works show a sublimity of genius, and who is esteemed by

---

[1] [The particular passage which excited this strong emotion was, as I have heard from my father, the third stanza, ''Tis night,' &c. J. Boswell.]

[2] The Honourable Horace Walpole, now Earl of Orford, thus bears testimony to this gentleman's merit as a writer: Mr. Chambers's 'Treatise on Civil Architecture' is the most sensible book, and the most exempt from prejudices, that ever was written on that science.—Preface to '*Anecdotes of Painting in England.*'

all who know him, for his social, hospitable, and generous qualities, submitted the manuscript of his 'Chinese Architecture' to Dr. Johnson's perusal. Johnson was much pleased with it, and said, 'It wants no addition nor correction, but a few lines of introduction;' which he furnished, and Sir William adopted.[1]

He said to Sir William Scott, 'The age is running mad after innovation; and all the business of the world is to be done in a new way; men are to be hanged in a new way; Tyburn itself is not safe from the fury of innovation.'[a] It having been argued that this was an improvement.—'No, Sir, (said he, eagerly,) it is *not* an improvement; they object, that the old method drew together a number of spectators. Sir, executions are intended to draw spectators. If they do not draw spectators, they don't answer their purpose. The old method was most satisfactory to all parties; the publick was gratified by a procession; the criminal was supported by it. Why is all this to be swept away?' I perfectly agree with Dr. Johnson upon this head, and am persuaded that executions now, the solemn procession being discontinued, have not nearly the effect which they formerly had. Magistrates both in London, and elsewhere, have, I am afraid, in this, had too much regard to their own ease.

Of Dr. Hurd, Bishop of Worcester, Johnson said to a friend,—'Hurd, Sir, is one of a set of men who account for every thing systematically; for instance, it has been a fashion to wear scarlet breeches; these men would tell you, that according to causes and effects, no other wear could at that time have been chosen.' He, however, said of him at another time to the same gentleman, 'Hurd, Sir, is a man whose acquaintance is a valuable acquisition.'[b]

That learned and ingenious Prelate it is well known published at one period of his life 'Moral and Political Dialogues,' with a woefully whiggish cast. Afterwards, his Lordship having thought better, came to see his errour, and

[a] *& Tyburn fell soon after this was said—It is now wholly forgotten. 1820.* [H]

[b] *So it might surely notwithstanding his Remark on Red Breeches.* [H]

---

[1] The introductory lines are these: 'It is difficult to avoid praising too little or too much. The boundless panegyricks which have been lavished upon the Chinese learning, policy, and arts, shew with what power novelty attracts regard, and how naturally esteem swells into admiration.

'I am far from desiring to be numbered among the exaggerators of Chinese excellence. I consider them as great, or wise, only in comparison

republished the work with a more constitutional spirit. Johnson, however, was unwilling to allow him full credit for his political conversion. I remember when his Lordship declined the honour of being Archbishop of Canterbury, Johnson said 'I am glad he did not go to Lambeth; for, after all, I fear he is a Whig in his heart.'

Johnson's attention to precision and clearness in expression was very remarkable. He disapproved of a parenthesis; and I believe in all his voluminous writings, not half a dozen of them will be found. He never used the phrases *the former* and *the latter*,[a] having observed, that they often occasioned obscurity; he therefore contrived to construct his sentences so as not to have occasion for them, and would even rather repeat the same words, in order to avoid them. Nothing is more common than to mistake surnames, when we hear them carelessly uttered for the first time. To prevent this, he used not only to pronounce them slowly and distinctly, but to take the trouble of spelling them; a practice which I have often followed, and which I wish were general.

Such was the heat and irritability of his blood,[b] that not only did he pare his nails to the quick, but scraped the joints of his fingers with a pen-knife, till they seemed quite red and raw.[c]

The heterogeneous composition of human nature was remarkably exemplified in Johnson. His liberality in giving his money to persons in distress was extraordinary. Yet there lurked about him a propensity to paltry saving. One day I owned to him, that 'I was occasionally troubled with a fit of *narrowness*.' 'Why, Sir, (said he,) so am I. *But I do not tell it*.' He has now and then borrowed a shilling of me; and when I asked him for it again, seemed to be rather out of humour. A droll little circumstance once occurred; as if he meant to reprimand my minute exactness as a creditor, he thus addressed me; — 'Boswell, *lend* me sixpence — *not to be repaid*.'

with the nations that surround them; and have no intention to place them in competition either with the antients or with the moderns of this part of the world; yet they must be allowed to claim our notice as a distinct and very singular race of men; as the inhabitants of a region divided by its situation from all civilized countries, who have formed their own manners, and invented their own arts, without the assistance of example.'[d]

[a] *They are very vulgar, & now grown very tedious.* [I]

[b] *was* that *the Reason? It is no better Reason than Hurd's for wearing red Breeches* [H]
underlined: *pen-knife* [I]

[c] *did he? I have seen him pick his Fingers but not scrape them with Knives.* [I]

[d] *A common Sailor's Reply to their vaunting was pointed very sharply. They were saying how they excelled the Europeans in this, that, & t'other. & Yet retorts the Fellow, if you have been as you say, pouring out Tea ever since the Flood—You never had Skill to make a Spout to your Teapot, till we taught you how.* [H]

This great man's attention to small things was very remarkable. As an instance of it, he one day said to me, 'Sir, when you get silver in change for a guinea, look carefully at it; you may find some curious piece of coin.'

Though a stern *true-born Englishman*, and fully prejudiced against all other nations, he had discernment enough to see, and candour enough to censure, the cold reserve too common among Englishmen towards strangers: 'Sir, (said he,) two men of any other nation who are shewn into a room together, at a house where they are both visitors, will immediately find some conversation. But two Englishmen will probably go each to a different window, and remain in obstinate silence. Sir, we as yet do not enough understand the common rights of humanity.'[a]

Johnson was at a certain period of his life a good deal with the Earl of Shelburne, now Marquis of Lansdown, as he doubtless could not but have a due value for that nobleman's activity of mind, and uncommon acquisitions of important knowledge, however much he might disapprove of other parts of his Lordship's character, which were widely different from his own.

Maurice Morgann, Esq. authour of the very ingenious 'Essay on the character of Falstaff,'[1] being a particular friend of his Lordship, had once an opportunity of entertaining Johnson for a day or two at Wycombe, when its Lord was absent, and by him I have been favoured with two anecdotes.

One is not a little to the credit of Johnson's candour. Mr. Morgann and he had a dispute pretty late at night, in which Johnson would not give up, though he had the wrong side; and in short, both kept the field. Next morning, when they met in the breakfasting-room, Dr. Johnson accosted Mr. Morgann thus: 'Sir, I have been thinking on our dispute last night—*You were in the right.*'

The other was as follows: Johnson, for sport perhaps, or from the spirit of contradiction, eagerly maintained that Derrick had merit as a writer. Mr. Morgann argued with him directly, in vain. At length he had recourse to this

[a] *It was much for him to confess—but obviously true & daily remarked: Lady Morgan's Observation that Talk was in England a Solemn Game at Chess—& in France a brisk Bout at Shuttlecock is new, & true, & pretty.* [H]

---

[1] Johnson being asked his opinion of this Essay, answered, 'Why, Sir, we shall have the man come forth again; and as he has proved Falstaff to be no coward, he may prove Iago to be a very good character.'

device. 'Pray, Sir, (said he) whether do you reckon Derrick or Smart the best poet?' Johnson at once felt himself roused; and answered, 'Sir, there is no settling the point of precedency between a louse and a flea.'

Once, when checking my boasting too frequently of myself in company, he said to me, 'Boswell, you often vaunt so much as to provoke ridicule. You put me in mind of a man who was standing in the kitchen of an inn with his back to the fire, and thus accosted the person next him, "Do you know, Sir, who I am?" "No, Sir, (said the other,) I have not that advantage." "Sir, (said he,) I am the *great* TWALMLEY, who invented the New Floodgate Iron."'[1] The Bishop of Killaloe, on my repeating the story to him, defended TWALMLEY, by observing that he was entitled to the epithet of *great;* for Virgil in his group of worthies in the Elysian fields—

Hic manus ob patriam pugnando vulnera passi; &c.

mentions

Inventas aut qui vitam excoluere per artes.

He was pleased to say to me one morning when we were left alone in his study, 'Boswell, I think, I am easier with you than with almost any body.'[a]

[a] *if not with Boswell —not with any one I suppose. A Man contented to be under his Feet.* [H]
two marginal lines: *remark, 'Sir ... their hearts* [H]

He would not allow Mr. David Hume any credit for his political principles, though similar to his own; saying of him, 'Sir, he was a Tory by chance.'

His acute observation of human life made him remark, 'Sir, there is nothing by which a man exasperates most people more, than by displaying a superior ability of brilliancy in conversation. They seem pleased at the time; but their envy makes them curse him at their hearts.'

My readers will probably be surprised to hear that the great Dr. Johnson could amuse himself with so slight and playful a species of composition as a *Charade.* I have recovered one which he made on Dr. Barnard, now Lord Bishop of Killaloe;[2] who has been pleased for many years to treat me with so much intimacy and social ease, that I may

---

[1] What the *great* TWALMLEY was so proud of having invented, was neither more nor less than a kind of box-iron for smoothing linen.

[2] [Afterwards translated to the see of Limerick. MALONE.]

presume to call him not only my Right Reverend, but my very dear, Friend. I therefore with peculiar pleasure give to the world a just and elegant compliment thus paid to his Lordship by Johnson.

CHARADE

'My *first*[1] shuts out thieves from your house or your room,
My *second*[2] expresses a Syrian perfume.
My *whole*[3] is a man in whose converse is shar'd
The strength of a Bar and the sweetness of Nard.'

Johnson asked Richard Owen Cambridge, Esq. if he had read the Spanish translation of Sallust, said to be written by a Prince of Spain, with the assistance of his tutor, who is professedly the authour of a treatise annexed, on the Phœnician language.

Mr. Cambridge commended the work, particularly as he thought the Translator understood his authour better than is commonly the case with Translators; but said, he was disappointed in the purpose for which he borrowed the book; to see whether a Spaniard could be better furnished with inscriptions from monuments, coins, or other antiquities, which he might more probably find on a coast, so immediately opposite to Carthage, than the Antiquaries of any other countries. JOHNSON. 'I am very sorry you were not gratified in your expectations.' CAMBRIDGE. 'The language would have been of little use, as there is no history existing in that tongue to balance the partial accounts which the Roman writers have left us.' JOHNSON. 'No, Sir. They have not been *partial*, they have told their own story, without shame or regard to equitable treatment of their injured enemy; they had no compunction, no feeling for a Carthaginian. Why, Sir, they would never have borne Virgil's description of Æneas's treatment of Dido, if she had not been a Carthaginian.'

I gratefully acknowledge this and other communications from Mr. Cambridge, whom, if a beautiful villa on the banks of the Thames, a few miles distant from London, a numerous and excellent library, which he accurately

---

[1] Bar.   [2] Nard.   [3] Barnard.

knows and reads, a choice collection of pictures, which he understands and relishes, an easy fortune, an amiable family, an extensive circle of friends and acquaintance, distinguished by rank, fashion, and genius, a literary fame, various, elegant and still increasing, colloquial talents rarely to be found, and with all these means of happiness, enjoying, when well advanced in years, health and vigour of body, serenity and animation of mind, do not entitle to be addressed *fortunate senex!* I know not to whom, in any age, that expression could with propriety have been used. Long may he live to hear and to feel it![1]

Johnson's love of little children, which he discovered upon all occasions, calling them 'pretty dears,' and giving them sweetmeats, was an undoubted proof of the real humanity and gentleness of his disposition.

His uncommon kindness to his servants, and serious concern, not only for their comfort in his world, but their happiness in the next, was another unquestionable evidence of what all, who were intimately acquainted with him, knew to be true.

Nor would it be just under this head, to omit the fondness which he shewed for animals which he had taken under his protection. I never shall forget the indulgence with which he treated Hodge, his cat; for whom he himself used to go out and buy oysters,[a] lest the servants, having that trouble, should take a dislike to the poor creature.[b] I am, unluckily, one of those who have an antipathy to a cat, so that I am uneasy when in the room with one; and I own, I frequently suffered a good deal from the presence of this same Hodge. I recollect him one day scrambling up Dr. Johnson's breast, apparently with much satisfaction, while my friend, smiling and half-whistling, rubbed down his back, and pulled him by the tail; and when I observed he was a fine cat, saying 'why, yes, Sir, but I have had cats whom I liked better than this;' and then as if perceiving Hodge to be out of countenance, adding, 'but he is a very fine cat, a very fine cat indeed.'

This reminds me of the ludicrous account which he gave

[a] *I used to joke him for getting* Valerian *to amuse Hodge in his last Hours.* [i]

[b] *no, it was lest they should consider him as degrading Humanity, by setting a Man to wait upon a Beast.* [H]

[c] *full of Family Fondness. How are the dear People? were his last Words.* [H]

[1] [Mr. Cambridge enjoyed all the blessings here enumerated for many years after this passage was written. He died at his seat near Twickenham, Sept. 17, 1802, in his eighty-sixth year.[c] MALONE.]

Mr. Langton, of the despicable state of a young gentleman of good family. 'Sir, when I heard of him last, he was running about town shooting cats.' And then in a sort of kindly reverie, he bethought himself of his own favourite cat, and said, 'But Hodge shan't be shot: no, no, Hodge shall not be shot.'

He thought Mr. Beauclerk made a shrewd and judicious remark to Mr. Langton, who, after having been for the first time in company with a well-known wit about town, was warmly admiring and praising him, — 'See him again,' said Beauclerk.[a]

[a] *it* was *well said.*
[H]

His respect for the Hierarchy, and particularly the Dignitaries of the Church, has been more than once exhibited in the course of this work. Mr. Seward saw him presented to the Archbishop of York, and described his *Bow to an* ARCH-BISHOP, as such a studied elaboration of homage, such an extension of limb, such a flexion of body, as have seldom or ever been equalled.

I cannot help mentioning with much regret, that by my own negligence I lost an opportunity of having the history of my family from its founder Thomas Boswell, in 1504, recorded and illustrated by Johnson's pen. Such was his goodness to me, that when I presumed to solicit him for so great a favour, he was pleased to say, 'Let me have all the materials you can collect, and I will do it both in Latin and English; then let it be printed, and copies of it be deposited in various places for security and preservation.' I can now only do the best I can to make up for this loss, keeping my great Master steadily in view. Family histories, like the *imagines majorum* of the ancients, excite to virtue: and I wish that they who really have blood, would be more careful to trace and ascertain its course. Some have affected to laugh at the history of the house of Yvery:[1] it would be well if many others would transmit their pedigrees to posterity, with the same accuracy and generous zeal, with which the Noble Lord who compiled that work has honoured and perpetuated his ancestry.

On Thursday, April 10, I introduced to him, at his house in Bolt-court, the Honourable and Reverend

[1] [Written by John, Earl of Egmont, and printed (but not published) in 1764. MALONE.]

William Stuart,[1] son of the Earl of Bute; a gentleman truly worthy of being known to Johnson; being, with all the advantages of high birth, learning, travel, and elegant manners, an exemplary parish-priest in every respect.

After some compliments on both sides, the tour which Johnson and I had made to the Hebrides was mentioned. —JOHNSON. 'I got an acquisition of more ideas by it than by any thing that I remember. I saw quite a different system of life.' BOSWELL. 'You would not like to make the same journey again?' JOHNSON. 'Why no, Sir; not the same: it is a tale told. Gravina, an Italian critick, observes, that every man desires to see that of which he has read; but no man desires to read an account of what he has seen: so much does description fall short of reality.[a] Description only excites curiosity; seeing satisfies it. Other people may go and see the Hebrides.' BOSWELL. 'I should wish to go and see some country totally different from what I have been used to; such as Turkey, where religion and every thing else are different.' JOHNSON. 'Yes, Sir; there are two objects of curiosity,—the Christian world, and the Mahometan world. All the rest may be considered as barbarous.' BOSWELL. 'Pray, Sir, is the "Turkish Spy" a genuine book?' JOHNSON. 'No, Sir. Mrs. Manley, in her Life, says, that her father wrote the first two volumes: and in another book, "Dunton's Life and Errours," we find that the rest was written by one *Sault*, at two guineas a sheet, under the direction of Dr. Midgeley.'[2]

BOSWELL. 'This has been a very factious reign, owing to the too great indulgence of Government.' JOHNSON. '*I* think so, Sir. What at first was lenity, grew timidity. Yet this is reasoning *à posteriori*, and may not be just. Supposing a few had at first been punished, I believe

[a] *very true indeed* [H]

[1] [At that time Vicar of Luton in Bedfordshire, where he lived for some years, and fully merited the character given of him in the text; now [1806] Lord Archbishop of Armagh, and Primate of Ireland. MALONE.]

[2] ['The Turkish Spy' was pretended to have been written originally in Arabick; from Arabick translated into Italian, and thence into English.[b] The real authour of the work, which was in fact originally written in Italian, was I. P. Marana, a Genoese, who died at Paris in 1693.

John Dunton in his Life says, that 'Mr. *William Bradshaw* received from Dr. Midgeley forty shillings a sheet for writing part of the "Turkish Spy;" but I do not find that he any where mentions *Sault* as engaged in that work.' MALONE.]

[b] *so it was—The* true *Acct. is in the Carpentariana: Charpentier gives the genuine Receipt for the Money paid.* [H]

There are many Italianisms in the Book [I]

faction would have been crushed; but it might have been said, that it was a sanguinary reign. A man cannot tell *à priori* what will be best for government to do. This reign has been very unfortunate. We have had an unsuccessful war; but that does not prove that we have been ill governed. One side or other must prevail in war, as one or other must win at play. When we beat Louis, we were not better governed; nor were the French better governed, when Louis beat us.'[a]

On Saturday, April 12, I visited him, in company with Mr. Windham, of Norfolk, whom, though a Whig, he highly valued. One of the best things he ever said was to this gentleman; who, before he set out for Ireland as Secretary to Lord Northington, when Lord Lieutenant, expressed to the Sage some modest and virtuous doubts, whether he could bring himself to practise those arts which it is supposed a person in that situation has occasion to employ. 'Don't be afraid, Sir, (said Johnson, with a pleasant smile,) you will soon make a very pretty rascal.'

He talked to-day a good deal of the wonderful extent and variety of London, and observed, that men of curious enquiry might see in it such modes of life as very few could even imagine. He in particular recommended to us to *explore Wapping*, which we resolved to do.[1]

Mr. Lowe, the painter, who was with him, was very much distressed that a large picture which he had painted was refused to be received into the Exhibition of the Royal Academy. Mrs. Thrale knew Johnson's character so superficially, as to represent him as unwilling to do small acts of benevolence; and mentions, in particular, that he would hardly take the trouble to write a letter in favour of his friends.[b] The truth, however, is, that he was remarkable, in an extraordinary degree, for what she denies to him; and, above all, for this very sort of kindness, writing letters for those to whom his solicitations might be of service. He now gave Mr. Lowe the following,[c] of which I was diligent

[a] *Oh that they were. Their King & Ministers were all excellent.* [H]

underlined: *Secretary* [H]

marginal line: *Don't be . . . pretty rascal* [H]

marginal line: *as very . . . which we* [H]

underlined: *favour of his* [1]

[b] *Yes, when his Friends like poor Lowe—were starving.* [1]

[c] *Yes—to get the Man a Dinner: he was a very poor Man. He would not have written Letters for Barry & Benjamin West.* [H]

[d] *There is nothing to be seen but Coarseness; True London Coarseness real Blackguardism* [1]

---

[1] We accordingly carried our scheme into execution, in October, 1792; but whether from that uniformity which has in modern times, in a great degree, spread through every part of the metropolis, or from our want of sufficient exertion, we were disappointed.[d]

enough, with his permission, to take copies at the next coffee-house, while Mr. Windham was so good as to stay by me.

'TO SIR JOSHUA REYNOLDS
'SIR,

'Mr. Lowe considers himself as cut off from all credit and all hope, by the rejection of his picture from the Exhibition. Upon this work he has exhausted all his powers, and suspended all his expectations: and, certainly, to be refused an opportunity of taking the opinion of the publick, is in itself a very great hardship. It is to be condemned without a trial.

'If you could procure the revocation of this incapacitating edict, you would deliver an unhappy man from great affliction. The Council has sometimes reversed its own determination; and I hope, that by your interposition this luckless picture may be got admitted.

'I am, &c.
'April 12, 1783.'   'SAM. JOHNSON'

'TO MR. BARRY
'SIR,

'Mr. Lowe's exclusion from the exhibition gives him more trouble than you and the other gentlemen of the Council could imagine or intend. He considers disgrace and ruin as the inevitable consequence of your determination.

'He says, that some pictures have been received after rejection; and if there be any such precedent, I earnestly entreat that you will use your interest in his favour. Of his work I can say nothing; I pretend not to judge of painting; and this picture I never saw: but I conceive it extremely hard to shut out any man from the possibility of success; and therefore I repeat my request that you will propose the re-consideration of Mr. Lowe's case; and if there be any among the Council with whom my name can have any weight, be pleased to communicate to them the desire of, Sir,

'Your most humble servant,
'April 12, 1783.'   'SAM. JOHNSON'

Such intercession was too powerful to be resisted; and Mr. Lowe's performance was admitted at Somerset Place. The subject, as I recollect, was the Deluge, at that point of time when the water was verging to the top of the last uncovered mountain.[a] Near to the spot was seen the last of the antediluvian race, exclusive of those who were saved in the ark of Noah. This was one of those giants, then the inhabitants of the earth, who had still strength to swim, and with one of his hands held aloft his infant child. Upon the small remaining dry spot appeared a famished lion, ready to spring at the child and devour it. Mr. Lowe told me that Johnson said to him, 'Sir, your picture is noble and probable.'—'A compliment, indeed, (said Mr. Lowe,) from a man who cannot lie, and cannot be mistaken.'

About this time he wrote to Mrs. Lucy Porter, mentioning his bad health, and that he intended a visit to Lichfield. 'It is (says he) with no great expectation of amendment that I make every year a journey into the country: but it is pleasant to visit those whose kindness has been often experienced.'

On April 18, (being Good Friday,) I found him at breakfast, in his usual manner upon that day, drinking tea without milk, and eating a cross bun to prevent faintness; we went to St. Clement's church, as formerly. When we came home from church, he placed himself on one of the stone-seats at his garden-door, and I took the other, and thus in the open air, and in a placid frame of mind, he talked away very easily. JOHNSON. 'Were I a country gentleman, I should not be very hospitable, I should not have crowds in my house.' BOSWELL. 'Sir Alexander Dick tells me, that he remembers having a thousand people in a year to dine at his house; that is, reckoning each person as one, each time that he dined there.' JOHNSON. 'That, Sir, is about three a-day.' BOSWELL. 'How your statement lessens the idea.' JOHNSON. 'That, Sir, is the good of counting. It brings every thing to a certainty, which before floated in the mind indefinitely.' BOSWELL. 'But *Omne ignotum pro magnifico est:* one is sorry to have this diminished.' JOHNSON. 'Sir, you should not allow yourself to be delighted with errour.' BOSWELL. 'Three a day seem but few.' JOHNSON. 'Nay, Sir, he who entertains

marginal line:
to the .... Near to [H]

[a] *It was a fine Idea, but poor Lowe could not paint it.* [H & I]

marginal line:
inhabitants of ... infant child [H]

marginal line:
drinking tea ... bun to [H]

three a day, does very liberally. And if there is a large family, the poor entertain those three, for they eat what the poor would get: there must be superfluous meat; it must be given to the poor, or thrown out.' BOSWELL. 'I observe in London, that the poor go about and gather bones, which I understand are manufactured.' JOHNSON. 'Yes, Sir; they boil them, and extract a grease from them for greasing wheels and other purposes. Of the best pieces they make a mock ivory, which is used for hafts to knives, and various other things; the coarser pieces they burn, and pound, and sell the ashes.' BOSWELL. 'For what purpose, Sir?' JOHNSON. 'Why, Sir, for making a furnace for the chemists for melting iron. A paste made of burnt bones will stand a stronger heat than any thing else. Consider, Sir; if you are to melt iron, you cannot line your pot with brass, because it is softer than iron, and would melt sooner; nor with iron, for though malleable iron is harder than cast-iron, yet it would not do; but a paste of burnt bones will not melt.' BOSWELL. 'Do you know, Sir, I have discovered a manufacture to a great extent, of what you only piddle at,—scraping and drying the peel of oranges.[1] At a place in Newgate-street, there is a prodigious quantity prepared, which they sell to the distillers.' JOHNSON. 'Sir, I believe they make a higher thing out of them than a spirit; they make what is called orange-butter, the oil of the orange inspissated, which they mix perhaps with common pomatum, and make it fragrant. The oil does not fly off in the drying.'

BOSWELL. 'I wish to have a good walled garden.' JOHNSON. 'I don't think it would be worth the expence to you. We compute, in England, a park-wall at a thousand pounds a mile; now a garden-wall must cost at least as much. You intend your trees should grow higher than a deer will leap. Now let us see;—for a hundred pounds you could only have forty-four square yards, which is very little; for two hundred pounds, you may have eighty-four square yards, which is very well. But when will you get

---

[1] It is suggested to me by an anonymous Annotator on my Work, that the reason why Dr. Johnson collected the peels of squeezed oranges, may be found, in the 358th Letter in Mrs. Piozzi's Collection, where it appears that he recommended 'dried orange-peel, finely powdered,' as a medicine.

the value of two hundred pounds of walls, in fruit, in your climate? No, Sir, such contention with Nature is not worth while. I would plant an orchard, and have plenty of such fruit as ripen well in your country. My friend, Dr. Madden, of Ireland, said, that "in an orchard there should be enough to eat, enough to lay up, enough to be stolen, and enough to rot upon the ground." Cherries are an early fruit, you may have them; and you may have the early apples and pears.' BOSWELL. 'We cannot have nonpareils.'— JOHNSON. 'Sir, you can no more have nonpareils, than you can have grapes.' BOSWELL. 'We have them, Sir; but they are very bad.' JOHNSON. 'Nay, Sir, never try to have a thing, merely to shew that you *cannot* have it. From ground that would let for forty shillings you may have a large orchard; and you see it costs you only forty shillings. Nay, you may graze the ground, when the trees are grown up; you cannot, while they are young.' BOSWELL. 'Is not a good garden a very common thing in England, Sir?' JOHNSON. 'Not so common, Sir, as you imagine. In Lincolnshire there is hardly an orchard; in Staffordshire very little fruit.' BOSWELL. 'Has Langton no orchard?' JOHNSON. 'No, Sir.' BOSWELL. 'How so, Sir?' JOHNSON, 'Why, Sir, from the general negligence of the county. He has it not, because nobody else has it.' BOSWELL. 'A hot-house is a certain thing; I may have that.' JOHNSON. 'A hot-house is pretty certain; but you must first build it, then you must keep fires in it, and you must have a gardener to take care of it.' BOSWELL. 'But if I have a gardener at any rate?'—JOHNSON. 'Why, yes.' BOSWELL. 'I'd have it near my house; there is no need to have it in the orchard.' JOHNSON. 'Yes, I'd have it near my house.—I would plant a great many currants; the fruit is good, and they make a pretty sweetmeat.'

I record this minute detail, which some may think trifling, in order to shew clearly how this great man, whose mind could grasp such large and extensive subjects, as he has shewn in his literary labours, was yet well-informed in the common affairs of life, and loved to illustrate them.

Mr. Walker, the celebrated master of elocution, came in, and then we went up stairs into the study. I asked him if he had taught many clergymen. JOHNSON. 'I hope not.'

WALKER. 'I have taught only one, and he is the best reader I ever heard, not by my teaching, but by his own natural talents.' JOHNSON. 'Were he the best reader in the world, I would not have it told that he was taught.' Here was one of his peculiar prejudices. Could it be any disadvantage to the clergyman to have it known that he was taught an easy and graceful delivery? BOSWELL. 'Will you not allow, Sir, that a man may be taught to read well?' JOHNSON. 'Why, Sir, so far as to read better than he might do without being taught, yes. Formerly it was supposed that there was no difference in reading, but that one read as well as another.'[a] BOSWELL. 'It is wonderful to see old Sheridan as enthusiastick about oratory as ever.' WALKER. 'His enthusiasm as to what oratory will do, may be too great: but he reads well.' JOHNSON. 'He reads well, but he reads low; and you know it is much easier to read low than to read high; for when you read high, you are much more limited, your loudest note can be but one, and so the variety is less in proportion to the loudness. Now some people have occasion to speak to an extensive audience, and must speak loud to be heard.' WALKER. 'The art is to read strong, though low.'

Talking of the origin of language;—JOHNSON. 'It must have come by inspiration. A thousand, nay, a million of children could not invent a language. While the organs are pliable, there is not understanding enough to form a language; by the time that there is understanding enough, the organs are become stiff. We know that after a certain age we cannot learn to pronounce a new language. No foreigner, who comes to England when advanced in life, ever pronounces English tolerably well; at least such instances are very rare. When I maintain that language must have come by inspiration, I do not mean that inspiration is required for rhetorick, and all the beauties of language; for when once man has language, we can conceive that he may gradually form modifications of it. I mean only that inspiration seems to me to be necessary to give man the faculty of speech; to inform him that he may have speech; which I think he could no more find out without inspiration, than cows or hogs would think of

underlined:
was supposed [H]

[a] so it was: *The People did read shamefully —Yet Mr. Lee the Poet—many Years before Johnson was born; read so gracefully, The Players would not accept his Tragedies till they had heard them from other Lips, his own (they said) sweeten'd all which proceeded from them.* [H]

So it was the people did read shamefully—
[I]

such a faculty.' WALKER. 'Do you think, Sir, that there are any perfect synonimes in any language?' JOHNSON. 'Originally there were not; but by using words negligently, or in poetry, one word comes to be confounded with another.'

He talked of Dr. Dodd. 'A friend of mine, (said he,) came to me and told me, that a lady wished to have Dr. Dodd's picture in a bracelet, and asked me for a motto. I said, I could think of no better than *Currat Lex*. I was very willing to have him pardoned, that is, to have the sentence changed to transportation: but, when he was once hanged, I did not wish he should be made a saint.'

Mrs. Burney, wife of his friend Dr. Burney, came in, and he seemed to be entertained with her conversation.

Garrick's funeral was talked of as extravagantly expensive. Johnson, from his dislike to exaggeration, would not allow that it was distinguished by any extraordinary pomp. 'Were there not six horses to each coach?' said Mrs. Burney. JOHNSON. 'Madam, there were no more six horses than six phœnixes.'

Mrs. Burney wondered that some very beautiful new buildings should be erected in Moorfields, in so shocking a situation as between Bedlam and St. Luke's Hospital; and said she could not live there. JOHNSON. 'Nay, Madam, you see nothing there to hurt you. You no more think of madness by having windows that look to Bedlam, than you think of death by having windows that look to a church-yard.'[a] MRS. BURNEY. We may look to a church-yard, Sir; for it is right that we should be kept in mind of death.' JOHNSON. 'Nay, Madam, if you go to that, it is right that we should be kept in mind of madness, which is occasioned by too much indulgence of imagination. I think a very moral use may be made of these new buildings: I would have those who have heated imaginations live there, and take warning.' MRS. BURNEY. 'But, Sir, many of the poor people that are mad, have become so from disease, or from distressing events. It is, therefore, not their fault, but their misfortune; and, therefore, to think of them, is a melancholy consideration.'

Time passed on in conversation till it was too late for the service of the church at three o'clock. I took a walk,

[a] & in Italy they would think of no thing else if they lookd into a Churchyard [H]

and left him alone for some time; then returned, and we had coffee and conversation again by ourselves.

I stated the character of a noble friend of mine, as a curious case for his opinion:—'He is the most inexplicable man to me that I ever knew. Can you explain him, Sir? He is, I really believe, noble-minded, generous, and princely. But his most intimate friends may be separated from him for years, without his ever asking a question concerning them. He will meet them with a formality, a coldness, a stately indifference; but when they come close to him, and fairly engage him in conversation, they find him as easy, pleasant, and kind, as they could wish. One then supposes that what is so agreeable will soon be renewed; but stay away from him for half a year, and he will neither call on you, nor send to enquire about you.' JOHNSON. 'Why, Sir, I cannot ascertain his character exactly, as I do not know him; but I should not like to have such a man for my friend. He may love study, and wish not to be interrupted by his friends; *Amici fures temporis*. He may be a frivolous man, and be so much occupied with petty pursuits that he may not want friends. Or he may have a notion that there is dignity in appearing indifferent, while he in fact may not be more indifferent at his heart than another.'

We went to evening prayers at St. Clement's, at seven, and then parted.[1]

[1] [The reader will recollect, that in the year 1775, when Dr. Johnson visited France, he was kindly entertained by the English Benedictine Monks at Paris. (See vol. ii. p. 201.) One of that body, the Reverend James Compton, in the course of some conversation with him at that time, asked him if any of them should become converts to the Protestant faith, and should visit England, whether they might hope for a friendly reception from him; to which he warmly replied, 'that he should receive such a convert most cordially.' In consequence of this conversation, Mr. Compton, a few years afterwards, having some doubts concerning the religion in which he had been bred, was induced, by reading the 110th Number of THE RAMBLER (on REPENTANCE,) to consider the subject more deeply; and the result of his inquiries was, a determination to become a protestant. With this in view, in the summer of 1782, he returned to his native country, from whence he had been absent from his sixth to his thirty-fifth year; and on his arrival in London, very scantily provided with the means of subsistence, he immediately repaired to Bolt-court, to visit Dr. Johnson; and having informed him of his desire to be admitted into the Church of England, for this purpose solicited his aid to procure for him an introduction to the Bishop of London (Dr. Lowth). At the time of his first visit, Johnson was so much

On Sunday, April 20, being Easter-day, after attending
solemn service at St. Paul's, I came to Dr. Johnson, and
found Mr. Lowe, the painter, sitting with him. Mr. Lowe
mentioned the great number of new buildings of late in
London, yet that Dr. Johnson had observed, that the
number of inhabitants was not increased. JOHNSON.
'Why, Sir, the bills of mortality prove that no more people
die now than formerly; so it is plain no more live. The
register of births proves nothing, for not one-tenth of the
people of London are born there.' BOSWELL. 'I believe,
Sir, a great many of the children born in London die early.'
JOHNSON. 'Why, yes, Sir.' BOSWELL. 'But those who do
live, are as stout and strong people as any: Dr. Price says,
they must be naturally strong to get through.' JOHNSON.
'That is system, Sir. A great traveller observes, that it is
said there are no weak or deformed people among the
Indians; but he with much sagacity assigns the reason of
this, which is, that the hardship of their life as hunters and

marginal line:
life as . . . been an [H]

indisposed, that he could allow him only a short conversation of a few
minutes; but he desired him to call again in the course of the following week.
When Mr. Compton visited him a second time, he was perfectly recovered
from his indisposition; received him with the utmost cordiality; and not only
undertook the management of the business in which his friendly interposition
had been requested, but with great kindness exerted himself in this gentleman's favour, with a view to his future subsistence, and immediately
supplied him with the means of present support.

Finding that the proposed introduction to the Bishop of London had from
some accidental causes been deferred, lest Mr. Compton, who then lodged at
Highgate, should suppose himself neglected, he wrote him the following note:

'SIR,   'TO THE REVEREND MR. COMPTON

'I HAVE directed Dr. Vyse's letter to be sent to you, that you may
know the situation of your business. Delays are incident to all affairs; but
there appears nothing in your case of either superciliousness or neglect. Dr.
Vyse seems to wish you well.

'I am, Sir, your most humble servant,

Oct. 6, 1782.'   'SAM. JOHNSON'

Mr. Compton having, by Johnson's advice, quitted Highgate, and settled
in London, had now more frequent opportunities of visiting his friend, and
profiting by his conversation and advice. Still, however, his means of subsistence being very scanty, Dr. Johnson kindly promised to afford him a
decent maintenance, until by his own exertions he should be able to obtain
a livelihood; which benevolent offer he accepted, and lived entirely at
Johnson's expence till the end of January, 1783, in which month, having
previously been introduced to Bishop Lowth, he was received into our
communion in St. James's parish-church. In the following April, the place
of Under-Master of St. Paul's school having become vacant, his friendly

fishers, does not allow weak or diseased children to grow up. Now had I been an Indian, I must have died early; my eyes would not have served me to get food. I indeed now could fish, give me English tackle; but had I been an Indian, I must have starved, or they would have knocked me on the head, when they saw I could do nothing.' BOSWELL. 'Perhaps they would have taken care of you; we are told they are fond of oratory,—you would have talked to them.' JOHNSON. 'Nay, Sir, I should not have lived long enough to be fit to talk; I should have been dead before I was ten years old. Depend upon it, Sir, a savage, when he is hungry, will not carry about with him a looby of nine years old, who cannot help himself. They have no affection, Sir.' BOSWELL. 'I believe natural affection, of which we hear so much, is very small.'

protector did him a more essential service, by writing the following letter in his favour, to the Mercers' Company, in whom the appointment of the new Under-Master lay:

'TO THE WORSHIPFUL COMPANY OF THE MERCERS

'GENTLEMEN,

'AT the request of the Reverend Mr. James Compton, who now solicits your votes to be elected Under-Master of St. Paul's School, I testify, with great sincerity, that he is in my opinion, a man of abilities sufficient, and more than sufficient, for the duties of the office for which he is a candidate.

'I am, Gentlemen,

'Bolt-court, Fleet-street,   'Your most humble servant,

April 19, 1783.'   'SAM. JOHNSON'

Though this testimony in Mr. Compton's favour was not attended with immediate success, the Reverend Mr. Edwards, who had been bred in St. Paul's School, having been elected to fill the vacant office, yet Johnson's kindness was not without effect; and the result of his recommendation shews how highly he was estimated in the great commercial city of London; for his letter procured Mr. Compton so many well-wishers in the respectable company of Mercers, that he was honoured, by the favour of several of its members, with more applications to teach Latin and French, than he could find time to attend to.—In 1796, the Reverend Mr. Gibert, one of his Majesty's French Chaplains, having accepted a living in Guernsey, nominated Mr. Compton as his substitute at the French Chapel of St. James's; which appointment in April 1811, he relinquished for a better in the French Chapel at Bethnal Green.—By the favour of Dr. Porteus, the late excellent Bishop of London, he was also appointed, in 1802, Chaplain of the Dutch Chapel at St. James's, a station which he still holds.

The preceding account of this gentleman's conversion, and of Johnson's

ª I remember however that the Acct. of Mr. Compton's Marriage disgusted him [H]

subsequent liberality to him, would doubtless have been embodied by our authour in his work, had he been apprized of the circumstances above related; which add one more proof to those which Mr. Boswell has accumulated, of Johnson's uniform and unbounded benevolence.ª MALONE.]

JOHNSON. 'Sir, natural affection is nothing: but affection from principle and established duty, is sometimes wonderfully strong.' LOWE. 'A hen, Sir, will feed her chickens in preference to herself.' JOHNSON. 'But we don't know that the hen is hungry; let the hen be fairly hungry, and I'll warrant she'll peck the corn herself. A cock, I believe, will feed hens instead of himself; but we don't know that the cock is hungry.' BOSWELL. 'And that, Sir, is not from affection but gallantry. But some of the Indians have affection.' JOHNSON. 'Sir, that they help some of their children is plain; for some of them live, which they could not do without being helped.'

queried:
natural affection etc.
[H]

I dined with him; the company were, Mrs. Williams, Mrs. Desmoulins, and Mr. Lowe. He seemed not to be well, talked little, grew drowsy soon after dinner, and retired; upon which I went away.

Having next day gone to Mr. Burke's seat in the country, from whence I was recalled by an express, that a near relation of mine had killed his antagonist in a duel, and was himself dangerously wounded, I saw little of Dr. Johnson till Monday, April 28, when I spent a considerable part of the day with him, and introduced the subject, which then chiefly occupied my mind. JOHNSON. 'I do not see, Sir, that fighting is absolutely forbidden in Scripture; I see revenge forbidden, but not self-defence.' BOSWELL. 'The Quakers say it is; "Unto him that smiteth thee on one cheek, offer him also the other."' JOHNSON. 'But stay, Sir; the text is meant only to have the effect of moderating passion; it is plain that we are not to take it in a literal sense. We see this from the context, where there are other recommendations, which I warrant you the Quaker will not take literally; as, for instance, "From him that would borrow of thee, turn thou not away." Let a man whose credit is bad, come to a Quaker, and say, "Well, Sir, lend me a hundred pounds;" he'll find him as unwilling as any other man. No, Sir, a man may shoot the man who invades his character, as he may shoot him who attempts to break into his house.[1] So in

[1] I think it necessary to caution my readers against concluding that in this or any other conversation of Dr. Johnson, they have his serious and deliberate opinion on the subject of duelling. In my Journal of a Tour to the Hebrides,

1745, my friend, Tom Cumming the Quaker, said he would not fight, but he would drive an ammunition cart; and we know that the Quakers have sent flannel waistcoats to our soldiers, to enable them to fight better.' BOSWELL. 'When a man is the aggressor, and by ill-usage forces on a duel in which he is killed, have we not little ground to hope that he is gone to a state of happiness?' JOHNSON. 'Sir, we are not to judge determinately of the state in which a man leaves this life. He may in a moment have repented effectually, and it is possible may have been accepted of GOD. There is in "Camden's Remains," an epitaph upon a very wicked man, who was killed by a fall from his horse, in which he is supposed to say,

"Between the stirrup and the ground,
I mercy ask'd, I mercy found."' [1]

BOSWELL. 'Is not the expression in the Burial-service,— "in the *sure* and *certain* hope[a] of a blessed resurrection,"— too strong to be used indiscriminately, and, indeed, sometimes when those over whose bodies it is said, have been notoriously profane?' JOHNSON. 'It is sure and certain *hope*, Sir; not *belief*.' I did not insist further; but cannot help thinking that less positive words would be more proper. [2]

Talking of a man who was grown very fat, so as to be

a *certain Hope is a Contradiction in Terms. if it is Hope it is not Certainty—and vice versa.* [I]

marginal line:
that he . . . owned he [H]

3 edit. p. 386, it appears that he made this frank confession: 'Nobody at times, talks more laxly than I do;' and, ibid. p. 231, 'He fairly owned he could not explain the rationality of duelling.' We may, therefore, infer, that he could not think that justifiable, which seems so inconsistent with the spirit of the Gospel. At the same time it must be confessed, that from the prevalent notions of honour, a gentleman who receives a challenge is reduced to a dreadful alternative. A remarkable instance of this is furnished by a clause in the will of the late Colonel Thomas, of the Guards, written the night before he fell in a duel, September 3, 1783: 'In the first place, I commit my soul to Almighty GOD, in hopes of his mercy and pardon for the irreligious step I now (in compliance with the unwarrantable customs of this wicked world) put myself under the necessity of taking.'

[1] [In repeating this epitaph Johnson improved it. The original runs thus:
'*Betwixt* the stirrup and the ground,
Mercy I ask'd, mercy I found.' MALONE.]

[2] Upon this objection the Reverend Mr. Ralph Churton, Fellow of Brazennose College, Oxford, has favoured me with the following satisfactory observation. 'The passage in the Burial-service does not mean the resurrection of the person interred, but the general resurrection;[b] it is in sure and certain hope of *the* resurrection; not *his* resurrection. Where the deceased is really spoken of, the expression is very different,—"as our hope is this our brother doth" [rest in Christ;] a mode of speech consistent with every

underlined:
general [H]
b *Certainly* [H]

incommoded with corpulency; he said, 'He eats too much, Sir.' BOSWELL. 'I don't know, Sir; you will see one man fat, who eats moderately, and another lean, who eats a great deal.' JOHNSON. 'Nay, Sir, whatever may be the quantity that a man eats, it is plain that if he is too fat, he has eaten more than he should have done. One man may have a digestion that consumes food better than common; but it is certain that solidity is encreased by putting something to it.' BOSWELL. 'But may not solids swell and be distended?' JOHNSON. 'Yes, Sir, they may swell and be distended; but that is not fat.'

We talked of the accusation against a gentleman for supposed delinquencies in India. JOHNSON. 'What foundation there is for accusation I know not, but they will not get at him. Where bad actions are committed at so great a distance, a delinquent can obscure the evidence till the scent becomes cold; there is a cloud between, which cannot be penetrated: therefore all distant power is bad. I am clear that the best plan for the government of India is a despotick governour; for if he be a good man, it is evidently the best government; and supposing him to be a bad man, it is better to have one plunderer than many. A governour, whose power is checked, lets others plunder, that he himself may be allowed to plunder; but if despotick, he sees that the more he lets others plunder, the less there will be for himself, so he restrains them; and though he himself plunders, the country is a gainer, compared with being plundered by numbers.'[a]

[a] *excellently said.* [H]

I mentioned the very liberal payment which had been received for reviewing; and, as evidence of this, that it had been proved in a trial, that Dr. Shebbeare had received six guineas a sheet for that kind of literary labour. JOHNSON. 'Sir, he might get six guineas for a particular sheet, but not *communibus sheetibus*.' BOSWELL. 'Pray, Sir, by a sheet of review is it meant that it shall be all of the writer's

thing but absolute certainty that the person departed doth *not* rest in Christ, which no one can be assured of, without immediate revelation from Heaven. In the first of these places also, "eternal life" does not necessarily mean eternity of bliss, but merely the eternity of the state, whether in happiness or in misery, to ensue upon the resurrection; which is probably the sense of "the life everlasting," in the Apostles Creed. See Wheatly and Bennet on the Common Prayer.'

own composition? or are extracts, made from the book reviewed, deducted?' JOHNSON. 'No, Sir; it is a sheet, no matter of what.' BOSWELL. 'I think, that is not reasonable.' JOHNSON. 'Yes, Sir, it is. A man will more easily write a sheet all his own, than read an octavo volume to get extracts.' To one of Johnson's wonderful fertility of mind, I believe writing was really easier than reading and extracting; but with ordinary men the case is very different. A great deal, indeed, will depend upon the care and judgement with which extracts are made. I can suppose the operation to be tedious and difficult; but in many instances we must observe crude morsels cut out of books as if at random; and when a large extract is made from one place, it surely may be done with very little trouble. One, however, I must acknowledge, might be led, from the practice of reviewers, to suppose that they take a pleasure in original writing; for we often find, that instead of giving an accurate account of what has been done by the authour whose work they are reviewing, which is surely the proper business of a literary journal, they produce some plausible and ingenious conceits of their own, upon the topicks which have been discussed.

marginal lines: *giving an . . . have been* [H]

Upon being told that old Mr. Sheridan, indignant at the neglect of his oratorical plans, had threatened to go to America;—JOHNSON. 'I hope he will go to America.' BOSWELL. 'The Americans don't want oratory.' JOHNSON. 'But we can want Sheridan.'

On Monday, April 28, I found him at home in the morning, and Mr. Seward with him. Horace having been mentioned;—BOSWELL. 'There is a great deal of thinking in his works. One finds there almost every thing but religion.' SEWARD. 'He speaks of his returning to it, in his Ode *Parcus Deorum cultor et infrequens*.' JOHNSON. 'Sir, he was not in earnest; this was merely poetical.' BOSWELL. 'There are, I am afraid, many people who have no religion at all.' SEWARD. 'And sensible people too.' JOHNSON. 'Why, Sir, not sensible in that respect. There must be either a natural or a moral stupidity, if one lives in a total neglect of so very important a concern.' SEWARD. 'I wonder that there should be people without religion.' JOHNSON. 'Sir, you need not wonder at this, when you consider how large a proportion of almost every man's life is passed without thinking of it. I myself was for some years totally regardless of religion. It had dropped out of my mind. It was at an early part of my life. Sickness brought it back, and I hope I have never lost it since.' BOSWELL. 'My dear Sir, what a man must you have been without religion! Why you must have gone on drinking, and swearing, and—' JOHNSON. (with a smile) 'I drank enough and swore enough to be sure.' SEWARD. 'One should think that sickness, and the view of death would make more men religious.' JOHNSON. 'Sir, they do not know how to go about it: they have not the first notion. A man who has never had religion before, no more grows religious when he is sick, than a man who has never learnt figures can count, when he has need of calculation.'

I mentioned a worthy friend of ours[a] whom we valued much, but observed that he was too ready to introduce religious discourse upon all occasions. JOHNSON. 'Why, yes, Sir, he will introduce religious discourse without seeing whether it will end in instruction and improvement, or produce some profane jest. He would introduce it in the company of Wilkes, and twenty more such.'

[a] *Langton* [H & I]

I mentioned Dr. Johnson's excellent distinction between liberty of conscience and liberty of teaching. JOHNSON. 'Consider, Sir; if you have children whom you wish to educate in the principles of the Church of England, and there comes a Quaker who tries to pervert them to his principles, you would drive away the Quaker. You would not trust to the predomination of right; which you believe is in your opinions; you will keep wrong out of their heads. Now the vulgar are the children of the State. If any one attempts to teach them doctrines contrary to what the State approves, the magistrate may and ought to restrain him.' SEWARD. 'Would you restrain private conversation, Sir?' JOHNSON. 'Why, Sir, it is difficult to say where private conversation begins, and where it ends. If we three should discuss even the great question concerning the existence of a Supreme Being by ourselves, we should not be restrained; for that would be to put an end to all improvement. But if we should discuss it in the presence of ten boarding-school girls, and as many boys, I think

marginal line:
*improvement. But . . .
in the* [H]

the magistrate would do well to put us in the stocks, to finish the debate there.'

Lord Hailes had sent him a present of a curious little printed poem, on repairing the University of Aberdeen, by David *Malloch*, which he thought would please Johnson, as affording clear evidence that Mallet had appeared even as a literary character by the name of *Malloch;* his changing which to one of softer sound, had given Johnson occasion to introduce him into his Dictionary, under the article *Alias*.[1] This piece was, I suppose, one of Mallet's first essays. It is preserved in his works, with several variations. Johnson having read aloud, from the beginning of it, where there were some common-place assertions as to the superiority of ancient times;—'How false (said he) is all this, to say that "in ancient times learning was not a disgrace to a Peer, as it is now." In ancient times a Peer was as ignorant as any one else. He would have been angry to have it thought he could write his name. Men in ancient times dared to stand forth with a degree of ignorance with which nobody would now dare to stand forth. I am always angry, when I hear ancient times praised at the expence of modern times. There is now a great deal more learning in the world than there was formerly; for it is universally diffused. You have, perhaps, no man who knows as much Greek and Latin as Bentley; no man who knows as much mathematicks as Newton: but you have many more men who know Greek and Latin, and who know mathematicks.'

On Thursday, May 1, I visited him in the evening along with young Mr. Burke. He said, 'It is strange that there should be so little reading in the world, and so much

marginal line:
*introduce him . . .
article* Alias [H]

[1] [Malloch, as Mr. Bindley observes to me, 'continued to write his name thus, *after he came to London.* His verses prefixed to the second edition of Thomson's "Winter," are so subscribed, and so are his Letters written in London, and published a few years ago in "the European Magazine;" but he soon afterwards adopted the alteration to Mallet, for he is so called in the list of Subscribers to Savage's Miscellanies printed in 1726; and thenceforward uniformly *Mallet,* in all his writings.' MALONE.]

[A notion has been entertained, that no such exemplification of *Alias* is to be found in Johnson's Dictionary, and that the whole story was waggishly fabricated by Wilkes in the NORTH BRITON.[a] The real fact is, that it is not to be found in the Folio, or Quarto editions, but was added by Johnson in his own *Octavo* Abridgement, in 1756. J. BOSWELL.]

marginal line:
The real . . . Octavo Abridgement [H]
[a] *Britain* crossed out; *Briton* written in [I]

writing. People in general do not willingly read, if they can have any thing else to amuse them. There must be an external impulse; emulation, or vanity, or avarice. The progress which the understanding makes through a book, has more pain than pleasure in it. Language is scanty, and inadequate to express the nice gradations and mixtures of our feelings. No man reads a book of science from pure inclination. The books that we do read with pleasure are light compositions, which contain a quick succession of events. However, I have this year read all Virgil through. I read a book of the Æneid every night, so it was done in twelve nights, and I had a great delight in it. The Georgicks did not give me so much pleasure, except the fourth book. The Eclogues I have almost all by heart. I do not think the story of the Æneid interesting. I like the story of the Odyssey much better;[a] and this not on account of the wonderful things which it contains; for there are wonderful things enough[b] in the Æneid;—the ships of the Trojans turned to sea-nymphs,—the tree at Polydorus's tomb dropping blood. The story of the Odyssey is interesting, as a great part of it is domestick.—It has been said, there is pleasure in writing, particularly in writing verses. I allow, you may have pleasure from writing, after it is over, if you have written well;[1] but you don't go willingly to it again. I know when I have been writing verses, I have run my finger down the margin, to see how many I had made, and how few I had to make.'

He seemed to be in a very placid humour, and although I have no note of the particulars of young Mr. Burke's[2] conversation, it is but justice to mention in general, that it was such that Dr. Johnson said to me afterwards, 'He did very well indeed; I have a mind to tell his father.'

'TO SIR JOSHUA REYNOLDS

'DEAR SIR,

'THE gentleman who waits on you with this, is Mr. Cruikshanks, who wishes to succeed his friend Dr. Hunter,

[1] [Dum pingit, fruitur arte; postquam pinxerat, fruitur fructu artis. SENECA. KEARNEY.]

[2] [This gentleman, to the inexpressible grief of his parents, died, Aug. 2, 1794, in his thirty-fifth year.[c] MALONE.]

Marginal notes:

marginal line: *a book . . . done in* [1]

[a] *wisely said: so do I.* [H]

[b] not *enough.* [H]

marginal lines: *writing verses . . . and how* [H]
underlined: *after it . . . written well* [H]

underlined: *parents* [H]

[c] *yes; but I think no one else thought very highly of him. Burke never recover'd from the Blow.* [H]

as Professor of Anatomy in the Royal Academy. His qualifications are very generally known, and it adds dignity to the institution that such men[1] are candidates.

I am Sir,

'Your most humble servant,

'May 2, 1783.'   'SAM. JOHNSON'

I have no minute of any interview with Johnson till Thursday, May 15th, when I find what follows: BOSWELL. 'I wish much to be in Parliament, Sir.' JOHNSON. 'Why, Sir, unless you come resolved to support any administration, you would be the worse for being in Parliament, because you would be obliged to live more expensively.'— BOSWELL. 'Perhaps, Sir, I should be the less happy for being in Parliament. I never would sell my vote, and I should be vexed if things went wrong.' JOHNSON. 'That's cant, Sir. It would not vex you more in the house, than in the gallery: publick affairs vex no man.' BOSWELL. 'Have not they vexed yourself a little, Sir? Have not you been vexed by all the turbulence of this reign, and by that absurd vote of the House of Commons, "That the influence of the Crown has increased, is increasing, and ought to be diminished"?' JOHNSON. 'Sir, I have never slept an hour less, nor eat an ounce less meat. I would have knocked the factious dogs on the head, to be sure; but I was not *vexed*.' BOSWELL. 'I declare, Sir, upon my honour, I did imagine I was vexed, and took a pride in it; but it *was*, perhaps, cant; for I own I neither eat less, nor slept less.' JOHNSON. 'My dear friend, clear your *mind* of cant. You may *talk* as other people do: you may say to a man, "Sir, I am your most humble servant." You are *not* his most humble servant. You may say, "These are bad times; it is a melancholy thing to be reserved to such times." You don't mind the times. You tell a man, "I am sorry you had such bad weather the last day of your journey, and were so much wet." You don't care six-pence whether he is wet or dry. You may *talk* in this manner; it is a mode of talking in Society: but don't *think* foolishly.'

[1] Let it be remembered by those who accuse Dr. Johnson of illiberality, that both were *Scotchmen*.

I talked of living in the country. JOHNSON. 'Don't set up for what is called hospitality: it is a waste of time, and a waste of money; you are eaten up, and not the more respected for your liberality. If your house be like an inn, nobody cares for you. A man who stays a week with another, makes him a slave for a week.' BOSWELL. 'But there are people, Sir, who make their houses a home to their guests, and are themselves quite easy.' JOHNSON. 'Then, Sir, home must be the same to the guests, and they need not come.'

Here he discovered a notion common enough in persons not much accustomed to entertain company, that there must be a degree of elaborate attention, otherwise company will think themselves neglected; and such attention is no doubt very fatiguing. He proceeded: 'I would not, however, be a stranger in my own country; I would visit my neighbours, and receive their visits; but I would not be in haste to return visits. If a gentleman comes to see me, I tell him he does me a great deal of honour. I do not go to see him perhaps for ten weeks; then we are very complaisant to each other. No, Sir, you will have much more influence by giving or lending money where it is wanted, than by hospitality.'

On Saturday, May 17, I saw him for a short time. Having mentioned that I had that morning been with old Mr. Sheridan, he remembered their former intimacy with a cordial warmth, and said to me, 'Tell Mr. Sheridan, I shall be glad to see him, and shake hands with him.' BOSWELL. 'It is to me very wonderful that resentment should be kept up so long.' JOHNSON. 'Why, Sir, it is not altogether resentment that he does not visit me; it is partly falling out of the habit,—partly disgust, such as one has at a drug that has made him sick. Besides, he knows that I laugh at his oratory.'

Another day I spoke of one of our friends, of whom he, as well as I, had a very high opinion. He expatiated in his praise; but added, 'Sir, he is a cursed Whig, a *bottomless* Whig, as they all are now.'

I mentioned my expectations from the interest of an eminent person then in power; adding, 'but I have no claim but the claim of friendship; however, some people will go a great way from that motive.' JOHNSON. 'Sir, they will go all the way from that motive.' A gentleman talked of retiring. 'Never think of that,' said Johnson. The gentleman urged, 'I should then do no ill.' JOHNSON. 'Nor no good either. Sir, it would be a civil suicide.'

On Monday, May 26, I found him at tea, and the celebrated Miss Burney, the authour of 'Evelina' and 'Cecilia,' with him. I asked, if there would be any speakers in Parliament, if there were no places to be obtained. JOHNSON. 'Yes, Sir. Why do you speak here? Either to instruct and entertain, which is a benevolent motive; or for distinction, which is a selfish motive.' I mentioned 'Cecilia.' JOHNSON. (with an air of animated satisfaction) 'Sir, if you talk of "Cecilia," talk on.'

We talked of Mr. Barry's exhibition of his pictures. JOHNSON. 'Whatever the hand may have done, the mind has done its part. There is a grasp of mind there, which you find no where else.'[1]

I asked, whether a man naturally virtuous, or one who has overcome wicked inclinations, is the best. JOHNSON. 'Sir, to *you*, the man who has overcome wicked inclinations, is not the best. He has more merit to *himself*. I would rather trust my money to a man who has no hands, and so a physical impossibility to steal, than to a man of the most honest principles. There is a witty satirical story of Foote. He had a small bust of Garrick placed upon his bureau. "You may be surprised (said he) that I allow him to be so near my gold;—but you will observe, he has no hands."'

On Friday,[2] May 29, being to set out for Scotland next morning, I passed a part of the day with him in more than usual earnestness; as his health was in a more precarious state than at any time when I had parted from him. He, however, was quick and lively, and critical, as usual. I mentioned one who was a very learned man. JOHNSON. 'Yes, Sir, he has a great deal of learning; but it never lies straight. There is never one idea by the side of another; 'tis all entangled: and then he drives it so aukwardly upon conversation!'

marginal line:
was a . . . lies straight
[H]

[1] In Mr. Barry's printed analysis, or description of these pictures, he speaks of Johnson's character in the highest terms.

[2] [Boswell's mistake for Thursday. F.]

I stated to him an anxious thought, by which a sincere Christian might be disturbed, even when conscious of having lived a good life, so far as is consistent with human infirmity; he might fear that he should afterwards fall away, and be guilty of such crimes as would render all his former religion vain. Could there be, upon this awful subject, such a thing as balancing of accounts? Suppose a man who has led a good life for seven years, commits an act of wickedness, and instantly dies; will his former good life have any effect in his favour? JOHNSON. 'Sir, if a man has led a good life for seven years, and then is hurried by passion to do what is wrong, and is suddenly carried off, depend upon it he will have the reward of his seven years' good life: GOD will not take a catch of him. Upon this principle Richard Baxter believes that a Suicide may be saved.[a] "If (says he) it should be objected that what I maintain may encourage suicide, I answer, I am not to tell a lie to prevent it."' BOSWELL. 'But does not the text say, "As the tree falls, so it must lie"?' JOHNSON. 'Yes, Sir; as the tree falls: but,—(after a little pause)—that is meant as to the general state of the tree, not what is the effect of a sudden blast.' In short, he interpreted the expression as referring to condition, not to position. The common notion, therefore, seems to be erroneous; and Shenstone's witty remark on Divines trying to give the tree a jerk upon a death-bed, to make it lie favourably, is not well founded.

I asked him what works of Richard Baxter's I should read. He said, 'Read any of them; they are all good.'

He said, 'Get as much force of mind as you can. Live within your income. Always have something saved at the end of the year. Let your imports be more than your exports, and you'll never go far wrong.'

I assured him, that in the extensive and various range of his acquaintance there never had been any one who had a more sincere respect and affection for him than I had. He said, 'I believe it, Sir. Were I in distress, there is no man to whom I should sooner come than to you. I should like to come and have a cottage in your park, toddle about, live mostly on milk, and be taken care of by Mrs. Boswell.[b] She and I are good friends now; are we not?'

[a] *The 26th. Verse of the 18th. Chapter of Ezekiel says—When a Righteous Man turneth away from his Righteousness, and committeth Iniquities — & dieth in them;—for his Iniquity that he hath done, shall he die. The next Verse is better known, it opens our Liturgy — our Common Prayer. Now if Richd. Baxter or Saml. Johnson know of any softner in the New Testament to set against this Chapter in the Old, their Opinions are sound Opinions; but I recollect none such. The 24th. Verse of the same Chapter in Ezekiel is still fuller & stronger; but here is not Room to insert it . . . it says All his Righteousness that he hath done shall not be mention'd &c &c* [H]

[b]—*Ah! but then Bozzy would not have cared a Pin for him.* [H]

Talking of devotion, he said, 'Though it be true that "GOD dwelleth not in Temples made with hands," yet in this state of being, our minds are more piously affected in places appropriated to divine worship, than in others. Some people have a particular room in their house, where they say their prayers; of which I do not disapprove, as it may animate their devotion.'

He embraced me, and gave me his blessing, as usual when I was leaving him for any length of time. I walked from his door to-day, with a fearful apprehension of what might happen before I returned.

'TO THE RIGHT HONOURABLE WILLIAM WINDHAM

'SIR,

'The bringer of this letter is the father of Miss Philips,[1] a singer, who comes to try her voice on the stage at Dublin.

'Mr. Philips is one of my old friends; and as I am of opinion that neither he nor his daughter will do any thing that can disgrace their benefactors, I take the liberty of entreating you to countenance and protect them so far as may be suitable to your station[2] and character; and shall consider myself as obliged by any favourable notice which they shall have the honour of receiving from you.

'I am Sir,

'Your most humble servant,

'London, May 31, 1783.'   'SAM. JOHNSON'

The following is another instance of his active benevolence:

'TO SIR JOSHUA REYNOLDS

'DEAR SIR,

'I HAVE sent you some of my god-son's[3] performances, of which I do not pretend to form any opinion. When I took the liberty of mentioning him to you, I did not know

---

[1] Now the celebrated Mrs. Crouch.

[2] Mr. Windham was at this time in Dublin, Secretary to the Earl of Northington, then Lord Lieutenant of Ireland.

[3] Son of Mr. Samuel Paterson.

what I have since been told, that Mr. Moser had admitted him among the Students of the Academy. What more can be done for him, I earnestly entreat you to consider; for I am very desirous that he should derive some advantage from my connection with him. If you are inclined to see him, I will bring him to wait on you, at any time that you shall be pleased to appoint.

'I am, Sir,
'Your most humble servant,
'June 2, 1783.'   'SAM. JOHNSON'

My anxious apprehensions at parting with him this year, proved to be but too well founded; for not long afterwards he had a dreadful stroke of the palsy, of which there are very full and accurate accounts in letters written by himself, to shew with what composure of mind, and resignation to the Divine Will, his steady piety enabled him to behave.

'TO MR. EDMUND ALLEN

'DEAR SIR,
'IT has pleased GOD, this morning, to deprive me of the powers of speech; and as I do not know but that it may be his further good pleasure to deprive me soon of my senses, I request you will on the receipt of this note, come to me, and act for me, as the exigencies of my case may require.   'I am,
'Sincerely your's,
'June 17, 1783.   'SAM. JOHNSON'

'TO THE REVEREND DR. JOHN TAYLOR

'DEAR SIR,
'IT has pleased GOD, by a paralytick stroke in the night, to deprive me of speech.
'I am very desirous of Dr. Heberden's assistance, as I think my case is not past remedy. Let me see you as soon as it is possible. Bring Dr. Heberden with you, if you can; but come yourself at all events. I am glad you are so well, when I am so dreadfully attacked.

'I think that by a speedy application of stimulants much may be done. I question if a vomit, vigorous and rough, would not rouse the organs of speech to action. As it is too early to send, I will try to recollect what I can, that can be suspected to have brought on this dreadful distress.

'I have been accustomed to bleed frequently for an asthmatick complaint; but have forborne for some time by Dr. Pepys's persuasion, who perceived my legs beginning to swell. I sometimes alleviate a painful, or more properly an oppressive, constriction of my chest, by opiates; and have lately taken opium frequently, but the last, or two last times, in smaller quantities. My largest dose is three grains, and last night I took but two. You will suggest these things (and they are all that I can call to mind) to Dr. Heberden.

'I am, &c.

'June 17, 1783.'   'SAM. JOHNSON'

Two days after he wrote thus to Mrs. Thrale:[1]

'On Monday, the 16th, I sat for my picture, and walked a considerable way with little inconvenience. In the afternoon and evening I felt myself light and easy, and began to plan schemes of life. Thus I went to bed, and in a short time waked and sat up, as has been long my custom, when I felt a confusion and indistinctness in my head, which lasted, I suppose, about half a minute. I was alarmed, and prayed GOD, that however he might afflict my body, he would spare my understanding. This prayer, that I might try the integrity of my faculties, I made in Latin verse. The lines were not very good, but I knew them not to be very good: I made them easily, and concluded myself to be unimpaired in my faculties.

'Soon after I perceived that I had suffered a paralytick stroke, and that my speech was taken from me. I had no pain, and so little dejection in this dreadful state, that I wondered at my own apathy, and considered that perhaps death itself, when it should come, would excite less horrour than seems now to attend it.

[1] Vol. ii. p. 268, of Mrs. Thrale's Collection.

'In order to rouse the vocal organs, I took two drams. Wine has been celebrated for the production of eloquence. I put myself into violent motion, and I think repeated it; but all was vain. I then went to bed, and strange as it may seem, I think slept. When I saw light, it was time to contrive what I should do. Though GOD stopped my speech, he left me my hand; I enjoyed a mercy which was not granted to my dear friend Lawrence, who now perhaps overlooks me as I am writing, and rejoices that I have what he wanted. My first note was necessarily to my servant, who came in talking, and could not immediately comprehend why he should read what I put into his hands.

'I then wrote a card to Mr. Allen, that I might have a discreet friend at hand, to act as occasion should require. In penning this note, I had some difficulty; my hand, I knew not how nor why, made wrong letters. I then wrote to Dr. Taylor to come to me, and bring Dr. Heberden: and I sent to Dr. Brocklesby, who is my neighbour. My physicians are very friendly, and give me great hopes; but you may imagine my situation. I have so far recovered my vocal powers, as to repeat the Lord's Prayer with no very imperfect articulation. My memory, I hope, yet remains as it was! but such an attack produces solicitude for the safety of every faculty.'

'TO MR. THOMAS DAVIES

'DEAR SIR,

'I HAVE had, indeed, a very heavy blow; but GOD, who yet spares my life, I humbly hope will spare my understanding, and restore my speech. As I am not at all helpless, I want no particular assistance, but am strongly affected by Mrs. Davies's tenderness; and when I think she can do me good, shall be very glad to call upon her. I had ordered friends to be shut out; but one or two have found the way in; and if you come you shall be admitted; for I know not whom I can see, that will bring more amusement on his tongue, or more kindness in his heart.

I am, &c.

'June 18, 1783.'　　　　　　　　'SAM. JOHNSON'

exclamation point: *my dear friend Lawrence* etc. [H]

It gives me great pleasure to preserve such a memorial of Johnson's regard for Mr. Davies, to whom I was indebted for my introduction to him.[1] He indeed loved Davies cordially, of which I shall give the following little evidence. One day when he had treated him with too much asperity, Tom, who was not without pride and spirit, went off in a passion; but he had hardly reached home, when Frank, who had been sent after him, delivered this note:—'Come, come, dear Davies, I am always sorry when we quarrel; send me word that we are friends.'

'TO JAMES BOSWELL, ESQ.

'DEAR SIR,

'Your anxiety about my health is very friendly, and very agreeable with your general kindness. I have, indeed, had a very frightful blow. On the 17th of last month, about three in the morning, as near as I can guess, I perceived myself almost totally deprived of speech. I had no pain. My organs were so obstructed that I could say *no*, but could scarcely say *yes*. I wrote the necessary directions, for it pleased GOD to spare my hand, and sent for Dr. Heberden and Dr. Brocklesby. Between the time in which I discovered my own disorder, and that in which I sent for the doctors, I had, I believe, in spite of my surprize and solicitude, a little sleep, and Nature began to renew its operations. They came and gave the directions which the disease required, and from that time I have been continually improving in articulation. I can now speak, but the nerves are weak, and I cannot continue discourse long; but strength, I hope, will return. The physicians consider me as cured. I was last Sunday at Church. On Tuesday I took an airing to Hampstead, and dined with THE CLUB, where Lord Palmerston was proposed, and, against my opinion, was rejected.[2] I designed to go next week with Mr. Langton to Rochester, where I purpose to stay about ten days, and then try some other air. I have

---

[1] Poor Derrick, however, though he did not himself introduce me to Dr. Johnson as he promised, had the merit of introducing me to Davies, the immediate introductor.

[2] His Lordship was soon after chosen, and is now a member of THE CLUB.

many kind invitations. Your brother has very frequently enquired after me. Most of my friends have, indeed, been very attentive. Thank dear Lord Hailes for his present.

'I hope you found at your return every thing gay and prosperous, and your lady, in particular, quite recovered and confirmed. Pay her my respects.

I am, dear Sir,
'Your most humble servant,

'London, July 3, 1783.'   'SAM. JOHNSON'

'TO MRS. LUCY PORTER, IN LICHFIELD

'DEAR MADAM,

'The account which you give of your health is but melancholy. May it please GOD to restore you. My disease affected my speech, and still continues, in some degree, to obstruct my utterance; my voice is distinct enough for a while; but the organs being still weak are quickly weary: but in other respects I am, I think, rather better than I have lately been: and can let you know my state without the help of any other hand.

'In the opinion of my friends, and in my own, I am gradually mending. The physicians consider me as cured, and I had leave four days ago, to wash the cantharides from my head. Last Tuesday I dined at THE CLUB.

'I am going next week into Kent, and purpose to change the air frequently this summer; whether I shall wander so far as Staffordshire I cannot tell. I should be glad to come. Return my thanks to Mrs. Cobb, and Mr. Pearson,[1] and all that have shewn attention to me.

'Let us, my dear, pray for one another, and consider our sufferings as notices mercifully given us to prepare ourselves for another state.

'I live now but in a melancholy way. My old friend Mr. Levett is dead, who lived with me in the house, and was useful and companionable; Mrs. Desmoulins is gone away; and Mrs. Williams is so much decayed, that she can add little to another's gratifications. The world passes away,

---

[1] [The Reverend Mr. Pearson, to whom Mrs. Lucy Porter bequeathed the greater part of her property. MALONE.]

and we are passing with it; but there is, doubtless, another world, which will endure for ever. Let us all fit ourselves for it. I am, &c.

'London, July 5, 1783.'   'SAM. JOHNSON'

Such was the general vigour of his constitution, that he recovered from this alarming and severe attack with wonderful quickness; so that in July he was able to make a visit to Mr. Langton at Rochester, where he passed about a fortnight, and made little excursions as easily as at any time of his life. In August he went as far as the neighbourhood of Salisbury, to Heale, the seat of William Bowles, Esq. a gentleman whom I have heard him praise for exemplary religious order in his family. In his diary I find a short but honourable mention of this visit:— 'August 28, I came to Heale without fatigue. 30. I am entertained quite to my mind.'[1]

'TO DR. BROCKLESBY

'DEAR SIR,   'Heale, near Salisbury, Aug. 29, 1783

'WITHOUT appearing to want a just sense of your kind attention, I cannot omit to give an account of the day which seemed to appear in some sort perilous. I rose

---

[1] [In his letter to Mrs. Thrale, written on the 13th of August, we find the following melancholy paragraph:

'I am now broken with disease, without the alleviation of familiar friendship or domestick society: I have no middle state between clamour and silence, between general conversation and self-tormenting solitude. Levett is dead, and poor Williams is making haste to die: I know not if she will ever more come out of her chamber.'

In a subsequent letter (August 26) he adds, 'Mrs. Williams fancies now and then that she grows better,[a] but her vital powers appear to be slowly burning out. Nobody thinks, however, that she will very soon be quite wasted, and as she suffers me to be of very little use to her, I have determined to pass some time with Mr. Bowles near Salisbury, and have taken a place for Thursday.

'Some benefit may be perhaps received from change of air, some from change of company, and some from mere change of place. It is not easy to grow well in a chamber where one has long been sick, and where every thing seen, and every person speaking, revives and impresses images of pain. Though it may be true, that no man can run away from himself, yet he may escape from many causes of useless uneasiness. That *the mind is its own place*, is the boast of a fallen angel that had learned to lie. External locality has great effects, at least upon all embodied beings. I hope this little journey will afford me at least some suspense of melancholy.' MALONE.]

a Life to the last—like harden'd Felons lies. [H]

marginal line:
place. It . . . it may [H]

at five, and went out at six; and having reached Salisbury about nine, went forward a few miles in my friend's chariot. I was no more wearied with the journey, though it was a high-hung, rough coach, than I should have been forty years ago. We shall now see what air will do. The country is all a plain; and the house in which I am, so far as I can judge from my window, for I write before I have left my chamber, is sufficiently pleasant.

'Be so kind as to continue your attention to Mrs. Williams; it is great consolation to the well, and still greater to the sick, that they find themselves not neglected; and I know that you will be desirous of giving comfort, even where you have no great hope of giving help.

'Since I wrote the former part of the letter, I find that by the course of the post I cannot send it before the thirty-first. I am, &c.

'SAM. JOHNSON'

While he was here, he had a letter from Dr. Brocklesby, acquainting him of the death of Mrs. Williams,[1] which affected him a good deal. Though for several years her temper had not been complacent, she had valuable qualities, and her departure left a blank in his house. Upon this occasion he, according to his habitual course of piety, composed a prayer.[2]

I shall here insert a few particulars concerning him, with which I have been favoured by one of his friends.

'He had once conceived the design of writing the Life of Oliver Cromwell, saying, that he thought it must be

---

[1] [In his letter to Miss Susannah Thrale, Sept. 9, 1783, he thus writes: 'Pray shew Mamma this passage of a letter from Dr. Brocklesby. "Mrs. Williams, from mere inanition, has at length paid the great debt to nature about three o'clock this morning (Sept. 6.) She died without a struggle, retaining her faculties to the very last, and as she expressed it, having set her house in order, was prepared to leave it at the last summons of nature." '

In his letter to Mrs. Thrale, Sept. 22, he adds, 'Poor Williams has, I hope, seen the end of her afflictions. She acted with prudence and she bore with fortitude. She has left me.

"Thou thy weary task hast done,
Home art gone, and ta'en thy wages."

Had she had good humour and prompt elocution, her universal curiosity and comprehensive knowledge would have made her the delight of all that knew her. She has left her little to your charity-school.' MALONE.]

[2] Prayers and Meditations, p. 226.

highly curious to trace his extraordinary rise to the supreme power, from so obscure a beginning. He at length laid aside his scheme, on discovering that all that can be told of him is already in print; and that it is impracticable to procure any authentick information in addition to what the world is already possessed of.'[1]

'He had likewise projected, but at what part of his life is not known, a work to shew how small a quantity of REAL FICTION there is in the world;[a] and that the same images, with very little variation, have served all the authours who have ever written.'

'His thoughts in the latter part of his life were frequently employed on his deceased friends. He often muttered these, or such like sentences: "Poor man! and then he died."'

'Speaking of a certain literary friend, "He is a very pompous puzzling fellow, (said he); he lent me a letter once that somebody had written to him, no matter what it was about; but he wanted to have the letter back, and expressed a mighty value for it; he hoped it was to be met with again, he would not lose it for a thousand pounds. I layed my hand upon it soon afterwards, and gave it him. I believe I said I was very glad to have met with it. O, then he did not know that it signified any thing. So you see, when the letter was lost it was worth a thousand pounds, and when it was found it was not worth a farthing."'

'The style and character of his conversation is pretty generally known; it was certainly conducted in conformity with a precept of Lord Bacon, but it is not clear, I apprehend, that this conformity was either perceived or intended by Johnson. The precept alluded to is as follows: "In all

[a] *That would have been pretty. Johnson used to say that He believed no Combination & few Sentiments, that might not be traced up to Homer Shakespeare & Richardson.* [H]

[1] Mr. Malone observes, 'This, however, was entirely a mistake, as appears from the Memoirs published by Mr. Noble. Had Johnson been furnished with the materials which the industry of that gentleman has procured, and with others which, it is believed, are yet preserved in manuscript, he would, without doubt, have produced a most valuable and curious history of Cromwell's life.'

[I may add, that, had Johnson given us a Life of Cromwell, we should not have been disgusted in numberless instances with—'My Lord Protector' and 'My Lady PROTECTRESS;' and certainly the brutal ruffian who presided in the bloody assembly that murdered their sovereign, would have been characterized by very different epithets than those which are applied to him in this work, where we find him described as 'the BOLD and DETERMINED Bradshaw.' MALONE.]

kinds of speech, either pleasant, grave, severe, or ordinary, it is convenient to speak leisurely, and rather drawlingly than hastily: because hasty speech confounds the memory, and oftentimes, besides the unseemliness, drives a man either to stammering, a non-plus, or harping on that which should follow; whereas a slow speech confirmeth the memory, addeth a conceit of wisdom to the hearers, besides a seemliness of speech and countenance."[1] Dr. Johnson's method of conversation was certainly calculated to excite attention, and to amuse and instruct, (as it happened,) without wearying or confusing his company. He was always most perfectly clear and perspicuous; and his language was so accurate, and his sentences so neatly constructed, that his conversation might have been all printed without any correction. At the same time, it was easy and natural; the accuracy of it had no appearance of labour, constraint, or stiffness; he seemed more correct than others, by the force of habit, and the customary exercises of his powerful mind.'

'He spoke often in praise of French literature. "The French are excellent in this, (he would say,) they have a book on every subject." From what he had seen of them he denied them the praise of superior politeness, and mentioned, with very visible disgust, the custom they have of spitting on the floors of their apartments.[a] "This, (said the Doctor) is as gross a thing as can well be done; and one wonders how any man, or set of men, can persist in so offensive a practice for a whole day together; one should expect that the first effort towards civilization would remove it even among savages."'

a *The Floor is never cover'd with Carpeting—it is commonly Brick.* [H]

'Baxter's "Reasons of the Christian religion," he thought contained the best collection of the evidences of the divinity of the Christian system.'

'Chymistry was always an interesting pursuit with Dr. Johnson. Whilst he was in Wiltshire, he attended some experiments that were made by a physician at Salisbury, on the new kinds of air. In the course of the experiments frequent mention being made of Dr. Priestley, Dr. Johnson knit his brows, and in a stern manner enquired, "Why do

[1] [Hints for Civil Conversation.—Bacon's Works, 4to. vol. i. p. 571. MALONE.]

we hear so much of Dr. Priestley!"[1] He was very properly answered, "Sir, because we are indebted to him for these important discoveries." On this Dr. Johnson appeared well content; and replied, "Well, well, I believe we are; and let every man have the honour he has merited." '

'A friend was one day, about two years before his death, struck with some instance of Dr. Johnson's great candour. "Well, Sir, (said he,) I will always say that you are a very candid man." —"Will you, (replied the Doctor,) I doubt then you will be very singular. But, indeed, Sir, (continued he,) I look upon myself to be a man very much misunderstood. I am not an uncandid, nor am I a severe

[1] I do not wonder at Johnson's displeasure when the name of Dr. Priestley was mentioned; for I know no writer who has been suffered to publish more pernicious doctrines. I shall instance only three. First, *Materialism;* by which *mind* is denied to human nature; which, if believed, must deprive us of every elevated principle. Secondly, *Necessity;* or the doctrine that every action, whether good or bad, is included in an unchangeable and unavoidable system; a notion utterly subversive of moral government. Thirdly, that we have no reason to think that the *future* world, (which, as he is pleased to *inform* us, will be adapted to our *merely improved* nature,) will be materially different from *this;* which, if believed, would sink wretched mortals into despair, as they could no longer hope for the 'rest that remaineth for the people of GOD,' or for that happiness which is revealed to us as something beyond our present conceptions; but would feel themselves doomed to a continuation of the uneasy state under which they now groan. I say nothing of the petulant intemperance with which he dares to insult the venerable establishments of his country.

As a specimen of his writings, I shall quote the following passage, which appears to me equally absurd and impious, and which might have been retorted upon him by the men who were prosecuted for burning his house. 'I cannot, (says he,) as a *necessarian,* [meaning *necessitarian,*] hate *any man;* because I consider him as *being,* in all respects, just what GOD has *made him to be;* and also as *doing with respect to me,* nothing but what he was *expressly designed* and *appointed* to do: GOD being the *only cause,* and men nothing more than the *instruments* in his hands to *execute all his pleasure.*'—Illustrations of Philosophical Necessity, p. 111.

The Reverend Dr. Parr, in a late tract, appears to suppose that *Dr. Johnson not only endured, but almost solicited, an interview with Dr. Priestley.* In justice to Dr. Johnson, I declare my firm belief that he never did. My illustrious friend was particularly resolute in not giving countenance to men whose writings he considered as pernicious to society. I was present at Oxford when Dr. Price, even before he had rendered himself so generally obnoxious by his zeal for the French revolution, came into a company where Johnson was, who instantly left the room. Much more would he have reprobated Dr. Priestley.

Whoever wishes to see a perfect delineation of this *Literary Jack of all Trades,* may find it in an ingenious tract, entitled, 'A SMALL WHOLE-LENGTH OF DR. PRIESTLEY,' printed for Rivingtons in St. Paul's Church-Yard.

man. I sometimes say more than I mean, in jest; and
people are apt to believe me serious: however, I am more
candid than I was when I was younger. As I know more
of mankind, I expect less of them, and am ready now to
call a man *a good man*, upon easier terms than I was
formerly." ' ª

ª *Oh so am I now
every day. 1817.* [H]

On his return from Heale he wrote to Dr. Burney. —'I
came home on the 18th of September, at noon, to a very
disconsolate house. You and I have lost our friends; but
you have more friends at home. My domestick companion
is taken from me. She is much missed, for her acquisitions
were many, and her curiosity universal; so that she partook
of every conversation. I am not well enough to go much
out; and to sit, and eat, or fast alone, is very wearisome.
I always mean to send my compliments to all the ladies.'

His fortitude and patience met with severe trials during
this year. The stroke of the palsy has been related circum-
stantially; but he was also afflicted with the gout, and was
besides troubled with a complaint which not only was
attended with immediate inconvenience, but threatened
him with a chirurgical operation, from which most men
would shrink. The complaint was a *sarcocele*, which Johnson
bore with uncommon firmness, and was not at all frightened while he looked forward to amputation. He was
attended by Mr. Pott and Mr. Cruikshank. I have before
me a letter of the 30th of July this year, to Mr. Cruikshank,
in which he says, 'I am going to put myself into your
hands:' and another, accompanying a set of his 'Lives of
the Poets,' in which he says, 'I beg your acceptance of these
volumes, as an acknowledgement of the great favours
which you have bestowed on, Sir, your most obliged and
most humble servant.' I have in my possession several
more letters from him to Mr. Cruikshank, and also to
Dr. Mudge at Plymouth, which it would be improper to
insert, as they are filled with unpleasing technical details.
I shall, however, extract from his letters to Dr. Mudge,
such passages as shew either a felicity of expression, or the
undaunted state of his mind.

'My conviction of your skill, and my belief of your
friendship, determine me to entreat your opinion and

advice.'—'In this state I with great earnestness desire you
to tell me what is to be done. Excision is doubtless necessary
to the cure, and I know not any means of palliation. The
operation is doubtless painful; but is it dangerous? The
pain I hope to endure with decency; but I am loth to put
life into much hazard.'—'By representing the gout as an
antagonist to the palsy, you have said enough to make it
welcome. This is not strictly the first fit, but I hope it is as
good as the first; for it is the second that ever confined me;
and the first was ten years ago, much less fierce and fiery
than this.'—'Write, dear Sir, what you can to inform or
encourage me. The operation is not delayed by any fears
or objections of mine.'

'TO BENNET LANGTON, ESQ.

'DEAR SIR,

'YOU may very reasonably charge me with insensibility of your kindness, and that of lady Rothes, since I
have suffered so much time to pass without paying any
acknowledgement. I now, at last, return my thanks; and
why I did it not sooner I ought to tell you. I went into
Wiltshire as soon as I well could, and was there much
employed in palliating my own malady. Disease produces
much selfishness. A man in pain is looking after ease; and
lets most other things go as chance shall dispose of them.
In the mean time I have lost a companion,[1] to whom I
have had recourse for domestick amusement for thirty
years, and whose variety of knowledge never was exhausted;
and now return to a habitation vacant and desolate. I
carry about a very troublesome and dangerous complaint,
which admits no cure but by the chirurgical knife. Let me
have your prayers. I am, &c.

'London, Sept. 29, 1783.'   'SAM. JOHNSON'

Happily the complaint abated without his being put
to the torture of amputation. But we must surely admire
the manly resolution which he discovered, while it hung
over him.

In a letter to the same gentleman he writes, 'The gout
has within these four days come upon me with a violence

[1] Mrs. Anna Williams.

which I never experienced before. It made me helpless as an infant.'—And in another, having mentioned Mrs. Williams, he says,—'whose death following that of Levett, has now made my house a solitude. She left her little substance to a charity-school. She is, I hope, where there is neither darkness, nor want, nor sorrow.'

I wrote to him, begging to know the state of his health, and mentioned that 'Baxter's Anacreon, which is in the library at Auchinleck, was, I find, collated by my father in 1727, with the MS. belonging to the University of Leyden, and he has made a number of Notes upon it. Would you advise me to publish a new edition of it?'

His answer was dated September 30.—'You should not make your letters such rarities, when you know, or might know, the uniform state of my health. It is very long since I heard from you; and that I have not answered is a very insufficient reason for the silence of a friend.—Your Anacreon is a very uncommon book; neither London nor Cambridge can supply a copy of that edition. Whether it should be reprinted, you cannot do better than consult Lord Hailes.—Besides my constant and radical disease, I have been for these ten days much harassed with the gout; but that has now remitted. I hope GOD will yet grant me a little longer life, and make me less unfit to appear before him.'

He this autumn received a visit from the celebrated Mrs. Siddons. He gives this account of it in one of his letters to Mrs. Thrale [October 27]:—'Mrs. Siddons, in her visit to me, behaved with great modesty and propriety, and left nothing behind her to be censured or despised. Neither praise nor money, the two powerful corrupters of mankind, seem to have depraved her. I shall be glad to see her again. Her brother Kemble calls on me, and pleases me very well. Mrs. Siddons and I talked of plays; and she told me her intention of exhibiting this winter the characters of Constance, Catharine, and Isabella, in Shakspeare.'

Mr. Kemble has favoured me with the following minute of what passed at this visit.

'When Mrs. Siddons came into the room, there happened to be no chair ready for her, which he observing, said with a smile, "Madam, you who so often occasion a

marginal line:
Mrs. Siddons . . . nothing behind [H]

marginal line:
observing, said . . . one yourself [H]

want of seats to other people, will the more easily excuse
the want of one yourself."

'Having placed himself by her, he with great good
humour entered upon a consideration of the English
drama; and, among other enquiries, particularly asked
her which of Shakspeare's characters she was most pleased
with. Upon her answering that she thought the character
of Queen Catharine, in Henry the Eighth, the most natural:—"I think so too, Madam, (said he;) and whenever
you perform it, I will once more hobble out to the theatre
myself." Mrs. Siddons promised she would do herself the
honour of acting his favourite part for him; but many
circumstances happened to prevent the representation of
King Henry the Eighth during the Doctor's life.

'In the course of the evening he thus gave his opinion
upon the merits of some of the principal performers whom
he remembered to have seen upon the stage. "Mrs. Porter,
in the vehemence of rage, and Mrs. Clive in the sprightliness of humour, I have never seen equalled. What Clive
did best, she did better than Garrick; but could not do
half so many things well; she was a better romp than any
I ever saw in nature.—Pritchard, in common life, was a
vulgar ideot; she would talk of her *gownd;* but, when she
appeared upon the stage, seemed to be inspired by gen-
tility and understanding.—I once talked with Colley
Cibber, and thought him ignorant of the principles of his
art.—Garrick, Madam, was no declaimer; there was not
one of his own scene-shifters who could not have spoken
To be, or not to be, better than he did;[a] yet he was the only
actor I ever saw, whom I could call a master both in
tragedy and comedy; though I liked him best in comedy.
A true conception of character, and natural expression of
it, were his distinguished excellencies." Having expatiated,
with his usual force and eloquence, on Mr. Garrick's extraordinary eminence as an actor, he concluded with this
compliment to his social talents: "And after all, Madam,
I thought him less to be envied on the stage than at the
head of a table."'

Johnson, indeed, had thought more upon the subject
of acting than might be generally supposed. Talking of it
one day to Mr. Kemble, he said, 'Are you, Sir, one of

[a] *or than Mr. Kean*
[H]

those enthusiasts who believe yourself transformed into the very character you represent?' Upon Mr. Kemble's answering—that he had never felt so strong a persuasion himself;[a] 'To be sure not, Sir, (said Johnson;) the thing is impossible. And if Garrick really believed himself to be that monster, Richard the Third, he deserved to be hanged every time he performed it.'[1]

[a] *I dare say not* [1]
marginal line:
And if . . be hanged [H]

[TO MRS. LUCY PORTER, IN LICHFIELD

'DEAR MADAM,

'THE death of poor Mr. Porter, of which your maid has sent an account, must have very much surprised you. The death of a friend is almost always unexpected: we do not love to think of it, and therefore are not prepared for its coming. He was, I think, a religious man, and therefore that his end was happy.

'Death has likewise visited my mournful habitation. Last month died Mrs. Williams, who had been to me for thirty years in the place of a sister: her knowledge was great, and her conversation pleasing. I now live in cheerless solitude.

'My two last years have past under the pressure of

---

[1] My worthy friend, Mr. John Nichols, was present when Mr. Henderson, the actor, paid a visit to Dr. Johnson, and was received in a very courteous manner.—See 'Gentleman's Magazine,' June 1791.

I found among Dr. Johnson's papers, the following letter to him, from the celebrated Mrs. Bellamy:

'SIR,   'TO DR. JOHNSON

'The flattering remembrance of the partiality you honoured me with some years ago, as well as the humanity you are known to possess, has encouraged me to solicit your patronage at my Benefit.

'By a long Chancery suit, and a complicated train of unfortunate events, I am reduced to the greatest distress; which obliges me, once more, to request the indulgence of the publick.

'Give me leave to solicit the honour of your company, and to assure you, if you grant my request, the gratification I shall feel, from being patronized by Dr. Johnson, will be infinitely superiour to any advantage that may arise from the Benefit; as I am, with the profoundest respect, Sir,

'Your most obedient, humble servant,
'No. 10, Duke-street, St. James's,   'G. A. BELLAMY'
      May 11, 1783.'

I am happy in recording these particulars, which prove that my illustrious friend lived to think much more favourably of Players than he appears to have done in the early part of his life.

successive diseases. I have lately had the gout with some severity. But I wonderfully escaped the operation which I mentioned, and am upon the whole restored to health beyond my own expectation.

'As we daily see our friends die round us, we that are left must cling closer, and, if we can do nothing more, at least pray for one another; and remember, that as others die we must die too, and prepare ourselves diligently for the last great trial.

'I am, Madam,
'Your's affectionately,

'Bolt-court, Fleet-street,   'SAM. JOHNSON']
    Nov. 10, 1783.'

A pleasing instance of the generous attention of one of his friends has been discovered by the publication of Mrs. Thrale's collection of Letters. In a letter to one of the Miss Thrales,[1] he writes, 'A friend, whose name I will tell when your mamma has tried to guess it, sent to my physician to enquire whether this long train of illness had brought me into difficulties for want of money, with an invitation to send to him for what occasion required. I shall write this night to thank him, having no need to borrow.' And afterwards, in a letter to Mrs. Thrale, 'Since you cannot guess, I will tell you, that the generous man was Gerard Hamilton. I returned him a very thankful and respectful letter.'[2]

I applied to Mr. Hamilton, by a common friend, and he has been so obliging as to let me have Johnson's letter to him upon this occasion, to adorn my collection.

'TO THE RIGHT HONOURABLE WILLIAM GERARD
HAMILTON

'DEAR SIR,

'YOUR kind enquiries after my affairs, and your generous offers, have been communicated to me by Dr. Brocklesby. I return thanks with great sincerity, having lived long enough to know what gratitude is due to such friendship; and entreat that my refusal may not be imputed to sullenness or pride. I am, indeed, in no want. Sickness is, by the generosity of my physicians, of little

[1] 'Letters to Mrs. Thrale,' vol. ii. p. 328.   [2] Ibid. vol. ii. p. 342.

expence to me. But if any unexpected exigence should press me, you shall see, dear Sir, how cheerfully I can be obliged to so much liberality.

'I am, Sir,
'Your most obedient
'And most humble servant,

'November 19, 1783.'   'SAM. JOHNSON'

I find in this, as in former years, notices of his kind attention to Mrs. Gardiner, who, though in the humble station of a tallow-chandler upon Snow-hill, was a woman of excellent good sense, pious, and charitable.[1] She told me, she had been introduced to him by Mrs. Masters, the poetess,[a] whose volumes he revised, and, it is said, illuminated here and there with a ray of his own genius. Mrs. Gardiner was very zealous for the support of the Ladies' charity-school, in the parish of St. Sepulchre. It is confined to females; and, I am told, it afforded a hint for the story of *Betty Broom* in 'The Idler.' Johnson this year, I find, obtained for it a sermon from the late Bishop of St. Asaph, Dr. Shipley, whom he, in one of his letters to Mrs. Thrale, characterises as 'knowing and conversible;' and whom all who knew his Lordship, even those who differed from him in politicks, remember with much respect.

underlined:
Masters [H]
underlined:
Mrs. Masters, the poetess [I]
[a] *Of her I never heard but in this Book.* [H]
of whom I never heard [I]

The Earl of Carlisle having written a tragedy, entitled 'THE FATHER'S REVENGE,' some of his Lordship's friends applied to Mrs. Chapone, to prevail on Dr. Johnson to read and give his opinion of it, which he accordingly did, in a letter to that lady. Sir Joshua Reynolds having informed me that this letter was in Lord Carlisle's possession, though I was not fortunate enough to have the honour of being known to his Lordship, trusting to the general courtesy of literature, I wrote to him, requesting the favour of a copy of it, and to be permitted to insert it in my life of Dr. Johnson. His Lordship was so good as to comply with my request, and has thus enabled me to enrich my work with a very fine piece of writing, which

[1] [In his Will Dr. Johnson left her a book 'at her election, to keep as a token of remembrance.' MALONE.]

[This excellent woman died September 13, 1789, aged 74.
A. CHALMERS]

displays both the critical skill and politeness of my illustrious friend; and perhaps the curiosity which it will excite, may induce the noble and elegant Authour to gratify the world by the publication[1] of a performance, of which Dr. Johnson has spoken in such terms.

'TO MRS. CHAPONE

'MADAM,

'By sending the tragedy to me a second time,[2] I think that a very honourable distinction has been shewn me, and I did not delay the perusal, of which I am now to tell the effect.

'The construction of the play is not completely regular; the stage is too often vacant, and the scenes are not sufficiently connected. This, however, would be called by Dryden only a mechanical defect; which takes away little from the power of the poem, and which is seen rather than felt.

'A rigid examiner of the fiction might, perhaps, wish some words changed, and some lines more vigorously terminated. But from such petty imperfections what writer was ever free?

'The general form and force of the dialogue is of more importance. It seems to want that quickness of reciprocation which characterises the English drama, and is not always sufficiently fervid or animated.

'Of the sentiments, I remember not one that I wished omitted. In the imagery I cannot forbear to distinguish the comparison of joy succeeding grief to light rushing on the eye accustomed to darkness.[3] It seems to have all that can be desired to make it please. It is new, just, and delightful.

[1] A few copies only of this tragedy have been printed, and given to the authour's friends.

[2] Dr. Johnson having been very ill when the tragedy was first sent to him, had declined the consideration of it.

[3] 'I could have borne my woes; that stranger Joy
Wounds while it smiles:—The long-imprison'd wretch,
Emerging from the night of his damp cell,
Shrinks from the sun's bright beams ; and that which flings
Gladness o'er all, to him is agony.'

'With the characters, either as conceived or preserved, I have no fault to find; but was much inclined to congratulate a writer, who, in defiance of prejudice and fashion, made the Archbishop a good man, and scorned all thoughtless applause, which a vicious churchman would have brought him.

'The catastrophe is affecting. The Father and Daughter both culpable, both wretched, and both penitent, divide between them our pity and our sorrow.

'Thus, Madam, I have performed what I did not willingly undertake, and could not decently refuse. The noble writer will be pleased to remember that sincere criticism ought to raise no resentment, because judgement is not under the controul of will; but involuntary criticism, as it has still less of choice, ought to be more remote from possibility of offence.

'I am, &c.

'November 28, 1783.'   'SAM. JOHNSON'

I consulted him on two questions of a very different nature: one, whether the unconstitutional influence exercised by the Peers of Scotland in the election of the representatives of the Commons, by means of fictitious qualifications, ought not to be resisted;—the other, What in propriety and humanity, should be done with old horses unable to labour. I gave him some account of my life at Auchinleck; and expressed my satisfaction that the gentlemen of the county had, at two publick meetings, elected me their *Præses*, or Chairman.

'TO JAMES BOSWELL, ESQ.

'DEAR SIR,

'LIKE all other men who have great friends, you begin to feel the pangs of neglected merit; and all the comfort that I can give you is, by telling you that you have probably more pangs to feel, and more neglect to suffer. You have, indeed, begun to complain too soon; and I hope I am the only confidant of your discontent. Your friends have not yet had leisure to gratify personal kindness; they have hitherto been busy in strengthening their ministerial interest. If a vacancy happens in Scotland, give them early intelligence: and as you can serve Government as powerfully as any of your probable competitors, you may make in some sort a warrantable claim.

'Of the exaltations and depressions of your mind you delight to talk, and I hate to hear. Drive all such fancies from you.

'On the day when I received your letter, I think, the foregoing page was written; to which one disease or another has hindered me from making any additions. I am now a little better. But sickness and solitude press me very heavily. I could bear sickness better, if I were relieved from solitude.

marginal line:
*hereditary possessions
... an hour* [H]

'The present dreadful confusion of the publick ought to make you wrap yourself up in your hereditary possessions, which, though less than you may wish, are more than you can want; and in an hour of religious retirement return thanks to GOD, who has exempted you from any strong temptation to faction, treachery, plunder, and disloyalty.

'As your neighbours distinguish you by such honours as they can bestow, content yourself with your station, without neglecting your profession. Your estate and the Courts will find you full employment, and your mind well occupied will be quiet.

'The usurpation of the nobility, for they apparently usurp all the influence they gain by fraud and misrepresentation, I think it certainly lawful, perhaps your duty, to resist. What is not their own, they have only by robbery.

'Your question about the horses gives me more perplexity. I know not well what advice to give you. I can only recommend a rule which you do not want;—give as little pain as you can. I suppose that we have a right to their service while their strength lasts; what we can do with them afterwards, I cannot so easily determine. But let us consider. Nobody denies that man has a right first to milk the cow, and to sheer the sheep, and then to kill them for his table. May he not, by parity of reason, first work a horse, and then kill him the easiest way, that he may have the means of another horse, or food for cows and sheep? Man is influenced in both cases by different motives of self-interest. He that rejects the one must reject the other.   'I am, &c.

'London, Dec. 24, 1783.'   'SAM. JOHNSON'

'A happy and pious Christmas; and many happy years to you, your lady, and children.'

The late ingenious Mr. Mickle, some time before his death, wrote me a letter concerning Dr. Johnson, in which he mentions, 'I was upwards of twelve years acquainted with him, was frequently in his company, always talked with ease to him, and can truly say, that I never received from him one rough word.'

In this letter he relates his having, while engaged in translating the Lusiad, had a dispute of considerable length with Johnson, who, as usual, declaimed upon the misery and corruption of a sea life, and used this expression:—'It had been happy for the world, Sir, if your hero Gama, Prince Henry of Portugal, and Columbus, had never been born, or that their schemes had never gone farther than their own imaginations.'—'This sentiment, (says Mr. Mickle,) which is to be found in his "Introduction to the World displayed," I, in my Dissertation prefixed to the Lusiad, have controverted; and though authours are said to be bad judges of their own works, I am not ashamed to own to a friend, that that dissertation is my favourite above all that I ever attempted in prose. Next year, when the Lusiad was published, I waited on Dr. Johnson, who addressed me with one of his good-humoured smiles:— "Well, you have remembered our dispute about Prince Henry, and have cited me too. You have done your part very well indeed: you have made the best of your argument; but I am not convinced yet."

'Before publishing the Lusiad, I sent Mr. Hoole a proof of that part of the introduction, in which I make mention of Dr. Johnson, yourself, and other well-wishers to the work, begging it might be shewn to Dr. Johnson. This was accordingly done; and in place of the simple mention of him which I had made, he dictated to Mr. Hoole the sentence as it now stands.

'Dr. Johnson told me in 1772, that, about twenty years before that time, he himself had a design to translate the Lusiad, of the merit of which he spoke highly, but had been prevented by a number of other engagements.'

Mr. Mickle reminds me in this letter, of a conversation at dinner one day at Mr. Hoole's with Dr. Johnson, when Mr. Nicol, the King's Bookseller, and I, attempted to controvert the maxim, 'better that ten guilty should escape, than one innocent person suffer;' and were answered by Dr. Johnson with great power of reasoning and eloquence. I am very sorry that I have no record of that day: but I well recollect my illustrious friend's having ably shewn, that unless civil institutions ensure protection to the innocent, all the confidence which mankind should have in them would be lost.

marginal line: that unless . . . mankind should [H]

I shall here mention what, in strict chronological arrangement, should have appeared in my account of last year; but may more properly be introduced here, the controversy having not been closed till this. The Reverend Mr. Shaw, a native of one of the Hebrides, having entertained doubts of the authenticity of the poems ascribed to Ossian, divested himself of national bigotry; and having travelled in the Highlands and Islands of Scotland, and also in Ireland, in order to furnish himself with materials for a Gaelick Dictionary, which he afterwards compiled, was so fully satisfied that Dr. Johnson was in the right upon the question, that he candidly published a pamphlet, stating his conviction, and the proofs and reasons on which it was founded. A person at Edinburgh, of the name of Clark, answered this pamphlet with much zeal, and much abuse of its authour. Johnson took Mr. Shaw under his protection, and gave him his assistance in writing a reply, which has been admired by the best judges, and by many been considered as conclusive. A few paragraphs, which sufficiently mark their great Authour, shall be selected.

'My assertions are, for the most part, purely negative: I deny the existence of Fingal, because in a long and curious peregrination through the Gaelick regions I have never been able to find it. What I could not see myself, I suspect to be equally invisible to others; and I suspect with

the more reason, as among all those who have seen it no
man can shew it.

'Mr. Clark compares the obstinacy of those who dis-
believe the genuineness of Ossian to a blind man, who
should dispute the reality of colours, and deny that the
British troops are cloathed in red. The blind man's doubt
would be rational, if he did not know by experience that
others have a power which he himself wants: but what
perspicacity has Mr. Clark which Nature has withheld
from me or the rest of mankind?

'The true state of the parallel must be this. Suppose a
man, with eyes like his neighbours, was told by a boasting
corporal, that the troops, indeed, wore red clothes for their
ordinary dress, but that every soldier had likewise a suit
of black velvet, which he puts on when the King reviews
them. This he thinks strange, and desires to see the fine
clothes, but finds nobody in forty thousand men that can
produce either coat or waistcoat. One, indeed, has left
them in his chest at Port Mahon; another has always heard
that he ought to have velvet clothes somewhere; and a
third has heard somebody say, that soldiers ought to wear
velvet. Can the enquirer be blamed if he goes away
believing that a soldier's red coat is all that he has?

'But the most obdurate incredulity may be shamed or
silenced by facts. To overpower contradictions, let the
soldier shew his velvet coat, and the Fingalist the original
of Ossian.

'The difference between us and the blind man is this:
the blind man is unconvinced, because he cannot see; and
we, because, though we can see, we find nothing that can
be shewn.'

Notwithstanding the complication of disorders under
which Johnson now laboured, he did not resign himself to
despondency and discontent, but with wisdom and spirit
endeavoured to console and amuse his mind with as many
innocent enjoyments as he could procure. Sir John Hawkins has mentioned the cordiality with which he insisted
that such of the members of the old club in Ivy-lane as
survived, should meet again and dine together, which they
did twice at a tavern, and once at his house: and in order
to ensure himself society in the evening for three days in

the week, he instituted a club at the Essex Head, in Essex-street, then kept by Samuel Greaves, an old servant of
Poor Sam & Molly Mr. Thrale's.[a]
& they gone too !! [1]

'TO SIR JOSHUA REYNOLDS

'DEAR SIR,

'IT is inconvenient to me to come out; I should else have waited on you with an account of a little Evening-Club which we are establishing in Essex-street, in the Strand, and of which you are desired to be one. It will be held at the Essex Head, now kept by an old servant of Thrale's. The company is numerous, and, as you will see by the list, miscellaneous. The terms are lax, and the expences light. Mr. Barry was adopted by Dr. Brocklesby, who joined with me in forming the plan. We meet thrice a week, and he who misses forfeits two-pence.

'If you are willing to become a member, draw a line under your name. Return the list. We meet for the first time on Monday at eight.

'I am, &c.

'Dec. 4, 1783.'   'SAM. JOHNSON'

It did not suit Sir Joshua to be one of this Club. But
index sign: when I mention only Mr. Daines Barrington, Dr. Brockles-
Mr. Cooke . . . Dr.   by, Mr. Murphy, Mr. John Nichols, Mr. Cooke, Mr.
Horsley [1]   Joddrel, Mr. Paradise, Dr. Horsley, Mr. Windham,[1] I shall sufficiently obviate the misrepresentation of it by Sir John Hawkins, as if it had been a low ale-house association, by which Johnson was degraded. Johnson himself, like his namesake Old Ben, composed the Rules of his Club.[2]

[1] I was in Scotland when this Club was founded, and during all the winter. Johnson, however, declared I should be a member, and invented a word upon the occasion: 'Boswell, (said he) is a very *clubable* man.' When I came to town I was proposed by Mr. Barrington, and chosen. I believe there are few societies where there is better conversation or more decorum. Several of us resolved to continue it after our great founder was removed by death. Other members were added; and now, above eight years since that loss, we go on happily.

[2] RULES
'To-day deep thoughts with me resolve to drench
    In mirth, which after no repenting draws.'—MILTON.
'The Club shall consist of four-and-twenty.'

In the end of this year he was seized with a spasmodic asthma of such violence, that he was confined to the house in great pain, being sometimes obliged to sit all night in his chair, a recumbent posture being so hurtful to his respiration, that he could not endure lying in bed; and there came upon him at the same time that oppressive and fatal disease, a dropsy. It was a very severe winter, which probably aggravated his complaints; and the solitude in which Mr. Levett and Mrs. Williams had left him, rendered his life very gloomy. Mrs. Desmoulins, who still lived, was herself so very ill, that she could contribute very little to his relief. He, however, had none of that unsocial shyness which we commonly see in people afflicted with sickness. He did not hide his head from the world, in

'The meetings shall be on the Monday, Thursday, and Saturday of every week; but in the week before Easter there shall be no meeting.

'Every member is at liberty to introduce a friend once a week, but not oftener.

'Two members shall oblige themselves to attend in their turn every night from eight to ten, or to procure two to attend in their room.

'Every member present at the Club shall spend at least six-pence; and every member who stays away shall forfeit three-pence.

'The master of the house shall keep an account of the absent members: and deliver to the President of the night a list of the forfeits incurred.

'When any member returns after absence, he shall immediately lay down his forfeits; which if he omits to do, the President shall require.

'There shall be no general reckoning, but every man shall adjust his own expences.

'The night of indispensable attendance will come to every member once a month. Whoever shall for three months together omit to attend himself, or by substitution, nor shall make any apology in the fourth month, shall be considered as having abdicated the Club.

'When a vacancy is to be filled, the name of the candidate, and of the member recommending him, shall stand in the Club-room three nights. On the fourth he may be chosen by ballot; six members at least being present, and two-thirds of the ballot being in his favour; or the majority, should the numbers not be divisible by three.

'The master of the house shall give notice, six days before, to each of those members whose turn of necessary attendance is come.

'The notice may be in these words:—"Sir, On———— the ———— of ————, will be your turn of presiding at the Essex-Head. Your company is therefore earnestly requested."

'One penny shall be left by each member for the waiter.'

Johnson's definition of a Club in this sense, in his Dictionary, is 'An assembly of good fellows, meeting under certain conditions.'

solitary abstraction; he did not deny himself to the visits of his friends and acquaintances; but at all times, when he was not overcome by sleep, was ready for conversation as in his best days.

'TO MRS. LUCY PORTER, IN LICHFIELD

'DEAR MADAM,

'YOU may perhaps think me negligent that I have not written to you again upon the loss of your brother; but condolences and consolations are such common and such useless things, that the omission of them is no great crime: and my own diseases occupy my mind and engage my care. My nights are miserably restless, and my days, therefore, are heavy. I try, however, to hold up my head as high as I can.

'I am sorry that your health is impaired: perhaps the spring and the summer may, in some degree, restore it; but if not, we must submit to the inconveniences of time, as to the other dispensations of Eternal Goodness. Pray for me, and write to me, or let Mr. Pearson write for you.

'I am, &c.

'London, Nov. 29, 1783.'   'SAM. JOHNSON'

And now I am arrived at the last year of the life of SAMUEL JOHNSON, a year in which, although passed in severe indisposition, he nevertheless gave many evidences of the continuance of those wondrous powers of mind, which raised him so high in the intellectual world. His conversation and his letters of this year were in no respect inferiour to those of former years.

The following is a remarkable proof of his being alive to the most minute curiosities of literature.

'TO MR. DILLY, BOOKSELLER, IN THE POULTRY

'SIR,

'THERE is in the world a set of books which used to be sold by the booksellers on the bridge, and which I must entreat you to procure me. They are called,

Burton's Books;[1] the title of one is *Admirable Curiosities, Rarities, and Wonders in England.* I believe there are about five or six of them; they seem very proper to allure backward readers; be so kind as to get them for me, and send me them with the best printed edition of "Baxter's Call to the Unconverted."

                                                'I am, &c.

'Jan. 6, 1784.'   'SAM. JOHNSON'

                         'TO MR. PERKINS
'DEAR SIR,

   'I WAS very sorry not to see you, when you were so kind as to call on me; but to disappoint friends, and if they

---

[1] [These books are much more numerous than Johnson supposed. The following list comprises several of them; but probably is incomplete:

  1. Historical Rarities in London and Westminster..............1681
  2. Wars in England, Scotland, and Ireland....................1681
  3. Wonderful Prodigies of Judgement and Mercy................1681
  4. Strange and prodigious religious Customs and Manners of sundry Nations...1683
  5. English Empire in America................................1685
  6. Surprising Miracles of Nature and Art....................1685
     [Admirable Curiosities of Nature, &c. 1681.—Probably the same book with a different title.]
  7. History of Scotland......................................1685
  8. History of Ireland.......................................1685
  9. Two Journies to Jerusalem................................1685
 10. Nine Worthies of the World...............................1687
 11. Winter's Evenings' Entertainments........................1687
 12. The English Hero, or the Life of Sir Francis Drake...........1687
 13. Memorable Accidents and unheard-of Transactions..........1693
 14. History of the House of Orange...........................1693
 15. Burton's Acts of the Martyrs (or, of Martyrs in flames)........1695
 16. Curiosities of England 1697
 17. History of Oliver Cromwell...............................1698
 18. Unparalleled Varieties...................................1699
 19. Unfortunate Court Favourites of England..................1706
 20. History of the Lives of English Divines..................1709
 21. Ingenious Riddles ....——
 22. Unhappy Princesses, or the History of Anne Boleyn and Lady Jane Gray 1710
 23. Æsop's Fables, in prose and verse........................1712
 24. History of Virginia......................................1722
 25. English Acquisitions in Guinea and the East Indies 1726
 26. Female Excellency, or the Ladies' Glory..................1728
 27. General History of Earthquakes...........................1736
 28. The English Heroine, or the Life and Adventures of Mrs. Christian Davis, commonly called Mother Ross[a]...........——
 29. Youth's Divine Pastime...................................——
                                                MALONE.]

[a] *Legitimate Parent of Ferdinand Count Fathom—* [H]

are not very good-natured, to disoblige them, is one of the evils of sickness. If you will please to let me know which of the afternoons in this week I shall be favoured with another visit by you and Mrs. Perkins, and the young people, I will take all the measures that I can to be pretty well at that time. I am, dear Sir,

'Your most humble servant,

'Jan. 21, 1784.'   'SAM. JOHNSON'

His attention to the Essex-Head Club appears from the following letter to Mr. Alderman Clark, a gentleman for whom he deservedly entertained a great regard.

'TO RICHARD CLARK, ESQ.

'DEAR SIR,

'YOU will receive a requisition, according to the rules of the Club, to be at the house as President of the night. This turn comes once a month, and the member is obliged to attend, or send another in his place. You were enrolled in the Club by my invitation, and I ought to introduce you; but as I am hindered by sickness, Mr. Hoole will very properly supply my place as introductor, or yours as President. I hope in milder weather to be a very constant attendant.

'I am, Sir, &c.

'Jan. 27, 1784.'   'SAM. JOHNSON'

'You ought to be informed that the forfeits began with the year, and that every night of non-attendance incurs the mulct of three-pence, that is, nine-pence a week.'

On the 8th of January I wrote to him, anxiously enquiring as to his health, and enclosing my 'Letter to the People of Scotland, on the present state of the nation.'—'I trust, (said I,) that you will be liberal enough to make allowance for my differing from you on two points, [the Middlesex Election, and the American War,] when my general principles of government are according to your own heart, and when, at a crisis of doubtful event, I stand forth with honest zeal as an ancient and faithful Briton. My reason for introducing those two points was, that as my opinions with regard to them had been declared at the periods when they were least favourable, I might have the credit of a man who is not a worshipper of ministerial power.'

'TO JAMES BOSWELL, ESQ.

'DEAR SIR,

'I HEAR of many enquiries which your kindness has disposed you to make after me. I have long intended you a long letter, which perhaps the imagination of its length hindered me from beginning. I will, therefore, content myself with a shorter.

'Having promoted the institution of a new Club in the neighbourhood, at the house of an old servant of Thrale's, I went thither to meet the company, and was seized with a spasmodick asthma, so violent, that with difficulty I got to my own house, in which I have been confined eight or nine weeks, and from which I know not when I shall be able to go even to church. The asthma, however, is not the worst. A dropsy gains ground upon me: my legs and thighs are very much swollen with water, which I should be content if I could keep there, but I am afraid that it will soon be higher. My nights are very sleepless and very tedious. And yet I am extremely afraid of dying.

'My physicians try to make me hope, that much of my malady is the effect of cold, and that some degree at least of recovery is to be expected from vernal breezes and summer suns. If my life is prolonged to autumn, I should be glad to try a warmer climate; though how to travel with a diseased body, without a companion to conduct me, and with very little money, I do not well see. Ramsay has recovered his limbs in Italy; and Fielding was sent to Lisbon, where, indeed, he died; but he was, I believe, past hope when he went. Think for me what I can do.

'I received your pamphlet, and when I write again may perhaps tell you some opinion about it; but you will forgive a man struggling with disease his neglect of disputes, politicks, and pamphlets. Let me have your prayers. My compliments to your lady, and young ones. Ask your

physicians about my case: and desire Sir Alexander Dick
to write me his opinion.

'I am, dear Sir, &c.

'Feb. 11, 1784.' 'SAM. JOHNSON'

'TO MRS. LUCY PORTER IN LICHFIELD

'MY DEAREST LOVE,

'I HAVE been extremely ill of an asthma and dropsy,
but received by the mercy of GOD, sudden, and unexpected
relief last Thursday, by the discharge of twenty pints of
water. Whether I shall continue free, or shall fill again,
cannot be told. Pray for me.

'Death, my dear, is very dreadful; let us think nothing
worth our care but how to prepare for it: what we know
amiss in ourselves let us make haste to amend, and put our
trust in the mercy of GOD, and the intercession of our
SAVIOUR.

'I am, dear Madam,
'Your most humble servant,

'Feb. 23, 1784.' 'SAM. JOHNSON'

'TO JAMES BOSWELL, ESQ.

'DEAR SIR,

'I HAVE just advanced so far towards recovery as to
read a pamphlet; and you may reasonably suppose that
the first pamphlet which I read was yours. I am very much
of your opinion, and, like you, feel great indignation at the
indecency with which the King is every day treated. Your
paper contains very considerable knowledge of history and
of the constitution, very properly produced and applied.
It will certainly raise your character,[1] though perhaps it
may not make you a Minister of State.

* * * * * *

'I desire you to see Mrs. Stewart once again, and tell
her, that in the letter-case was a letter relating to me, for

[1] I sent it to Mr. Pitt, with a letter, in which I thus expressed myself: 'My
principles may appear to you too monarchical: but I know and am persuaded, they are not inconsistent with the true principles of liberty. Be this
as it may, you, Sir, are now the Prime Minister, called by the Sovereign to
maintain the rights of the Crown, as well as those of the people, against a

which I will give her, if she is willing to give it me, another guinea. The letter is of consequence only to me.

'I am, dear Sir, &c.

'London, Feb. 27, 1784.'   'SAM. JOHNSON'

In consequence of Johnson's request that I should ask our physicians about his case, and desire Sir Alexander Dick to send his opinion, I transmitted him a letter from that very amiable Baronet, then in his eighty-first year, with his faculties as entire as ever: and mentioned his expressions to me in the note accompanying it,—'With my most affectionate wishes for Dr. Johnson's recovery, in which his friends, his country, and all mankind have so deep a stake;' and at the same time a full opinion upon his case by Dr. Gillespie, who, like Dr. Cullen, had the advantage of having passed through the gradations of surgery and pharmacy, and by study and practice had attained to such skill, that my father settled on him two hundred pounds a year for five years, and fifty pounds a year during his life, as an *honorarium* to secure his particular attendance. The opinion was conveyed in a letter to me, beginning, 'I am sincerely sorry for the bad state of health your very learned and illustrious friend, Dr. Johnson, labours under at present.'

'TO JAMES BOSWELL, ESQ.

'DEAR SIR,

'PRESENTLY after I had sent away my last letter, I received your kind medical packet. I am very much obliged both to you and to your physicians for your kind attention to my disease. Dr. Gillespie has sent me an excellent *consilium medicum*, all solid practical experimental knowledge. I am at present in the opinion of my physicians, (Dr. Heberden and Dr. Brocklesby,) as well as my own, going on very hopefully. I have just begun to take vinegar of squills. The powder hurt my stomach so much, that it could not be continued.

violent faction. As such, you are entitled to the warmest support of every good subject in every department.' He answered, 'I am extremely obliged to you for the sentiments you do me the honour to express, and have observed with great pleasure the *zealous and able support* given to the CAUSE OF THE PUBLICK in the work you were so good to transmit to me.'

'Return Sir Alexander Dick my sincere thanks for his kind letter; and bring with you the rhubarb[1] which he so tenderly offers me.

'I hope dear Mrs. Boswell is now quite well, and that no evil, either real or imaginary, now disturbs you.

'I am, &c.

'London, March 2, 1784.'   'SAM. JOHNSON'

I also applied to three of the eminent physicians who had chairs in our celebrated school of medicine at Edinburgh, Doctors Cullen, Hope, and Munro, to each of whom I sent the following letter:

'DEAR SIR,

'DR. JOHNSON has been very ill for some time; and in a letter of anxious apprehension he writes to me, "Ask your physicians about my case."

'This, you see, is not authority for a regular consultation: but I have no doubt of your readiness to give your advice to a man so eminent, and who, in his Life of Garth, has paid your profession a just and elegant compliment: "I believe every man has found in physicians great liberality and dignity of sentiment, very prompt effusions of beneficence, and willingness to exert a lucrative art, where there is no hope of lucre."

'Dr. Johnson is aged seventy-four. Last summer he had a stroke of the palsy, from which he recovered almost entirely. He had, before that, been troubled with a catarrhous cough. This winter he was seized with a spasmodick asthma, by which he has been confined to his house for about three months. Dr. Brocklesby writes to me, that upon the least admission of cold, there is such a constriction upon his breast, that he cannot lie down in his bed, but is obliged to sit up all night, and gets rest and sometimes sleep, only by means of laudanum and syrup of poppies; and that there are œdematous tumours in his legs and thighs. Dr. Brocklesby trusts a good deal to the return of mild weather. Dr. Johnson says, that a dropsy

[1] From his garden at Prestonfield, where he cultivated that plant with such success, that he was presented with a gold medal by the Society of London for the Encouragement of Arts, Manufactures, and Commerce.

gains ground upon him; and he seems to think that a warmer climate would do him good. I understand he is now rather better, and is using vinegar of squills. I am, with great esteem, dear Sir,

'Your most obedient humble servant,
'March 7, 1784.'   'JAMES BOSWELL'

All of them paid the most polite attention to my letter, and its venerable object. Dr. Cullen's words concerning him were, 'It would give me the greatest pleasure to be of any service to a man whom the publick properly esteem, and whom I esteem and respect as much as I do Dr. Johnson.' Dr. Hope's, 'Few people have a better claim on me than your friend, as hardly a day passes that I do not ask his opinion about this or that word.' Dr. Munro's, 'I most sincerely join you in sympathising with that very worthy and ingenious character, from whom his country has derived much instruction and entertainment.'

Dr. Hope corresponded with his friend Dr. Brocklesby. Doctors Cullen and Munro wrote their opinions and prescriptions to me, which I afterwards carried with me to London, and, so far as they were encouraging, communicated to Johnson. The liberality on one hand, and grateful sense of it on the other, I have great satisfaction in recording.

'TO JAMES BOSWELL, ESQ.

'DEAR SIR,

'I AM too much pleased with the attention which you and your dear lady[1] show to my welfare, not to be diligent in letting you know the progress which I make towards health. The dropsy, by GOD's blessing, has now run almost totally away by natural evacuation: and the asthma, if not irritated by cold, gives me little trouble. While I am writing this, I have not any sensation of debility or disease. But I do not yet venture out, having been confined to the house from the thirteenth of December, now a quarter of a year.

'When it will be fit for me to travel as far as Auchinleck, I am not able to guess; but such a letter as Mrs. Boswell's might draw any man, not wholly motionless, a great way.

[1] Who had written him a very kind letter.

Pray tell the dear lady how much her civility and kindness have touched and gratified me.

'Our parliamentary tumults have now begun to subside, and the King's authority is in some measure re-established. Mr. Pitt will have great power; but you must remember, that what he has to give, must, at least for some time, be given to those who gave, and those who preserve, his power. A new minister can sacrifice little to esteem or friendship; he must, till he is settled, think only of extending his interest.

* * * * * *

'If you come hither through Edinburgh, send for Mrs. Stewart, and give from me another guinea for the letter in the old case, to which I shall not be satisfied with my claim, till she gives it me.

'Please to bring with you Baxter's Anacreon; and if you procure heads of Hector Boece, the historian, and Arthur Johnston, the poet, I will put them in my room; or any other of the fathers of Scottish literature.

'I wish you an easy and happy journey, and hope I need not tell you that you will be welcome to, dear Sir,

'Your most affectionate humble servant,

'London, March 18, 1784.'   'SAM. JOHNSON'

I wrote to him, March 28, from York, informing him that I had a high gratification in the triumph of monarchical principles over aristocratical influence, in that great county, in an address to the King; that I was thus far on my way to him, but that news of the dissolution of Parliament having arrived, I was to hasten back to my own county, where I had carried an Address to his Majesty by a great majority, and had some intention of being a candidate to represent the county in Parliament.

'TO JAMES BOSWELL, ESQ.

'DEAR SIR,

'YOU could do nothing so proper as to hasten back when you found the Parliament dissolved. With the influence which your address must have gained you, it may reasonably be expected that your presence will be of importance, and your activity of effect.

'Your solicitude for me gives me that pleasure which every man feels from the kindness of such a friend; and it is with delight I relieve it by telling, that Dr. Brocklesby's account is true, and that I am, by the blessing of GOD, wonderfully relieved.

'You are entering upon a transaction which requires much prudence. You must endeavour to oppose without exasperating; to practise temporary hostility, without producing enemies for life. This is, perhaps, hard to be done; yet it has been done by many, and seems most likely to be effected by opposing merely upon general principles, without descending to personal or particular censures or objections. One thing I must enjoin you, which is seldom observed in the conduct of elections;—I must entreat you to be scrupulous in the use of strong liquors. One night's drunkenness may defeat the labours of forty days well employed. Be firm, but not clamorous; be active, but not malicious; and you may form such an interest, as may not only exalt yourself, but dignify your family.

'We are, as you may suppose, all busy here. Mr. Fox resolutely stands for Westminster, and his friends say will carry the election. However that be, he will certainly have a seat. Mr. Hoole has just told me, that the city leans towards the King.

'Let me hear, from time to time, how you are employed, and what progress you make.

'Make dear Mrs. Boswell, and all the young Boswells, the sincere compliments of, Sir, your affectionate humble servant,

'London, March 30, 1784.'   'SAM. JOHNSON'

To Mr. Langton he wrote with that cordiality which was suitable to the long friendship which had subsisted between him and that gentleman.

March 27. 'Since you left me, I have continued in my own opinion, and in Dr. Brocklesby's, to grow better with respect to all my formidable and dangerous distempers; though to a body battered and shaken as mine has lately been, it is to be feared that weak attacks may be sometimes mischievous. I have, indeed, by standing carelessly at an open window, got a very troublesome cough, which it has been necessary to appease by opium, in larger quantities than I like to take, and I have not found it give way so readily as I expected; its obstinacy, however, seems at last disposed to submit to the remedy, and I know not whether I should then have a right to complain of any morbid sensation. My asthma is, I am afraid, constitutional and incurable; but it is only occasional, and unless it be excited by labour or by cold, gives me no molestation, nor does it lay very close siege to life; for Sir John Floyer, whom the physical race consider as authour of one of the best books upon it, panted on to ninety, as was supposed; and why were we content with supposing a fact so interesting, of a man so conspicuous? because he corrupted, at perhaps seventy or eighty, the register, that he might pass for younger than he was. He was not much less than eighty, when to a man of rank who modestly asked his age, he answered, "Go look;" though he was in general a man of civility and elegance.

'The ladies, I find, are at your house all well, except Miss Langton, who will probably soon recover her health by light suppers. Let her eat at dinner as she will, but not take a full stomach to bed.—Pay my sincere respects to dear Miss Langton in Lincolnshire, let her know that I mean not to break our league of friendship, and that I have a set of Lives for her, when I have the means of sending it.'

April 8. 'I am still disturbed by my cough; but what thanks have I not to pay, when my cough is the most painful sensation that I feel? and from that I expect hardly to be released, while winter continues to gripe us with so much pertinacity. The year has now advanced eighteen days beyond the equinox, and still there is very little remission of the cold. When warm weather comes, which surely must come at last, I hope it will help both me and your young lady.

'The man so busy about addresses is neither more nor less than our own Boswell, who had come as far as York towards London, but turned back on the dissolution, and is said now to stand for some place. Whether to wish him success, his best friends hesitate.

'Let me have your prayers for the completion of my

recovery: I am now better than I ever expected to have been. May GOD add to his mercies the grace that may enable me to use them according to his will. My compliments to all.'

April 13. 'I had this evening a note from Lord Port-more,[1] desiring that I would give you an account of my health. You might have had it with less circumduction. I am, by GOD's blessing, I believe, free from all morbid sensations, except a cough, which is only troublesome. But I am still weak, and can have no great hope of strength till the weather shall be softer. The summer, if it be kindly, will, I hope, enable me to support the winter. GOD, who has so wonderfully restored me, can preserve me in all seasons.

'Let me enquire in my turn after the state of your family, great and little. I hope Lady Rothes and Miss Langton are both well. That is a good basis of content. Then how goes George on with his studies? How does Miss Mary? And how does my own Jenny? I think I owe Jenny a letter, which I will take care to pay. In the mean time tell her that I acknowledge the debt.

'Be pleased to make my compliments to the ladies. If Mrs. Langton comes to London, she will favour me with a visit, for I am not well enough to go out.'

'TO OZIAS HUMPHRY,[2] ESQ.

'SIR,

'MR. HOOLE has told me with what benevolence you listened to a request which I was almost afraid to

---

[1] To which Johnson returned this answer:

'TO THE RIGHT HONOURABLE EARL OF PORTMORE

'DR. JOHNSON acknowledges with great respect the honour of Lord Portmore's notice. He is better than he was; and will, as his Lordship directs, write to Mr. Langton.

'Bolt-court, Fleet-street,
    Apr. 13, 1784.'

[2] The eminent painter, representative of the ancient family of Homfrey (now Humphry) in the west of England; who, as appears from their arms which they have invariably used, have been, (as I have seen authenticated by the best authority,) one of those among the Knights and Esquires of honour who are represented by Holinshed as having issued from the Tower of London on coursers apparelled for the justes, accompanied by ladies of honour, leading every one a Knight, with a chain of gold, passing through

make, of leave to a young painter[1] to attend you from time to time in your painting-room, to see your operations, and receive your instructions.

'The young man has perhaps good parts, but has been without a regular education. He is my god-son, and therefore I interest myself in his progress and success, and shall think myself much favoured if I receive from you a permission to send him.

'My health is, by GOD's blessing, much restored, but I am not yet allowed by my physicians to go abroad; nor, indeed, do I think myself yet able to endure the weather.

'I am, Sir,

'Your most humble servant,

'April 5, 1784.'   'SAM. JOHNSON'

TO THE SAME

'SIR,

'THE bearer is my god-son, whom I take the liberty of recommending to your kindness; which I hope he will deserve by his respect to your excellence, and his gratitude for your favours.

'I am, Sir,

'Your most humble servant,

'April 10, 1784.'   'SAM. JOHNSON'

TO THE SAME

'SIR,

'I AM very much obliged by your civilities to my god-son, but must beg of you to add to them the favour of permitting him to see you paint, that he may know how a picture is begun, advanced, and completed.

'If he may attend you in a few of your operations, I hope he will shew that the benefit has been properly conferred,

a In this Vol. he re-commends him to Rey-nolds: how did that Recommendation suc-ceed I wonder ! & how this to Mr. Humphries became necessary after that. [H]

the streets of London into Smithfield, on Sunday, at three o'clock in the afternoon, being the first Sunday after Michaelmas, in the fourteenth year of King Richard the Second. This family once enjoyed large possessions, but, like others, have lost them in the progress of ages. Their blood, however, remains to them well ascertained; and they may hope in the revolution of events, to recover that rank in society for which, in modern times, fortune seems to be an indispensable requisite.

[1] Son of Mr. Samuel Paterson, eminent for his knowledge of books.[a]

both by his proficiency and his gratitude. At least I shall consider you as enlarging your kindness to, Sir,

'Your humble servant,

'May 31, 1784.'   'SAM. JOHNSON'

'TO THE REVEREND DR. TAYLOR, ASHBOURNE,
DERBYSHIRE
'DEAR SIR,

'WHAT can be the reason that I hear nothing from you? I hope nothing disables you from writing. What I have seen, and what I have felt, gives me reason to fear every thing. Do not omit giving me the comfort of knowing, that after all my losses I have yet a friend left.

'I want every comfort. My life is very solitary and very cheerless. Though it has pleased GOD wonderfully to deliver me from the dropsy, I am yet very weak, and have not passed the door since the 13th of December. I hope for some help from warm weather, which will surely come in time.

'I could not have the consent of the physicians to go to church yesterday; I therefore received the holy sacrament at home, in the room where I communicated with dear Mrs. Williams, a little before her death. O! my friend, the approach of death is very dreadful. I am afraid to think on that which I know I cannot avoid. It is vain to look round and round for that help which cannot be had. Yet we hope and hope, and fancy that he who has lived to-day may live to-morrow. But let us learn to derive our hope only from GOD.

'In the mean time, let us be kind to one another. I have no friend now living but you[1] and Mr. Hector,[a] that was the friend of my youth. Do not neglect, dear Sir,

'Yours affectionately,

'London, Easter-Monday,   'SAM. JOHNSON'
April 12, 1784.'

[a] to whom he perpetually turned . . . not to his Flatterers & Admirers. Ever sighing for the Tea & Bread & Butter of Life, when satiated with the Turtle & Burgundy of it. [H]

[TO MRS. LUCY PORTER, IN LICHFIELD

'MY DEAR,

'I WRITE to you now, to tell you that I am so far recovered that on the 21st. I went to church, to return

[1] [This friend of Johnson's youth survived him somewhat more than three years, having died Feb. 19, 1788. MALONE.]

thanks, after a confinement of more than four long months.

'My recovery is such as neither myself nor the physicians at all expected, and is such as that very few examples have been known of the like. Join with me, my dear love, in returning thanks to GOD.

'Dr. Vyse has been with [me] this evening: he tells me that you likewise have been much disordered, but that you are now better. I hope that we shall sometime have a cheerful interview. In the mean time let us pray for one another.
                                    'I am, Madam,
                                    'Your humble servant,
'London, April 26, 1784.'   'SAM. JOHNSON']

What follows is a beautiful specimen of his gentleness and complacency to a young lady his god-child, one of the daughters of his friend Mr. Langton, then I think in her seventh year. He took the trouble to write it in a large round hand, nearly resembling printed characters, that she might have the satisfaction of reading it herself. The original lies before me, but shall be faithfully restored to her; and I dare say will be preserved by her as a jewel, as long as she lives.

'TO MISS JANE LANGTON, IN ROCHESTER, KENT

'MY DEAREST MISS JENNY,

'I AM sorry that your pretty letter has been so long
^a *like his Letters to* without being answered; but, when I am not pretty well,
Mr. Thrale's Daugh- I do not always write plain enough for young ladies.^a I am
ters—exactly. [H] glad, my dear, to see that you write so well, and hope that you mind your pen, your book, and your needle, for they are all necessary. Your books will give you knowledge, and make you respected; and your needle will find you useful employment when you do not care to read. When you are a little older, I hope you will be very diligent in learning arithmetick; and, above all, that through your whole life you will carefully say your prayers, and read your Bible.
                                    'I am, my dear,
                                    'Your most humble servant,
'May 10, 1784.'   'SAM. JOHNSON'

On Wednesday, May 5, I arrived in London, and next morning had the pleasure to find Dr. Johnson greatly recovered. I but just saw him; for a coach was waiting to carry him to Islington, to the house of his friend the Reverend Mr. Strahan, where he went sometimes for the benefit of good air, which, notwithstanding his having formerly laughed at the general opinion upon the subject, he now acknowledged was conducive to health.

One morning afterwards, when I found him alone, he communicated to me, with solemn earnestness, a very remarkable circumstance which had happened in the course of his illness, when he was much distressed by the dropsy. He had shut himself up, and employed a day in particular exercises of religion—fasting, humiliation, and prayer. On a sudden he obtained extraordinary relief, for which he looked up to Heaven with grateful devotion. He made no direct inference from this fact; but from his manner of telling it, I could perceive that it appeared to him as something more than an incident in the common course of events. For my own part, I have no difficulty to avow that cast of thinking, which, by many modern pretenders to wisdom, is called *superstitious*. But here I think even men of dry rationality may believe, that there was an intermediate interposition of Divine Providence, and that 'the fervent prayer of this righteous man' availed.[1]

On Sunday, May 9, I found Colonel Vallancy, the celebrated Antiquary, and Engineer of Ireland, with him. On Monday, the 10th, I dined with him at Mr. Paradise's, where was a large company; Mr. Bryant, Mr. Joddrel,

---

[1] Upon this subject there is a very fair and judicious remark in the Life of Dr. Abernethy, in the first edition of the *Biographia Britannica*, which I should have been glad to see in his Life which has been written for the second edition of that valuable work. 'To deny the exercise of a particular providence in the Deity's government of the world, is certainly impious, yet nothing serves the cause of the scorner more than an incautious forward zeal in determining the particular instances of it.'

In confirmation of my sentiments, I am also happy to quote that sensible and elegant writer Mr. *Melmoth*, in Letter VIII. of his collection, published under the name of *Fitzosborne*. 'We may safely assert, that the belief of a particular Providence is founded upon such probable reasons as may well justify our assent. It would scarce, therefore, be wise to renounce an opinion which affords so firm a support to the soul, in those seasons wherein she stands in most need of assistance, merely because it is not possible, in questions of this kind, to solve every difficulty which attends them.'

Mr. Hawkins Browne, &c. On Thursday the 13th, I dined with him at Mr. Joddrel's, with another large company; the Bishop of Exeter, Lord Monboddo,[1] Mr. Murphy, &c.

On Saturday, May 15, I dined with him at Dr. Brocklesby's, where were Colonel Vallancy, Mr. Murphy, and that ever-cheerful companion Mr. Devaynes, apothecary to his Majesty. Of these days, and others on which I saw him, I have no memorials, except the general recollection of his being able and animated in conversation, and appearing to relish society as much as the youngest man. I find only these three small particulars:—When a person was mentioned, who said, 'I have lived fifty-one years in this world, without having had ten minutes of uneasiness;' he exclaimed, 'The man who says so, lies: he attempts to impose on human credulity.' The Bishop of Exeter[2] in vain observed, that men were very different. His Lordship's manner was not impressive; and I learnt afterwards, that Johnson did not find out that the person who talked to him was a Prelate; if he had, I doubt not that he would have treated him with more respect; for once talking of George Psalmanazar, whom he reverenced for his piety, he said, 'I should as soon think of contradicting a Bishop.' One of the company provoked him greatly by doing what he could least of all bear, which was quoting something of his own writing, against what he then maintained. 'What, Sir, (cried the gentleman,) do you say to

"The busy day, the peaceful night,
Unfelt, uncounted, glided by"?'[3]

Johnson finding himself thus presented as giving an instance of a man who had lived without uneasiness, was much offended, for he looked upon such a quotation as unfair, his anger burst out in an unjustifiable retort,

[1] I was sorry to observe Lord Monboddo avoid any communication with Dr. Johnson. I flattered myself that I had made them very good friends, (see 'Journal of a Tour to the Hebrides,' third edition, page 67,) but unhappily his Lordship had resumed and cherished a violent prejudice against my illustrious friend, to whom I must do the justice to say, there was on his part not the least anger, but a good humoured sportiveness. Nay, though he knew of his Lordship's indisposition towards him, he was even kindly; as appeared from his enquiring of me after him, by an abbreviation of his name, 'Well, how does *Monny?*'

[2] [Dr. John Ross.]   [3] Verses on the death of Mr. Levett.

insinuating that the gentleman's remark was a sally of ebriety; 'Sir, there is one passion I would advise you to command: when you have drunk out that glass, don't drink another.' Here was exemplified what Goldsmith said of him, with the aid of a very witty image from one of Cibber's Comedies: 'There is no arguing with Johnson: for if his pistol misses fire, he knocks you down with the butt end of it.'

Another was this: when a gentleman of eminence in the literary world was violently censured for attacking people by anonymous paragraphs in news-papers; he, from the spirit of contradiction as I thought, took up his defence and said, 'Come, come, this is not so terrible a crime; he means only to vex them a little. I do not say that I should do it; but there is a great difference between him and me; what is fit for Hephæstion is not fit for Alexander.' — Another, when I told him that a young and handsome Countess had said to me, 'I should think that to be praised by Dr. Johnson would make one a fool all one's life;' and that I answered, 'Madam, I shall make him a fool to-day, by repeating this to him;' he said, 'I am too old to be made a fool; but if you say I am made a fool I shall not deny it. I am much pleased with a compliment, especially from a pretty woman.'

On the evening of Saturday, May 15, he was in fine spirits at our Essex-Head Club. He told us, 'I dined yesterday at Mrs. Garrick's with Mrs. Carter,[1] Miss Hannah More, and Miss Fanny Burney. Three such women are not to be found: I know not where I could find a fourth, except Mrs. Lennox, who is superiour to them all.' BOSWELL. 'What! had you them all to yourself, Sir?' JOHNSON. 'I had them all, as much as they were had; but it might have been better had there been more company there.' BOSWELL. 'Might not Mrs. Montague have been a fourth?' JOHNSON. 'Sir, Mrs. Montague does not make a trade of her wit; but Mrs. Montague is a very extraordinary woman: she has a constant stream of conversation, and it is always impregnated; it has always

[1] [This learned and excellent lady, who has been often mentioned in these volumes, died at her house in Clarges-street, Feb. 19, 1806, in her eighty-ninth year. MALONE.]

meaning.' BOSWELL. 'Mr. Burke has a constant stream of conversation.' JOHNSON. 'Yes, Sir; if a man were to go by chance at the same time with Burke under a shed, to shun a shower, he would say—"this is an extraordinary man." If Burke should go into a stable to see his horse drest, the ostler would say—"we have had an extraordinary man here." ' BOSWELL. 'Foote was a man who never failed in conversation. If he had gone into a stable—' JOHNSON. 'Sir, if he had gone into the stable, the ostler would have said, here has been a comical fellow; but he would not have respected him.' BOSWELL. 'And, Sir, the ostler would have answered him, would have given him as good as he brought, as the common saying is.' JOHNSON. 'Yes, Sir; and Foote would have answered the ostler. ——When Burke does not descend to be merry, his conversation is very superiour indeed. There is no proportion between the powers which he shews in serious talk and in jocularity. When he lets himself down to that, he is in the kennel.' I have in another place[1] opposed, and I hope with success, Dr. Johnson's very singular and erroneous notion as to Mr. Burke's pleasantry. Mr. Windham now said low to me, that he differed from our great friend in this observation; for that Mr. Burke was often very happy in his merriment. It would not have been right for either of us to have contradicted Johnson at this time, in a Society all of whom did not know and value Mr. Burke as much as we did. It might have occasioned something more rough, and at any rate would probably have checked the flow of Johnson's good-humour. He called to us with a sudden air of exultation, as the thought started into his mind, 'O! Gentlemen, I must tell you a very great thing. The Empress of Russia has ordered the "Rambler" to be translated into the Russian language;[2] so I shall be read on the banks of the Wolga. Horace boasts that his fame would extend as far as the banks of the Rhone; now the Wolga is farther from me than the Rhone was from Horace.' BOSWELL. 'You must certainly be pleased with this, Sir.'

[1] 'Journal of a Tour to the Hebrides,' third edition, p. 20.

[2] I have since heard that the report was not well founded; but the elation discovered by Johnson in the belief that it was true, shewed a noble ardour for literary fame.

JOHNSON. 'I am pleased, Sir, to be sure.[a] A man is pleased to find he has succeeded in that which he has endeavoured to do.'

One of the company mentioned his having seen a noble person driving in his carriage, and looking exceedingly well, notwithstanding his great age. JOHNSON. 'Ah, Sir; that is nothing. Bacon observes, that a stout healthy old man is like a tower undermined.'

On Sunday, May 16, I found him alone; he talked of Mrs. Thrale with much concern, saying, 'Sir, she has done every thing wrong, since Thrale's bridle was off her neck;' and was proceeding to mention some circumstances which have since been the subject of public discussion, when he was interrupted by the arrival of Dr. Douglas, now Bishop of Salisbury.

Dr. Douglas, upon this occasion, refuted a mistaken notion which is very common in Scotland, that the ecclesiastical discipline of the Church of England, though duly enforced, is insufficient to preserve the morals of the clergy, inasmuch as all delinquents may be screened by appealing to the Convocation, which being never authorized by the King to sit for the dispatch of business, the appeal never can be heard. Dr. Douglas observed, that this was founded upon ignorance; for that the Bishops have sufficient power to maintain discipline, and that the sitting of the Convocation was wholly immaterial in this respect, it being not a Court of judicature, but like a parliament, to make canons and regulations as times may require.

Johnson, talking of the fear of death, said, 'Some people are not afraid, because they look upon salvation as the effect of an absolute decree, and think they feel in themselves the marks of sanctification. Others, and those the most rational in my opinion, look upon salvation as conditional; and as they never can be sure that they have complied with the conditions, they are afraid.'[b]

In one of his little manuscript diaries, about this time, I find a short notice, which marks his amiable disposition more certainly than a thousand studied declarations.— 'Afternoon spent cheerfully and elegantly, I hope without offence to GOD or man; though in no holy duty, yet in the general exercise and cultivation of benevolence.'

[a] *Had he not the Turtle & Champagne of Human Life? Oh!* that he had *Yet pined for the Tea & Bread & Bread & Butter of it.* [H & I; I version; H omits the second '& Bread']

[b] *St. Paul himself was (in this Sense) afraid, & Paschal died in Terror if he did not die of Terror.* [H]

'On Monday, May 17, I dined with him at Mr. Dilly's, where were Colonel Vallancy, the Reverend Dr. Gibbons, and Mr. Capel Lofft, who, though a most zealous Whig, has a mind so full of learning and knowledge, and so much exercised in various departments, and withal so much liberality, that the stupendous powers of the literary Goliath, though they did not frighten this little David of popular spirit, could not but excite his admiration. There was also Mr. Braithwaite of the Post-office, that amiable and friendly man, who, with modest and unassuming manners, has associated with many of the wits of the age. Johnson was very quiescent to-day. Perhaps too I was indolent. I find nothing more of him in my notes, but that when I mentioned that I had seen in the King's library sixty-three editions of my favourite Thomas à Kempis, — amongst which it was in eight languages, Latin, German, French, Italian, Spanish, English, Arabick, and Armenian, —he said, he thought it unnecessary to collect many editions of a book, which were all the same, except as to the paper and print; he would have the original, and all the translations, and all the editions which had any variations in the text. He approved of the famous collection of editions of Horace by Douglas, mentioned by Pope, who is said to have had a closet filled with them; and he added, 'every man should try to collect one book in that manner, and present it to a publick library.'

On Tuesday, May 18, I saw him for a short time in the morning. I told him that the mob had called out, as the King passed, 'No Fox—No Fox,' which I did not like. He said, 'They were right, Sir.' I said, I thought not; for it seemed to be making Mr. Fox the King's competitor. There being no audience, so that there could be no triumph in a victory, he fairly agreed with me. I said it might do very well, if explained thus: 'Let us have no Fox;' understanding it as a prayer to his Majesty not to appoint that gentleman minister.

On Wednesday, May 19, I sat a part of the evening with him, by ourselves. I observed, that the death of our friends might be a consolation against the fear of our own dissolution, because we might have more friends in the other world than in this. He perhaps felt this as a reflection

marginal line:
being no . . . said it [H]

upon his apprehension as to death; and said, with heat, 'How can a man know *where* his departed friends are,[a] or whether they will be his friends in the other world. How many friendships have you known formed upon principles of virtue? Most friendships are formed by caprice or by chance, mere confederacies in vice or leagues in folly.'[b]

We talked of our worthy friend Mr. Langton. He said, 'I know not who will go to Heaven if Langton does not. Sir, I could almost say, *Sit anima mea cum Langtono.*' I mentioned a very eminent friend as a virtuous man. JOHNSON. 'Yes, Sir; but ——— has not the evangelical virtue of Langton. ———, I am afraid, would not scruple to pick up a wench.'

He however charged Mr. Langton with what he thought want of judgement upon an interesting occasion. 'When I was ill, (said he) I desired he would tell me sincerely in what he thought my life was faulty. Sir, he brought me a sheet of paper, on which he had written down several texts of Scripture, recommending christian charity.[c] And when I questioned him what occasion I had given for such an animadversion, all that he could say amounted to this, — that I sometimes contradicted people in conversation. Now what harm does it do to any man to be contradicted?' BOSWELL. 'I suppose he meant the *manner* of doing it; roughly,—and harshly.' JOHNSON. 'And who is the worse for that?' BOSWELL. 'It hurts people of weaker nerves.' JOHNSON. 'I know no such weak-nerved people.' Mr. Burke, to whom I related this conference, said, 'It is well, if when a man comes to die, he has nothing heavier upon his conscience than having been a little rough in conversation.'

Johnson, at the time when the paper was presented to him, though at first pleased with the attention of his friend, whom he thanked in an earnest manner, soon exclaimed in a loud and angry tone, 'What is your drift, Sir?' Sir Joshua Reynolds pleasantly observed, that it was a scene for a comedy, to see a penitent get into a violent passion and belabour his confessor.[1]

---

[1] After all, I cannot but be of opinion, that as Mr. Langton was seriously requested by Dr. Johnson to mention what appeared to him erroneous in the character of his friend, he was bound as an honest man, to intimate what he really thought, which he certainly did in the most delicate manner; so that Johnson himself, when in a quiet frame of mind, was pleased with it.

[a] *Ay truly:* where *indeed?* [H]

[b] *oh wisely & truly said!* [H]

[c] *very Comical* [H]

I have preserved no more of his conversation at the times when I saw him during the rest of this month, till Sunday, the 30th of May, when I met him in the evening at Mr. Hoole's, where there was a large company both of ladies and gentlemen. Sir James Johnston happened to say that he paid no regard to the arguments of counsel at the bar of the House of Commons, because they were paid for speaking. JOHNSON. 'Nay, Sir, argument is argument. You cannot help paying regard to their arguments, if they are good. If it were testimony, you might disregard it, if you knew that it were purchased. There is a beautiful image in Bacon[1] upon this subject: testimony is like an arrow shot from a long bow; the force of it depends on the strength of the hand that draws it. Argument is like an arrow from a cross-bow, which has equal force though shot by a child.'

He had dined that day at Mr. Hoole's, and Miss Helen Maria Williams being expected in the evening, Mr. Hoole put into his hands her beautiful 'Ode on the Peace:'[2] Johnson read it over, and when this elegant and accomplished young lady[3] was presented to him, he took her by

marginal line: speaking. JOHNSON . . . Bacon upon [H]

The texts suggested are now before me, and I shall quote a few of them. 'Blessed are the meek, for they shall inherit the earth.' *Mat.* v. 5.—'I therefore, the prisoner of the LORD, beseech you, that ye walk worthy of the vocation wherewith ye are called, with all lowliness and meekness, with long-suffering, forbearing one another in love.' *Ephes.* v. 1, 2.—'And above all these things put on charity, which is the bond of perfectness.' *Col.* iii. 14. —'Charity suffereth long, and is kind: charity envieth not, charity vaunteth not itself, is not puffed up: doth not behave itself unseemly, is not easily provoked.' 1 *Cor.* xiii. 4, 5.

marginal line: Dr. Johnson's . . . with a [H]

[1] [Dr. Johnson's memory deceived him. The passage referred to is not Bacon's, but Boyle's: and may be found, with a slight variation, in Johnson's Dictionary, under the word—CROSSBOW.—So happily selected are the greater part of the examples in that incomparable work, that if the most striking passages found in it were collected by one of our modern book-makers, under the title of THE BEAUTIES OF JOHNSON'S DICTIONARY, they would form a very pleasing and popular volume. MALONE.]

[2] The Peace made by that very able statesman, the Earl of Shelburne, now Marquis of Lansdowne, which may fairly be considered as the foundation of all the prosperity of Great Britain since that time.

[3] In the first edition of my Work, the epithet *amiable* was given. I was sorry to be obliged to strike it out; but I could not in justice suffer it to remain, after this young lady had not only written in favour of the savage Anarchy with which France has been visited, but had (as I have been informed by good authority,) walked, without horrour, over the ground at the Thuilleries when it was strewed with the naked bodies of the faithful Swiss Guards, who

the hand in the most courteous manner, and repeated the
finest stanza of her poem; this was the most delicate and
pleasing compliment he could pay. Her respectable friend,
Dr. Kippis, from whom I had this anecdote, was standing
by, and was not a little gratified.

Miss Williams told me, that the only other time she was
fortunate enough to be in Dr. Johnson's company, he
asked her to sit down by him, which she did, and upon her
enquiring how he was, he answered, 'I am very ill indeed,
Madam. I am very ill even when you are near me; what
should I be were you at a distance?'

He had now a great desire to go to Oxford, as his first
jaunt after his illness; we talked of it for some days, and I
had promised to accompany him. He was impatient and
fretful to-night, because I did not at once agree to go with
him on Thursday. When I considered how ill he had been,
and what allowance should be made for the influence of
sickness upon his temper, I resolved to indulge him, though
with some inconvenience to myself, as I wished to attend
the musical meeting in honour of Handel, in Westminster-
Abbey, on the following Saturday.

In the midst of his own diseases and pains, he was ever
compassionate to the distresses of others, and actively
earnest in procuring them aid, as appears from a note to
Sir Joshua Reynolds, of June 1, in these words: 'I am
ashamed to ask for some relief for a poor man, to whom, I
hope, I have given what I can be expected to spare. The
man importunes me, and the blow goes round. I am going
to try another air on Thursday.'

On Thursday, June 3, the Oxford post-coach took us
up in the morning at Bolt-court. The other two passengers
were Mrs. Beresford and her daughter, two very agreeable
ladies from America; they were going to Worcestershire,
where they then resided. Frank had been sent by his master
the day before to take places for us; and I found from the
way-bill that Dr. Johnson had made our names be put
down. Mrs. Beresford, who had read it, whispered me, 'Is
this the great Dr. Johnson?' I told her it was; so she was

were barbarously massacred for having bravely defended, against a crew of
ruffians, the Monarch whom they had taken an oath to defend. From Dr.
Johnson she could now expect not endearment but repulsion.

then prepared to listen. As she soon happened to mention in a voice so low that Johnson did not hear it, that her husband had been a member of the American Congress, I cautioned her to beware of introducing that subject, as she must know how very violent Johnson was against the people of that country. He talked a great deal. But I am sorry I have preserved little of the conversation. Miss Beresford was so much charmed, that she said to me aside, 'How he does talk! Every sentence is an essay.' She amused herself in the coach with knotting; he would scarcely allow this species of employment any merit. 'Next to mere idleness (said he) I think knotting is to be reckoned in the scale of insignificance; though I once attempted to learn knotting. Dempster's sister (looking to me) endeavoured to teach me it; but I made no progress.'

I was surprised at his talking without reserve in the publick post-coach of the state of his affairs; 'I have (said he) about the world I think above a thousand pounds, which I intend shall afford Frank an annuity of seventy pounds a-year.' Indeed his openness with people at a first interview was remarkable. He said once to Mr. Langton, 'I think I am like Squire Richard in "The Journey to London," *I'm never strange in a strange place.*' He was truly *social.* He strongly censured what is much too common in England among persons of condition,—maintaining an absolute silence, when unknown to each other; as for instance when occasionally brought together in a room before the master or mistress of the house has appeared. 'Sir, that is being so uncivilized as not to understand the common rights of humanity.'

At the inn where we stopped he was exceedingly dissatisfied with some roast mutton which we had for dinner. The ladies, I saw, wondered to see the great philosopher, whose wisdom and wit they had been admiring all the way, get into ill-humour from such a cause. He scolded the waiter, saying, 'It is as bad as bad can be: it is ill-fed, ill-killed, ill-kept, and ill-drest.'

He bore the journey very well, and seemed to feel himself elevated as he approached Oxford, that magnificent and venerable seat of Learning, Orthodoxy, and Toryism. Frank came in the heavy coach, in readiness to attend him;

index sign:
It is etc. [H]

and we were received with the most polite hospitality at
the house of his old friend Dr. Adams, Master of Pembroke
College, who had given us a kind invitation. Before we
were set down, I communicated to Johnson, my having
engaged to return to London directly, for the reason I
have mentioned, but that I would hasten back to him
again. He was pleased that I had made this journey merely
to keep him company. He was easy and placid, with Dr.
Adams, Mrs. and Miss Adams, and Mrs. Kennicot, widow
of the learned Hebræan, who was here on a visit. He soon
dispatched the enquiries which were made about his illness
and recovery, by a short and distinct narrative; and then
assuming a gay air, repeated from Swift,

> 'Nor think on our approaching ills,
> And talk of spectacles and pills.'

Dr. Newton, the Bishop of Bristol, having been mentioned, Johnson, recollecting the manner in which he had
been censured by that Prelate,[1] thus retaliated:—'Tom
knew he should be dead before what he has said of me
would appear.[a] He durst not have printed it while he
was alive.' DR. ADAMS. 'I believe his "Dissertations on the
Prophecies" is his great work.' JOHNSON. 'Why, Sir, it is

[a] *comical enough! &
true I doubt not* [H]

[1] Dr. Newton, in his Account of his own Life, after animadverting upon
Mr. Gibbon's History, says, 'Dr. Johnson's "Lives of the Poets" afforded
more amusement; but candour was much hurt and offended at the male-
volence that predominates in every part. Some passages, it must be allowed,
are judicious and well written, but make not sufficient compensation for so
much spleen and ill-humour. Never was any biographer more sparing of his
praise, or more abundant in his censures. He seemingly delights more in
exposing blemishes, than in recommending beauties; slightly passes over
excellencies, enlarges upon imperfections, and not content with his own
severe reflections, revives old scandal, and produces large quotations from
the forgotten works of former criticks. His reputation was so high in the
republick of letters, that it wanted not to be raised upon the ruins of others.
But these Essays, instead of raising a higher idea than was before entertained of his understanding, have certainly given the world a worse opinion
of his temper.'—The Bishop was therefore the more surprized and concerned
for his townsman, for '*he respected him not only for his genius and learning, but
valued him much for the more amiable part of his character, his humanity and charity,
his morality and religion.*' The last sentence we may consider as the general and
permanent opinion of Bishop Newton; the remarks which precede it must
by all who have read Johnson's admirable work, be imputed to the disgust
and peevishness of old age.[b] I wish they had not appeared, and that Dr.
Johnson had not been provoked by them to express himself not in respectful
terms, of a Prelate, whose labours were certainly of considerable advantage
both to literature and religion.

underlined:
last [H]
underlined:
*disgust, peevishness of
old age* [H]
[b] *comical enough!* [H]

ᵃ very good—Bravo!
[H]

Tom's great work; but how far it is great, or how much of it is Tom's, are other questions.ᵃ I fancy a considerable part of it was borrowed.' DR. ADAMS. 'He was a very successful man.' JOHNSON. 'I don't think so, Sir.—He did not get very high. He was late in getting what he did get; and he did not get it by the best means. I believe he was a gross flatterer.'

I fulfilled my intention by going to London, and returned to Oxford on Wednesday the 9th of June, when I was happy to find myself again in the same agreeable circle at Pembroke College, with the comfortable prospect of making some stay. Johnson welcomed my return with more than ordinary glee.

He talked with great regard of the Honourable Archibald Campbell, whose character he had given at the Duke of Argyll's table, when we were at Inverary;[1] and at this time wrote out for me, in his own hand, a fuller account of that learned and venerable writer, which I have published in its proper place. Johnson made a remark this evening which struck me a good deal. 'I never (said he) knew a nonjuror who could reason.'[2] Surely he did not mean to deny that faculty to many of their writers; to Hickes, Brett, and other eminent divines of that persuasion; and did not recollect that the seven Bishops, so justly celebrated for their magnanimous resistance of arbitrary power, were yet Nonjurors to the new Government. The nonjuring clergy of Scotland, indeed, who, excepting a few, have lately, by a sudden stroke, cut off all ties of allegiance to the house of Stuart, and resolved to pray for our present lawful Sovereign by name, may be thought to have confirmed this remark; as it may be said, that the divine

---

[1] 'Journal of a Tour to the Hebrides,' third edit. p. 371.

[2] The Rev. Mr. Agutter has favoured me with a note of a dialogue between Mr. John Henderson and Dr. Johnson on this topick, as related by Mr. Henderson, and it is evidently so authentick that I shall here insert it:— HENDERSON. 'What do you think, Sir, of William Law?' JOHNSON. 'William Law, Sir, wrote the best piece of Parenetick Divinity; but William Law was no reasoner.' HENDERSON. 'Jeremy Collier, Sir?' JOHNSON. 'Jeremy Collier fought without a rival, and therefore could not claim the victory.' Mr. Henderson mentioned Kenn and Kettlewell; but some objections were made; at last he said, 'But, Sir, what do you think of Lesley?' JOHNSON. 'Charles Lesley I had forgotten. Lesley *was* a reasoner, and *a reasoner who was not to be reasoned against.*'

indefeasible hereditary right which they professed to believe, if ever true, must be equally true still. Many of my readers will be surprized when I mention, that Johnson assured me he had never in his life been in a nonjuring meeting-house.

Next morning at breakfast, he pointed out a passage in Savage's 'Wanderer,' saying 'These are fine verses.'— 'If (said he)I had written with hostility of Warburton in my Shakspeare, I should have quoted this couplet:

> "Here Learning, blinded first, and then beguil'd,
> Looks dark as Ignorance, as Frenzy wild."

You see they'd have fitted him to a *T*,' (smiling.) DR. ADAMS. 'But you did not write against Warburton.' JOHNSON. 'No, Sir, I treated him with great respect both in my Preface and in my Notes.'

Mrs. Kennicot spoke of her brother, the Reverend Mr. Chamberlayne, who had given up great prospects in the Church of England on his conversion to the Roman Catholick faith. Johnson, who warmly admired every man who acted from a conscientious regard to principle, erroneous or not, exclaimed fervently, 'GOD bless him.'

Mrs. Kennicot, in confirmation of Dr. Johnson's opinion, that the present was not worse than former ages, mentioned that her brother assured her, there was now less infidelity on the Continent than there had been; Voltaire and Rousseau were less read. I asserted, from good authority, that Hume's infidelity was certainly less read. JOHNSON. 'All infidel writers drop into oblivion, when personal connections and the floridness of novelty are gone; though now and then a foolish fellow, who thinks he can be witty upon them, may bring them again into notice. There will sometimes start up a College joker, who does not consider that what is a joke in a College will not do in the world. To such defenders of Religion I would apply a stanza of a poem which I remember to have seen in some old collection:

> "Henceforth be quiet and agree,
>   Each kiss his empty brother;
> Religion scorns a foe like thee,
>   But dreads a friend like t'other."

ᵃ *That may be true here but not in their own Country—not in Italy.* [H]

so strenuously will they insist on your renouncing your own Faith, that no Conformity will prevail on them to call You a Christian, or bury you like a Christian. This I know better than Dr. Johnson could. [I]

marginal line:
Heaven. I . . . prevents me [H]

The point is well, though the expression is not correct; *one*, and not *thee*, should be opposed to *t'other.*[1]

On the Roman Catholick religion he said, 'If you join the Papists externally, they will not interrogate you strictly as to your belief in their tenets.ᵃ No reasoning Papist believes every article of their faith. There is one side on which a good man might be persuaded to embrace it. A good man of a timorous disposition, in great doubt of his acceptance with GOD, and pretty credulous, may be glad to be of a church where there are so many helps to get to Heaven. I would be a Papist if I could. I have fear enough; but an obstinate rationality prevents me. I shall never be a Papist, unless on the near approach of death, of which I have a very great terrour. I wonder that women are not all Papists.' BOSWELL. 'They are not more afraid of death than men are.' JOHNSON. 'Because they are less wicked.' DR. ADAMS. 'They are more pious.' JOHNSON. 'No, hang 'em, they are not more pious. A wicked fellow is the most pious when he takes to it. He'll beat you all at piety.'

He argued in defence of some of the peculiar tenets of the Church of Rome. As to the giving the bread only to the laity, he said, 'They may think, that in what is merely ritual, deviations from the primitive mode may be admitted on the ground of convenience; and I think they are

ᵇ *Oh certainly . . . besides when our Saviour said—Drink ye all of this—He might mean merely the 12 Apostles—who were all the People present* [H]

Certainly: he is quite right. [I]

marginal line:
Foundling Hospital . . . as follows [H]

as well warranted to make this alteration, as we are to substitutes prinkling in the room of the ancient baptism.'ᵇ As to the invocation of saints, he said, 'Though I do not think it authorised, it appears to me, that "the communion of saints" in the Creed means the communion with the saints in Heaven, as connected with "The holy catholick

[1] I have inserted the stanza as Johnson repeated it from memory; but I have since found the poem itself, in 'The Foundling Hospital for Wit,' printed at London, 1749. It is as follows:

'EPIGRAM, *occasioned by a religious dispute at Bath.*

'On Reason, Faith, and Mystery high,
     Two wits harangue the table;
B ————————y believes he knows not why,
     N ——— swears 'tis all a fable.

Peace, coxcombs, peace, and both agree,
     N————————, kiss thy empty brother;
Religion laughs at foes like thee,
     And dreads a friend like t'other.'

church." [1] He admitted the influence of evil spirits upon
our minds, and said, 'Nobody who believes the New
Testament can deny it.'[a]

I brought a volume of Dr. Hurd, the Bishop of Worcester's Sermons, and read to the company some passages
from one of them, upon this text, '*Resist the Devil*,[b] *and he
will fly from you*.' James iv. 7. I was happy to produce so
judicious and elegant a supporter[2] of a doctrine, which, I
know not why, should, in this world of imperfect knowledge, and, therefore, of wonder and mystery in a thousand

[a] *The Pater Noster
prays against it ex-
presly.* [I]

[b] *The* evil one. [I]

---

[1] Waller, in his 'Divine Poesie,' Canto first, has the same thought finely
expressed:

> 'The Church triumphant, and the Church below,
> In songs of praise their present union show;
> Their joys are full; our expectation long,
> In life we differ, but we join in song;
> Angels and we assisted by this art,
> May sing together, though we dwell apart.'

[2] The Sermon thus opens:—'That there are angels and spirits good and
bad; that at the head of these last there is ONE more considerable and
malignant than the rest, who, in the form, or under the name of a *serpent*,
was deeply concerned in the fall of man, and whose *head*, as the prophetick
language is, the son of man was one day to *bruise;* that this evil spirit, though
that prophecy be in part completed, has not yet received his death's wound,
but is still permitted, for ends unsearchable to us, and in ways which we
cannot particularly explain, to have a certain degree of power in this world
hostile to its virtue and happiness, and sometimes exerted with too much
success; all this is so clear from Scripture, that no believer, unless he be first
of all *spoiled by philosophy and vain deceit*, can possibly entertain a doubt of it.'

Having treated of *possessions*, his Lordship says, 'As I have no authority
to affirm that there *are* now any such, so neither may I presume to say with
confidence, that there are *not* any.'

'But then with regard to the influence of evil spirits at this day upon the
SOULS of men, I shall take leave to be a great deal more peremptory.—
[Then, having stated the various proofs, he adds,] All this, I say, is so
manifest to every one who reads the Scriptures, that, if we respect their
authority, the question concerning the reality of the demoniack influence
upon the minds of men is clearly determined.'

Let it be remembered, that these are not the words of an antiquated or
obscure enthusiast, but of a learned and polite Prelate now alive; and were
spoken, not to a vulgar congregation, but to the Honourable Society of
Lincoln's Inn. His Lordship in this Sermon explains the words, 'deliver us
from evil,' in the Lord's Prayer, as signifying a request to be protected from
'the evil one,' that is, the Devil.[c] This is well illustrated in a short but
excellent Commentary by my late worthy friend, the Reverend Dr. Lort,
of whom it may truly be said, *Multis ille bonis flebilis occidit*. It is remarkable
that Waller in his 'Reflections on the several Petitions,' in that sacred form
of devotion, has understood this in the same sense:

'Guard us from all temptations of the FOE.'[d]

[c] *la Malin in every
French Pater Noster* [H]

*oh very true; here is
the Observation* [I]

[d] *He knew that the
Word Satan means Ad-
versary. Otway knew it
—he says
To meet the Foe of
Mankind in his
Walk.* [H]

instances, be contested by some with an unthinking assurance and flippancy.

After dinner, when one of us talked of there being a great enmity between Whig and Tory:—JOHNSON. 'Why, not so much, I think, unless when they come into competition with each other. There is none when they are only common acquaintance, none when they are of different sexes. A Tory will marry into a Whig family, and a Whig into a Tory family, without any reluctance. But, indeed, in a matter of much more concern than political tenets, and that is religion, men and women do not concern themselves much about difference of opinion; and ladies set no value on the moral character of men who pay their addresses to them; the greatest profligate will be as well received as the man of the greatest virtue, and this by a very good woman, by a woman who says her prayers three times a day.' Our ladies endeavoured to defend their sex from this charge; but he roared them down! 'No, no, a lady will take Jonathan Wild as readily as St. Austin, if he has threepence more; and, what is worse, her parents will give her to him. Women have a perpetual envy of our vices; they are less vicious than we, not from choice, but because we restrict them; they are the slaves of order and fashion; their virtue is of more consequence to us than our own, so far as concerns this world.'

Miss Adams mentioned a gentleman of licentious character, and said, 'Suppose I had a mind to marry that gentleman, would my parents consent?' JOHNSON. 'Yes, they'd consent, and you'd go. You'd go, though they did not consent.' MISS ADAMS. 'Perhaps their opposing might make me go.' JOHNSON. 'O, very well; you'd take one whom you think a bad man, to have the pleasure of vexing your parents. You put me in mind of Dr. Barrowby, the physician, who was very fond of swine's flesh. One day, when he was eating it, he said, "I wish I was a Jew."— "Why so? (said somebody,) the Jews are not allowed to eat your favourite meat."—"Because (said he,) I should then have the gust of eating it, with the pleasure of sinning."'— Johnson then proceeded in his declamation.

Miss Adams soon afterwards made an observation that I do not recollect, which pleased him much; he said with

marginal line:
themselves much . . . *of*
men [H]

marginal line:
go.' JOHNSON . . .
of Dr. [H]

exclamation point
and marginal line:
Because (said he etc.
[H]

a good-humoured smile, 'That there should be so much excellence united with so much *depravity*, is strange.'

Indeed, this lady's good qualities, merit, and accomplishments, and her constant attention to Dr. Johnson, were not lost upon him. She happened to tell him that a little coffee-pot, in which she had made him coffee, was the only thing she could call her own. He turned to her with a complacent gallantry, 'Don't say so, my dear; I hope you don't reckon my heart as nothing.'

marginal line:
made him . . . you don't
[H]

I asked him if it was true as reported, that he had said lately, 'I am for the King against Fox; but I am for Fox against Pitt.' JOHNSON. 'Yes, Sir; the King is my master; but I do not know Pitt; and Fox is my friend.'

'Fox, (added he,) is a most extraordinary man: here is a man (describing him in strong terms of objection in some respects according as he apprehended, but which exalted his abilities the more) who has divided the kingdom with Cæsar: so that it was a doubt whether the nation should be ruled by the sceptre of George the Third, or the tongue of Fox.'

Dr. Wall, physician at Oxford, drank tea with us. Johnson had in general a peculiar pleasure in the company of physicians, which was certainly not abated by the conversation of this learned, ingenious, and pleasing gentleman. Johnson said, 'It is wonderful how little good Radcliffe's travelling fellowships have done. I know nothing that has been imported by them; yet many additions to our medical knowledge might be got in foreign countries. Inoculation, for instance, has saved more lives than war destroys; and the cures performed by the Peruvian-bark are innumerable. But it is in vain to send our travelling physicians to France, and Italy, and Germany, for all that is known there is known here; I'd send them out of Christendom; I'd send them among barbarous nations.'

On Friday, June 11, we talked at breakfast, of forms of prayer. JOHNSON. 'I know of no good prayers but those in the "Book of Common Prayer."' DR. ADAMS, (in a very earnest manner): 'I wish, Sir, you would compose some family prayers.' JOHNSON. 'I will not compose prayers for you, Sir, because you can do it for yourself.

But I have thought of getting together all the books of prayers which I could, selecting those which should appear to me the best, putting out some, inserting others, adding some prayers of my own, and prefixing a discourse on prayer. We all now gathered about him, and two or three of us at a time joined in pressing him to execute this plan. He seemed to be a little displeased at the manner of our importunity, and in great agitation called out, 'Do not talk thus of what is so awful. I know not what time GOD will allow me in this world. There are many things which I wish to do.' Some of us persisted, and Dr. Adams said, 'I never was more serious about any thing in my life.' JOHNSON. 'Let me alone, let me alone; I am overpowered.' And then he put his hands before his face, and reclined for some time upon the table.

I mentioned Jeremy Taylor's using, in his forms of prayer, 'I am the chief of sinners,' and other such self-condemning expressions. 'Now, (said I) this cannot be said with truth by every man, and therefore is improper for a general printed form. I myself cannot say that I am the worst of men: I *will* not say so.' JOHNSON. 'A man may know, that physically, that is, in the real state of things, he is not the worst man; but that morally he may be so. Law observes, "that every man knows something worse of himself, than he is sure of in others."[a] You may not have committed such crimes as some men have done; but you do not know against what degree of light they have sinned. Besides, Sir, "the chief of sinners" is a mode of expression for "I am a great sinner." So St. Paul, speaking of our SAVIOUR's having died to save sinners, says, "of whom I am the chief:" yet he certainly did not think himself so bad as Judas Iscariot.'[b] BOSWELL. 'But, Sir, Taylor means it literally, for he founds a conceit upon it. When praying for the conversion of sinners, and of himself in particular, he says, "LORD, thou wilt not leave thy *chief* work undone." ' JOHNSON. 'I do not approve of figurative expressions in addressing the Supreme Being; and I never use them. Taylor gives a very good advice: "Never lie in your prayers; never confess more than you really believe; never promise more than you mean to perform." '

[a] *O Dear! no sure.* [I]

underlined:
Judas Iscariot [H]

[b] *Judas Iscariot was dead & gone.* [H]

I recollected this precept in his 'Golden Grove;' but his *example* for prayer contradicts his *precept.*[a]

index sign:
Golden Grove [H]

[a] *so it does.* [H]

Dr. Johnson and I went in Dr. Adams's coach to dine with Mr. Nowell, Principal of St. Mary Hall, at his beautiful villa at Iffley, on the banks of the Isis, about two miles from Oxford. While we were upon the road, I had the resolution to ask Johnson whether he thought that the roughness of his manner had been an advantage or not, and if he would not have done more good if he had been more gentle. I proceeded to answer myself thus: 'Perhaps it has been of advantage, as it has given weight to what you said; you could not, perhaps, have talked with such authority without it.' JOHNSON. 'No, Sir; I have done more good as I am. Obscenity and Impiety have always been repressed in my company.' BOSWELL. 'True, Sir; and that is more than can be said of every Bishop. Greater liberties have been taken in the presence of a Bishop, though a very good man, from his being milder, and therefore not commanding such awe. Yet, Sir; many people who might have been benefited by your conversation, have been frightened away. A worthy friend of ours has told me, that he has often been afraid to talk to you.' JOHNSON. 'Sir, he need not have been afraid, if he had any thing rational to say.[1] If he had not, it was better he did not talk.'

two marginal lines:
have been . . . not talk
[H]

Dr. Nowell is celebrated for having preached a sermon before the House of Commons, on the 30th of January, 1772, full of high Tory sentiments, for which he was thanked as usual, and printed it at their request; but, in the midst of that turbulence and faction which disgraced a part of the present reign, the thanks were afterwards ordered to be expunged. This strange conduct sufficiently exposes itself; and Dr. Nowell will ever have the honour which is due to a lofty friend of our monarchical constitution. Dr. Johnson said to me, 'Sir, the Court will be very much to blame, if he is not promoted.' I told this to Dr. Nowell; and asserting my humbler, though not less zealous

---

[1] [The words of Erasmus (as my learned friend Archdeacon Kearney observes to me,) may be applied to Johnson: 'Qui ingenium, sensum, dictionem hominis noverant, multis non offenduntur, quibus graviter erant offendendi, qui hæc ignorarunt.' MALONE.]

exertions in the same cause, I suggested, that whatever
return we might receive, we should still have the consolation of being like Butler's steady and generous Royalist,

> 'True as the dial to the sun,
> Although it be not shone upon.'

We were well entertained and very happy at Dr.
Nowell's, where was a very agreeable company; and we
drank 'Church and King' after dinner, with true Tory
cordiality.

We talked of a certain clergyman of extraordinary
character, who, by exerting his talents in writing on temporary topicks, and displaying uncommon intrepidity, had
raised himself to affluence.[a] I maintained that we ought
not to be indignant at his success; for merit of every sort
was entitled to reward. JOHNSON. 'Sir, I will not allow
this man to have merit. No, Sir; what he has is rather the
contrary; I will, indeed, allow him courage, and on this
account we so far give him credit. We have more respect
for a man who robs boldly on the highway, than for a
fellow who jumps out of a ditch, and knocks you down
behind your back. Courage is a quality so necessary for
maintaining virtue, that it is always respected, even when
it is associated with vice.'

I censured the coarse invectives which were become
fashionable in the House of Commons, and said, that if
members of parliament must attack each other personally
in the heat of debate, it should be done more genteelly.
JOHNSON. 'No, Sir; that would be much worse. Abuse
is not so dangerous when there is no vehicle of wit or
delicacy, no subtle conveyance. The difference between
coarse and refined abuse is as the difference between being
bruised by a club, and wounded by a poisoned arrow.' —
I have since observed his position elegantly expressed by
Dr. Young:

> 'As the soft plume gives swiftness to the dart,
> Good breeding sends the satire to the heart.'

On Saturday, June 12, there drank tea with us at Dr.
Adams's, Mr. John Henderson, student of Pembroke-
College, celebrated for his wonderful acquirements in

[a] *I guess not who this was.* [H]
*Who could this be?
I have not a Guess.* [I]

Alchymy, Judicial Astrology, and other abstruse and curious learning;[1] and the Reverend Herbert Croft, who, I am afraid, was somewhat mortified by Dr. Johnson's not being highly pleased with some 'Family Discourses,' which he had printed; they were in too familiar a style to be approved of by so manly a mind. I have no note of this evening's conversation, except a single fragment. When I mentioned Thomas Lord Lyttleton's vision, the prediction of the time of his death, and its exact fulfilment;— JOHNSON. 'It is the most extraordinary thing that has happened in my day. I heard it with my own ears, from his uncle, Lord Westcote.[2][a] I am so glad to have every evidence of the spiritual world, that I am willing to believe it.' DR. ADAMS. 'You have evidence enough; good evidence, which needs not such support.' JOHNSON. 'I like to have more.'

Mr. Henderson, with whom I had sauntered in the venerable walks of Merton-College, and found him a very learned and pious man, supped with us. Dr. Johnson surprised him not a little, by acknowledging with a look of horrour, that he was much oppressed by the fear of death. The amiable Dr. Adams suggested that G O D was infinitely good. JOHNSON. 'That he is infinitely good, as far as the perfection of his nature will allow, I certainly believe; but it is necessary for good upon the whole, that individuals should be punished. As to an *individual*, therefore, he is not infinitely good; and as I cannot be *sure* that I have fulfilled the conditions on which salvation is granted, I am afraid I may be one of those who shall be damned.' (looking dismally.) DR. ADAMS. 'What do you mean by damned?' JOHNSON. (passionately and loudly) 'Sent to Hell, Sir, and punished everlastingly.' DR. ADAMS. 'I don't believe that doctrine.' JOHNSON. 'Hold, Sir, do you believe that some will be punished at all?' DR. ADAMS. 'Being excluded from Heaven will be a punishment; yet there may be no great positive suffering.' JOHNSON. 'Well, Sir; but, if you admit any degree of punishment, there is an end of

[a] *So he did at Mr. Thrale's house Streatham Park.* [H]

[b] *I should like to read that because I Think I know most of the Story —I heard of the Fact from Ld Westcote & Lord Sandys.* [I]

---

[1] See an account of him, in a sermon by the Reverend Mr. Agutter.

[2] [A correct account of Lord Lyttleton's supposed Vision may be found in Nashe's 'History of Worcestershire;'—ADDITIONS AND CORRECTIONS, p. 36.[b] MALONE.]

your argument for infinite goodness simply considered; for, infinite goodness would inflict no punishment whatever. There is not infinite goodness physically considered; morally there is.' BOSWELL. 'But may not a man attain to such a degree of hope as not to be uneasy from the fear of death?' JOHNSON. 'A man may have such a degree of hope as to keep him quiet. You see I am not quiet, from the vehemence with which I talk; but I do not despair.' MRS. ADAMS. 'You seem, Sir, to forget the merits of our Redeemer.' JOHNSON. 'Madam, I do not forget the merits of my Redeemer; but my Redeemer has said that he will set some on his right hand and some on his left.'—He was in gloomy agitation, and said, 'I'll have no more on't.'— If what has now been stated should be urged by the enemies of Christianity, as if its influence on the mind were not benignant, let it be remembered, that Johnson's temperament was melancholy, of which such direful apprehensions of futurity are often a common effect. We shall presently see, that when he approached nearer to his awful change, his mind became tranquil, and he exhibited as much fortitude as becomes a thinking man in that situation.

From the subject of death we passed to discourse of life, whether it was upon the whole more happy or miserable. Johnson was decidedly for the balance of misery:[1] in

---

[1] The Reverend Mr. Ralph Churton, Fellow of Brazen-Nose College, Oxford, has favoured me with the following remarks on my Work, which he is pleased to say, 'I have hitherto extolled, and cordially approve.'

'The chief part of what I have to observe is contained in the following transcript from a letter to a friend, which, with his concurrence, I copied for this purpose; and, whatever may be the merit or justness of the remarks, you may be sure that being written to a most intimate friend, without any intention that they ever should go further, they are the genuine and undisguised sentiments of the writer:

'Jan. 6, 1792

'LAST week, I was reading the second volume of Boswell's Johnson, with increasing esteem for the worthy authour, and increasing veneration of the wonderful and excellent man who is the subject of it. The writer throws in, now and then, very properly, some serious religious reflections; but there is one remark, in my mind an obvious and just one, which I think he has not made, that Johnson's "morbid melancholy," and constitutional infirmities, were intended by Providence, like St. Paul's thorn in the flesh, to check intellectual conceit and arrogance; which the consciousness of his extraordinary talents, awake as he was to the voice of praise, might otherwise have generated in a very culpable degree. Another observation strikes me, that in consequence of the same natural indisposition, and habitual sickliness, (for he says he scarcely passed one day without pain after his twentieth year,) he

confirmation of which I maintained, that no man would choose to lead over again the life which he had experienced. Johnson acceded to that opinion in the strongest terms. This is an enquiry often made; and its being a subject of disquisition is a proof that much misery presses upon human feelings; for those who are conscious of a felicity

considered and represented human life, as a scene of much greater misery than is generally experienced. There may be persons bowed down with affliction all their days; and there are those, no doubt, whose iniquities rob them of rest; but neither calamities nor crimes, I hope and believe, do so much and so generally abound, as to justify the dark picture of life which Johnson's imagination designed, and his strong pencil delineated. This I am sure, the colouring is far too gloomy for what I have experienced, though as far as I can remember, I have had more sickness, (I do not say more severe, but only more in quantity,) than falls to the lot of most people. But then daily debility and occasional sickness were far overbalanced by intervenient days, and, perhaps, weeks void of pain, and overflowing with comfort. So that in short, to return to the subject, human life, as far as I can perceive from experience or observation, is not that state of constant wretchedness which Johnson always insisted it was: which misrepresentation, (for such it surely is,) his Biographer has not corrected, I suppose, because, unhappily, he has himself a large portion of melancholy in his constitution, and fancied the portrait a faithful copy of life.'

The learned writer then proceeds thus in his letter to me:

'I have conversed with some sensible men on this subject, who all seem to entertain the same sentiments respecting life with those which are expressed or implied in the foregoing paragraph. It might be added, that as the representation here spoken of, appears not consistent with fact and experience, so neither does it seem to be countenanced by Scripture There is, perhaps, no part of the sacred volume which at first sight promises so much to lend its sanction to these dark and desponding notions as the book of Ecclesiastes, which so often, and so emphatically, proclaims the vanity of things sublunary. But "the design of this whole book, (as it has been justly observed,) is not to put us out of conceit with life, but to cure our vain expectations of a compleat and perfect happiness in this world; to convince us, that there is no such thing to be found in mere external enjoyments;—and to teach us to seek for happiness in the practice of virtue, in the knowledge and love of GOD, and in the hopes of a better life." For this is the application of all: *Let us hear*, &c. xii. 13. Not only his duty, but his happiness too: *For* GOD, &c. v. 14.— See "Sherlock on Providence," p. 299.

'The New Testament tells us, indeed, and most truly, that "sufficient unto the day is the evil thereof:"[a] and, therefore, wisely forbids us to increase our burden by forebodings of sorrows; but I think it no where says, that even our ordinary afflictions are not consistent with a very considerable degree of positive comfort and satisfaction. And, accordingly, one whose sufferings as well as merits were conspicuous, assures us, that in proportion "as the sufferings of Christ abounded in them, so their consolation also abounded by Christ." 2 Cor. i. 5. It is needless to cite, as indeed it would be endless even to refer to, the multitude of passages in both Testaments holding out, in the strongest language, promises of blessings, even in this world, to the faithful servants of GOD. I will only refer to St. Luke, xviii. 29, 30, and 1 Tim. iv. 8.

underlined:
unto the . . . evil thereof
[1]

[a] *meaning of Care for this World.* [1]

of existence, would never hesitate to accept of a repetition of it. I have met with very few who would. I have heard Mr. Burke make use of a very ingenious and plausible argument on this subject; 'Every man (said he), would lead his life over again; for, every man is willing to go on and take an addition to his life, which, as he grows older,

'Upon the whole, setting aside instances of great and lasting bodily pain, of minds peculiarly oppressed by melancholy, and of severe temporal calamities, from which extraordinary cases we surely should not form our estimate of the general tenour and complexion of life; excluding these from the account, I am convinced that as well the gracious constitution of things which Providence has ordained, as the declarations of Scripture and the actual experience of individuals, authorize the sincere Christian to hope that his humble and constant endeavours to perform his duty, chequered as the best life is with many failings, will be crowned with a greater degree of present peace, serenity, and comfort, than he could reasonably permit himself to expect, if he measured his views and judged of life from the opinion of Dr. Johnson, often and energetically expressed in the Memoirs of him, without any animadversion or censure by his ingenious Biographer. If he himself, upon reviewing the subject, shall see the matter in this light, he will, in an octavo edition, which is eagerly expected, make such additional remarks or corrections as he shall judge fit; lest the impressions which these discouraging passages may leave on the reader's mind, should in any degree hinder what otherwise the whole spirit and energy of the work tends, and, I hope, successfully, to promote,—pure morality and true religion.'

Though I have, in some degree, obviated any reflections against my illustrious friend's dark views of life, when considering, in the course of this Work, his 'Rambler' and his 'Rasselas,' I am obliged to Mr. Churton for complying with my request of his permission to insert his Remarks, being conscious of the weight of what he judiciously suggests as to the melancholy in my own constitution. His more pleasing views of life, I hope, are just. *Valeant quantum valere possunt.*

Mr. Churton concludes his letter to me in these words: 'Once, and only once, I had the satisfaction of seeing your illustrious friend; and as I feel a particular regard for all whom he distinguished with his esteem and friend-ship, so I derive much pleasure from reflecting that I once beheld, though but transiently near our College-gate, one whose works will for ever delight and improve the world, who was a sincere and zealous son of the Church of England, an honour to his country, and an ornament to human nature.'

His letter was accompanied with a present from himself of his 'Sermons at the Bampton Lecture,' and from his friend, Dr. Townson, the venerable Rector of Malpas, in Cheshire, of his 'Discourses on the Gospels,' together with the following extract of a letter from that excellent person, who is now gone to receive the reward of his labours: 'Mr. Boswell is not only very entertaining in his works, but they are so replete with moral and religious sentiments, without an instance, as far as I know, of a contrary tendency, that I cannot help having a great esteem for him; and if you think such a trifle as a copy of the Discourses, *ex dono authoris,* would be acceptable to him, I should be happy to give him this small testimony of my regard.'

Such spontaneous testimonies of approbation from such men, without any personal acquaintance with me, are truly valuable and encouraging.

he has no reason to think will be better, or even so good as what has preceded.' I imagine, however, the truth is, that there is a deceitful hope that the next part of life will be free from the pains, and anxieties, and sorrows, which we have already felt. We are for wise purposes 'Condemn'd to Hope's delusive mine,' as Johnson finely says; and I may also quote the celebrated lines of Dryden, equally philosophical and poetical:

> 'When I consider life, 'tis all a cheat,
> Yet, fool'd with hope, men favour the deceit;
> Trust on, and think to-morrow will repay;
> To-morrow's falser than the former day;
> Lies worse; and while it says we shall be blest
> With some new joys, cuts off what we possest.
> Strange cozenage! none would live past years again;
> Yet all hope pleasure in what yet remain;
> And from the dregs of life think to receive,
> What the first sprightly running could not give.'[1]

It was observed to Dr. Johnson, that it seemed strange that he, who has so often delighted his company by his lively and brilliant conversation, should say he was miserable. JOHNSON. 'Alas! it is all outside; I may be cracking my joke, and cursing the sun. *Sun, how I hate thy beams!*' I knew not well what to think of this declaration; whether to hold it as a genuine picture of his mind,[2] or as the effect of his persuading himself contrary to fact, that the position which he had assumed as to human unhappiness, was true. We may apply to him a sentence in Mr. Greville's 'Maxims, Characters, and Reflections;'[3] a book which is entitled to much more praise than it has received:[a] 'ARIS-   [a] *so it is.* [H]
TARCHUS is charming: how full of knowledge, of sense, of sentiment. You get him with difficulty to your supper; and after having delighted every body and himself for a few hours, he is obliged to return home;—he is finishing his treatise, to prove that unhappiness is the portion of man.'

[1] AURENGZEBE, Act iv. Sc. 1.

[2] Yet there is no doubt that a man may appear very gay in company, who is sad at heart. His merriment is like the sound of drums and trumpets in a battle, to drown the groans of the wounded and dying.

[3] Page 139.

On Sunday, June 13, our philosopher was calm at breakfast. There was something exceedingly pleasing in our leading a College life, without restraint, and with superiour elegance, in consequence of our living in the Master's House, and having the company of ladies. Mrs. Kennicot related, in his presence, a lively saying of Dr. Johnson to Miss Hannah More, who had expressed a wonder that the poet who had written 'Paradise Lost,' should write such poor Sonnets:—'Milton, Madam, was a genius that could cut a Colossus from a rock, but could not carve heads upon cherry-stones.'

We talked of the casuistical question, 'Whether it was allowable at any time to depart from *Truth?*' JOHNSON. 'The general rule is, that Truth should never be violated, because it is of the utmost importance to the comfort of life, that we should have a full security by mutual faith; and occasional inconveniences should be willingly suffered, that we may preserve it. There must, however, be some exceptions. If, for instance, a murderer should ask you which way a man is gone, you may tell him what is not true, because you are under a previous obligation not to betray a man to a murderer.' BOSWELL. 'Supposing the person who wrote *Junius* were asked whether he was the author, might he deny it?' JOHNSON. 'I don't know what to say to this. If you were *sure* that he wrote *Junius*, would you, if he denied it, think as well of him afterwards? Yet it may be urged, that what a man has no right to ask, you may refuse to communicate; and there is no other effectual mode of preserving a secret and an important secret, the discovery of which may be very hurtful to you, but a flat denial; for if you are silent, or hesitate, or evade, it will be held equivalent to a confession. But stay, Sir, here is another case. Supposing the authour had told me confidentially that he had written *Junius*, and I were asked if he had, I should hold myself at liberty to deny it, as being under a previous promise, express or implied, to conceal it. Now what I ought to do for the authour, may I not do for myself? But I deny the lawfulness of telling a lie to a sick man, for fear of alarming him. You have no business with consequences; you are to tell the truth. Besides, you are not sure, what effect your telling him that he is in danger may have. It may bring his distemper to a crisis, and that may cure him. Of all lying, I have the greatest abhorrence of this, because I believe it has been frequently practised on myself.'

I cannot help thinking that there is much weight in the opinion of those who have held, that Truth, as an eternal and immutable principle, ought, upon no account whatever, to be violated, from supposed previous or superiour obligations, of which every man being to judge for himself, there is great danger that we too often, from partial motives, persuade ourselves that they exist; and probably whatever extraordinary instances may sometimes occur, where some evil may be prevented by violating this noble principle, it would be found that human happiness would, upon the whole, be more perfect, were Truth universally preserved.

In the notes to the 'Dunciad,' we find the following verses, addressed to Pope:[1]

> 'While malice, Pope, denies thy page
>   Its own celestial fire;
> While criticks, and while bards in rage,
>   Admiring, won't admire:
>
> While wayward pens thy worth assail,
>   And envious tongues decry;
> These times, though many a friend bewail,
>   These times bewail not I.
>
> But when the world's loud praise is thine,
>   And spleen no more shall blame:
> When with thy Homer thou shalt shine
>   In one establish'd fame!
>
> When none shall rail, and every lay
>   Devote a wreath to thee;
> That day (for come it will) that day
>   Shall I lament to see.'

It is surely not a little remarkable, that they should appear without a name. Miss Seward, knowing Dr. Johnson's almost universal and minute literary information, signified

[1] The annotator calls them 'amiable verses.'

a desire that I should ask him who was the authour. He was prompt with his answer:—'Why, Sir, they were written by one Lewis, who was either under-master or an usher of Westminster-school, and published a Miscellany, in which "Grongar Hill" first came out.'[1] Johnson praised them highly, and repeated them with a noble animation. In the twelfth line, instead of 'one establish'd fame,' he repeated 'one unclouded flame,' which he thought was the reading in former editions: but I believe was a flash of his own genius. It is much more poetical than the other.

On Monday, June 14, and Tuesday, 15, Dr. Johnson and I dined, on one of them, I forget which, with Mr. Mickle,

[1] [Lewis's Verses addressed to Pope, (as Mr. Bindley suggests to me,) were first published in a collection of Pieces in verse and prose on occasion of 'the Dunciad,' 8vo. 1732. They are there called an Epigram.—'Grongar Hill,' the same gentleman observes, was first printed in Savage's Miscellanies, as an *Ode*, (it is singular that Johnson should not have recollected this,) and was *reprinted* in the same year, (1726,) in Lewis's Miscellany, in the form it now bears.

In that Miscellany, (as the Reverend Mr. Blakeway observes to me,) 'the beautiful poem, "Away, let nought to love displeasing," &c. (reprinted in Percy's RELIQUES, vol. i. b. iii. No. 14,) first appeared.' It is there said to be a translation from the ancient British.

Lewis was authour of 'Philip of Macedon,' a tragedy, published in 1727, and dedicated to Pope: and in 1730, he published a second volume of miscellaneous poems.

As Dr. Johnson settled in London not long after the Verses addressed to Pope first appeared, he probably then obtained some information concerning their authour, David Lewis, whom he has described as an Usher of Westminster-school: yet the Dean of Westminster, who has been pleased at my request to make some enquiry on this subject, has not found any vestige of his having ever been employed in this situation. A late writer ('Environs of London,' iv. 171,) supposed that the following inscription in the church-yard of the church of Low Leyton in Essex, was intended to commemorate this poet:

'Sacred to the memory of David Lewis, Esq. who died the 8th day of April, 1760, aged 77 years; a great favourite of the Muses, as his many excellent pieces in poetry sufficiently testify.

'Inspired verse may on this marble live,
But can no honour to thy ashes give.'

'. . . Also Mary, the wife of the above-named David Lewis, fourth daughter of Newdigate Owsley, Esq. who departed this life the 10th of October, 1774, aged 90 years.'

But it appears to me improbable that this monument was erected for the authour of the Verses to Pope, and of the Tragedy already mentioned: the language both of the dedication prefixed to that piece, and of the dedication addressed to the Earl of Shaftesbury, and prefixed to the Miscellanies, 1730, denoting a person who moved in a lower sphere than this Essex 'Squire seems to have done. MALONE.]

translator of the 'Lusiad,' at Wheatley, a very pretty country place a few miles from Oxford; and on the other with Dr. Wetherell, Master of University College. From Dr. Wetherell's he went to visit Mr. Sackville Parker, the bookseller; and when he returned to us, gave the following account of his visit, saying, 'I have been to see my old friend, Sack. Parker; I find he has married his maid; he has done right. She had lived with him many years in great confidence, and they had mingled minds; I do not think he could have found any wife that would have made him so happy. The woman was very attentive and civil to me; she pressed me to fix a day for dining with them, and to say what I liked, and she would be sure to get it for me. Poor Sack! He is very ill, indeed.[1] We parted as never to meet again. It has quite broke me down.' This pathetick narrative was strangely diversified with the grave and earnest defence of a man's having married his maid. I could not but feel it as in some degree ludicrous.

In the morning of Tuesday, June 15, while we sat at Dr. Adams's, we talked of a printed letter from the reverend Herbert Croft, to a young gentleman who had been his pupil, in which he advised him to read to the end of whatever books he should begin to read. JOHNSON. 'This is surely a strange advice; you may as well resolve that whatever men you happen to get acquainted with, you are to keep to them for life. A book may be good for nothing; or there may be only one thing in it worth knowing; are we to read it all through? These Voyages, (pointing to the three large volumes of "Voyages to the South Sea," which were just come out) *who* will read them through? A man had better work his way before the mast, than read them through; they will be eaten by rats and mice, before they are read through. There can be little entertainment in such books; one set of Savages is like another.' BOSWELL. 'I do not think the people of Otaheité can be reckoned Savages.' JOHNSON. 'Don't cant in defence of Savages.' BOSWELL. 'They have the art of navigation.'—JOHNSON. 'A dog or cat can swim.' BOSWELL. 'They carve very ingeniously.' JOHNSON. 'A cat can scratch, and a child

[1] [He died at Oxford in his 89th year, Dec. 10, 1796. MALONE.]

with a nail can scratch.' I perceived this was none of the *mollia tempora fandi;* so desisted.

Upon his mentioning that when he came to College he wrote his first exercise twice over, but never did so afterwards; MISS ADAMS. 'I suppose, Sir, you could not make them better?' JOHNSON. 'Yes, Madam, to be sure, I could make them better. Thought is better than no thought.' MISS ADAMS. 'Do you think, Sir, you could make your Ramblers better?' JOHNSON. 'Certainly I could.' BOSWELL. 'I'll lay a bet, Sir, you cannot.' JOHNSON. 'But I will, Sir, if I choose. I shall make the best of them you shall pick out, better.'—BOSWELL. 'But you may add to them. I will not allow of that.' JOHNSON. 'Nay, Sir, there are three ways of making them better;—putting out,—adding,—or correcting.'

During our visit at Oxford, the following conversation passed between him and me on the subject of my trying my fortune at the English bar. Having asked, whether a very extensive acquaintance in London, which was very valuable, and of great advantage to a man at large, might not be prejudicial to a lawyer, by preventing him from giving sufficient attention to his business?—JOHNSON. 'Sir, you will attend to business, as business lays hold of you. When not actually employed, you may see your friends as much as you do now. You may dine at a Club every day, and sup with one of the members every night; and you may be as much at publick places as one who has seen them all would wish to be. But you must take care to attend constantly in Westminster Hall; both to mind your business, as it is almost all learnt there, (for nobody reads now,) and to shew that you want to have business. And you must not be too often seen at publick places, that competitors may not have it to say, "He is always at the Playhouse or at Ranelagh, and never to be found at his chambers." And, Sir, there must be a kind of solemnity in the manner of a professional man. I have nothing particular to say to you on the subject. All this I should say to any one; I should have said it to Lord Thurlow twenty years ago.'

THE PROFESSION may probably think this representation of what is required in a Barrister who would hope for success, to be much too indulgent; but certain it is, that as

'The wits of Charles found easier ways to fame,'

some of the lawyers of this age who have risen high, have by no means thought it absolutely necessary to submit to that long and painful course of study which a Plowden, a Coke, and a Hale, considered as requisite. My respected friend, Mr. Langton, has shewn me in the hand-writing of his grandfather, a curious account of a conversation which he had with Lord Chief Justice Hale, in which that great man tells him, 'That for two years after he came to the inn of court, he studied sixteen hours a day; however, (his Lordship added,) that by this intense application he almost brought himself to his grave, though he were of a very strong constitution, and after reduced himself to eight hours; but that he would not advise any body to so much; that he thought six hours a day, with attention and constancy, was sufficient; that a man must use his body as he would his horse, and his stomach; not tire him at once, but rise with an appetite.'

On Wednesday, June 16, Dr. Johnson and I returned to London; he was not well to-day, and said very little, employing himself chiefly in reading Euripides. He expressed some displeasure at me, for not observing sufficiently the various objects upon the road. 'If I had your eyes, Sir, (said he,) I should count the passengers.' It was wonderful how accurate his observations of visual objects were, not-withstanding his imperfect eyesight, owing to a habit of attention.—That he was much satisfied with the respect paid to him at Dr. Adams's is thus attested by himself: 'I returned last night from Oxford, after a fortnight's abode with Dr. Adams, who treated me as well as I could expect or wish; and he that contents a sick man, a man whom it is impossible to please, has surely done his part well.'[1]

After his return to London from this excursion, I saw him frequently, but have few memorandums; I shall therefore here insert some particulars which I collected at various times.

[1] 'Letters to Mrs. Thrale,' vol. ii. p. 372.

The Reverend Mr. Astle, of Ashbourne, in Derbyshire, brother to the learned and ingenious Thomas Astle, Esq. was from his early years known to Dr. Johnson, who obligingly advised him as to his studies and recommended to him the following books, of which a list which he has been pleased to communicate, lies before me, in Johnson's own hand-writing:—*Universal History (ancient.)—Rollin's Ancient History.—Puffendorf's Introduction to History.—Vertot's History of Knights of Malta.—Vertot's Revolution of Portugal.—Vertot's Revolution of Sweden.—Carte's History of England.—Present State of England.—Geographical Grammar.—Prideaux's Connection.—Nelson's Feasts and Fasts.—Duty of Man.—Gentleman's Religion.—Clarendon's History.—Watts's Improvement of the Mind.—Watts's Logick.—Nature Displayed.—Lowth's English Grammar.—Blackwell on the Classicks.—Sherlock's Sermons.—Burnet's Life of Hale.—Dupin's History of the Church.—Shuckford's Connections.—Law's Serious Call.—Walton's Complete Angler.—Sandys's Travels.—Sprat's History of the Royal Society.—England's Gazeteer.—Goldsmith's Roman History.—Some Commentaries on the Bible.*

It having been mentioned to Dr. Johnson that a gentleman who had a son whom he imagined to have an extreme degree of timidity, resolved to send him to a publick school, that he might acquire confidence;—'Sir, (said Johnson,) this is a preposterous expedient for removing his infirmity; such a disposition should be cultivated in the shade. Placing him at a publick school is forcing an owl upon day.'

Speaking of a gentleman whose house was much frequented by low company;[a] 'Rags, Sir, (said he,) will always make their appearance, where they have a right to do it.'

a *Who in the World was this?* [1]

Of the same gentleman's mode of living, he said, 'Sir, the servants, instead of doing what they are bid, stand round the table in idle clusters, gaping upon the guests; and seem as unfit to attend a company as to steer a man of war.'

A dull country magistrate gave Johnson a long, tedious account of his exercising his criminal jurisdiction, the result of which was his having sentenced four convicts to transportation. Johnson, in an agony of impatience to get rid of such a companion, exclaimed, 'I heartily wish, Sir,

two marginal lines: *exclaimed,'I ... a fifth* [H]

that I were a fifth.' Johnson was present when a tragedy
was read, in which there occurred this line:

'Who rules o'er freemen should himself be free.'

The company having admired it much, 'I cannot agree
with you (said Johnson:) It might as well be said,

"Who drives fat oxen should himself be fat." '

He was pleased with the kindness of Mr. Cator, who was
joined with him in Mr. Thrale's important trust, and thus
describes him:[1] 'There is much good in his character, and
much usefulness in his knowledge.' He found a cordial
solace at that gentleman's seat at Beckenham, in Kent,
which is indeed one of the finest places at which I ever was
a guest; and where I find more and more a hospitable
welcome.

Johnson seldom encouraged general censure of any
profession; but he was willing to allow a due share of merit
to the various departments necessary in civilised life. In a
splenetick, sarcastical, or jocular frame of mind, however,
he would sometimes utter a pointed saying of that nature.
One instance has been mentioned,[2] where he gave a
sudden satirical stroke to the character of an *attorney*.
The too indiscriminate admission to that employment,
which requires both abilities and integrity, has given rise
to injurious reflections, which are totally inapplicable to
many very respectable men who exercise it with reputation
and honour.

Johnson having argued for some time with a pertinacious
gentleman; his opponent, who had talked in a very
puzzling manner, happened to say, 'I don't understand
you, Sir;' upon which Johnson observed, 'Sir, I have
found you an argument; but I am not obliged to find you
an understanding.'

marginal line:
observed, 'Sir . . . an
understanding [H]

Talking to me of Harry[a] Walpole, (as Horace, now Earl
of Orford, was often called,) Johnson allowed that he got
together a great many curious little things, and told them in
an elegant manner. Mr. Walpole thought Johnson a more
amiable character after reading his Letters to Mrs. Thrale:

[a] *Harry* corrected to
Horry [H]

---

[1] 'Letters to Mrs. Thrale,' vol. ii. p. 284.   [2] See vol. i. p. 449.

but never was one of the true admirers of that great man.[1] We may suppose a prejudice conceived, if he ever heard Johnson's account to Sir George Staunton, that when he made the speeches in parliament for the Gentleman's Magazine, 'he always took care to put Sir Robert Walpole in the wrong, and to say every thing he could against the electorate of Hanover.' The celebrated Heroick Epistle, in which Johnson is satyrically introduced, has been ascribed both to Mr. Walpole and Mr. Mason. One day at Mr. Courtenay's, when a gentleman expressed his opinion that there was more energy in that poem than could be expected from Mr. Walpole; Mr. Warton, the late Laureat, observed, 'It may have been written by Walpole, and *buckram'd* by Mason.'[2]

He disapproved of Lord Hailes, for having modernised the language of the ever memorable John Hales of Eton, in an edition which his Lordship published of that writer's works. 'An authour's language, Sir, (said he,) is a characteristical part of his composition, and is also characteristical of the age in which he writes. Besides, Sir, when the language is changed we are not sure that the sense is the same. No, Sir: I am sorry Lord Hailes has done this.'

Here it may be observed, that his frequent use of the expression, *No, Sir*, was not always to intimate contradiction: for he would say so when he was about to enforce an affirmative proposition which had not been denied, as in the instance last mentioned. I used to consider it as a kind of flag of defiance: as if he had said, 'Any argument you may offer against this, is not just. No, Sir, it is not.' It was like Falstaff's 'I deny your Major.'

Sir Joshua Reynolds having said that he took the altitude of a man's taste by his stories and his wit, and of his understanding by the remarks which he repeated; being always sure that he must be a weak man, who quotes common things with an emphasis as if they were oracles;[a]— Johnson agreed with him; and Sir Joshua having also observed that the real character of a man was found out

Marginal notes (left column):

queried:
he always took care etc. [H]

marginal line:
Walpole and . . . by Mason [H]

underlined:
weak [H]

[a] *rather an* Ignorant Man than a weak one. The strongest Mind might admire a Joe Miller Joke had he lived long abroad; or in a remote Province where he had never heard of Joe Miller. [H]

[1] [In his Posthumous Works, he has spoken of Johnson in the most contemptuous manner! MALONE.]

[2] [It is now (1804) *known*, that the 'Heroick Epistle' was written by Mason. MALONE.]

by his amusements,—Johnson added, 'Yes, Sir; no man is a hypocrite in his pleasures.'

I have mentioned Johnson's general aversion to a pun. He once, however, endured one of mine. When we were talking of a numerous company in which he had distinguished himself highly, I said, 'Sir, you were a COD surrounded by smelts. Is not this enough for you? at a time too when you were not *fishing* for a compliment?' He laughed at this with a complacent approbation. Old Mr. Sheridan observed, upon my mentioning it to him, 'He liked your compliment so well, he was willing to take it with *pun sauce*.' For my own part I think no innocent species of wit or pleasantry should be suppressed: and that a good pun may be admitted among the smaller excellencies of lively conversation.

Had Johnson treated at large *De Claris Oratoribus*, he might have given us an admirable work. When the Duke of Bedford attacked the ministry as vehemently as he could, for having taken upon them to extend the time for the importation of corn, Lord Chatham, in his first speech in the House of Lords, boldly avowed himself to be an adviser of that measure. 'My colleagues, (said he,) as I was confined by indisposition, did me the signal honour of coming to the bed-side of a sick man, to ask his opinion. But, had they not thus condescended, I should have *taken up my bed and walked*, in order to have delivered that opinion at the Council-Board.' Mr. Langton, who was present, mentioned this to Johnson, who observed, 'Now, Sir, we see that he took these words as he found them; without considering, that though the expression in Scripture, *take up thy bed and walk*, strictly suited the instance of the sick man restored to health and strength, who would of course be supposed to carry his bed with him, it could not be proper in the case of a man who was lying in a state of feebleness, and who certainly would not add to the difficulty of moving at all, that of carrying his bed.'

When I pointed out to him in the news-paper one of Mr. Grattan's animated and glowing speeches, in favour of the freedom of Ireland, in which this expression occurred (I know not if accurately taken): 'We will persevere, till there is not one link of the English chain left to clank upon

two marginal lines:
*Johnson,) don't . . .
cannot clank* [H]

the rags of the meanest beggar in Ireland;'—'Nay, Sir, (said Johnson,) don't you perceive that *one* link cannot clank?'

Mrs. Thrale has published,[1] as Johnson's, a kind of parody or counterpart of a fine poetical passage in one of Mr. Burke's speeches on American Taxation. It is vigorously but somewhat coarsely executed; and I am inclined to suppose, is not quite correctly exhibited. I hope he did not use the words '*vile agents*' for the Americans in the House of Parliament;[a] and if he did so, in an extempore effusion, I wish the lady had not committed it to writing.

[a] *had he* not *used the Words,* The Lady *could never have invented them: I knew not at the Moment that Burke was meant.* [H]

Mr. Burke uniformly shewed Johnson the greatest respect; and when Mr. Townshend, now Lord Sydney, at a period when he was conspicuous in opposition, threw out some reflection in parliament upon the grant of a pension to a man of such political principles as Johnson; Mr. Burke, though then of the same party with Mr. Townshend, stood warmly forth in defence of his friend, to whom, he justly observed, the pension was granted solely on account of his eminent literary merit. I am well assured, that Mr. Townshend's attack upon Johnson was the occasion of his 'hitching in a rhyme;' for, that in the original copy of Goldsmith's character of Mr. Burke, in his 'Retaliation,' another person's name stood in the couplet where Mr. Townshend is now introduced:

'Though fraught with all learning, kept straining his throat,
To persuade *Tommy Townshend* to lend him a vote.'

It may be worth remarking, among the *minutiæ* of my collection, that Johnson was once drawn to serve in the militia, the Trained Bands of the City of London, and that Mr. Rackstrow, of the Museum in Fleet-street, was his Colonel. It may be believed he did not serve in person; but the idea, with all its circumstances, is certainly laughable. He upon that occasion provided himself with a musket, and with a sword and belt, which I have seen hanging in his closet.

He was very constant to those whom he once employed, if they gave him no reason to be displeased. When somebody talked of being imposed on in the purchase of tea

[1] 'Anecdotes,' p. 43.

and sugar, and such articles: 'That will not be the case, (said he,) if you go to a *stately shop*, as I always do. In such a shop it is not worth their while to take a petty advantage.'

queried: *if you go* etc. [H]

An authour of most anxious and restless vanity being mentioned, 'Sir, (said he,) there is not a young sapling upon Parnassus more severely blown about by every wind of criticism than that poor fellow.'

The difference, he observed, between a well-bred and an ill-bred man is this: 'One immediately attracts your liking, the other your aversion. You love the one till you find reason to hate him; you hate the other till you find reason to love him.'

The wife of one of his acquaintance had fraudulently made a purse for herself out of her husband's fortune.[a] Feeling a proper compunction in her last moments, she confessed how much she had secreted; but before she could tell where it was placed, she was seized with a convulsive fit and expired. Her husband said, he was more hurt by her want of confidence in him, than by the loss of his money. 'I told him, (said Johnson,) that he should console himself: for *perhaps* the money might be *found*, and he was *sure* that his wife was *gone*.'

[a] *yes, I remember* that *Story; but have lost the Names*. [I]

index sign: *she was seized* etc. [H]

A foppish physician once reminded Johnson of his having been in company with him on a former occasion, 'I do not remember it, Sir.' The physician still insisted; adding that he that day wore so fine a coat that it must have attracted his notice. 'Sir, (said Johnson,) had you been dipt in Pactolus, I should not have noticed you.'

marginal line: *Sir, (said . . . noticed you* [H]

He seemed to take a pleasure in speaking in his own style; for when he had carelessly missed it, he would repeat the thought translated into it. Talking of the Comedy of 'The Rehearsal,' he said, 'It has not wit enough to keep it sweet.' This was easy;—he therefore caught himself, and pronounced a more round sentence; 'It has not vitality enough to preserve it from putrefaction.'

marginal line: *Talking of . . . he said* [H]

He censured a writer of entertaining Travels for assuming a feigned character, saying, (in his sense of the word,) 'He carries out one lye; we know not how many he brings back.' At another time, talking of the same person, he observed, 'Sir, your assent to a man whom you have never known to falsify, is a debt: but after you have known a man

marginal line:
*Though he . . . he ad-
mired* [H]

to falsify, your assent to him then is a favour.'

Though he had no taste for painting, he admired much the manner in which Sir Joshua Reynolds treated of his art, in his 'Discourses to the Royal Academy.' He observed one day of a passage in them, 'I think I might as well have said this myself:' and once when Mr. Langton was sitting by him, he read one of them very eagerly, and expressed himself thus: 'Very well, Master Reynolds; very well, indeed. But it will not be understood.'

When I observed to him that Painting was so far inferiour to Poetry, that the story or even emblem which it communicates must be previously known, and mentioned as a natural and laughable instance of this, that a little Miss on seeing a picture of Justice with the scales, had exclaimed to me, 'See, there's a woman selling sweetmeats;' he said, 'Painting, Sir, can illustrate, but cannot inform.'

No man was more ready to make an apology when he had censured unjustly, than Johnson. When a proof-sheet of one of his works was brought to him, he found fault with the mode in which a part of it was arranged, refused to read it, and in a passion desired that the compositor[1] might be sent to him. The compositor was Mr. Manning, a decent sensible man, who had composed about one half of his 'Dictionary,' when in Mr. Strahan's printing-house; and a great part of his 'Lives of the Poets,' when in that of Mr. Nichols; and who (in his seventy-seventh year) when in Mr. Baldwin's printing-house, composed a part of the first edition of this work concerning him. By producing the manuscript, he at once satisfied Dr. Johnson that he was not to blame. Upon which Johnson candidly and earnestly said to him, 'Mr. Compositor, I ask your pardon; Mr. Compositor, I ask your pardon, again and again.'

His generous humanity to the miserable was almost beyond example. The following instance is well attested: Coming home late one night, he found a poor woman lying in the street, so much exhausted that she could not walk;

---

[1] Compositor in the Printing-house means, the person who adjusts the types in the order in which they are to stand for printing; and arranges what is called a *form*, from which an impression is taken.

he took her upon his back, and carried her to his house, where he discovered that she was one of those wretched females who had fallen into the lowest state of vice, poverty, and disease. Instead of harshly unbraiding her, he had her taken care of with all tenderness for a long time, at a considerable expence, till she was restored to health, and endeavoured to put her into a virtuous way of living.[1]

He thought Mr. Caleb Whitefoord singularly happy in hitting on the signature of *Papyrius Cursor*, to his ingenious and diverting cross readings of the news-papers;[a] it being a real name of an ancient Roman, and clearly expressive of the thing done in this lively conceit.

He once in his life was known to have uttered what is called a *bull:* Sir Joshua Reynolds, when they were riding together in Devonshire, complained that he had a very bad horse, for that even when going down hill he moved slowly step by step. 'Ay (said Johnson,) and when he *goes* up hill, he *stands still.*'

He had a great aversion to gesticulating in company. He called once to a gentleman who offended him in that point, 'Don't *attitudenise.*' And when another gentleman thought he was giving additional force to what he uttered, by expressive movements of his hands, Johnson fairly seized them, and held them down.[b]

An authour of considerable eminence having engrossed a good share of the conversation in the company of Johnson, and having said nothing but what was trifling and insignificant; Johnson when he was gone, observed to us, 'It is wonderful what a difference there sometimes is between a man's powers of writing and of talking. ****** writes with great spirit, but is a poor talker; had he held his tongue, we might have supposed him to have been restrained by modesty; but he has spoken a great deal to-day; and you have heard what stuff it was.'

A gentleman having said that a *congé d'élire* has not, perhaps, the force of a command, but may be considered only as a strong recommendation;—'Sir, (replied Johnson, who overheard him,) it is such a recommendation, as if I

underlined: *singularly* [H]

a *not singularly happy, because the same Trick was played in Queen Anne's Time: I have it in an old Edition of the Tatler . . . The Signature however is new & pretty —& original.* [H]

So he was—but The Trick had been played before 'tis in a Spurious Edition of The Tatler—I bought the odd Vol: for that very Reason [I]

b *This was Sir W. W. Pepys when reading Jephson's Braganza*[H]

That was Pepys reading Braganza. [I]

---

[1] The circumstance therefore alluded to in Mr. Courtenay's 'Poetical Character' of him is strictly true. My informer was Mrs. Desmoulins, who lived many years in Dr. Johnson's house.

should throw you out of a two pair of stairs window, and recommend to you to fall soft.'[1]

Mr. Steevens, who passed many a social hour with him during their long acquaintance, which commenced when they both lived in the Temple, has preserved a good number of particulars concerning him, most of which are to be found in the department of Apophthegms, &c. in the Collection of 'Johnson's Works.' But he has been pleased to favour me with the following, which are original:

'One evening, previous to the trial of Baretti, a consultation of his friends was held at the house of Mr. Cox, the solicitor, in Southampton-buildings, Chancery-lane. Among others present were, Mr. Burke and Dr. Johnson, who differed in sentiments concerning the tendency of some part of the defence the prisoner was to make. When the meeting was over, Mr. Steevens observed, that the question between him and his friend had been agitated with rather too much warmth. "It may be so, Sir, (replied the Doctor,) for Burke and I should have been of one opinion, if we had had no audience."'

'Dr. Johnson once assumed a character in which perhaps even Mr. Boswell never saw him. His curiosity having been excited by the praises bestowed on the celebrated Torré's fireworks at Marybone-Gardens, he desired Mr. Steevens to accompany him thither. The evening had proved showery; and soon after the few people present were assembled, publick notice was given, that the conductors to the wheels, suns, stars, &c. were so thoroughly water-soaked, that it was impossible any part of the exhibition should be made. "This is a mere excuse, (says the Doctor,) to save their crackers for a more profitable company. Let us both hold up our sticks, and threaten to break those coloured lamps that surround the Orchestra, and we shall soon have our wishes gratified. The core of the fire-works cannot be injured; let the different pieces be touched in their respective centers, and they will do their offices as well as ever." —Some young men who overheard

---

[1] This has been printed in other publications, 'fall *to the ground.*' But Johnson himself gave me the true expression which he had used as above; meaning that the recommendation left as little choice in the one case as the other.

him, immediately began the violence he had recommended,
and an attempt was speedily made to fire some of the
wheels which appeared to have received the smallest
damage; but to little purpose were they lighted, for most
of them completely failed.—The authour of "The Rambler," however, may be considered on this occasion, as the
ringleader of a successful riot, though not as a skilful
pyrotechnist.'

'It has been supposed that Dr. Johnson, so far as fashion
was concerned, was careless of his appearance in publick.
But this is not altogether true, as the following slight
instance may show:—Goldsmith's last Comedy was to be
represented during some court-mourning; and Mr. Steevens
appointed to call on Dr. Johnson, and carry him to the
tavern where he was to dine with others of the Poet's
friends. The Doctor was ready dressed, but in coloured
cloaths; yet being told that he would find every one else
in black, received the intelligence with a profusion of
thanks, hastened to change his attire,[a] all the while repeating his gratitude for the information that had saved him
from an appearance so improper in the front row of a front
box. "I would not (added he,) for ten pounds have seemed
so retrograde to any general observance."'

'He would sometimes found his dislikes on very slender
circumstances. Happening one day to mention Mr. Flex-
man, a Dissenting Minister, with some compliment to his
exact memory in chronological matters; the Doctor replied,
"Let me hear no more of him, Sir. That is the fellow who
made the Index to my Ramblers, and set down the name
of Milton thus:—Milton, *Mr.* John."'

Mr. Steevens adds this testimony: 'It is unfortunate, however, for Johnson, that his particularities and frailties can
be more distinctly traced than his good and amiable
exertions. Could the many bounties he studiously concealed, the many acts of humanity he performed in private,
be displayed with equal circumstantiality, his defects
would be so far lost in the blaze of his virtues, that the
latter only would be regarded.'

Though from my very high admiration of Johnson, I
have wondered that he was not courted by all the great

[a] *Yes—& when the
fine Show called Cox's
Museum was exhibited,
I well remember his
violently-express'd In-
dignation at the Man
who shewed us Gilded
Dragons that spit up
Diamonds, & Hum-
ming Birds that fed
their Young with Pearls;
& suffer'd his Son to
walk the Rooms in a
Colour'd Coat when
everyone else was in
Mourning—* [H]
marginal line:
to my . . . Mr. John
[H]

and all the eminent persons of his time, it ought fairly to
be considered, that no man of humble birth, who lived
entirely by literature, in short no authour by profession,
ever rose in this country into that personal notice which
he did. In the course of this work a numerous variety of
names has been mentioned, to which many might be added.
I cannot omit Lord and Lady Lucan, at whose house he
often enjoyed all that an elegant table and the best company can contribute to happiness; he found hospitality
united with extraordinary accomplishments, and embel-
lished with charms of which no man could be insensible.

On Tuesday, June 22, I dined with him at THE
LITERARY CLUB, the last time of his being in that respectable society. The other members present were the Bishop
of St. Asaph, Lord Eliot, Lord Palmerston, Dr. Fordyce,
and Mr. Malone. He looked ill; but had such a manly
fortitude, that he did not trouble the company with melancholy complaints. They all shewed evident marks of kind
concern about him, with which he was much pleased, and
he exerted himself to be as entertaining as his indisposition
allowed him.

The anxiety of his friends to preserve so estimable a life,
as long as human means might be supposed to have
influence, made them plan for him a retreat from the
severity of a British winter, to the mild climate of Italy.
This scheme was at last brought to a serious resolution at
General Paoli's, where I had often talked of it. One essential matter, however, I understood was necessary to be
previously settled, which was obtaining such an addition
to his income, as would be sufficient to enable him to defray
the expence in a manner becoming the first literary
character of a great nation, and, independent of all his
other merits, the Authour of THE DICTIONARY OF THE
ENGLISH LANGUAGE. The person to whom I above all
others thought I should apply to negociate this business,
was the Lord Chancellor,[1] because I knew that he highly
valued Johnson, and that Johnson highly valued his Lordship; so that it was no degradation of my illustrious friend

---

[1] [Edward Lord Thurlow, who was devested of the great seal a second
time in 1793, and died Sept. 12, 1806, in the seventy-first year of his age.
MALONE.]

to solicit for him the favour of such a man. I have mentioned
what Johnson said of him to me when he was at the bar;
and after his Lordship was advanced to the seals, he said of
him, 'I would prepare myself for no man in England but
Lord Thurlow. When I am to meet with him, I should
wish to know a day before.' How he would have prepared
himself, I cannot conjecture. Would he have selected
certain topicks, and considered them in every view, so as to
be in readiness to argue them at all points? and what may
we suppose those topicks to have been? I once started
the curious enquiry to the great man who was the subject
of this compliment: he smiled, but did not pursue it.

I first consulted with Sir Joshua Reynolds, who perfectly
coincided in opinion with me; and I therefore, though
personally very little known to his Lordship, wrote to him,[1]
stating the case, and requesting his good offices for Dr.
Johnson. I mentioned that I was obliged to set out for
Scotland early in the following week, so that if his Lordship should have any commands for me as to this pious
negociation, he would be pleased to send them before
that time; otherwise Sir Joshua Reynolds would give all
attention to it.

This application was made not only without any suggestion on the part of Johnson himself, but was utterly
unknown to him, nor had he the smallest suspicion of it.
Any insinuations, therefore, which since his death have
been thrown out, as if he had stooped to ask what was
superfluous, are without any foundation. But, had he
asked it, it would not have been superfluous; for though the
money he had saved proved to be more than his friends
imagined, or than I believe he himself, in his carelessness
concerning worldly matters, knew it to be, had he travelled
upon the Continent, an augmentation of his income would
by no means have been unnecessary.[a]

On Wednesday, June 23, I visited him in the morning,
after having been present at the shocking sight of fifteen
men executed before Newgate. I said to him, I was sure

[a] *certainly;   If he
would needs leave the
Black so much Money:
otherwise there was
enough for all Pur-
poses.* [H]

---

[1] It is strange that Sir John Hawkins should have related that the application was made by Sir Joshua Reynolds, when he could so easily have been
informed of the truth by enquiring of Sir Joshua. Sir John's carelessness to
ascertain facts is very remarkable.

that human life was not machinery, that is to say, a chain of fatality planned and directed by the Supreme Being, as it had in it so much wickedness and misery, so many instances of both, as that by which my mind was now clouded.

Were it machinery, it would be better than it is in these respects, though less noble, as not being a system of moral government. He agreed with me now, as he always did, upon the great question of the liberty of the human will, which has been in all ages perplexed with so much sophistry, 'But, Sir, as to the doctrine of Necessity, no man believes it. If a man should give me arguments that I do not see, though I could not answer them, should I believe that I do not see?' It will be observed, that Johnson at all times made the just distinction between doctrines *contrary* to reason, and doctrines *above* reason.

Talking of the religious discipline proper for unhappy convicts, he said, 'Sir, one of our regular clergy will probably not impress their minds sufficiently: they should be attended by a Methodist preacher;[1] or a Popish priest.' Let me however observe, in justice to the Reverend Mr. Vilette, who has been Ordinary of Newgate for no less than eighteen years, in the course of which he has attended many hundreds of wretched criminals, that his earnest and humane exhortations have been very effectual. His extraordinary diligence is highly praise-worthy, and merits a distinguished reward.[2]

On Thursday, June 24, I dined with him at Mr. Dilly's, where were the Rev. Mr. (now Dr.) Knox, master of Tunbridge-school, Mr. Smith, Vicar of Southill, Dr. Beattie, Mr. Pinkerton, authour of various literary performances, and the Rev. Dr. Mayo. At my desire old Mr. Sheridan was invited, as I was earnest to have Johnson and him brought together again by chance, that a reconciliation might be effected. Mr. Sheridan happened to come early,

[1] A friend of mine happened to be passing by a *field congregation* in the environs of London, when a Methodist preacher quoted this passage with triumph.

[2] I trust that THE CITY OF LONDON, now happily in unison with THE COURT, will have the justice and generosity to obtain preferment for this Reverend Gentleman, now a worthy old servant of that magnificent Corporation.

and having learnt that Dr. Johnson was to be there, went away; so I found, with sincere regret, that my friendly intentions were hopeless. I recollect nothing that passed this day, except Johnson's quickness, who, when Dr. Beattie observed, as something remarkable which had happened to him, that he had chanced to see both No. 1, and No. 1000, of the hackney-coaches, the first and the last; 'Why, Sir, (said Johnson,) there is an equal chance for one's seeing those two numbers as any other two.' He was clearly right; yet the seeing of the two extremes, each of which is in some degree more conspicuous than the rest, could not but strike one in a stranger manner than the sight of any other two numbers.—Though I have neglected to preserve his conversation, it was perhaps at this inter- view that Dr. Knox formed the notion of it which he has exhibited in his 'Winter Evenings.'

On Friday, June 25, I dined with him at General Paoli's, where, he says in one of his letters to Mrs. Thrale, 'I love to dine.' There was a variety of dishes much to his taste, of all which he seemed to me to eat so much, that I was afraid he might be hurt by it; and I whispered to the General my fear, and begged he might not press him. 'Alas! (said the General,) see how very ill he looks; he can live but a very short time. Would you refuse any slight gratifications to a man under sentence of death? There is a humane custom in Italy, by which persons in that melan- choly situation are indulged with having whatever they like best to eat and drink, even with expensive delicacies.'

I shewed him some verses on Lichfield by Miss Seward, which I had that day received from her, and had the pleasure to hear him approve of them. He confirmed to me the truth of a high compliment which I had been told he had paid to that lady, when she mentioned to him 'The Colombiade,' an epick poem, by Madame du Boccage:— 'Madam, there is not any thing equal to your description of the sea round the North Pole, in your Ode on the death of Captain Cooke.'

On Sunday, June 27, I found him rather better. I men- tioned to him a young man who was going to Jamaica with his wife and children, in expectation of being provided for by two of her brothers settled in that island, one a clergyman, and the other a physician. JOHNSON. 'It is a wild scheme, Sir, unless he has a positive and deliberate invitation. There was a poor girl, who used to come about me, who had a cousin in Barbadoes, that, in a letter to her, expressed a wish she should come out to that Island, and expatiated on the comforts and happiness of her situation. The poor girl went out: her cousin was much surprized, and asked her how she could think of coming. "Because, (said she,) you invited me."—"Not I," answered the cousin. The letter was then produced. "I see it is true, (said she,) that I did invite you: but I did not think you would come." They lodged her in an out-house, where she passed her time miserably; and as soon as she had an opportunity she returned to England. Always tell this, when you hear of people going abroad to relations, upon a notion of being well received. In the case which you mention, it is probable the clergyman spends all he gets, and the physician does not know how much he is to get.'

We this day dined at Sir Joshua Reynolds's, with General Paoli, Lord Eliot, (formerly Mr. Eliot, of Port Eliot,) Dr. Beattie, and some other company. Talking of Lord Chesterfield;—JOHNSON. 'His manner was exquisitely elegant, and he had more knowledge than I expected.' BOSWELL. 'Did you find, Sir, his conversation to be of a superiour style?' JOHNSON. 'Sir, in the conversation which I had with him I had the best right to superiority, for it was upon philology and literature.' Lord Eliot, who had travelled at the same time with Mr. Stanhope, Lord Chesterfield's natural son, justly observed, that it was strange that a man who shewed he had so much affection for his son as Lord Chesterfield did, by writing so many long and anxious letters to him, almost all of them when he was Secretary of State, which certainly was a proof of great goodness of disposition, should endeavour to make his son a rascal. His Lordship told us, that Foote had intended to bring on the stage a father who had thus tutored his son, and to shew the son an honest man to every one else, but practising his father's maxims upon him, and cheating him. JOHNSON. 'I am much pleased with this design; but I think there was no occasion to make the son honest at all. No; he should be a consummate rogue: the contrast between honesty and knavery would be the stronger. It should be contrived so that the father should be the only sufferer by the son's villainy, and thus there would be poetical justice.'

He put Lord Eliot in mind of Dr. Walter Harte. 'I know, (said he,) Harte was your Lordship's tutor, and he was also tutor to the Peterborough family. Pray, my Lord, do you recollect any particulars that he told you of Lord Peterborough? He is a favourite of mine, and is not enough known; his character has been only ventilated in party pamphlets.' Lord Eliot said, if Dr. Johnson would be so good as to ask him any questions, he would tell what he could recollect. Accordingly some things were mentioned. 'But, (said his Lordship,) the best account of Lord Peterborough that I have happened to meet with, is in "Captain Carleton's Memoirs." Carleton was descended of an ancestor who had distinguished himself at the siege of Derry. He was an officer; and, what was rare at that time, had some knowledge of engineering.' Johnson said, he had never heard of the book. Lord Eliot had it at Port Eliot; but, after a good deal of enquiry, procured a copy in London, and sent it to Johnson, who told Sir Joshua Reynolds that he was going to bed when it came, but was so much pleased with it, that he sat up till he had read it through, and found in it such an air of truth, that he could not doubt of its authenticity; adding, with a smile, (in allusion to Lord Eliot's having recently been raised to the peerage,) I did not think a *young Lord* could have mentioned to me a book in the English history that was not known to me.'

An addition to our company came after we went up to the drawing-room; Dr. Johnson seemed to rise in spirits as his audience increased. He said, 'He wished Lord Orford's pictures, and Sir Ashton Lever's Museum, might be purchased by the publick, because both the money, and the pictures, and the curiosities would remain in the country; whereas if they were sold into another kingdom, the nation would indeed get some money, but would lose the pictures and curiosities, which it would be desirable we should have, for improvement in taste and natural history. The only question was, as the nation was much in want of money, whether it would not be better to take a large price from a foreign state?'

He entered upon a curious discussion of the difference between intuition and sagacity; one being immediate in its effect, the other requiring a circuitous process; one he observed was the *eye* of the mind, the other the *nose* of the mind.

A young gentleman present took up the argument against him, and maintained that no man ever thinks of the *nose of the mind*, not adverting that though that figurative sense seems strange to us, as very unusual, it is truly not more forced than Hamlet's 'In my *mind's eye*, Horatio.' He persisted much too long, and appeared to Johnson as putting himself forward as his antagonist with too much presumption: upon which he called to him in a loud tone, 'What is it you are contending for, if you *be* contending?'— And afterwards imagining that the gentleman retorted upon him with a kind of smart drollery, he said, 'Mr. *****, it does not become you to talk so to me. Besides, ridicule is not your talent; you have *there* neither intuition

^a *pretty severe surely.* [H]

nor sagacity.'^a—The gentleman protested that he had intended no improper freedom, but had the greatest respect for Dr. Johnson. After a short pause, during which we were somewhat uneasy.—JOHNSON. 'Give me your

^b *Quere who was the Man?* [H]

hand, Sir. You were too tedious, and I was too short.'^b MR. *****. 'Sir, I am honoured by your attention in any way.' JOHNSON. 'Come, Sir, let's have no more of it. We offended one another by our contention; let us not offend

^c *That was very good.* [I]

the company by our compliments.'^c

He now said, 'He wished much to go to Italy, and that he dreaded passing the winter in England.' I said nothing; but enjoyed a secret satisfaction in thinking that I had taken the most effectual measures to make such a scheme practicable.

On Monday, June 28, I had the honour to receive from the Lord Chancellor the following letter:

'SIR,   'TO JAMES BOSWELL, ESQ.

'I SHOULD have answered your letter immediately; if, (being much engaged when I received it) I had not put it in my pocket, and forgot to open it till this morning.

'I am much obliged to you for the suggestion; and I will adopt and press it as far as I can. The best argument, I am sure, and I hope it is not likely to fail, is Dr. Johnson's merit.—But it will be necessary, if I should be so unfortunate as to miss seeing you, to converse with Sir Joshua on the sum it will be proper to ask,—in short, upon the means of setting him out. It would be a reflection on us all, if such a man should perish for want of the means to take care of his health.

'Your's, &c.

'THURLOW'

This letter gave me a very high satisfaction; I next day went and shewed it to Sir Joshua Reynolds, who was exceedingly pleased with it. He thought that I should now communicate the negociation to Dr. Johnson, who might afterwards complain if the attention with which he had been honoured, should be too long concealed from him. I intended to set out for Scotland next morning; but Sir Joshua cordially insisted that I should stay another day, that Johnson and I might dine with him, that we three might talk of his Italian Tour, and, as Sir Joshua expressed himself, 'have it all out.' I hastened to Johnson, and was told by him that he was rather better to-day. BOSWELL. 'I am very anxious about you, Sir, and particularly that you should go to Italy for the winter, which I believe is your own wish.' JOHNSON. 'It is, Sir.' BOSWELL. 'You have no objection, I presume, but the money it would require.' JOHNSON. 'Why, no, Sir.'—Upon which I gave him a particular account of what had been done, and read to him the Lord Chancellor's letter.—He listened with much attention; then warmly said, 'This is taking prodigious pains about a man.'—'O, Sir, (said I, with most sincere affection) your friends would do every thing for you.' He paused,—grew more and more agitated,—till tears started into his eyes, and he exclaimed with fervent emotion, 'GOD bless you all.' I was so affected that I also shed tears.—After a short silence, he renewed and extended his grateful benediction, 'GOD bless you all, for JESUS CHRIST's sake.' We both remained for some time unable to speak.—He rose suddenly and quitted the room, quite melted in tenderness. He staid but a short time, till he had recovered his firmness; soon after he returned I left him, having first engaged him to dine at Sir Joshua Reynolds's next day.—I never was again under that roof which I had so long reverenced.

On Wednesday, June 30, the friendly confidential dinner with Sir Joshua Reynolds took place, no other company being present. Had I known that this was the last time that I should enjoy in this world, the conversation of a friend whom I so much respected, and from whom I derived so much instruction and entertainment, I should have been deeply affected. When I now look back to it, I am vexed that a single word should have been forgotten.

Both Sir Joshua and I were so sanguine in our expectations, that we expatiated with confidence on the liberal provision which we were sure would be made for him, conjecturing whether munificence would be displayed in one large donation, or in an ample increase of his pension. He himself catched so much of our enthusiasm, as to allow himself to suppose it not impossible that our hopes might in one way or other be realised. He said that he would rather have his pension doubled than a grant of a thousand pounds; 'For, (said he,) though probably I may not live to receive as much as a thousand pounds, a man would have the consciousness that he should pass the remainder of his life in splendour, how long soever it might be.' Considering what a moderate proportion an income of six hundred pounds a-year bears to innumerable fortunes in this country, it is worthy of remark, that a man so truly great should think it splendour.

As an instance of extraordinary liberality of friendship, he told us, that Dr. Brocklesby had upon this occasion offered him a hundred a-year for his life. A grateful tear started into his eye, as he spoke this in a faultering tone.

Sir Joshua and I endeavoured to flatter his imagination with agreeable prospects of happiness in Italy. 'Nay, (said he,) I must not expect much of that; when a man goes to Italy merely to feel how he breathes the air, he can enjoy very little.'

Our conversation turned upon living in the country, which Johnson, whose melancholy mind required the dissipation of quick successive variety, had habituated himself to consider as a kind of mental imprisonment. 'Yet, Sir, (said I,) there are many people who are content to live in the country.' JOHNSON. 'Sir, it is in the intellectual world as in the physical world: we are told by natural philosophers that a body is at rest in the place that is fit for it; they who are content to live in the country, are *fit* for the country.'

marginal line: *philosophers that . . . country, are* [H]

Talking of various enjoyments, I argued that a refinement of taste was a disadvantage, as they who have attained to it must be seldomer pleased than those who have no nice discrimination, and are therefore satisfied with every thing that comes in their way. JOHNSON. 'Nay, Sir; that is a paltry notion. Endeavour to be as perfect as you can in every respect.'

I accompanied him in Sir Joshua Reynolds's coach, to the entry of Bolt-court. He asked me whether I would not go with him to his house; I declined it, from an apprehension that my spirits would sink. We bade adieu to each other affectionately in the carriage. When he had got down upon the foot-pavement, he called out, 'Fare you well;' and without looking back, sprung away with a kind of pathetick briskness, if I may use that expression, which seemed to indicate a struggle to conceal uneasiness, and impressed me with a foreboding of our long, long separation.

I remained one day more in town, to have the chance of talking over my negociation with the Lord Chancellor; but the multiplicity of his Lordship's important engagements did not allow of it; so I left the management of the business in the hands of Sir Joshua Reynolds.

Soon after this time Dr. Johnson had the mortification of being informed by Mrs. Thrale, that, 'what she supposed he never believed,'[1] was true; namely, that she was actually going to marry Signor Piozzi, an Italian musickmaster. He endeavoured to prevent it; but in vain. If she would publish the whole of the correspondence that passed between Dr. Johnson and her on the subject, we should have a full view of his real sentiments. As it is, our judgement must be biassed by that characteristick specimen which Sir John Hawkins has given us: 'Poor Thrale, I

[1] 'Letters to Mrs. Thrale,' vol. ii. page 375.

thought that either her virtue or her vice would have restrained her from such a marriage. She is now become a subject for her enemies to exult over; and for her friends, if she has any left, to forget, or pity.'[1]

It must be admitted that Johnson derived a considerable portion of happiness from the comforts and elegancies which he enjoyed in Mr. Thrale's family; but Mrs. Thrale assures us he was indebted for these to her husband alone, who certainly respected him sincerely. Her words are, '*Veneration for his virtue, reverence for his talents*, delight *in his conversation, and* habitual endurance of a yoke my husband first put upon me, *and of which he contentedly bore his share for sixteen or seventeen years, made me go on so long with* Mr. Johnson; *but the perpetual confinement I will own to have been* terrifying *in the first years of our friendship, and* irksome *in the last; nor could I pretend to* support *it without help, when my coadjutor was no more.*'[2] Alas! how different is this from the declarations which I have heard Mrs. Thrale make in his life-time, without a single murmur against any peculiarities, or against any one circumstance which attended their intimacy.

As a sincere friend of the great man whose Life I am writing, I think it necessary to guard my readers against the mistaken notion of Dr. Johnson's character, which this Lady's 'Anecdotes' of him suggest; for from the very nature and form of her book, it 'lends deception lighter wings to fly.'

^a *Who was this?* [I]

'Let it be remembered, (says an eminent critick,[3])^a that she has comprised in a small volume all that she could recollect of Dr. Johnson in *twenty years*, during which period, doubtless, some severe things were said by him; and they who read the book in *two hours*, naturally enough suppose that his whole conversation was of this complexion. But the fact is, I have been often in his company, and never once heard him say a severe thing to any one;^b and many others can attest the same. When he did say a severe thing, it was generally extorted by ignorance pretending to knowledge, or by extreme vanity or affectation.

exclamation point: *never* once etc. [H]

^b *What was that Speech he made some Man? recorded in this Volume at bottom of Page 363?* [p. 392 of this volume] [H]

[1] Dr. Johnson's Letter to Sir John Hawkins, 'Life,' p. 570.
[2] 'Anecdotes,' p. 293.
[3] Who has been pleased to furnish me with his remarks.

'Two instances of inaccuracy, (adds he,) are peculiarly worthy of notice:

'It is said,[1] "*That natural roughness of his manner so often mentioned, would, notwithstanding the regularity of his notions, burst through them all from time to time; and he once bade a very celebrated lady, who praised him with too much zeal perhaps, or perhaps too strong an emphasis, (which always offended him,) consider what her flattery was worth, before she choaked* him *with it.*"

marginal line:
consider what . . .
with it [H]

'Now let the genuine anecdote be contrasted with this. — The person thus represented as being harshly treated, though a very celebrated lady, was *then* just come to London[a] from an obscure situation in the country. At Sir Joshua Reynolds's one evening, she met Dr. Johnson. She very soon began to pay her court to him in the most fulsome strain. "Spare me, I beseech you, dear Madam," was his reply. She still *laid it on.* "Pray, Madam, let us have no more of this;" he rejoined. Not paying any attention to these warnings, she continued still her eulogy. At length, provoked by this indelicate and *vain* obtrusion of compliment, he exclaimed, "Dearest lady, consider with yourself what your flattery is worth, before you bestow it so freely."

a *Hannah More* [1]

'How different does this story appear, when accompanied with all these circumstances which really belong to it, but which Mrs. Thrale either did not know, or has suppressed.

'She says, in another place,[2] "*One gentleman, however, who dined at a nobleman's house*[b] *in his company, and that of* Mr. Thrale, *to whom I was obliged for the anecdote, was willing to enter the lists in defence of* King William's *character; and having opposed and contradicted* Johnson *two or three times, petulantly enough, the master of the house began to feel uneasy, and expect disagreeable consequences; to avoid which he said, loud enough for the Doctor to hear,—Our friend here has no meaning now in all this, except just to relate at club to-morrow how he teazed* Johnson *at dinner to-day; this is all to do himself* honour. — *No, upon my word, (replied the other,) I see no* honour *in it, whatever you may do.—Well, Sir, (returned* Mr. Johnson, *sternly,) if you do not* see *the honour, I am sure I* feel *the disgrace.*"

underlined:
nobleman's [1]

b *Fitzmaurice's in Pall Mall* [1]

marginal line:
you may . . . sure I
[H]

---

[1] 'Anecdotes,' p. 183.   [2] Ibid. p. 242.

'This is all sophisticated. Mr. Thrale was *not* in the company,[a] though he might have related the story to Mrs. Thrale. A friend, from whom I had the story, was present; and it was *not* at the house of a nobleman.[b] On the observation being made by the master of the house on a gentleman's contradicting Johnson, that he had talked for the honour, &c. the gentleman muttered in a low voice, "I see no honour in it;" and Dr. Johnson said nothing: so all the rest, (though *bien trouvée*) is mere garnish.'

I have had occasion several times, in the course of this work, to point out the incorrectness of Mrs. Thrale, as to particulars which consisted with my own knowledge. But indeed she has, in flippant terms enough, expressed her disapprobation of that anxious desire of authenticity which prompts a person who is to record conversations, to write them down *at the moment*.[1] Unquestionably, if they are to be recorded at all, the sooner it is done the better. This lady herself says,[2] '*To recollect, however, and to repeat the sayings of Dr. Johnson, is almost all that can be done by the writers of his Life; as his life, at least since my acquaintance with him, consisted in little else than talking, when he was not employed in some serious piece of work.*' She boasts of her having kept a common-place book; and we find she noted, at one time or other, in a very lively manner, specimens of the conversation of Dr. Johnson, and of those who talked with him; but had she done it recently, they probably would have been less erroneous; and we should have been relieved from those disagreeable doubts of their authenticity, with which we must now pursue them.

She says of him:[3] '*He was the most charitable of mortals, without being what we call an* active *friend. Admirable at giving counsel; no man saw his way so clearly; but he would not stir a finger for the assistance of those to whom he was willing enough to give advice.*' And again on the same page, '*If you wanted a slight favour, you must apply to people of other dispositions; for not a step would Johnson move to obtain a man a vote in a society, to repay a compliment which might be useful or pleasing, to write a letter of request, &c. or to obtain a hundred pounds a year more for a friend who perhaps had already two or three.*'

[a] *Mr. Thrale was in Company & the Gentleman—Mr Pottinger was his particular Friend—1808.* [I]

[b] *It was the House of Thos. Fitzmaurice Son to Ld. Shelburne, & Pottinger the Hero.* [H]

Fitzmaurice was noble enough—on one Side at least [I]

[1] 'Anecdotes,' p. 44. [2] Ibid. p. 23.
[3] Ibid. p. 51.

No force could urge him to diligence, no importunity could conquer his resolution to stand still.'

It is amazing that one who had such opportunities of knowing Dr. Johnson, should appear so little acquainted with his real character. I am sorry this lady does not advert, that she herself contradicts the assertion of his being obstinately defective in the *petites morales*, in the little endearing charities of social life, in conferring smaller favours; for she says,[1] 'Dr. Johnson *was liberal enough in granting literary assistance to others, I think; and innumerable are the Prefaces, Sermons, Lectures, and Dedications which he used to make for people who begged of him.'* I am certain that a *more active friend* has rarely been found in any age. This work, which I fondly hope will rescue his memory from obloquy, contains a thousand instances of his benevolent exertions in almost every way that can be conceived; and particularly in employing his pen with a generous readiness for those to whom its aid could be useful. Indeed his obliging activity in doing little offices of kindness, both by letters and personal application, was one of the most remarkable features in his character; and for the truth of this I can appeal to a number of his respectable friends: Sir Joshua Reynolds, Mr. Langton, Mr. Hamilton, Mr. Burke, Mr. Windham, Mr. Malone, the Bishop of Dromore, Sir William Scott, Sir Robert Chambers.—And can Mrs. Thrale forget the advertisements which he wrote for her husband at the time of his election contest; the epitaphs on him and her mother; the playful and even trifling verses, for the amusement of her and her daughters; his corresponding with her children, and entering into their minute concerns, which shews him in the most amiable light?

She relates,[2] That Mr. Ch—lm—ley unexpectedly rode up to Mr. Thrale's carriage, in which Mr. Thrale and she, and Dr. Johnson were travelling; that he paid them all his proper compliments, but observing that Dr. Johnson, who was reading, did not see him, '*tapt him gently on the shoulder.* "'*Tis Mr. Ch—lm—ley;" says my husband. "Well, Sir—and what if it is Mr. Ch—lm—ley;" says the other, sternly, just lifting his eyes a moment from his book, and returning to it again with renewed avidity.'* This surely conveys a notion of Johnson,

[1] 'Anecdotes,' p. 193.   [2] Ibid. p. 258.

as if he had been grossly rude to Mr. Cholmondeley,[1] a gentleman whom he always loved and esteemed. If, therefore, there was an absolute necessity for mentioning the story at all, it might have been thought that her tenderness for Dr. Johnson's character would have disposed her to state any thing that could soften it. Why then is there a total silence as to what Mr. Cholmondeley told her?[a]— that Johnson, who had known him from his earliest years, having been made sensible of what had doubtless a strange appearance, took occasion, when he afterwards met him, to make a very courteous and kind apology. There is another little circumstance which I cannot but remark. Her book was published in 1785, she had then in her possession a letter from Dr. Johnson, dated in 1777,[2] which begins thus: 'Cholmondeley's story shocks me, if it be true, which I can hardly think, for I am utterly unconscious of it: I am very sorry, and very much ashamed.' Why then publish the anecdote? Or if she did, why not add the circumstances, with which she was well acquainted!

In his social intercourse she thus describes him:[3] '*Ever musing till he was called out to converse, and conversing till the fatigue of his friends, or the promptitude of his own temper to take offence, consigned him back again to silent meditation.*' Yet, in the same book,[4] she tells us, '*He was, however, seldom inclined to be silent, when any moral or literary question was started; and it was on such occasions that, like the Sage in "Rasselas," he spoke, and attention watched his lips; he reasoned, and conviction closed his periods.*'—His conversation, indeed, was so far from ever *fatiguing* his friends, that they regretted when it was interrupted or ceased, and could exclaim in Milton's language,

'With thee conversing, I forget all time.'

I certainly, then, do not claim too much in behalf of my illustrious friend in saying, that however smart and entertaining Mrs. Thrale's 'Anecdotes' are, they must not be held as good evidence against him; for wherever an

[a] *look at a Letter of his own Saying what you tell me of Cholmondeley* shocks me. [1]

[1] George James Cholmondeley, Esq. grandson of George, third Earl of Cholmondeley, and one of the Commissioners of Excise; a gentleman respected for his abilities, and elegance of manners.

[2] 'Letters to Mrs. Thrale,' vol. ii. p. 12.

[3] 'Anecdotes,' p. 23.   [4] Ibid. p. 302.

instance of harshness and severity is told, I beg leave to doubt its perfect authenticity; for though there may have been *some* foundation for it, yet, like that of his reproof to the 'very celebrated lady,' it may be so exhibited in the narration as to be very unlike the real fact.

The evident tendency of the following anecdote[1] is to represent Dr. Johnson as extremely deficient in affection, tenderness, or even common civility. '*When I one day lamented the loss of a first cousin killed in* America,—"*Prithee, my dear, (said he,) have done with canting; how would the world be the worse for it, I may ask, if all your relations were at once spitted like larks, and roasted for* Presto's *supper?*"—Presto *was the dog that lay under the table while we talked.*'—I suspect this too of exaggeration and distortion. I allow that he made her an angry speech; but let the circumstances fairly appear, as told by Mr. Baretti, who was present:[a]

'Mrs. Thrale, while supping very heartily upon larks, laid down her knife and fork, and abruptly exclaimed, "Oh, my dear Johnson,[b] do you know what has happened? The last letters from abroad have brought us an account that our poor cousin's head was taken off by a cannon-ball." Johnson, who was shocked both at the fact, and her light unfeeling manner of mentioning it, replied, "Madam, it would give *you* very little concern if all your relations were spitted like those larks, and drest for Presto's supper."'[2]

It is with concern that I find myself obliged to animadvert on the inaccuracies of Mrs. Piozzi's 'Anecdotes,' and perhaps I may be thought to have dwelt too long upon her little collection. But as from Johnson's long residence under Mr. Thrale's roof, and his intimacy with her, the

[a] *Boswell appealing to* Baretti *for a Testimony of the* Truth *is comical enough.* [H]

[b] *I never address'd him so familiarly in my Life. I never did eat any Supper:—& there were no Larks to eat.* [H]

Mrs. Thrale never saw a Supper in those Days, never eat a Lark for Supper in England; & dar'd as well have swallow'd the Lark alive as have said O my dear Johnson! She never address'd him with any such familiarity. [I]

[c] *very like my hearty Supper of Larks—who never eat Supper at all: nor was ever a hot dish seen on the Table after Dinner at Streatham Park.* [H]

---

[1] 'Anecdotes,' p. 63.

[2] Upon mentioning this to my friend Mr. Wilkes, he, with his usual readiness, pleasantly matched it with the following *sentimental anecdote*. He was invited by a young man of fashion at Paris, to sup with him and a lady, who had been for some time his mistress, but with whom he was going to part. He said to Mr. Wilkes that he really felt very much for her, she was in such distress; and that he meant to make her a present of two hundred louis-d'ors. Mr. Wilkes observed the behaviour of Mademoiselle, who sighed indeed very piteously, and assumed every pathetick air of grief; but eat no less than three French pigeons, which are as large as English partridges, besides other things.[c] Mr. Wilkes whispered the gentleman, 'We often say in England, *Excessive sorrow is exceeding dry*, but I never heard *Excessive sorrow is exceeding hungry*. Perhaps *one* hundred will do.' The gentleman took the hint.

account which she has given of him may have made an unfavourable and unjust impression, my duty, as a faithful biographer, has obliged me reluctantly to perform this unpleasing task.

Having left the *pious negociation*, as I called it, in the best hands, I shall here insert what relates to it. Johnson wrote to Sir Joshua Reynolds on July 6, as follows: 'I am going, I hope, in a few days, to try the air of Derbyshire, but hope to see you before I go. Let me, however, mention to you what I have much at heart.—If the Chancellor should continue his attention to Mr. Boswell's request, and confer with you on the means of relieving my languid state, I am very desirous to avoid the appearance of asking money upon false pretences. I desire you to represent to his Lordship, what, as soon as it is suggested, he will perceive to be reasonable,—That, if I grow much worse, I shall be afraid to leave my physicians, to suffer the inconveniences of travel, and pine in the solitude of a foreign country;—That, if I grow much better, of which indeed there is now little appearance, I shall not wish to leave my friends and my domestick comforts; for I do not travel for pleasure or curiosity; yet if I should recover, curiosity would revive.—In my present state, I am desirous to make a struggle for a little longer life, and hope to obtain some help from a softer climate. Do for me what you can.' He wrote to me July 26: 'I wish your affairs could have permitted a longer and continued exertion of your zeal and kindness. They that have your kindness may want your ardour. In the mean time I am very feeble, and very dejected.'

By a letter from Sir Joshua Reynolds I was informed, that the Lord Chancellor had called on him, and acquainted him that the application had not been successful; but that his Lordship, after speaking highly in praise of Johnson, as a man who was an honour to his country, desired Sir Joshua to let him know, that on granting a mortgage of his pension, he should draw on his Lordship to the amount of five or six hundred pounds; and that his Lordship explained the meaning of the mortgage to be, that he wished the business to be conducted in such a manner, that Dr. Johnson should appear to be under the least possible obligation. Sir Joshua mentioned, that he had by the same post communicated all this to Dr. Johnson.

How Johnson was affected upon the occasion will appear from what he wrote to Sir Joshua Reynolds:

'Ashbourne, Sept. 9. Many words I hope are not necessary between you and me, to convince you what gratitude is excited in my heart by the Chancellor's liberality, and your kind offices. * * * * * *

'I have enclosed a letter to the Chancellor, which, when you have read it, you will be pleased to seal with a head, or any other general seal, and convey it to him: had I sent it directly to him, I should have seemed to overlook the favour of your intervention.'

'TO THE LORD HIGH CHANCELLOR[1]

'MY LORD,

'AFTER a long and not inattentive observation of mankind, the generosity of your Lordship's offer raises in me not less wonder than gratitude. Bounty, so liberally bestowed, I should gladly receive, if my condition made it necessary; for, to such a mind, who would not be proud to own his obligations? But it has pleased GOD to restore me to so great a measure of health, that if I should now appropriate so much of a fortune destined to do good, I could not escape from myself the charge of advancing a false claim. My journey to the continent, though I once thought it necessary, was never much encouraged by my physicians; and I was very desirous that your Lordship should be told of it by Sir Joshua Reynolds, as an event very uncertain; for if I grew much better, I should not be willing, if much worse, not able, to migrate.—Your Lordship was first solicited without my knowledge; but, when I was told that you were pleased to honour me with your

---

[1] Sir Joshua Reynolds, on account of the excellence both of the sentiment and expression of this letter, took a copy of it, which he shewed to some of his friends: one of whom, who admired it, being allowed to peruse it leisurely at home, a copy was made, and found its way into the news-papers and magazines. It was transcribed with some inaccuracies. I print it from the original draft in Johnson's own hand-writing.

patronage, I did not expect to hear of a refusal; yet, as I have had no long time to brood hope, and have not rioted in imaginary opulence, this cold reception has been scarce a disappointment; and, from your Lordship's kindness, I have received a benefit, which only men like you are able to bestow. I shall now live *mihi carior*, with a higher opinion of my own merit.

> 'I am, my Lord,
> > 'Your Lordship's most obliged,
> > > 'Most grateful, and
> > > > 'Most humble servant,

'September, 1784.'   'SAM. JOHNSON'

underlined:
failure [H]

[a] *failure of what?* [H]

[b] *What is supposed to have been the Reason? I never heard any Cause suggested.* [I]

Upon this unexpected failure[a] I abstain from presuming to make any remarks,[b] or to offer any conjectures.

Having, after repeated reasonings, brought Dr. Johnson to agree to my removing to London, and even to furnish me with arguments in favour of what he had opposed; I wrote to him requesting he would write them for me; he was so good as to comply, and I shall extract that part of his letter to me of June 11, as a proof how well he could exhibit a cautious yet encouraging view of it.

'I remember, and intreat you to remember, that *virtus est vitium fugere;* the first approach to riches is security from poverty. The condition upon which you have my consent to settle in London is, that your expence never exceeds your annual income. Fixing this basis of security, you cannot be hurt, and you may be very much advanced. The loss of your Scottish business, which is all that you can lose, is not to be reckoned as any equivalent to the hopes and possibilities that open here upon you. If you succeed, the question of prudence is at an end; every body will think that done right which ends happily; and though your expectations, of which I would not advise you to talk too much, should not be totally answered, you can hardly fail to get friends who will do for you all that your present situation allows you to hope; and if, after a few years, you should return to Scotland, you will return with a mind supplied by various conversation, and many opportunities of enquiry, with much knowledge, and materials for reflection and instruction.'

Let us now contemplate Johnson thirty years after the death of his wife, still retaining for her all the tenderness of affection.

'TO THE REVEREND MR. BAGSHAW, AT BROMLEY[1]

'SIR,

'Perhaps you may remember, that in the year 1753, you committed to the ground my dear wife. I now entreat your permission to lay a stone upon her; and have sent the inscription, that, if you find it proper, you may signify your allowance.

'You will do me a great favour by showing the place where she lies, that the stone may protect her remains.

'Mr. Ryland will wait on you for the inscription,[2] and procure it to be engraved. You will easily believe that I shrink from this mournful office. When it is done, if I have strength remaining, I will visit Bromley once again, and pay you part of the respect to which you have a right from, Reverend Sir,

'Your most humble servant,

'July 12, 1784.'   'SAM. JOHNSON'

On the same day he wrote to Mr. Langton: 'I cannot but think that in my languid and anxious state, I have some reason to complain that I receive from you neither enquiry nor consolation. You know how much I value your friendship, and with what confidence I expect your kindness, if I wanted any act of tenderness that you could perform; at least, if you do not know it, I think your ignorance is your own fault. Yet how long is it that I have lived almost in your neighbourhood without the least notice. —I do not, however, consider this neglect as particularly shown to me; I hear two of your most valuable friends make the same complaint. But why are all thus overlooked? You are not oppressed by sickness, you are not distracted by business; if you are sick, you are sick of leisure:—And allow yourself to be told, that no disease is more to be dreaded or avoided. Rather to do nothing than

---

[1] See vol. ii. p. 88.   [2] Printed in his Works.

to do good, is the lowest state of a degraded mind. Boileau says to his pupil,

> "*Que les vers ne soient pas vôtre eternel emploi,*
> *Cultivez vos amis.*"——

That voluntary debility, which modern language is content to term indolence, will, if it is not counteracted by resolution, render in time the strongest faculties lifeless, and turn the flame to the smoke of virtue. —I do not expect nor desire to see you, because I am much pleased to find that your mother stays so long with you, and I should think you neither elegant nor grateful, if you did not study her gratification. You will pay my respects to both the ladies, and to all the young people. —I am going Northward for a while, to try what help the country can give me; but, if you will write, the letter will come after me.'

Next day he set out on a jaunt to Staffordshire and Derbyshire, flattering himself that he might be in some degree relieved.

During his absence from London he kept up a correspondence with several of his friends, from which I shall select what appears to me proper for publication, without attending nicely to chronological order.

To Dr. BROCKLESBY, he writes, Ashbourne, July 20. 'The kind attention which you have so long shewn to my health and happiness, makes it as much a debt of gratitude as a call of interest, to give you an account of what befalls me, when accident recovers[1] me from your immediate care. —The journey of the first day was performed with very little sense of fatigue; the second day brought me to Lichfield, without much lassitude; but I am afraid that I could not have borne such violent agitation for many days together. Tell Dr. Heberden, that in the coach I read "Ciceronianus," which I concluded as I entered Lichfield. My affection and understanding went along with Erasmus, except that once or twice he somewhat unskilfully entangles Cicero's civil or moral, with his rhetorical character. —I staid five days at Lichfield, but being unable to walk, had no great pleasure, and yesterday (19th) I came hither,

---

[1] [This is probably an errour either of the transcript or the press. *Removes* seems to be the word intended. MALONE.]

where I am to try what air and attention can perform.—
Of any improvement in my health I cannot yet please
myself with the perception. * * * * * *.—The asthma
has no abatement. Opiates stop the fit, so as that I can sit
and sometimes lie easy, but they do not now procure me
the power of motion; and I am afraid that my general
strength of body does not encrease. The weather indeed is
not benign; but how low is he sunk whose strength depends
upon the weather!—I am now looking into Floyer, who
lived with his asthma to almost his ninetieth year. His
book by want of order is obscure; and his asthma, I think,
not of the same kind with mine. Something however I
may perhaps learn.—My appetite still continues keen
enough; and what I consider as a symptom of radical
health, I have a voracious delight in raw summer fruit, of
which I was less eager a few years ago.—You will be pleased
to communicate this account to Dr. Heberden, and if any
thing is to be done, let me have your joint opinion.—Now
—*abite curæ;*—let me enquire after the Club.'[1]

July 31. 'Not recollecting that Dr. Heberden might be
at Windsor, I thought your letter long in coming. But,
you know, *nocitura petuntur*, the letter which I so much
desired, tells me that I have lost one of my best and
tenderest friends.[2] My comfort is, that he appeared to live
like a man that had always before his eyes the fragility of
our present existence, and was therefore, I hope, not unprepared to meet his judge.—Your attention, dear Sir, and
that of Dr. Heberden, to my health, is extremely kind.
I am loth to think that I grow worse; and cannot fairly
prove even to my own partiality, that I grow much better.'

August 5. 'I return you thanks, dear Sir, for your un-
wearied attention, both medicinal and friendly, and hope
to prove the effect of your care by living to acknowledge it.'

August 12. 'Pray be so kind as to have me in your
thoughts, and mention my case to others as you have
opportunity. I seem to myself neither to gain nor lose
strength. I have lately tried milk, but have yet found no
advantage, and am afraid of it merely as a liquid. My
appetite is still good, which I know is dear Dr. Heberden's
criterion of the *vis vitæ*.—As we cannot now see each other,

---

[1] At the Essex Head, Essex-street.   [2] Mr. Allen the printer.

do not omit to write, for you cannot think with what warmth of expectation I reckon the hours of a post-day.'

August 14. 'I have hitherto sent you only melancholy letters, you will be glad to hear some better account. Yesterday the asthma remitted, perceptibly remitted, and I moved with more ease than I have enjoyed for many weeks. May GOD continue his mercy.—This account I would not delay, because I am not a lover of complaints or complainers, and yet I have, since we parted, uttered nothing till now but terrour and sorrow. Write to me, dear Sir.'

August 16. 'Better I hope, and better. My respiration gets more and more ease and liberty. I went to church yesterday, after a very liberal dinner, without any inconvenience; it is indeed no long walk, but I never walked it without difficulty, since I came, before. * * * * * * the intention was only to overpower the seeming *vis inertiæ* of the pectoral and pulmonary muscles.—I am favoured with a degree of ease that very much delights me, and do not despair of another race upon the stairs of the Academy.— If I were, however, of a humour to see, or to show the state of my body, on the dark side, I might say,

^a *True enough poor Thing!* [H]

"Quid te exempta juvat spinis de pluribus una?" ^a

The nights are still sleepless, and the water rises, though it does not rise very fast. Let us, however, rejoice in all the good that we have. The remission of one disease will enable nature to combat the rest.—The squills I have not neglected; for I have taken more than a hundred drops a day, and one day took two hundred and fifty, which, according to the popular equivalent of a drop to a grain, is more than half an ounce.—I thank you, dear Sir, for your attention in ordering the medicines; your attention to me has never failed. If the virtue of medicines could be enforced by the benevolence of the prescriber, how soon should I be well.'

August 19. 'The relaxation of the asthma still continues, yet I do not trust it wholly to itself, but soothe it now and then with an opiate. I not only perform the perpetual act of respiration with less labour, but I can walk with fewer intervals of rest, and with greater freedom of motion.—I never thought well of Dr. James's compounded medicines; his ingredients appear to me sometimes inefficacious and trifling, and sometimes heterogeneous and destructive of each other. This prescription exhibits a composition of about three hundred and thirty grains, in which there are four grains of emetick tartar, and six drops [of] thebaick tincture. He that writes thus surely writes for show. The basis of his medicine is the gum ammoniacum, which dear Dr. Lawrence used to give, but of which I never saw any effect. We will, if you please, let this medicine alone. The squills have every suffrage, and in the squills we will rest for the present.'

August 21. 'The kindness which you show by having me in your thoughts upon all occasions, will, I hope, always fill my heart with gratitude. Be pleased to return my thanks to Sir George Baker, for the consideration which he has bestowed upon me.—Is this the balloon that has been so long expected, this balloon to which I subscribed, but without payment? it is pity that philosophers have been disappointed, and shame that they have been cheated; but I know not well how to prevent either. Of this experiment I have read nothing; where was it exhibited? and who was the man that ran away with so much money?—Continue, dear Sir, to write often and more at a time; for none of your prescriptions operate to their proper uses more certainly than your letters operate as cordials.'

August 26. 'I suffered you to escape last post without a letter, but you are not to expect such indulgence very often; for I write not so much because I have any thing to say, as because I hope for an answer; and the vacancy of my life here makes a letter of great value.—I have here little company and little amusement, and thus abandoned to the contemplation of my own miseries, I am something gloomy and depressed; this too I resist as I can, and find opium, I think, useful; but I seldom take more than one grain.—Is not this strange weather? Winter absorbed the spring, and now autumn is come before we have had summer. But let not our kindness for each other imitate the inconstancy of the seasons.'

Sept. 2. 'Mr. Windham has been here to see me; he came, I think, forty miles out of his way, and staid about a day and a half; perhaps I make the time shorter than it was. Such conversation I shall not have again till I come back to the regions of literature; and there Windham is, *inter stellas*[1] *Luna minores.*' He then mentions the effects of certain medicines, as taken; that 'Nature is recovering its original powers, and the functions returning to their proper state. God continue his mercies, and grant me to use them rightly.'

Sept. 9. 'Do you know the Duke and Duchess of Devonshire? And have you ever seen Chatsworth? I was at Chatsworth on Monday; I had seen it before, but never when its owners were at home; I was very kindly received, and honestly pressed to stay; but I told them that a sick man is not a fit inmate of a great house. But I hope to go again some time.'

Sept 11. 'I think nothing grows worse, but all rather better, except sleep, and that of late has been at its old pranks. Last evening, I felt what I had not known for a long time, an inclination to walk for amusement; I took a short walk, and came back again neither breathless nor fatigued.—This has been a gloomy, frigid, ungenial summer; but of late it seems to mend: I hear the heat sometimes mentioned, but I do not feel it;

> "*Præterea minimus gelido jam in corpore sanguis*
> *Febre calet solâ.*"——

I hope, however, with good help, to find means of supporting a winter at home, and to hear and tell at the Club what is doing, and what ought to be doing in the world. I have no company here, and shall naturally come home hungry for conversation.—To wish you, dear Sir, more leisure, would not be kind; but what leisure you have, you must bestow upon me.'

Sept. 16. 'I have now let you alone for a long time, having indeed little to say. You charge me somewhat unjustly with luxury. At Chatsworth, you should remember, that I have eaten but once; and the Doctor, with whom I live, follows a milk diet. I grow no fatter, though my

[a] *He did not mean it as a* Verse *but a* Sentiment; & *thought Ignes too great a Compliment to his Competitors. 1820.* [H]

but the Moon is no Fire if She may be called a Star. [J]

[1] It is remarkable that so good a Latin scholar as Johnson, should have been so inattentive to the metre, as by mistake to have written *stellas* instead of *ignes.*[a]

stomach, if it be not disturbed by physick, never fails me. —
I now grow weary of solitude, and think of removing next
week to Lichfield, a place of more society, but otherwise of
less convenience. When I am settled, I shall write again. —
Of the hot weather that you mentioned, we have [not] had
in Derbyshire very much, and for myself I seldom feel
heat, and suppose that my frigidity is the effect of my
distemper; a supposition which naturally leads me to hope
that a hotter climate may be useful. But I hope to stand
another English winter.'

Lichfield, Sept. 29. 'On one day I had three letters
about the air balloon: yours was far the best, and has
enabled me to impart to my friends in the country an idea
of this species of amusement. In amusement, mere amusement, I am afraid it must end, for I do not find that its
course can be directed so as that it should serve any purposes of communication: and it can give no new intelligence of the state of the air at different heights, till they
have ascended above the height of mountains, which they
seem never likely to do. —I came hither on the 27th. How
long I shall stay, I have not determined. My dropsy is
gone, and my asthma much remitted, but I have felt
myself a little declining these two days, or at least to-day;
but such vicissitudes must be expected. One day may be
worse than another; but this last month is far better than
the former; if the next should be as much better than this,
I shall run about the town on my own legs.'

October 6. 'The fate of the balloon I do not much
lament: to make new balloons, is to repeat the jest again.
We now know a method of mounting into the air, and, I
think, are not likely to know more. The vehicles can serve
no use till we can guide them; and they can gratify no
curiosity till we mount with them to greater heights than
we can reach without; till we rise above the tops of the
highest mountains, which we have yet not done.[a] We know
the state of the air in all its regions, to the top of Teneriffe,
and therefore, learn nothing from those who navigate a
balloon below the clouds. The first experiment, however,
was bold, and deserved applause and reward. But since it
has been performed, and its event is known, I had rather
now find a medicine that can ease an asthma.'

[a] *& when we did
What came on't? No-
thing* [1]

October 25. 'You write to me with a zeal that animates, and a tenderness that melts me. I am not afraid either of a journey to London, or a residence in it. I came down with little fatigue, and am now not weaker. In the smoky atmosphere I was delivered from the dropsy, which I consider as the original and radical disease. The town is my element;[1] there are my friends, there are my books, to which I have not yet bid farewell, and there are my amusements. Sir Joshua told me long ago, that my vocation was to publick life, and I hope still to keep my station, till GOD shall bid me *Go in peace.*'

To MR. HOOLE. Ashbourne, Aug. 7. 'Since I was here, I have two little letters from you, and have not had the gratitude to write. But every man is most free with his best friends, because he does not suppose that they can suspect him of intentional incivility.—One reason for my omission is, that being in a place to which you are wholly a stranger, I have no topicks of correspondence. If you had any knowledge of Ashbourne, I could tell you of two Ashbourne men, who, being last week condemned at Derby to be hanged for a robbery, went and hanged themselves in their cell. But this, however it may supply us with talk, is nothing to you.—Your kindness, I know, would make you glad to hear some good of me, but I have not much good to tell; if I grow not worse it is all that I can say.—I hope Mrs. Hoole receives more help from her migration. Make her my compliments, and write again to, dear Sir, your affectionate servant.'

Aug. 13. 'I thank you for your affectionate letter. I hope we shall both be the better for each other's friendship, and I hope we shall not very quickly be parted.—Tell Mr.

---

[1] His love of London continually appears. In a letter from him to Mrs. Smart, wife of his friend the Poet, which is published in a well-written Life of him, prefixed to an edition of his Poems, in 1791, there is the following sentence: 'To one that has passed so many years in the pleasures and opulence of London, there are few places that can give much delight.'

Once, upon reading that line in the curious epitaph quoted in 'The Spectator.' 'Born in New-England, did in London die:'

he laughed and said, 'I do not wonder at this. It would have been strange, if, born in London, he had died in New-England.'

Nichols that I shall be glad of his correspondence, when his business allows him a little remission; though to wish him less business, that I may have more pleasure, would be too selfish. To pay for seats at the balloon is not very necessary, because in less than a minute, they who gaze at a mile's distance will see all that can be seen. About the wings I am of your mind; they cannot at all assist it, nor I think regulate its motion. I am now grown somewhat easier in my body, but my mind is sometimes depressed.— About the Club I am in no great pain. The forfeitures go on, and the house, I hear, is improved for our future meetings. I hope we shall meet often and sit long.'

Sept. 4. 'Your letter was, indeed, long in coming, but it was very welcome. Our acquaintance has now subsisted long, and our recollection of each other involves a great space, and many little occurrences which melt the thoughts to tenderness.—Write to me, therefore, as frequently as you can.—I hear from Dr. Brocklesby and Mr. Ryland, that the Club is not crowded. I hope we shall enliven it when winter brings us together.'

To Dr. Burney. August 2. 'The weather, you know, has not been balmy; I am now reduced to think, and am at last content to talk of the weather. Pride must have a fall.[1]—I have lost dear Mr. Allen; and wherever I turn, the dead or the dying meet my notice, and force my attention upon misery and mortality. Mrs. Burney's escape from so much danger, and her ease after so much pain, throws, however, some radiance of hope upon the gloomy prospect. May her recovery be perfect, and her continuance long.—I struggle hard for life. I take physick, and take air; my friend's chariot is always ready. We have run this morning twenty-four miles, and could run forty-eight more. *But who can run the race with Death?*'

---

[1] [There was no information for which Dr. Johnson was less grateful than for that which concerned the weather. It was in allusion to his impatience with those who were reduced to keep conversation alive by observations on the weather, that he applied the old proverb to himself. If any one of his intimate acquaintance told him it was hot or cold, wet or dry, windy or calm, he would stop them, by saying, 'Poh! poh! you are telling us that of which none but men in a mine or a dungeon can be ignorant. Let us bear with patience, or enjoy in quiet, elementary changes, whether for the better or the worse, as they are never secrets.' Burney.]

Sept. 4. [Concerning a private transaction, in which his opinion was asked, and after giving it, he makes the following reflections, which are applicable on other occasions.] 'Nothing deserves more compassion than wrong conduct with good meaning; than loss or obloquy suffered by one, who, as he is conscious only of good intentions, wonders why he loses that kindness which he wishes to preserve; and not knowing his own fault, if, as may sometimes happen, nobody will tell him, goes on to offend by his endeavours to please.—I am delighted by finding that our opinions are the same.—You will do me a real kindness by continuing to write. A post-day has now been long a day of recreation.'

Nov. 1. 'Our correspondence paused for want of topicks. I had said what I had to say on the matter proposed to my consideration, and nothing remained but to tell you, that I waked or slept; that I was more or less sick. I drew my thoughts in upon myself, and supposed yours employed upon your book.—That your book has been delayed I am glad, since you have gained an opportunity of being more exact.—Of the caution necessary in adjusting narratives there is no end. Some tell what they do not know, that they may not seem ignorant, and others from mere indifference about truth. All truth is not, indeed, of equal importance; but, if little violations are allowed, every violation will in time be thought little; and a writer should keep himself vigilantly on his guard against the first temptations to negligence or supineness.—I had ceased to write, because respecting you I had no more to say, and respecting myself could say little good. I cannot boast of advancement, and in case of convalescence it may be said, with few exceptions, *non progredi, est regredi.* I hope I may be excepted.—My great difficulty was with my sweet Fanny,[1] who, by her artifice of inserting her letter in yours, had given me a precept of frugality which I was not at liberty to neglect; and I know not who were in town under whose cover I could send my letter. I rejoice to hear that you are so well, and have a delight particularly sympathetick in the recovery of Mrs. Burney.'

[1] The celebrated Miss Fanny Burney.

To Mr. Langton. Aug. 25. 'The kindness of your
last letter, and my omission to answer it, begins to give
you, even in my opinion, a right to recriminate, and to
charge me with forgetfulness for the absent. I will, therefore, delay no longer to give an account of myself, and
wish I could relate what would please either myself or my
friend.—On July 13, I left London, partly in hope of help
from new air and change of place, and partly excited by
the sick man's impatience of the present. I got to Lichfield
in a stage vehicle, with very little fatigue, in two days, and
had the consolation[1] to find, that since my last visit my
three old acquaintance are all dead.—July 20, I went to
Ashbourne, where I have been till now; the house in which
we live is repairing. I live in too much solitude, and am
often deeply dejected: I wish we were nearer, and rejoice
in your removal to London. A friend, at once cheerful
and serious, is a great acquisition. Let us not neglect one
another for the little time which providence allows us to
hope.—Of my health I cannot tell you, what my wishes
persuaded me to expect, that it is much improved by the
season or by remedies. I am sleepless; my legs grow weary
with a very few steps, and the water breaks its boundaries
in some degree. The asthma, however, has remitted; my
breath is still much obstructed, but is more free than it
was. Nights of watchfulness produce torpid days; I read
very little, though I am alone; for I am tempted to supply
in the day what I lost in bed. This is my history; like all
other histories, a narrative of misery. Yet am I so much
better than in the beginning of the year, that I ought to be
ashamed of complaining. I now sit and write with very
little sensibility of pain or weakness; but when I rise, I
shall find my legs betraying me. Of the money which you
mentioned, I have no immediate need; keep it, however,
for me, unless some exigence requires it. Your papers I will
shew you certainly, when you would see them; but I am
a little angry at you for not keeping minutes of your own
acceptum et expensum, and think a little time might be spared

---

[1] [Probably some word has been here omitted before *consolation;* perhaps
sad, or *miserable;* or the word *consolation* has been printed by mistake, instead
of *mortification:*—but the original letter not being now [1798] in Mr.
Langton's hands, the errour (if it be one) cannot be corrected. Malone.]

from Aristophanes, for the *res familiares*. Forgive me, for I mean well. I hope, dear Sir, that you and Lady Rothes, and all the young people, too many to enumerate, are well and happy. GOD bless you all.'

To MR. WINDHAM. August. 'The tenderness with which you have been pleased to treat me, through my long illness, neither health nor sickness can, I hope, make me forget; and you are not to suppose, that after we parted you were no longer in my mind. But what can a sick man say, but that he is sick? His thoughts are necessarily concentered in himself: he neither receives nor can give delight; his enquiries are after alleviations of pain, and his efforts are to catch some momentary comfort.—Though I am now in the neighbourhood of the Peak, you must expect no account of its wonders, of its hills, its waters, its caverns, or its mines; but I will tell you, dear Sir, what I hope you will not hear with less satisfaction, that, for about a week past, my asthma has been less afflictive.'

Lichfield, October 2. 'I believe you had been long enough acquainted with the *phænomena* of sickness, not to be surprised that a sick man wishes to be where he is not, and where it appears to every body but himself that he might easily be, without having the resolution to remove. I thought Ashbourne a solitary place, but did not come hither till last Monday.—I have here more company, but my health has for this last week not advanced; and in the languor of disease how little can be done? Whither or when I shall make my next remove, I cannot tell; but I entreat you, dear Sir, to let me know from time to time, where you may be found, for your residence is a very powerful attractive to, Sir, your most humble servant.'

'TO MR. PERKINS

'DEAR SIR,

'I cannot but flatter myself that your kindness for me will make you glad to know where I am, and in what state.

'I have been struggling very hard with my diseases. My breath has been very much obstructed, and the water has attempted to encroach upon me again. I passed the first part of the summer at Oxford, afterwards I went to

Lichfield, thence to Ashbourne, in Derbyshire, and a week ago I returned to Lichfield.

'My breath is now much easier, and the water is in a great measure run away, so that I hope to see you again before winter.

'Please make my compliments to Mrs. Perkins, and to Mr. and Mrs. Barclay. I am, dear Sir,

'Your most humble servant,

'Lichfield, Oct. 4, 1784.'   'SAM. JOHNSON'

'TO THE RIGHT HON. WILLIAM GERARD HAMILTON

'DEAR SIR,

'CONSIDERING what reason you gave me in the spring to conclude that you took part in whatever good or evil might befall me, I ought not to have omitted so long the account which I am now about to give you.—My diseases are an asthma and a dropsy, and, what is less curable, seventy-five. Of the dropsy, in the beginning of the summer, or in the spring, I recovered to a degree which struck with wonder both me and my physicians: the asthma now is likewise for a time very much relieved. I went to Oxford, where the asthma was very tyrannical, and the dropsy began again to threaten me; but seasonable physick stopped the inundation: I then returned to London, and in July took a resolution to visit Staffordshire and Derbyshire, where I am yet struggling with my disease. The dropsy made another attack, and was not easily ejected, but at last gave way. The asthma suddenly remitted in bed, on the 13th of August, and though now very oppressive, is, I think, still something gentler than it was before the remission. My limbs are miserably debilitated, and my nights are sleepless and tedious.—When you read this, dear Sir, you are not sorry that I wrote no sooner. I will not prolong my complaints. I hope still to see you *in a happier hour*, to talk over what we have often talked, and perhaps to find new topicks of merriment, or new incitements to curiosity.

'I am, dear Sir, &c.

'Lichfield, Oct. 20, 1784.'   'SAM. JOHNSON'

'TO JOHN PARADISE, ESQ.[1]

'DEAR SIR,

'THOUGH in all my summer's excursion I have given you no account of myself, I hope you think better of me than to imagine it possible for me to forget you, whose kindness to me has been too great and too constant not to have made its impression on a harder breast than mine. — Silence is not very culpable, when nothing pleasing is suppressed. It would have alleviated none of your complaints to have read my vicissitudes of evil. I have struggled hard with very formidable and obstinate maladies; and though I cannot talk of health, think all praise due to my Creator and Preserver for the continuance of my life. The dropsy has made two attacks, and has given way to medicine; the asthma is very oppressive, but that has likewise once remitted. I am very weak, and very sleepless; but it is time to conclude the tale of misery. — I hope, dear Sir, that you grow better, for you have likewise your share of human evil, and that your lady and the young charmers are well.   'I am, dear Sir, &c.

'Lichfield, Oct. 27, 1784.'   'SAM. JOHNSON'

'TO MR. GEORGE NICOL[2]

'DEAR SIR,

'SINCE we parted, I have been much oppressed by my asthma, but it has lately been less laborious. When I sit I am almost at ease, and I can walk, though yet very little, with less difficulty for this week past, than before. I hope I shall again enjoy my friends, and that you and I shall have a little more literary conversation. — Where I now am, every thing is very liberally provided for me but conversation. My friend is sick himself, and the reciprocation of complaints and groans afford not much of either

[1] Son of the late Peter Paradise, Esq. his Britannick Majesty's Consul at Salonica, in Macedonia, by his lady, a native of that country. He studied at Oxford, and has been honoured by that University with the degree of LL.D. He is distinguished not only by his learning and talents, but by an amiable disposition, gentleness of manners, and a very general acquaintance with well-informed and accomplished persons of almost all nations.

[Mr. Paradise died, December 12, 1795. MALONE.]

[2] Bookseller to his Majesty.

pleasure or instruction. What we have not at home this town does not supply, and I shall be glad of a little imported intelligence, and hope that you will bestow, now and then, a little time on the relief and entertainment of, Sir,

'Your's, &c.

'Ashbourne, Aug. 19, 1784.'   'SAM. JOHNSON'

'TO MR. CRUIKSHANK

'DEAR SIR,

'Do not suppose that I forget you; I hope I shall never be accused of forgetting my benefactors. I had, till lately, nothing to write but complaints upon complaints, of miseries upon miseries; but within this fortnight I have received great relief.—Have your Lectures any vacation? If you are released from the necessity of daily study, you may find time for a letter to me.—[In this letter he states the particulars of his case.]—In return for this account of my health let me have a good account of yours, and of your prosperity in all your undertakings.

'I am, dear Sir, yours, &c.

'Ashbourne, Sept. 4, 1784.'   'SAM. JOHNSON'

TO MR. THOMAS DAVIES. August 14.—'The tenderness with which you always treat me, makes me culpable in my own eyes for having omitted to write in so long a separation; I had, indeed, nothing to say that you could wish to hear. All has been hitherto misery accumulated upon misery, disease corroborating disease, till yesterday my asthma was perceptibly and unexpectedly mitigated. I am much comforted with this short relief, and am willing to flatter myself that it may continue and improve. I have at present, such a degree of ease, as not only may admit the comforts, but the duties of life. Make my compliments to Mrs. Davies.—Poor dear Allen, he was a good man.'

TO SIR JOSHUA REYNOLDS. Ashbourne, July 21. 'The tenderness with which I am treated by my friends, makes it reasonable to suppose that they are desirous to know the state of my health, and a desire so benevolent ought to be gratified. —I came to Lichfield in two days without any painful fatigue, and on Monday came hither, where I purpose to stay and try what air and regularity will effect. I cannot yet persuade myself that I have made much progress in recovery. My sleep is little, my breath is very much encumbered, and my legs are very weak. The water has encreased a little, but has again run off. The most distressing symptom is want of sleep.'

August 19. 'Having had since our separation, little to say that could please you or myself by saying, I have not been lavish of useless letters; but I flatter myself that you will partake of the pleasure with which I can now tell you that about a week ago, I felt suddenly a sensible remission of my asthma, and consequently a greater lightness of action and motion. —Of this grateful alleviation I know not the cause, nor dare depend upon its continuance; but while it lasts I endeavour to enjoy it, and am desirous of communicating, while it lasts, my pleasure to my friends. —Hitherto, dear Sir, I had written before the post, which stays in this town but a little while, brought me your letter. Mr. Davies seems to have represented my little tendency to recovery in terms too splendid. I am still restless, still weak, still watery, but the asthma is less oppressive. —Poor Ramsay![1] On which side soever I turn, mortality presents its formidable frown. I left three old friends at Lichfield, when I was last there, and now found them all dead. I no sooner lost sight of dear Allan, than I am told that I shall see him no more. That we must all die, we always knew; I wish I had sooner remembered it. Do not think me intrusive or importunate, if I now call, dear Sir, on you to remember it.'

Sept. 2. 'I am glad that a little favour from the court has intercepted your furious purposes. I could not in any case have approved such publick violence of resentment, and should have considered any who encouraged it, as rather seeking sport for themselves, than honour for you. Resentment gratifies him who intended an injury, and pains him unjustly who did not intend it. But all this is now superfluous. —I still continue by GOD's mercy to mend. My

a *I think he died at Dover, on his way home from a Journey in Search of Health.* [H]

[1] Allan Ramsay, Esq. painter to his Majesty, who died August 10, 1784, in the 71st year of his age, much regretted by his friends.[a]

breath is easier, my nights are quieter, and my legs are less in bulk, and stronger in use. I have, however, yet a great deal to overcome, before I can yet attain even an old man's health.—Write, do write to me now and then; we are now old acquaintance, and perhaps few people have lived so much and so long together, with less cause of complaint on either side. The retrospection of this is very pleasant, and I hope we shall never think on each other with less kindness.'

Sept. 9. 'I could not answer your letter before this day, because I went on the sixth to Chatsworth, and did not come back till the post was gone.—Many words, I hope, are not necessary between you and me to convince you what gratitude is excited in my heart, by the Chancellor's liberality and your kind offices. I did not indeed expect that what was asked by the Chancellor would have been refused, but since it has, we will not tell that any thing has been asked.—I have enclosed a letter to the Chancellor, which when you have read it, you will be pleased to seal with a head, or other general seal, and convey it to him; had I sent it directly to him, I should have seemed to overlook the favour of your intervention.—My last letter told you of my advance in health, which, I think, in the whole still continues. Of the hydropick tumour there is now very little appearance; the asthma is much less troublesome, and seems to remit something day after day. I do not despair of supporting an English winter.—At Chatsworth, I met young Mr. Burke, who led me very commodiously into conversation with the Duke and Duchess. We had a very good morning. The dinner was publick.'

Sept. 18. 'I flattered myself that this week would have given me a letter from you, but none has come. Write to me now and then, but direct your next to Lichfield.—I think, and I hope am sure, that I still grow better; I have sometimes good nights; but am still in my legs weak, but so much mended, that I go to Lichfield in hope of being able to pay my visits on foot, for there are no coaches.—I have three letters this day, all about the balloon; I could have been content with one. Do not write about the balloon, whatever else you may think proper to say.'

October 2. 'I am always proud of your approbation, and therefore was much pleased that you liked my letter. When you copied it, you invaded the Chancellor's right rather than mine.—The refusal I did not expect, but I had never thought much about it, for I doubted whether the Chancellor had so much tenderness for me as to ask. He, being keeper of the King's conscience, ought not to be supposed capable of an improper petition.—All is not gold that glitters, as we have often been told; and the adage is verified in your place and my favour; but if what happens does not make us richer, we must bid it welcome, if it makes us wiser.—I do not at present grow better, nor much worse; my hopes, however, are somewhat abated, and a very great loss is the loss of hope, but I struggle on as I can.'

To Mr. John Nichols. Lichfield, Oct. 20. 'When you were here, you were pleased, as I am told, to think my absence an inconvenience. I should certainly have been very glad to give so skilful a lover of antiquities any information about my native place, of which, however, I know not much, and have reason to believe that not much is known.—Though I have not given you any amusement, I have received amusement from you. At Ashbourne, where I had very little company, I had the luck to borrow "Mr. Bowyer's Life;" a book so full of contemporary history, that a literary man must find some of his old friends. I thought that I could, now and then, have told you some hints worth your notice; and perhaps we may talk a life over. I hope we shall be much together; you must now be to me what you were before, and what dear Mr. Allen was, besides. He was taken unexpectedly away, but I think he was a very good man.—I have made little progress in recovery. I am very weak, and very sleepless: but I live on and hope.'

This various mass of correspondence, which I have thus brought together, is valuable, both as an addition to the store which the publick already has of Johnson's writings, and as exhibiting a genuine and noble specimen of vigour and vivacity of mind, which neither age nor sickness could impair or diminish.

It may be observed, that his writing in every way, whether for the publick, or privately to his friends, was by fits and starts; for we see frequently, that many letters are written on the same day. When he had once overcome his aversion to begin, he was, I suppose, desirous to go on, in order to relieve his mind from the uneasy reflection of delaying what he ought to do.

While in the country, notwithstanding the accumulation of illness which he endured, his mind did not lose its powers. He translated an Ode of Horace, which is printed in his works, and composed several prayers. I shall insert one of them, which is so wise and energetick, so philosophical and so pious, that I doubt not of its affording consolation to many a sincere Christian, when in a state of mind to which I believe the best are sometimes liable.[1]

And here I am enabled fully to refute a very unjust reflection, by Sir John Hawkins, both against Dr. Johnson, and his faithful servant, Mr. Francis Barber; as if both of them had been guilty of culpable neglect towards a person of the name of Heely, whom Sir John chooses to call a *relation* of Dr. Johnson's. The fact is, that Mr. Heely was not his relation; he had indeed been married to one of his cousins, but she had died without having children, and he had married another woman; so that even the slight connection which there once had been by *alliance* was dissolved. Dr. Johnson, who had shewn very great liberality to this man while his first wife was alive, as has appeared in a former part of this work,[2] was humane and charitable enough to continue his bounty to him

---

[1] *Against inquisitive and perplexing thoughts.* 'O LORD, my Maker and Protector, who hast graciously sent me into this world to work out my salvation, enable me to drive from me all such unquiet and perplexing thoughts as may mislead or hinder me in the practice of those duties which Thou hast required. When I behold the works of thy hands, and consider the course of thy providence, give me grace always to remember that thy thoughts are not my thoughts, nor thy ways my ways. And while it shall please Thee to continue me in this world, where much is to be done, and little to be known, teach me by thy Holy Spirit, to withdraw my mind from unprofitable and dangerous enquiries, from difficulties vainly curious, and doubts impossible to be solved. Let me rejoice in the light which Thou hast imparted, let me serve Thee with active zeal and humble confidence, and wait with patient expectation for the time in which the soul which Thou receivest shall be satisfied with knowledge. Grant this, O LORD, for JESUS CHRIST's sake. Amen.'

[2] Vol. i. p. 380.

occasionally; but surely there was no strong call of duty upon him or upon his legatee, to do more. The following letter, obligingly communicated to me by Mr. Andrew Strahan, will confirm what I have stated:

'TO MR. HEELY, NO. 5, IN PYE-STREET,
WESTMINSTER

'SIR,

'As necessity obliges you to call so soon again upon me, you should at least have told the smallest sum that will supply your present want; you cannot suppose that I have much to spare. Two guineas is as much as you ought to be behind with your creditor.—If you wait on Mr. Strahan, in New-street, Fetter-lane, or in his absence, on Mr. Andrew Strahan, show this, by which they are entreated to advance you two guineas, and to keep this as a voucher.

       'I am, Sir,

        'Your humble servant,

'Ashbourne, Aug. 12, 1784.'   'SAM. JOHNSON'

Indeed it is very necessary to keep in mind that Sir John Hawkins has unaccountably viewed Johnson's character and conduct in almost every particular, with an unhappy prejudice.[1] [a]

a So he did every body's. [H]

We now behold Johnson for the last time, in his native city, for which he ever retained a warm affection, and

[1] I shall add one instance only to those which I have thought it incumbent on me to point out. Talking of Mr. Garrick's having signified his willingness to let Johnson have the loan of any of his books to assist him in his edition of Shakspeare; Sir John says (page 444,) 'Mr. Garrick knew not what risque he ran by this offer. Johnson had so strange a forgetfulness of obligations of this sort, that few who lent him books ever saw them again.' This surely conveys a most unfavourable insinuation, and has been so understood. Sir John mentions the single case of a curious edition of Politian, which he tells us, appeared to belong to Pembroke College, and which, probably, had been considered by Johnson as his own, for upwards of fifty years. Would it not be fairer to consider this as an inadvertence, and draw no general inference? The truth is, that Johnson was so attentive, that in one of his manuscripts in my possession, he has marked in two columns, books borrowed, and books lent.

In Sir John Hawkins's compilation, there are, however, some passages concerning Johnson which have unquestionable merit. One of them I shall transcribe, in justice to a writer whom I have had too much occasion to censure, and to shew my fairness as the biographer of my illustrious friend: 'There was wanting in his conduct and behaviour, that dignity which results from a regular and orderly course of action, and by an irresistible power commands esteem. He could not be said to be a stayed man, nor so to have

which, by a sudden apostrophe, under the word *Lich*, he introduces with reverence, into his immortal work, THE ENGLISH DICTIONARY:—*Salve, magna parens!*[1] While here, he felt a revival of all the tenderness of filial affection, an instance of which appeared in his ordering the gravestone and inscription over Elizabeth Blaney[2] to be substantially and carefully renewed.

To Mr. Henry White, a young clergyman, with whom he now formed an intimacy, so as to talk to him with great freedom, he mentioned that he could not in general accuse himself of having been an undutiful son. 'Once, indeed, (said he,) I was disobedient; I refused to attend my father to Uttoxeter-market. Pride was the source of that refusal, and the remembrance of it was painful. A few years ago I desired to atone for this fault. I went to Uttoxeter in very bad weather, and stood for a considerable time bareheaded in the rain, on the spot where my father's stall used to stand. In contrition I stood, and I hope the penance was expiatory.'[a]

[a] very *like a Romanist; but we must all go to the old Shop for* something. [H]

'I told him (says Miss Seward) in one of my latest visits to him, of a wonderful learned pig, which I had seen at Nottingham; and which did all that we have observed exhibited by dogs and horses. The subject amused him. "Then, (said he,) the pigs are a race unjustly calumniated.

adjusted in his mind the balance of reason and passion, as to give occasion to say what may be observed of some men, that all they do is just, fit, and right.' Yet a judicious friend well suggests, 'It might, however, have been added, that such men are often merely just, and rigidly correct, while their hearts are cold and unfeeling; and that Johnson's virtues were of a much higher tone than those of the *stayed, orderly man*, here described.'

[1] The following circumstance, mutually to the honour of Johnson and the Corporation of his native city, has been communicated to me by the reverend Dr. Vyse, from the Town-Clerk: 'Mr. Simpson has now before him, a record of the respect and veneration which the Corporation of Lichfield, in the year 1767, had for the merits and learning of Dr. Johnson. His father built the corner house in the market-place, the two fronts of which, towards Market and Broad-market street, stood upon waste land of the Corporation, under a forty years' lease, which was then expired. On the 15th of August, 1767, at a common-hall of the bailiffs and citizens, it was ordered (and that without any solicitation,) that a lease should be granted to Samuel Johnson, Doctor of Laws, of the encroachments at his house, for the term of ninety-nine years, at the old rent, which was five shillings. Of which, as Town-Clerk, Mr. Simpson had the honour and pleasure of informing him, and that he was desired to accept it, without paying any fine on the occasion, which lease was afterwards granted, and the Doctor died possessed of this property.'

[2] See vol. i. p. 10.

Pig has, it seems, not been wanting to *man*, but *man* to *pig*. We do not allow *time* for his education, we kill him at a year old." Mr. Henry White, who was present, observed that if this instance had happened in or before Pope's time, he would not have been justified in instancing the swine as the lowest degree of groveling instinct. Dr. Johnson seemed pleased with the observation, while the person who made it proceeded to remark, that great torture must have been employed, ere the indocility of the animal could have been subdued.—"Certainly, (said the Doctor;) but, (turning to me) how old is your pig?" I told him, three years old. "Then (said he,) the pig has no cause to complain; he would have been killed the first year if he had not been *educated*, and protracted existence is a good recompence for very considerable degrees of torture." '

As Johnson had now very faint hopes of recovery, and as Mrs. Thrale was no longer devoted to him, it might have been supposed that he would naturally have chosen to remain in the comfortable house of his beloved wife's daughter, and end his life where he began it. But there was in him an animated and lofty spirit,[1] and however complicated diseases might depress ordinary mortals, all who saw him beheld and acknowledged the *invictum animum Catonis*.[2] Such was his intellectual ardour even at this time, that he said to one friend, 'Sir, I look upon every day to be lost, in which I do not make a new acquaintance;' and to another, when talking of his illness, 'I will be conquered; I will not capitulate.' And such was his love of London, so high a relish had he of its magnificent extent, and variety of intellectual entertainment, that he languished when absent from it, his mind having become quite luxurious from the long habit of enjoying the metropolis; and, therefore, although at Lichfield, surrounded with friends who

---

[1] Mr. Burke suggested to me as applicable to Johnson, what Cicero, in his CATO MAJOR, says of *Appius*: '*Intentum enim animum, tanquam arcum, habebat, nec languescens succumbebat senectuti;*' repeating at the same time the following noble words in the same passage: '*Ita enim senectus honesta est, si se ipsa defendit, si jus suum retinet, si nemini emancipata est, si usque ad extremum vitæ spiritum vindicet jus suum.*'

[2] [*Atrocem* animum Catonis, are Horace's words, and it may be doubted whether *atrox* is used by any other original writer in the same sense. *Stubborn* is perhaps the most correct translation of this epithet.[a] MALONE.]

[a] *Stubborn is expressive of passive, Atrox of active Quality—but I can find no better Word for it than dear Mr. Malone's; which however I do not like— would Stern do? 1820.* [H]

loved and revered him, and for whom he had a very sincere affection, he still found that such conversation as London affords, could be found nowhere else. These feelings, joined, probably, to some flattering hopes of aid from the eminent physicians and surgeons in London, who kindly and generously attended him without accepting fees, made him resolve to return to the capital.

From Lichfield he came to Birmingham, where he passed a few days with his worthy old schoolfellow, Mr. Hector, who thus writes to me: 'He was very solicitous with me to recollect some of our most early transactions, and transmit them to him, for I perceived nothing gave him greater pleasure than calling to mind those days of our innocence. I complied with his request, and he only received them a few days before his death. I have transcribed for your inspection, exactly the minutes I wrote to him.' This paper having been found in his repositories after his death, Sir John Hawkins has inserted it entire, and I have made occasional use of it and other communications from Mr. Hector,[1] in the course of this Work. I have both visited and corresponded with him since Dr. Johnson's death, and by my enquiries concerning a great variety of particulars have obtained additional information. I followed the same mode with the Reverend Dr. Taylor, in whose presence I wrote down a good deal of what he could tell; and he, at my request, signed his name to give it authenticity. It is very rare to find any person who is able to give a distinct account of the life even of one whom he has known intimately, without questions being put to them. My friend Dr. Kippis has told me, that on this account it is a practice with him to draw out a biographical catechism.

[1] It is a most agreeable circumstance attending the publication of this Work, that Mr. Hector has survived his illustrious school-fellow so many years; that he still retains his health and spirits; and has gratified me with the following acknowledgement: 'I thank you, most sincerely thank you, for the great and long continued entertainment your Life of Dr. Johnson has afforded me, and others, of my particular friends.' Mr. Hector, besides setting me right as to the verses on a sprig of Myrtle, (see vol. i. p. 50, note,) has favoured me with two English odes, written by Dr. Johnson, at an early period of his life, which will appear in my edition of his Poems.

[This early and worthy friend of Johnson died at Birmingham, September 2, 1794. MALONE.]

Johnson then proceeded to Oxford, where he was again kindly received by Dr. Adams,[1] who was pleased to give me the following account in one of his letters, (Feb. 17th, 1785:) 'His last visit was, I believe, to my house, which he left, after a stay of four or five days. We had much serious talk together, for which I ought to be the better as long as I live. You will remember some discourse which we had in the summer upon the subject of prayer, and the difficulty of this sort of composition. He reminded me of this, and of my having wished him to try his hand, and to give us a specimen of the style and manner that he approved. He added that he was now in a right frame of mind, and as he could not possibly employ his time better, he would in earnest set about it. But I find upon enquiry, that no papers of this sort were left behind him, except a few short ejaculatory forms suitable to his present situation.'

Dr. Adams had not then received accurate information

[1] [This amiable and excellent man survived Dr. Johnson about four years, having died in January 1789, at Gloucester, where a Monument is erected to his memory, with the following inscription:—

Sacred to the Memory of

WILLIAM ADAMS, D.D.

Master of Pembroke College, Oxford,
Prebendary of this Cathedral, and
Archdeacon of Landaff.

Ingenious, Learned, Eloquent,
He ably defended the Truth of Christianity;
Pious, Benevolent, and Charitable,
He successfully inculcated its sacred Precepts.
Pure, and undeviating in his own Conduct,
He was tender and compassionate to the Failings of others,
Ever anxious for the welfare and happiness of Mankind,
He was on all occasions forward to encourage
Works of public Utility, and extensive Beneficence.
In the Government of the College over which he presided,
His vigilant Attention was uniformly exerted
To promote the important Objects of the institution:
Whilst the mild Dignity of his Deportment,
His gentleness of Disposition, and urbanity of Manners,
Inspired Esteem, Gratitude, and Affection.

Full of Days, and matured in Virtue,
He died Jan. 13th, 1789, aged 82.

A very just character of Dr. Adams may also be found in 'The Gentleman's Magazine,' for 1789, Vol. LIX. p. 214. His only daughter (see p. 355,) was married in July 1788, to B. Hyatt, of Painswick in Gloucestershire. Esq. MALONE.]

on this subject; for it has since appeared that various
prayers had been composed by him at different periods,
which intermingled with pious resolutions, and some short
notes of his life, were entitled by him 'Prayers and Meditations,' and have, in pursuance of his earnest requisition,
in the hopes of doing good, been published, with a judicious well-written Preface, by the reverend Mr. Strahan,
to whom he delivered them. This admirable collection, to
which I have frequently referred in the course of this Work,
evinces, beyond all his compositions for the publick, and
all the eulogies of his friends and admirers, the sincere
virtue and piety of Johnson. It proves with unquestionable
authenticity, that amidst all his constitutional infirmities,
his earnestness to conform his practice to the precepts
of Christianity was unceasing, and that he habitually
endeavoured to refer every transaction of his life to the
will of the Supreme Being.

He arrived in London on the 16th of November, and
next day sent to Dr. Burney the following note, which I
insert as the last token of his remembrance of that ingenious and amiable man, and as another of the many proofs
of the tenderness and benignity of his heart:

'MR. JOHNSON, who came home last night, sends
his respects to dear Dr. Burney, and all the dear Burneys,
little and great.'

'TO MR. HECTOR, IN BIRMINGHAM

'DEAR SIR,

'I DID not reach Oxford until Friday morning, and
then I sent Francis to see the balloon fly, but could not go
myself. I staid at Oxford till Tuesday, and then came in
the common vehicle easily to London. I am as I was, and
having seen Dr. Brocklesby, am to ply the squills; but,
whatever be their efficacy, this world must soon pass away.
Let us think seriously on our duty.—I send my kindest
respects to dear Mrs. Careless: let me have the prayers of
both. We have all lived long, and must soon part. GOD
have mercy on us, for the sake of our LORD JESUS
CHRIST. Amen.   'I am, &c.

'London, Nov. 17, 1784.'   'SAM. JOHNSON'

His correspondence with me, after his letter on the subject of my settling in London, shall now, so far as is proper,
be produced in one series.

July 26, he wrote to me from Ashbourne: 'On the 14th
I came to Lichfield, and found every body glad enough to
see me. On the 20th, I came hither, and found a house
half-built, of very uncomfortable appearance; but my own
room has not been altered. That a man worn with diseases,
in his seventy-second or third year, should condemn part
of his remaining life to pass among ruins and rubbish, and
that no inconsiderable part, appears to me very strange. —
I know that your kindness makes you impatient to know
the state of my health, in which I cannot boast of much
improvement. I came through the journey without much
inconvenience, but when I attempt self-motion I find my
legs weak, and my breath very short; this day I have been
much disordered. I have no company; the Doctor[1] is
busy in his fields, and goes to bed at nine, and his whole
system is so different from mine, that we seem formed for
different elements; I have, therefore, all my amusement to
seek within myself.'

Having written to him in bad spirits, a letter filled with
dejection and fretfulness, and at the same time expressing
anxious apprehensions concerning him, on account of a
dream which had disturbed me; his answer was chiefly
in terms of reproach, for a supposed charge of 'affecting
discontent, and indulging the vanity of complaint.' It,
however, proceeded, 'Write to me often, and write like a
man. I consider your fidelity and tenderness as a great
part of the comforts which are yet left me, and sincerely
wish we could be nearer to each other. — * * * * * * *.
My dear friend, life is very short, and very uncertain; let
us spend it as well as we can. My worthy neighbour, Allen,
is dead. Love me as well as you can. Pay my respects to
dear Mrs. Boswell. — Nothing ailed me at that time; let
your superstition at last have an end.'

Feeling very soon, that the manner in which he had
written might hurt me, he two days afterwards, July 28,
wrote to me again, giving me an account of his sufferings;
after which, he thus proceeds: 'Before this letter, you will

[1] The Rev. Dr. Taylor.

have had one which I hope you will not take amiss; for it contains only truth, and that truth kindly intended. * * * * * * *. *Spartam quam nactus es orna;* make the most and best of your lot, and compare yourself not with the few that are above you, but with the multitudes which are below you. * * * * * *. Go steadily forwards with lawful business or honest diversions. "*Be,* (as Temple says of the Dutchmen,) *well when you are not ill, and pleased when you are not angry.*"—* * * * * *. This may seem but an ill return for your tenderness; but I mean it well, for I love you with great ardour and sincerity. Pay my respects to dear Mrs. Boswell, and teach the young ones to love me.'

I unfortunately was so much indisposed during a considerable part of the year, that it was not, or at least I thought it was not, in my power to write to my illustrious friend as formerly, or without expressing such complaints as offended him. Having conjured him not to do me the injustice of charging me with affectation, I was with much regret long silent. His last letter to me then came, and affected me very tenderly:

'TO JAMES BOSWELL, ESQ.

'DEAR SIR,

'I HAVE this summer sometimes amended, and sometimes relapsed, but, upon the whole, have lost ground very much. My legs are extremely weak, and my breath very short, and the water is now encreasing upon me. In this uncomfortable state your letters used to relieve; what is the reason that I have them no longer? Are you sick, or are you sullen? Whatever be the reason, if it be less than necessity, drive it away; and of the short life that we have, make the best use for yourself and for your friends. * * * * * *. I am sometimes afraid that your omission to write has some real cause, and shall be glad to know that you are not sick, and that nothing ill has befallen dear Mrs. Boswell, or any of your family.

'I am, Sir, your, &c.

'Lichfield, Nov. 5, 1784.'   'SAM. JOHNSON'

Yet it was not a little painful to me to find, that in a paragraph of this letter, which I have omitted, he still

persevered in arraigning me as before, which was strange
in him who had so much experience of what I suffered.
I, however, wrote to him two as kind letters as I could; the
last of which came too late to be read by him, for his illness
encreased more rapidly upon him than I had apprehended; but I had the consolation of being informed that he
spoke of me on his death-bed with affection, and I look
forward with humble hope of renewing our friendship in
a better world.

I now relieve the readers of this Work from any farther
personal notice of its authour; who, if he should be
thought to have obtruded himself too much upon their
attention, requests them to consider the peculiar plan of
his biographical undertaking.

Soon after Johnson's return to the metropolis, both the
asthma and dropsy became more violent and distressful.
He had for some time kept a journal in Latin of the state
of his illness, and the remedies which he used, under the
title of *Ægri Ephemeris*, which he began on the 6th of July,
but continued it no longer than the 8th of November;
finding, I suppose, that it was a mournful and unavailing
register. It is in my possession: and is written with great
care and accuracy.

Still his love of literature[1] did not fail. A very few days

[1] It is truly wonderful to consider the extent and constancy of Johnson's
literary ardour, notwithstanding the melancholy which clouded and em-
bittered his existence. Besides the numerous and various works which he
executed, he had, at different times, formed schemes of a great many more,
of which the following catalogue was given by him to Mr. Langton, and by
that gentleman presented to his Majesty:

'DIVINITY

'A small book of precepts and directions for piety; the hint taken from
the directions in Morton's exercise.

'PHILOSOPHY, HISTORY, and LITERATURE in general.

'History of Criticism, as it relates to judging of authours, from Aristotle to
the present age. An account of the rise and improvements of that art: of the
different opinions of authours, ancient and modern.

'Translation of the History of Herodian.

'New edition of Fairfax's Translation of Tasso, with notes, glossary, &c.

'Chaucer, a new edition of him, from manuscripts and old editions, with
various readings, conjectures, remarks on his language, and the changes it
had undergone from the earliest times to his age, and from his to the present;
with notes explanatory of customs, &c. and references to Boccace, and other
authours, from whom he has borrowed, with an account of the liberties he

before his death he transmitted to his friend Mr. John
Nichols, a list of the authors of the Universal History,

has taken in telling the stories; his life, and an exact etymological glossary.
'Aristotle's Rhetorick, a translation of it into English.
'A collection of Letters, translated from the modern writers, with some
account of the several authours.
'Oldham's Poems, with notes, historical and critical.
'Roscommon's Poems, with notes.
'Lives of the Philosophers, written with a polite air, in such a manner as
may divert as well as instruct.
'History of the Heathen Mythology, with an explication of the fables,
both allegorical and historical; with references to the poets.
'History of the State of Venice, in a compendious manner.
'Aristotle's Ethics, an English translation of them, with notes.
'Geographical Dictionary, from the French.
'Hierocles upon Pythagoras, translated into English, perhaps with notes.
This is done by Norris.
'A book of Letters, upon all kinds of subjects.
'Claudian, a new edition of his works, *cum notis variorum*, in the manner of
Burman.
'Tully's Tusculan Questions, a translation of them.
'Tully's De Naturâ Deorum, a translation of those books.
'Benzo's New History of the New World, to be translated.
'Machiavel's History of Florence, to be translated.
'History of the Revival of Learning in Europe, containing an account of
whatever contributed to the restoration of literature; such as controversies,
printing, the destruction of the Greek empire, the encouragement of great
men, with the lives of the most eminent patrons, and most eminent early
professors of all kinds of learning in different countries.
'A Body of Chronology, in verse, with historical notes.
'A Table of the Spectators, Tatlers, and Guardians, distinguished by
figures into six degrees of value, with notes, giving the reasons of preference
or degradation.
'A Collection of Letters from English authours, with a preface giving some
account of the writers; with reasons for selection, and criticism upon styles;
remarks on each letter, if needful.
'A Collection of Proverbs from various languages. Jan. 6,—53.
'A Dictionary to the Common Prayer, in imitation of Calmet's Dictionary
of the Bible. March,—52.
'A Collection of Stories and Examples, like those of Valerius Maximus.
Jan. 10,—53.
'From Ælian, a volume of select Stories, perhaps from others. Jan. 28,—53.
'Collection of Travels, Voyages, Adventures, and Descriptions of
Countries.
'Dictionary of Ancient History and Mythology.
'Treatise on the Study of Polite Literature, containing the history of
learning, directions for editions, commentaries, &c.
'Maxims, Characters, and Sentiments, after the manner of Bruyère,
collected out of ancient authours, particularly the Greek, with Apophthegms.
'Classical Miscellanies, Select Translations from ancient Greek and Latin
authours.
'Lives of Illustrious Persons, as well of the active as the learned, in
imitation of Plutarch.

mentioning their several shares in that work. It has, according to his direction, been deposited in the British

'Judgement of the learned upon English authours.
'Poetical Dictionary of the English tongue.
'Considerations upon the present state of London.
'Collection of Epigrams, with notes and observations.
'Observations on the English language, relating to words, phrases, and modes of Speech.
'Minutiæ Literariæ, Miscellaneous reflections, criticisms, emendations, notes.
'History of the Constitution.
'Comparison of Philosophical and Christian Morality, by sentences collected from the moralists and fathers.
'Plutarch's Lives, in English, with notes.

'POETRY and works of IMAGINATION

'Hymn to Ignorance.
'The Palace of Sloth,—a vision.
'Coluthus, to be translated.
'Prejudice,—a poetical essay.
'The Palace of Nonsense,—a vision.'

Johnson's extraordinary facility of composition, when he shook off his constitutional indolence, and resolutely sat down to write, is admirably described by Mr. Courtenay, in his 'Poetical Review,' which I have several times quoted:

> 'While through life's maze he sent a piercing view,
> His mind expansive to the object grew.
> With various stores of erudition fraught,
> The lively image, the deep-searching thought,
> Slept in repose ;—but when the moment press'd,
> The bright ideas stood at once confess'd;
> Instant his genius sped its vigorous rays,
> And o'er the letter'd world diffus'd a blaze:
> As womb'd with fire the cloud electrick flies,
> And calmly o'er th' horizon seems to rise:
> Touch'd by the pointed steel, the lightning flows,
> And all th' expanse with rich effulgence glows.'

We shall in vain endeavour to know with exact precision every production of Johnson's pen. He owned to me that he had written about forty sermons: but as I understood that he had given or sold them to different persons, who were to preach them as their own, he did not consider himself at liberty to acknowledge them. Would those who were thus aided by him, who are still alive, and the friends of those who are dead, fairly inform the world, it would be obligingly gratifying a reasonable curiosity, to which there should, I think, now be no objection. Two volumes of them, published since his death, are sufficiently ascertained: see vol. ii. p. 405. I have before me, in his hand-writing, a fragment of twenty quarto leaves, of a translation into English of Sallust, *De Bello Catilinario*. When it was done I have no notion; but it seems to have no very superiour merit to mark it as his. Besides the publications heretofore mentioned, I am satisfied, from internal evidence, to admit also as genuine the following, which, notwithstanding all my chronological care, escaped me in the course of this Work:

Museum, and is printed in the Gentleman's Magazine for December, 1784.[1]

During his sleepless nights he amused himself by translating into Latin verse, from the Greek, many of the epigrams in the *Anthologia*. These translations, with some other poems by him in Latin, he gave to his friend Mr. Langton,

'Considerations on the Case of Dr. Trapp's Sermons,'† published in 1739, in the Gentleman's Magazine. It is a very ingenious defence of the right of *abridging* an authour's work, without being held as infringing his property. This is one of the nicest questions in the *Law of Literature;* and I cannot help thinking, that the indulgence of abridging is often exceedingly injurious to authours and booksellers, and should in very few cases be permitted. At any rate, to prevent difficult and uncertain discussion, and give an absolute security to authours in the property of their labours, no abridgement whatever should be permitted, till after the expiration of such a number of years as the Legislature may be pleased to fix.

But, though it has been confidently ascribed to him, I cannot allow that he wrote a Dedication to both Houses of Parliament of a book entitled 'The Evangelical History Harmonized.' He was no *croaker;* no declaimer against *the times.* He would not have written, 'That we are fallen upon an age in which corruption is not barely universal, is universally confessed.'[a] Nor, 'Rapine preys on the publick without opposition, and perjury betrays it without inquiry.' Nor would he, to excite a speedy reformation, have conjured up such phantoms of terrour as these: 'A few years longer, and perhaps all endeavours will be in vain. We may be swallowed by an earthquake; we may be delivered to our enemies.' This is not Johnsonian.[b]

[a] *I think he* would. [H]

[b] *no more it is.* [H]

There are, indeed, in this Dedication several sentences constructed upon the model of those of Johnson. But the imitation of the form, without the spirit of his style, has been so general, that this of itself is not sufficient evidence. Even our news-paper writers aspire to it. In an account of the funeral of Edwin, the comedian, in ''The Diary' of Nov. 9, 1790, that son of drollery is thus described: 'A man who had so often cheered the sullenness of vacancy, and suspended the approaches of sorrow.'[c] And in 'The Dublin Evening Post,' August 16, 1791, there is the following paragraph: 'It is a singular circumstance, that in a city like this, containing 200,000 people, there are three months in the year during which no place of public amusement is open. Long vacation is here a vacation from pleasure, as well as business; nor is there any mode of passing the listless evenings of declining summer, but in the riots of a tavern, or the stupidity of a coffee-house.'

[c] *very pretty.* [H]

I have not thought it necessary to specify every copy of verses written by Johnson, it being my intention to publish an authentick edition of all his Poetry, with notes.

[1] [As the letter accompanying this list, (which fully supports the observation in the text,) was written but a week before Dr. Johnson's death, the reader may not be displeased to find it here preserved:

'TO MR. NICHOLS

'The late learned Mr. Swinton, having one day remarked that one man, meaning, I suppose, no man but himself, could assign all the parts of the Ancient Universal History to their proper authours, at the request of Sir Robert Chambers, or of myself, gave the account which I now transmit to you in his own hand; being willing that of so great a work the history should

who, having added a few notes, sold them to the book-sellers for a small sum to be given to some of Johnson's relations, which was accordingly done; and they are printed in the collection of his works.

A very erroneous notion has circulated as to Johnson's deficiency in the knowledge of the Greek language, partly owing to the modesty with which, from knowing how much there was to be learnt, he used to mention his own comparative acquisitions. When Mr. Cumberland[1] talked to him of the Greek fragments which are so well illustrated in 'The Observer,' and of the Greek dramatists in general, he candidly acknowledged his insufficiency in that particular branch of Greek literature. Yet it may be said, that though

be known, and that each writer should receive his due proportion of praise from posterity.

'I recommend to you to preserve this scrap of literary intelligence in Mr. Swinton's own hand, or to deposit it in the Museum, that the veracity of this account may never be doubted.   'I am, Sir,

'Your most humble servant,

'Dec. 6, 1784.'   'SAM. JOHNSON'

Mr. S———n.

The History of the Carthaginians.
——————— Numidians.
——————— Mauritanians.
——————— Gætulians.
——————— Garamanthes.
——————— Melano Gætulians.
——————— Nigritæ.
——————— Cyrenaica.
——————— Marmarica.
——————— the Regio Syrtica.
——————— Turks, Tartars, and Moguls.
——————— Indians.
——————— Chinese.
Dissertation on the peopling of America.
——————— independency of the Arabs.—
The Cosmogony, and a small part of the History immediately following; by Mr. Sale.
To the birth of Abraham; chiefly by Mr. Shelvock.
History of the Jews, Gauls, and Spaniards; by Mr. Psalmanazar.
Xenophon's Retreat; by the same.
History of the Persians and the Constantinopolitan Empire; by Dr. Campbell.
History of the Romans; by Mr. Bower.]

[1] Mr. Cumberland assures me, that he was always treated with great courtesy by Dr. Johnson, who, in his 'Letters to Mrs. Thrale,' vol. ii. p. 68, thus speaks of that learned, ingenious, and accomplished gentleman: 'The want of company is an inconvenience, but Mr. Cumberland is a million.'

not a great, he was a good Greek scholar. Dr. Charles Burney, the younger, who is universally acknowledged by the best judges, to be one of the few men of this age who are very eminent for their skill in that noble language, has assured me, that Johnson could give a Greek word for almost every English one; and that although not sufficiently conversant in the niceties of the language, he, upon some occasions discovered, even in these, a considerable degree of critical acumen. Mr. Dalzel, Professor of Greek at Edinburgh, whose skill in it is unquestionable, mentioned to me, in very liberal terms, the impression which was made upon him by Johnson, in a conversation which they had in London concerning that language. As Johnson, therefore, was undoubtedly one of the first Latin scholars in modern times, let us not deny to his fame some additional splendour from Greek.[a]

I shall now fulfil my promise of exhibiting specimens of various sorts of imitation of Johnson's style.

In the 'Transactions of the Royal Irish Academy, 1787,' there is an 'Essay on the Style of Dr. Samuel Johnson,' by the Reverend Robert Burrowes, whose respect for the great object of his criticism[1] is thus evinced in the concluding paragraph: 'I have singled him out from the whole body of English writers, because his universally-acknowledged beauties would be most apt to induce imitation; and I have treated rather on his faults, than his perfections, because an essay might comprize all the observations I could make upon his faults, while volumes would not be sufficient for a treatise on his perfections.'

MR. BURROWES has analysed the composition of Johnson, and pointed out its peculiarities with much acuteness; and I would recommend a careful perusal of his Essay to those, who being captivated by the union of perspicuity and splendour which the writings of Johnson contain, without having a sufficient portion of his vigour of mind, may be in danger of becoming bad copyists of his manner. I, however, cannot but observe, and I observe

[a] *He was one of the first Conversers; & dazzled his Hearers till they believed whatever he wished them to do.* [H]

---

[1] We must smile at a little inaccuracy of metaphor in the Preface to the Transactions, which is written by Mr. Burrowes. The *critick of the style of* JOHNSON having, with a just zeal for literature, observed, that the whole nation are called on to exert themselves, afterwards says: 'They are *called on* by every *tye* which can have a laudable influence on the heart of man.'

underlined: *laudable influence* [H]

it to his credit, that this learned gentleman has himself caught no mean degree of the expansion and harmony, which, independent of all other circumstances, characterise the sentences of Johnson. Thus, in the Preface to the volume in which the Essay appears, we find, 'If it be said that in societies of this sort, too much attention is frequently bestowed on subjects barren and speculative, it may be answered, that no one science is so little connected with the rest, as not to afford many principles whose use may extend considerably beyond the science to which they primarily belong; and that no proposition is so purely theoretical as to be totally incapable of being applied to practical purposes. There is no apparent connection between duration and the cycloidal arch, the properties of which duly attended to, have furnished us with our best regulated methods of measuring time: and he who had made himself master of the nature and affections of the logarithmick curve, is not aware that he has advanced considerably towards ascertaining the proportionable density of the air at its various distances from the surface of the earth.'

The ludicrous imitators of Johnson's style are innumerable. Their general method is to accumulate hard words, without considering, that, although he was fond of introducing them occasionally, there is not a single sentence in all his writings where they are crowded together, as in the first verse of the following imaginary Ode by him to Mrs. Thrale,[1] which appeared in the news-papers:

> '*Cervisial coctor's viduate* dame,
> *Opins't* thou this gigantick frame,
>   *Procumbing* at thy shrine;
> Shall, *catenated* by thy charms,
> A captive in thy *ambient* arms,
>   *Perennially* be thine?'[a]

[a] *Whose silly Fun was this? Soame Jenyns's?* [H]

This, and a thousand other such attempts, are totally unlike the original, which the writers imagined they were

underlined: *I believe* [H]

[b] *I believe so too!!* [H]

[1] Johnson's wishing to unite himself with this rich widow, was much talked of, but I believe without foundation.[b] The report, however, gave occasion to a poem, not without characteristical merit, entitled, 'Ode to Mrs. Thrale, by Samuel Johnson, LL.D. on their supposed approaching Nuptials;'

turning into ridicule. There is not similarity enough for burlesque, or even for caricature.

Mr. COLMAN, in his 'Prose on several Occasions,' has 'A Letter from LEXIPHANES; containing Proposals for a *Glossary* or *Vocabulary* of the *Vulgar Tongue:* intended as a Supplement to a larger DICTIONARY.' It is evidently meant as a sportive sally of ridicule on Johnson, whose style is thus imitated, without being grossly overcharged. 'It is easy to foresee, that the idle and illiterate will complain that I have increased their labours by endeavouring to diminish them; and that I have explained what is more easy by what is more difficult—*ignotum per ignotius*. I expect, on the other hand, the liberal acknowledgements of the learned. He who is buried in scholastick retirement, secluded from the assemblies of the gay, and remote from the circles of the polite, will at once comprehend the definitions, and be grateful for such a seasonable and necessary elucidation of his mother-tongue. Annexed to this letter is a short specimen of the work, thrown together in a vague and desultory manner, not even adhering to aphabetical concatenation.'[1]

printed for Mr. Faulder, in Bond-street.—I shall quote as a specimen, the first three stanzas:

> 'If e'er my fingers touch'd the lyre,
>   In satire fierce, in pleasure gay;
> Shall not my THRALIA's smiles inspire?
>   Shall SAM refuse the sportive lay?
>
> My dearest Lady! view your slave,
>   Behold him as your very *Scrub;*
> Eager to write as authour grave,
>   Or govern well, the brewing-tub.
>
> To rich felicity thus raised,
>   My bosom glows with amorous fire,
> Porter no longer shall be praised,
>   'Tis I MYSELF am *Thrale's Entire.*'[a]

[a] *whose Fun was this? It is better than the other.* [H]

[1]'HIGGLEDY-PIGGLEDY,—Conglomeration and confusion.

'HODGE-PODGE,—A culinary mixture of heterogeneous ingredients; applied metaphorically to all discordant combinations.

'TIT FOR TAT,—Adequate retaliation.

'SHILLY SHALLY,—Hesitation and irresolution.

'FEE! FA! FUM!—Gigantick intonations.

'RIGMAROLE,—Discourse, incoherent and rhapsodical.

'CRINCUM-CRANCUM,—Lines of irregularity and involution.

'DING-DONG,—Tintinabulary chimes, used metaphorically to signify dispatch and vehemence.'

The serious imitators of Johnson's style, whether intentionally or by the imperceptible effect of its strength and animation, are, as I have had already occasion to observe, so many, that I might introduce quotations from a numerous body of writers in our language, since he appeared in the literary world. I shall point out the following:

WILLIAM ROBERTSON, D.D.

'In other parts of the globe, man, in his rudest state, appears as Lord of the creation, giving law to various tribes of animals which he has tamed and reduced to subjection. The Tartar follows his prey on the horse which he has reared, or tends his numerous herds which furnish him both with food and clothing; the Arab has rendered the camel docile, and avails himself of its persevering strength; the Laplander has formed the rein-deer to be subservient to his will; and even the people of Kamschatka have trained their dogs to labour. This command over the inferiour creatures is one of the noblest prerogatives of man, and among the greatest efforts of his wisdom and power. Without this, his dominion is incomplete. He is a monarch who has no subjects; a master without servants; and must perform every operation by the strength of his own arm.'[1]

EDWARD GIBBON, ESQ.

'Of all our passions and appetites, the love of power is of the most imperious and unsociable nature, since the pride of one man requires the submission of the multitude. In the tumult of civil discord the laws of society lose their force, and their place is seldom supplied by those of humanity. The ardour of contention, the pride of victory, the despair of success, the memory of past injuries, and the fear of future dangers, all contribute to inflame the mind, and to silence the voice of pity.'[2]

MISS BURNEY

'My family, mistaking ambition for honour, and rank for dignity, have long planned a splendid connection for

[1] 'History of America:' vol. i. quarto, p. 332.
[2] 'Decline and Fall of the Roman Empire,' vol. i. chap. iv.

me, to which, though my invariable repugnance has stopped any advances, their wishes and their views immoveably adhere. I am but too certain they will now listen to no other. I dread, therefore, to make a trial where I despair of success; I know not how to risk a prayer with those who may silence me by a command.'[1]

REVEREN MR. NARES[2]

'In an enlightened and improving age, much perhaps is not to be apprehended from the inroads of mere caprice; at such a period it will generally be perceived, that needless irregularity is the worst of all deformities, and that nothing is so truly elegant in language as the simplicity of unviolated analogy.—Rules will, therefore, be observed so far as they are known and acknowledged: but, at the same time, the desire of improvement having been once excited will not remain inactive; and its efforts, unless assisted by knowledge, as much as they are prompted by zeal, will not unfrequently be found pernicious; so that the very persons whose intention it is to perfect the instrument of reason, will deprave and disorder it unknowingly. At such a time, then, it becomes peculiarly necessary that the analogy of language should be fully examined and understood; that its rules should be carefully laid down; and that it should be clearly known how much it contains, which being already right should be defended from change and violation; how much it has that demands amendment; and how much that, for fear of greater inconveniencies, must, perhaps, be left, unaltered, though irregular.'

A distinguished authour in 'THE MIRROR,'[3] a periodical paper, published at Edinburgh, has imitated Johnson

---

[1] 'Cecilia,' Book VII. chap. i.

[2] The passage which I quote is taken from that gentleman's 'ELEMENTS OF ORTHOEPY; containing a distinct view of the whole Analogy of the ENGLISH LANGUAGE, so far as relates to *Pronunciation, Accent, and Quantity*,' London, 1784. I beg leave to offer my particular acknowledgements to the authour of a work of uncommon merit and great utility. I know no book which contains, in the same compass, more learning, polite literature, sound sense, accuracy of arrangement, and perspicuity of expression.

[3] That collection was presented to Dr. Johnson, I believe by its authours; and I heard him speak very well of it.

very closely. Thus, in No. 16,—'The effects of the return
of spring have been frequently remarked as well in relation
to the human mind as to the animal and vegetable world.
The reviving power of this season has been traced from
the fields to the herds that inhabit them, and from the
lower classes of beings up to man. Gladness and joy are
described as prevailing through universal Nature, ani-
mating the low of the cattle, the carol of the birds, and the
pipe of the shepherd.'

The Reverend Dr. Knox, master of Tunbridge-school,
appears to have the *imitari aveo* of Johnson's style perpetually in his mind: and to his assiduous, though not
servile, study of it, we may partly ascribe the extensive
popularity of his writings.[1]

In his 'Essays, Moral and Literary,' No. 3, we find the
following passage:—'The polish of external grace may
indeed be deferred till the approach of manhood. When
solidity is obtained by pursuing the modes prescribed by
our fore-fathers, then may the file be used. The firm
substance will bear attrition, and the lustre then acquired
will be durable.'

There is, however, one in No. 11, which is blown up
into such tumidity, as to be truly ludicrous. The writer
means to tell us, that Members of Parliament, who have
run in debt by extravagance, will sell their votes to avoid

[1] It were to be wished, that he had imitated that great man in every
respect, and had not followed the example of Dr. Adam Smith, in un-
graciously attacking his venerable *Alma Mater*, Oxford. It must, however,
be observed, that he is much less to blame than Smith: he only objects to
certain particulars; Smith to the whole institution; though indebted for
much of his learning to an exhibition which he enjoyed, for many years at
Balliol College. Neither of them, however, will do any hurt to the noblest
university in the world. While I animadvert on what appears to me excep-
tionable in some of the works of Dr. Knox, I cannot refuse due praise to
others of his productions; particularly his sermons, and to the spirit with
which he maintains, against presumptuous hereticks, the consolatory
doctrines peculiar to the Christian Revelation. This he has done in a manner
equally strenuous and conciliating. Neither ought I to omit mentioning a
remarkable instance of his candour: Notwithstanding the wide difference of
our opinions, upon the important subject of University education, in a letter
to me concerning this Work, he thus expresses himself: 'I thank you for the
very great entertainment your Life of Johnson gives me. It is a most valuable
work. Yours is a new species of biography. Happy for Johnson, that he had
so able a recorder of his wit and wisdom.'

an arrest,[1] which he thus expresses:—'They who build houses and collect costly pictures and furniture, with the money of an honest artisan or mechanick, will be very glad of emanicipation from the hands of a bailiff, by a sale of their senatorial suffrage.'

But I think the most perfect imitation of Johnson is a professed one, entitled 'A Criticism on Gray's Elegy in a Country Church-Yard,' said to be written by Mr. YOUNG, Professor of Greek, at Glasgow, and of which let him have the credit, unless a better title can be shewn. It has not only the particularities of Johnson's style, but that very species of literary discussion and illustration for which he was eminent. Having already quoted so much from others, I shall refer the curious to this performance, with an assurance of much entertainment.

Yet whatever merit there may be in any imitations of Johnson's style, every good judge must see that they are obviously different from the original; for all of them are either deficient in its force, or overloaded with its peculiarities; and the powerful sentiment to which it is suited is not to be found.

Johnson's affection for his departed relations seemed to grow warmer as he approached nearer to the time when he might hope to see them again.[a] It probably appeared to him that he should upbraid himself with unkind inattention, were he to leave the world without having paid a tribute of respect to their memory.

[a] *So does every Man's.* [H]

'TO MR. GREEN, APOTHECARY, AT LICHFIELD[2]

'DEAR SIR,

'I HAVE enclosed the Epitaph for my Father, Mother, and Brother, to be all engraved on the large size, and laid in the middle aisle in St. Michael's-church, which I request the clergyman and churchwardens to permit.

'The first care must be to find the exact place of interment, that the stone may protect the bodies. Then let the

[1] Dr Knox, in his 'Moral and Literary' abstraction, may be excused for not knowing the political regulations of his country. No senator can be in the hands of a bailiff.

[2] See vol. ii. p. 251.

stone be deep, massy, and hard; and do not let the difference of ten pounds, or more, defeat our purpose.

'I have enclosed ten pounds, and Mrs. Porter will pay you ten more, which I gave her for the same purpose. What more is wanted shall be sent; and I beg that all possible haste may be made, for I wish to have it done while I am yet alive. Let me know, dear Sir, that you receive this.   'I am, Sir,

'Your most humble servant,

'Dec. 2, 1784.'   'SAM. JOHNSON'

'TO MRS. LUCY PORTER, IN LICHFIELD[1]

'DEAR MADAM,

'I AM very ill, and desire your prayers. I have sent Mr. Green the Epitaph, and a power to call on you for ten pounds.

'I laid this summer a stone over Tetty, in the chapel of Bromley, in Kent. The inscription is in Latin, of which this is the English. [Here a translation.]

'That this is done, I thought it fit that you should know. What care will be taken of us, who can tell? May GOD pardon and bless us, for JESUS CHRIST'S sake.

'I am, &c.

'Dec. 2, 1784.'   'SAM. JOHNSON'

My readers are now, at last, to behold SAMUEL JOHN-SON preparing himself for that doom, from which the most exalted powers afford no exemption to man. Death had always been to him an object of terrour; so that, though by no means happy, he still clung to life with an eagerness at which many have wondered. At any time when he was ill, he was very much pleased to be told that he looked better. An ingenious member of the *Eumelian Club*[2] informs me,

___

[1] [This lady, whose name so frequently occurs in the course of this work, survived Dr. Johnson just thirteen months. She died at Lichfield in her 71st year, January 13, 1786, and bequeathed the principal part of her fortune to the Rev. Mr. Pearson, of Lichfield. MALONE.]

[2] A Club in London, founded by the learned and ingenious physician, Dr. Ash, in honour of whose name it was called *Eumelian*, from the Greek Εὐμέλιος: though it was warmly contended, and even put to a vote, that it should have the more obvious appellation of *Fraxinean*, from the Latin.

that upon one occasion, when he said to him that he saw health returning to his cheek, Johnson seized him by the hand and exclaimed, 'Sir, you are one of the kindest friends I ever had.'[a]

[a] *Seward I suppose.*
[H]

His own statement of his views of futurity will appear truly rational; and may, perhaps, impress the unthinking with seriousness.

'You know, (says he,)[1] I never thought confidence with respect to futurity, any part of the character of a brave, a wise, or a good man. Bravery has no place where it can avail nothing; wisdom impresses strongly the consciousness of those faults, of which it is, perhaps, itself an aggravation; and goodness, always wishing to be better, and imputing every deficience to criminal negligence, and every fault to voluntary corruption, never dares to suppose the condition of forgiveness fulfilled, nor what is wanting in the crime supplied by penitence.

'This is the state of the best; but what must be the condition of him whose heart will not suffer him to rank himself among the best, or among the good? Such must be his dread of the approaching trial, as will leave him little attention to the opinion of those whom he is leaving for ever; and the serenity that is not felt, it can be no virtue to feign.'

His great fear of death, and the strange dark manner in which Sir John Hawkins imparts the uneasiness which he expressed on account of offences with which he charged himself, may give occasion to injurious suspicions, as if there had been something of more than ordinary criminality weighing upon his conscience. On that account, therefore, as well as from the regard to truth which he inculcated,[2] I am to mention, (with all possible respect and delicacy, however,) that his conduct, after he came to London, and had associated with Savage and others, was not so strictly virtuous, in one respect, as when he was a younger man. It was well known, that his amorous inclinations were uncommonly strong and impetuous. He owned to many of his friends, that he used to take women of the town to taverns, and hear them relate their history.—In short, it

---

[1] Mrs. Thrale's Collection, March 10, 1784. Vol. ii. p. 3.
[2] See what he said to Mr. Malone, pp. 165, 166 of this volume.

must not be concealed, that like many other good and pious men, among whom we may place the apostle Paul upon his own authority, Johnson was not free from propensities which were ever 'warring against the law of his mind,'—and that in his combats with them, he was sometimes overcome.

Here let the profane and licentious pause; let them not thoughtlessly say that Johnson was an *hypocrite*, or that his *principles* were not firm, because his *practice* was not uniformly conformable to what he professed.

Let the question be considered independent of moral and religious associations; and no man will deny that thousands, in many instances, act against conviction. Is a prodigal, for example, an *hypocrite*, when he owns he is satisfied that his extravagance will bring him to ruin and misery? We are *sure* he *believes* it; but immediate inclination, strengthened by indulgence, prevails over that belief in influencing his conduct. Why then shall credit be refused to the *sincerity* of those who acknowledge their persuasion of moral and religious duty, yet sometimes fail of living as it requires? I heard Dr. Johnson once observe, 'There is something noble in publishing truth, though it condemns one's self.'[1a] And one who said in his presence, 'he had no notion of people being in earnest in their good professions, whose practice was not suitable to them,' was thus reprimanded by him:—'Sir, are you so grossly ignorant of human nature as not to know that a man may be very sincere in good principles, without having good practice?'[2]

a *he often quoted the Lines*
  Pyrrhus will ne'er approve his own Injustice,
  Or form Excuses while his Heart condemns him. [H]

But let no man encourage or soothe himself in 'presumptuous sin,' from knowing that Johnson was sometimes hurried into indulgences which he thought criminal. I have exhibited this circumstance as a shade in so great a character, both from my sacred love of truth, and to shew that he was not so weakly scrupulous as he has been represented by those who imagine that the sins, of which a deep

[1] Journal of a Tour to the Hebrides, 3d. edit. p. 209. On the same subject, in his Letter to Mrs. Thrale, dated Nov. 29, 1783, he makes the following just observation: 'Life, to be worthy of a rational being, must be always in progression; we must always purpose to do more or better than in time past. The mind is enlarged and elevated by mere purposes, though they end as they began, by airy contemplation. We compare and judge, though we do not practise.'   [2] Ibid. p. 374.

sense was upon his mind, were merely such little venial
trifles as pouring milk into his tea on Good-Friday. His
understanding will be defended by my statement, if his
consistency of conduct be in some degree impaired. But
what wise man would, for momentary gratifications,
deliberately subject himself to suffer such uneasiness as we
find was experienced by Johnson in reviewing his conduct
as compared with his notion of the ethicks of the gospel?
Let the following passages be kept in remembrance: 'O,
GOD, giver and preserver of all life, by whose power I was
created, and by whose providence I am sustained, look
down upon me with tenderness and mercy; grant that
I may not have been created to be finally destroyed; that
I may not be preserved to add wickedness to wickedness.'[1]—
'O, LORD, let me not sink into total depravity; look down
upon me, and rescue me at last from the captivity of sin.'[2]
—'Almighty and most merciful Father, who hast continued
my life from year to year, grant that by longer life I may
become less desirous of sinful pleasures, and more careful
of eternal happiness.'[3]—'Let not my years be multiplied
to increase my guilt; but as my age advances, let me
become more pure in my thoughts, more regular in my
desires, and more obedient to thy laws.'[4] 'Forgive, O
merciful LORD, whatever I have done contrary to thy
laws. Give me such a sense of my wickedness as may
produce true contrition and effectual repentance; so
that when I shall be called into another state, I may
be received among the sinners to whom sorrow and
reformation have obtained pardon, for JESUS CHRIST's
sake. Amen.'[5]

Such was the distress of mind, such the penitence
of Johnson, in his hours of privacy, and in his devout
approaches to his Maker. His *sincerity*, therefore, must
appear to every candid mind unquestionable.

It is of essential consequence to keep in view, that there
was in this excellent man's conduct no false principle of
commutation, no *deliberate* indulgence in sin, in consideration
of a counterbalance of duty. His offending, and his

---

[1] Prayers and Meditations, p. 47.   [2] Ibid. p. 68.
[3] Ibid. p. 84.   [4] Ibid. p. 120.
[5] Ibid. p. 130.

repenting, were distinct and separate:[1] and when we consider his almost unexampled attention to truth, his inflexible integrity, his constant piety, who will dare to 'cast a stone' at him? Besides, let it never be forgotten, that he cannot be charged with any offence, indicating badness of *heart*, any thing dishonest, base, or malignant; but, that, on the contrary, he was charitable in an extraordinary degree: so that even in one of his own rigid judgements of himself, (Easter-eve, 1781,) while he says, 'I have corrected no external habits;' he is obliged to own, 'I hope that since my last communion I have advanced, by pious reflections, in my submission to GOD, and my benevolence to man.'[2]

I am conscious that this is the most difficult and dangerous part of my biographical work, and I cannot but be very anxious concerning it. I trust that I have got through it, preserving at once my regard to truth,—to my friend,—and to the interests of virtue and religion. Nor can I apprehend that more harm can ensue from the knowledge of the irregularities of Johnson, guarded as I have stated it, than from knowing that Addison and Parnell were intemperate in the use of wine; which he himself, in his Lives of those celebrated writers and pious men, has not forborne to record.

It is not my intention to give a very minute detail of the particulars of Johnson's remaining days, of whom it was now evident, that the crisis was fast approaching, when he must '*die like men, and fall like one of the Princes*.' Yet it will be instructive, as well as gratifying to the curiosity of my readers, to record a few circumstances, on the authenticity of which they may perfectly rely, as I have been at the utmost pains to obtain an accurate account of his last illness, from the best authority.

Dr. Heberden, Dr. Brocklesby, Dr. Warren, and Dr. Butter, physicians, generously attended him, without accepting any fees, as did Mr. Cruikshank, surgeon; and all that could be done from professional skill and ability,

---

[1] Dr. Johnson related, with very earnest approbation, a story of a gentleman, who, in an impulse of passion, overcame the virtue of a young woman. When she said to him, 'I am afraid we have done wrong!' he answered, 'Yes, we have done wrong:—for I would not *debauch her mind*.'

[2] Prayers and Meditations, p. 192.

was tried, to prolong a life so truly valuable. He himself, indeed, having, on account of his very bad constitution, been perpetually applying himself to medical inquiries, united his own efforts with those of the gentlemen who attended him; and imagining that the dropsical collection of water which oppressed him might be drawn off by making incisions in his body, he, with his usual resolute defiance of pain, cut deep, when he thought that his surgeon had done it too tenderly.[1]

About eight or ten days before his death, when Dr. Brocklesby paid him his morning visit, he seemed very low and desponding, and said, 'I have been as a dying man all night.' He then emphatically broke out in the words of Shakspeare,

> 'Can'st thou not minister to a mind diseas'd;
> Pluck from the memory a rooted sorrow;
> Raze out the written troubles of the brain;
> And, with some sweet oblivious antidote,
> Cleanse the stuff'd bosom of that perilous stuff,
> Which weighs upon the heart?'

To which Dr. Brocklesby readily answer'd, from the same great poet:

> '————————— therein the patient
> Must minister to himself.'

Johnson expressed himself much satisfied with the application.

On another day after this, when talking on the subject of prayer, Dr. Brocklesby repeated from Juvenal,

> '*Orandum est, ut sit mens sana in corpore sano,*'

and so on to the end of the tenth satire; but in running it quickly over, he happened, in the line,

> '*Qui spatium vitæ extremum inter munera ponat,*'

to pronounce *supremum* for *extremum;* at which Johnson's

---

[1] This bold experiment, Sir John Hawkins has related in such a manner as to suggest a charge against Johnson of intentionally hastening his end; a charge so very inconsistent with his character in every respect, that it is injurious even to refute it, as Sir John has thought it necessary to do. It is evident, that what Johnson did in hopes of relief, indicated an extraordinary eagerness to retard his dissolution.[a]

[a] *Yes, Yes—apparently so.* [H]

critical ear instantly took offence, and discoursing vehemently on the unmetrical effect of such a lapse, he shewed
himself as full as ever of the spirit of the grammarian.[a]

[a] *Bravo.* [H]

Having no other relations,[1] it had been for some time
Johnson's intention to make a liberal provision for his
faithful servant, Mr. Francis Barber, whom he looked upon
as particularly under his protection, and whom he had all
along treated truly as an humble friend. Having asked Dr.
Brocklesby what would be a proper annuity to a favourite
servant, and being answered that it must depend on the
circumstances of the master; and, that in the case of a
nobleman, fifty pounds a-year was considered as an
adequate reward for many years' faithful service;—'Then,
(said Johnson,) shall I be *nobilissimus*, for I mean to leave
Frank seventy pounds a-year, and I desire you to tell him
so.' It is strange, however, to think, that Johnson was not
free from that general weakness of being averse to execute
a will, so that he delayed it from time to time; and had it
not been for Sir John Hawkins's repeatedly urging it, I
think it is probable that his kind resolution would not
have been fulfilled. After making one, which, as Sir John
Hawkins informs us, extended no further than the

[1] [The authour in a former page has shewn the injustice of Sir John
Hawkins's charge against Johnson, with respect to a person of the name of
Heely, whom he has inaccurately represented as a relation of Johnson's.
See pp. 423, 424.—That Johnson was anxious to discover whether any of
his relations were living, is evinced by the following letter, written not long
before he made his Will:

'TO THE REV. DR. VYSE, IN LAMBETH
'SIR,

'I AM desirous to know whether Charles Scrimshaw, of Woodsease (I
think,) in your father's neighbourhood, be now living; what is his condition,
and where he may be found. If you can conveniently make any inquiry about
him, and can do it without delay, it will be an act of great kindness to me,
he being very nearly related to me. I beg [you] to pardon this trouble.

I am, Sir,

'Your most humble servant,
'Bolt-court, Fleet-street,   'SAM JOHNSON'
    Nov. 29, 1784.'

In conformity to the wish expressed in the preceding letter, an inquiry
was made, but no descendants of Charles Scrimshaw, or of his sisters, were
discovered to be living. Dr. Vyse informs me, that Dr. Johnson told him,
'he was disappointed in the inquiries he had made after his relations.' There
is therefore no ground whatsoever for supposing that he was unmindful of
them, or neglected them. MALONE.]

promised annuity, Johnson's final disposition of his property was established by a Will and Codicil, of which copies are subjoined.[1]

[1] 'IN THE NAME OF GOD. AMEN. I, SAMUEL JOHNSON, being in full possession of my faculties, but fearing this night may put an end to my life, do ordain this my last Will and Testament. I bequeath to GOD, a soul polluted by many sins, but I hope purified by JESUS CHRIST.—I leave seven hundred and fifty pounds in the hands of Bennet Langton, Esq.; three hundred pounds in the hands of Mr. Barclay and Mr. Perkins, brewers; one hundred and fifty pounds in the hands of Dr. Percy, Bishop of Dromore; one thousand pounds, three *per cent.* annuities in the publick funds; and one hundred pounds now lying by me in ready money: all these before-mentioned sums and property I leave, I say, to Sir Joshua Reynolds, Sir John Hawkins, and Dr. William Scott, of Doctors Commons, in trust, for the following uses:—That is to say, to pay to the representatives of the late William Innys, bookseller, in St. Paul's Church-yard, the sum of two hundred pounds; to Mrs. White, my female servant, one hundred pounds stock in the three *per cent.* annuities aforesaid. The rest of the aforesaid sums of money and property, together with my books, plate, and household furniture, I leave to the before-mentioned Sir Joshua Reynolds, Sir John Hawkins, and Dr. William Scott, also in trust, to be applied, after paying any debts, to the use of Francis Barber, my man-servant, a negro, in such manner as they shall judge most fit and available to his benefit. And I appoint the aforesaid Sir Joshua Reynolds, Sir John Hawkins, and Dr. William Scott, sole executors of this my last will and testament, hereby revoking all former wills and testaments whatever. In witness whereof I hereunto subscribe my name, and affix my seal, this eighth day of December, 1784.

'SAM. JOHNSON, (L. S.)

'Signed, sealed, published, declared, and delivered, by the said testator, as his last will and testament, in the presence of us, the word *two* being first inserted in the opposite page.

'GEORGE STRAHAN
'JOHN DESMOULINS'

'By way of Codicil to my last Will and Testament, I, SAMUEL JOHNSON, give, devise, and bequeath, my messuage or tenement situate at Lichfield, in the county of Stafford, with the appurtenances in the tenure and occupation of Mrs. Bond, of Lichfield aforesaid, or of Mr. Hinchman, her under-tenant, to my executors, in trust, to sell and dispose of the same; and the money arising from such sale I give and bequeath as follows, viz. to Thomas and Benjamin, the sons of Fisher Johnson, late of Leicester, and ———— Whiting, daughter of Thomas Johnson, late of Coventry, and the grand-daughter of the said Thomas Johnson, one full and equal fourth part each; but in case there shall be more grand-daughters than one of the said Thomas Johnson, living at the time of my decease, I give and bequeath the part or share of that one to and equally between such grand-daughters. I give and bequeath to the Rev. Mr. Rogers, of Berkley, near Froom, in the county of Somerset, the sum of one hundred pounds, requesting him to apply the same towards the maintenance of Elizabeth Herne, a lunatick. I also give and bequeath to my godchildren, the son and daughter of Mauritius Lowe, painter, each of them, one hundred pounds of my stock in the three *per cent.* consolidated annuities, to be applied and disposed of by and at the discretion

The consideration of numerous papers of which he was possessed, seems to have struck Johnson's mind, with a

of my executors, in the education or settlement in the world of them my said legatees. Also I give and bequeath to Sir John Hawkins, one of my Executors, the Annales Ecclesiastici of Baronius, and Holinshed's and Stowe's Chronicles, and also an octavo Common Prayer-Book. To Bennet Langton, Esq. I give and bequeath my Polyglot Bible. To Sir Joshua Reynolds, my great French Dictionary, my Martiniere, and my own copy of my folio English Dictionary, of the last revision. To Dr. William Scott, one of my Executors, the Dictionnaire de Commerce, and Lectius's edition of the Greek Poets. To Mr. Windham, Poetæ Græci Heroici per Henricum Stephanum. To the Rev. Mr. Strahan, vicar of Islington, in Middlesex, Mill's Greek Testament, Beza's Greek Testament, by Stephens, all my Latin Bibles, and my Greek Bible, by Wechelius. To Dr. Heberden, Dr. Brocklesby, Dr. Butter, and Mr. Cruikshank, the surgeon who attended me, Mr. Holder, my apothecary, Gerard Hamilton, Esq. Mrs. Gardiner, of Snow-hill, Mrs. Frances Reynolds, Mr. Hoole, and the Reverend Mr. Hoole, his son, each a book at their election, to keep as a token of remembrance. I also give and bequeath to Mr. John Desmoulins, two hundred pounds consolidated three *per cent.* annuities: and to Mr. Sastres, the Italian Master, the sum of five pounds, to be laid out in books of piety for his own use. And whereas the said Bennet Langton hath agreed in consideration of the sum of seven hundred and fifty pounds mentioned in my Will to be in his hands, to grant and secure an annuity of seventy pounds payable during the life of me and my servant, Francis Barber, and the life of the survivor of us, to Mr. George Stubbs, in trust for us; my mind and will is, that in case of my decease before the said agreement shall be perfected, the said sum of seven hundred and fifty pounds, and the bond for securing the said sum, shall go to the said Francis Barber; and I hereby give and bequeath to him the same, in lieu of the bequest in his favour, contained in my said Will. And I hereby empower my Executors to deduct and retain all expences that shall or may be incurred in the execution of my said Will, or of this Codicil thereto, out of such estate and effects as I shall die possessed of. All the rest, residue, and remainder, of my estate and effects I give and bequeath to my said Executors, in trust for the said Francis Barber, his Executors, and Administrators. Witness my hand and seal, this ninth day of December, 1784.

'SAM JOHNSON, (L. S.)

'Signed, sealed, published, declared, and delivered, by the said Samuel Johnson, as, and for a Codicil to his last Will and Testament, in the presence of us, who, in his presence, and at his request, and also in the presence of each other, have hereto subscribed our names as witnesses.

'JOHN COPLEY.
'WILLIAM GIBSON.
'HENRY COLE.'

Upon these testamentary deeds it is proper to make a few observations.

His express declaration with his dying breath as a Christian, as it had been often practised in such solemn writings, was of real consequence from this great man, for the conviction of a mind equally acute and strong, might well overbalance the doubts of others who were his contemporaries. The expression *polluted*, may, to some, convey an impression of more than ordinary contamination; but that is not warranted by its genuine meaning, as appears

sudden anxiety, and as they were in great confusion, it is much to be lamented that he had not entrusted some

from 'The Rambler,' No. 42. The same word is used in the will of Dr. Sanderson, Bishop of Lincoln, who was piety itself.

His legacy of two hundred pounds to the representatives of Mr. Innys, bookseller, in St. Paul's Church-yard, proceeded from a very worthy motive. He told Sir John Hawkins that his father having become a bankrupt, Mr. Innys had assisted him with money or credit to continue his business. 'This, (said he,) I consider as an obligation on me to be grateful to his descendants.'

The amount of his property proved to be considerably more than he had supposed it to be. Sir John Hawkins estimates the bequest to Francis Barber at a sum little short of fifteen hundred pounds, including an annuity of seventy pounds to be paid to him by Mr. Langton, in consideration of seven hundred and fifty pounds, which Johnson had lent to that gentleman. Sir John seems not a little angry at this bequest, and mutters 'a caveat against ostentatious bounty and favour to negroes.' But surely when a man has money entirely of his own acquisition, especially when he has no near relations, he may, without blame, dispose of it as he pleases, and with great propriety to a faithful servant. Mr. Barber, by the recommendation of his master, retired to Lichfield, where he might pass the rest of his days in comfort.[a]

underlined: *days in comfort* [H]

[a] *I fancy he had very little Comfort: some one told me he lived to be much distress'd.* [H]

It has been objected that Johnson has omitted many of his best friends, when leaving books to several as tokens of his last remembrance. The names of Dr. Adams, Dr. Taylor, Dr. Burney, Mr. Hector, Mr. Murphy, the Authour of this Work, and others who were intimate with him, are not to be found in his Will. This may be accounted for by considering, that as he was very near his dissolution at the time, he probably mentioned such as happened to occur to him; and that he may have recollected, that he had formerly shewn others such proofs of his regard, that it was not necessary to crowd his Will with their names. Mrs. Lucy Porter was much displeased that nothing was left to her; but besides what I have now stated, she should have considered, that she had left nothing to Johnson by her Will, which was made during his life time, as appeared at her decease.[b]

[b] *well said Bozzy.* [H]

His enumerating several persons in one group, and leaving them 'each a book at their election,' might possibly have given occasion to a curious question as to the order of choice, had they not luckily fixed on different books. His library, though by no means handsome in its appearance, was sold by Mr. Christie, for two hundred and forty-seven pounds, nine shillings; many people being desirous to have a book which had belonged to Johnson. In many of them he had written little notes: sometimes tender memorials of his departed wife; as, 'This was dear Tetty's book:' sometimes occasional remarks of different sorts. Mr. Lysons, of Clifford's Inn, has favoured me with the two following:

In 'Holy Rules and Helps to Devotion,' by Bryan Duppa, Lord Bishop of Winton, '*Preces quidam videtur diligenter tractasse; spero non inauditus.*'

In 'The Rosicrucian infallible Axiomata, by John Heydon, Gent.' prefixed to which are some verses addressed to the authour, signed Ambr. Waters, A.M. Coll. Ex. Oxon. '*These Latin verses were written to Hobbes by Bathurst, upon his Treatise on Human Nature, and have no relation to the book.——— An odd fraud.*'

[Francis Barber, Dr. Johnson's principal legatee, died in the infirmary at Stafford, after undergoing a painful operation, Feb. 13, 1801. MALONE.]

faithful and discreet person with the care and selection of them; instead of which, he, in a precipitate manner, burnt large masses of them, with little regard, as I apprehend, to discrimination. Not that I suppose we have thus been deprived of any compositions which he had ever intended for the publick eye; but from what escaped the flames I judge that many curious circumstances, relating both to himself and other literary characters, have perished.

Two very valuable articles, I am sure, we have lost, which were two quarto volumes, containing a full, fair, and most particular account of his own life, from his earliest recollection. I owned to him, that having accidentally seen them, I had read a great deal in them; and apologizing for the liberty I had taken, asked him if I could help it. He placidly answered. 'Why, Sir, I do not think you could have helped it.' I said that I had, for once in my life, felt half an inclination to commit theft. It had come into my mind to carry off those two volumes, and never see him more. Upon my enquiring how this would have affected him, 'Sir, (said he,) I believe I should have gone mad.'[1a]

During his last illness, Johnson experienced the steady and kind attachment of his numerous friends. Mr. Hoole has drawn up a narrative of what passed in the visits which he paid him during that time, from the 10th of November to the 13th of December, the day of his death, inclusive, and has favoured me with a perusal of it, with permission to make extracts, which I have done. Nobody was more

underlined:
you [H]

two exclamation points:
an inclination etc. [H]

[a] *What a Project it was! & to tell of too!!* [H]

[1] One of these volumes, Sir John Hawkins informs us, he put into his pocket; for which the excuse he states is, that he meant to preserve it from falling into the hands of a person whom he describes so as to make it sufficiently clear who is meant; 'having strong reasons, (said he,) to suspect that this man might find and make an ill use of the book.' Why Sir John should suppose that the gentleman alluded to would act in this manner, he has not thought fit to explain. But what he did was not approved of by Johnson; who, upon being acquainted of it without delay by a friend, expressed great indignation, and warmly insisted on the book being delivered up; and, afterwards, in the supposition of his missing it, without knowing by whom it had been taken, he said, 'Sir, I should have gone out of the world distrusting half mankind.' Sir John next day wrote a letter to Johnson, assigning reasons for his conduct; upon which Johnson observed to Mr. Langton, 'Bishop Sanderson could not have dictated a better letter. I could almost say, *Melius est sic penituisse quam non errâsse.*' The agitation into which Johnson was thrown by this incident, probably made him hastily burn those precious records which must ever be regretted.[b]

[b] *It was enough to make him do so,— surely.* [H]

attentive to him than Mr. Langton,[1] to whom he tenderly said, *Te teneam moriens deficiente manu*. And I think it highly to the honour of Mr. Windham, that his important occupations as an active statesman did not prevent him from paying assiduous respect to the dying Sage whom he revered. Mr. Langton informs me, that, 'one day he found Mr. Burke and four or five more friends sitting with Johnson. Mr. Burke said to him, "I am afraid, Sir, such a number of us may be oppressive to you." —"No, Sir, (said Johnson,) it is not so; and I must be in a wretched state, indeed, when your company would not be a delight to me." Mr. Burke, in a tremulous voice, expressive of being very tenderly affected, replied, "My dear Sir, you have always been too good to me." Immediately afterwards he went away. This was the last circumstance in the acquaintance of these two eminent men.'

The following particulars of his conversation within a few days of his death, I give on the authority of Mr. John Nichols:[2]

[1] [Mr. Langton, whose name so often occurs in these volumes, survived Johnson several years. He died at Southampton, Dec. 18, 1801, aged sixty-five. MALONE.]

[2] On the same undoubted authority, I give a few articles, which should have been inserted in chronological order; but which, now that they are before me, I should be sorry to omit:

'In 1736, Dr. Johnson had a particular inclination to have been engaged as an assistant to the Reverend Mr. Budworth, then head master of the Grammar-school, at Brewood, in Staffordshire, "an excellent person, who possessed every talent of a perfect instructor of youth, in a degree which, (to use the words of one of the brightest ornaments of literature, the Reverend Dr. Hurd, Bishop of Worcester,) has been rarely found in any of that profession since the days of Quintilian." Mr. Budworth, "who was less known in his life-time, from that obscure situation to which the caprice of fortune oft condemns the most accomplished characters, than his highest merit deserved," had been bred under Mr. Blackwell, at Market Bosworth, where Johnson was some time an usher; which might naturally lead to the application. Mr. Budworth was certainly no stranger to the learning or abilities of Johnson, as he more than once lamented his having been under the necessity of declining the engagement, from an apprehension that the paralytick affection, under which our great Philologist laboured through life, might become the object of imitation or of ridicule, among his pupils.'— Captain Budworth, his grandson, has confirmed to me this anecdote.'

'Among the early associates of Johnson, at St. John's Gate, was Samuel Boyse, well known by his ingenious productions; and not less noted for his imprudence. It was not unusual for Boyse to be a customer to the pawnbroker. On one of these occasions, Dr. Johnson collected a sum of money to redeem

'He said, that the Parliamentary Debates were the only part of his writings which then gave him any compunction: but that at the time he wrote them, he had no conception he was imposing upon the world, though they were frequently written from very slender materials, and often from none at all,—the mere coinage of his own imagination. He never wrote any part of his works with equal velocity. Three columns of the Magazine, in an hour, was no uncommon effort, which was faster than most persons could have transcribed that quantity.

'Of his friend Cave, he always spoke with great affection. "Yet, (said he,) Cave, (who never looked out of his window, but with a view to the Gentleman's Magazine,) was a penurious pay-master; he would contract for lines by the hundred, and expect the long hundred; but he was a good man, and always delighted to have his friends at his table."

'When talking of a regular edition of his own works, he said, "that he had power, [from the booksellers,] to print such an edition, if his health admitted it; but had no power to assign over any edition, unless he could add notes, and so alter them as to make them new works;

his friend's clothes, which in two days after were pawned again. "The sum, (said Johnson) was collected by sixpences, at a time when to me sixpence was a serious consideration."

'Speaking one day of a person for whom he had a real friendship, but in whom vanity was somewhat too predominant, he observed, that "Kelly was so fond of displaying on his side-board the plate which he possessed, that he added to it his spurs. For my part, (said he,) I never was master of a pair of spurs, but once; and they are now at the bottom of the ocean. By the carelessness of Boswell's servant, they were dropped from the end of the boat, on our return from the Isle of Sky." '

The late Reverend Mr. Samuel Badcock, having been introduced to Dr. Johnson, by Mr. Nichols, some years before his death, thus expressed himself in a letter to that gentleman:

'How much I am obliged to you for the favour you did me in introducing me to Dr. Johnson! *Tantùm vidi Virgilium.* But to have seen him, and to have received a testimony of respect from him, was enough. I recollect all the conversation, and shall never forget one of his expressions.—Speaking of Dr. P******, (whose writings, I saw, he estimated at a low rate,) he said, "You have proved him as deficient in *probity* as he is in learning."—I called him an "*Index-scholar;*" but he was not willing to allow him a claim even to that merit. He said, "that he borrowed from those who had been borrowers themselves, and did not know that the mistakes he adopted had been answered by others."—I often think of our short, but precious, visit to this great man. I shall consider it as a kind of an *æra* in my life.'

which his state of health forbade him to think of. I may possibly live, (said he) or rather breathe, three days, or perhaps three weeks; but find myself daily and gradually weaker."

'He said at another time, three or four days only before his death, speaking of the little fear he had of undergoing a chirurgical operation, "I would give one of these legs for a year more of life, I mean of comfortable life, not such as that which I now suffer;"—and lamented much his inability to read during his hours of restlessness. "I used formerly, (he added,) when sleepless in bed, *to read like a Turk*."

marginal line: *hours of . . . he added* [H]

'Whilst confined by his last illness, it was his regular practice to have the church service read to him, by some attentive and friendly Divine. The Rev. Mr. Hoole performed this kind office in my presence for the last time, when, by his own desire, no more than the litany was read; in which his responses were in the deep and sonorous voice which Mr. Boswell has occasionally noticed, and with the most profound devotion that can be imagined. His hearing not being quite perfect, he more than once interrupted Mr. Hoole, with, "Louder, my dear Sir, louder, I entreat you, or you pray in vain!"—and, when the service was ended, he, with great earnestness, turned round to an excellent lady who was present,[a] saying, "I thank you, Madam, very heartily, for your kindness in joining me in this solemn exercise. Live well, I conjure you; and you will not feel the compunction at the last, which I now feel." So truly humble were the thoughts which this great and good man entertained of his own approaches to religious perfection.

[a] *who was She?* [H]

'He was earnestly invited to publish a volume of *Devotional Exercises;* but this, (though he listened to the proposal with much complacency, and a large sum of money was offered for it,) he declined, from motives of the sincerest modesty.

'He seriously entertained the thought of translating *Thuanus*. He often talked to me on the subject; and once, in particular, when I was rather wishing that he would favour the world, and gratify his Sovereign, by a Life of Spenser, (which he said that he would readily have done,

had he been able to obtain any new materials for the purpose,) he added, "I have been thinking again, Sir, of
Thuanus: it would not be the laborious task which you have
supposed it. I should have no trouble but that of dictation,
which would be performed as speedily as an amanuensis
could write." '

It is to the mutual credit of Johnson and Divines of
different communions, that although he was a steady
Church-of-England man, there was, nevertheless, much
agreeable intercourse between him and them. Let me
particularly name the late Mr. La Trobe, and Mr. Hutton,
of the Moravian profession. His intimacy with the English
Benedictines, at Paris, has been mentioned; and as an
additional proof of the charity in which he lived with
good men of the Romish Church, I am happy in this
opportunity of recording his friendship with the Reverend
Thomas Hussey, D.D. His Catholick Majesty's Chaplain
of Embassy at the Court of London, that very respectable
man, eminent not only for his powerful eloquence as a
preacher, but for his various abilities and acquisitions.—
Nay, though Johnson loved a Presbyterian the least of all,
this did not prevent his having a long and uninterrupted
social connection with the Reverend Dr. James Fordyce,
who, since his death, hath gratefully celebrated him in a
warm strain of devotional composition.

Amidst the melancholy clouds which hung over the
dying Johnson, his characteristical manner shewed itself
on different occasions.

When Dr. Warren, in his usual style, hoped that he was
better; his answer was, 'No, Sir; you cannot conceive with
what acceleration I advance towards death.'

A man whom he had never seen before was employed
one night to sit up with him. Being asked next morning how he liked his attendant, his answer was, 'Not
at all, Sir: the fellow's an ideot; he is as aukward as a
turn-spit when first put into the wheel, and as sleepy as
a dormouse.'

marginal line:
was, 'Not . . . a dor-
mouse [H]

Mr. Windham having placed a pillow conveniently to
support him, he thanked him for his kindness, and said,
'That will do,—all that a pillow can do.'

He repeated with great spirit a poem, consisting of

several stanzas, in four lines, in alternate rhyme, which
he said he had composed some years before,[1] on occasion
of a rich, extravagant young gentleman's coming of age:
saying he had never repeated it but once since he composed it, and had given but one copy of it. That copy was
given to Mrs. Thrale, now Piozzi, who has published it in
a Book which she entitles 'British Synonimy,' but which
is truly a collection of entertaining remarks and stories,
no matter whether accurate or not. Being a piece of
exquisite satire, conveyed in a strain of pointed vivacity
and humour, and in a manner of which no other instance
is to be found in Johnson's writings, I shall here insert it:

> Long-expected one-and-twenty,
>   Ling'ring year, at length is flown;
> Pride and pleasure, pomp and plenty,
>   Great *** ****, are now your own.
>
> Loosen'd from the Minor's tether,
>   Free to mortgage or to sell,
> Wild as wind, and light as feather,
>   Bid the sons of thrift farewell.
>
> Call the Betseys, Kates, and Jennies,
>   All the names that banish care;
> Lavish of your grandsire's guineas,
>   Shew the spirit of an heir.
>
> All that prey on vice and folly
>   Joy to see their quarry fly;
> There the gamester, light and jolly,
>   There the lender, grave and sly.
>
> Wealth, my lad, was made to wander,
>   Let it wander as it will;
> Call the jockey, call the pander,
>   Bid them come and take their fill.

---

[1] [In 1730. See his Letter to Mrs. Thrale, dated August 8, 1780. 'You have
heard in the papers how *** is come to age: I have enclosed a short song of
congratulation, which you must not shew to any body.—It is odd that it
should come into any body's head. I hope you will read it with candour; it
is, I believe, one of the authour's first essays in that way of writing, and a
beginner is always to be treated with tenderness.' MALONE.]

When the bonny blade carouses,
    Pockets full, and spirits high—
What are acres? what are houses?
    Only dirt, or wet or dry.

Should the guardian friend or mother
    Tell the woes of wilful waste:
Scorn their counsels, scorn their pother,—
    You can hang or drown at last.

As he opened a note which his servant brought to him, he said, 'An odd thought strikes me:—we shall receive no letters in the grave.'

He requested three things of Sir Joshua Reynolds:—To forgive him thirty pounds which he had borrowed of him;[a]—to read the Bible;—and never to use his pencil on a Sunday. Sir Joshua readily acquiesced.

a & why? He had Money enough to pay every Debt. [H]

Indeed he shewed the greatest anxiety for the religious improvement of his friends, to whom he discoursed of its infinite consequence. He begged of Mr. Hoole to think of what he had said, and to commit it to writing; and, upon being afterwards assured that this was done, pressed his hands, and in an earnest tone thanked him. Dr. Brocklesby having attended him with the utmost assiduity and kindness as his physician and friend, he was peculiarly desirous that this gentleman should not entertain any loose speculative notions, but be confirmed in the truths of Christianity, and insisted on his writing down in his presence, as nearly as he could collect it, the import of what passed on the subject: and Dr. Brocklesby having complied with the request, he made him sign the paper, and urged him to keep it in his own custody as long as he lived.

Johnson, with that native fortitude, which, amidst all his bodily distress and mental sufferings, never forsook him, asked Dr. Brocklesby, as a man in whom he had confidence, to tell him plainly whether he could recover. 'Give me (said he) a direct answer.' The Doctor having first asked him if he could bear the whole truth, which way soever it might lead, and being answered that he could, declared that, in his opinion, he could not recover without a miracle. 'Then (said Johnson,) I will take no more

physick, not even my opiates: for I have prayed that I
may render up my soul to GOD unclouded.' In this resolution he persevered, and, at the same time, used only the
weakest kinds of sustenance. Being pressed by Mr. Windham to take somewhat more generous nourishment, lest
too low a diet should have the very effect which he dreaded,
by debilitating his mind, he said, 'I will take any thing but
inebriating sustenance.'

The Reverend Mr. Strahan, who was the son of his
friend, and had been always one of his great favourites,
had, during his last illness, the satisfaction of contributing
to soothe and comfort him. That gentleman's house, at
Islington, of which he is Vicar, afforded Johnson, occasionally and easily, an agreeable change of place and fresh air;
and he attended also upon him in town in the discharge
of the sacred offices of his profession.

Mr. Strahan has given me the agreeable assurance, that,
after being in much agitation, Johnson became quite
composed, and continued so till his death.

Dr. Brocklesby, who will not be suspected of fanaticism,
obliged me with the following accounts:

'For some time before his death, all his fears were calmed
and absorbed by the prevalence of his faith, and his trust
in the merits and *propitiation* of JESUS CHRIST.

'He talked often to me about the necessity of faith in
the *sacrifice* of Jesus, as necessary beyond all good works
whatever, for the salvation of mankind.[a]

[a] *Ay Sure; there is our Sheet Anchor.* [H]

'He pressed me to study Dr. Clarke and to read his
Sermons. I asked him why he pressed Dr. Clarke, an
Arian.[1] "Because, (said he,) he is fullest on the *propitiatory
sacrifice.*"'

[1] The change of his sentiments with regard to Dr. Clarke, is thus mentioned
to me in a letter from the late Dr. Adams, Master of Pembroke College,
Oxford.—'The Doctor's prejudices were the strongest, and certainly in
another sense the weakest, that ever possessed a sensible man. You know his
extreme zeal for orthodoxy. But did you ever hear what he told me himself?
That he had made it a rule not to admit Dr. Clarke's name in his Dictionary.
This, however, wore off. At some distance of time he advised with me what
books he should read in defence of the Christian Religion. I recommended
"Clarke's Evidences of Natural and Revealed Religion," as the best of the
kind; and I find in what is called his "Prayers and Meditations," that he
was frequently employed in the latter part of his time in reading Clarke's
Sermons.'

Johnson having thus in his mind the true Christian scheme, at once rational and consolatory, uniting justice and mercy in the DIVINITY, with the improvement of human nature, previous to his receiving the Holy Sacrament in his apartment, composed and fervently uttered this prayer:[1]

'Almighty and most merciful Father, I am now, as to human eyes it seems, about to commemorate, for the last time, the death of thy Son JESUS CHRIST, our Saviour and Redeemer. Grant, O LORD, that my whole hope and confidence may be in his merits, and thy mercy; enforce and accept my imperfect repentance; make this commemoration available to the confirmation of my faith, the establishment of my hope, and the enlargement of my charity; and make the death of thy Son JESUS CHRIST effectual to my redemption. Have mercy upon me, and pardon the multitude of my offences. Bless my friends; have mercy upon all men. Support me, by thy Holy Spirit, in the days of weakness, and at the hour of death; and receive me, at my death, to everlasting happiness, for the sake of JESUS CHRIST. Amen.'

Having, as has been already mentioned, made his will on the 8th and 9th of December, and settled all his worldly affairs, he languished till Monday, the 13th of that month, when he expired, about seven o'clock in the evening, with so little apparent pain that his attendants hardly perceived when his dissolution took place.

Of his last moments, my brother, Thomas David, has furnished me with the following particulars:

'The Doctor, from the time that he was certain his death was near, appeared to be perfectly resigned, was seldom or never fretful or out of temper, and often said to his faithful servant, who gave me this account, "Attend, Francis, to the salvation of your soul, which is the object of greatest importance:" he also explained to him passages in the scripture, and seemed to have pleasure in talking upon religious subjects.

'On Monday, the 13th of December, the day on which he died, a Miss Morris, daughter to a particular friend of

[1] The Reverend Mr. Strahan took care to have it preserved, and has inserted it in 'Prayers and Meditations,' p. 216.

his, called, and said to Francis, that she begged to be permitted to see the Doctor, that she might earnestly request him to give her his blessing. Francis went into his room, followed by the young lady, and delivered the message. The Doctor turned himself in the bed, and said, "GOD bless you, my dear!" These were the last words he spoke.—His difficulty of breathing increased till about seven o'clock in the evening, when Mr. Barber and Mrs. Desmoulins, who were sitting in the room, observing that the noise he made in breathing had ceased, went to the bed, and found he was dead.'

About two days after his death, the following very agreeable account was communicated to Mr. Malone, in a letter by the honourable John Byng, to whom I am much obliged for granting me permission to introduce it in my work.

'DEAR SIR,

'Since I saw you, I have had a long conversation with Cawston,[1] who sat up with Dr. Johnson, from nine o'clock on Sunday evening, till ten o'clock on Monday morning. And, from what I can gather from him, it should seem, that Dr. Johnson was perfectly composed, steady in hope, and resigned to death. At the interval of each hour, they assisted him to sit up in his bed, and move his legs, which were in much pain; when he regularly addressed himself to fervent prayer; and though, sometimes, his voice failed him, his sense never did, during that time. The only sustenance he received, was cyder and water. He said his mind was prepared, and the time to his dissolution seemed long. At six in the morning, he enquired the hour, and, on being informed, said that all went on regularly, and he felt he had but a few hours to live.

'At ten o'clock in the morning, he parted from Cawston, saying, "You should not detain Mr. Windham's servant:— I thank you; bear my remembrance to your master." Cawston says, that no man could appear more collected, more devout, or less terrified at the thoughts of the approaching minute.

[1] Servant to the Right Honourable William Windham.

marginal line: *time. The . . . and the* [H]

'This account, which is so much more agreeable than, and somewhat different from, yours, has given us the satisfaction of thinking that that great man died as he lived, full of resignation, strengthened in faith, and joyful in hope.'

A few days before his death, he had asked Sir John Hawkins, as one of his executors, where he should be buried; and on being answered, 'Doubtless, in Westminster-Abbey,' seemed to feel a satisfaction, very natural to a Poet; and indeed in my opinion very natural to every man of any imagination, who has no family sepulchre in which he can be laid with his fathers. Accordingly, upon Monday, December 20, his remains were deposited in that noble and renowned edifice; and over his grave was placed a large blue flag-stone, with this inscription:

'SAMUEL JOHNSON, LL.D.
Obiit XIII *die Decembris,*
Anno Domini
M. DCC. LXXXIV.
Ætatis suæ LXXV.'

His funeral was attended by a respectable number of his friends, particularly such of the members of THE LITERARY CLUB as were then in town; and was also honoured with the presence of several of the Reverend Chapter of Westminster. Mr. Burke, Sir Joseph Banks, Mr. Windham, Mr. Langton, Sir Charles Bunbury, and Mr. Colman, bore his pall. His school-fellow, Dr. Taylor, performed the mournful office of reading the burial service.

I trust, I shall not be accused of affectation, when I declare, that I find myself unable to express all that I felt upon the loss of such a 'Guide, Philosopher, and Friend.'[1] I shall, therefore, not say one word of my own, but adopt

[1] On the subject of Johnson I may adopt the words of Sir John Harrington, concerning his venerable Tutor and Diocesan, Dr. John Still, Bishop of Bath and Wells; 'who hath given me some helps, more hopes, all encouragements in my best studies: to whom I never came but I grew more religious; from whom I never went, but I parted better instructed. Of him therefore, my acquaintance, my friend, my instructor, if I speak much, it were not to be marvelled; if I speak frankly, it is not to be blamed; and though I speak partially, it were to be pardoned.' *Nugæ Antiquæ*, Vol. I. p. 136. There is one circumstance in Sir John's character of Bishop Still, which is peculiarly

those of an eminent friend,[1] which he uttered with an abrupt felicity, superiour to all studied compositions:— 'He has made a chasm, which not only nothing can fill up, but which nothing has a tendency to fill up.—Johnson is dead.—Let us go to the next best:—there is nobody; no man can be said to put you in mind of Johnson.'

As Johnson had abundant homage paid to him during his life,[2] so no writer in this nation ever had such an

applicable to Johnson: 'He became so famous a disputer, that the learnedest were even afraid to dispute with him: and he finding his own strength, could not stick to warn them in their arguments to take heed to their answers, like a perfect fencer that will tell aforehand in which button he will give the venew, or like a cunning chess-player that will appoint aforehand with which pawn and in what place he will give the mate.' *Ibid.*

[1] [The late Right Hon. William Gerard Hamilton, who had been intimately acquainted with Dr. Johnson near thirty years. He died in London, July 16, 1796, in his sixty-eighth year. MALONE.]

[2] Beside the Dedications to him by Dr. Goldsmith, the Reverend Dr. Franklin, and the Reverend Mr. Wilson, which I have mentioned according to their dates, there was one by a lady, of a versification of 'Aningait and Ajut,' and one by the ingenious Mr. Walker, of his 'Rhetorical Grammar.' I have introduced into this work several compliments paid to him in the writings of his contemporaries; but the number of them is so great, that we may fairly say that there was almost a general tribute.

Let me not be forgetful of the honour done to him by Colonel Myddleton, of Gwaynynog, near Denbigh; who, on the banks of a rivulet in his park, where Johnson delighted to stand and repeat verses, erected an urn with the following inscription:

'This spot was often dignified by the presence of
SAMUEL JOHNSON, LL.D.
Whose moral writings, exactly conformable to the precepts of
Christianity,
Give ardour to Virtue and confidence to Truth.'

As no inconsiderable circumstance of his fame, we must reckon the extraordinary zeal of the artists to extend and perpetuate his image. I can enumerate a bust by Mr. Nollekens, and the many casts which are made from it; several pictures by Sir Joshua Reynolds; from one of which, in the possession of the Duke of Dorset, Mr. Humphry executed a beautiful miniature in enamel: one by Mrs. Frances Reynolds, Sir Joshua's sister: one by Mr. Zoffani;[a] and one by Mr. Opie; and the following engravings of his portrait: 1. One by Cooke, from Sir Joshua, for the Proprietors' edition of his folio Dictionary.—2. One from ditto, by ditto, for their quarto edition.— 3. One from Opie, by Heath, for Harrison's edition of his Dictionary.— 4. One from Nollekens' bust of him, by Bartolozzi, for Fielding's quarto edition of his Dictionary.—5. One small, from Harding, by Trotter, for his 'Beauties.'—6. One small, from Sir Joshua, by Trotter, for his 'Lives of the Poets.'—7. One small, from Sir Joshua, by Hall, for 'The Rambler.'—8. One small, from an original drawing, in the possession of Mr. John Simco, etched by Trotter, for another edition of his 'Lives of the Poets.'—9. One small, no

underlined:
one, Mr. Zoffani [H]

[a] *I should like to see that before I follow him.* [H]

accumulation of literary honours after his death. A sermon upon that event was preached in St. Mary's church, Oxford, before the University, by the Reverend Mr. Agutter, of Magdalen College.[1] The Lives, the Memoirs, the Essays, both in prose and verse, which have been published concerning him, would make many volumes. The numerous attacks too upon him, I consider as part of his consequence, upon the principle which he himself so well knew and asserted. Many who trembled at his presence were forward in assault, when they no longer apprehended danger. When one of his little pragmatical foes was invidiously snarling at his fame, at Sir Joshua Reynolds's table, the Reverend Dr. Parr exclaimed, with his usual bold animation, 'Ay, now that the old lion is dead, every ass thinks he may kick at him.'

A monument for him, in Westminster-Abbey, was resolved upon soon after his death, and was supported by

painter's name, etched by Taylor, for his 'Johnsoniana.'—10. One folio whole-length, with his oak-stick, as described in Boswell's 'Tour,' drawn and etched by Trotter.—11. One large mezzotinto, from Sir Joshua, by Doughty.—12. One large Roman Head, from Sir Joshua, by Marchi.—13. One octavo, holding a book to his eye, from Sir Joshua, by Hall, for his works.—14. One small, from a drawing from the life, and engraved by Trotter, for his Life published by Kearsley.—15. One large, from Opie, by Mr. Townley, (brother of Mr. Townley, of the Commons,) an ingenious artist, who resided some time at Berlin, and has the honour of being engraver to his Majesty the King of Prussia. This is one of the finest mezzotintos that ever was executed; and what renders it of extraordinary value, the plate was destroyed after four or five impressions only were taken off. One of them is in the possession of Sir William Scott. Mr. Townley has lately been prevailed with to execute and publish another of the same, that it may be more generally circulated among the admirers of Dr. Johnson.—16. One large, from Sir Joshua's first picture of him, by Heath, for this work, in quarto.— 17. One octavo, by Baker, for the octavo edition.—18. And one for 'Lavater's Essays on Physiognomy,' in which Johnson's countenance is analysed upon the principles of that fanciful writer.—There are also several seals with his head cut on them, particularly a very fine one by that eminent artist, Edward Burch, Esq. R. A. in the possession of the younger Dr. Charles Burney.[a]

Let me add, as a proof of the popularity of his character, that there are copper pieces struck at Birmingham, with his head impressed on them, which pass current as half-pence there, and in the neighbouring parts of the country.

[1] It is not yet published.—In a letter to me, Mr. Agutter says, 'My sermon before the University was more engaged with Dr. Johnson's *moral* than his *intellectual* character. It particularly examined his fear of death, and sug-gested several reasons for the apprehensions of the good, and the indifference of the infidel in their last hours; this was illustrated by contrasting the death of Dr. Johnson and Mr. Hume: the text was Job xxi. 22-26.'

[a] *To a Quarto Volume however of the Life of Richard Owen Cambridge Esq. & his Works perhaps; There is annex'd a Print of many People—I forget all but Doctor Johnson: and it must have been done from some Portrait in his early Days— long, oh very, very long indeed,—before his Person was known to me: yet exceedingly like. H. L. P. 1820.* [H]

a most respectable contribution; but the Dean and Chapter of St. Paul's having come to a resolution of admitting monuments there, upon a liberal and magnificent plan, that Cathedral was afterwards fixed on, as the place in which a cenotaph should be erected to his memory: and in the cathedral of his native city of Lichfield, a smaller one is to be erected.[1] To compose his epitaph, could not but excite the warmest competition of genius.[2] If *laudari à*

[1] [This monument has been since erected. It consists of a Medallion, with a tablet beneath, on which is this inscription:

'The friends of SAMUEL JOHNSON, LL.D.
A Native of Lichfield,
Erected this Monument,
As a tribute of respect
To the Memory of a man of extensive learning,
A distinguished moral writer, and a sincere Christian.
He died Dec. 13, 1784, aged 75.'
MALONE.]

[2] The Reverend Dr. Parr, on being requested to undertake it, thus expressed himself in a letter to William Seward, Esq.:

'I leave this mighty task to some hardier and some abler writer. The variety and splendour of Johnson's attainments, the peculiarities of his character, his private virtues, and his literary publications, fill me with confusion and dismay, when I reflect upon the confined and difficult species of composition, in which alone they can be expressed, with propriety, upon his monument.'

But I understand that this great scholar, and warm admirer of Johnson, has yielded to repeated solicitations, and executed the very difficult undertaking.

[Dr. Johnson's Monument, consisting of a Colossal Figure leaning against a column, (but not very strongly resembling him,) has since the death of our authour been placed in St. Paul's Cathedral, having been first opened to publick view, Feb. 23, 1796. The Epitaph was written by the Rev. Dr. Parr, and is as follows:

A ☧ ω

SAMVELI · IOHNSON
GRAMMATICO · ET · CRITICO
SCRIPTORVM · ANGLICORVM · LITTERATE · PERITO
POETAE · LVMINIBVS · SENTENTIARVM
ET · PONDERIBVS · VERBORVM · ADMIRABILI
MAGISTRO · VIRTVTIS · GRAVISSIMO
HOMINI · OPTIMO · ET · SINGVLARIS · EXEMPLI

———

QVI · VIXIT · ANN · lxxv. · MENS · iI. DIEB · xiiiI.
DECESSIT · IDIB · DECEMBR · ANN · CHRIST · cIɔ · Iɔcc · LxxxiiiI
SEPVLT · IN · AED · SANCT · PETR · WESTMONASTERIENS.
xiiI · KAL · IANVAR · ANN · CHRIST · cIɔ · Iɔcc · lxxxv
AMICI · ET · SODALES · LITTERARII
PECVNIA · CONLATA
H · M · FACIVND · CVRAVER.

laudato viro be praise which is highly estimable, I should not forgive myself were I to omit the following sepulchral verses on the authour of THE ENGLISH DICTIONARY, written by the Right Honourable Henry Flood:[1]

> 'No need of Latin or of Greek to grace
>   Our JOHNSON's memory, or inscribe his grave;
> His native language claims this mournful space,
>   To pay the Immortality he gave.'

The character of SAMUEL JOHNSON has, I trust, been so developed in the course of this work, that they who have honoured it with a perusal, may be considered as well acquainted with him. As, however, it may be expected that I should collect into one view the capital and distinguishing features of this extraordinary man, I shall endeavour to acquit myself of that part of my biographical undertaking,[2] however difficult it may be to do that which many of my readers will do better for themselves.

On a scroll in his hand are the following words:
ΕΝΜΑΚΑΡΕΣΣΙΠΟΝΩΝΑΝΤΑΞΙΟΣΕΙΗΑΜΟΙΒΗ

On one side of the monument—FACIEBAT JOHANNES BACON,
        SCVLPTOR ANN. CHRIST. M.DCC.LXXXXV.

The Subscription for this monument, which cost eleven hundred guineas, was begun by the LITERARY CLUB, and completed by the aid of Dr. Johnson's other friends and admirers. MALONE.]

[1] To prevent any misconception on this subject, Mr. Malone, by whom these lines were obligingly communicated, requests me to add the following remark:
'In justice to the late Mr. Flood, now himself wanting, and highly meriting, an epitaph from his country, to which his transcendent talents did the highest honour, as well as the most important service; it should be observed, that these lines were by no means intended as a regular monumental inscription for Dr. Johnson. Had he undertaken to write an appropriate and discriminative epitaph for that excellent and extraordinary man, those who knew Mr. Flood's vigour of mind, will have no doubt that he would have produced one worthy of his illustrious subject. But the fact was merely this: In Dec. 1789, after a large subscription had been made for Dr. Johnson's monument, to which Mr. Flood liberally contributed, Mr. Malone happened to call on him at his house, in Berners-street, and the conversation turning on the proposed monument, Mr. Malone maintained that the epitaph, by whomsoever it should be written, ought to be in Latin. Mr. Flood thought differently. The next morning, in a postscript to a note on another subject, he mentioned that he continued of the same opinion as on the preceding day, and subjoined the lines above given.'

[2] As I do not see any reason to give a different character of my illustrious friend now, from what I formerly gave, the greatest part of the sketch of him in my 'Journal of a Tour to the Hebrides,' is here adopted.

His figure was large and well formed, and his countenance of the cast of an ancient statue; yet his appearance
was rendered strange and somewhat uncouth, by convulsive cramps, by the scars of that distemper which it was
once imagined the royal touch could cure, and by a
slovenly mode of dress. He had the use only of one eye; yet
so much does mind govern, and even supply the deficiency
of organs, that his visual perceptions, as far as they extended, were uncommonly quick and accurate. So morbid
was his temperament, that he never knew the natural joy
of a free and vigorous use of his limbs: when he walked, it
was like the struggling gait of one in fetters; when he rode,
he had no command or direction of his horse, but was
carried as if in a balloon. That with his constitution and
habits of life he should have lived seventy-five years, is a
proof that an inherent *vivida vis* is a powerful preservative
of the human frame.

marginal line:
*command or . . . con-
stitution and* [H]

two marginal lines:
is a . . . human frame
[H]

Man is, in general, made up of contradictory qualities;
and these will ever shew themselves in strange succession,
where a consistency in appearance at least, if not in reality,
has not been attained by long habits of philosophical
discipline. In proportion to the native vigour of the mind,
the contradictory qualities will be the more prominent,
and more difficult to be adjusted; and, therefore, we are
not to wonder, that Johnson exhibited an eminent example of this remark which I have made upon human
nature. At different times, he seemed a different man, in
some respects; not, however, in any great or essential
article, upon which he had fully employed his mind, and
settled certain principles of duty, but only in his manners,
and in the display of argument and fancy in his talk. He
was prone to superstition, but not to credulity. Though
his imagination might incline him to a belief of the mar-
vellous and the mysterious, his vigorous reason examined
the evidence with jealousy. He was a sincere and zealous
Christian, of high Church-of-England and monarchical
principles, which he would not tamely suffer to be questioned; and had, perhaps, at an early period, narrowed his
mind somewhat too much, both as to religion and politicks.
His being impressed with the danger of extreme latitude
in either, though he was of a very independent spirit,

occasioned his appearing somewhat unfavourable to the prevalence of that noble freedom of sentiment which is the best possession of man. Nor can it be denied, that he had many prejudices; which, however, frequently suggested many of his pointed sayings, that rather shew a playfulness of fancy than any settled malignity. He was steady and inflexible in maintaining the obligations of religion and morality; both from a regard for the order of society, and from a veneration for the GREAT SOURCE of all order; correct, nay stern in his taste; hard to please, and easily offended; impetuous and irritable in his temper, but of a most humane and benevolent heart,[1] which shewed itself not only in a most liberal charity, as far as his circumstances would allow, but in a thousand instances of active benevolence. He was afflicted with a bodily disease, which made him often restless and fretful; and with a constitutional melancholy, the clouds of which darkened the brightness of his fancy, and gave a gloomy cast to his whole course of thinking: we, therefore, ought not to wonder at his sallies of impatience and passion at any time; especially when provoked by obtrusive ignorance, or presuming petulance; and allowance must be made for his uttering hasty and satirical sallies even against his best friends. And, surely, when it is considered, that 'amidst sickness and sorrow,' he exerted his faculties in so many works for the benefit of mankind, and particularly that he atchieved the great and admirable DICTIONARY of our language, we must be astonished at his resolution. The solemn text, 'of him to whom much is given, much will be required,' seems to have been ever present to his mind, in a rigorous sense, and to have made him dissatisfied with his labours and acts of goodness, however comparatively great; so that the unavoidable consciousness of his superiority was, in that respect, a cause of disquiet. He suffered so much from this, and from the gloom which

marginal line:
provoked by . . . his
uttering [H]

[1] In the 'OLLA PODRIDA,' a collection of Essays published at Oxford, there is an admirable paper upon the character of Johnson written by the Reverend Dr. Horne, the late excellent Bishop of Norwich. The following passage is eminently happy:—'To reject wisdom, because the person of him who communicates it is uncouth, and his manners are inelegant;—what is it, but to throw away a pine-apple, and assign for a reason the roughness of its coat?'

perpetually haunted him, and made solitude frightful, that it may be said of him, 'If in this life only he had hope, he was of all men most miserable.' He loved praise, when it was brought to him; but was too proud to seek for it. He was somewhat susceptible of flattery. As he was general and unconfined in his studies, he cannot be considered as master of any one particular science; but he had accumulated a vast and various collection of learning and knowledge, which was so arranged in his mind, as to be ever in readiness to be brought forth. But his superiority over other learned men consisted chiefly in what may be called the art of thinking, the art of using his mind; a certain continual power of seizing the useful substance of all that he knew, and exhibiting it in a clear and forcible manner; so that knowledge, which we often see to be no better than lumber in men of dull understanding, was, in him, true, evident, and actual wisdom. His moral precepts are practical; for they are drawn from an intimate acquaintance with human nature. His maxims carry conviction: for they are founded on the basis of common sense, and a very attentive and minute survey of real life. His mind was so full of imagery, that he might have been perpetually a poet; yet it is remarkable, that, however rich his prose is in this respect, his poetical pieces, in general, have not much of that splendour, but are rather distinguished by strong sentiment, and acute observation, conveyed in harmonious and energetick verse, particularly in heroick couplets. Though usually grave, and even awful in his deportment, he possessed uncommon and peculiar powers of wit and humour; he frequently indulged himself in colloquial pleasantry; and the heartiest merriment was often enjoyed in his company; with this great advantage, that, as it was entirely free from any poisonous tincture of vice or impiety, it was salutary to those who shared in it. He had accustomed himself to such accuracy in his common conversation[1] that he at all times expressed his

marginal line:
men most . . . for it [H]

[1] Though a perfect resemblance of Johnson is not to be found in any age, parts of his character are admirably expressed by Clarendon, in drawing that of Lord Falkland, whom the noble and masterly historian describes at his seat near Oxford:—'Such an immenseness of wit, such a solidity of judgement, so infinite a fancy, bound in by a most logical ratiocination.—His acquaintance was cultivated by the most polite and accurate men, so that

thoughts with great force, and an elegant choice of language, the effect of which was aided by his having a loud voice, and a slow deliberate utterance. In him were united a most logical head with a most fertile imagination, which gave him an extraordinary advantage in arguing: for he could reason close or wide, as he saw best for the moment. Exulting in his intellectual strength and dexterity, he could, when he pleased, be the greatest sophist that ever contended in the lists of declamation; and, from a spirit of contradiction, and a delight in shewing his powers, he would often maintain the wrong side with equal warmth and ingenuity; so that, when there was an audience, his real opinions could seldom be gathered from his talk; though when he was in company with a single friend, he would discuss a subject with genuine fairness; but he was too conscientious to make errour permanent and pernicious, by deliberately writing it; and, in all his numerous

his house was an University in less volume, whither they came, not so much for repose as study, and to examine and refine those grosser propositions, which laziness and consent made current in conversation.'

Bayle's account of *Menage* may also be quoted as exceedingly applicable to the great subject of this work.—'His illustrious friends erected a very glorious monument to him in the collection entitled *Menagiana*. Those who judge of things aright, will confess that this collection is very proper to shew the extent of genius and learning which was the character of Menage. And I may be bold to say, that *the excellent works he published will not distinguish him from other learned men so advantageously as this*. To publish books of great learning, to make Greek and Latin verses exceedingly well turned, is not a common talent, I own; neither is it extremely rare. It is incomparably more difficult to find men who can furnish discourse about an infinite number of things, and who can diversify them an hundred ways. How many authours are there, who are admired for their works, on account of the vast learning that is displayed in them, who are not able to sustain a conversation. Those who know Menage only by his books, might think he resembled those learned men: but if you shew the MENAGIANA, you distinguish him from them, and make him known by a talent which is given to very few learned men. There it appears that he was a man who spoke off-hand a thousand good things. His memory extended to what was ancient and modern; to the court and to the city; to the dead and to the living languages; to things serious and things jocose; in a word, to a thousand sorts of subjects. That which appeared a trifle to some readers of the *Menagiana*, who did not consider circumstances, caused admiration in other readers, who minded the difference between what a man speaks without preparation, and that which he prepares for the press. And, therefore, we cannot sufficiently commend the care which his illustrious friends took to erect a monument so capable of giving him immortal glory. They were not obliged to rectify what they had heard him say; for, in so doing, they had not been faithful historians of his conversation.'

works, he earnestly inculcated what appeared to him to be the truth; his piety being constant, and the ruling principle of all his conduct.

Such was SAMUEL JOHNSON, a man whose talents, acquirements, and virtues, were so extraordinary, that the more his character is considered, the more he will be regarded by the present age, and by posterity, with admiration and reverence.

FINIS